To my H

Happy 41st.

all my love

Sally

xxx

BRITISH VESSELS LOST AT SEA 1914-18 and 1939-45

BRITISH VESSELS LOST AT SEA 1914-18 and 1939-45

Facsimile reprints of four HMSO official publications: *Navy Losses* and *Merchant Shipping (Losses)*, published in 1919, and *Ships of the Royal Navy: Statement of Losses during the Second World War* and *British Merchant Vessels Lost or Damaged by Enemy Action during Second World War*, published in 1947.

Patrick Stephens

Navy Losses and *Merchant Shipping
(Losses)* first published 1919 by His
Majesty's Stationery Office, London.

*Ships of the Royal Navy: Statement of
Losses during the Second World War* and
*British Merchant Vessels Lost or Damaged
by Enemy Action during Second World War*
Crown copyright: first published in 1947 by
His Majesty's Stationery Office, London.
Reprinted by permission of the Controller
of Her Majesty's Stationery Office.

First published by Patrick Stephens Limited
in two volumes in 1976-77
This combined edition first published 1988

War Diaries © Patrick Stephens Limited
1976 and 1988

**British Library Cataloguing in Publication
Data**
British vessels lost at sea, 1914-18 and
   1939-45.
   1. British ships. Losses, 1914-1918
   2. British ships. Losses, 1939-1945 –
   Lists. Early works
   940.4'5

   ISBN 1-85260-134-5

Patrick Stephens Limited is part of the
Thorsons Publishing Group,
Wellingborough, Northamptonshire
NN8 2RQ, England.

Printed in Great Britain

10 9 8 7 6 5 4 3 2 1

Publisher's introduction

In August 1919, less than a year after the First World War ended, HMSO issued two important House Of Commons papers. One was entitled *Navy Losses* and the other *Merchant Shipping (Losses)*. After the Second World War, in 1947, two further publications appeared, *Ships of the Royal Navy: Statement of Losses During The Second World War* and *British Merchant Vessels Lost or Damaged by Enemy Action during Second World War*. For many years, the original editions of all these volumes were extremely hard to find, yet they contain a wealth of important historical data on the Royal and Merchant Navies during two World Wars.

In 1976 and 1977, these excellent and highly detailed books were combined in two case-bound volumes, and reprinted by PSL exactly as they first appeared but in a smaller, more practical format. They soon became standard works of reference, and to them was later added supplementary material in the form of month-by-month diaries of the two conflicts to help the reader put the events recorded into their historical perspective.

Both volumes are now reprinted here in a new, combined edition so that all four of these invaluable publications are available within a single volume.

The information is presented in clear and concise tabular form for ease of reference. Sections I and III, for instance, which deal with Royal Navy losses in the two World Wars, give the following data on warships and auxiliary vessels: class, name, tonnage, date of completion, date of loss, and how lost and where. Sections II and IV give similar information on merchant vessels, which, together with many other details as recorded in the originals, has made the books eagerly sought after by keen naval historians and shipping enthusiasts.

Acknowledgements
The publishers would like to thank the following for their help and assistance with this reprint: Her Majesty's Stationery Office, London; the Central Library of the Department of Trade and Industry, London (in particular Mr G. Cook); and Mr R. Perry.

Special note
The four sections of this book are separately numbered and indexed, as were the original papers.

Contents

Section III: Ships of the Royal Navy: Statement of Losses during the Second World War

Section IV: British Merchant Vessels Lost or Damaged by Enemy Action during Second World War

War diary, 1914-18

1914
June
28 At Sarajevo, the Bosnian capital, Slav nationalists assassinated Archduke Ferdinand, heir to the Austrian crown. As a result, Austria delivered an ultimatum to Serbia.
July
28 Austria declared war on Serbia; Russia aligned itself behind Serbia, and Germany behind Austria. Germany delivered an ultimatum to France to see where the French stood in a German-Russian war.
29 The Royal Navy's Grand Fleet sailed from Portland bound for Scapa Flow, its war base.
30 German troops, on patrol, crossed into France.
August
2 Germany delivered an ultimatum to Belgium, demanding a free passage for her troops.
3 Germany declared war on France.
4 Great Britain declared war on Germany. German troops invaded Belgium. Britain responded by delivering an ultimatum that Germany should respect Belgian neutrality. At 11 pm, the ultimatum expired.
5 In the North Sea, the German auxiliary minelayer *Koningin Louise* was sunk by gunfire from the scout cruiser *Amphion* and destroyers. The next morning, the *Amphion* ran on to mines laid by the German ship and sank.
9 The RN Grand Fleet was on patrol in the northern North Sea when the advance cruisers ran into a group of German U-boats returning home after a sortie to the British coast. The cruiser *Birmingham* rammed *U-15* twice and the submarine sank with all her crew.
20 German troops entered Brussels.
26 The German auxiliary cruiser *Kaiser Wilhelm der Grosse* was bunkering off Rio del Oro, Spanish West Africa, when she was surprised by the cruiser *Highflyer*. The two ships exchanged gunfire and then the auxiliary cruiser ran out of ammunition and was scuttled. The 14,349-ton transatlantic passenger liner had been the first German ship to capture the Blue Riband for the

fastest Atlantic crossing.
In the Gulf of Finland, the German cruiser *Magdeburg* went aground and was destroyed by two Russian warships. Among the bodies recovered was that of a signalman, and on the body was the German Navy's cipher signal book which reached London at the end of October.
28 A RN force attacked German warships in the Heligoland Bight. This was essentially a fight between light cruisers and destroyers, but a squadron of RN battlecruisers, held in reserve, joined in. Early in the morning, the cruiser *Arethusa*, the scout cruiser *Fearless*, and two destroyer flotillas engaged a number of German cruisers and torpedo vessels. Gunfire from the *Arethusa* damaged the German light cruiser *Ariadne*, and the *Arethusa* was also damaged. The German light cruiser *Mainz* was seriously damaged later that morning and was sunk by cruiser gunfire; shortly after noon, RN battlecruisers arrived and sank the *Ariadne* and the light cruiser *Koln*.
September
5 Off the Firth of Forth, the destroyer *Pathfinder* was torpedoed by the German submarine *U-21*. The destroyer's forward magazine blew up and she sank with the loss of over 250 crew.
9 On the Western Front, German troops began retreating in the battle of the Marne.
13 South of Heligoland, the submarine *E-9* sank the German light cruiser *Hela*, the first RN submarine success of the war.
14 Off the small Brazilian island of Trinidade in the South Atlantic, the armed merchant cruiser *Carmania* encountered the German auxiliary cruiser *Cap Trafalgar*. In a fierce engagement, the German ship was sunk and the *Carmania* was damaged. The Cunard SS Co passenger liner was one of several RN warships hunting German warships and auxiliary cruisers on commerce raiding voyages in the South Atlantic. Some reports said that the *Cap Trafalgar* was disguised as the *Carmania* with one of her three funnels removed.
20 The cruiser *Pegasus* was sunk in an action with the German light cruiser *Konigsberg* at Zanzibar. The *Pegasus* was

hunting German cruisers off East Africa.

22 On patrol in the North Sea off the Dutch coast, the cruisers *Cressy*, *Aboukir* and *Hogue* were torpedoed by the German submarine *U-9*. The *Aboukir* was the first to be hit and as she sank her sister ships went to pick up survivors. First the *Hogue*, then the *Cressy* were torpedoed and sank. A total of 1,460 seamen died on the three cruisers.

30 In the Pacific, a German raiding squadron, led by the heavy cruisers *Scharnhorst* and *Gneisenau*, shelled French installations at Papeete, Tahiti.

October

9 Antwerp fell to the Germans.

17 In a running fight off the Dutch coast, the cruiser *Undaunted* and a squadron of destroyers sank the German destroyers *T-115*, *T-117*, *T-118* and *T-119*.

18 Two RN submarines, *E-1* and *E-9*, entered the Baltic. Operating from Russian bases, they were joined by other submarines and posed serious problems for the German Navy. (In 1917, following a peace treaty between the Bolsheviks and the Germans, the submarines put to sea and were scuttled.)

20 Off the coast of Norway, the steamer *Glitra*, 866 tons, was stopped by the German submarine *U-17*, and after her crew had taken to the boats, the German boarding party scuttled the ship—the first merchant ship to be sunk by a submarine in the war.

26 On a voyage from Buenos Aires to New York, the Lamport & Holt Line passenger-cargo liner *Vandyck* was intercepted by the German light cruiser *Karlsruhe* in the South Atlantic. The crew and passengers were put aboard the German auxiliary ship *Asuncion* and then the 10,328-ton liner was sunk.

27 Eight RN battleships sailed from their anchorage for firing practice and were about 20 miles off Tory Island when the *Audacious* hit a mine. Despite salvage attempts, the battleship sank.

30 The hospital ship *Rohilla*, 7,400 tons (British India SN Co), was driven ashore in a gale at Saltwick Nab, near Whitby. She was on passage from the Firth of Forth to Dunkirk and carried 229 crew and medical staff. RNLI lifeboats carried out three dramatic rescues in raging seas to save the crew.

31 On the Western Front came a turning point in the first battle of Ypres when British troops halted the German advance.

Turkey entered the war against the Allies.

November

1 A German squadron, led by the heavy cruisers *Scharnhorst* and *Gneisenau*, disappeared in the Pacific. Off Coronel, Chile, the German ships were surprised by a RN force of cruisers. In the ensuing action, the British ships were shown up against the sunset while the German ships were almost hidden against the black of the land. The *Good Hope* was set on fire, blew up and sank; the *Monmouth* was set on fire and was sunk by gunfire from the light cruiser *Nurnberg*; and the damaged cruiser *Glasgow* and auxiliary cruiser *Otranto* (Orient Line) managed to escape.

3 German battlecruisers bombarded Lowestoft.

9 Off the Cocos Islands, the Australian cruiser *Sydney* intercepted the German light cruiser *Emden*. In the chase, the *Emden* was set on fire and beached on North Keeling Island. The cruiser had been operating against merchant ships in the East Indies, the Bay of Bengal and the Indian Ocean.

11 The end of the first Battle of Ypres on the Western Front.

21 Indian troops captured Basrah in a campaign to safeguard the Persian Gulf oilfields.

December

8 After their victory in the Battle of Coronel (November 1), the German squadron sailed round into the South Atlantic and headed for the Falkland Islands. The RN battlecruisers *Invincible* and *Inflexible* and other warships were coaling in Port William and Port Stanley in the Falklands when the German squadron approached. The Germans were surprised to find the RN warships, which had been ordered south to hunt the victors of Coronel. The RN battlecruisers put to sea to engage the enemy ships, the heavy cruisers *Scharnhorst* and *Gneisenau* and the light cruisers *Nurnberg*, *Leipzig* and *Dresden*. In the action, the *Scharnhorst* and the *Gneisenau* were sunk by the *Invincible* and the *Inflexible*; the *Nurnberg* was sunk by the cruiser *Kent*; and the *Leipzig* was sunk by the cruisers *Glasgow* and *Cornwall*. The *Dresden* escaped but was hunted down and on 14 Mar 1915 was attacked by the cruisers *Glasgow* and *Kent* in Cumberland Bay, Chile and was blown up by her crew on March 14, 1915.

13 The RN submarine *B-11* penetrated the heavily defended Straits at the Dardanelles and torpedoed and sank the Turkish ironclad *Messudieh*, which was moored as a stationary guardship off Charnak, above The Narrows.

16 German battlecruisers bombarded Scarborough, Hartlepool and Whitby.

25 Seven Royal Naval Air Service Short seaplanes carried out a successful attack on Cuxhaven and along the Kiel Canal.

1915

January

24 A German squadron put to sea to bombard towns on the east coast of England when they were trapped by a RN squadron off the Dogger Bank. The RN light cruisers gave chase and the battlecruisers eventually overhauled the Germans. The RN force consisted of the battlecruisers *Lion, Tiger, Princess Royal, New Zealand* and *Indomitable*, accompanied by seven light cruisers and a destroyer flotilla; the German force comprised the battlecruisers *Seydlitz, Derfflinger* and *Moltke*, together with the heavy cruiser *Blucher*, six light cruisers and a number of destroyers. In the action, the *Blucher* was set on fire and sank and the *Seydlitz* was set on fire but reached port safely; the *Lion* was the most seriously damaged of the RN ships.

February

4 Germany declared a war zone around the British Isles, announcing that ships would be sunk without warning in the zone.

19 The Dardanelles campaign began with a naval bombardment of the Turkish forts by British and French ships. The campaign was to help relieve Turkish pressure on Russian forces in the Caucasus.

25 British and French warships again bombarded the outer forts in the Dardanelles.

26 Allied troops were landed to destroy the guns in the outer forts at the entrance to the Dardanelles. Further landings were made the next day.

March

3 Allied troops were landed at the entrance to the Dardanelles and a further landing was carried out the next day, but the troops were withdrawn after meeting opposition.

18 British and French warships tried to force the Straits in the Dardanelles. Ten battleships went up the Straits, engaged and subsequently silenced the forts of The Narrows. Six more battleships then sailed into the Straits, and in the ensuing action the French battleship *Bouvet* struck a mine, her magazine blew up and she sank with the loss of over 600 men. Of the RN forces, the *Inflexible* was damaged by mine, the *Irresistable* hit a mine, drifted towards the Asiatic shore and foundered during the night, and the *Ocean*, going to the aid of the *Irresist-*

able, hit a mine and sank.

Off the Pentland Firth, the battleship *Dreadnought*, exercising with ships of a Battle Squadron, rammed and sank the German submarine *U-12*.

April

22 German forces used chlorine gas in an offensive against Allied positions in the second Battle of Ypres on the Western Front.

25 In a major operation, British, Australian and French troops landed on the Gallipoli peninsula, the object being to eliminate enemy opposition so that Allied warships could force their way through the heavily guarded Narrows. Supported by Allied warships, the landing was made at several points but it turned into a disaster.

26 The RN submarine *E-14* sailed through the Straits of the Dardanelles and into the Sea of Marmora where, for three weeks, she caused chaos. Among her victims was the Turkish transport *Gul Djemal*, which was carrying 2,000 troops bound for the front.

May

7 The Cunard passenger liner *Lusitania*, 31,550 tons, on passage from New York, was torpedoed by the German submarine *U-20* off the entrance to Cork harbour. She was about 12 miles off the Old Head of Kinsale and sank within 20 minutes. 1,198 out of the 1,959 passengers and crew on board died. Among them were a number of Americans and the sinking caused an international outcry.

15 During the night, the RN battleship the *Goliath* was sunk by a German-manned Turkish destroyer *Mauvenet* off Cape Helles, Dardanelles.

27 Off Gaba Tepe, Dardanelles, the RN battleship *Majestic*, carrying out a bombardment of shore positions, was torpedoed by the German submarine *U-21* and sank.

July

11 The RN monitors *Mersey* and *Severn* attacked the German cruiser *Konigsberg* in the Rufiji River delta in German East Africa, south of Dar-es-Salaam. The cruiser was set alight by gunfire and then disabled by her crew. The two monitors had been transferred from the Mediterranean for this mission.

August

6 The reinforcement of troops in the Dardanelles culminated in the Suvla Bay landings.

8 The Turkish battleship *Hairreddin Barbarousse* was sunk by a torpedo from the RN submarine *E-11* at the end of the submarine's second incursion into the Sea of Marmora, both being highly successful. In the first, *E-11* had sailed into the Golden Horn at Constantinople.

12 A British seaplane gained the distinction of being the first to torpedo a ship in action. The Short 182 plane had flown from the seaplane carrier *Ben-My-Chree* and torpedoed an enemy transport in the Sea of Marmora.

14 The Canadian Northern Steamships liner *Royal Edward*, 10,864 tons, on a trooping voyage, was sunk in the Aegean by the German submarine *UB-14*; 935 died.

19 Off the Old Head of Kinsale, near Cork, a German submarine sank another passenger liner; *U-24* torpedoed the White Star Line's *Arabic*, 15,800 tons, which sank with the loss of 44.

23 The RN monitors *Lord Clive*, *Prince Rupert* and *Sir John Moore* bombarded the locks of the Zeebrugge Canal.

30 As a result of pressure from the US after several Americans had died in British ships that had been sunk, German submarines were ordered not to attack passenger liners without prior warning.

September

21 On the Western Front, British and French troops launched an offensive at Loos and used gas against the German positions; the offensive failed.

October

6 In an attack on Serbia, Austro-German armies attacked southwards across the Danube. With Serbia in danger, British and French troops were sent from Gallipoli to Salonika.

December

19 During the night, the evacuation of troops from Suvla and Anzac on the Gallipoli peninsula was completed.

1916

January

6 The RN battleship *King Edward VII* was sunk by a mine off Cape Wrath. The minefield had been laid by the German raider *Mowe*.

8 During the night, the evacuation of troops from Helles on the Gallipoli peninsula, Dardanelles, was completed.

February

10 The RN sloop *Arabis*, taking part in a minesweeping exercise, was sunk by German destroyers east of the Dogger Bank. That night, ships of the Harwich Light Force were returning after a rescue attempt when the cruiser *Arethusa* hit a mine and grounded, then broke in two.

21 On the Western Front, German troops launched a major offensive at Verdun.

29 In the northern North Sea, the German auxiliary cruiser *Greif*, disguised as the Norwegian steamer *Reno*, was intercepted by the auxiliary cruiser *Alcantara* (Royal Mail Lines). During the action, the auxiliary cruiser *Andes* (Royal Mail Lines) arrived and shortly afterwards the blazing *Alcantara* sank. The *Greif* was sunk by the *Andes*, with the cruiser *Comus* and the destroyer *Munster*.

March

24 The French passenger steamer *Sussex*, on a passage from Dieppe to Folkestone, was sunk by the German submarine *UB-29*. A number of Americans were among those killed or injured and, after US pressure, U-boats were ordered to attack ships only after a warning, examining the ship's papers and cargo and ensuring the safety of those on board.

April

25 German battlecruisers bombarded Lowestoft and Great Yarmouth in the early hours. Ships of the Harwich Light Force attacked the battlecruisers which, with units of the German High Seas Fleet, headed back to Germany; the *Seydlitz* was badly damaged by a mine as she returned home.

May

31 The Battle of Jutland, the only major encounter between the Royal Navy and the German Navy main fleets; it was an inconclusive action.

The RN Battlecruiser Fleet was at sea bound for a mission in the Skagerrak when an intercepted German signal indicated that the German High Seas Fleet was planning an operation. The RN Grand Fleet sailed to rendezvous with the Battlecruiser Fleet to form a fleet of 37 dreadnoughts; the German fleet comprised 27 battleships and battlecruisers. The battle comprised a series of incidents that day and during the early hours of 1 June.

The opening shots were fired in the afternoon when the cruisers *Galatea* and *Phaeton* fired on the German light cruiser *Elbing*, which was accompanied by three destroyers.

In an action between the battlecruisers, the *Indefatigable* was sunk by gunfire from the German battlecruiser *Von der Tann*.

The battlecruiser *Queen Mary* blew up and sank after being hit by shells from the *Derfflinger* and the *Seydlitz*; there were few survivors from her crew of 1,266 and the *Lion* was seriously damaged.

In an action between destroyers, both sides lost two ships each.

The Grand Fleet scouting cruisers located the German High Seas Fleet of 22 battleships and their escorting cruisers and destroyers and in an engagement the *Malaya* was damaged, as was the *Seydlitz*.

In an action between the battlecruisers *Indomitable*, *Inflexible* and their escorting cruisers and destroyers and German cruisers, the *Wiesbaden* was sunk and the *Pillau* and the *Frankfurt* were seriously damaged; on the RN side, the cruiser *Chester* was damaged and the destroyer *Shark* was sunk.

The cruisers *Defence* and *Warrior* were sunk by German battlecruisers and battleships. The *Invincible* blew up after being hit by shells from German battleships with the loss of 1,026 crew.

RN battlecruisers damaged the *Seydlitz* and the *Lutzow*, the latter later sinking. The cruiser *Southampton* sank the cruiser *Frauenlob* but was seriously damaged herself.

Four RN destroyers were lost in attacking German battleships, damaging the Dreadnought *Nassau* and sinking the cruiser *Rostock*; the cruiser *Elbing* was sunk in a collision. RN destroyers attacked German battleships, sinking the *Pommern*.

The cruiser *Black Prince* was set on fire by shells from the *Thuringen* and blew up and sank.

By 3.30 am, the German High Seas Fleet was safely on its way back home and arrived in the Jade by 6.30 am.

June
5 The cruiser *Hampshire* was sunk by a mine off the Orkney Islands while on her way to Russia. Among the casualties was Field Marshall Lord Kitchener.

July
1 On the Western Front, the Somme offensive was opened, the final phase being launched on 25 Sept.

August
19 The German High Seas Fleet sailed on a planned raid to bombard Sunderland but it returned to harbour once it was known that the RN Grand Fleet was at sea in force. The German fleet did not venture out again until the surrender. The cruiser *Falmouth* was sunk by the German submarine *U-63* and the cruiser *Nottingham* by *U-52*, both cruisers being part of the RN force that had put to sea to counter the planned German raid.

September
15 On the Western Front, the first tank went into action with the British forces on the Somme.

November
21 In the Aegean, the hospital ship *Britannic*, 48,158 tons (White Star Line), was sunk by a mine west of Port St Nikolo. She was carrying 1,134 people; 21 died.

1917

January
25 The White Star Line passenger liner *Laurentic*, 14,890 tons, on a voyage from Liverpool to Halifax, ran on to a minefield off Malin Head. The ship sank quickly; 354 of the 475 people on board died. The ship was carrying £5 million in gold.

February
1 The Kaiser's order for unrestricted submarine warfare came into effect and the number of sinkings of British merchant ships rose dramatically over the next few months.

March
11 British troops entered Baghdad.
16 On the Western Front, German troops began to pull back to the Hindenburg (or Siegfried) Line.

April
6 America entered the war against Germany.
9 On the Western Front, the Allied spring offensive was launched at Arras, with British troops capturing Vimy ridge.
20 On patrol in the Channel, the RN destroyers *Swift* and *Broke* encountered a German force of five destroyers. The *Broke* sank the destroyers *G-24* and *G-85*.

May
10 After pressure to cut losses to merchant ships by German submarines, the Admiralty introduced the convoy system; the first convoy left Gibraltar bound for the UK. The system drastically cut the toll of British ships.

June
7 On the Western Front, British troops attacked and captured German positions on the Messines Ridge.

July
9 During the night, aircraft of the Royal Naval Air Service attacked the Turkish fleet lying in the Golden Horn off Constantinople. The battlecruiser *Yavuz Sultan Selim* was set on fire, hits were observed on other warships, and the War Office building was hit.
31 On the Western Front, the third Battle of Ypres.

October
16 In Russia, the Bolsheviks took over; the revolution had begun in the March, and in December a peace treaty was reached with the Germans.
24 German forces launched a major offensive in northern Italy.

November
4 On the Western Front, the village of Passchendaele was occupied after a four-month long campaign.

20 British troops carried out a major offensive at Cambrai, the attack being led by nearly 400 tanks.
30 The Germans counter-attacked and drove the British forces back at Cambrai.
December
9 British troops captured Jerusalem.

1918
January
20 The RN monitors *Raglan* and *M-28* were sunk by the Turkish battlecruiser *Yavuz Sultan Selim* and the light cruiser *Midilli* at Kusu Bay, Imbros island, off the Gallipoli peninsula. The two Turkish ships were the former German *Goeben* and *Breslau* respectively, which had arrived in the Dardanelles in 1914 and were sold to Turkey.
31 Units of the RN Grand Fleet sailed from Rosyth for the Norwegian coast. The Fleet comprised battleships, battlecruisers, cruisers, destroyers, and two flotillas of K-class submarines. In the dark, after a steering gear failure, *K-14* hit *K-22*; the battlecruiser *Inflexible* hit *K-14*; the cruiser *Fearless* hit and sank *K-17*; and *K-6* rammed *K-4* which sank.
March
21 On the Western Front, German troops attacked the British lines on the Somme in great strength.
April
23 A RN force attacked Zeebrugge in a bid to blockade the port and put it out of action to submarines. The cruiser *Vindictive* and the River Mersey ferries *Daffodil* and *Iris* landed Marines and Navy men who stormed the guns before the arrival of the blockships. The *Vindictive* was badly damaged by gunfire as she lay alongside the mole. The old submarines *C-1* and *C-3* were used as part of the blockships force but only *C-3* reached her position; the other blockships were the cruiser *Brilliant* and the minelayers *Thetis*, *Intrepid* and *Iphigenia*.

May
10 A RN force attempted to block the port of Ostend; the cruisers *Vindictive* and *Sirius* were sunk as blockships.
July
15 The last German offensive on the Western Front; the second Battle of the Marne, around Reims. After three days, the German troops were in retreat.
August
8 On the Western Front, British troops achieved a major victory at Amiens.
September
19 British troops launched a major offensive in Palestine and soon had the Turkish troops trapped.
October
5 On the Western Front, British troops broke through the German's Hindenburg (or Siegfried) Line.
6 In the Irish Sea, the Orient Line passenger liner *Otranto*, acting as a convoy escort and troop transport, was in collision with the P&O liner *Kashmir*; the *Otranto* was run aground off Islay; 431 people died.
29 There was a mutiny among sailors of ships of the German High Seas Fleet at Wilhelmshaven; the action spread to ships in other ports.
30 The Austrian offensive in Italy failed and turned into a retreat.
  Turkey capitulated.
November
3 The Armistice was signed with Austria.
11 The Allies and Germany signed the Armistice agreement in a railway carriage in the Forest of Compeigne, following Germany's acceptance of the Allies' surrender conditions.
21 In the North Sea, ships of the German High Seas Fleet rendezvoused with RN warships and surrendered, both fleets sailing for the Firth of Forth. Crews of the High Seas Fleet scuttled their ships in Scapa Flow on June 21, 1919.

War diary, 1939-45

1939
August
Between mid-August and the end of the month, 16 German U-boats were on station in the North Atlantic and the North Sea and the German pocket battleships *Admiral Graf Spee* and *Deutschland* had sailed into the Atlantic. By the end of the month, all ships of the Royal Navy's Home Fleet had moved or were moving to their war stations.

September
1 German forces invaded Poland.
2 First British convoy, eight ships, left Gibraltar for Cape Town.
3 Britain declared war on Germany, and a blockade of Germany was immediately ordered.
Passenger liner *Athenia*, 13,581 grt, Donaldson Line, sunk by *U-30* south of Rockall, 112 died, 1,300 survivors. The U-boat gave no warning.
5 First major British troop convoy, 11 ships, left the Clyde for Gibraltar.
6 RN's Northern Patrol, used in contraband control, became operational between the Faroes and Iceland.
Convoys from the Thames to the east coast ports up to the Firth of Forth started.
7 First British trans-Atlantic convoys set out from the Channel and from Liverpool.
9 First troop transport convoys of the British Expeditionary Force across the Channel from Southampton and the Bristol Channel to Cherbourg, Nantes and St Nazaire.
10 The first British ship to be sunk in the war in the North Sea, the steamer *Goodwood*, 2,796 grt, mined off Flamborough Head.
16 First British homeward convoy, 18 ships, sailed from Halifax, Nova Scotia, across the Atlantic.
17 RN aircraft carrier *Courageous*, 22,500 tons, torpedoed by *U-29* and sank within 15 minutes in the Western Approaches. 519 of her crew died.
30 The *Admiral Graf Spee* achieved her first success, the steamer *Clement*, 5,051 grt, Booth SS Co, sunk by gunfire off Pernambuco.

October
14 Royal Navy battleship *Royal Oak*, at anchor in Scapa Flow, torpedoed by *U-47* and sank with the loss of 833 lives.
November
23 While part of the Northern Patrol, the armed merchant cruiser *Rawalpindi*, 16,697 grt, a P&O liner, was sunk in action with the German battlecruisers *Scharnhorst* and *Gneisenau*, south-east of Iceland. Only 37 of her crew were rescued.
On the Shoeburyness mudflats, Lieutenant-Commander J.G.D. Ouvry de-fused a German magnetic mine, enabling countermeasures to be taken on Allied ships.
December
13 The cruisers *Exeter*, *Ajax* and *Achilles* engaged the German pocket battleship *Admiral Graf Spee* in the South Atlantic in the Battle of the River Plate. The damaged German warship put into Montevideo, while the cruisers waited outside. On December 17 the *Admiral Graf Spee* was scuttled off the port.

1940
January
24 First mines of the east coast mine barrier were laid off Spurn Point by the minelayer *Princess Victoria*.
February
16 299 British prisoners taken from ships sunk by the *Admiral Graf Spee* were rescued from the German supply tanker *Altmark* in Jossing Fjord, Norway, by the RN destroyer *Cossack*.
March
2 In great secrecy, the new Cunard liner *Queen Elizabeth*, 83,000 tons, left the UK on her first trans-Atlantic voyage to New York. She had left Clydebank for trials on February 26.
31 German raider *Atlantis*, the first of her type to be ordered to sea, sailed on a commerce raiding voyage into the Atlantic, Pacific and Indian Ocean. The raider was sunk in the Indian Ocean by the cruiser HMS *Devonshire* on November 22 1941.
April
9 Germany invaded Denmark and Norway.

10 The first Battle of Narvik, when RN force attacked German ships in the confined waters at Narvik. Two RN destroyers were lost while two German destroyers and several ore-carriers were sunk.

13 Second Battle of Narvik, with the British force including the battleship *Warspite*. Eight German destroyers were lost.

May

5 RN minelaying submarine *Seal* captured after being disabled by a German aircraft in the Kattegat. She became a German UB.

10 Germany invaded the Netherlands, Belgium and Luxembourg.

Britain's Prime Minister, Neville Chamberlain, resigned and was succeeded by Winston Churchill.

28 As the German advance swept across Europe into France, and Allied troops retreated to French ports, evacuation of the BEF started. Between May 28 and June 4, 338,226 Allied troops were transported from the Dunkirk area safely across the Channel to England. An armada of 'little ships' helped in the evacuation.

June

1 In the evacuation from Southern France, the Orient Line passenger ship *Orford*, 20,043 grt, was lost when she was bombed and set on fire off Toulon.

4 The Allied evacuation from Norway began: between June 4 and June 9, 245,000 troops were evacuated in transports.

8 Operating off the Norwegian coast, the German battlecruisers *Scharnhorst* and *Gneisenau* sank the aircraft carrier *Glorious* and her escorting destroyers *Acasta* and *Ardent*.

A second German naval force, including the heavy cruiser *Admiral Hipper*, sank the Orient Line passenger ship *Orama*, 19,977 grt, on passage to England.

10 Italy declared war on Britain and France.

14 Paris surrendered.

17 Cunard Liner *Lancastria*, anchored about three miles off-shore from St Nazaire, was attacked by dive-bombers. The ship was carrying evacuated troops and the exact numbers on board were not known. Estimates vary between 4,000 and 9,000 and over 2,000 died (again the exact figure was not known).

19 On anti-submarine patrol from Aden, the naval trawler *Moonstone* forced the Italian submarine *Galileo Galilei* to the surface and her crew surrendered. The captured submarine was towed to Aden.

22 France signed surrender documents with Germany at Compiègne, the ceasefire

taking place on June 25.

25 Operations to evacuate Allied troops from France ended.

July

3 Royal Navy attacked French warships at Mers El-Kebir, Oran, naval base.

On passage from the Mersey to St John's, Newfoundland, the Blue Star Line passenger ship *Arandora Star* was torpedoed by *U-47* about 75 miles off Bloody Foreland. On board were nearly 1,300 German and Italian internees bound for Canada, plus a guard of 200 and 174 crew. 805 died.

10 Start of the Battle of Britain when RAF aircraft defeated the Luftwaffe over Britain. The air battle officially ended on October 31 1940.

16 Hitler ordered Operation Seeloewe, the invasion of Britain.

September

2 Agreement signed between Britain and the United States under which 50 old USN destroyers were transferred to the Royal Navy and the Royal Canadian Navy in exchange for use of various bases.

17 Hitler postponed Operation Seeloewe.

23–25 British naval force attacked Vichy-controlled Dakar in a bid to persuade the French warships there to come over to the Free French cause.

October

26 The Canadian Pacific liner *Empress of Britain*, 42,348 grt, in service as a troopship, was set on fire in bombing attacks by a Focke-Wulf Condor aircraft, about 70 miles north west of Ireland while on passage from Cape Town to Liverpool, carrying 223 passengers and 419 crew. After being abandoned, the burning ship was taken in tow but shortly before midnight on October 27, she was hit by two torpedoes from *U-32*. The liner capsized and sank early the next day.

November

5 The German pocket battleship *Admiral Scheer*, hunting for Allied shipping in the North Atlantic, came across a convoy of 38 ships. The convoy escort, the armed merchant cruiser *Jervis Bay*, 14,164 grt, Aberdeen & Commonwealth Line, turned to attack the superior-armed warship while the merchant ships in the convoy scattered. The *Jervis Bay* was sunk with the loss of 191 men but her action allowed most of the ships to escape, only five of the merchant ships being sunk.

11–12 Twenty-one Fleet Air Arm Swordfish aircraft, flying from the carrier *Illustrious*, attacked the Italian naval base of Taranto. The battleship *Conte de Cavour* was sunk and among the warships severely damaged were the battleships *Littorio* and *Caio Duilio*. Two aircraft were lost.

1941

January

10 Part of the naval force giving protection to two convoys heading for the beleaguered island of Malta, the aircraft carrier *Illustrious* was attacked by German aircraft about 80 miles from the island. On fire, badly damaged and with heavy casualties, the carrier arrived in Malta harbour on the evening of January 10.

17 The Blue Star Line steamer *Almeda Star*, 14,935 grt, was torpedoed and sunk by *U-96* about 220 miles west of the Outer Hebrides. All 360 people on board died.

February

13 The German heavy cruiser *Admiral Hipper* returned to Brest after a commerce raiding voyage into the Atlantic. She had left Brest on February 1.

March

4 British-Norwegian commando raid on Lofoten Islands.

11 The Lend-Lease agreement was given US Presidential assent. Under this agreement, the US supplied military equipment to Britain.

22 The German battlecruisers *Scharnhorst* and *Gneisenau* arrived at Brest after a commerce raiding voyage into the Atlantic. They had left Kiel on January 23 and despite efforts by the Royal Navy to intercept them, the two German ships sank or captured 22 ships.

28 In the Battle of Matapan, Royal Navy warships engaged a superior Italian naval force which lost three heavy cruisers and two destroyers.

April

1 The German pocket battleship *Admiral Scheer* arrived at Kiel after a commerce raiding voyage into the Atlantic and Indian Ocean. The ship had left Brunsbuttel in October, 1940, and during her voyage sank 17 ships.

6 Germany invaded Greece and Yugoslavia.

9 The Lamport and Holt Line steamer *Voltaire*, 13,301 grt, converted into an armed merchant cruiser and used as a convoy escort, was on passage from Halifax NS to Freetown when she was intercepted by the German raider *Thor*. After a fierce battle, during which 75 of her crew were killed, the *Voltaire* sank.

11 The eight-month siege of Tobruk began. Allied ships kept the garrison supplied until its relief in December.

16 In the central Mediterranean, the RN destroyers *Janus, Jervis, Mohawk* and *Nubian* attacked an Italian convoy of five ships escorted by three destroyers taking supplies to North Africa. The eight Italian ships were sunk. The *Mohawk* was torpedoed and sank.

25 Off Piraeus, the troopship *Pennland*, 16,322 grt, was helping in the evacuation of Greece when she was bombed by German aircraft and sank after being abandoned.

May

3 In a German air attack on Liverpool, the T&J Brocklebank steamer *Malakand*, 7,649 grt, loaded with ammunition, was set on fire and blew up.

9 In the North Atlantic, the German submarine *U-110* was captured by the RN corvette *Aubretia* and destroyers *Bulldog* and *Broadway*. Vital equipment recovered included the Enigma coding machine and the relevant documents, enabling a major breakthrough into cracking German codes. The U-boat sank under tow.

17 Elder Dempster Lines' *Aba*, operating as a hospital ship and clearly marked with red crosses, was bombed and attacked by German and Italian aircraft off the Crete coast. There were casualties on board and the ship was damaged in the attacks.

20 German troops landed in Crete. The evacuation of Allied troops began on May 27 and ended on June 1 by which time over 18,000 troops had been evacuated by sea.

21 The German battleship *Bismarck* and the heavy cruiser *Prinz Eugen* sailed from Norwegian waters on a commerce raiding sortie into the North Atlantic. The Royal Navy began searching for the two ships.

23 The *Bismarck* and *Prinz Eugen* were sighted by the cruiser *Suffolk* which, with her sister ship, the *Norfolk*, shadowed the two German ships while the new battleship *Prince of Wales* and the battlecruiser *Hood* sailed into position to intercept.

24 In an exchange of gunfire, the *Bismarck* hit the *Hood* which blew up. There were only three survivors from her crew of 1,419. The *Bismarck* had been damaged and later that day, the *Prinz Eugen* was detached to make her own way to Brest.

25 Contact with the *Bismarck* was lost.

26 After the *Bismarck* had been located by an RAF Catalina, Fleet Air Arm Swordfish torpedo bombers attacked the battleship, one torpedo seriously damaging her steering gear.

27 By now, the RN had a sizeable naval force and after daylight, in an engagement of just under two hours with the battleships *King George V* and *Rodney*, the *Bismarck* was reduced to a wreck. She was sunk by torpedoes from the cruiser *Devonshire*. There were 110 survivors.

June

1 The German heavy cruiser *Prinz Eugen*, which had sailed with the *Bismarck*, arrived at Brest, where she remained until February 1942.

22 Germany invaded Russia. By early December, German troops were 25 miles from Moscow.

July

5 Booth SS Co liner *Anselm*, 5,954 grt, was torpedoed and sunk 300 miles north of the Azores while in a convoy. She was serving as a troopship and there were a large number of casualties.

14 Cunard-White Star Line's *Georgic*, 27,759 grt, bombed by German aircraft and set on fire at Port Tewfik. After an epic salvage operation, the liner, which was serving as a troopship, arrived at Liverpool on March 1 1942. After a major refit, she re-entered service in December 1944.

25–26 Attack by Italian explosive-carrying motor boats on Malta harbour. The attack was unsuccessful.

August

10 Britain's Prime Minister Winston Churchill and US President Roosevelt met in Placentia Bay, Newfoundland, for historic Atlantic Charter talks. The Prime Minister sailed to Newfoundland and returned home on the battleship *Prince of Wales*.

24 British-Canadian raid on Spitsbergen when the mines were destroyed. Troops were withdrawn on September 2.

27 The German submarine *U-570* was damaged by depth charges from an RAF Hudson off Iceland, and was forced to the surface, unable to dive. Trawlers were the first naval ships on the scene and the captured U-boat was taken in tow to Iceland. The U-boat entered RN service as HMS *Graph*, being wrecked, while under tow, on the west coast of Islay, March 20 1944.

September

20 The oil hulk *Fiona Shell*, 2,198 tons, which had been at Gibraltar since 1925, was sunk by explosives planted by the crew of an Italian human torpedo operating from the submarine *Sirce*.

29 The first Russian PQ convoy sailed from Iceland, the first homeward bound convoy having left the day before.

October

31 The first US Navy loss in the North Atlantic. The destroyer *Reuben James*, escorting convoy HX 156, was torpedoed by *U-552* and sank.

November

9 An Italian convoy on the way to North Africa was attacked by an RN force from Malta. All seven cargo ships and two of the escorting ten destroyers were sunk.

14 After being 'sunk' by German propaganda on several occasions, the aircraft carrier *Ark Royal* was torpedoed by *U-81* on November 13. Taken in tow, she sank early the next day about 25 miles from Gibraltar.

19 The German commerce raider *Kormoran*, which left Gotenhafen in December 1940, was challenged by the cruiser HMAS *Sydney*, about 200 miles off the western coast of Australia. In a 2½-hour engagement, both ships were set on fire and drew apart. After being abandoned, the blazing *Kormoran* blew up. The *Sydney*, on fire, had disappeared over the horizon and no trace of her or any of her crew was ever found.

22 In the South Atlantic, west of Ascension, the German commerce raider *Atlantis*, which left Germany in March 1940, was sunk by the cruiser HMS *Devonshire*.

25 On passage from Alexandria to support patrols against an Italian convoy, the battleship *Barham*, 31,000 tons, was torpedoed by *U-331* and blew up with the loss of 862 of her crew.

December

7 In a surprise attack, Japanese carrier-based aircraft bombed the US Navy base at Pearl Harbor, Hawaii. Over an hour earlier (but a day difference due to the International Date Line) Japanese troops landed in Malaya and Siam and attacks were made on Hong Kong and the Philippines.

10 The battleship *Prince of Wales* and the battlecruiser *Repulse*, which had been sent from Singapore to intercept the Japanese forces, were attacked by Japanese aircraft and sank off Kuantan with the loss of 840 men.

13 One Dutch and three RN destroyers sank the Italian cruisers *Alberto di Giussano* and *Alberico da Barbiano* off Cap Bon, Tunisia.

25 Hong Kong surrendered. British forces had put up stout resistance to the Japanese attacks since December 8.

26 British commando raid on Vaagso and Lofoten.

30 The first of over 2,700 US 'Liberty' Class ships was delivered. She was the *Patrick Henry*, 7,176 grt.

1942

February

12 With a heavy escort, the German battle-cruisers *Scharnhorst* and *Gneisenau* and the heavy cruiser *Prinz Eugen* sailed up the Channel and through the Straits of Dover on passage from Brest to Germany. British aircraft and ships made determined but unsuccessful attacks.

15 Surrender of Singapore to Japanese.

27 British paratroopers raided the German radar site at Bruneval, on the French Channel coast, and removed vital radar equipment.

27–March 1 In the Java Sea, Japanese warships defeated a British-US-Dutch force. The Allied losses included the Dutch cruisers *De Ruyter* and *Java* and the RN cruiser *Exeter.*

March

7 Japanese forces captured Rangoon, Burma.

8 Dutch East Indies surrendered to Japanese forces.

27 British commando raid on St Nazaire to stop the Germans using the port's huge dry dock for their large ships. The old destroyer *Campbeltown* rammed the lock gates and was then blown up, putting the dock out of action.

April

5 The RN cruisers *Cornwall* and *Dorsetshire* were sunk by Japanese aircraft near Ceylon.

7 The hospital ship *Somersetshire*, 7,456 grt, with Red Cross markings, was hit by a torpedo from a U-boat in the Mediterranean. The ship was holed but reached Alexandria safely.

9 South of Ceylon, Japanese carrier-based aircraft sank the aircraft carrier *Hermes* and the corvette *Hollyhock.*

18 US bombers, taking off from the aircraft carrier *Hornet* about 800 miles from Japan, raided five Japanese cities.

May

2 The cruiser *Edinburgh*, which had loaded 5½ tons of Russian gold, was sunk by the RN to avoid capture. The cruiser had remained afloat for two days after being torpedoed in the Barentz Sea and was part of the escort for a homeward-bound convoy.

6 After a five-month siege, US forces at Corregidor surrendered.

8 The Battle of the Coral Sea, when the US carrier *Lexington* was sunk by Japanese aircraft.

30 First RAF 1,000-aircraft bombing raid against Germany. The target was Cologne.

June

4 Battle of Midway when aircraft from four Japanese carriers attacked the US base on Midway in the Pacific. Three of the carriers were sunk by aircraft from US carriers.

17 In North Africa, British forces withdrew to Egypt, leaving the garrison at Tobruk, which fell on June 21. By June 24, German troops, commanded by Field-Marshal Rommel, were in Egypt.

27 Convoy PQ-17, 35 merchant ships, sailed from Iceland for North Russia.

July

2 The first battle of El Alamein, Egypt.

4 In the belief that convoy PQ-17 was to be attacked off the Norwegian coast by a large German surface force, including the battleship *Tirpitz*, the order was given for the merchant ships to scatter. German aircraft and U-boats sank 24 of the 35 merchant ships.

9 Off Beirut, the RN corvette *Hyacinth* captured the Italian submarine *Perla*, which became the RN's *P-712* and then served in the Greek Navy.

August

7 US Marines invaded Guadalcanal, Southern Solomons. The battle went on until February 1943.

11 The aircraft carrier *Eagle* was torpedoed by *U-73* and sank. She was part of the escort for Operation Pedestal, a specially formed Malta convoy.

15 The tanker *Ohio* arrived in Malta harbour. The tanker had been bombed and was in danger of sinking, being supported by two destroyers. She was part of Operation Pedestal, other losses included the merchant ships *Glenorchy, Wairangi, Dorset, Waimarama, Clan Ferguson, Deucalion* and *Empire Hope* and the cruisers *Cairo* and *Manchester* and the destroyer *Foresight.*

19 British-Canadian troops raided Dieppe, suffering heavy casualties.

September

12 The Cunard liner *Laconia*, 19,695 grt, in service as a troopship, was torpedoed by *U-156* off Freetown. On board were over 1,500 prisoners-of-war. There was a heavy loss of life.

13 The George Cross was presented to the people of Malta in recognition of their heroism during the siege of the island.

27 In the South Atlantic, the German raider *Steir* was sunk in an action with the US Liberty ship *Stephen Hopkins*, which was also lost.

October

9 The Orient Line's *Oronsay*, 20,043 grt, serving as a troopship, was torpedoed by the Italian submarine *Archimede* about 500 miles West-South-West of Freetown. The main party of survivors was picked up after eight days in nine lifeboats.

10 The Canadian Pacific liner *Duchess of Atholl*, 20,119 grt, in service as a troopship, was torpedoed by *U-178* and sank about 200 miles east of Ascension Isle.

The Orient Line's *Orcades*, 23,456 grt, homeward bound from Cape Town with 1,000 troops and civilians, was torpedoed by *U-172*. She was not in danger of sinking so the liner headed back to Cape Town, about 220 miles away. She was torpedoed again and abandoned. Some of the crew remained to try and save her but she was torpedoed yet again and sank. 48 lives were lost.

23 Montgomery launched the British offensive against Rommel at El Alamein. The Eighth Army took only 80 days to reach Tripoli, a distance of 1,500 miles.

29 The Elder Dempster liner *Abosso*, 11,329 grt, in service as a transport, was on her way from Cape Town to Liverpool, with 100 passengers and 182 crew when, about 700 miles north of the Azores, she was torpedoed by *U-575* and sank. 83 passengers and 168 crew died.

30 In the Mediterranean, the German submarine *U-559* was captured by Royal Navy ships. All the confidential books were recovered.

November

7 An Anglo-US force landed in Morocco and Algeria, North Africa.

11 In North Africa, three liners being used as troopships were lost. At Bougie, the P&O liner *Cathay*, 15,225 grt, and the *Awatea*, 13,482 grt, owned by the Union Steam Ship Co of New Zealand, were bombed and sunk, and off Oran, the P&O liner *Viceroy Of India*, 19,627 grt, was torpedoed by *U-407* and sank.

15 In the Pacific, the US Navy achieved a decisive victory over a Japanese force in the Battle of Guadalcanal.

27 At the Toulon naval base in Vichy France, ships of the French fleet were scuttled by their crews to stop them falling into the hands of the Germans who had invaded France.

30 The German supply tanker *Uckermark* (ex-*Altmark*), which had been supplying commerce raiders, blew up and sank while berthed at Yokohama, Japan. The raider *Thor* and the captured British ship *Nankin* were set on fire and lost.

December

1 Soviet forces launched a major offensive between the Don and the Volga rivers.

5 Three naval trawlers, the *Canna*, *Bengali* and *Spaniard* were lost and about 200 people, including dockyard workers, died in a fire and explosion at Lagos. The cause was petrol that had been accidentally discharged from a tanker in the harbour and caught

alight, the flames enveloping the trawlers. A fourth trawler, the *Kelt*, was badly damaged.

6 Shaw Savill & Albion Line's *Ceramic*, 18,750 grt, was torpedoed west of the Azores. There were 656 passengers and crew on board but there was only one survivor, a soldier who was taken on board the submarine.

1943

January

3 In a raid on Palermo harbour, British human torpedoes—or chariots, carrying two men—sank the Italian light cruiser *Ulpio Traiana* and damaged other ships.

14–24 The Casablanca conference between Prime Minister Winston Churchill and US President Roosevelt.

23 The Eighth Army, advancing from Egypt, entered Tripoli. Allied naval force and commandos raided the Norwegian island of Stord and wrecked the iron pyrites mine, putting it out of action for over a year.

March

1–5 In the Battle of the Bismarck Sea, New Guinea, US and Australian aircraft sank 10 Japanese warships and 12 transports in a convoy.

13 The submarine *Thunderbolt* was lost when depth-charged by the Italian corvette *Cicogna* north of Sicily. (The submarine was originally the *Thetis* which sank on trials in Liverpool Bay, June 1 1939, and was salvaged.)

14 Sailing independently from the Middle East to the UK, via the Cape, the Canadian Pacific liner *Empress of Canada*, 21,516 grt, in service as a troopship, was torpedoed by the Italian submarine *Leonardo da Vinci* in the South Atlantic and sank. She was carrying around 1,890 passengers and crew, of which around 1,520 were picked up. Several of the survivors died on board the rescue ships from shark bites.

23 The Union-Castle liner *Windsor Castle*, 19,141 grt, was one of the ships in a large troop convoy about 100 miles north-west of Algiers when she was torpedoed by aircraft and sank.

April

7 In North Africa, British troops advancing from the east linked up with American troops moving from the west in Tunisia.

May

14 The Ocean SS Co passenger-cargo ship *Centaur*, 3,222 grt, which had been converted into a hospital ship, was torpedoed by a Japanese submarine and sank within minutes, about 50 miles from Brisbane. At the time, the ship was fully illuminated with

the Red Cross markings lit-up.

15 In four separate incidents, four German submarines, *U-175, U-182, U-463* and *U-753* were lost.

17 Successful raid by RAF Lancasters of 617 Squadron on the Möhne and Eider dams in the German Ruhr.

June

16 The Eagle Oil & Shipping Co's tanker *San Ernesto*, 8,078 grt, was torpedoed about 1,000 miles south of Colombo by a Japanese submarine and the derelict drifted 2,000 miles before running aground.

July

10 Allied troops landed in Sicily. The seaborne landings were on a 100-mile stretch of coast in south-east Sicily. Among the ships in the invasion fleet lost was the hospital ship *Talamba*, 8,018 grt. A converted British India cargo liner, she was sunk by bombs.

11 Two troopships, the Canadian Pacific liner Duchess of York, 20,021 grt, and the Anchor Line's *California*, 16,792 grt, were sunk by German aircraft off the Moroccan coast.

24 Mussolini was defeated in the Grand Council and was arrested the next day. He was freed from a hotel 6,000 ft up in the Gran Sasso mountains in a daring raid by German troops on September 12 and set up the Social Republic of Italy on September 23.

30 In separate incidents, six German submarines, *U-43, U-375, U-461, U-462, U-504* and *U-591* were lost.

September

8 Italy surrendered.

9 Allied troops landed at Salerno.

11 The Italian fleet arrived in Grand Harbour, Malta.

19 The steamer *Fort Longueuil*, 7,128 grt, owned by the Ministry of War Transport, London, was torpedoed by a submarine south of Chagos Island in the Indian Ocean and sank within minutes. Two survivors on a raft landed on Sumatra on February 1 1944.

22 RN X-craft midget submarines attacked the German battleship *Tirpitz* in Kaafjord, North Norway, causing serious damage.

October

9 In use as a hospital ship at the U-boat base at Gotenhafen, Gdynia, the German 'Strength Through Joy' cruise ship *Stuttgart*, was bombed by Allied aircraft and set on fire. There were few survivors and the wreck was towed out into the Baltic and sunk with the bodies of the victims still on board.

13 Italy declared war on Germany.

23 In an action with German torpedo boats off North France, the RN cruiser *Charybdis* was torpedoed and sank and the destroyer

Limbourne was so badly damaged she had to be sunk by RN forces. 500 men died in the action.

November

20 In the Pacific, US Marines invaded Tarawa, which fell on November 24, this being the latest victory in their island-hopping campaign against Japanese forces.

26 Off Oran, the British India steamer *Rohna*, 8,602 grt, became the first merchant ship to be sunk by a German radio-controlled guided missile. She was carrying US troops and over 1,000 of those on board died.

28 In Teheran, Britain's Prime Minister Winston Churchill, US President Roosevelt and the Soviet leader Jozef Stalin met in a conference, which ended on December 1.

December

2 In a German air raid on the harbour of Bari, Sicily, 17 ships were lost. Several were carrying ammunition and blew up, causing extensive damage to nearby ships. Among those hit was the US cargo ship *John Harvey*, which was carrying mustard gas bombs. Over 1,000 men died as a result of the air attack.

26 Off Norway, a Royal Navy force comprising the battleship *Duke of York*, the cruiser *Jamaica* and four destroyers engaged and sank the German battleship *Scharnhorst*.

1944

January

15 Soviet forces launched a major offensive against the Germans on the Leningrad front.

22 Allied forces landed at Anzio, only 30 miles from Rome. The landing was not the success that had been hoped for, because it was not until May 23 that the troops were able to break out of the beachhead. There were heavy casulaties.

24 Among the ships anchored off the Anzio beachhead was the hospital ship *St David*, brightly lit to show off her Red Cross markings. She was hit by a glider bomb, guided to the target from a German aircraft, and sank.

February

5 In the Pacific, the US advance took another step forward with the capture of Kwajalein, in the Marshall Islands.

28 The first of the US 'Victory' type ships was delivered. She was the *United Victory*, 7,600 grt, and had been launched on January 12 1944. She was the first of over 500 Victory ships.

March

5 In Burma, troops led by Major General Orde Wingate launched an offensive against Japanese forces.

April

14 At Bombay, the Ministry of War Transport cargo ship *Fort Stikine*, 7,142 grt, her cargo including explosives, caught fire while being unloaded. The fire spread to the explosives and the ship blew up sinking many other ships and causing extensive damage to the port area and the city. Thousands of people were killed or injured.

May

27 US and Australian troops invaded Biak Island, in the Schouten group, which eventually fell on September 1.

June

4 Allied troops entered Rome.

The German submarine *U-505* was captured by USN escort carrier *Guadalcanal* and three destroyer escorts north-west of Dakar. (She became a museum exhibit in Chicago.)

6 Allied invasion of France when troops landed in Normandy. The invasion fleet was the biggest the world had ever seen. Over the following weeks, there was a steady build-up of troops and supplies as the Allied forces advanced into France.

9 The first ships that were part of the breakwater for the artificial harbours at Arromanches, Normandy, were sunk in position. Warships and merchant ships were used for this purpose, either being old or damaged.

12 Germany launched the first V-1 rocket attack on London.

15 In the Pacific, US Marines invaded Saipan.

19–20 The Battle of the Philippine Sea, when a US task force defeated a Japanese force, sinking three aircraft carriers.

July

20 Attempted assassination of Hitler by senior Army officers in a conference room at the HQ near Rostenburg, East Prussia. Hitler was slightly injured. The conspirators were executed.

August

15 Allied invasion of the south of France, between Nice and Marseilles.

18 The German hospital ship *Tubingen* was sunk by RAF aircraft in the Adriatic.

22 In Italy, Allied troops liberated the northern city of Florence.

25 Allied troops re-occupied Paris.

27 Off Cap d'Antifer on the French Channel coast, the Royal Navy minesweepers *Jason, Britomart, Hussar* and *Salamander* and the trawlers *Colsay* and *Lord Ashfield* were working on a minefield when they were attacked by RAF Typhoons. The *Britomart* and *Hussar* were lost and the *Salamander* had her stern blown off. 78 men died and

nearly 150 were wounded. The aircraft had mistaken the ships for German warships.

September

17 The Battle of Arnhem began with the launching of the greatest single airborne operation of the war, Operation Market Garden, the capture of three vital river bridges in Holland. Arnhem was the furthest of the three bridges but the British paratroopers were outnumbered and fought a gallant action.

October

4 British and Greek troops landed in Greece, near Patras.

November

1 British commando raid on the Belgian island of Walcheren to open the way to use the port of Antwerp.

12 RAF Lancaster bombers attacked the German battleship *Tirpitz* at Tromso, Norway. The battleship capsized and sank.

22 The Norwegian Bergen Line passenger ship *Rigel*, 3,828 grt, which the Germans were using as a troop transport, was attacked by RAF aircraft off the Norwegian coast and sank. She was carrying 5,100 prisoners-of-war. Only 400 were rescued.

December

16 German troops launched a counter-offensive in the Ardennes, the start of the 10-day Battle of the Bulge.

1945

January

1 Germany began evacuating German nationals fleeing from the advancing Russian troops. Ships sailed between Pillau or Gotenhafen and Lubeck, Kiel or Hamburg.

30 The German cruise ship *Wilhelm Gustloff*, 25,500 grt, which had been used at Gotenhafen as an accommodation ship for U-boat crews, was torpedoed by the Soviet submarine *S-13*. Over 7,000 people she was carrying died.

February

4–12 Britain's Prime Minister Winston Churchill, US President Roosevelt and the Soviet leader Jozef Stalin met at Yalta.

10 Over 3,000 people died when the German cruise ship *Steuben*, 14,690 grt, being used in the Baltic ports evacuation, was torpedoed by a Soviet submarine off Stolpmunde.

19 In the Pacific, US Marines landed on Iwo Jima, Japanese resistance ending on March 16.

March

23 British troops, under General Montgomery, crossed the Rhine between Rees and Wesel.

29 Soviet troops entered Austria.

April

1 In the Pacific, US Marines invaded Okinawa, Japanese resistance ending on June 21.

7 The world's biggest battleship, the Japanese Navy's *Yamato*, 65,000 tons, was attacked by US carrier-based aircraft as she headed a task force towards Okinawa. The battleship blew up with the loss of nearly 2,500 lives.

16 The German cargo liner *Goya*, 5,230 grt, being used by the Germans in the evacuation of the Baltic ports, was torpedoed by a Soviet submarine and sank off Stolpmunde. It was not known for certain how many people she was carrying but the death toll has been put at nearly 7,000.

26 Italian partisans seized Mussolini, and executed him on April 28.

29 German forces in Italy and the Austrian Tyrol surrendered.

May

2 Berlin fell to Soviet troops.

British and Indian troops landed 25 miles south-east of Rangoon, the largest amphibious operation in that war theatre.

3 5,000 people died when RAF aircraft sank the German liner *Cap Arcona*, 27,561 grt, in Lubeck Bay. She was being used in the evacuation of Baltic ports.

4 All German forces in North-west Germany, Holland and Denmark surrendered unconditionally at Luneburg.

7 The unconditional surrender of Germany to the Western Allies and the Soviet Union was signed at Rheims.

8 VE Day.

July

26 Winston Churchill resigned as Prime Minister after the Labour Party won the General Election.

August

6 A US B-29 dropped the first atomic bomb on the Japanese city of Hiroshima. Over 150,000 people died.

8 The Soviet Union declared war on Japan.

9 Another US B-29 dropped the second atomic bomb on the Japanese city of Nagasaki. Over 40,000 people died.

14 The unconditional surrender of Japan was announced by the Allies.

September

2 The formal surrender of Japan was signed on board the US battleship *Missouri*, moored in Tokyo Bay.

Section I
NAVY LOSSES, 1914-18

NAVY LOSSES.

RETURN to an Order of the Honourable the House of Commons,
dated 1 August 1919 ;— *for*,

RETURN " showing the losses of ships of the ROYAL NAVY during the period 4th day of August 1914 to 11th day of November 1918, distinguishing Battleships, Cruisers, Light Cruisers, Torpedo Gunboats, Coast Defence Ships, Monitors, Sloops, River Gunboats, Flotilla Leaders, Torpedo Boat Destroyers, Torpedo Boats, Submarines, Coastal Motor Boats, Patrol Boats, Armed Merchant Cruisers, Minelayers, Aircraft Carriers and Armed Boarding Steamers ; to show, as far as is known, Name, Class, Displacement, Date of Launch, Date of Completion, and Date, Place and Method of Loss.

" And showing the losses of AUXILIARY SHIPS of the ROYAL NAVY during the period 4th day of August 1914 to 11th day of November 1918, distinguishing Hospital Ships, Store Carriers, Mine Sweepers, Auxiliary Patrol Paddlers, Mine Carriers, Fleet Messengers, Commissioned Escort Ships, Miscellaneous Craft, Colliers, Oilers, Special Service Ships, Tugs, Yachts, and other Auxiliary Craft; to show, as far as is known, Name, Class, Gross Tonnage, whether or not commissioned, and Date, Place and Method of Loss."

ADMIRALTY,
August, 1919.

O. A. R. MURRAY,
Secretary.

(*Lieutenant-Colonel Burgoyne.*)

Ordered, by The House of Commons, *to be Printed*,
19 *August* 1919.

Losses of H.M. Ships and Auxiliaries during the War from 4th August 1914 to 11th November 1918.

CONTENTS.

PART I.—WARSHIPS.

I.—List of Losses arranged according to Year and Class.—Warships.

Class.	Name.	Displacement.	Date of Launch.	Date of Completion.	Date of Loss.	How Lost and Where.
		Tons.			**1914.**	
BATTLESHIPS - -	Audacious	23,000	14 Sept. 1912	Oct. 1913	27 Oct.	Sunk by mine off N. Coast of Ireland.
	Bulwark	15,000	18 Oct. 1899	March 1902	26 Nov.	Internal explosion off Sheerness.
CRUISERS - - -	Aboukir	12,000	16 May 1900	Feb. 1902	22 Sept.	
	Cressy	12,000	4 Dec 1899	May 1901	22 Sept.	Sunk by submarine in North Sea.
	Hogue	12,000	13 Aug. 1900	Sept. 1902	22 Sept.	
	Hawke	7,350	11 March 1891	March 1893	15 Oct.	
	Good Hope	14,100	21 Feb. 1901	Nov. 1902	1 Nov.	Sunk by "Scharnhorst" and "Gneisenau" off Valparaiso.
	Monmouth	9,800	13 Nov. 1901	Nov. 1903	1 Nov.	
LIGHT CRUISERS -	Amphion	3,440	4 Dec. 1911	April 1913	6 Aug.	Sunk by mine in North Sea.
	Pathfinder	2,940	16 July 1904	July 1905	5 Sept.	Sunk by submarine in North Sea.
	Pegasus	2,135	4 March 1897	Dec. 1898	20 Sept.	Sunk by "Königsberg" off Zanzibar.
TORPEDO GUNBOATS	Speedy	810	18 May 1893	March 1894	3 Sept.	Sunk by mine off the Humber.
	Niger	810	17 Dec. 1892	July 1893	11 Nov.	Sunk by submarine off Deal.
DESTROYER - -	Success	385	21 March 1901	May 1902	27 Dec.	Wrecked off Fifeness.
SUBMARINES - -	A.E. 1	791	18 June 1913	Jan. 1914	19 Sept.	Accident — cause unknown. Lost off Bismarck Archipelago.
	D. 5	620	28 Aug. 1911	Jan. 1912	3 Oct.	Sunk by mine in North Sea.
	E. 3	791	29 Oct. 1912	June 1914	18 Oct.	Sunk in North Sea—cause unknown.
	D. 2	600	25 May 1910	March 1911	25 Nov.	
AIRCRAFT CARRIER	Hermes	5,600	7 April 1898	Oct. 1899	31 Oct.	Sunk by submarine in Straits of Dover.
ARMED MERCHANT CRUISER.	Oceanic	17,274 (gross).	—	*Built* 1899	8 Sept.	Wrecked off Shetland Islands.
					1915.	
BATTLESHIPS - -	Formidable	15,000	17 Nov. 1898	Sept. 1901	1 Jan.	Sunk by submarine in the English Channel.
	Irresistible	15,000	15 Dec. 1898	Feb. 1902	18 March	Sunk by mine in the Dardanelles.
	Ocean	12,950	5 July 1898	Feb. 1900	18 March	
	Goliath	12,950	23 March 1898	March 1900	13 May	Sunk by T.B. off Cape Helles.
	Triumph	11,985	15 Jan. 1903	June 1904	25 May	Sunk by submarine off Gaba Tepe.
	Majestic	14,900	31 Jan. 1895	Dec. 1895	27 May	Sunk by submarine off Cape Helles.
CRUISERS - - -	Argyll	10,850	3 March 1904	Dec. 1905	28 Oct.	Wrecked on East Coast of Scotland.
	Natal	13,550	30 Sept. 1905	April 1907	31 Dec.	Internal explosion, Cromarty Firth.
RIVER GUNBOATS	Shaitan		No particulars available.		28 Nov.	Grounded in River Tigris.
	Comet				1 Dec.	
DESTROYERS - -	Erne	550	14 Jan. 1903	Feb. 1904	6 Feb.	Wrecked off Rattray Head.
	Goldfinch	747	12 July 1910	Feb. 1911	18/19 Feb.	Wrecked off Orkney Islands.
	Recruit	385	22 Aug. 1896	Oct. 1900	1 May	Sunk by submarine off Galloper.
	Maori	1,035	24 May 1909	Nov. 1909	7 May	Sunk by mine in North Sea.
	Lightning	320	10 April 1895	Jan. 1896	30 June	Do. do.
	Lynx	935	20 March 1913	Jan. 1914	9 Aug.	Mined off Moray Firth.
	Velox	420	11 Feb. 1902	Feb. 1904	25 Oct.	Mined off Nab Light Vessel.
	Louis	965	30 Dec. 1913	May 1914	31 Oct.	Wrecked in Suvla Bay.
TORPEDO BOATS -	064	87	—	Sept. 1886	21 March	Do. Ægean Sea.
	10	245	13 Feb. 1907	May 1907	10 June	Sunk by submarine in North Sea.
	12	263	15 March 1907	May 1907	10 June	
	96	130	—	April 1896	1 Nov.	Sunk in collision off Gibraltar.
	046	79	—	July 1886	27 Dec.	Wrecked by heavy weather while in tow in Eastern Mediterranean.
SUBMARINES - -	C. 31	321	2 Sept. 1909	Nov. 1909	4 Jan.	Lost off Belgian coast—cause unknown.
	E. 10	805	29 Dec. 1913	Aug. 1914	18 Jan.	Lost in North Sea—cause unknown.
	E. 15	805	23 April 1914	Oct. 1914	15 April	Wrecked in Dardanelles.
	A.E. 2	791	22 May 1913	Feb. 1914	30 April	Sunk in action in Sea of Marmora.
	C. 33	321	10 May 1910	Aug. 1910	4 Aug.	Lost in North Sea—cause unknown.
	E. 13	791	22 Sept. 1914	Dec. 1914	18 Aug.	Wrecked off Saltholm, and interned.
	C. 29	321	19 June 1909	Sept. 1909	29 Aug.	Sunk by mine in North Sea.
	E. 7	791	2 Oct. 1913	March 1914	4 Sept.	Sunk in Dardanelles.
	E. 20	807	12 June 1915	Aug. 1915	6 Nov.	Sunk by submarine in Dardanelles.
	E. 6	791	12 Nov. 1912	Oct. 1913	26 Dec.	Sunk by mine in North Sea.
MINELAYER - -	Princess Irene	6,000 (gross)	—	*Built* 1914	27 May	Internal explosion, Sheerness.
ARMED MERCHANT CRUISERS.	Viknor	5,386 (gross)	—	„ 1888	13 Jan.	Lost off Irish Coast.
	Clan MacNaughton	4,985 (gross)	—	„ 1911	3 Feb.	Believed to have foundered in North Atlantic.
	Bayano	5,948 (gross)	—	„ 1913	11 March	Sunk by submarine off Clyde.
	India	7,940 (gross)	—	„ 1896	8 Aug.	Sunk by submarine off Norwegian Coast.

Class.	Name.	Displacement.	Date of Launch.	Date of Completion.	Date of Loss.	How Lost and Where.
		Tons.			**1915,**	
ARMED BOARDING STEAMERS.	The Ramsey	1,443 (gross)	—	*Built* 1895	8 Aug.	Sunk by German auxiliary mine-layer "Meteor" in North Sea.
	Tara	1,862 (gross)	—	„ 1900	5 Nov.	Sunk by submarine in Eastern Mediterranean.
					1916.	
BATTLESHIPS - -	King Edward VII.	16,350	23 July 1903	Feb. 1905	6 Jan.	Sunk by mine off North of Scotland.
	Russell	14,000	19 Feb. 1901	Feb. 1903	27 April	Sunk by mine off Malta.
BATTLE CRUISERS	Indefatigable	18,750	28 Oct. 1909	April 1911	31 May	
	Invincible	17,250	13 April 1907	March 1909	31 May	
	Queen Mary	27,000	20 March 1912	August 1913	31 May	
CRUISERS - - -	Black Prince	13,550	8 Nov. 1904	March 1906	31 May	Sunk in action in North Sea.
	Defence	14,600	27 April 1907	Feb. 1909	31 May	
	Warrior	13,550	25 Nov. 1905	May 1907	31 May	
	Hampshire	10,850	24 Sept. 1903	Aug. 1905	5 June	Sunk by mine off Orkneys.
LIGHT CRUISERS -	Arethusa	3,500	25 Oct. 1913	Aug. 1914	11 Feb.	Sunk by mine in North Sea.
	Falmouth	5,250	20 Sept. 1910	Sept. 1911	19 Aug.	Sunk by submarine in North Sea.
	Nottingham	5,440	18 April 1913	April 1914	19 Aug.	
MONITOR - - -	M. 30	355	23 June 1915	June 1915	13 May'	Sunk in action in Gulf of Smyrna.
SLOOPS - - -	Arabis	1,250	6 Nov. 1915	Dec. 1915	10 Feb.	Sunk by T.B.D. in North Sea.
	Primula	1,250	6 Dec. 1915	Jan. 1916	1 March	Sunk by submarine in Mediterranean.
	Nasturtium	1,250	21 Dec. 1915	Feb. 1916	27 April	Sunk by mine in Mediterranean.
	Genista	1,250	26 Feb. 1916	April 1916	23 Oct.	Sunk by submarine in Atlantic.
FLOTILLA LEADERS	Tipperary	1,737	5 March 1915	May 1915	31 May	Sunk in action in North Sea.
	Hoste	1,666	16 Aug. 1916	Nov. 1916	21 Dec.	Sunk in collision in North Sea.
DESTROYERS - -	Coquette	355	25 Nov. 1897	Nov. 1899	7 March	Sunk by mine in North Sea.
	Medusa	1,007	27 March 1915	June 1915	25 March	Sunk by collision in North Sea.
	Ardent	981	8 Sept. 1913	Feb. 1914	31 May	
	Fortune	1,000	17 May 1913	Dec. 1913	31 May	
	Nestor	1,025	22 Dec. 1915	April 1916	31 May	
	Nomad	1,025	7 Feb. 1916	April 1916	31 May	Sunk in action in North Sea.
	Shark	935	30 July 1912	April 1913	31 May	
	Sparrowhawk	935	12 Oct. 1912	May 1913	31 May	
	Turbulent	1,080	5 Jan. 1916	May 1916	31 May	
	Eden	540	14 March 1903	June 1904	18 June	Sunk in collision in English Channel.
	Lassoo	1,010	24 Aug. 1915	Oct. 1915	13 Aug.	Sunk by mine in North Sea.
	Flirt	380	15 May 1897	April 1899	27 Oct.	Sunk in action in Straits of Dover.
	Zulu	1,027	16 Sept. 1909	March 1910	27 Oct.	Damaged in action and afterwards made into one ship named "Zubian."
	Nubian	1,062	20 April 1909	Sept. 1909		
	Negro	1,025	8 March 1916	May 1916	21 Dec.	Sunk by collision in North Sea.
TORPEDO BOATS -	13	270	10 July 1907	May 1908	26 Jan.	
	11	263	29 Jan. 1907	May 1907	7 March	Sunk by mine in North Sea.
	9	247	18 March 1907	June 1907	26 July	Sunk by collision in North Sea.
SUBMARINES - -	E. 17	805	16 Jan. 1915	April 1915	6 Jan.	Wrecked on Dutch Coast.
	H. 6	434	—	June 1915	18 Jan.	Wrecked on Dutch Coast and interned.
	E. 5	791	17 May 1912	June 1913	7 March	Lost in North Sea—cause unknown.
	E. 24	807	9 Dec. 1915	Jan. 1916	24 March	Do. do.
	E. 22	807	27 Aug. 1915	Nov. 1915	25 April	Sunk by submarine in North Sea.
	E. 18	805	4 March 1915	June 1915	24 May	Lost in Baltic—cause unknown.
	E. 26	807	11 Nov. 1915	Dec. 1915	6 July	Lost in North Sea—cause unknown.
	H. 3	434	—	June 1915	15 July	Lost in Adriatic—cause unknown.
	B. 10	316	7 March 1906	May 1906	9 Aug.	Sunk by bomb from aircraft at Venice.
	E. 16	805	23 Sept. 1914	Feb. 1915	22 Aug.	Lost in North Sea—cause unknown.
	E. 30	807	29 June 1915	Dec. 1915	22 Nov.	
	E. 37	807	25 Sept. 1915	March 1916	1 Dec.	
ARMED MERCHANT CRUISER.	Alcantara	15,300 (gross)	—	*Built* 1913	29 Feb.	Sunk in action in North Sea.
ARMED BOARDING STEAMERS.	Fauvette	2,544 (gross)	—	„ 1912	9 March	Sunk by mine in North Sea.
	Marcella	127 (gross)	—	„ 1887	24 March	Sunk by collision in North Sea.
	Duke of Albany.	1,997 (gross)	—	„ 1907	25 Aug.	Sunk by submarine in North Sea.
					1917.	
BATTLESHIPS - -	Cornwallis	14,000	17 July 1901	Feb. 1904	11 Jan.	Sunk by submarine off Malta.
	Vanguard	19,250	22 Feb. 1909	Feb. 1910	9 July	Blown up by internal explosion at Scapa.
CRUISER - - -	Drake	14,100	5 March 1901	Jan. 1903	2 Oct.	Sunk by submarine in North Channel.
TORPEDO GUNBOAT	Jason	810	14 May 1892	June 1893	7 April	Sunk by mine off West Coast of Scotland.
MONITOR - - -	M. 15	540	28 April 1915	May 1915	11 Nov.	Sunk by submarine off Coast of Palestine.
SLOOPS - - -	Mignonette	1,250	26 Jan. 1916	March 1916	17 March	Sunk by mine off S.W. Coast of Ireland.
	Alyssum	1,250	5 Nov. 1915	Dec. 1915	18 March	
	*Tulip	1,250	15 July 1916	Sept. 1916	30 April	Sunk by submarine in Atlantic.

* Employed as Special Service Ship.

Class.	Name.	Displacement.	Date of Launch.	Date of Completion.	Date of Loss.	How Lost and Where.
		Tons.			**1917.**	
SLOOPS—*continued*	Lavender	1,200	12 June 1915	Aug. 1915	5 May	Sunk by submarine in English Channel.
	*Salvia	1,250	16 June 1916	Oct. 1916	20 June	Sunk by submarine off W. Coast of Ireland.
	Aster	1,200	1 May 1915	June 1915	4 July	Sunk by mine in Mediterranean.
	*Bergamot	1,290	5 May 1917	July 1917	13 Aug.	Sunk by submarine in Atlantic.
	*Begonia	1,200	26 Aug. 1915	Oct. 1915	— Oct.	Probably sunk by submarine in Atlantic.
	*Candytuft	1,290	19 May 1917	Aug. 1917	18 Nov.	Sunk by submarine in Mediterranean.
	*Arbutus	1,290	8 Sept. 1917	Nov. 1917	16 Dec.	Sunk by submarine off Bristol Channel.
DESTROYERS	Simoon	1,072	30 Oct. 1916	Dec. 1916	23 Jan.	Sunk in action in North Sea.
	Ghurka	880	29 April 1907	Dec. 1908	8 Feb.	Sunk by mine in English Channel.
	Pheasant	1,025	23 Oct. 1916	Nov. 1916	1 March	Sunk off Orkneys, apparently by floating mine.
	Foyle	550	25 Feb. 1903	March 1904	15 March	Sunk by mine in Dover Straits.
	Paragon	917	21 Feb. 1913	Dec. 1913	18 March	Sunk in action in Dover Straits.
	Laforey	995	22 Aug. 1913	Feb. 1914	23 March	Sunk by mine in English Channel.
	Myrmidon	370	26 May 1900	May 1901	26 March	
	Derwent	555	14 Feb. 1903	July 1904	2 May	
	Setter	1,040	18 Aug. 1916	Feb. 1917	17 May	Sunk by collision in North Sea.
	Cheerful	370	14 July 1897	Feb. 1900	30 June	Sunk by mine off Shetland Islands.
	Itchen	550	17 March 1903	Jan. 1904	6 July	Sunk by submarine in North Sea.
	Recruit	1,075	9 Dec. 1916	April 1917	9 Aug.	Sunk by mine in North Sea.
	Contest	957	7 Jan. 1913	June 1913	18 Sept.	Sunk by submarine in English Channel.
	Mary Rose	1,017	8 Oct. 1915	March 1916	17 Oct.	Sunk in action in North Sea.
	Strongbow	898	30 Sept. 1916	Nov. 1916	17 Oct.	
	Marmion	1,029	28 May 1915	Sept. 1915	21 Oct.	Sunk by collision in North Sea.
	Staunch	748	29 Oct. 1910	March 1916	11 Nov.	Sunk by submarine off Coast of Palestine.
	Partridge	1,016	4 March 1916	June 1916	12 Dec.	Sunk in action in North Sea.
	Wolverine	986	15 Jan. 1910	Sept. 1910	12 Dec.	Sunk by collision off Irish Coast.
	Surprise	910	25 Nov. 1916	Jan. 1917	23 Dec.	Sunk by mine in North Sea.
	Tornado	1,091	4 Aug. 1917	Nov. 1917		
	Torrent	1,069	26 Nov. 1916	Feb. 1917		
	Attack	785	21 Dec. 1911	May 1912	30 Dec.	Sunk by mine off Alexandria.
TORPEDO BOATS	24	319	19 March 1908	June 1909	28 Jan.	Wrecked off Dover breakwater.
	117	197	18 Feb. 1904	Sept. 1904	10 June	Sunk by collision in English Channel.
SUBMARINE	E. 36	807	16 Sept. 1916	Nov. 1916	19 Jan.	Lost in North Sea—cause unknown.
	E. 49	807	18 Sept. 1916	Dec. 1916	12 March	Mined off Shetland Islands.
	C. 34	321	8 June 1910	Sept. 1910	21 July	Sunk by submarine off Shetland Islands.
	E. 47	807	29 May 1916	Oct. 1916	20 Aug.	Lost in North Sea—cause unknown.
	G. 9	965	15 June 1916	Aug. 1916	16 Sept.	Accidentally sunk in North Sea.
	C. 32	321	29 Sept. 1909	Nov. 1909	24 Oct.	Ran ashore and was blown up in Baltic Sea.
	K. 1	2,650	14 Nov. 1916	April 1917	18 Nov.	Sunk by collision in North Sea.
AIRCRAFT CARRIER	Ben-my-Chree	3,888	—	— 1908	11 Jan.	Sunk in action off Asia Minor.
PATROL BOAT	P. 26	613	22 Dec. 1915	May 1916	10 April	Sunk by mine in English Channel.
MINELAYER	Ariadne	11,000	22 April 1898	Nov. 1899	26 July	Sunk by submarine in English Channel.
ARMED MERCHANT CRUISERS.	Laurentic	14,892 (gross)	—	*Built* 1908	23 Jan.	Sunk by mine off Irish Coast.
	Hilary	6,329 (gross)	—	„ 1908	25 May	Sunk by submarine in Atlantic.
	Avenger	15,000 (gross)	—	„ 1915	14 June	Sunk by submarine in N. Atlantic.
	Otway	12,077 (gross)	—	„ 1909	23 July	
	Champagne	5,360 (gross)	—	„ 1895	9 Oct.	Sunk by submarine in Atlantic.
	Orama	12,927 (gross)	—	„ 1911	19 Oct.	
ARMED BOARDING STEAMERS.	Dundee	2,187 (gross)	—	„ 1911	3 Sept.	Sunk by submarine in entrance to English Channel.
	Fiona	1,611 (gross)	—	„ 1905	6 Sept.	Wrecked off Pentland Skerries.
	Stephen Furness	1,712 (gross)	—	„ 1910	13 Dec.	Sunk by submarine in Irish Sea.
	Grive	2,037 (gross)	—	„ 1905	24 Dec.	Torpedoed in North Sea 8th December and foundered 24th December.
COASTAL MOTOR BOATS.	No. 1	5	—	„ 1916	19 June	Sunk in action off Ostend.
	No. 8	5	—	„ 1916	27 Sept.	Sunk off Belgian Coast to avoid capture.
	No. 11	5	—	„ 1916	2 Nov.	Caught fire in Dover Straits after collision.

* Employed as Special Service Ships.

Class.	Name.	Displace-ment.	Date of Launch.	Date of Completion.	Date of Loss. **1918.**	How Lost and Where.
		Tons.				
BATTLESHIPS - -	Britannia	16,350	10 Dec. 1904	Sept. 1906	9 Nov.	Sunk by submarine off Cape Trafalgar.
LIGHT CRUISERS -	Brilliant	3,600	24 June 1891	April 1893	23 April	Sunk as blockship at Ostend.
	Intrepid	3,600	20 June 1891	Nov. 1892	23 April	Sunk as blockship at Zeebrugge.
	Iphigenia	3,600	19 Nov. 1891	May 1893	23 April	Do. do.
	Sirius	3,600	27 Oct. 1890	April 1892	23 April	Sunk as blockship at Ostend.
	Thetis	3,400	13 Dec. 1890	April 1892	23 April	Sunk as blockship at Zeebrugge
	Vindictive	5,750	9 Dec. 1897	Oct. 1898	10 May	Sunk as blockship at Ostend.
TORPEDO GUN-BOATS.	Hazard	1,070	17 Feb. 1894	Sept. 1894	28 Jan.	Sunk by collision in English Channel.
	Seagull	735	31 May 1889	Dec. 1890	30 Sept.	Sunk in collision in Firth of Clyde.
COAST DEFENCE SHIP.	Glatton	5,700	8 Aug. 1914	Sept. 1918	16 Sept.	Sunk by internal explosion in Dover Harbour.
MONITORS - -	Raglan	6,150	29 April 1915	June 1915	20 Jan.	⎱ Sunk at Imbros in action with
	M. 28	540	28 June 1915	Aug. 1915	20 Jan.	⎰ "Goeben" and "Breslau."
	M. 21	540	27 May 1915	July 1915	20 Oct.	Mined off Ostend.
SLOOPS - - -	Gaillardia	1,290	19 May 1917	Nov. 1917	22 Mar.	Sunk by mine in North Sea.
	Cowslip	1,290	19 Oct. 1917	Dec. 1917	25 April	Sunk by submarine off Cape Spartel.
	Rhododendron	1,290	15 Oct. 1917	Feb. 1918	5 May	Sunk by submarine in North Sea.
	Anchusa	1,290	21 April 1917	June 1917	16 July	Sunk by submarine off North Coast of Ireland.
FLOTILLA LEADER	Scott	1,801	18 Oct. 1917	Jan. 1918	15 Aug.	Sunk by submarine in North Sea.
DESTROYERS - -	Racoon	913	15 Feb. 1910	Oct. 1910	9 Jan.	Wrecked on Irish Coast.
	Narbrough	1,010	2 March 1916	April 1916	12 Jan.	⎱ Wrecked off Orkneys.
	Opal	1,000	11 Sept. 1915	April 1916	12 Jan.	⎰
	Boxer	280	28 Nov. 1894	June 1895	8 Feb.	Sunk by collision in English Channel.
	Arno	550		June 1915	23 March	Sunk by collision off Darda-nelles.
	Kale	545	8 Nov. 1904	Aug. 1905	27 March	Sunk by mine in North Sea.
	Falcon	408	29 Dec. 1899	Dec. 1901	1 April	Sunk by collision in North Sea.
	Bittern	360	1 Feb. 1897	April 1899	4 April	Sunk by collision in English Channel.
	North Star	1,042	9 Nov. 1916	Feb. 1917	23 April	Sunk in action at Zeebrugge.
	Phoenix	765	9 Oct. 1911	May 1912	14 May	Sunk by submarine in Adriatic.
	Fairy	380	29 May 1897	Aug. 1898	31 May	Sunk after ramming and destroying enemy submarine in North Sea.
	Pincher	975	15 March 1910	Sept. 1910	24 July	Wrecked on Seven Stones.
	Vehement	1,300	6 July 1917	Oct. 1917	2 Aug.	Sunk by mine in North Sea.
	Ariel	763	26 Sept. 1911	March 1912	2 Aug.	Do. do.
	Comet	747	23 June 1910	Jan. 1911	6 Aug.	Sunk by submarine in Mediter-ranean.
	Ulleswater	923	4 Aug. 1917	Sept. 1917	15 Aug.	Sunk by submarine in North Sea.
	Nessus	1,022	24 Aug. 1915	Nov. 1915	8 Sept.	Sunk by collision in North Sea.
	Ulysses	1,090	24 March 1917	June 1917	29 Oct.	Sunk by collision in Firth of Clyde.
TORPEDO BOAT -	90	130	—	Nov. 1895	25 April	Capsized and sank in Straits of Gibraltar.
SUBMARINES - -	G. 8	965	1 May 1916	June 1916	14 Jan.	Lost in North Sea—cause unknown.
	H. 10	434	—	June 1915	19 Jan.	Do. Do.
	E 14	795	7 July 1914	Dec. 1914	28 Jan.	Sunk in action in Darda-nelles.
	K. 4	2,650	15 July 1916	Dec. 1916	} 31 Jan.	Sunk in collision in North Sea.
	K. 17	2,650	10 April 1917	Sept. 1917		
	E. 50	807	14 Nov. 1916	Jan 1917	31 Jan.	Lost in North Sea—cause unknown.
	H. 5	434		June 1915	6 March	Sunk by collision in Irish Sea.
	D. 3	620	17 Oct. 1910	Sept. 1911	15 March	Accidentally sunk in English Channel.
	E. 1	795	9 Nov. 1912	April 1913	⎫	
	E. 8	795	30 Oct. 1913	June 1914		
	E. 9	807	29 Nov. 1913	June 1914	3 & 4 April	Destroyed at Helsingfors to avoid capture.
	E. 19	807	13 May 1915	July 1915		
	C. 26	321	20 March 1909	May 1909		
	C. 27	321	22 April 1909	Aug. 1909		
	C. 35	321	2 Nov. 1909	Feb. 1910	⎭	
	C. 3	316	3 Oct. 1906	Feb. 1907	23 April	Blown up at Zeebrugge Mole.
	D. 6	620	23 Oct. 1911	April 1912	28 June	Sunk by German submarine off North Coast of Ireland.
	E. 34	807	27 Jan. 1917	March 1917	20 July	Lost in North Sea—cause unknown.
	L. 10	1,070	24 Jan. 1918	June 1918	3-4 Oct.	Sunk in action in North Sea.
	J. 6	1,900	9 Sept. 1915	July 1916	15 Oct.	Accidentally sunk in North Sea.
	G. 7	965	4 March 1916	Aug. 1916	1 Nov.	Lost in North Sea—cause unknown.
AIRCRAFT CARRIER	Campania	18,000	—	April 1915*	5 Nov.	Sunk by collision in Firth of Forth.
PATROL BOAT - -	P. 12	613	4 Dec. 1915	Feb. 1916	4 Nov.	Sunk by collision in English Channel.
ARMED MERCHANT CRUISERS.	Calgarian	17,515 (gross)	—	Built 1914	1 March	Sunk by submarine off Irish Coast.
	Moldavia	9,500 (gross)	—	„ 1903	23 May	Sunk by submarine in English Channel.

* Date of completion of reconstruction as Aircraft Carrier.

Class.	Name.	Displacement.	Date of Launch.	Date of Completion.	Date of Loss.	How Lost and Where.
ARMED MERCHANT CRUISERS—*cont.*	Patia	Tons. 6,103 (gross)	—	*Built* 1913	**1918.** 13 June	Sunk by submarine in Bristol Channel.
	Marmora	10,509 (gross)	—	„ 1903	23 July	Sunk by submarine off South Coast of Ireland.
	Otranto	12,124 (gross)	—	„ 1909	6 Oct.	Wrecked off Islay after collision.
ARMED BOARDING STEAMERS.	Louvain	1,830 (gross)	—	„ 1897	20 Jan.	Sunk by submarine in Mediterranean.
	Tithonus (late Titania)	3,463 (gross)	—	„ 1908	28 March	Sunk by submarine in North Sea.
	Snaefell	1,368 (gross)	—	„ 1910	5 June	} Sunk by submarine in Mediterranean.
	Sarnia	1,498 (gross)	—	„ 1910	12 Sept.	
COASTAL MOTOR BOATS.	No. 18A	10 (disp.)	—	„ 1917	12 April	Sunk by collision off Belgian coast.
	No. 33A	10 (disp.)	—	„ 1918	12 April	Sunk in action off Ostend.
	No. 39B	10 (disp.)	—	„ 1918	28 April	Accidentally burnt at Dunkirk.
	No. 10	5 (disp.)	—	„ 1916	7 May	Accidentally burnt at Dover.
	No. 2	5 (disp.)	—	„ 1916	9 July	Accidentally burnt in Portsmouth Harbour.
	No. 50	5 (disp.)	—	„ 1918	19 July	Sunk in Heligoland Bight to avoid capture.
	No. 40	5 (disp.)	—	„ 1918	11 Aug.	} Sunk in action with aircraft off Frisian Islands.
	No. 42	5 (disp.)	—	„ 1918	11 Aug.	
	No. 47	5 (disp.)	—	„ 1918	11 Aug.	Caught fire during action off Frisian Islands and sank.
	No. 71A	10 (disp.)	—	„ 1918	15 Oct.	Missing, believed foundered off Belgian coast as result of collision.

II.—Summary of Losses.—Warships.

Class.	Period. 4 Aug. 1914 to 31 Dec. 1914.	1915.	1916.	1917.	1 Jan. 1918 to 11 Nov. 1918.	Total Number lost.	Total Displacement Tonnage lost (gross tonnage in *italics* is additional).
	No.	No.	No.	No.	No.	No.	Tons.
Battleships - - -	2	6	2	2	1	13	200,735
Battle Cruisers - -	—	—	3	—	—	3	63,000
Cruisers - - -	6	2	4	1	—	13	158,300
Light Cruisers - -	3	—	3	—	6†	12†	46,255
Torpedo Gunboats - -	2	—	—	1	2	5	4,235
River Gunboats - -	—	2	—	—	—	2	—‡
Coast Defence Ships -	—	—	—	—	1	1	5,700
Monitors - - -	—	—	1	1	3	5	8,125
Sloops - - -	—	—	4	10	4	18	22,630
Flotilla Leaders - -	—	—	2	—·	1	3	5,204
Torpedo Boat Destroyers	1	8	14*	23	18	64*	52,045
Torpedo Boats - -	—	5	3	2	1	11	2,230
Submarines - -	4	10	12	7	21§	54§	43,649
Aircraft Carriers - -	1	—	—	1	1	3	27,488
Patrol Boats - -	—	—	—	1	1	2	1,226
Minelayers - - -	—	1	—	1	—	2	{ 11,000 *6,000*
Armed Merchant Cruisers	1	4	1	6	5	17	*179,169*
Armed Boarding Steamers	—	2	3	4	4	13	*23,779*
Coastal Motor Boats -	—	—	—	3	10	13	85
Total—Nos. - -	20	40	52	63	79	254	—
Tons Displacement.	124,172	119,890	190,378	103,785	113,682	—	651,907‡
Tons Gross -	*17,274*	*33,564*	*20,068*	*74,132*	*63,910*	—	*208,948*

* Including "Zulu" and "Nubian," damaged in action and afterwards made into one ship named "Zubian" (counted as one lost of 1,027 tons displacement).
† Six Light Cruisers sunk as blockships at Zeebrugge and Ostend.
‡ River Gunboats "Comet" and "Shaitan," tonnage uncertain.
§ Including seven destroyed at Helsingfors to avoid capture.

III.—Analysis of Causes of Loss.—Warships.

Class.	Action.	Submarine.	Mine.	Destruction to avoid Capture.	Used as Blockships.	Internal Explosion.	Collision.	Wrecked.	Accident.	Unknown.	Total.
Battleships	1	5	5	—	—	2	—	—	—	—	13
Battle Cruisers	3	—	—	—	—	—	—	—	—	—	3
Cruisers	5	5	1	—	—	1	—	1	—	—	13
Light Cruisers	1	3	2	—	6	—	—	—	—	—	12
Torpedo Gunboats	—	1	2	—	—	—	2	—	—	—	5
River Gunboats	—	—	—	—	—	—	—	2	—	—	2
Coast Defence Ship	—	—	—	—	—	1	—	—	—	—	1
Monitors	3	1	1	—	—	—	—	—	—	—	5
Sloops	1	11	5	—	—	—	—	—	—	1	18
Flotilla Leaders	1	1	—	—	—	—	1	—	—	—	3
Torpedo Boat Destroyers	16*	7	20	—	—	—	12	8	—	1	64*
Torpedo Boats	—	2	1	—	—	—	4	4	—	—	11
Submarines	3	4	4	9	1†	—	4	4	4	21	54
Aircraft Carriers	1	1	—	—	—	—	1	—	—	—	3
Patrol Boats	—	—	1	—	—	—	1	—	—	—	2
Minelayers	—	1	—	—	—	1	—	—	—	—	2
Armed Merchant Cruisers	1	11	1	—	—	—	—	2	—	2	17
Armed Boarding Steamers	1	9	1	—	—	—	1	1	—	—	13
Coastal Motor Boats	5	—	—	2	—	—	2	—	3	1	13
Total	42	62	44	11	7	5	28	22	7	26	254

* " Nubian " and " Zulu " counted as 1. (*See* Note, p. 7.)
† Blown up at Zeebrugge Mole.

IV.—Classified Nominal List of Losses.—Warships.

BATTLESHIPS.

Audacious.
Britannia.
Bulwark.
Cornwallis.
Formidable.
Goliath.
Irresistible.
King Edward VII.
Majestic.
Ocean.
Russell.
Triumph.
Vanguard.
(13)

BATTLE CRUISERS.

Indefatigable.
Invincible.
Queen Mary.
(3)

CRUISERS.

Aboukir.
Argyll.
Black Prince.
Cressy.
Defence.
Drake.
Good Hope.
Hampshire.
Hawke.
Hogue.
Monmouth.
Natal.
Warrior.
(13)

LIGHT CRUISERS.

Amphion.
Arethusa.
Brilliant.
Falmouth.
Intrepid.
Iphigenia.
Nottingham.
Pathfinder.
Pegasus.
Sirius.
Thetis.
Vindictive.
(12)

TORPEDO GUNBOATS.

Hazard.
Jason.
Niger.
Seagull.
Speedy.
(5)

RIVER GUNBOATS.

Comet.
Shaitan.
(2)

COAST DEFENCE SHIP.

Glatton.

MONITORS.

M. 15.
M. 21.
M. 28.
M. 30.
Raglan.
(5)

SLOOPS.

Alyssum.
Anchusa.
Arabis.
*Arbutus.
Aster.
*Begonia.
*Bergamot.
*Candytuft.
Cowslip.
Gaillardia.
Genista.
Lavender.
Mignonette.
Nasturtium.
Primula.
Rhododendron.
*Salvia.
*Tulip.
(18)

FLOTILLA LEADERS.

Hoste.
Scott.
Tipperary.
(3)

TORPEDO BOAT DESTROYERS.

Ardent.
Ariel.
Arno.
Attack.
Bittern.
Boxer.
Cheerful.
Comet.
Contest.
Coquette.
Derwent.
Eden.
Erne.
Fairy.
Falcon.
Flirt.
Fortune.
Foyle.
Ghurka.
Goldfinch.
Itchen.
Kale.
Laforey.
Lassoo.
Lightning.
Louis.
Lynx.
Maori.
Marmion.
Mary Rose.
Medusa.
Myrmidon.
Narbrough.
Negro.
Nessus.

* Employed as special Service Ships.

TORPEDO BOAT DESTROYERS—cont.	SUBMARINES.	SUBMARINES—cont.	ARMED MERCHANT CRUISERS—cont.
Nestor.	A.E. 1.	H. 6.	Laurentic.
Nomad.	A.E. 2.	H. 10.	Marmora.
North Star.	B. 10.	J. 6.	Moldavia.
*Nubian.	C. 3.	K. 1.	Oceanic.
Opal.	C. 26.	K. 4.	Orama.
Paragon.	C. 27.	K. 17.	Otranto.
Partridge.	C. 29.	L. 10.	Otway.
Pheasant.	C. 31.	(54)	Patia.
Phœnix.	C. 32.		Viknor.
Pincher.	C. 33.		(17)
Racoon.	C. 34.	AIRCRAFT CARRIERS.	
Recruit (1).	C. 35.		ARMED BOARDING STEAMERS.
Recruit (2).	D. 2.	Ben-my-Chree.	
Setter.	D. 3.	Campania.	
Shark.	D. 5.	Hermes.	Duke of Albany.
Simoon.	D. 6.	(3)	Dundee.
Sparrowhawk.	E. 1.		Fauvette.
Staunch.	E. 3.		Fiona.
Strongbow.	E. 5.		Grive.
Success.	E. 6.	PATROL BOATS.	Louvain.
Surprise.	E. 7.		Marcella.
Tornado.	E. 8.	P. 12.	Sarnia.
Torrent.	E. 9.	P. 26.	Snaefell.
Turbulent.	E. 10.	(2)	Stephen Furness.
Ulleswater.	E. 13.		Tara.
Ulysses.	E. 14.		The Ramsey.
Vehement.	E. 15.		Tithonus.
Velox.	E. 16.	MINELAYERS.	(13)
Wolverine.	E. 17.		
*Zulu.	E. 18.	Ariadne.	COASTAL MOTOR BOATS.
(64)*	E. 19.	Princess Irene.	
	E. 20.	(2)	
	E. 22.		No. 1.
TORPEDO BOATS.	E. 24.		No. 2.
	E. 26.		No. 8.
046.	E. 30.	ARMED MERCHANT CRUISERS.	No. 10.
064.	E. 34.		No. 11.
9.	E. 36.		No. 18A.
10.	E. 37.	Alcantara.	No. 33A.
11.	E. 47.	Avenger.	No. 39B.
12.	E. 49.	Bayano.	No. 40.
13.	E. 50.	Calgarian.	No. 42.
24.	G. 7.	Champagne.	No. 47.
90.	G. 8.	Clan MacNaughton.	No. 5Q.
96.	G. 9.	Hilary.	No. 71A.
117.	H. 3.	India.	(13)
(11)	H. 5.		

* "Nubian" and "Zulu" counted as 1. (*See* Note, p. 7.)

PART II.—AUXILIARIES ON ADMIRALTY SERVICE.

V.—List of Losses arranged according to Year and Class.—Auxiliaries.

From 4th August 1914 to 11th November 1918, comprising the following classes :—

Hospital Ships.	Fleet Messengers.	Special Service Ships.
Store Carriers.	Commissioned Escort Ships.	Tugs.
Minesweepers.	Miscellaneous Craft.	Yachts.
Auxiliary Patrol Paddlers.	Colliers.	Other Auxiliary Patrol Craft.
Mine Carriers.	Oilers.	

Class.	Name.	Gross Tonnage.	Date Lost.	How Lost and Where.	C = Commissioned. NC = Not Commiss⁴.
				1914.	
Hospital Ship	Rohilla	7,891	30.10.14	Wrecked off Whitby	NC
Colliers	Buresk	4,337	27.9.14	Captured by "Emden" and sunk by H.M.A.S. "Sydney," 9.11.14, at Cocos Isles.	NC
	North Wales	3,691	16.11.14	Sunk by "Dresden" 360 miles S.W. ¼ W. (true) from Valparaiso.	NC
Admiralty Trawler.	Spider	271	21.11.14	Wrecked at Lowestoft	C

Class.	Name.	Gross Tonnage.	Date Lost.	How Lost and Where.	C = Commissioned. NC = Not Commiss⁴.

				1914.	
Hired Trawlers	Thomas W. Irvin	201	27.8.14	Sunk by mine off River Tyne -	C
	Crathie - -	210	27.8.14		
	Princess Beatrice	214	5.10.14	Sunk by mine off Belgian coast -	
	Drumoak - -	208	5.10.14		
	Ivanhoe - -	190	3.11.14	Wrecked in Firth of Forth - -	C
	Mary - -	256	5.11.14	Sunk by mine off Yarmouth - -	C
	Condor - -	227	22.11.14	Wrecked off Lowestoft - - -	C
	Lorenzo - -	173	17.12.14	Wrecked at Hoy Sound - -	C
	Orianda - -	273	19.12.14		
	Garmo - -	203	20.12.14	Sunk by mine off Scarborough -	C
	Night Hawk -	287	25.12.14		
	Tom Tit -	169	26.12.14	Wrecked at Peterhead - - -	C
	Fair Isle -	192	26.12.14	Wrecked at Sinclair Bay - -	C
Hired Drifters	Eyrie - -	84	2.9.14	Sunk by mine off Outer Dowsing -	C
	Lindsell - -	88	3.9.14		

				1915.	
Ammunition Ship.	Combe - -	2,030	12.10.15	Lost on voyage from United Kingdom to Archangel—cause not recorded.	NC
Store Carrier -	Immingham -	2,083	6.6.15	Sunk in collision off Mudros - -	NC
Minesweepers -	Roedean (ex Roebuck).	1,094	13.1.15	Sunk at Longhope—cause not recorded.	C
	Brighton Queen	553	6.10.15	Sunk by mine off Nieuport - -	C
	Hythe - -	509	28.10.15	Sunk by collision with "Sarnia" near Cape Helles.	C
	Duchess of Hamilton.	553	29.11.15	Sunk by mine near Galloper - -	C
	Lady Ismay -	495	21.12.15	Sunk by mine near Longsand Light Vessel.	C
Fleet Messengers.	Nugget - -	405	31.7.15	Sunk by submarine 45 miles S.W. from Scilly Isles.	C
	Turquoise -	486	31.7.15	Sunk by submarine 60 miles S.W. from Scilly Isles.	C
	Portia - -	494	2.8.15	Sunk by submarine 70 miles South from Scilly Isles.	C
Colliers - -	Ben Cruachan -	3,092	30.1.15	Sunk by submarine 15 miles N.W. of Morecambe Light.	NC
	Oakby - -	1,976	23.2.15	Sunk by submarine 4 miles E. by N. from Royal Sovereign Light Vessel.	NC
	Branksome Chine	2,026	23.2.15	Sunk by submarine 6 miles E. by S. ¾ S. from Beachy Head.	NC
	Bengrove - -	3,840	7.3.15	Sunk by submarine 5 miles N.N.E. from Ilfracombe.	NC
	Invergyle - -	1,794	12.3.15	Sunk by submarine 12 miles N.N.E. from Tyne,	NC
	Lochwood -	2,042	2.4.15	Sunk by submarine 25 miles S.W. from Start Point.	NC
	Mobile - -	1,950	28.4.15	Sunk by submarine 25 miles N.W. from Butt of Lewis.	NC
	Cherbury - -	3,220	29.4.15	Sunk by submarine 27 miles W.N.W. from Eagle Island, Co. Mayo.	NC
	Fulgent - -	2,008	30.4.15	Sunk by submarine 20 miles W.N.W. from Blaskets.	NC
	Don - - -	939	8.5.15	Sunk by submarine 7 miles E. from Coquet Isle.	NC
	Spennymoor -	2,733	28.5.15	Sunk by submarine 50 miles S.W. ¼ W. from Start Point.	NC
	Strathcarron -	4,347	8.6.15	Sunk by submarine 60 miles W. of Lundy Island.	NC
	Inglemoor -	4,331	1.7.15	Sunk by submarine 75 miles S.W. by W. from the Lizard.	NC
	African Monarch	4,003	6.7.15	Sunk by mine entrance White Sea.	NC
	Glenby - -	2,196	17.8.15	Sunk by submarine 30 miles N. from the Smalls.	NC
	The Queen -	557	17.8.15	Sunk by submarine 40 miles N.N.E. from the Smalls.	NC

Class.	Name.	Gross Tonnage.	Date Lost.	How Lost and Where.	C = Commissioned. NC = Not Commiss⁴.
				1915.	
Colliers—*cont.*	Kirkby - -	3,034	17.8.15	Sunk by submarine 23 miles W. by S. from Bardsey Isle.	NC
	Ben Vrackie -	3,908	19.8.15	Sunk by submarine 55 miles N.W. by N. from Scilly Isles.	NC
	Churston - -	2,470	3.9.15	Sunk by mine $2\frac{1}{2}$ miles S. from Orfordness.	NC
	Linkmoor - -	4,306	20.9.15	Sunk by submarine 50 miles W. from Cape Matapan.	NC
	Craigston - -	2,617	4.10.15	Sunk by submarine 35 miles W. from Ovo Island.	NC
	Burrsfield - -	4,037	5.10.15	Sunk by submarine 70 miles W. from Cape Matapan.	NC
	Thorpwood -	3,184	8.10.15	Sunk by submarine 122 miles S. from Cape Martello, Crete.	NC
	Apollo - -	3,774	9.10.15	Sunk by submarine 63 miles S. from Gavdo Island, Crete.	NC
	Monitoria - -	1,904	21.10.15	Sunk by mine $1\frac{3}{4}$ miles N. by E. $\frac{3}{4}$ E. from Sunk Head Buoy.	NC
	Cape Antibes -	2,549	21.10.15	Sunk by mine entrance to White Sea.	NC
	Enosis - -	3,409	18.11.15	Sunk by submarine 150 miles E.S.E. from Malta.	NC
	Hallamshire -	4,420	19.11.15	Sunk by submarine 20 miles S.W. by S. from Cerigotto Island.	NC
	Lemnos - -	1,530	16.12.15	Wrecked at entrance to River Tees	NC
	Knarsdale -	1,641	21.12.15	Sunk by mine $2\frac{3}{4}$ miles E. by S. of Orfordness.	NC
	Lady Iveagh -	2,286	24.12.15	Wrecked at entrance to St. Valery of Cayaux.	NC
	Satrap - -	2,234	31.12.15	Left Barry—not since heard of -	NC
	Tynemouth -	2,222	31.12.15	Left Cardiff—not since heard of -	NC
Oilers - -	Desabla - -	6,047	12.6.15	Sunk by submarine 12 miles E. from Tod Head.	NC
	Caucasian -	4,656	1.7.15	Sunk by submarine 80 miles S. from the Lizard.	NC
	Silvia - -	5,268	23.8.15	Sunk by submarine 47 miles W. from the Fastnet.	NC
	Cymbeline -	4,505	4.9.15	Sunk by submarine 96 miles W. by S. from the Fastnet.	NC
	Balakani - -	3,696	9.9.15	Sunk by mine $\frac{1}{2}$ mile S.W. from S. Longsand Buoy.	NC
	H. C. Henry -	4,219	28.9.15	Sunk by submarine 59 miles S. $\frac{1}{2}$ E. from Cape Matapan.	NC
	Lumina - -	5,950	6.11.15	Sunk by submarine 120 miles S. by E. from Cape Martello, Crete.	NC
	El Zorro - -	5,989	28.12.15	Sunk by submarine 10 miles S. from Old Head of Kinsale.	NC
Tugs - -	Char (ex Stranton)	149	16.1.15	Sunk by collision in the Downs -	C
	Alexandra -	168	28.10.15	Wrecked, Hoxa Sound - - -	C
	Marsden - -	131	1.11.15	Stranded at Suvla Bay - -	C
Yachts - -	Rhiannon - -	137	20.7.15	Sunk by mine off Longsand - -	C
	Clementina -	625	5.8.15	Beached after collision off Tor Cor Point. Salvage abandoned.	C
	Sanda - -	351	25.9.15	Sunk by gunfire off Belgian coast -	C
	Aries - -	268	31.10.15	Sunk by mine off Leathercoat -	C
	Resource II. -	1,000	12.11.15	Destroyed by fire in Southampton Harbour.	C
Admiralty Trawlers.	Jasper - -	221	26.8.15	Sunk by mine in Moray Forth -	C
	Javelin - -	205	17.10.15	Sunk by mine off Longsand -	C
Hired Trawlers	Banyers - -	448	6.1.15	Do. do. Scarborough -	C
	Bedouin - -	188	13.2.15	Do. do. Tory Island -	C
	Blakedown -	207	19.2.15	Wrecked at Crudensgeir - -	C
	Corcyra - -	225	20.2.15	Do. Bacton - -	C
	Tern - -	199	23.2.15	Do. Loch Erribol -	C
	Rondo - -	117	3.3.15	Wrecked, Shetland Islands -	C
	John Sherburn -	244	6.3.15	Wrecked near Dover - -	C
	Okino - -	241	8.3.15	Sunk by mine in Dardanelles -	C
	Manx Hero -	221	10.3.15	Sunk by mine in Mediterranean -	C
	Orlando - -	276	14.3.15	Wrecked at Stornoway -	C
	Trygon - -	289	30.3.15	Sunk by collision in Clyde -	C
	Rhodesia - -	155	19.4.15	Wrecked at Stornoway -	C

Class.	Name.	Gross Tonnage.	Date Lost.	How Lost and Where.	C = Commissioned. NC = Not Commiss⁴.
				1915.	
Hired Trawlers —cont.	Balmedie - -	205	27.4.15	Sunk after collision in Dardanelles	C
	Columbia - -	266	1.5.15	Torpedoed by enemy T.B.D. off Foreness.	C
	Berkshire - -	133	15.5.15	Sunk after collision off Red Bay -	C
	Rolulo - -	170	27.5.15	Wrecked on Obb Rock, Isle of Lewis.	C
	Schiehallion -	198	9.6.15	Sunk by mine in Mediterranean -	C
	Quail III. -	162	23.6.15	Sunk after collision off Portland -	C
	Edison - -	196	6.7.15	Wrecked, Isle of Lewis -	C
	Strathgarry -	202	6.7.15	Sunk after collision at Scapa -	C
	Agamemnon II.	225	15.7.15	Sunk by mine off Shipwash - -	C
	Briton - -	196	21.7.15	Do. do. Longsand - -	C
	Leandros - -	276	6.8.15	Do. do. North Knock -	C
	Ben Ardna -	187	8.8.15	Sunk by mine near Elbow Buoy -	C
	Worsley - -	309	14.8.15	Do. off Aldeburgh -	C
	Japan - -	205	16.8.15	Do. off the Shipwash -	C
	Lundy - -	188	16.8.15	Sunk by collision in Suvla Bay -	C
	Poonah - -	171	18.8.15	Sunk by collision - - -	
	Miura - -	257	23.8.15	Sunk by mine off Yarmouth - -	C
	Dane - -	265	28.8.15	Do. do. Aldeburgh - -	C
	Nadine -	150	1.9.15	Do. do. N. Shipwash Buoy	C
	Malta - -	138	1.9.15	Do. do. N. Shipwash Buoy	C
	City of Dundee -	269	14.9.15	Sunk after collision off Folkestone -	C
	Lydian - -	244	18.9.15	Sunk by mine off South Foreland -	C
	Erin II. -	181	19.10.15	Do. do. Nab - - -	C
	Scott - -	288	22.10.15	Do. do. Tongue - -	C
	Lord Denman -	309	22.10.15	Sunk after collision in White Sea -	C
	Bonar Law -	284	27.10.15	Do. do. off S. Goodwin	C
	Othello II. -	206	31.10.15	Sunk by mine off Leathercoat -	C
	John G. Watson	196	31.10.15	Sunk after collision at Stornoway -	C
	Princess Victoria	272	7.11.15	Do. do. near Ushant -	C
	Xerxes - -	243	16.11.15	Do. do. off Girdleness -	C
	Falmouth III. -	198	19.11.15	Sunk by mine off Dover -	C
	Ruby - -	198	24.11.15	Wrecked in Grandes Bay, Crete -	C
	William Morrison	211	28.11.15	Sunk by mine near Sunk Head Buoy.	C
	Etoile Polaire -	278	3.12.15	Sunk by mine off S. Goodwin -	C
	Carilon - -	226	24.12.15	Do. do. near Margate - -	C
	Resono - -	230	26.12.15	Do. do. near Sunk Light -	C
	Speeton - -	205	31.12.15	Do. do. off Lowestoft -	C
	Responso - -	228	31.12.15	Wrecked at Sanday Island - -	C
Hired Drifters -	G.M.V. - -	94	13.3.15	Sunk after collision off Larne -	C
	Thistle IV. -	71	30.6.15	Sunk after collision off Great Orme's Head.	C
	Waterlily -	82	23.7.15	Sunk after collision off St. Alban's Head.	C
	Great Heart -	78	24.9.15	Sunk off Dover. Cause unknown (probably explosion own mine).	C
	Restore - -	93	12.10.15	Sunk by submarine in Adriatic -	C
	Frons Oliviae -	98	12.10.15	Sunk by mine off Elbow Buoy -	C
	Star of Buchan -	81	20.10.15	Do. do. Nab - - -	C
	Charity - -	102	24.10.15	Disappeared on passage from Great Yarmouth to Poole.	C
	Silvery Wave -	96	13.11.15	Wrecked in Crow Sound - -	C
	Susanna - -	83	14.12.15	Foundered off Milford - - -	C
	Lottie Leask -	94	18.12.15	Sunk by submarine off Saseno Island.	C
	Ladysmith -	89	27.12.15	Disappeared in gale off Milford -	C
	Ferndale - -	75	27.12.15	Wrecked on St. Ann's Head - -	C
Motor Boats -	Dorothea - -	33	21.7.15	Destroyed by fire in E. Mediterranean.	C
	Dolores - -	12	28.8.15	Destroyed by fire, Douglas Harbour, Isle of Man.	C
	Nita Pita - -	—	2.12.15	Destroyed by fire at Poole - -	C
				1916.	
Store Carrier -	Leicester - -	1,001	12.2.16	Sunk by mine 2½ miles S.E. by E. from Folkestone Pier.	NC

Class.	Name.	Gross Tonnage.	Date Lost.	How Lost and Where.	C = Commissioned. NC = Not Commiss⁴.
				1916.	
Minesweepers -	Clacton - -	820	3.8.16	Sunk by submarine at Chai Aghizi	C
	Fair Maid -	430	9.11.16	Sunk by mine near Cross Saud Buoy.	C
	Ludlow - -	810†	29.12.16	Sunk by mine off Shipwash Light Vessel.	C
Auxy. Patrol Paddlers.	Majestic II. -	408	28.7.16	Sprang a leak and sank near Oran -	C
	Stirling Castle -	271	26.9.16	Sunk by explosion, cause unknown, off West Coast of Malta.	C
Fleet Messenger	Clifford - -	487	16.5.16	Sunk by submarine in Lat. 34° 2' N., Long. 27° 32' E.	C
Colliers - -	Dromonby -	3,627	13.1.16	Sunk by raider " Möwe " 220 miles W. (true) from Lisbon.	NC
	Larchwood -	689	14.1.16	Sunk in collision off Bull Point -	NC
	Ashby - -	1,947	15.2.16	Wrecked off Ushant - - -	NC
	Wilston - -	2,611	15.2.16	Sunk by mine 20 miles E.N.E from Wick.	NC
	Duckbridge -	1,491	22.2.16	Sunk by mine 6 miles N. from Straithie Point.	NC
	Kilbride - -	3,712	1.3.16	Sunk by submarine 30 miles E. from Galita Islands, Tunis.	NC
	Rio Tiete - -	7,464	28.3.16	Sunk by submarine 140 miles W. from Ushant.	NC
	Sneaton - -	3,470	3.4.16	Sunk by submarine 35 miles N.N.E. from Cap de Garde. Tunis.	NC
	Adamton - -	2,304	8.4.16	Sunk by submarine 15 miles S. from Skerryvore.	NC
	Zafra - -	3,578	8.4.16	Sunk by submarine 44 miles N. from Oran.	NC
	Margam Abbey -	4,471	10.4.16	Sunk by submarine 55 miles S.W. ¼ S. from the Lizard.	NC
	Ribston - -	3,048	23.4.16	Sunk by submarine 66 miles W. by S. from Ushant.	NC
	Trunkby - -	2,635	27.5.16	Sunk by submarine 50 miles S. by E. from Port Mahon, Minorca.	NC
	Lincairn - -	3,638	27.5.16	Sunk by mine 8 miles N. by E. of the Shipwash.	NC
	Silverton - -	2,682	13.7.16	Sunk by submarine 14 miles N.E. from Canae Rocks.	NC
	Swift Wings -	4,465	1.9.16	Sunk by submarine 18 miles E. from Cape Bengut, Algeria.	NC
	Butetown - -	3,789	8.9.16	Sunk by submarine 55 miles W.S.W. from Cape Matapan.	NC
	Inververbie -	4,309	14.9.16	Sunk by submarine 17 miles S. by W. from Cape Rizzuto, Italy.	NC
	Etton - -	2,831	20.9.16	Sunk by mine in entrance to White Sea.	NC
	St. Gothard -	2,788	26.9.16	Sunk by submarine 12 miles N. by W. from Fair Isle.	NC
	Lotusmere -	3,911	2.10.16	Sunk by submarine 48 miles N.N.E. from Teriberski Lighthouse.	NC
	J. Y. Short -	2,193	4.10.16	Sunk by submarine 80 miles E. from Vardo.	NC
	Iolo - - -	3,903	11.10.16	Sunk by submarine 153 miles N. from Vardo.	NC
	Ethel Duncan -	2,510	18.10.16	Sunk by submarine 40 miles W.N.W. from Noop Head, Orkneys,	NC
	Penylan - -	3,875	19.10.16	Sunk by submarine 5 miles W. by N. from Cape Bougaroni.	NC
	Polruan - -	3,692	25.10.16	Foundered off Whitby - - -	NC
	Oola - -	2,494	26.10.16	Sunk by submarine 22 miles N.E. by N. from North Cape.	NC
	Adriatic - -	3,028	31.10.16	Left Newport (Mon.)—not since heard of.	NC
	Kilellan - -	1,971	8.11.16	Sunk by submarine 17 miles S.W. by S. ¼ S. from Colbart Light Vessel.	NC
	Sarah Radcliffe -	3,333	11.11.16	Sunk by submarine 170 miles S.W. from Ushant.	NC

† Displacement tonnage.

Class.	Name.	Gross Tonnage.	Date Lost	How Lost and Where.	C = Commissioned. NC = Not Commiss⁴.
				1916.	
Colliers—*cont.*	Lady Carrington	3,269	12.11.16	Sunk by submarine 98 miles N. by W. from Cape Ortegal.	NC
	Corinth - -	3,669	13.11.16	Sunk by submarine 28 miles S. ¾ E. from Flamborough Head.	NC
	F. Matarazzo -	2,823	15.11.16	Sunk by submarine 26 miles E.N.E. from Linosa Island.	NC
	Canganian -	1,142	17.11.16	Left Methil for Scapa—not since heard of.	NC
	Mansuri - -	3,227	17.11.16	Left S. Shields for St. Nazaire—not since heard of.	NC
	Reapwell - -	3,417	27.11.16	Sunk by submarine 148 miles N.W. by N. from Alexandria.	NC
	Luciston - -	2,948	29.11.16	Sunk by mine 4 miles E. from Dellamara Point, Malta.	NC
	Zoroaster - -	3,803	29.12.16	Sunk by mine 1¾ miles E.N.E. from Sunk Light Vessel, Harwich.	NC
Oilers - -	Prudentia - -	2,781	12.1.16	Sunk in collision with s.s. " Hermione " of Scapa.	NC
	Goldmouth -	7,446	31.3.16	Sunk by submarine 60 miles W.N.W. from Ushant.	NC
	Elax - -	3,980	10.10.16	Sunk by submarine 70 miles W.S.W. from Cape Matapan.	NC
	Clearfield - -	4,229	21.10.16	Left Invergordon for Hampton Roads—not since heard of.	NC
	Ponus - -	5,077	3.11.16	Wrecked in Falmouth Bay - -	NC
	Murex -	3,564	21.12.16	Sunk by submarine 94 miles N.W. from Port Said.	NC
Special Service Ships.	King Stephen -	162	25.4.16	Sunk by submarine in North Sea -	C
	Remembrance -	3,660	14.8.16	Do. do. in Mediterranean	C
	Fame - -	22 (net)	19.11.16	Sunk by collision in North Sea -	C
	Perugia - -	4,348	3.12.16	Sunk by submarine in Gulf of Genoa.	C
	Kent County -	86	8.12.16	Sunk by mine off Cross Sand, Lowestoft.	C
Yachts - -	Hersilia - -	454	6.1.16	Wrecked on Eilean Chuai, Hebrides	C
	Mekong - -	899	12.3.16	Do. Christthorpe Cliff -	C
	Ægusa - -	1,242	28.4.16	Sunk by mine or submarine near Malta.	C
	Zaida - -	350	17.8.16	Sunk by submarine in Gulf of Alexandretta.	C
	Conqueror II. -	526	26.9.16	Sunk by submarine N. of Fair Isle.	C
Admiralty Trawlers.	Crownsin (prize)	137	4.5.16	Probably sunk by mine near Malta	C
	Carbineer -	276	18.5.16	Wrecked on Crebawethan Point -	C
Hired Trawlers	Mediator -	178	2.1.16	Sunk by mine off Hornsea - -	C
	Courtier - -	181	6.1.16	Do. do. Kilnsea - -	C
	Albion II. -	240	13.1.16	Sunk by mine off St. Catherine's Point.	C
	Rosy Morn -	181	13.1.16	Sunk by mine near Dogger Bank -	C
	Fulmar - -	231	17.1.16	Disappeared off Gulf of Sollum. Probably sunk by British mine.	C
	De la Pole -	255	4.2.16	Wrecked on Goodwin Sands - -	C
	Carlton - -	266	21.2.16	Sunk by mine off Folkestone -	C
	Angelus - -	304	28.2.16	Do. do. Dover - -	C
	Weigelia - -	262	28.2.16	Do. do. Dover - -	C
	Chester II. -	143	29.2.16	Sunk after collision in Firth of Forth.	C
	Manx Queen -	234	1.3.16	Wrecked on Filey Brig - -	C
	Flicker - -	192	4.3.16	Sunk by mine off Dover - -	C
	Calliope II. -	240	5.3.16	Sunk after collision off Butt of Lewis.	C
	Ameer - -	216	18.3.16	Sunk by mine off Felixstowe -	C
	Valpa - -	230	19.3.16	Sunk by mine off Spurn Head -	C
	Corona - -	212	23.3.16	Sunk by mine near Ramsgate -	C
	Saxon Prince -	237	28.3.16	Disappeared in storm off Dover -	C
	Commandant -	207	2.4.16	Sunk by mine off Sunk Light -	C
	Alberta - -	209	14.4.16	Sunk by mine off Grimsby - -	C
	Orcades - -	270	14.4.16	Sunk by mine off Grimsby - -	C
	Lena Melling -	274	23.4.16	Sunk by mine near Elbow Light Buoy.	C

Class.	Name.	Gross. Tonnage.	Date Lost.	How Lost and Where,	C = Commissioned. NC = Not Commiss⁴.
				1916.	
Hired Trawlers —cont.	Klondyke -	155	4.6.16	Sunk after collision near Owers Light Vessel.	C
	Kaphreda - -	245	8.6.16	Sunk by mine near Corton Light Vessel.	C
	Tugela - -	233	26.6.16	Sunk by mine off Lowestoft - -	C
	Hirose - -	275	29.6.16	Sunk by mine off Aldborough Napes	C
	Whooper - -	302	30.6.16	Sunk by mine off Lowestoft - -	C
	Onward - -	266	11.7.16	} Sunk by submarines off Aberdeen	C
	Nellie Nutten -	184	11.7.16		C
	Era - - -	168	11.7.16		C
	John High -	228	7.8.16	Sunk by mine off Mt. Sozonova, White Sea.	C
	Irawadi - -	238	10.8.16	Wrecked on Tigani Rocks, E. Mediterranean.	C
	Neath Castle -	225	14.8.16	Sank after collision with Dutch steamship off Orkneys.	C
	Birch - -	215	23.8.16	Sunk by mine off Yarmouth - -	C
	Italy - -	145	3.9.16	Sunk after collision off Sunderland	C
	Jessie Nutten -	187	4.9.16	Sunk by mine off Lowestoft - -	C
	Loch Garry -	176	13.9.16	Foundered at her moorings at Kirkwall.	C
	Loch Shiel -	216	26.9.16	Sunk by mine off Milford Haven -	C
	Sarah Alice -	299	26.9.16	Sunk by submarine north of Fair Isle.	C
	Orsino - -	172	28.9.16	Sunk by submarine between Loch Erribol and Stromness.	C
	Filey - -	226	2.10.16	Wrecked at Camusmore Bay, Tory Island.	C
	Lord Roberts -	293	26.10.16	Sunk by mine off the Shipwash -	C
	Bradford - -	163	28.10.16	Foundered in gale near Old Head of Kinsale.	C
	Glenprosen -	224	3.11.16	Sunk by mine off Cross Sand Light Vessel.	C
	Knot - -	168	5.11.16	Wrecked on North Carr Rock -	C
	Cantatrice -	302	5.11.16	Sunk by mine near Yarmouth -	C
	Benton Castle -	283	10.11.16	Sunk by mine off Dartmouth -	C
	Anthony Hope -	288	16.11.16	Sunk by mine off Havre - -	C
	Dhoon - -	275	24.11.16	Sunk by mine near Newarp Light Vessel, Great Yarmouth.	C
	Burnley - -	275	25.11.16	Sunk by mine off Orfordness - -	C
	Narval - -	211	26.11.16	Disappeared between Grimsby and Harwich.	C
	Lord Airedale -	215	29.11.16	Sunk by mine near Sunk Light Vessel, Harwich.	C
	Remarko - -	245	3.12.16	Sunk by mine off Lowestoft - -	C
	Tervani - -	457	5.12.16	Sunk by mine off Orfordness - -	C
	Dagon - -	250	8.12.16	Sunk by mine off Royal Sovereign Light Vessel.	C
	Crathie - -	225	16.12.16	Wrecked on Nizam Point, Barra Head.	C
	St. Ives - -	325	21.12.16	Sunk by mine off St. Anthony, Falmouth.	C
	Abelard - -	187	24.12.16	Wrecked off Plymouth Breakwater	C
	Relevo - -	176	30.12.16	Wrecked off El Arish - - -	C
Hired Drifters	Freuchny - -	84	8.1.16	} Sunk by mine off Brindisi - -	C
	Morning Star -	97	8.1.16		C
	Everard - -	82	15.1.16	Sunk after collision off Tuskar -	C
	Chance - -	92	26.1.16	Sunk in collision off Orkneys -	C
	Persistive -	82	9.2.16	Sunk by mine off Dover - -	C
	Gavenwood -	88	20.2.16	Sunk by mine off Brindisi - -	C
	Lily Reaich -	88	26.2.16	Sunk by mine off Durazzo - -	C
	Boy Harold -	74	3.3.16	} Sunk by mine off Brindisi - -	C
	Enterprise II. -	84	8.3.16		C
	Grateful - -	107	25.3.16	Wrecked off Torr Head - -	C
	Hilary II. -	78	25.3.16	Sunk by mine near Spit Buoy -	C
	Lerwick - -	86	27.3.16	Wrecked in Yarmouth Roads -	C
	Pecheur - -	67	3.4.16	Sunk after collision off Smalls Light	C
	Clover Bank -	78	24.4.16	Sunk in action off Zeebrugge -	C
	Au Fait - -	83	25.4.16	Captured by German T.B.D. off Zeebrugge.	C
	Beneficent -	80	1.6.16	Sunk by gunfire near Sarnichey Light Vessel, Adriatic.	C

Class.	Name.	Gross Tonnage.	Date Lost.	How Lost and Where.	C = Commissioned. NC = Not Commiss^d.
				1916.	
Hired Drifters —cont.	Laurel Crown -	81	2.6.16	Sunk by mine west of Orkneys -	C
	Astrum Spei -	82	9.7.16	} Sunk by enemy in Adriatic - -	C
	Clavis - -	87	9.7.16		
	White Rose - -	79	26.7.16	Sunk after collision off Dover -	C
	Rooke - -	84	3.8.16	Sunk after collision off Deal -	C
	Rosie - -	84	26.8.16	Sunk by bomb from enemy seaplane in Adriatic.	C
	Ocean Plough -	99	27.8.16	} Sunk by mine off Lowestoft -	C
	Tuberose - -	67	31.8.16		
	Manzanita -	93	6.9.16	Wrecked on Ugenti Rocks, Adriatic	C
	Girl Eva - -	76	2.10.16	Sunk by mine off Elbow Light Buoy.	C
	Fame - -	68	22.10.16	Wrecked on Hook Sand, Poole -	C
	Waveney II. -	58	27.10.16	Disabled by German T.B.D.'s in Dover Straits and subsequently sank.	C
	Ajax II. - -	81	27.10.16		
	Datum - -	90	27.10.16		
	Gleaner of the Sea.	91	27.10.16	Sunk by German T.B.D.'s in Dover Straits.	C
	Launch Out -	67	27.10.16		
	Roburn - -	83	27.10.16		
	Spotless Prince	85	27.10.16		
	Speedwell V. -	92	28.10.16	Stranded on Splaugh Rock near Greenore Point.	C
	Michaelmas Daisy	99	26.11.16	Sunk by mine near Santa Maria di Leuca, Mediterranean.	C
	Finross - -	78	26.11.16	Wrecked near Gallipoli, Adriatic -	C
	Pelagia - -	84	28.11.16	Sunk by mine off Nab Light Vessel.	C
	Eskburn - -	90	30.11.16	Sunk after collision off Dover -	C
	Adequate - -	90*	2.12.16	Sunk after collision off Kirkabista Light.	C
Motor Launches	M.L. 19 - -	25	31.1.16	Destroyed by fire at Harwich -	C
	M.L. 40 - -	25	18.5.16	Destroyed by fire, Suez Canal -	C
	M.L. 149 - -	37	10.9.16	Destroyed by fire at Taranto -	C
	M.L. 230 - -	37	14.9.16		
	M.L. 253 - -	37	14.9.16	} Sunk in Gulf of Squillace when "Inververbie" was torpedoed.	C
	M.L. 255 - -	37	14.9.16		
Motor Boats -	Allegro - -	7	8.9.16		
	Doreen - -	9	8.9.16	} Lost when "Achaia" was torpedoed outside Oran.	C
	Griffin - -	—	8.9.16		
				1917.	
Store Carriers -	Charles Goodanew.	791	17.4.17	Sunk by mine 3½ miles E.N.E. from Rattray Head.	NC
	Hebble - -	904	6.5.17	Sunk by mine 1½ miles E. from Roker Pier, Sunderland.	NC
Minesweepers	Duchess of Montrose.	322	18.3.17	Sunk by mine off Dunkirk - -	C
	Nepaulin - -	314	20.4.17	Sunk by mine near Dyck Light Vessel, Dunkirk.	C
	Kempton - -	810†	24.6.17	} Sunk by mine off Dover - -	C
	Redcar - -	810†	24.6.17		
	Newmarket -	833	16.7.17	Proceeded to sea (E. Mediterranean). Not heard of since.	C
	Queen of the North.	590	20.7.17	Sunk by mine off Orfordness - -	C
	Marsa - -	317	18.11.17	Sunk by collision at entrance to Harwich Harbour.	C
Fleet Messengers.	Princess Alberta	1,586	21.2.17	Sunk by mine en route from Stavros to Mudros.	C
	Redbreast -	1,313	15.7.17	Sunk by submarine in Mediterranean.	C
	Ermine - -	1,777	2.8.17	Sunk by mine or submarine in Ægean Sea.	C
	Osmanieh - -	4,041	31.12.17	Sunk by mine in entrance to Alexandria.	C

* Estimated.   † Displacement tonnage.

Class.	Name.	Gross Tonnage.	Date Lost.	How Lost and Where.	C = Commissioned. NC = Not Commiss⁴.
				1917.	
Commissioned Escort Ships.	Quernmore	7,302	31.7.17	Sunk by submarine 160 miles W. by N. ¾ N. from Tory Island.	C
	Bostonian	5,736	10.10.17	Sunk by submarine 34 miles S. by E. ½ E. from Start Point.	C
Miscellaneous -	White Head	1,172	15.10.17	Sunk by submarine 40 miles N.N.E. from Suda Bay.	C
Colliers - -	Lynfield - -	3,023	8.1.17	Sunk by submarine 32 miles S.E. by S. from Malta.	NC
	Minieh - -	3,806	9.1.17	Sunk by raider " Möwe " 170 miles E.N.E. (true) from Peruambuco.	NC
	Excellent - -	1,944	9.1.17	Sunk by submarine 40 miles N.W. from Noop Head, Orkneys.	NC
	Garfield - -	3,838	15.1.17	Sunk by submarine 60 miles N.E. by N. ½ N. from Alexandria.	NC
	Artist -	3,570	27.1.17	Sunk by submarine 58 miles W. ½ S. from the Smalls.	NC
	Eavestone -	1,858	3.2.17	Sunk by submarine 95 miles W. from the Fastnet.	NC
	Cliftonian -	4,303	6.2.17	Sunk by submarine 4½ miles S. ¾ E. from Galley Head.	NC
	Lullington -	2,816	8.2.17	Sunk by mine 3 miles E. from Royal Sovereign Light Vessel.	NC
	Foreland - -	1,960	12.2.17	Sunk by mine 6 miles S. ¾ W. from Shipwash Light Vessel.	NC
	Cilicia -	3,750	12.2.17	Sunk by mine 5 miles S. from Dassen Island, Cape of Good Hope.	NC
	Lucent - -	1,409	12.2.17	Sunk by submarine 20 miles E. from the Lizard.	NC
	Okement - -	4,349	17.2.17	Sunk by submarine 140 miles S.E. by S. from Malta.	NC
	Romsdalen -	2,548	17.2.17	Sunk by submarine 10 miles S.W. from Portland Bill,	NC
	Iser - - -	2,160	23.2.17	Sunk by submarine 14 miles N.W. from Belle Ile.	NC
	Burnby - -	3,665	26.2.17	Sunk by submarine 20 miles N. from Cape Falcone.	NC
	Munificent -	3,270	1.3.17	Sunk by submarine 3½ miles N.N.W. from Cape Gris Nez.	NC
	Meldon - -	2,514	3.3.17	Sunk by mine, Firth of Lorne -	NC
	Craigendoran -	2,789	3.3.17	Sunk by submarine 6 miles E. from Cape Sigli, Algeria.	NC
	River Forth -	4,421	3.3.17	Sunk by submarine 60 miles S. by E. from Malta.	NC
	Kincardine -	4,108	3.3.17	Sunk by submarine 20 miles N.E. from Tearagh Island.	NC
	Tandil - -	2,897	12.3.17	Sunk by submarine 20 miles W. by N. ½ N. from Portland.	NC
	Bilswood - -	3,097	12.3.17	Sunk by mine 8 miles N.W. from Alexandria.	NC
	Ambient - -	1,517	12.3.17	Sunk by mine off Aldeburgh - -	NC
	Rose Lea - -	2,830	14.3.17	Sunk by submarine 230 miles W. from Bishop Rock.	NC
	Pola - -	3,061	18.3.17	Sunk by submarine 280 miles W.N.W. from Ushant.	NC
	Trevose - -	3,112	18.3.17	Sunk by submarine 230 miles W. by N. ½ N. from Ushant.	NC
	Vellore - -	4,926	25.3.17	Sunk by submarine 21 miles N.W. by N. from Alexandria.	NC
	Don Benito -	3,749	27.3.17	Sunk by collision in Lat. 49° 35' N., Long. 6° 44' W.	NC
	Wychwood -	1,985	28.3.17	Sunk by submarine 4 miles S.S.W. from S. Arklow Light Vessel.	NC
	Zambesi - -	3,759	1.4.17	Sunk by submarine 15 miles N. by W. from Alexandria.	NC
	Margit - -	2,490	4.4.17	Sunk by submarine 80 miles S.W. ½ W. from Cape Matapan.	NC
	Trefusis - -	2,642	7.4.17	Sunk by submarine 30 miles S.E. from Cape Pula, Sardinia.	NC
	Lowdale - -	2,660	20.4.17	Sunk by submarine 90 miles W. by N. from Gibraltar.	NC
	Plutus - -	1,189	24.4.17	Sunk by submarine 9 miles N.N.W. from Trevose Head.	NC

Class.	Name.	Gross Tonnage.	Date Lost.	How Lost and Where.	C = Commissioned. NC = Not Commiss⁴.
				1917.	
Colliers—*cont.*	Chertsey - -	3,264	26.4.17	Sunk by submarine 4 miles N. from Algiers.	NC
	Beemah - -	4,750	27.4.17	Sunk by submarine 30 miles S.W. by S. from Bishop Rock.	NC
	Alfalfa - -	2,993	27(?)4.17	Sunk by submarine, position not known.	NC
	Hurlford - -	444	29.4.17	Wrecked on south coast of Tiree -	NC
	Gena - -	2,784	1.5.17	Sunk by enemy seaplane off Southwold.	NC
	Herrington -	1,258	4.5.17	Sunk by mine $\frac{3}{4}$ mile E.S.E. from Red Head, Forfar.	NC
	Repton - -	2,881	7.5.17	Sunk by submarine 45 miles S.S.E. from Cape Matapan.	NC
	Broomhill -	1,392	10.5.17	Sunk by submarine 9 miles S.W. from Portland Bill.	NC
	Lady Charlotte -	3,593	11.5.17	Wrecked off Scilly Isles - -	NC
	Millicent Knight	3,563	18.5.17	Sunk by submarine 130 miles E. by S. $\frac{1}{2}$ S. from Malta.	NC
	Porthkerry -	1,920	20.5.17	Sunk by submarine 16 miles W. by S. from Beachy Head.	NC
	Ampleforth -	3,873	21.5.17	Sunk by submarine 15 miles W.S.W. from Gozo.	NC
	Milo - -	1,475	22.5.17	Foundered 10 miles S. from St. Albans Head.	NC
	England - -	3,798	23.5.17	Sunk by submarine 40 miles S. by E. from Cape Bon.	NC
	Holmesbank -	3,051	26.5.17	Sunk by submarine 90 miles N. by W. from Alexandria.	NC
	Boldwell - -	3,118	27.5.17	Sunk by submarine 35 miles N.E. from Linosa Island.	NC
	Islandmore -	3,046	3.6.17	Sunk by submarine 20 miles N.W. from Cape Falcon, Algeria.	NC
	New Zealand Transport.	4,481	14.6.17	Sunk by submarine 8 miles S.E. from Serpho Pulo, Ægean.	NC
	Longbenton -	924	27.6.17	Sunk by submarine 12 miles S. by W. from Flamborough Head.	NC
	Southina - -	3,506	7.7.17	Sunk by submarine 6 miles W.N.W. from Cape Sigli, Algeria.	NC
	Calliope - -	2,883	14(?)7.17	Sunk by submarine in Atlantic -	NC
	Valentia - -	3,242	16.7.17	Sunk by submarine 70 miles W. $\frac{1}{2}$ S. from Bishop Rock.	NC
	Clan McLachlan	4,729	19.7.17	Sunk by collision near Gibraltar -	NC
	Huelva - -	4,867	23.7.17	Sunk by submarine 270 miles S.W. from the Fastnet.	NC
	Purley - -	4,500	25.7.17	Sunk by submarine 210 miles S.W. $\frac{1}{4}$ S. from the Fastnet.	NC
	Monkstone -	3,097	25.7.17	Sunk by submarine 240 miles W. from Scilly Isles.	NC
	Bestwood - -	2,248	29.7.17	Sunk by collision when on passage from Cardiff to Loch Ewe.	NC
	Snowdonian -	3,870	31.7.17	Sunk by submarine 245 miles S. by E. from Sta. Maria, Azores.	NC
	Maston - -	3,881	13.8.17	Sunk by submarine 35 miles E.N.E. from Cape Spartivento, Italy.	NC
	Glocliffe - -	2,211	19.8.17	Sunk by submarine 9 miles E.N.E. from Berry Head.	NC
	Norhilda - -	1,175	21.8.17	Sunk by submarine 5 miles S.E. from Scarborough.	NC
	Winlaton - -	3,270	23.8.17	Sunk by submarine 25 miles W. from Cape Spartel.	NC
	Kilwinning -	3,071	24.8.17	Sunk by submarine 94 miles E.S.E. from Malta.	NC
	Mountpark -	1,376	21.8.17	Sunk by collision 1$\frac{1}{2}$ miles N. of Lundy Island.	NC
	Heatherside -	2,767	24(?)8.17	Probably sunk by submarine in Atlantic.	NC
	Nairn - -	3,627	27.8.17	Sunk by submarine 125 miles N. by W. $\frac{1}{4}$ W. from Ben Ghazi.	NC
	Westbury -	3,097	31.8.17	Sunk by submarine 8 miles S.S.E. from the Fastnet.	NC
	Clan Ferguson -	4,808	6.9.17	Sunk by submarine 15 miles N.W. from Cape Spartel.	NC

Class.	Name.	Gross Tonnage.	Date Lost.	How Lost and Where.	C = Commissioned. NC = Not Commiss⁴.
				1917.	
Colliers—*cont.*	Huusbridge -	3,424	7.9.17	Sunk by submarine 60 miles S.W. by W. ¾ W. from Cape Spartel.	NC
	Hockwold -	1,472	9.9.17	Sunk by collision off the Lizard -	NC
	Sandsend - -	3,814	16.9.17	Sunk by submarine 6 miles S.E. by E. from Mine Head.	NC
	Polar Prince -	3,611	18.9.17	Sunk by submarine 8 miles W. by S. from Cape Spartel.	NC
	Etal Manor -	1,875	19.9.17	Sunk by submarine 7 miles S. by W. from Hook Point, Waterford.	NC
	Kurdistan - -	3,720	20.9.17	Sunk by submarine 27 miles E.S.E. from Pantellaria.	NC
	Rosehill - -	2,788	23.9.17	Sunk by submarine 5 miles S.W. by S. from Fowey.	NC
	Cydonia - -	3,085	27.9.17	Wrecked when on passage from Methil to Brest.	NC
	Nuceria - -	4,702	2.10.17	Sunk by submarine 120 miles W. ½ N. from Cape Spartel.	NC
	Ellerslie - -	299	3.10.17	Wrecked - - - - -	NC
	Bedale - -	2,116	6.10.17	Sunk by submarine 25 miles S.E. by S. from Mine Head.	NC
	Poldown - -	1,370	9.10.17	Sunk by mine 2 miles W.S.W. from Trevose Head.	NC
	Eskmere - -	2,293	13.10.17	Sunk by submarine 15 miles W.N.W. from South Stack.	NC
	Elsiston - -	2,908	19.10.17	Sunk by submarine 150 miles E. by S. ½ S. from Malta.	NC
	Pera - -	7,635	19.10.17	Sunk by submarine 105 miles E. ¾ N. from Marsa Susa.	NC
	Collegian - -	7,520	20.10.17	Sunk by submarine 100 miles N.W. by N. ¼ N. from Alexandria.	NC
	Seistan - -	4,238	23.10.17	Sunk by submarine 3½ miles N. by W. ¼ W. from Flamborough Head.	NC
	Euston - -	2,841	24.10.17	Sunk by submarine 37 miles S.W. from Cape Matapan.	NC
	Redesmere -	2,123	28.10.17	Sunk by submarine 6 miles W.S.W. from St. Catherine's Point.	NC
	Axminster -	1,905	13.11.17	Sunk by submarine off Pakefield Gat.	NC
	Trowbridge -	3.712	14.11.17	Sunk by submarine 12 miles S.E. from Cape de Gata.	NC
	Prophet - -	3,230	14.11.17	Sunk by submarine 3 miles S.E. from Antikithera Island.	NC
	Gasconia - -	3,801	16.11.17	Sunk by submarine 12 miles N.E. ½ E. from Shershel.	NC
	Western Coast -	1,394	17.11.17	Sunk by submarine 10 miles W.S.W. from the Eddystone.	NC
	Gisella - -	2,502	18.11.17	Sunk by submarine 2 miles S.W. by S. from Skokham Island.	NC
	Bilbster - -	4,478	21.11.17	Sunk by collision in Lat. 43° 30′ N., Long. 13° 24′ W.	NC
	Eastfield - -	2,145	27.11.17	Sunk by submarine 7 miles E.S.E. from Dedman Point.	NC
	Groeswen -	3,570	27.11.17	Sunk by mine 3 miles N.E. ½ E. from Sunk Light Vessel, Harwich.	NC
	Bleamoor - -	3,755	27.11.17	Sunk by submarine 4 miles S.S.E. from Berry Head.	NC
	Jane Radcliffe -	4,074	28.11.17	Sunk by submarine 2 miles S.W. from Antimilo.	NC
	Ilvington Court	4,217	6.12.17	Sunk by submarine 8 miles N.W. by N. from Shershel.	NC
	Venetia - -	3,596	9.12.17	Sunk by submarine 3 miles N.N.W. from Whitby Rock buoy.	NC
	Persier - -	3,874	11.12.17	Sunk by submarine 50 miles E. from Cape Spartivento, Italy.	NC
	Charleston -	1,866	12.12.17	Sunk by submarine 30 miles W. from the Smalls.	NC
	Bangarth - -	1,872	13.12.17	Sunk by submarine 13 miles N.N.E. from the Tyne.	NC
	Arnewood -	2,259	13.12.17	Sunk by mine 4 miles E.S.E. from Sleat Point, Skye.	NC
	Greenhill - -	1,900	16.12.17	Sunk by collision off Long Sand -	NC

Class.	Name.	Gross Tonnage.	Date Lost.	How Lost and Where.	C = Commissioned. NC = Not Commiss⁴.
				1917.	
Colliers—*cont.*	Argo -	3,071	24.12.17	Sunk by submarine 18 miles N.W. from Cape Tenez.	NC
	Turnbridge -	2,874	24.12.17	Sunk by submarine 34 miles N.E. by N. from Cape Ivi.	NC
	Cliftondale -	3,811	25.12.17	Sunk by submarine 36 miles E. by N. $\frac{1}{2}$ N. from Cape Tenez.	NC
	Lord Derby -	3,757	28.12.17	Sunk by submarine 7 miles S.W. by S. from St. Ann's Head.	NC
	Clara -	2,425	28.12.17	Sunk by submarine 1$\frac{1}{2}$ miles S.S.W. from the Runnelstone.	NC
	Hercules - -	1,295	30.12.17	Sunk by submarine 3 miles E.N.E. from Whitby.	NC
Oilers - -	El Toro - -	5,958	2.1.17	Wrecked on Blasket Island - -	NC
	Palmleaf -	5,489	4.2.17	Sunk by submarine 230 miles W. from the Fastnet.	NC
	Turritella - -	5,528	27.2.17	Captured by raider "Wolf." Scuttled 4.4.17 Indian Ocean.	NC
	Gafsa -	3,974	28.3.17	Sunk by submarine 10 miles S.E. $\frac{1}{2}$ S. from Kinsale Head.	NC
	Rosalind -	6,535	6.4.17	Sunk by submarine 180 miles W.N.W. from the Fastnet.	NC
	Powhatan -	6,117	6.4.17	Sunk by submarine 25 miles N. by W. from N. Rona.	NC
	Telena -	4,778	21.4.17	Sunk by submarine 170 miles W.N.W. from the Fastnet.	NC
	Bullmouth -	4,018	28.4.17	Sunk by submarine 125 miles N.W. by N. from Tory Island.	NC
	Teakwood -	5,315	28.4.17	Sunk by submarine 26 miles S.W. by W. from Sapienza Island.	NC
	British Sun -	5,565	1.5.17	Sunk by submarine 230 miles E.S.E. from Malta.	NC
	Sebastian - -	3,110	10.5.17	Lost by fire off Nantucket - -	NC
	San Onofre	9,717	12.5.17	Sunk by submarine 64 miles N.W. $\frac{1}{2}$ N. from the Skelligs.	NC
	Ashleaf -	5,768	29.5.17	Sunk by submarine 150 miles W. from Bishop Rock.	NC
	Wapello -	5,576	15.6.17	Sunk by submarine 14 miles W.S.W. from Owers Light Vessel.	NC
	Fornebo -	4,259	17.6.17	Sunk by submarine 4 miles N. from Cape Wrath.	NC
	Batoun -	4,054	19.6.17	Sunk by submarine 6 miles S. from the Fastnet.	NC
	Oakleaf -	8,106	25.7.17	Sunk by submarine 64 miles N.W. $\frac{1}{4}$ N. from Butt of Lewis.	NC
	Bulysses -	6,127	20.8.17	Sunk by submarine 145 miles W.N.W. from the Butt of Lewis.	NC
	Echunga -	6,285	5.9.17	Sunk by submarine 40 miles N. by E. from Ushant.	NC
	Mira -	3,700	11.10.17	Sunk by mine 4 miles S.W. $\frac{1}{2}$ W. from Beachy Head.	NC
	Derbent -	3,178	30.11.17	Sunk by submarine 6 miles N E. by E. from Lynas Point.	NC
Special Service Ships.	Lady Olive -	701	19.2.17	Sunk by submarine in English Channel.	C
	Warner -	1,273	13.3.17	Sunk by submarine off West Coast of Ireland.	C
	Lady Patricia -	1,372	20.5.17	Sunk by submarine in Atlantic -	C
	Zylpha -	2,917	15.6.17	Sunk by submarine off S.W. of Ireland.	C
	Bayard -	220	29.6.17	Sunk by collision in English Channel.	C
	Mona -	Not known	4.7.17	Blown up to avoid capture in Mediterranean off Cape Passaro.	C
	Asama -	284	16.7.17	Sunk by submarine west of Ushant	C
	Bracondale -	2,095	7.8.17	Sunk by submarine in Atlantic -	C
	Dunraven -	3,117	10.8.17	Torpedoed by submarine, then sunk in tow at entrance to English Channel.	C
	Else -	227	14.8.17	Sunk by submarine in Atlantic -	C
	Ethel and Millie	Not known	15.8.17	Sunk by submarine in North Sea -	C
	Nelson - -	34	15.8.17	Sunk by submarine in North Sea -	C
	Bradford City -	3,683	16.8.17	Sunk by submarine in Straits of Messina.	C

Class.	Name.	Gross Tonnage.	Date Lost.	How Lost and Where.	C = Commissioned. NC = Not Commiss⁴.
Special Service Ships—*cont.*	Vala - -	1,016	21.8.17	1917. Probably sunk by submarine ; last reported Lat. 47° N., Long. 9° 32′ W.	C
	Glenfoyle - -	1,680	18.9.17	Sunk by submarine in Atlantic -	C
	Peveril - -	1,459	6.11.17	Sunk by submarine outside Straits of Gibraltar.	C
	Penshurst -	1,191	25.12.17	Sunk by submarine off Bristol Channel.	C
Tug - -	Jack - -	360	9.8.17	Stranded off River Tyne - -	C
Yachts - -	Verona - -	437	24.2.17	Sunk by mine off Portmahomack -	C
	Zarefah - -	279	8.5.17	Sunk by mine off Mull Head, Deer Ness.	C
	Kethailes -	611	11.10.17	Sunk after collision off Blackwater Lightship.	C
Admiralty Trawlers.	Charles Astie -	295	26.6.17	Sunk by mine off Fanad Point, Lough Swilly.	C
	Benjamin Stevenson.	255	18.8.17	Sunk by submarine 40 miles E. of Fetlar, Shetlands.	C
	James Seckar -	255	25.9.17	Disappeared at sea ; last seen Lat. 46° 30′ N., Long. 12° 00′ W	C
	Charlsin (prize)	241	30.9.17	Sunk by submarine 8 miles N. of Marsa Matruh, Mediterranean.	C
Hired Trawlers	Sapper - -	276	29.12.17	Disappeared off Owers Light Vessel	C
	Teal - -	165	2.1.17	Wrecked off Buckie - - -	C
	Donside - -	182	7.1.17	Sunk by mine off Lowestoft - -	C
	Amplify - -	342	17.1.17	Wrecked at Skeirascape, Castlebay	C
	New Comet -	177	20.1.17	Sunk by mine off Orfordness -	C
	Jacamar - -	293	28.1.17	Sunk after collision off Folkestone Southgate Light Vessel.	C
	Holdene - -	274	2.2.17	Sunk by mine off Orfordness - -	C
	Cotsmuir - -	242	2.2.17	Disappeared on passage from Tyne to Humber.	C
	Longset - -	275	6.2.17	Sunk by mine off Nells Point -	C
	Yesso - -	229	9.2.17	Sunk by mine off Aberdeen - -	C
	Euston - -	209	12.2.17	Sunk by mine off Hartlepool - -	C
	Sisters Melville	260	13.2.17	Sunk by mine near Aldeburgh -	C
	Recepto - -	245	16.2.17	Sunk by mine off Longscar Buoy, Tees Bay.	C
	Clifton - -	242	18.2.17	Sunk by mine off Daunt Light Vessel.	C
	Hawk - -	243	17.2.17	Sunk by submarine 120 miles S.E. of Malta.	C
	Picton Castle -	245	19.2.17	Sunk by mine off Dartmouth Harbour.	C
	Evadne - -	189	27.2.17	Sunk by mine off Owers Light Vessel	C
	Northumbria -	211	3.3.17	Sunk by mine near May Island, Firth of Forth.	C
	Vivanti - -	226	7.3.17	Foundered off Fairlight, Hastings -	C
	Caledonia -	161	17.3 17	Sunk by submarine off Newton, Northumberland.	NC
	Evangel - -	197	25.3.17	Sunk by mine off Milford Haven -	C
	Christopher -	316	30.3.17	Sunk by mine off Southwold -	C
	Strathrannoch -	215	6.4.17	Sunk by mine off St. Abbs Head -	C
	Orthos - -	218	9.4.17	Sunk by mine off Lowestoft - -	C
	Amy - -	270	11.4.17	Sunk by mine off Havre - -	C
	Pitstruan - -	206	13.4.17	Sunk by mine off Nosshead Light-house, Wick.	C
	Star of Freedom	258	19.4.17	Sunk by mine off Trevose Head -	C
	Lobelia II. -	184	19.4.17	Sunk by mine off Fanad Point, Lough Swilly.	C
	Loch Eye -	225	20.4.17	Sunk by mine off Dunmore - -	C
	Othonna - -	180	20.4.17	Sunk by mine off Fife Ness - -	C
	Ruthin Castle -	275	21.4.17	Sunk by mine off Skinningrove, Yorkshire.	C
	Rose II. -	213	23.4.17	Sunk by mine in Belfast Lough -	C
	Margate - -	161	24.4.17	Sunk by submarine off Spurn Point	C
	Repro - -	230	26.4.17	Sunk by mine off Tod Head - -	C
	Agile - -	246	27.4.17	Sunk by mine off Sunk Head Light Vessel, Harwich.	C
	Arfon - -	227	30.4.17	Sunk by mine off St. Albans Head	C
	Lord Salisbury -	285	4.5.17	Sunk by mine off Eros Island, Salonika.	C

Class.	Name.	Gross Tonnage.	Date Lost.	How Lost and Where.	C = Commissioned. NC = Not Commiss^{d.}
				1917.	
Hired Trawlers —cont.	Lord Ridley	215	10.5.17	Sunk by mine off Whitby	C
	Bracklyn	303	11.5.17	Sunk by mine off Yarmouth	C
	Lucknow	171	18.5.17	Sunk by mine off Portsmouth	C
	Senator	211	21.5.17	Sunk by mine off Tory Island	C
	Epworth	223	22.5.17	Sunk after collision off East Coast	C
	Merse	296	22.5.17	Sunk by mine off Garroch Head, Bute.	C
	Tettenhall	227	23.5.17	Sunk by mine off Lowestoft	C
	Ina William	337	30.5.17	Sunk by mine off Bull Light, Berehaven.	C
	Carew Castle	256	12.6.17	Sunk by mine off Hartland Point	C
	Towhee	199	15.6.17	Disappeared while on escort duty in English Channel.	C
	Fraser	310	17.6.17	Sunk by mine off Boulogne	C
	Bega	318	18.6.17	Sunk by submarine 40 miles N. of Muckle Flugga.	C
	Borneo	211	18.6.17	Sunk by mine off Beachy Head	C
	Corientes	280	23.6.17	Sunk by mine off Malin Head	C
	Taipo	247	24.6.17	Sunk by mine off Royal Sovereign Light Vessel.	C
	Gelsina	227	25.6.17	Sunk by mine off Girdleness	C
	Drake II.	207	3.7.17	Wrecked in Garinish Bay, Kenmare River.	C
	Kelvin	322	7.7.17	Sunk by mine off Harwich	C
	Vale of Leven	223	10.7.17	Sunk after collision off Worthing	C
	George Milburn	235	12.7.17	Sunk by mine off Dunmore	C
	Robert Smith	211	20.7.17	Disappeared in Lat. 59° 14′ N., Long. 9° 40′ W. (approx.).	C
	Orphesia	273	22.7.17	Sank after striking submerged wreck off Alexandria.	C
	Bovic	162	5.8.17	Sunk after collision 3 miles S.E. of Souter Point.	C
	Jay	144	11.8.17	Sunk by submarine off Southwold	C
	Kirkland	224	20.8.17	Sunk by mine off Fugla Skerry, Papastour, Shetlands.	C
	Sophron	195	22.8.17	Sunk by mine off Firth of Tay	C
	Eros	286	5.9.17	Sunk by mine off Felixstowe	C
	Helgian	220	6.9.17	Sunk by mine in Gulf of Ruphani, Ægean Sea.	C
	By George	225	7.9.17	Sunk by mine in Gulf of Ruphani, Ægean Sea.	C
	Loch Ard	225	10.9.17	Sunk by mine off Lowestoft	C
	Asia	309	12.9.17	Sunk by mine off Bressay Islands, Shetlands.	C
	Ben Heilem	196	8.10.17	Wrecked off Berwick	C
	Waltham	161	10.10.17	Disappeared off Isle of Man (presumed sunk by submarine).	C
	Clyde	146	14.10.17	Sunk after collision off Sidmouth	C
	Ruby	251	17.10.17	Sunk by submarine off Ushant	C
	Vitality	262	20.10.17	Sunk by mine off Orfordness	C
	Thomas Stratten	309	20.10.17	Sunk by mine off Butt of Lewis	C
	Earl Lennox	226	23.10.17	Sunk by mine off entrance to Sound of Islay.	C
	Strymon	198	27.10.17	Sunk by mine off Shipwash Light Vessel.	C
	Thuringia	297	11.11.17	Blown up off Youghal (presumed torpedoed).	C
	Newbridge	228	19.11.17	Sunk after collision off Prawle Point.	C
	Morococola	265	19.11.17	Sunk by mine off Daunt Rock Light Vessel.	C
	Lord Grey	215	2.12.17	Wrecked on La Barrier Shoal, Cape Gris Nez.	C
	Apley	250	6.2.17	Sunk by mine off E. end of Isle of Wight.	C
	Commander Fullerton.	227	12.12.17	⎫ Sunk by enemy destroyer in North Sea.	
	Livingstone	213	12.12.17	⎬	C
	Lord Alverstone	247	12.12.17	⎪	
	Tokio	295	12.12.17	⎭	
	Duster	192	17.12.17	Wrecked off Scratten Cove near Portreath.	C

Class.	Name.	Gross Tonnage.	Date Lost.	How Lost and Where.	C = Commissioned. NC = Not Commiss⁴.
				1917.	
Hired Trawlers —cont.	Ocean Scout I. -	200	21.12.17	Sunk after collision off Inisheer Light, W. Coast of Ireland.	C
Hired Drifters -	Cape Colony -	82	8.1.17	Sunk by mine off Harwich - -	C
	G. S. P. - -	100	2.2.17	Sunk after collision 6 miles south of Owers Light Vessel.	C
	Aivern - -	72	8.2.17	Foundered in English Channel while on passage from Mediterranean.	C
	Gracie - -	83	10.2.17	Sunk after collision off Tongue Light Vessel.	C
	Campania II. -	90	5.3.17	Disappeared in gale off St. Abbs Head.	C
	Energy - -	45	5.3.17	Wrecked in Peterhead Bay - -	NC
	Protect - -	98	16.3.17	Sunk by mine off Dover - -	C
	Gowan - -	45	17.3.17	Sunk by submarine off Newton, Northumberland.	NC
	Forward III. -	89	31.3.17	Sunk by mine off the Shipwash -	C
	Plantin - -	84	26.4.17	Sunk by mine off Staudfast Point -	C
	Admirable -	90	15.5.17		C
	Avondale - -	80	15.5.17		C
	Coral Haven -	82	15.5.17		C
	Craignoon -	77	15.5.17		C
	Felicitas - -	67	15.5.17		C
	Girl Gracie -	95	15.5.17		C
	Girl Rose - -	86	15.5.17	Lost in action in Adriatic - -	C
	Helenora - -	88	15.5.17		C
	Quarry Knowe -	98	15.5.17		C
	Selby - -	75	15.5.17		C
	Serene - -	86	15.5.17		C
	Taits - -	93	15.5.17		C
	Transit - -	83	15.5.17		C
	Young Linnett -	93	15.5.17		C
	Rosevine - -	100	24.5.17	Sunk after collision off Great Yarmouth.	C
	George V. -	67	3.6.17	Sunk after E.C. mine explosion near Dover.	C
	Southesk - -	93	7.7.17	Sunk by mine in Auskerry Sound -	C
	Betsy Sim -	53	18.7.17	Sunk after collision near Haisboro' Light Vessel.	C
	Nina - -	83	2.8.17	Sunk after explosion off Prawle Point.	C
	Dewey - -	83	12.8.17	Sunk after collision off Royal Sovereign Light Vessel.	C
	Ocean's Gift II.	50	30.8.17	Destroyed by fire off the Wash -	C
	Hastfen - -	77	24.9.17	Sunk by mine off Longsand - -	C
	Ocean Star -	92	26.9.17	Disappeared off the Nab Light (presumed mined).	C
	Active III. -	81	15.10.17	Sunk by mine off Milford Haven -	C
	Jean - -	94	17.10.17	Sunk by mine off Cape Santa Maria di Leuca.	C
	Comrades - -	63	18.10.17	Sunk by mine off Cape d'Antifer -	C
	Deliverer - -	79	3.11.17	Disappeared outside Dublin Bay (presumed sunk by submarine).	C
	John Mitchell -	89	14.11.17	Sunk after collision off St. Albans Head.	C
	Bounteous -	63	4.12.17	Wrecked on North Shore, Rhum -	C
	Helen Wilson -	44	5.12.17	Destroyed by fire at Oban - -	C
	Annie - -	94	19.12.17	Destroyed after grounding off Enos	C
	Piscatorial II. -	93	29.12.17	Disappeared off Newhaven - -	C
Motor Launches	M.L. 197 - -	37	31.1.17	Wrecked near Ballincourty Lighthouse.	C
	M.L. 534 - -	37	13.4.17	Destroyed by fire at Taranto - -	C
	M.L. 431 - -	37	22.4.17	Destroyed by fire at Poole - -	C
	M.L. 540 - -	37	8.6.17	Lost in " Hunstrick," which was torpedoed by submarine off Tangier.	C
	M.L. 541 - -	37	8.6.17		
	M.L. 474 - -	37	23.7.17	Destroyed by fire after being struck by enemy shell near Chios.	C
	M.L. 52 - -	37	29.11.17	Destroyed by fire in Sandown Bay	

Class.	Name.	Gross Tonnage.	Date Lost.	How Lost and Where.	C = Commissioned. NC = Not Commiss⁴.
				1918.	
Hospital Ship -	Rewa - -	7,308	4.1.18	Sunk by submarine W. ¼ S. from Hartland Point.	NC
Frozen Meat Ship.	Romeo - -	1,730	3.3.18	Sunk by submarine 7 miles S. from Mull of Galloway.	NC
Mine Carriers -	Eleanor - -	1,980	12.2.18	Sunk by submarine 9 miles W. by S. ⅓ S. from St. Catherine's Point.	C
	Lady Cory-Wright.	2,516	26.3.18	Sunk by submarine 14 miles S.S.W. from the Lizard.	C
Minesweepers -	St. Seiriol -	928	25.4.18	Sunk by mine off the Shipwash -	C
	Blackmorevale -	750*	1.5.18	Sunk by mine off Montrose - -	C
	Ascot - -	810*	10.11.18	Blown up off Farn Islands (presumed torpedoed).	C
Fleet Messenger	Chesterfield -	1,013	18.5.18	Sunk by submarine 42 miles N.E. by E. ½ E. from Malta.	C
Commissioned Escort Ship.	Mechanician -	9,044	20.1.18	Sunk by submarine 8 miles W. from St. Catherine's Point.	C
Miscellaneous -	Lowtyne - -	3,231	10.6.18	Sunk by submarine 3½ miles E.S.E. from Whitby.	C
	Puruni - -	295	29.8.18	Wrecked off W. point of Mayers Islands, Grenadines.	C
Colliers - -	Birchwood -	2,756	3.1.18	Sunk by submarine 25 miles E. from Blackwater Light Vessel.	NC
	Gartland - -	2,613	3.1.18	Sunk by submarine 5 miles E.S.E. from Owers Light Vessel.	NC
	Steelville - -	3,649	3.1.18	} Sunk by submarine 20 miles N. from Cape Bon.	} NC
	Allanton - -	4,253	3.1.18		
	Birtley - -	1,438	4.1.18	Sunk by submarine (?) 8 miles N. from Flamborough Head.	NC
	Knightsgarth -	2,889	5.1.18	Sunk by submarine 5 miles W.N.W. from Bull Point, Rathlin Island.	NC
	Rose Marie -	2,220	5.1.18	Sunk by submarine 13 miles S.E. from N. Arklow Light Vessel.	NC
	Taiyabi - -	3,157	9.1.18	Foundered when on passage from Cardiff to Malta.	NC
	West Wales -	4,331	21.1.18	Sunk by submarine 140 miles S.E. ¾ S. from Malta.	NC
	Hartley - -	1,150	26.1.18	Sunk by submarine 2 miles N.E. from Skinningrove, Yorkshire.	NC
	Butetown - -	1,829	29.1.18	Sunk by submarine 1½ miles S. from Dodman Point.	NC
	Towneley - -	2,476	31.1.18	Sunk by submarine 18 miles N.E. ¼ E. from Trevose Head.	NC
	Standish Hall -	3,996	4.2.18	Sunk by submarine 38 miles W. by N. from Alexandria.	NC
	Lydie - -	2,599	9.2.18	Sunk by submarine 1 mile E. by S. from Manacles Buoy.	NC
	Dorisbrook -	3,431	9.2.18	Sunk by collision in South Pacific -	NC
	Pinewood -	2,219	17.2.18	Sunk by submarine 15 miles S. from Mine Head.	NC
	Northville . -	2,472	17.2.18	Sunk by submarine 3½ miles S.E. by E. from Berry Head.	NC
	Remus - -	1,079	23.2.18	Sunk by submarine 6 miles S.S.W. from Copinsay, Orkneys.	NC
	Rubio - -	2,395	25.2.18	Sunk by mine 4 miles N. ½ E. from Shipwash Light Vessel.	NC
	Maltby - -	3,977	26.2.18	Sunk by submarine 10 miles S.W. by S. from Pantellaria.	NC
	Greavesash -	1,263	26.2.18	Sunk by submarine 10 miles N.E. from Cape Barfleur.	NC
	Dalewood -	2,420	26.2.18	Sunk by submarine 10 miles S.W. from the Isle of Man.	NC
	Largo - -	1,764	27.2.18	Sunk by submarine 12 miles W. from Calf of Man.	NC
	Northfield -	2,099	3.3.18	Sunk by submarine 25 miles S.W. from Lundy Island.	NC
	Castle Eden -	1,949	4.3.18	Sunk by submarine 4 miles S.S.E. from Inistrahull Lighthouse.	NC
	Intent - -	1,564	8.3.18	Sunk by submarine 4 miles E. by N. from Seaham.	NC
	Tweed - -	1,025	13.3.18	Sunk by submarine 10 miles S. by W. ¼ W. from St. Catherine's Pt.	NC

* Displacement tonnage.

Class.	Name.	Gross Tonnage.	Date Lost.	How Lost and Where.	C = Commissioned. NC = Not Commiss⁴.
				1918.	
Colliers—*cont.*	Ardandearg -	3,237	14.3.18	Sunk by submarine 86 miles E. ¼ N. from Malta.	NC
	Ellaston - -	3,192	16.3.18	Sunk by submarine 180 miles W. by S. (true) from Palma, Canary Islands.	NC
	Burnstone -	2,340	19.3.18	Sunk by submarine 44 miles N. from Farn Islands.	NC
	Begonia - -	3,070	21.3.18	Sunk by submarine 44 miles S. by W. from Wolf Rock.	NC
	Boscastle - -	2,346	7.4.18	Sunk by submarine 14 miles N.N.W. from Strumble Head.	NC
	Marstonmoor -	2,744	14.4.18	Sunk by submarine 55 miles N.N.E. from Cape Wrath.	NC
	Gregynog -	1,701	18.4.18	Sunk by submarine 16 miles S.W. from Hartland Point.	NC
	Bellview - -	3,567	21.4.18	Sunk by submarine 16 miles E.N.E. from Cape Bon.	NC
	Eric Calvert -	1,862	22.4.18	Sunk by submarine 4 miles S.S.W. from St. Anthony Point.	NC
	Dronning Maud -	2,663	22.4.18	Sunk by submarine 65 miles N. by E. ¾ E. from Cape Sigli, Algeria.	NC
	Llwyngwair -	1,304	26.4.18	Sunk by submarine 5 miles S.S.E. from Seaham Harbour.	NC
	Ellis Sayer -	2,549	29.4.18	Sunk by submarine 15 miles E. by N. from Royal Sovereign Light Vessel.	NC
	Baron Ailsa -	1,836	9.5.18	Sunk by submarine 18 miles W.N.W. from the Smalls.	NC
	Heron Bridge -	2,420	16.5.18	Sunk by submarine 320 miles E. by N. (true) from San Miguel, Azores.	NC
	Mavisbrook -	3,152	17.5.18	Sunk by submarine 50 miles S.E. by S. ½ S. from Cape de Gata.	NC
	Snowdon - -	3,189	19.5.18	Sunk by submarine 84 miles S. ½ W. from Malta.	NC
	Clan Forbes -	3,946	9.6.18	Sunk by submarine 115 miles W.N.W. from Alexandria.	NC
	Waitemata -	5,432	14.7.18	Sunk by submarine 100 miles E. ¾ N. from Marsa Susa.	NC
	Marie Suzanne -	3,106	19.8.18	Sunk by submarine 47 miles W. ¾ S. from Mudros Bay.	NC
	Boscawen - -	1,936	21.8.18	Sunk by submarine 23 miles W.N.W. from Bardsey Isle.	NC
	Milly - -	2,964	6.9.18	Sunk by submarine 2¼ miles W. ¾ S. from Tintagel Head.	NC
	Madryn - -	2,244	16.9.18	Sunk by submarine 5 miles N.N.E. from Trevose Head.	NC
	Lord Stewart -	1,445	16.9.18	Sunk by submarine 6 miles E. ½ N. from Hope's Nose.	NC
	Muriel - -	1,831	17.9.18	Sunk by submarine 3½ miles N.E. from Peterhead.	NC
	John O'Scott -	1,235	18.9.18	Sunk by submarine 9 miles W. by N. from Trevose Head.	NC
	Gorsemore -	3,079	22.9.18	Sunk by submarine 44 miles S.E. ½ E. from Cape Colonne.	NC
	Hebburn - -	1,938	25.9.18	Sunk by submarine 14 miles S. from Mine Head.	NC
	Westwood -	1,968	3.10.18	Sunk by submarine 5 miles S.W. ½ W. from the Lizard.	NC
	War Council -	5,875	16.10.18	Sunk by submarine 85 miles W.S.W. from Cape Matapan.	NC
Oilers - -	Trecas - -	4,129	19.1.18	Sunk by submarine 10 miles N.E. from Skyros Lighthouse.	NC
	Baku Standard -	3,708	11.2.18	Sunk by submarine 5 miles S. by W. ½ W. from Tod Head.	NC
	Beacon Light -	2,768	19.2.18	Sunk by submarine 15 miles S.E. from Butt of Lewis.	NC
	British Viscount	3,287	23.2.18	Sunk by submarine off Holyhead -	NC
	Oilfield - -	4,000	16.3.18	Sunk by submarine 15 miles N.W. from Cape Wrath.	NC
	Samoset - -	5,251	20.3.18	Sunk by submarine 50 miles N. by E. ¾ E. from Port Said.	NC

Class.	Name.	Gross Tonnage.	Date Lost.	How Lost and Where.	C = Commissioned. NC = Not Commiss⁴.
				1918.	
Oilers—*cont.*	Waneta - -	1,683	30.5.18	Sunk by submarine 42 miles S.S.E. from Kinsale Head.	NC
	Tatarrax - -	6,216	11.8.18	Sunk by internal explosion off Alexandria.	NC
	Arca - -	4,839	2.10.18	Sunk by submarine 40 miles N.W. by W. from Tory Island.	NC
Special Service Ships.	Wellholme -	113	30.1.18	Sunk by submarine in English Channel.	C
	Westphalia -	1,467	11.2.18	Sunk by submarine in Irish Sea -	C
	Brown Mouse -	42	28.2.18	Caught fire and blew up in Lyme Bay.	C
	Willow Branch -	3,314	25.4.18	Sunk by submarine probably off W. Coast of Africa, E. of Cape Verde.	C
	Ocean Fisher -	96	16.6.18	Sunk by mine in North Sea - -	C
	Stockforce -	732	30.7.18	Sunk by submarine in English Channel.	C
	M. J. Hedley -	449	4.10.18	Capsized and sank while coaling in Barry Docks, Cardiff.	C
Tugs - -	Blackcock -	253	18.1.18	Wrecked in White Sea - -	C
	Desire - -	165	24.1.18	Sunk by submarine off Yorkshire Coast.	NC
	Guiana - -	166	29.1.18	Sunk by collision off East Coast -	C
	Ludgate - -	165	15.2.18	Stranded in Wigtown Bay - -	C
	Thames - -	32	16.2.18	Foundered off E. Coast of Scotland	C
	David Gillies -	375	5.5.18	Stranded in Mediterranean - -	C
	Dalkeith - -	741	18.5.18	Sunk by enemy action in Mediterranean.	C
	Oceana - -	337	18.10.18	Stranded at Scapa - - -	C
	George R. Gray	268	27.10.18	Stranded at Farn Islands - -	C
	Blazer - -	283	9.11.18	Stranded at Scilly Islands - -	C
Whalers - -	Hirpa - -	110	2.1.18	Wrecked near Buckie - - -	C
	Blackwhale -	237	3.1.18	Sunk by mine off Fife Ness - -	C
Admiralty Trawlers.	Nathaniel Cole -	275	6.2.18	Sprung a leak off Buncrana - -	C
	James Pond -	275	15.2.18	Lost in action off Dover - -	C
	Thos. Collard -	215	1.3.18	Sunk by submarine N. of Rathlin Island.	C
	Antares II. -	275*	2.5.18	Sunk by gunfire after collision off Gibraltar.	C
	Lancer II. -	275*	18.7.18	Sunk after collision off Brighton Light Vessel.	C
	Michael Clements	324	8.8.18	Sunk after collision off St. Catharine's Point.	C
	Thos. Cornwall -	324	29.10.18	Sunk after collision off Flamborough Head.	C
	Charles Hammond	324	2.11.18	Sunk after collision with H.M.S. " Marksman " off Kirkcaldy.	C
Hired Trawlers	Miranda III. -	173	14.1.18	Wrecked in Pelwick Bay - -	C
	John E. Lewis -	253	16.1.18	Sunk by mine off Cork Light Vessel, Harwich.	C
	Gambri - -	274	18.1.18	Sunk by mine off Royal Sovereign Light Vessel.	C
	Drumtochty -	211	29.1.18	Sunk by mine off Dover - -	C
	Cleon - -	266	1.2.18	Sunk by mine off Folkestone Gate Buoy.	C
	Remindo - -	256	2.2.18	Lost off Portland. Cause unknown	C
	Idena - -	270	5.2.18	Abandoned and sunk by gunfire, Lat. 71° N., Long. 17° E.	C
	Sardius II. -	206	13.2.18	Wrecked in Pendower Cove (near Tolpenden Penwith).	C
	Marion - -	128	23.2.18	Sunk by mine off Malta - -	C
	Nerissa II. -	173	28.2.18	Wrecked off end of Valanidhi Shoal, Lemnos.	C
	Princess Alice -	225	6.3.18	Sunk after collision off Alexandria	C
	Columba - -	138	10.3.18	Sunk by mine off May Island -	C
	Endeavour -	156	10.3.18	Sunk after collision at Kirkwall Boom.	C
	Adrian - -	199	13.3.18	Sunk after collision off Harwich -	C
	Agate - -	248	14.3.18	Sunk by mine off Royal Sovereign Light Vessel.	C
	Vulture II. -	190	16.3.18	Sunk after collision in Eriboll wreck.	C

* Approximate.

Class.	Name.	Gross Tonnage	Date Lost.	How Lost and Where.	C = Commissioned. NC = Not Commiss⁴.
				1918.	
Hired Trawlers —cont.	Swallow - -	243	29.3.18	Sunk after collision off Whitby -	C
	Lord Hardinge -	212	9.4.18	Sunk after collision off Daunt Light Vessel.	C
	Numitor - -	242	20.4.18	Sunk by mine off Orfordness -	C
	Plethos - -	210	23.4.18	Sunk by mine off Montrose - -	C
	Emley - -	223	28.4.18	Sunk by mine off May Island -	C
	Loch Naver -	216	13.5.18	Sunk by mine near Mandili Point Ægean Sea.	C
	Balfour - -	285	13.5.18	Sunk after collision off Royal Sovereign Light Vessel.	C
	Gabir - -	219	24.5.18	} Sunk by mine off Lowestoft -	C
	Yucca - -	198	24.5.18		
	Dirk - -	181	28.5.18	Sunk by submarine off Flamborough Head.	C
	St. John's -	208	3.6.18	Sunk by submarine 45 miles N. of Tory Island.	C
	Princess Olga -	245	14.6.18	Sunk by mine off Havre - -	C
	Achilles II. -	225	26.6.18	Sunk by mine off Shipwash Light Vessel.	C
	Loch Tummel -	228	14.7.18	Foundered in Mediterranean, Lat. 33° 35' N., Long. 21° 45' E. Cause unknown.	C
	Speedwell II. -	273	15.7.18	Ran ashore in Mounts Bay and broke up.	C
	Ijuim - -	257	22.7.18	Sunk by gunfire of enemy submarine.	C
	Lochiel - -	241	24.7.18	Sunk by mine or torpedo off Whitby.	C
	Elise - -	239	22.9.18	Blown up 2 miles N.E. of St. Mary's Lighthouse, Blyth (presumed torpedoed).	C
	Sealark II. -	182	30.9.18	Sunk after collision off St. John's Point.	C
	Kalmia - -	189	7.10.18	Destroyed by fire at Stavros - -	C
	Neptunian -	315	27.10.18	Sunk after collision 5 miles N.N.W. of Albacarry Lighthouse.	C
	Riparvo - -	230	2.11.18	Sunk after collision, Lat. 35° 08' N., Long. 18° 54' E.	C
	Renarro - -	230	10.11.18	Sunk by mine in Dardanelles -	C
Hired Drifters	Golden Sunset -	85	4.1.18	Sunk after collision off Shambles Light Vessel.	C
	Ethnee - -	86	15.1.18	Wrecked on Goodwin Sands - -	C
	Christina Craig	86	15.2.18		
	Clover Bank -	92	15.2.18		
	Cosmos - -	91	15.2.18		
	Jeannie Murray	90	15.2.18	} Lost in action off Dover - -	C
	Silver Queen -	84	15.2.18		
	Veracity - -	96	15.2.18		
	W. Elliott -	60	15.2.18		
	William Tennant	93	5.3.18	Sunk after collision off Humber -	C
	Frigate Bird -	84	11.3.18	Sunk after collision off Marsa Scirocco, Mediterranean.	C
	Nexus - -	86	13.3.18	Sunk by mine in Thames Estuary -	C
	J. C. P. - -	73	22.3.18	Sunk after collision off Green Flash Buoy.	C
	New Dawn -	93	23.3.18	Sunk by mine at entrance to Needles Channel.	C
	Border Lads -	86	25.3.18	Blown up off Tyne (believed torpedoed).	C
	J. and A. - -	98	4.4.18	Sunk after collision off Scarborough	C
	Annie Smith -	84	9.4.18	Sunk after collision off Lundy Island.	C
	Select - -	74	16.4.18	Sunk after collision off St. Govans Light Buoy.	C
	Sunbeam I. -	75	16.4.18	Sunk after collision at Inchkeith -	NC
	Pursuit - -	79	22.4.18	Sunk after collision at Penzance -	C
	Holly III. -	93	11.5.18	Sunk after collision off Lands End -	C
	Silvery Harvest	86	16.5.18	Sunk after collision off Berry Head	C
	Clara and Alice	79	26.5.18	Sprang a leak off Palermo - -	C
	City of Liverpool	88	31.7.18	Believed sunk by mine off South Foreland.	C
	Scania - -	88	2.8.18	Sunk by collision in Dover Straits -	C

Class.	Name.	Gross Tonnage.	Date Lost.	How Lost and Where.	C = Commissioned. NC = Not Commiss⁴.
				1918.	
Hired Drifters —*cont.*	Strathmore -	56	20.8.18	Destroyed by fire off Buncrana -	C
	Tulip II. - -	88	23.8.18	Sunk after collision off St. Anthony	C
	Guide Me II. -	100	29.8.18	Sunk after collision off the Muglins	C
	Lustring - -	71	3.10.18	Sunk after collision off Hellier Holm.	C
	Coleus - -	102	4.10.18	Sunk by mine off Dover - -	C
	Ocean Foam -	90	7.10.18	Sunk after collision in Penzance Bay.	C
	Calceolaria -	92	27.10.18	Sunk by mine off Elbow Light Buoy.	C
	Falkirk - -	56	29.10.18	Sunk in collision off Kinnaird Head⁻	C
Motor Launches	M.L. 278 - -	37	15.1.18	Wrecked on Dunkirk Pier - -	C
	M.L. 55 - -	37	28.1.18	Destroyed by fire at yard of Messrs. Wills and Packham, Sittingbourne.	C
	M.L. 421 - -	37	6.4.18	Wrecked in Seaford Bay - -	C
	M.L. 356 - -	37	11.4.18	Sunk after collision off Dover -	C
	M.L. 110 - -	37	23.4.18	Lost in action off Zeebrugge - -	C
	M.L. 424 ·	37	23.4.18	Lost in action off Zeebrugge - -	C
	M.L. 254 - -	37	10.5.18	Sunk off Ostend to avoid capture -	C
	M.L. 64 ·	37	10.6.18	Destroyed by fire in Granton Harbour.	C
	M.L. 403 - -	37	22.8.18	Blown up in Runswick Bay while endeavouring to salve German torpedo.	C
	M.L. 247 - -	37	29.9.18	Wrecked on Oar Rock, West of Clodgy Point, St. Ives.	C
	M.L. 561 -	37	21.10.18	Sunk by mine off Ostend.	

VI.—Summary of Losses of Auxiliary Vessels.

Class.	Period.					Total Number lost.	Total Tonnage lost (Gross Tonnage in *italics*, Displacement Tonnage in ordinary type).
	4 Aug. 1914 to 31 Dec. 1914.	1915.	1916.	1917.	1 Jan. 1918 to 11 Nov. 1918.		
	No.	No.	No.	No.	No.	No.	Tons.
Hospital Ships - -	1	—	—	—	1	2	*15,199*
Frozen Meat Ship - -	—	—	—	—	1	1	*1,730*
Store Carriers - -	—	1	1	2	—	4	*4,779*
Ammunition Ship - -	—	1	—	—	—	1	*2,030*
Mine Carriers - -	—	—	—	—	2	2	*4,496*
Minesweepers - -	—	5	3	7	3	{ 5 { 13	3,990 *7,758*
Auxiliary Patrol Paddlers	—	—	2	—	—	2	*679*
Fleet Messengers - -	—	3	1	4	1	9	*11,602*
Commissioned Escort Ships.	—	—	—	2	1	3	*22,082*
Miscellaneous	—	—	—	1	2	3	*4,698*
Colliers - - - -	2	33	38	115	56	244	*714,613*
Oilers - - - -	—	8	6	21	9	44	*216,445*
Special Service Ships -	—	—	5	17	7	29	*35,760*
Tugs - - - -	—	3	—	1	10	14	*3,593*
Yachts - - - -	—	5	5	3	—	13	*7,179*
Whalers - - - -	—	—	—	—	2	2	*347*
Admiralty Trawlers -	1	2	2	5	8	18	*4,719*
Hired Trawlers - -	13	50	58	86	39	246	*56,300*
Hired Drifters - -	2	13	40	42	33	130	*10,809*
Motor Launches - -	—	—	6	7	11	24	*864*
Motor Boats - -	—	3	3	—	—	6	*61*
Total { Nos. - -	19	127	170	313	186	815	—
Total { Tons Displacement.	—	—	810	1,620	1,560	—	3,990
Total { Tons Gross.	*19,165*	*155,222*	*180,444*	*538,322*	*232,590*	—	*1,125,743**

* Excluding two Motor Boats and two Special Service Ships whose Tonnage is uncertain.

VII.—Analysis of Causes of Loss—Auxiliary Vessels.

Class.	Cause of Loss.									
	Action.	Submarine.	Mine.	Destruction to avoid Capture.	Fire.	Collision.	Wrecked.	Various	Unknown.	Total.
Hospital Ships - - - -	—	1	—	—	—	—	1	—	—	2
Frozen Meat Ships - - -	—	1	—	—	—	—	—	—	—	1
Store Carriers - - - -	—	—	3	—	—	1	—	—	—	4
Ammunition Ships - - -	—	—	—	—	—	—	—	—	1	1
Mine Carriers - - - -	—	2	—	—	—	—	—	—	—	2
Minesweepers - - - -	—	1	12	—	—	2	—	2	1	18
Auxiliary Patrol Paddlers - -	—	—	—	—	—	—	—	2	—	2
Fleet Messengers - - -	—	6	2	—	—	—	—	1	—	9
Commissioned Escort Ships - -	—	3	—	—	—	—	—	—	—	3
Miscellaneous - - - -	—	2	—	—	—	—	1	—	—	3
Colliers - - - - -	—	193	22	—	—·	9	10	5	5	244
Oilers - - - - -	—	35	2	—	1	1	2	1	2	44
Special Service Ships - - -	—	22	2	1	1	2	—	1	—	29
Tugs - - - - - -	1	1	—	—	—	2	9	1	—	14
Yachts - - - - -	1	2	4	—	1	2	2	1	—	13
Whalers - - - - -	—	—	1	—	—	—	1	—	—	2
Admiralty Trawlers - - -	1	3	4	—	—	5	2	1	2	18
Hired Trawlers - - - -	5	14	140	—	1	35	34	9	8	246
Hired Drifters - - - -	32	3	32	—	3	33	11	8	8	130
Motor Launches - - - -	3	—	1	—	8	1	4	7	—	24
Motor Boats - - - -	—	—	—	—·	3	—	—	3	—	6
Total - - -	43	289	225	1	18	93	77	38	31	815

VIII.—Classified Nominal List of Losses—Auxiliary Ships.

AMMUNITION SHIP.

Combe.
(1)

AUXILIARY PATROL
PADDLERS.

Majestic II.
Stirling Castle.
(2)

COLLIERS.

Adamton.
Adriatic.
African Monarch.
Alfalfa.
Allanton.
Ambient.
Ampleforth.
Apollo.
Ardandearg.
Argo.
Arnewood.
Artist.
Ashby.
Axminster.
Baron Ailsa.
Bedale.
Beemah.
Begonia.
Bellview.
Ben Cruachan.
Bengarth.
Bengrove.
Ben Vrackie.
Bestwood.
Bilbster.

COLLIERS—continued.

Bilswood.
Birchwood.
Birtley.
Bleamoor.
Boldwell.
Boscastle.
Boscawen.
Branksome Chine.
Broomhill.
Buresk.
Burnby.
Burnstone.
Burrsfield.
Butetown (1).
Butetown (2).
Calliope.
Canganian.
Cape Antibes.
Castle Eden.
Charleston.
Cherbury.
Chertsey.
Churston.
Cilicia.
Clan Ferguson.
Clan Forbes.
Clan McLachlan.
Clara.
Cliftondale.
Cliftonian.
Collegian.
Corinth.
Craigendoran.
Craigston.
Cydonia.
Dalewood.
Don.

COLLIERS—continued.

Don Benito.
Dorisbrook.
Dromonby.
Dronning Maud.
Duckbridge.
Eastfield.
Eavestone.
Ella Sayers.
Ellaston.
Ellerslie.
Elsiston.
England.
Enosis.
Eric Calvert.
Eskmere.
Etal Manor.
Ethel Duncan.
Etton.
Euston.
Excellent.
F. Matarazzo.
Foreland.
Fulgent.
Garfield.
Gartland.
Gasconia.
Gena.
Gisella.
Glenby.
Glocliffe.
Gorsemore.
Greavesash.
Greenhill.
Gregynog.
Groeswen.
Hallamshire.
Hartley.

COLLIERS—continued.

Heatherside.
Hebburn.
Hercules.
Heron Bridge.
Herrington.
Hockwold.
Holmesbank.
Huelva.
Hunsbridge.
Hurlford.
Ilvington Court.
Inglemoor.
Intent.
Invergyle.
Inververbie.
Iolo.
Iser.
Islandmore.
Jane Radcliffe.
John O'Scott.
J. Y. Short.
Kilbride.
Kilellan.
Kilwinning.
Kincardine.
Kirkby.
Knarsdale.
Knightgarth.
Kurdistan.
Lady Carrington.
Lady Charlotte.
Lady Iveagh.
Larchwood.
Largo.
Lemnos.
Lincairn.
Linkmoor.

COLLIERS—*continued.*

Llwyngwair.
Lochwood.
Longbenton.
Lord Derby.
Lord Stewart.
Lotusmere.
Lowdale.
Lucent.
Luciston.
Lullington.
Lydie.
Lynfield.
Madryn.
Maltby.
Mansuri.
Margam Abbey.
Margit.
Marie Suzanne.
Marstonmoor.
Maston.
Mavisbrook.
Meldon.
Millicent Knight.
Milly.
Milo.
Minieh.
Mobile.
Monitoria.
Monkstone.
Mountpark.
Munificent.
Muriel.
Nairn.
New Zealand Transport.
Norhilda.
Northfield.
Northville.
North Wales.
Nuceria.
Oakby.
Okement.
Oola.
Penylan.
Pera.
Persier.
Pinewood.
Plutus.
Pola.
Polar Prince.
Poldown.
Polruan.
Porthkerry.
Prophet.
Purley.
Reapwell.
Redesmere.
Remus.
Repton.
Ribston.
Rio Tiete.
River Forth.
Romsdalen.
Rosehill.
Rose Lea.
Rose Marie.
Rubio.
St. Gothard.
Sandsend.
Sarah Radcliffe.
Satrap.
Seistan.
Silverton.
Sneaton.
Snowdon.
Snowdonian.
Southina.
Spennymoor.

COLLIERS—*continued.*

Standish Hall.
Steelville.
Strathcarron.
Swift Wings.
Taiyabi.
Tandil.
The Queen.
Thorpwood.
Towneley.
Trefusis.
Trevose.
Trowbridge.
Trunkby.
Turnbridge.
Tweed.
Tynemouth.
Valentia.
Vellore.
Venetia.
Waitemata.
War Council.
Westbury.
Western Coast.
West Wales.
Westwood.
Wilston.
Winlaton.
Wychwood.
Zafra.
Zambesi.
Zoroaster.

(244)

COMMISSIONED ESCORT SHIPS.
———

Bostonian.
Mechanician.
Quernmore.

(3)

DRIFTERS (HIRED).
———

Active III.
Adequate.
Admirable.
Aivern.
Ajax II.
Annie.
Annie Smith.
Astrum Spei.
Au Fait.
Avondale.
Beneficent.
Betsy Sim.
Border Lads.
Bounteous.
Boy Harold.
Calceolaria.
Campania II.
Cape Colony
Chance.
Charity.
Christina Craig.
City of Liverpool.
Clara and Alice.
Clavis.
Clover Bank (1).
Clover Bank (2).
Coleus.
Comrades.
Coral Haven.
Cosmos.
Craignoon.
Datum.
Deliverer.
Dewey.

DRIFTERS (HIRED)— *continued.*
———

Energy.
Enterprise.
Eskburn.
Ethnee.
Everard.
Eyrie.
Falkirk.
Fame.
Felicitas.
Ferndale.
Finrose.
Forward III.
Freuchny.
Frigate Bird.
Frons Oliviae.
Gavenwood.
George V.
Girl Eva.
Girl Gracie.
Girl Rose.
Gleaner of the Sea.
G.M.V.
Golden Sunset.
Gowan.
Gracie.
Grateful.
Great Heart.
G.S.P.
Guide Me II.
Hastfen.
Helenora.
Helen Wilson.
Hilary II.
Holly III.
J. and A.
J.C.P.
Jean.
Jeannie Murray.
John Mitchell.
Ladysmith.
Launch Out.
Laurel Crown.
Lerwick.
Lily Reaich.
Lindsell.
Lottie Leask.
Lustring.
Manzanita.
Michaelmas Daisy.
Morning Star.
New Dawn.
Nexus.
Nina.
Ocean Foam.
Ocean Plough.
Ocean Gift II.
Ocean Star.
Pecheur.
Pelagia.
Persistive.
Piscatorial II.
Plantin.
Protect.
Pursuit.
Quarry Knowe.
Restore.
Roburn.
Rooke.
Rosevine.
Rosie.
Scania.
Selby.
Select.
Serene
Silver Queen.
Silvery Harvest.

DRIFTERS (HIRED)— *continued.*
———

Silvery Wave.
Southesk.
Speedwell V.
Spotless Prince.
Star of Buchan.
Strathmore.
Sunbeam I.
Susanna.
Taits.
Thistle IV.
Transit.
Tuberose.
Tulip II.
Veracity.
Waterlily.
Waveney II.
W. Elliott.
White Rose.
William Tennant.
Young Linnett.

(130)

FLEET MESSENGERS.
———

Chesterfield.
Clifford.
Ermine.
Nugget.
Osmanieh.
Portia.
Princess Alberta.
Redbreast.
Turquoise.

(9)

FROZEN MEAT SHIPS.
———

Romeo.

(1)

HOSPITAL SHIPS.
———

Rewa.
Rohilla.

(2)

MINE CARRIERS.
———

Eleanor.
Lady Cory-Wright.

(2)

MINESWEEPERS.
———

Ascot.
Blackmorevale.
Brighton Queen.
Clacton.
Duchess of Hamilton.
Duchess of Montrose.
Fair Maid.
Hythe.
Kempton.
Lady Ismay.
Ludlow.
Marsa.
Nepaulin.
Newmarket.
Queen of the North.
Redcar.
Roedean (ex Roebuck).
St. Seiriol.

(18)

MISCELLANEOUS.

Lowtyne.
Puruni.
White Head.
(3)

MOTOR BOATS.

Allegro.
Dolores.
Doreen.
Dorothea.
Griffiu.
Nita Pita.
(6)

MOTOR LAUNCHES.

M.L. 19.
M.L. 40.
M.L. 52.
M.L. 55.
M.L. 64.
M.L. 110.
M.L. 149.
M.L. 197.
M.L. 230.
M.L. 247.
M.L. 253.
M.L. 254.
M.L. 255.
M.L. 278.
M.L. 356.
M.L. 403.
M.L. 421.
M.L. 424.
M.L. 431.
M.L. 474.
M.L. 534.
M.L. 540.
M.L. 541.
M.L. 561.
(24)

OILERS.

Arca.
Ashleaf.
Baku Standard.
Balakani.
Batoum.
Beacon Light.
British Sun.
British Viscount.
Bullmouth.
Bulysses.
Caucasian.
Clearfield.
Cymbeline.
Derbent.
Desabla.
Echunga.
Elax.
El Toro.
El Zorro.
Fornebo.
Gafsa.
Goldmouth.
H. C. Henry.
Lumina.
Mira.
Murex.
Oakleaf.
Oilfield.
Palmleaf.
Ponus.
Powhatan.
Prudentia.

OILERS—continued.

Rosalind.
Samoset.
San Onofre.
Sebastian.
Silvia.
Tatarrax.
Teakwood.
Telena.
Trocas.
Turritella.
Waneta.
Wapello.
(44)

SPECIAL SERVICE SHIPS.

Asama.
Bayard.
Bracondale.
Bradford City.
Brown Mouse.
Dunraven.
Else.
Ethel and Millie.
Fame.
Glenfoyle.
Kent County.
King Stephen.
Lady Olive.
Lady Patricia.
M. J. Hedley.
Mona.
Nelson.
Ocean Fisher.
Penshurst.
Perugia.
Peveril.
Remembrance.
Stockforce.
Vala.
Warner.
Wellholme.
Westphalia.
Willow Branch.
Zylpha.
(29)

STORE CARRIERS.

Charles Goodanew.
Hebble.
Immingham.
Leicester.
(4)

TRAWLERS (ADMIRALTY).

Antares II.
Benjamin Stevenson.
Carbineer.
Charles Astie.
Charles Hammond.
Charlsin.
Crownsin.
James Pond.
James Seckar.
Jasper.
Javelin.
Lancer II.
Michael Clements.
Nathaniel Cole.
Sapper.
Spider.
Thos. Collard.
Thos. Cornwall.
(18)

TRAWLERS (HIRED).

Abelard.
Achilles II.
Adrian.
Agamemnon II.
Agate.
Agile.
Alberta.
Albion II.
Ameer.
Amplify.
Amy.
Angelus.
Anthony Hope.
Apley.
Arfon.
Asia.
Balfour.
Balmedie.
Banyers.
Bedouin.
Bega.
Ben Ardna.
Ben Heilen.
Benton Castle.
Berkshire.
Birch.
Blakedown.
Bonar Law.
Borneo.
Bovic.
Bracklyn.
Bradford.
Briton.
Burnley.
By George.
Caledonia.
Calliope II.
Cantatrice.
Carew Castle,
Carilon.
Carlton.
Chester II.
Christopher.
City of Dundee.
Cleon.
Clifton.
Clyde.
Columba.
Columbia.
Commandant.
Commander Fullerton.
Condor.
Corcyra.
Corientes.
Corona.
Cotsmuir.
Courtier.
Crathie (1).
Crathie (2).
Dagon.
Dane.
De la Pole.
Dhoon.
Dirk.
Donside.
Drake II.
Drumoak.
Drumtochty.
Duster.
Earl Lennox.
Edison.
Elise.
Emley.
Endeavour.
Epworth.
Era.
Erin II.

TRAWLERS (HIRED)—continued.

Eros.
Etoile Polaire.
Euston.
Evadne.
Evangel.
Fair Isle.
Falmouth III.
Filey.
Flicker.
Fraser.
Fulmar.
Gabir.
Gambri.
Garmo.
Gersina.
George Milburn.
Glenprosen.
Hawke.
Helgian.
Hirose.
Holdene.
Idena.
Ijuin.
Ina William.
Irawadi.
Italy.
Ivanhoe.
Jacamar.
Japan.
Jay.
Jessie Nutten.
John E. Lewis.
John G. Watson.
John High.
John Sherburn.
Kalmia.
Kaphreda.
Kelvin.
Kirkland.
Klondyke.
Knot.
Leandros.
Lena Melling.
Livingstone.
Lobelia II.
Loch Ard.
Loch Eye.
Loch Garry.
Lochiel.
Loch Naver.
Loch Shiel.
Loch Tummel.
Longset.
Lord Airedale.
Lord Alverstone.
Lord Denman.
Lord Grey.
Lord Hardinge.
Lord Ridley.
Lord Roberts.
Lord Salisbury.
Lorenzo.
Lucknow.
Lundy.
Lydian.
Malta.
Manx Hero.
Manx Queen.
Margate.
Marion.
Mary.
Mediator.
Merse.
Miranda III.
Miura.
Morococola.

TRAWLERS (HIRED)—
continued.

Nadine.
Narval.
Neath Castle.
Nellie Nutten.
Neptunian.
Nerissa II.
Newbridge.
New Comet.
Night Hawk.
Northumbria.
Numitor.
Ocean Scout I.
Okino.
Onward.
Orcades.
Orianda.
Orlando.
Orphesia.
Orsino.
Orthos.
Othello II.
Othonna.
Picton Castle.
Pitsruan.
Plethos.
Poonah.
Princess Alice.
Princess Beatrice.
Princess Olga.
Princess Victoria.
Quail III.
Recepto.
Relevo.
Remarko.

TRAWLERS (HIRED)—
continued.

Remindo.
Renarro.
Repro.
Resono.
Responso.
Rhodesia.
Riparvo.
Robert Smith.
Rolulo.
Rondo.
Rose II.
Rosy Morn.
Ruby (1).
Ruby (2).
Ruthin Castle.
St. Ives.
St. Johns.
Sarah Alice.
Sardius II.
Saxon Prince.
Schiehallion.
Scott.
Sealark II.
Senator.
Sisters Melville.
Sophron.
Speedwell II.
Speeton.
Star of Freedom.
Strathgarry.
Strathrannoch.
Strymon.
Swallow.
Taipo.

TRAWLERS (HIRED)—
continued.

Teal.
Tern.
Tervant.
Tettenhall.
Thomas Stretton.
Thomas W. Irvin.
Thuringia.
Tokio.
Tom Tit.
Towhee.
Trygon.
Tugela.
Vale of Leven.
Valpa.
Vitality.
Vivanti.
Vulture II.
Waltham.
Weigelia.
Whooper.
William Morrison.
Worsley.
Xerxes.
Yesso.
Yucca.

(246)

TUGS.

Alexandra.
Blackcock.
Blazer.
Char (*ex* Stranton).
Dalkeith.

TUGS—*continued.*

David Gillies.
Desire.
George R. Gray.
Guiana.
Jack.
Ludgate.
Marsden.
Oceana.
Thames.

(14)

WHALERS.

Blackwhale.
Hirpa.

(2)

YACHTS.

Ægusa.
Aries.
Clementina.
Conqueror II.
Hersilia.
Kethailes.
Mekong.
Resource II.
Rhiannon.
Sanda.
Verona.
Zaida.
Zarefah.

(13)

INDEX.

Black type = **Warships.**

Ordinary type = Auxiliary Vessels.

Section II
MERCHANT SHIPPING
(LOSSES), 1914-18

MERCHANT SHIPPING (LOSSES).

RETURN to an Order of the Honourable The House of Commons,
dated 1 August 1919 ;—*for,*

RETURN "showing separately, BRITISH MERCHANT and FISHING VESSELS captured
or destroyed by the ENEMY; also BRITISH MERCHANT VESSELS damaged or
molested by the ENEMY, but not sunk ; during the period 4th day of August
1914 to 11th day of November 1918 ; to show, as far as is known, Name,
Gross Tonnage, Date, Position, and Method of Attack, Cause of Loss or
Escape, and Number of Lives lost."

Admiralty,   }
   August 1919. }

O. A. R. MURRAY,
Secretary.

(Lieutenant-Colonel Burgoyne.)

Ordered, *by* The House of Commons, *to be Printed,*
19 *August* 1919.

CONTENTS.

A † before a vessel's name indicates that she was armed for defensive purposes. Vessels armed for offensive purposes are not included in these lists. Unless otherwise stated, all bearings given are magnetic. Crew and civilian passengers only are included in column headed "Lives lost."

I.—BRITISH MERCHANT VESSELS CAPTURED OR DESTROYED BY THE ENEMY.

Name.	Tons.	Date.	Position.	Cause of Loss.	How attacked.	How sunk.	Lives lost.
AUGUST 1914.		**1914.** Aug.					
San Wilfrido -	6,458	3	Off Cuxhaven -	Mine - - -	Mine - -	Mine - -	Crew made prisoners.
City of Winchester.	6,601	6	280 miles E. (true) from Aden.	Konigsberg - -	Captured -	Scuttled -	—
Frau Minna Petersen (S.V.).	176	7	5 miles N.W. from Osterems Port Buoy.	Torpedo Boat -	Captured -	Taken to Emden.	—
Hyades - -	3,352	15	180 miles N.E. ¼ N. (true) from Pernambuco.	Dresden - -	Captured -	Gunfire -	—
Kaipara - -	7,392	16	170 miles S. by W. (true) from Tenerife.	Kaiser Wilhelm der Grosse.	Captured -	Gunfire -	—
Nyanga - -	3,066	16	240 miles S. ¼ E. (true) from Tenerife.	Kaiser Wilhelm der Grosse.	Captured -	Scuttled -	—
Bowes Castle -	4,650	18	350 miles N. by W. ½ W. (true) from Cape Orange.	Karlsruhe - -	Captured -	Scuttled -	—
Holmwood - -	4,223	26	170 miles S. ½ W. (true) from Cape Santa Marta Grande.	Dresden - -	Captured -	Bombs -	—
Strathroy - -	4,336	31	100 miles N.N.E. (true) from Cape St. Roque.	Karlsruhe - -	Captured● -	Scuttled -	—
SEPTEMBER		**1914.** Sept.					
Maple Branch -	4,338	3	250 miles S.W. ¼ S. (true) from St. Paul Rocks.	Karlsruhe - -	Captured -	Bomb -	—
Indian Prince -	2,846	4	210 miles E. by N. ½ N. (true) from Pernambuco.	Kronprinz Wilhelm	Captured -	Bomb -	—
Runo - - -	1,679	5	About 22 miles E. by N. from Tyne.	Mine - - -	Mine - -	Mine -	29
Indus - -	3,413	10	240 miles S.E. by E. (true) from Madras.	Emden - -	Captured -	Gunfire -	—
Lovat - -	6,102	11	260 miles E. ½ N. (true) from Madras.	Emden - -	Captured -	Gunfire -	—
Elsinore - -	6,542	11	80 miles S.W. by W. (true) from Cape Corrientes.	Leipzig - -	Captured -	Gunfire -	—
Killin - -	3,544	13	410 miles N.E. by E. (true) from Madras.	Emden - -	Captured -	Gunfire -	—
Diplomat - -	7,615	13	480 miles N.E. ½ E. (true) from Madras.	Emden - -	Captured -	Gunfire -	—
Trabboch - -	4,028	14	70 miles S.W. by S. (true) from Pilots Lt.,Mouth of Hooghli.	Emden - -	Captured -	Gunfire -	—

Name.	Tons.	Date.	Position.	Cause of Loss.	How attacked.	How sunk.	Lives lost.
		1914. Sept.					
Clan Matheson -	4,775	14	60 miles S.W. by S. (true) from Pilots Lt.,Mouth of Hooghli.	Emson - -	Captured -	Bombs -	—
Highland Hope -	5,150	14	190 miles S.W. ½ W. (true) from St. Paul Rocks.	Karlsruhe - -	Captured -	Scuttled -	—
Indrani - -	5,706	17	145 miles N. by W. (true) from Cape St. Roque.	Karlsruhe - -	Captured -	Scuttled -	—
Cornish City -	3,816	21	245 miles S.W. ¼ S. (true) from St. Paul Rocks.	Karlsruhe - -	Captured -	Bombs -	—
Rio Iguassu -	3,817	22	155 miles S.W. ½ W. (true) from St. Paul Rocks.	Karlsruhe - -	Captured -	Bombs -	—
King Lud - -	3,650	25	25 miles S.S.W. (true) from Point de Galle.	Emden - -	Captured -	Bombs -	—
Tymeric - -	3,314	25	50 miles W. by N. (true) from Colombo.	Emden - -	Captured -	Bombs -	—
Bankfields - -	3,763	25	In Gulf of Guayaquil.	Leipzig - -	Captured -	Gunfire -	—
Buresk - -	4,337	27	180 miles W. by N. ¾ N. (true) from Colombo.	Emden - -	Captured -	By H.M.A.S. " Sydney " on 9th Nov. 1914.	—
Ribera - -	3,500	27	210 miles W. by N. (true) from Colombo.	Emden - -	Captured -	Gunfire -	—
Foyle - -	4,147	27	300 miles W. ¾ N. (true) from Colombo.	Emden - -	Captured -	Scuttled -	—
Selby - -	2,137	30	34 miles S.E. by S. from Newarp L.V.	Mine - - -	Mine - -	Mine - -	—
OCTOBER 1914.		Oct.					
Dawdon - -	1,310	3	10 miles N.W. by W. from Wandelaar L.V.	Mine - - -	Mine - -	Mine - -	10
Ardmount - -	3,510	5	3 miles E. by S. ½ S. from Wandelaar L.V.	Mine - - -	Mine - -	Mine - -	—
Niceto de Larrinaga.	5,018	6	100 miles S. by W. ¼ W. (true) from St. Paul Rocks.	Karlsruhe - -	Captured -	Bombs -	—
Lynrowan - -	3,384	7	90 miles S.S.W. (true) from St. Paul Rocks.	Karlsruhe - -	Captured -	Bombs -	—
La Correntina -	8,529	7	320 miles E. ½ N. (true) from Monte Video.	Kronprinz Wilhelm	Captured -	Scuttled -	—
Cervantes - -	4,635	8	100 miles S. ¾ W. (true) from St. Paul Rocks.	Karlsruhe - -	Captured -	Bombs -	—
Pruth - -	4,408	9	90 miles S. by W. ¼ W. (true) from St. Paul Rocks.	Karlsruhe - -	Captured -	Bombs -	—
Condor - -	3,053	11	215 miles N. by E. ¾ E. (true) from Cape St. Roque.	Karlsruhe - -	Captured -	Scuttled -	—
Clan Grant - -	3,948	16	150 miles W. ¼ S. (true) from Minikoi.	Emden - -	Captured -	Gunfire -	—
Benmohr - -	4,806	16	65 miles N.W. ½ W. (true) from Minikoi.	Emden - -	Captured -	Scuttled -	—

Name.	Tons.	Date.	Position.	Cause of Loss.	How attacked.	How sunk.	Lives lost.
		1914. **Oct.**					
Ponrabbel - - (Dredger).	473	16	20 miles N.W. (true) from Minikoi.	Emden - -	Captured -	Gunfire	—
Troilus - -	7,562	18	170 miles E. (true) from Minikoi.	Emden - -	Captured -	Gunfire -	—
Glanton - -	3,021	18	195 miles S.W. (true) from St. Paul Rocks.	Karlsruhe - -	Captured -	Bomb -	—
Chilkana - -	3,244	19	110 miles E.N.E. (true) from Minikoi.	Emden - -	Captured -	Gunfire -	—
Glitra - -	866	20	14 miles W.S.W. from Skudesnaes, Norway.	Submarine - -	Captured -	Scuttled -	—
Cormorant - -	1,595	21	4 miles E. from West Gabbard L.V.	Mine - - -	Mine - -	Mine - - -	—
Hurstdale - -	2,752	23	205 miles S.W. ¼ W. (true) from St. Paul Rocks.	Karlsruhe - -	Captured -	Scuttled -	—
Vandyk - -	10,328	26	690 miles W. by S. (true) from St. Paul Rocks.	Karlsruhe - -	Captured -	Not known	—
Manchester Commerce.	5,363	27	20 miles N. ¼ E. from Tory Island.	Mine - - -	Mine - -	Mine - - -	14 including Master.
NOVEMBER 1914.		**Nov.**					
Ayesha (S.V.) -	123	9	Off N. Keeling Island.	Emden * - -	Captured -	Scuttled 15th Dec. 1914.	—
North Wales -	3,661	16	360 miles S.W. ¼ W. (true) from Valparaiso.	Dresden - -	Captured -	Bombs -	—
Malachite - -	718	23	4 miles N. by W. from Cape la Hève.	Submarine - -	Captured -	Gunfire -	—
Primo - -	1,366	26	6 miles .NW. by N. from Cape Antifer.	Submarine - -	Captured -	Gunfire -	—
Khartoum - -	3,020	27	20 miles E.S.E. from Spurn Point.	Mine - - -	Mine - -	Mine - -	—
DECEMBER 1914.		**Dec.**					
Drummuir (S.V.)	1,844	2	70 miles E. by N. (true) from Cape Horn.	Liepzig - -	Captured -	Bombs -	—
Bellevue - -	3,814	4	460 miles N.E. ¼ E. (true) from Pernambuco.	Kronprinz Wilhelm	Captured -	Scuttled -	—
Charcas - -	5,067	5	70 miles S. by W. ½ W. (true) from Valparaiso.	Prinz Eitel Friedrich.	Captured -	Bombs -	—
Kildalton (S.V.)-	1,784	12	870 miles S.W. ¾ S. (true) from Valparaiso.	Prinz Eitel Friedrich.	Captured -	Bombs -	—
Elterwater - -	1,228	16	3 miles E. from Scarborough.	Mine - - -	Mine - -	Mine - -	6
Princess Olga -	998	16	5 miles E.N.E. from Scarborough.	Mine - - -	Mine - -	Mine - -	—
Tritonia - -	4,272	19	22 miles N.N.E. from Tory Island.	Mine - - -	Mine - -	Mine - -	—
Gem - - -	461	25	3½ miles S.E. by E. ¼ E. from Scarborough.	Mine - - -	Mine - -	Mine - - -	10 including Master.
Linaria - -	3,081	26	2½ miles N.N.E. from Filey.	Mine - - -	Mine - -	Mine - - -	—
Hemisphere -	3,486	28	400 miles N.E. by E. (true) from Pernambuco.	Kronprinz Wilhelm	Captured -	Scuttled -	—

Name.	Tons.	Date.	Position.	Cause of Loss.	How attacked.	How sunk.	Lives lost.
JANUARY 1915.	**915.**	1915. Jan.					
Elfrida - -	2,624	7	2 miles E.N.E. from Scarborough.	Mine - - -	Mine - -	Mine - -	—
Potaro - -	4,419	10	560 miles E. by N. ¼ N. (true) from Pernambuco.	Kronprinz Wilhelm	Captured -	Scuttled -	—
Highland Brae -	7,634	14	630 miles N.E. by E. ¼ E. (true) from Pernambuco.	Kronprinz Wilhelm	Captured -	Scuttled -	—
Wilfrid M. (S.V.)	251	14	625 miles N.E. by E. ¼ E. (true) from Pernambuco.	Kronprinz Wilhelm	Captured -	Rammed -	—
Durward - -	1,301	21	22 miles N.W. from Maas L.V.	Submarine - -	Captured -	Bombs -	—
Ben Cruachan -	3,092	30	15 miles N.W. from Morecambe Lt.	Submarine - -	Captured -	Bombs -	—
Linda Blanche -	369	30	18 miles N.W. ½ N. from Liverpool Bar L.V.	Submarine - -	Captured -	Bombs -	—
Kilcoan - -	456	30	18 miles N.W. from Liverpool Bar L.V.	Submarine - -	Captured -	Bombs -	—
Tokomaru _ -	6,084	30	7 miles N.W. from Havre L.V.	Submarine - -	No warning -	Torpedo -	—
Ikaria - -	4,335	30	25 miles N.W. from Havre.	Submarine - -	No warning -	Torpedo -	—
Oriole - -	1,489	30	English Channel -	Submarine - - (probably).	No warning -	Torpedo -	21 including Master.
FEBRUARY 1915.		Feb.					
Invercoe (S.V.) -	1,421	12	890 miles E. by S. ¼ S. (true) from Cape Frio.	Prinz Eitel Friedrich.	Captured -	Bombs -	—
Dulwich - -	3,289	15	27 miles N.N.E. from Cape la Hève.	Submarine - -	No warning -	Torpedo -	2
Membland - -	3,027	15 (?)	North Sea - -	Mine (?) - -	Mine (?) -	Mine (?) -	20 including Master.
Mary Ada Short -	3,605	18	400 miles E. by N. ¾ N. (true) from Pernambuco.	Prinz Eitel Friedrich.	Captured -	Bombs -	—
Willerby - -	3,630	20	490 miles N.E. by N. (true) from Pernambuco.	Prinz Eitel Friedrich.	Captured -	Bombs -	—
Cambank - -	3,112	20	10 miles E. from Point Lynas.	Submarine - -	No warning -	Torpedo -	4
Downshire - -	337	20	8 miles N.W. ½ W. from Calf of Man.	Submarine - -	Captured -	Bomb -	—
Oakby - -	1,976	23	4 miles E. by N. from Royal Sovereign L.V.	Submarine - -	No warning -	Torpedo -	—
Branksome Chine	2,026	23	6 miles E. by S. ¾ S. from Beachy Head.	Submarine - -	No warning -	Torpedo -	—
Rio Parana -	4,015	24	4 miles S.E. from Beachy Head.	Submarine - -	No warning -	Torpedo -	—
Western Coast -	1,165	24	8 miles S.E. by E. ½ E. from Beachy Head.	Submarine - -	No warning -	Torpedo -	—
Deptford - -	1,208	24	3 miles off Scarborough.	Mine - - -	Mine - -	Mine - -	1

Name.	Tons.	Date.	Position.	Cause of Loss.	How attacked.	How sunk.	Lives lost.
		1915. Feb.					
Harpalion - -	5,867	24	6½ miles W. from Royal . Sovereign L.V.	Submarine - -	No warning -	Torpedo -	3
Conway Castle (S.V.).	1,694	27	560 miles S.W. by W. ½ W. (true) from Valparaiso.	Drèsden - -	Captured -	Scuttled -	—

MARCH 1915.

		Mar.					
Bengrove - -	3,840	7	5 miles N.N.E. from Ilfracombe.	Submarine - -	No warning -	Torpedo -	—
Princess Victoria	1,108	9	16 miles N.W. by N. from Liverpool Bar L.V.	Submarine - -	No warning -	Torpedo -	—
Blackwood - -	1,230	9	18 miles S.W. by S. from Dungeness.	Submarine - -	No warning -	Torpedo -	—
Tangistan - -	3,738	9	9 miles N. from Flamborough Head.	Submarine - -	No warning -	Torpedo -	38 including Master.
Florazan - -	4,658	11	53 miles N.E. ½ E. from Longships.	Submarine - -	No warning -	Torpedo -	1
Headlands - -	2,988	12	8 miles S. from Scilly Isles.	Submarine - -	Chased -	Torpedo -	—
Indian City -	4,645	12	10 miles S. from St. Mary's, Scilly.	Submarine - -	Captured -	Torpedo -	—
Andalusian -	2,349	12	25 miles W.N.W. from Bishop Rock.	Submarine - -	Captured -	Scuttled -	—
Invergyle - -	1,794	12	12 miles N.N.E. from Tyne.	Submarine - -	No warning -	Torpedo -	—
Hartdale - -	3,839	13	7 miles S.E. by E. from South Rock, Co. Down.	Submarine - -	Chased -	Torpedo -	2
Fingal - -	1,562	15	6 miles E. by S. from Coquet Island.	Submarine - -	No warning -	Torpedo -	6
Leeuwarden -	990	17	4 miles W. by N. ½ N. from Maas L.V.	Submarine - -	Captured -	Gunfire -	—
Glenartney -	5,201	18	4 miles S. from Royal Sovereign L.V.	Submarine - -	No warning -	Torpedo -	1
Cairntorr - -	3,588	21	7 miles S. from Beachy Head.	Submarine - -	No warning -	Torpedo -	—
Concord - -	2,861	22	9 miles S.E. by E. ½ E. from Royal Sovereign L.V.	Submarine - -	No warning -	Torpedo -	—
Tamar - -	3,207	25	500 miles E.N.E. (true) from Pernambuco.	Kronprinz Wilhelm	Captured -	Gunfire -	—
Vosges - -	1,295	27	38 miles W. by N. from Trevose Head.	Submarine - -	Chased -	Gunfire -	1
South Point -	3,837	27	60 miles W. from Lundy Island.	Submarine - -	Captured -	Torpedo -	—
Aguila - -	2,114	27	47 miles S.W. from Smalls L.H.	Submarine - -	Captured -	Torpedo -	8
Coleby - -	3,824	27	460 miles N.E. ½ N. (true) from Pernambuco.	Kronprinz Wilhelm	Captured -	Gunfire -	—
Falaba - -	4,806	28	38 miles W. from Smalls L.H.	Submarine - -	Captured -	Torpedo -	104 including Master.
Flaminian - -	3,500	29	50 miles S.W. by W. from Scilly Isles.	Submarine - -	Captured -	Gunfire -	—
Crown of Castile	4,505	30	31 miles S.W. from Bishop Rock.	Submarine - -	Captured -	Bombs -	—

Name.	Tons.	Date.	Position.	Cause of Loss.	How attacked.	How sunk.	Lives lost.
APRIL 1915.		1915. April					
Seven Seas -	1,194	1	6 miles S. from Beachy Head.	Submarine -	No warning -	Torpedo -	9 including Master.
Lochwood -	2,042	2	25 miles S.W. from Start Point.	Submarine -	Captured -	Torpedo -	—
City of Bremen -	1,258	4	20 miles S. ¾ W. from Wolf Rock.	Submarine -	No warning -	Torpedo -	4
Olivine -	634	4	30 miles S. from St. Catherine's Point.	Submarine -	Captured -	Torpedo -	—
Northlands -	2,776	5	24 miles S.W. from Beachy Head.	Submarine -	Captured -	Torpedo -	—
Harpalyce -	5,940	10	7 miles E. by S. from N. Hinder L.V.	Submarine -	No warning -	Torpedo -	15 including Master.
The President -	647	10	14 miles S. by W. from Lizard.	Submarine -	Captured -	Bomb -	—
Ptarmigan -	784	15	6 miles W. by N. from N. Hinder L.V.	Submarine -	No warning -	Torpedo -	8
Mobile -	1,950	28	25 miles N.W. from Butt of Lewis.	Submarine -	Captured -	Gunfire -	—
Cherbury -	3,220	29	27 miles W.N.W. from Eagle Island.	Submarine -	Captured -	Bombs -	—
Fulgent -	2,008	30	20 miles W.N.W. from Blaskets.	Submarine -	Captured -	Bombs -	2 including Master.
MAY 1915.		May					
Edale -	3,110	1	45 miles N.W. by W. from Scilly Isles.	Submarine -	No warning -	Torpedo -	—
Minterne -	3,018	3	50 miles S.W. from Wolf Rock.	Submarine -	No warning -	Torpedo -	2
Earl of Lathom (S.V.).	132	5	8 miles S. by W. from Old Head of Kinsale.	Submarine -	Captured -	Gunfire -	—
Candidate -	5,858	6	13 miles S. by E. ¼ E. from Coningbeg L.V.	Submarine -	Captured -	Torpedo -	—
Centurion -	5,945	6	15 miles S. from Barrel L.V.	Submarine -	No.warning -	Torpedo -	—
Truro -	836	6	85 miles E.N.E. from St. Abb's Head.	Submarine -	Captured -	Torpedo -	—
Lusitania -	30,396	7	15 miles S. from Old Head of Kinsale.	Submarine -	No warning -	Torpedo -	1,198
Queen Wilhelmina.	3,590	8	20 miles S. by E. from Longstone.	Submarine -	Captured -	Torpedo -	—
Don -	939	8	7 miles E. from Coquet Island.	Submarine -	Captured -	Torpedo -	—
Drumcree -	4,052	18	11 miles N. by E. from Trevose Head.	Submarine -	No warning -	Torpedo -	—
Dumfries -	4,121	19	13 miles N. from Trevose Head.	Submarine -	No warning -	Torpedo -	2
Glenholm (S.V.) -	1,968	21	16 miles W.S.W. from Fastnet.	Submarine -	Captured -	Torpedo -	—
Morwenna -	1,414	26	72 miles S. by E. from Fastnet.	Submarine -	Captured -	Torpedo -	1
Cadeby -	1,130	27	20 miles S.W. by S. from Wolf Rock.	Submarine -	Captured -	Gunfire -	—
Spennymoor -	2,733	28	50 miles S.W. ¼ W. from Start Point.	Submarine -	Captured -	Torpedo -	5 including Master.

Name.	Tons.	Date.	Position.	Cause of Loss.	How attacked.	How sunk.	Lives lost.
		1915. May					
Ethiope - -	3,794	28	40 miles S.W. by S. from Start Point.	Submarine - -	Captured -	Torpedo -	—
Tullochmoor -	3,520	28	52 miles N. from Ushant.	Submarine - -	Captured -	Gunfire -	—
Dixiana - -	3,329	29	40 miles N. from Ushant.	Submarine - -	Captured -	Torpedo -	—
Glenlee - -	4,140	29	67 miles S.S.W. from Wolf Rock.	Submarine - -	Captured -	Torpedo -	—
JUNE 1915.		June					
Saidieh - -	3,303	1	·6 miles N.E. from Elbow Buoy.	Submarine - -	No warning -	Torpedo -	8
Iona - - -	3,344	3	22 miles S.S.E. from Fair Isle.	Submarine - -	Captured -	Torpedo -	—
Inkum - -	4,747	4	40 miles S.W. from Lizard.	Submarine - -	No warning -	Torpedo -	—
George and Mary (S.V.).	100	4	15 miles S.W. from Eagle Island.	Submarine - -	Captured -	Gunfire -	—
Dunnet Head -	343	4	35 miles E. by S. from Duncansby Head.	Submarine - -	Captured -	Torpedo -	—
Sunlight (S.V.) -	1,433	6	20 miles S.W. from Galley Head.	Submarine - -	Captured -	Torpedo -	—
Strathcarron -	4,347	8	60 miles W. from Lundy Island.	Submarine - -	No warning -	Torpedo -	—
Express (S.V.) -	115	8	44 miles S.S.W. ½ W. from Smalls.	Submarine - -	Captured -	Bomb -	—
Susannah (S.V.)	115	8	40 miles S.S.W. from Smalls.	Submarine - -	Captured -	Bombs -	—
Lady Salisbury -	1,446	9	1 mile N. from Sunk L.V.	Submarine - -	No warning -	Torpedo -	3
Erna Boldt -	1,731	9	½ mile N.E. by E. from Sunk L.V.	Submarine - -	No warning -	Torpedo -	—
Arndale - -	3,583	11	Entrance to White Sea.	Mine - - -	Mine - -	Mine - -	3
Desabla - -	6,047	12	15 miles E. from Tod Head.	Submarine - -	Captured -	Torpedo -	—
Leuctra - -	3,027	12	1½ miles S.E. by S. from Shipwash L.V.	Submarine - -	No warning -	Torpedo -	—
Crown of India (S.V.).	2,034	12	70 miles W.S.W. from St. Ann's Head.	Submarine - -	Captured -	Gunfire -	—
Hopemount -	3,300	13	70 miles W. by S. from Lundy Island.	Submarine - -	Captured -	Gunfire -	—
Pelham - -	3,534	13	30 miles N.W. from Scilly Isles.	Submarine - -	Captured -	Bombs -	—
Strathnairn -	4,336	15	25 miles N. by E. from Bishop and Clerks.	Submarine - -	No warning -	Torpedo -	21 including Master.
Trafford - -	215	16	30 miles W.S.W. from Tuskar.	Submarine - -	Captured -	Gunfire -	—
Ailsa - - -	876	18	30 miles E. by N. from Bell Rock.	Submarine - -	Captured -	Scuttled -	—
Dulcie - -	2,033	19	6 miles E. from Aldebergh.	Submarine - -	No warning -	Torpedo -	1
Carisbrook - -	2,352	21	70 miles S. ¾ W. from Start Point, Orkneys.	Submarine - -	Captured -	Gunfire -	—
Tunisiana - -	4,220	23	Off Lowestoft -	Submarine - -	No warning -	Torpedo -	—
Drumloist - -	3,118	24	Entrance to White Sea.	Mine - - -	Mine - -	Mine - -	—
Edith (S.V.) -	78	27	10 miles S.E. from Capel Island.	Submarine - -	Captured -	Gunfire -	—
Lucena - -	243	27	4 miles S. from Capel Island.	Submarine - -	Captured -	Gunfire -	—
Indrani - -	3,640	27	40 miles W. from Smalls.	Submarine - -	Captured -	Torpedo -	—

Name.	Tons.	Date.	Position.	Cause of Loss.	How attacked.	How sunk.	Lives lost.
		1915. June					
Dumfriesshire (S.V.).	2,622	28	25 miles S.W. from Smalls.	Submarine - -	No warning -	Torpedo -	—
Armenian - -	8,825	28	20 miles W. from Trevose Head.	Submarine - -	Captured -	Torpedo -	29
Scottish Monarch	5,043	29	40 miles S. from Ballycottin Light.	Submarine - -	Captured -	Gunfire -	15
Lomas - -	3,048	30	65 miles W. from Bishop Rock.	Submarine - -	Captured -	Torpedo -	1
JULY 1915.		July					
L. C. Tower (S.V.)	518	1	30 miles S. from Fastnet.	Submarine - -	Captured -	Set on fire -	—
Gadsby - -	3,497	1	33 miles S.S.W. from Wolf Rock.	Submarine - -	Captured -	Torpedo -	—
Caucasian - -	4,656	1	80 miles S. from Lizard.	Submarine - -	Captured -	Gunfire -	—
Inglemoor - -	4,331	1	75 miles S.W. by W. from Lizard.	Submarine - -	Captured -	Torpedo -	—
Welbury - -	3,591	1	40 miles W. from Fastnet.	Submarine - -	Captured -	Gunfire -	—
Craigard - -	3,286	1	50 miles S.W. by S. from Wolf Rock.	Submarine - -	Captured -	Torpedo -	—
Richmond - -	3,214	1	About 54 miles S.W. by S. from Wolf Rock.	Submarine - -	Captured -	Gunfire -	—
Renfrew - -	3,488	3	85 miles S.W. by S. from Wolf Rock.	Submarine - -	Captured -	Gunfire -	—
Larchmore - -	4,355	3	70 miles S.W. ½ S. from Wolf Rock.	Submarine - -	Captured -	Gunfire -	1
Sunbeam (S.V.) -	132	4	17 miles S. by E. from Wick.	Submarine - -	Captured -	Gunfire -	—
African Monarch	4,003	6	Entrance to White Sea.	Mine - - -	Mine - -	Mine - -	2
Guido - -	2,093	8	27 miles N.E. ¼ N. from Rattray Head.	Submarine - -	Captured -	Torpedo -	—
Meadowfield -	2,750	9	50 miles S.W. from Tuskar.	Submarine - -	Captured -	Gunfire -	1
Ellesmere - -	1,170	9	48 miles S.W. from Smalls.	Submarine - -	Captured -	Torpedo -	1
Grangewood -	3,422	25	20 miles E.N.E. from Flugga L.H., Shetland.	Submarine - -	Captured -	Torpedo -	—
Firth - - -	406	25	4 miles E. by S. from Aldborough Napes Buoy.	Submarine - -	No warning -	Torpedo -	4
Mangara - -	1,821	28	¼ mile E. from Sizewell Buoy, Aldeburgh.	Submarine - -	No warning -	Torpedo -	11
Iberian - -	5,223	30	9 miles S. by W. from Fastnet.	Submarine - -	Captured -	Torpedo -	7
Turquoise - -	486	31	60 miles S.W. from Scilly Isles.	Submarine - -	Captured -	Gunfire -	1
Nugget - -	405	31	45 miles S.W. from Scilly Isles.	Submarine - -	Captured -	Gunfire -	—
AUGUST 1915.		Aug.					
Clintonia - -	3,830	1	30 miles S.W. by W. from Ushant.	Submarine - -	Captured -	Torpedo -	10
Fulgens - -	2,512	1	1 mile off Palling, Norfolk.	Submarine - -	No warning -	Torpedo -	—
Benvorlich - -	3,381	1	50 miles S.W. from Ushant.	Submarine - -	Captured -	Torpedo -	—
Ranza - -	2,320	1	50 miles S.W. from Ushant.	Submarine - -	Captured -	Torpedo -	3
Portia - -	494	2	70 miles South from Scilly Isles.	Submarine - -	Captured -	Gunfire -	—

Name.	Tons.	Date.	Position.	Cause of Loss.	How attacked.	How sunk.	Lives lost.
		1915. Aug.					
Costello - -	1,591	3	95 miles W. by S. from Bishop.	Submarine - -	Captured -	Gunfire -	1
Midland Queen -	1,993	4	70 miles S.W. by W. from Fastnet.	Submarine - -	Captured -	Gunfire -	—
Glenravel - -	1,092	8	25 miles N. from Kinnaird Head.	Submarine - -	Captured -	Bombs -	—
Benarthur - -	2,029	8	8 miles S.E. from Orloff L.H.	Mine - - -	Mine - -	Beached ; wreck.	—
Rosalie - -	4,243	10	3 miles off Blakeney Buoy.	Submarine - -	No warning	Torpedo -	—
Utopia - -	155	10	12 miles E. from St. Abb's Hd.	Submarine - -	Captured -	Gunfire -	—
Oakwood - -	4,279	11	45 miles S.S.E. from Old Head of Kinsale.	Submarine - -	Captured -	Gunfire -	—
Osprey - -	310	12	40 miles N.E. by N. from Nush Terragh, Co. Kerry.	Submarine - -	Captured -	Gunfire -	—
Jacona - -	2,969	12	25 miles N.N.W. from Troupe Hd.	Mine - - -	Mine - -	Mine - -	29
Grodno - -	1,955	12	98 miles N.W. from Lofoten Islands.	Submarine - -	Captured -	Torpedo -	—
Summerfield -	687	13	2 miles East from Lowestoft.	Mine - - -	Mine - -	Mine - -	3
Royal Edward -	11,117	13	6 miles W. from Kandeliusa, Ægean Sea.	Submarine - -	No warning	Torpedo -	132 including Master.
Cairo - -	1,671	13	34 miles S.S.W. from Tuskar.	Submarine - -	Captured	Gunfire -	—
Princess Caroline	888	13	14 miles N. by E. ½ E. from Kinnaird Hd.	Mine - - -	Mine - -	Mine - -	4
Serbino - -	2,205	16	Off Worms Lt. Ho., Baltic.	Submarine - -	No warning	Torpedo -	—
Paros - -	3,596	17	30 miles W. by N. from Bardsey Id.	Submarine - -	Captured -	Torpedo -	—
Kirkby - -	3,034	17	23 miles W. by S. from Bardsey Id.	Submarine - -	Captured -	Torpedo -	—
Maggie - -	269	17	8 miles E. from S. Arklow L.V.	Submarine - -	Captured -	Gunfire -	—
Thornfield - -	488	17	25 miles N.N.E. from Smalls.	Submarine - -	Captured -	Gunfire -	—
Glenby - -	2,196	17	30 miles N. from Smalls.	Submarine - -	Captured -	Gunfire -	2
The Queen -	557	17	40 miles N.N.E. from Smalls.	Submarine - -	Captured -	Gunfire -	—
Bonney - -	2,702	17	16 miles S. by E. from Tuskar.	Submarine - -	Captured -	Gunfire -	—
Dunsley - -	4,930	19	48 miles S. by W. from Old Hd. of Kinsale.	Submarine - -	Captured -	Gunfire -	2
Restormel - -	2,118	19	28 miles N.N.W. from Bishop Rock.	Submarine - -	Captured -	Torpedo -	—
Gladiator - -	3,359	19	68 miles N. by W. from Bishop Rock.	Submarine - -	Captured -	Gunfire -	—
Baron Erskine -	5,585	19	25 miles N.N.W. from Bishop Rock.	Submarine - -	Captured -	Torpedo -	—
Arabic - -	15,801	19	50 miles S. by W. ½ W. from Old Hd. of Kinsale.	Submarine - -	No warning	Torpedo -	44
Ben Vrackie -	3,908	19	55 miles N.W. by N. from Scilly Is.	Submarine - -	Captured -	Gunfire -	—
Samara - -	3,172	19	35 miles W. from Bishop Rock.	Submarine - -	Captured -	Gunfire -	—

Name.	Tons.	Date.	Position.	Cause of Loss.	How attached.	How sunk.	Lives lost.
		1915. Aug.					
St. Olaf (S.V.) -	277	19	58 miles from Galley Hd.	Submarine - -	Captured -	Gunfire -	—
New York City -	2,970	19	44 miles S.S.E. from Fastnet.	Submarine - -	Captured -	Gunfire -	—
Bittern - -	1,797	20	50 miles N.W. from Ushant.	Submarine - -	Captured -	Gunfire -	—
Martha Edmonds (S.V.).	182	20	62 miles W.N.W. from Ushant.	Submarine - -	Captured -	Gunfire -	—
Carterswell -	4,308	20	65 miles N.W. from Ushant.	Submarine - -	Captured -	Gunfire -	—
Windsor - -	6,055	21	70 miles S.W. ½ S. fiom Wolf.	Submarine - -	Captured -	Gunfire -	—
Cober - -	3,060	21	45 miles S.S.W. from Scilly Is.	Submarine - -	Captured -	Torpedo -	—
William Dawson	284	21	Off Boulogne -	Mine - - -	Mine -	Mine - -	5
Ruel - - -	4,029	21	45 miles S.W. from Bishop Rock.	Submarine - -	Captured -	Gunfire -	1
Palmgrove -	3,100	22	46 miles W. by N. ½ N. from Bishop Rock.	Submarine - -	Captured -	Gunfire -	—
Diomed - -	4,672	22	57 miles W.N.W. from Scilly Is.	Submarine - -	Captured -	Gunfire -	10 including Master.
Trafalgar - -	4,572	23	54 miles S.W. by W. from Fastnet.	Submarine - -	Captured -	Bombs -	—
Silvia - -	5,268	23	47 miles West from Fastnet.	Submarine - -	Captured -	Gunfire -	—
Sir William Stephenson.	1,540	29	Off Cockle L.V. -	Mine - - -	Mine -	Mine -	2
Honiton - -	4,914	30	2½ miles E. from Longsand L.V.	Mine - - -	Mine -	Mine -	—
SEPTEMBER	**1915.**						
		Sept.					
Whitefield - -	2,422	1	95 miles N. by W. from Cape Wrath.	Submarine - -	Captured -	Gunfire -	—
Savona - -	1,180	1	½ mile from Shipwash L.V.	Mine - - -	Mine -	Mine -	3
Roumanie -	2,599	2	40 miles N.N.W. from St. Kilda.	Submarine - -	Captured -	Bombs -	—
Churston - -	2,470	3	2½ miles S. from Orfordness.	Mine - - -	Mine -	Mine -	4
Cymbeline - -	4,505	4	29 miles W. by S. from Fastnet.	Submarine - -	Captured -	Torpedo -	6
Mimosa - -	3,466	4	137 miles S.W. by W. from Fastnet.	Submarine - -	Captured -	Gunfire -	—
Natal Transport -	4,107	4	40 miles W. from Gavdo I., Crete.	Submarine - -	Captured	Gunfire -	—
†Hesperian -	10,920	4	85 miles S.W. by S. from Fastnet.	Submarine - -	No warning	Torpedo -	32
Dictator - -	4,116	5	135 miles S. by W. from Fastnet.	Submarine - -	Captured -	Gunfire -	—
Douro - -	1,604	5	79 miles S.W. by W. from Bishop Rock.	Submarine - -	Captured -	Gunfire -	1
John Hardie -	4,372	6	98 miles W. by S. from C. Finisterre.	Submarine - -	Captured -	Gunfire -	—
Caroni - -	2,652	7	15 miles West from Chassiron.	Submarine - -	Captured -	Torpedo -	—
Monarch - -	1,122	8	2½ miles S. from Folkestone.	Mine - - -	Mine -	Mine -	3
Mora - -	3,047	8	68 miles W. by S. from Belle Ile.	Submarine - -	Captured -	Gunfire -	—

Name.	Tons.	Date.	Position.	Cause of Loss.	How attacked.	How sunk.	Lives lost.
		1915. Sept.					
Cornubia - -	1,736	9	75 miles S.E. by S. from Cartagena.	Submarine - -	Captured -	Gunfire -	—
Balakani - -	3,696	9	½ mile S.W. from S. Longsand Buoy.	Mine - - -	Mine - -	Mine -	6
Ashmore - -	2,519	12	5 miles E. ½ N. from Kentish Knock L.V.	Submarine - -	No warning -	Torpedo -	4
Patagonia - -	6,011	15	10½ miles N.E. from Odessa.	Submarine - -	No warning -	Torpedo -	—
Africa - -	1,038	16	1½ miles off Kingsdown.	Mine - - -	Mine - -	Mine - -	2
Ramazan - -	3,477	19	55 miles S.W. from Cerigotto Island.	Submarine - -	Captured -	Gunfire -	1
Linkmoor - -	4,306	20	50 miles W. from C. Matapan.	Submarine - -	Captured -	Gunfire -	—
Horden - -	1,434	20	½ mile E. from Aldborough Napes Buoy.	Mine - - -	Mine - -	Mine - -	—
Groningen - -	988	23	1½ miles N. by E. from Sunk Head Buoy.	Mine - - -	Mine - -	Mine - -	1
Anglo-Colombian	4,792	23	79 miles S.E. from Fastnet.	Submarine - -	Captured -	Gunfire -	—
Chancellor - -	4,586	23	86 miles S. by E. from Fastnet.	Submarine - -	Captured -	Gunfire -	—
Hesione - -	3,663	23	86 miles S by E. from Fastnet.	Submarine - -	Captured -	Gunfire -	—
Urbino - -	6,651	24	67 miles S.W. by W. from Bishop Rock.	Submarine - -	Captured -	Gunfire -	—
Vigilant - - (Pilot Cutter).	69	26	Off Harwich -	Mine - - -	Mine - -	Mine - -	14 including Master.
H. C. Henry -	4,219	28	59 miles S. ½ E. from C. Matapan.	Submarine - -	Captured -	Gunfire -	—
Haydn - -	3,923	29	80 miles S. by E. ½ E. from Gavdo Is., Crete.	Submarine - -	Captured -	Bombs -	—
OCTOBER 1915.		Oct.					
Sailor Prince -	3,144	2	56 miles S.E. by S. from C. Sidero, Crete.	Submarine - -	Captured -	Gunfire -	2
Arabian - -	2,744	2	15 miles W. ½ S. from Cerigo I.	Submarine - -	Captured -	Gunfire -	—
Craigston - -	2,617	4	35 miles W. from Ovo Is.	Submarine - -	Captured -	Gunfire -	—
Bursfield - -	4,037	5	70 miles W. from C. Matapan.	Submarine - -	Captured -	Gunfire -	4 including Master.
Novocastrian -	1,151	5	3½ miles S.E. by E. from Lowestoft.	Mine - - -	Mine - -	Mine - -	—
Silverash -	3,753	6	184 miles E. from Malta.	Submarine - -	Captured -	Gunfire -	—
Scawby - -	3,658	6	220 miles E. from Malta.	Submarine - -	Captured -	Bomb -	—
Halizones - -	5,093	7	122 miles S.S.E.½ E. from C. Martello, Crete.	Submarine - -	Captured -	Gunfire -	—
Thorpwood -	3,184	8	122 miles S. from C. Martello, Crete.	Submarine - -	Captured -	Gunfire -	—
Apollo - -	3,774	9	63 miles S. from Gavdo I., Crete.	Submarine - -	Captured -	Gunfire -	—
Newcastle - -	3,403	10	4 miles S.W. from Folkestone Pier.	Mine - - -	Mine - -	Mine - -	—
Salerno - -	2,071	14	2½ miles S. from Longsand L.V.	Mine - - -	Mine - -	Mine - -	—
Monitoria - -	1,904	21	1¾ miles N. by E. ¾ E. from Sunk Head Buoy.	Mine - - -	Mine - -	Mine - -	—

Name.	Tons.	Date.	Position.	Cause of Loss.	How attacked.	How sunk.	Lives lost.
		1915. Oct.					
Cape Antibes -	2,549	21	Entrance to White Sea.	Mine - - -	Mine - -	Mine - -	6
Marquette - -	7,057	23	36 miles S. from Salonica Bay.	Submarine - . -	No warning -	Torpedo -	29
Ilaro - - -	2,799	23	4 miles E. from Dungeness.	Mine - - -	Mine - -	Mine - -	1
Toward - -	1,218	31	Off S. Foreland -	Mine - - -	Mine - -	Mine - -	—
NOVEMBER 1915.		Nov.					
†Woodfield -	3,584	3	40 miles E.S.E. from Ceuta.	Submarine - -	Captured -	Gunfire -	8
Woolwich - -	2,936	3	104 miles S. from C. Sidero, Crete.	Submarine - -	Captured -	Gunfire -	—
Friargate - -	264	3	4 miles E. from Orfordness.	Mine - - -	Mine - -	Mine - -	2
Moorina - -	4,994	5	105 miles S. from C. Martello (Crete).ı	Submarine - -	Captured -	Gunfire -	—
Buresk - -	3,673	5	30 miles N. by W. from C. Bengut (Algiers).	Submarine - -	Captured -	Gunfire -	—
Alastair - -	366	6	4 miles E. from Southwold.	Mine - - -	Mine - -	Mine - -	7 including Master.
†Lumina - -	5,950	6	120 miles S. by E. from C.Martello, (Crete).	Submarine - -	Captured -	Gunfire -	—
Caria - - -	3,032	6	120 miles S. by E. from C.Martello, Crete.	Submarine - -	Captured -	Gunfire -	—
Clan Macalister -	4,835	6	120 miles S. by E. from C.Martello (Crete).	Submarine - -	Captured -	Torpedo -	—
Glenmoor - -	3,075	6	5 miles N.E. from Cap de Fer (Tunis).	Submarine - -	Captured -	Torpedo -	—
Den of Crombie -	4,949	8	112 miles S. by W.from C. Martello (Crete).	Submarine - -	Captured -	Gunfire -	—
Sir Richard Awdry	2,234	8	72 miles S. by E. ½ E. from Gavdo I.	Submarine - -	Captured -	Torpedo -	1
Californian -	6,223	9	61 miles S.S.W. from C. Matapan.	Submarine - -	No warning -	Torpedo -	1
Irene (Trinity House Yacht).	543	9	1½ miles E.S.E. from Tongue L.V.	Mine - - -	Mine - -	Mine - -	21 including Master.
Rhineland - -	1,501	11	6½ miles S.E. ½ S. from Southwold.	Mine - - -	Mine - -	Mine - -	20 including Master.
Moorside - -	311	12	Off Boulogne -	Mine - - -	Mine - -	Mine - -	8 including Master.
Nigel - -	1,400	12	Off Boulogne -	Mine - - -	Mine - -	Mine - -	5
†Treneglos -	3,886	14	70 miles W.S.W. from Gavdo I.	Submarine - -	No warning -	Torpedo -	3
Orange Prince -	3,583	15	85 miles S.W. by W. from Gavdo I.	Submarine - -	No warning -	Torpedo -	3
Anglia (Hospital Ship).	1,862	17	1 mile E. from Folkestone Gate.	Mine - - -	Mine - -	Mine - -	25
Lusitania - -	1,834	17	1 mile E. from Folkestone Gate.	Mine - - -	Mine - -	Mine - -	—
Enosis - -	3,409	18	150 miles E.S.E. from Malta.	Submarine - -	Captured -	Torpedo -	1 (Master).
Hallamshire -	4,420	19	20 miles S.W.by S. from Cerigotto I.	Submarine - -	No warning -	Torpedo -	—

Name.	Tons.	Date.	Position.	Cause of Loss.	How attacked.	How sunk.	Lives lost.
		1915. Nov.					
Merganser - -	1,905	20	40 miles W.N.W. from Gozo I.	Submarine - -	Captured -	Gunfire -	—
Tringa - -	2,154	26	30 miles N.E. by N. from Galita Is.	Submarine - -	Captured -	Gunfire -	3
Tanis - -	3,655	27	3 miles N. from Zembra I.	Submarine - -	Captured -	Gunfire -	—
Kingsway - -	3,647	27	20 miles E.S.E. from Cape Bon, Tunis.	Submarine - -	Captured -	Gunfire -	—
Dotterel - -	1,596	29	4¾ miles N. by E. from Boulogne Pier.	Mine - - -	Mine - -	Mine - -	5
Malinehe - -	1,868	29	50 miles E. from Malta.	Submarine - -	Captured -	Torpedo -	—
Middleton - -	2,506	30	75 miles S.W. by W. from Gavdo I.	Submarine - -	Captured -	Gunfire -	4
Colenso - -	3,861	30	95 miles E.S.E. from Malta.	Submarine - -	Captured -	Gunfire -	1
Langton Hall -	4,437	30	112 miles E.S.E. from Malta.	Submarine - -	Captured -	Gunfire -	—

DECEMBER 1915.

Name.	Tons.	Date.	Position.	Cause of Loss.	How attacked.	How sunk.	Lives lost.
		Dec.					
Clan Macleod -	4,796	1	100 miles E.S.E. from Malta.	Submarine - -	Captured -	Gunfire -	12
Umeta - -	5,312	1	112 miles E.S.E. from Malta.	Submarine - -	Captured -	Gunfire -	2
Commodore -	5,858	2	160 miles E.S.E. from Malta.	Submarine - -	Captured -	Bombs -	1
Helmsmuir - -	4,111	3	66 miles S. by E. from Gavdo I.	Submarine - -	Captured -	Torpedo -	—
Veria - - -	3,229	7	24 miles N.W. by W. from Alexandria.	Submarine - -	Captured -	Bombs -	—
Ignis - - -	2,042	8	5½ miles N.E. from Aldeburgh.	Mine - - -	Mine - -	Mine - -	—
Busiris - -	2,705	9	190 miles W.N.W. from Alexandria.	Submarine - -	Captured -	Gunfire -	—
Orteric - -	6,535	9	140 miles S. by E. ½ E. from Gavdo I.	Submarine - -	Captured -	Torpedo -	—
Pinegrove - -	2,847	11	8 miles W. ½ S. from C. Grisnez.	Mine - - -	Mine - -	Mine - -	2
Huntly - -	1,153	20	Off Boulogne -	Submarine - -	No warning -	Torpedo -	2
Belford - -	516	20	Off Boulogne -	Submarine - -	No warning -	Torpedo -	—
Knarsdale - -	1,641	21	2¾ miles E. by S. from Orfordness.	Mine - - -	Mine - -	Mine - -	1
Yeddo - -	4,563	24	122 miles S.W. by S. from C. Matapan.	Submarine - -	Captured -	Bombs -	—
Embla - -	1,172	24	3 miles E.S.E. from Tongue L.V.	Mine - - -	Mine - -	Mine - -	—
Van Stirum -	3,284	25	8 miles S.S.W. from Smalls.	Submarine - -	Captured -	Torpedo -	2
Cottingham -	513	26	16 miles S.W. ½ W. from Lundy I.	Submarine - -	Captured -	Gunfire -	7
Hadley - -	1,777	27	3 miles S.E. ½ E. from Shipwash L.V.	Mine - - -	Mine - -	Mine - -	—
El Zorro - -	5,989	28	10 miles S. from Old Head of Kinsale.	Submarine - -	Captured -	Torpedo -	2
Abelia - -	3,650	30	152 miles W. from Gavdo I.	Submarine - -	Captured -	Gunfire -	—
†Persia - -	7,974	30	71 miles S.E. by S. from C. Martello, Crete.	Submarine - -	No warning -	Torpedo -	334 including Master.
†Clan Macfarlane	4,823	30	66 miles S.E. by S. from C. Martello, Crete.	Submarine - -	No warning -	Torpedo -	52 including Master.

Name.	Tons.	Date.	Position.	Cause of Loss.	How attacked.	How sunk.	Lives lost.
JANUARY 1916.		1916. Jan.					
†Glengyle - -	9,395	1	240 miles E. by S. from Malta.	Submarine - -	No warning -	Torpedo -	10
Coquet - -	4,396	4	200 miles E. from Malta.	Submarine - -	Captured -	Bombs -	17 10 made prisoners by Arabs.
Euterpe - -	1,522	7	North Sea - -	Mine (?) - -	Mine (?) -	Mine (?) -	19 including Master.
Farringford -	3,146	11	150 miles W. by N. ¾ N. (true) from C. Finisterre.	Möwe - - -	Captured -	Gunfire -	—
Corbridge - -	3,687	11	140 miles W. by N. ¾ N. (true) from C. Finisterre.	Möwe - - -	Captured -	Not known	—
Algerian - -	3,837	12	2½ miles S.W. from Needles.	Mine - - -	Mine - -	Mine -	—
Traquair - -	1,067	12	1 mile S.W. from Admiralty Pier, Dover.	Mine - - -	Mine - -	Mine -	—
Dromonby - -	3,627	13	220 miles W.(true) from Lisbon.	Möwe - - -	Captured -	Bombs .-	—
Author - -	3,496	13	225 miles W. ½ N. (true) from Lisbon.	Möwe - - -	Captured -	Bombs -	—
Trader - -	3,608	13	225 miles W. ½ N. (true) from Lisbon.	Möwe - - -	Captured -	Bombs -	—
Ariadne - -	3,035	15	140 miles E. by N. (true) from Funchal.	Möwe - - . -	Captured -	Torpedo -	—
†Clan Mactavish	5,816	16	120 miles S. by W. (true) from Funchal.	Möwe - - -	Captured -	Gunfire -	17 Master and 2 gunners made prisoners.
Sutherland - -	3,542	17	192 miles S.E. by E. from Malta.	Submarine - -	Captured -	Gunfire -	1
†Marere - -	6,443	18	236 miles E. from Malta.	Submarine - -	Captured -	Gunfire -	—
Trematon - -	4,198	20	180 miles E. by S. from Malta.	Submarine - -	Captured -	Gunfire -	—
Edinburgh (S.V.).	1,473	20	700 miles W. by S. ¾ S. (true) from St. Vincent C.V.	Möwe - - -	Captured -	Bombs -	—
FEBRUARY 1916.		Feb.					
Belle of France -	3,876	1	126 miles N.W. by W. from Alexandria.	Submarine - -	No warning -	Torpedo -	19
Franz Fischer -	970	1	2 miles S. from Kentish Knock.	Zeppelin - -	Bomb - -	Bomb -	13 including Master.
Flamenco - -	4,629	6	310 miles N.E. by N. (true) from Pernambuco.	Möwe - - -	Captured -	Bombs -	1
Balgownie - -	1,061	6	1¾ miles E.S.E. from Sunk Head Buoy.	Mine - - -	Mine - -	Mine -	1
Argo - - -	1,720	8	4½ miles N.W. from Boulogne Pier.	Mine - - -	Mine - -	Mine -	1
Westburn - -	3,300	8	530 miles N.N.E. (true) from Pernambuco.	Möwe - - -	Captured -	Scuttled -	Master and 2nd officer made prisoners.
Horace - -	3 335	9	610 miles N.N.E. (true) from Pernambuco,	Möwe - - -	Captured -	Bombs -	—

Name.	Tons.	Date.	Position.	Cause of Loss.	How attacked.	How sunk.	Lives lost.
		1916. Feb.					
†Springwell -	5,593	9	64 miles S.W. by W. from Gavdo Is.	Submarine - -	No warning -	Torpedo -	—
Cedarwood -	654	12	2½ miles E. from Aldborough Napes.	Mine - - -	Mine - -	Mine - -	6
Leicester - -	1,001	12	2½ miles S.E. by E. from Folkestone Pier.	Mine - - -	Mine - -	Mine -	17
Tergestea - -	4,308	13	8 miles E. by S. from Aldeburgh.	Mine - - -	Mine - -	Mine -	—
Wilston - -	2,611	15	20 miles E.N.E. from Wick.	Mine - - -	Mine - -	Mine -	8 including Master.
Dingle - -	593	20	10 miles S. by W. from Kentish Knock.	Mine - - -	Mine - -	Mine -	9 including Master.
Duckbridge -	1,491	22	6 miles N. from Straithie Point.	Mine - - -	Mine - -	Mine -	19 including Master.
Diadem - -	3,752	23	56 miles S.E. by S. from Porquerolles Is.	Submarine - -	Captured -	Gunfire -	—
Denaby - -	2,987	24	40 miles S.S.W. from Planier Island.	Submarine - -	Captured -	Gunfire -	1
Fastnet - -	2,227	24	55 miles S.W. from Planier Island.	Submarine - -	Captured -	Gunfire -	—
Tummel - -	531	24	7 miles S. from Kentish Knock.	Mine - - -	Mine - -	Mine - -	9
Saxon Prince -	3,471	25	620 miles W.(true) from Fastnet.	Möwe - - -	Captured -	Bombs -	Crew made prisoners.
Southford - -	963	25	4 miles E.S.E. from Southwold.	Mine - - -	Mine - -	Mine - -	4
Arbonne - -	672	25(?)	North Sea -	Submarine (?) -	No warning(?)	Torpedo (?)	14 including Master.
Dido - - -	4,769	26	4 miles N.N.E. from Spurn L.V.	Mine - - -	Mine - -	Mine - -	28 including Master.
†Maloja - -	12,431	27	2 miles S.W. from Dover Pier.	Mine - - -	Mine - -	Mine - -	122
Empress of Fort William.	2,181	27	2 miles S. from Dover Pier.	Mine - - -	Mine - -	Mine - -	—
Thornaby - -	1,782	28	2 miles N.E. from Shipwash L.V.	Mine - - -	Mine - -	Mine - -	19 including Master.
Masunda - -	4,952	28	106 miles S.W. ½ S. from Cape Matapan.	Submarine -	Captured -	Gunfire -	—
MARCH 1916.		Mar.					
Kilbride - -	3,712	1	30 miles E. from Galita Is., Tunis.	Submarine - -	Captured -	Gunfire -	—
Teutonian - -	4,824	4	36 miles S.W. by W. from Fastnet.	Submarine - -	Captured -	Torpedo -	—
Rothesay - -	2,007	5	30 miles S.W. from Bishop Rock.	Submarine - -	Captured -	Torpedo -	—
Harmatris - -	6,387	8	¼ mile N.E. by N. from Boulogne Breakwater.	Submarine - -	No warning -	Torpedo -	4
Willie (S.V.) -	185	16	60 miles N.W. by W. from Fastnet.	Submarine - -	Captured -	Gunfire -	—
Lowlands - -	1,789	18	8 miles N.E. by E. from N. Foreland.	Submarine - -	No warning -	Torpedo -	—
Port Dalhousie -	1,744	19	2 miles S. ½ W. from Kentish Knock L.V.	Submarine - -	No warning -	Torpedo -	12 including Master.

Name.	Tons.	Date.	Position.	Cause of Loss.	How attacked.	How sunk.	Lives lost.
		1916. Mar.					
Aranmore - -	1,050	21	24 miles E.N.E. from Eagle Island, Co. Mayo.	Submarine - -	Captured -	Torpedo -	—
Kelvinbank -	4,209	22	Havre Roads -	Submarine - -	No warning -	Torpedo -	1
Sea Serpent -	902	23	Off Folkestone Pier.	Mine - - -	Mine - -	Mine - -	14 including Master.
†Minneapolis -	13,543	23	195 miles E. ½ N. from Malta.	Submarine - -	No warning -	Torpedo -	12
Fulmar - -	1,270	24	7 miles N.E. from N. Foreland.	Mine - - -	Mine - -	Mine - -	1 (Master).
Englishman -	5,257	24	30 miles N.E. from Malin Head.	Submarine - -	Captured -	Torpedo -	10
Salybia - -	3,352	24	4 miles S.W. by W. from Dungeness.	Submarine - -	No warning -	Torpedo -	—
Fenay Bridge -	3,838	24	54 miles W. from Bishop Rock.	Submarine - -	Captured -	Torpedo -	—
Saint Cecilia -	4,411	26	4 miles from Folkestone L.V.	Mine - - -	Mine - -	Mine - -	—
Cerne - -	2,579	26	4 miles N.E. from Elbow Buoy.	Mine - - -	Mine - -	Mine - -	—
Manchester Engineer.	4,302	27	20 miles W. by S. from Coningbeg L.V.	Submarine - -	No warning -	Torpedo -	—
Empress of Midland.	2,224	27	9 miles S. from Kentish Knock L.V.	Mine - - -	Mine - -	Mine - -	—
†Eagle Point -	5,222	28	100 miles W.N.W. from Bishop Rock.	Submarine - -	Captured -	Torpedo -	—
Rio Tiete - -	7,464	28	140 miles West from Ushant.	Submarine - -	Captured -	Torpedo -	—
Lavinia Westoll -	3,131	28	33 miles S.E. by S. from Spurn L.V.	Mine - - -	Mine - -	Mine - -	—
John Pritchard (S.V.).	118	30	Off Santa Maura Is. (Greece).	Submarine - -	Captured -	Bombs -	—
†Goldmouth -	7,446	31	60 miles W.N.W. from Ushant.	Submarine - -	Captured -	Torpedo -	Master made prisoner.
†Achilles - -	7,043	31	90 miles W.N.W. from Ushant.	Submarine - -	No warning -	Torpedo -	5
Alacrity - -	1,080	—	North Sea - -	Mine - - -	Mine - -	Mine - -	14 including Master.

APRIL 1916.

		April.					
Ashburton - -	4,445	1	80 miles W.N.W. from Ushant.	Submarine - -	Captured -	Torpedo -	—
Perth - -	653	1	1 mile S.E. by E. from Cross Sand L.V.	Submarine - -	No warning -	Torpedo -	6
Bengairn (S.V.) -	2,127	1	165 miles W.S.W. from Fastnet.	Submarine - -	Captured -	Gunfire -	—
†Simla - -	5,884	2	45 miles N.W. ½ W. from Gozo Island.	Submarine - -	No warning -	Torpedo -	10
Sneaton - -	3,470	3	35 miles N.N.E. from Cap de Garde, Tunis.	Submarine - -	Captured -	Bombs -	—
†Clan Campbell -	5,897	3	29 miles S.E. from Cape Bon.	Submarine - -	No warning -	Torpedo -	—
Ellaston - -	3,796	3	65 miles N.W. by W. from Cape Serrat.	Submarine - -	Captured -	Torpedo -	—
Bendew - -	3,681	4	9 miles S. ½ E. from Kentish Knock.	Mine - - -	Mine - -	Mine - -	1
†Chantala - -	4,951	5	15 miles N. from C. Bengut.	Submarine - -	No warning -	Torpedo -	9
Zent - - -	3,890	5	28 miles W. by S. ½ S. from Fastnet.	Submarine - -	No warning -	Torpedo -	49

Name.	Tons.	Date.	Position.	Cause of Loss.	How attacked.	How sunk.	Lives lost.
		1916. April					
Vesuvio - -	1,391	6	6 miles E. from Owers L.V.	Mine - - -	Mine - -	Mine -	7 including Master.
Yonne - -	4,039	6	18 miles N.N.W. from Shershel, Algeria.	Submarine - -	No warning -	Torpedo -	—
Halcyon - -	1,319	7	3½ miles S.W. by S. from Folkestone Pier.	Mine - - -	Mine - -	Mine -	—
Clyde (S.V.) -	204	7	32 miles N. from Dieppe.	Submarine - -	Captured -	Bombs -	—
Braunton -	4,575	7	4½ miles S. by W. from Beachy Head.	Submarine - -	No warning -	Torpedo -	—
Zafra -	3,578	8	44 miles N. from Oran.	Submarine - -	Captured -	Bombs -	—
Adamton -	2,304	8	15 miles S. from Skerryvore.	Submarine - -	Captured -	Gunfire -	1
Avon -	1,574	9	2½ miles S.E. by S. from Tongue L.V.	Mine - - -	Mine - -	Mine	2
Eastern City	4,341	9	18 miles N. by W. from Ushant.	Submarine - -	Captured -	Gunfire -	—
Glenalmond -	2,888	9	27 miles N. from Ushant.	Submarine - -	Captured -	Torpedo -	—
Silksworth Hall -	4,777	10	1¼ miles N.E. from Corton L.V.	Submarine - -	No warning -	Torpedo -	3
Margam Abbey -	4,471	10	55 miles S.W. ¼ S. from Lizard.	Submarine - -	Captured -	Gunfire -	—
Robert Adamson -	2,978	10	3 miles N. by E. from Shipwash L.V.	Submarine - -	No warning -	Torpedo -	—
Inverlyon (S.V.) -	1,827	11	108 miles W.N.W. from Fastnet.	Submarine - -	Captured -	Gunfire -	—
Angus -	3,619	11	76 miles E. by N. from Valencia.	Submarine - -	Captured -	Gunfire -	—
Orlock Head -	1,945	12	65 miles S.E. from Barcelona.	Submarine - -	Captured -	Gunfire -	—
Chic - -	3,037	13	45 miles S.W. from Fastnet.	Submarine - -	Captured -	Torpedo -	9 including Master.
Shenandoah -	3,886	14	1½ miles W. from Folkestone Gate.	Mine - - -	Mine - -	Mine -	2
Fairport -	3,838	15	31 miles N. by W. from Bishop Rock.	Submarine - -	Captured -	Torpedo -	—
Harrovian -	4,309	16	60 miles W. from Bishop Rock.	Submarine - -	Captured -	Gunfire -	—
Cardonia (S.V.) -	2,169	16	20 miles S. from Fastnet.	Submarine - -	Captured -	Torpedo -	—
Ravenhill (S.V.) -	1,826	18	78 miles S.E. by S. from Fastnet.	Submarine - -	Captured -	Gunfire -	—
Cairngowan -	4,017	20	60 miles W. by N. from Fastnet.	Submarine - -	Captured -	Gunfire -	—
Sabbia -	2,802	20	7 miles S.E. by S. from May Island.	Mine - - -	Mine - -	Mine -	—
Whitgift -	4,397	20	Off Ushant -	Submarine - -	No warning -	Torpedo -	32 including Master.
Feliciana -	4,283	21	67 miles W. by N. ½ N. from Fastnet.	Submarine - -	No warning -	Torpedo -	—
Tregantle -	3,091	22	1½ miles E.S.E. from Corton L.V.	Submarine - -	No warning -	Torpedo -	—
Ross - -	2,666	22	108 miles W. by N. from Bishop Rock.	Submarine - -	Captured -	Torpedo -	—
Parisiana -	4,763	23	82 miles W. ½ S. from Ushant.	Submarine - -	Captured -	Torpedo -	—
Ribston -	3,048	23	66 miles W. by S. from Ushant.	Submarine - -	Captured -	Torpedo -	—

Name.	Tons.	Date.	Position.	Cause of Loss.	How attacked.	How sunk.	Lives lost.
		1916. April					
Industry -	4,044	27	120 miles W. by N. from Fastnet.	Submarine - -	Captured -	Torpedo -	—
Teal - - -	716	29	2 miles E. from Seaham Harhour.	Submarine - -	Captured -	Torpedo -	—
†City of Lucknow.	3,677	30	60 miles E. from Malta.	Submarine - -	No warning -	Torpedo -	—
MAY 1916.		May					
Hendonhall -	3,994	1	2 miles S. ½ E. from Inner Gabbard Buoy.	Mine - - -	Mine - -	Mine	—
Maud (S.V.) -	120	1	50 miles S.W. by W. from Ushant.	Submarine - -	Captured -	Gunfire -	—
Rochester City -	1,239	2	3 miles E. from Southwold.	Mine - - • -	Mine - -	Mine	1
Ruabon -	2,004	2	160 miles W. by S. ½ S. from Ushant.	Submarine - -	Captured -	Torpedo -	—
Galgate (S.V.) -	2,356	6	170 miles W. by N. from Ushant.	Submarine - -	Captured -	Gunfire -	—
Cymric -	13,370	8	140 miles W.N.W. from Fastnet.	Submarine - -	No warning -	Torpedo -	5
Dolcoath -	1,706	10	3¼ miles N.N.E. from N. Foreland.	Mine - - -	Mine - -	Mine	1
Eretria -	3,464	13	15 miles S.S.W. from Ile D'Yeu, Bay of Biscay.	Mine - - -	Mine - -	Mine	—
Rhenass -	285	22	Off Aldeburgh -	Mine - - -	Mine - -	Mine	6
†El Argentino -	6,809	26	7 miles S.E. by S. from Southwold.	Mine - - -	Mine - -	Mine	—
Denewood -	1,221	26	Off Aldeburgh -	Mine - - -	Mine - -	Mine	—
Lincairn -	3,638	27	8 miles N. by E. from Shipwash.	Mine - - -	Mine - -	Mine	—
Trunkby -	2,635	27	50 miles S. by E. from Port Mahon, Minorca.	Submarine - -	Captured -	Gunfire -	—
Lady Ninian -	4,297	28	106 miles N.E. ½ N. from Algiers.	Submarine - -	Captured -	Gunfire -	1
Elmgrove -	3,018	29	96 miles N.E. from Algiers.	Submarine - -	Captured -	Gunfire -	—
Southgarth -	2,414	29	60 miles N.N.E. from Algiers.	Submarine - -	Captured -	Bombs -	—
Baron Vernon -	1,779	29	56 miles N.E. ½ N. from Algiers.	Submarine - -	Captured -	Gunfire -	—
†Dalegarth -	2,265	30	12 miles N.E. from Cape Corbelin, Algiers.	Submarine - -	Captured -	Torpedo -	—
Julia Park -	2,900	30	10 miles N. from Cape Carbon, Algeria.	Submarine - -	Captured -	Torpedo -	—
Baron Tweedmouth.	5,007	30	25 miles N.E. by N. from Cape Carbon, Algeria.	Submarine - -	Captured -	Gunfire -	—
JUNE 1916.		1916. June					
Dewsland -	1,993	1	28 miles N.E. by E. from Cape Carbon, Algeria.	Submarine - -	Captured -	Gunfire -	—
Salmonpool -	4,905	1	30 miles N.E. by E. from Cape Carbon, Algeria.	Submarine - -	Captured -	Torpedo -	—
Golconda -	5,874	3	5 miles S.E. by E. from Aldeburgh.	Submarine - -	No warning -	Torpedo -	19
Sardinia -	1,119	15	38 miles W. ¼ N. from Gorgona Island.	Submarine - -	Captured -	Gunfire -	—

Name.	Tons.	Date.	Position.	Cause of Loss.	How attacked.	How sunk.	Lives lost.
		1916. June					
Gafsa - -	3,922	16	80 miles S.W. by S. from Genoa.	Submarine - -	Captured -	Gunfire -	—
Rona - - -	1,312	18	90 miles W. from Cape Falcone, Sardinia.	Submarine - -	Captured -	Gunfire -	—
Beachy - -	4,718	18	98 miles N.E. by E. from Port Mahon.	Submarine - -	Captured -	Torpedo -	—
Corton Light Vessel.	—	21	4 miles N.E. by E. from Lowestoft.	Mine - - -	Mine - -	Mine - -	5
Burma - -	706	23	5 miles N. by E. ½ E. from Shipwash L.V.	Mine - - -	Mine - -	Mine - -	7
Brussels - -	1,380	23	Off Dutch Coast -	Torpedo boat -	Captured -	Taken into Zeebrugge.	Crew made prisoners. Master subsequently shot.
Canford Chine -	2,398	24	5 miles off Calella, Spain.	Submarine - -	Captured -	Gunfire	—
Astrologer - -	912	26	5 miles S.S.E. from Lowestoft.	Mine - - -	Mine - -	Mine - -	11 including Master.
Windermere -	2,292	27	58 miles S.S.E. from Port Mahon.	Submarine - -	Captured -	Scuttled -	12 including Master.
Mercurius (Dredger).	129	28	3 miles S.E. from Lowestoft.	Mine - - -	Mine - -	Mine - -	6
Teano - -	1,907	29	24 miles N.W. by N. from Marittimo Island, Sicily.	Submarine - -	Captured -	Scuttled -	—
†Moeris - -	3,409	30	46 miles S.E. from Cape Sidero, Crete.	Submarine - -	No warning -	Torpedo -	3
JULY 1916.		1916. July					
Rockliffe - -	3,073	2	Black Sea - -	Submarine - -	—	—	—
Lestris - -	1,384	5	Between Maas L.V. and Schouwenbank.	Torpedo boat and submarine.	Captured - -	Taken into Zeebrugge.	Crew made prisoners. 8
Gannet - -	1,127	7	5 miles E.N.E. from Shipwash L.V.	Mine - - -	Mine - -	Mine -	—
Pendennis -	2,123	8	North Sea - -	Submarine - -	Captured -	Taken to Germany.	Crew made prisoners.
Kara - - -	2,338	10	Near Pakefield Gat Buoy.	Mine - - -	Mine - -	Mine - -	—
Calypso - -	2,876	10	North Sea - -	Submarine - -	No warning -	Torpedo -	30 including Master.
Silverton - -	2,682	13	14 miles N.E. from Canae Rocks.	Submarine - -	Captured -	Torpedo -	—
Ecclesia - -	3,714	14	11 miles N.W. from Bougaroni Point.	Submarine - -	Captured -	Gunfire -	—
Antigua - -	2,876	14	20 miles E. by N. from Jidjelli, Algeria.	Submarine - -	Captured -	Bombs -	—
Sylvie - -	1,302	15	15 miles from Cape Sigli, Algeria.	Submarine - -	Captured -	Gunfire -	—
Alto - - -	2,266	16	4 miles off Kessingland, Suffolk.	Mine - - -	Mine - -	Mine - -	—

Name.	Tons.	Date.	Position.	Cause of Loss.	How attacked.	How sunk.	Lives lost.
		1916. July					
Virginia - -	4,279	16	42 miles S.W. by W. from Cape Matapan.	Submarine - -	Captured -	Torpedo -	2
Mopsa - -	885	16	7 miles S. from Lowestoft.	Mine - - -	Mine - -	Mine - -	—
Wilton Hall -	3,387	16	65 miles N.W. from Algiers.	Submarine - -	Captured -	Bombs -	—
†Euphorbia -	3,837	16	56 miles N.E. from Algiers.	Submarine - -	No warning -	Torpedo -	11
Rosemoor - -	4,303	17	80 miles N.E. by N. from Algiers.	Submarine - -	Captured -	Bombs -	—
Llongwen - -	4,683	18	90 miles N.E. from Algiers.	Submarine - -	Captured -	Gunfire -	14
Grangemoor -	3,198	20	75 miles N.W. by W. from Algiers.	Submarine - -	Captured -	Gunfire -	—
Yzer - - -	3,538	20	56 miles N.W. ½ N. from Algiers.	Submarine - -	Captured -	Torpedo -	1
Karma - -	3,710	20	68 miles N.N.W. from Algiers.	Submarine - -	Captured -	Gunfire -	—
Wolff - - -	2,443	21	75 miles N.N.W. from Algiers.	Submarine - -	Captured -	Gunfire -	—
Knutsford - -	3,842	22	12 miles N.W. by N. from Cape Corbelin, Algeria.	Submarine - -	Captured -	Gunfire -	—
†Olive - -	3,678	22	10 miles N.W. by N. from Cape Corbelin, Algeaia.	Submarine - -	Captured -	Gunfire -	—
Badminton - -	3,847	23	63 miles N.E. by N. from Cape Carbon, Algeria.	Submarine - -	Captured -	Gunfire -	—
Eskimo - -	3,326	26	Off Risoer, in Norwegian territorial waters.	Auxiliary Cruiser -	Captured -	Taken to Germany.	Crew (except 1) made prisoners.
Claudia - -	1,144	30	8½ miles S.E. by S. ⅓ S. from Lowestoft.	Mine - - -	Mine - -	Mine - -	3
Ethelbryhta -	3,084	30	11 miles W.S.W. from Pantellaria.	Submarine - -	Captured -	Gunfire -	—
Britannic - -	3,487	30	20 miles E.S.E. from Cape Bon.	Submarine - -	Captured -	Gunfire -	—

AUGUST 1916.

		Aug.					
Aaro - - -	2,603	1	North Sea - -	Submarine - -	No warning -	Torpedo -	3 Remainder of crew made prisoners.
Heighington -	2,800	1	40 miles N.E. from Cape Serrat.	Submarine - -	Captured -	Torpedo -	—
G. C. Gradwell (S.V.).	156	2	20 miles N.W. from Cape Antifer.	Submarine - -	Captured -	Gunfire -	—
S.D. (barge) -	131	2	18 miles N.N.W. from Cape Antifer.	Submarine - -	Captured -	Gunfire -	—
Margaret Sutton (S.V.).	197	2	35 miles S.S.E. from St. Catherine's Point.	Submarine - -	Captured -	Bombs -	—
Sphene - -	740	3	26 miles S.W. from St. Catherine's Point.	Submarine - -	Captured -	Bombs -	—
Badger - -	89	3	30 miles S.W. ½ S. from St. Catherine's Point.	Submarine - -	Captured -	Gunfire -	—

Name.	Tons.	Date.	Position.	Cause of Loss.	How attacked.	How sunk.	Lives lost.
		1916. Aug.					
Fortuna (S.V.) -	131	3	15 miles S.S.W. from Portland Bill.	Submarine -	Captured -	Bombs -	—
Ermenilda (S.V.)	94	4	24 miles S.S.W. from Portland Bill.	Submarine -	Captured -	Bomb -	-
Demaris (S.V.) -	79	4	20 miles N. from Alderney.	Submarine -	Captured -	Bomb -	—
Spiral - -	1,342	4	40 miles W.S.W. from St. Catherine's Point.	Submarine -	Captured -	Bombs -	—
Favoniau - -	3,049	4	24 miles S.W. from Planier Island.	Submarine -	Captured -	Gunfire -	—
Tottenham - -	3,106	4	33 miles S.W. by W. from Marseilles.	Submarine -	Captured -	Gunfire -	—
Stamfordham	921	4	8 miles S. from Longstone.	Submarine -	Captured -	Gunfire -	—
Mount Coniston -	3,018	5	7 miles E. by S. from Meda Island, Spain.	Submarine -	Captured -	Bombs -	—
Trident - -	3,129	7	34 miles N. by E. ¾ E. from Dragonera Is., Majorca.	Submarine -	Captured -	Torpedo -	—
Newburn - -	3,554	7	34 miles N. by E. ¾ E. from Dragonera Is., Majorca.	Submarine -	Captured -	Torpedo -	—
Imperial - -	3,818	8	38 miles S.W. by W. from Planier Island.	Submarine -	Captured -	Gunfire - -	—
Antiope - -	2,973	9	88 miles S.W. by W. from Marseilles.	Submarine -	Captured -	Gunfire -	—
San Bernardo -	3,803	10	17 miles S.E. from Longstone.	Submarine -	Captured -	Bombs -	—
F. Stobart - -	801	11	½ mile N. from North Aldborough Napes Buoy.	Mine - -	Mine - -	Mine -	4
†Swedish Prince -	3,712	17	12 miles N.W. by W. from Pantellaria.	Submarine -	Captured -	Gunfire -	1 Master, Chief Engineer and Gunner made prisoners.
Duart - -	3,108	31	60 miles N. ¾ E. from Shershel, Algeria.	Submarine -	Captured -	Gunfire -	—
SEPTEMBER 1916.							
		Sept.					
Baron Yarborough.	1,784	1	27 miles N.W. from Dragonera Island, Majorca.	Submarine -	Captured -	Bombs -	—
†Swift Wings -	4,465	1	18 miles E. from Cape Bengut. Algeria.	Submarine -	No warning -	Torpedo -	2 Master made prisoner.
Kelvinia - -	5,039	2	9 miles S. by W. from Caldy Island, Bristol Channel.	Mine - -	Mine - -	Mine -	—
Strathallan -	4,404	2	20 miles N.E. from Philippeville.	Submarine -	Captured -	Gunfire -	Master made prisoner.
Teesbcrough -	308	3	30 miles N.E. by N. from Fecamp.	Submarine -	Captured -	Bombs -	—

Name.	Tons.	Date.	Position.	Cause of Loss.	How attacked.	How sunk.	Lives lost.
		1916. Sept.					
Mascotte - -	1,097	3	6½ miles S.E. from Southwold.	Mine - - -	Mine - -	Mine - -	1
Netta - -	370	3	35 miles N.E. ½ N. from Cape Antifer.	Submarine - -	Captured -	Bombs -	—
Rievaulx Abbey -	1,166	3	¾ mile E.N.E. from Rosse Spit Buoy, Humber.	Mine - - -	Mine - -	Mine - -	2
Laristan - -	3,675	4	30 miles W. from Gozo.	Submarine - -	Captured -	Torpedo -	Master prisoner.
City of Ghent	199	5	18 miles S.E. from Cape Barfleur.	Submarine - -	Captured -	Bombs -	—
Torridge - -	5,036	6	40 miles S.S.W. from Start Point.	Submarine - -	Captured -	Bombs -	—
Tagus - -	937	6	35 miles N.E. by E. ½ E. from Ushant.	Submarine - -	Captured -	Bombs -	—
Britannia (S.V.) -	39	6	12 miles N. from Alderney.	Submarine - -	Captured -	Bombs -	—
Strathtay - -	4,428	6	4 miles N. from Pontusval, Finistere.	Submarine - -	Captured -	Torpedo -	—
Heathdene - -	3,541	7	38 miles S.S.W. from the Lizard.	Submarine - -	Captured -	Scuttled -	—
†Achaia - -	2,733	7	300 yards E.N.E. from entrance to Oran Harbour.	Mine - - -	Mine - -	Mine -	—
†Llangorse - -	3,841	8	48 miles W.S.W. from Cape Matapan.	Submarine - -	No warning -	Torpedo -	—
†Butetown - -	3,789	8	55 miles W.S.W. from Cape Matapan.	Submarine - -	No warning -	Torpedo -	—
Lexie - -	3,778	10	42 miles S.W. from Ushant.	Submarine - -	Captured -	Torpedo -	—
†Italiana - -	2,663	14	112 miles E. from Malta.	Submarine - -	No warning -	Torpedo -	—
Counsellor - -	4,958	14	5 miles W. ½ S. from Galley Head.	Mine - - -	Mine - -	Mine - -	—
†Inverbervie -	4,309	14	17 miles S. by W. from Cape Rizzuto, Italy.	Submarine - -	No warning -	Torpedo -	6
Lord Tredegar -	3,856	17	51 miles S,E. by E. from Malta.	Submarine - -	No warning -	Torpedo -	4
†Dewa - -	3,802	17	45 miles E. ¾ N. from Malta.	Submarine - -	No warning -	Torpedo -	3
Etton - -	2,831	20	Entrance to White Sea.	Mine - - -	Mine - -	Mine - -	1
Colchester - -	964	22	North Sea - -	Torpedo Boats -	Captured -	Taken into Zeebrugge.	Crew prisoners.
Kennett - -	1,679	22	Baltic - -	Submarine - -	No warning -	Torpedo -	1 (Master).
†Charterhouse -	3,021	23	26 miles E. by S. ½ S. from S.E. point of Formentera.	Submarine - -	Captured -	Bombs -	Master and 2 gunners made prisoners.
Dresden - -	807	23	41 miles S. by E. ¼ E. from the Nab.	Submarine - -	Captured -	Bombs -	—
Pearl - - -	613	23	41 miles S. ¼ E. from the Nab.	Submarine - -	Captured -	Bombs -	—
†Bronwen - -	4,250	24	25 miles N. by E. from Dragonera Island.	Submarine - -	Captured -	Gunfire -	Master and 2 gunners made prisoners.
Stathe - -	2,623	26	50 miles E. by S. from Barcelona.	Submarine - -	Captured -	Gunfire -	—
Newby - -	2,168	26	53 miles E. from Barcelona.	Submarine - -	Captured -	Gunfire -	—

Name.	Tons.	Date.	Position.	Cause of Loss.	How attacked.	How sunk.	Lives lost.
		1916. Sept.					
Thelma - -	1,002	26	24 miles E. from Fair Isle.	Submarine -	Captured -	Torpedo -	—
†Boddam - -	3,218	26	76 miles E.S.E. from Barcelona.	Submarine - -	Captured -	Gunfire -	Master made prisoner.
St. Gothard -	2,788	26	12 miles N. by W. from Fair Isle.	Submarine - -	Captured -	Torpedo -	—
Thurso - -	1,244	27	60 miles N.E. by E. from Rattray Head.	Submarine - -	Captured -	Gunfire -	Master and Chief Engineer made prisoners.
†Secondo - -	3,912	27	40 miles N.N.E. from Dragonera Island.	Submarine - -	No warning -	Torpedo -	—
†Rallus - -	1,752	27	45 miles N.E. by N. from Dragonera Island.	Submarine - -	Captured -	Gunfire -	—
Maywood - -	1,188	30	1 mile W. from Whistle Buoy, Havre.	Mine - - -	Mine - -	Mine -	—
Pearl (S.V.) -	144	30	6 miles S.S.E. from Lizard.	Submarine - -	Captured -	Bombs -	—
William George (S.V.).	151	30	10 miles N.N.E. from Cap la Hague.	Submarine - -	Captured -	Gunfire -	—

OCTOBER 1916.

Name.	Tons.	Date. Oct.	Position.	Cause of Loss.	How attacked.	How sunk.	Lives lost.
†Vanellus - -	1,797	1	Havre Roads -	Mine - - -	Mine - -	Mine -	3
Lotusmere - -	3,911	2	48 miles N.N.E. from Teriberski L.H.	Submarine -	Captured -	Torpedo -	—
†Huntsfall - -	4,331	2	12 miles S.S.E. from Skyro.	Submarine - -	No warning -	Torpedo -	Master made prisoner.
†Franconia -	18,150	4	195 miles E. ½ S. from Malta.	Submarine - -	No warning -	Torpedo -	12
J. Y. Short -	2,193	4	80 miles E. from Vardo.	Submarine - -	Captured -	Gunfire -	—
Brantingham -	2,617	4	Arctic Ocean -	Submarine - -	No warning (probably).	Torpedo -	24 including Master
Isle of Hastings -	1,575	5	10 miles S. by W. from Ushant.	Submarine - -	Captured -	Bombs -	—
Lanterna - -	1,685	6	2½ miles N.E. ½ E. from Cromer.	Mine - - -	Mine - -	Mine -	—
Strathdene -	4,321	8	20 miles S. by E. from Nantucket L.V.	Submarine - -	Captured -	Torpedo -	—
West Point -	3,847	8	46 miles S.E. by E. from Nantucket L.V.	Submarine - -	Captured -	Bombs -	—
Stephano - -	3,449	8	2½ miles E.N.E. from Nantucket L.V.	Submarine - -	Captured -	Torpedo -	—
Astoria - -	4,262	9	120 miles N.W. by W. from Vardo.	Submarine - -	Captured •	Torpedo -	17
†Elax - -	3,980	10	70 miles W.S.W. from Cape Matapan.	Submarine - -	No warning -	Torpedo -	·—
Gardepee - -	1,633	10	70 miles N.N.E. from North Cape.	Submarine - -	Captured -	Bombs -	—
†Crosshill - -	5,002	11	60 miles W. from Malta.	Submarine - -	No warning -	Torpedo -	4
Iolo - -	3,903	11	153 miles N. from Vardo.	Submarine -	Captured •	Torpedo -	—

Name.	Tons.	Date.	Position.	Cause of Loss.	How attacked.	How sunk.	Lives lost.
		1916. Oct.					
Welsh Prince	4,934	13	33 miles S.W. from Cape Matapan.	Submarine	No warning	Torpedo	2
Ethel Duncan	2,510	18	40 miles W.N.W. from Noop Head, Orkney.	Submarine	Captured	Torpedo	—
†Penylan	3,875	19	5 miles W. by N. from Cape Bougaroni.	Submarine	No warning	Torpedo	—
Alaunia	13,405	19	2 miles S. from Royal Sovereign L.V.	Mine	Mine	Mine	2
Huguenot	1,032	20	4 miles N.E. ½ E. from Sunk L.V.	Mine	Mine	Mine	—
†Mombassa	4,689	20	8 miles N.W. by N. from Cape Corbelin.	Submarine	No warning	Torpedo	1
The Duke	376	20	40 miles N.N.E. from Havre.	Submarine	Captured	Gunfire	—
Cabotia	4,309	20	120 miles W.N.W. from Tory Island.	Submarine	Captured	Gunfire	32 including Master.
The Marchioness	553	20	30 miles N.W. from Fecamp.	Submarine	Captured	Gunfire	—
Cliburn	440	20	30 miles S.S.E. from St. Catherine's Point.	Submarine	Captured	Bombs	—
Barbara	3,740	20	25 miles S. from Isle of Wight.	Submarine	Captured	Gunfire	—
Midland	4,247	20	60 miles E. by N. ½ N. from Ushant.	Submarine	Captured	Bombs	—
Cock o' the Walk (S.V.).	111	21	30 miles N.W. by N. from Hanois, Guernsey.	Submarine	Captured	Gunfire	—
Grit (Motor Barge)	147	21	25 miles S. from Beachy Head.	Submarine	Captured	Gunfire	—
Princess May (S.V.).	104	21	25 miles S. from Beachy Head.	Submarine	Captured	Bomb	—
†Cluden	3,166	22	11 miles W. from Cape Tenez, Algeria.	Submarine	No warning	Torpedo	4
W. Harkess	1,185	22	17 miles W. from Cape Tenez, Algeria.	Submarine	Captured	Bombs	—
Sidmouth	4,045	24	22 miles S. from Wolf.	Submarine	Captured	Torpedo	—
Twig (S.V.)	128	24	15 miles N. from Alderney.	Submarine	Captured	Bomb	—
Framfield	2,510	24	3 miles N.E. from Sunk L.V.	Mine	Mine	Mine	6 including Master.
Rowanmore	10,320	26	128 miles W.N.W. from Fastnet.	Submarine	Captured	Torpedo	Master made prisoner.
The Queen	1,676	26	3 miles N.E. from Varne L.V.	Destroyers	Captured	—	—
Oola	2,494	26	22 miles N.E. by N. from North Cape.	Submarine	Captured	Bombs	—
Rappahannock	3,871	26	70 miles from Scilly Isles.	Submarine	Captured	Not known	37 including Master.
Sparta	480	28	3½ miles E. by N. from Southwold.	Mine	Mine	Mine	4
†Marina	5,204	28	30 miles W. from Fastnet.	Submarine	No warning	Torpedo	18
Rio Pirahy	3,561	28	60 miles S. from Cape St. Vincent.	Submarine	Captured	Bombs	—
Galeka (Hospital Ship).	6,772	28	5 miles N.W. from Cape la Hague.	Mine	Mine	Mine	—

Name.	Tons.	Date.	Position.	Cause of Loss.	How attacked.	How sunk.	Lives lost.
		1916. **Oct.**					
†Meroë - -	3,552	29	70 miles W. ½ N. from Cape Trafalgar.	Submarine - -	Captured -	Torpedo -	—
†Torino - -	1,850	29	70 miles W. ½ N. from Cape Trafalgar.	Submarine - -	Captured -	Torpedo -	1
†Marquis Bacque-hem.	4,396	29	50 miles S. by E. from Cape St. Vincent.	Submarine - -	No warning -	Torpedo -	
†Glenlogan -	5,838	31	10 miles S.E. from Stromboli.	Submarine - -	No warning -	Torpedo -	—
North Wales -	4,072	—	Off Scilly Islands	Submarine - - (reported).	No warning (probably).	Torpedo -	30 including Master.
NOVEMBER 1916.		**Nov.**					
Brierley Hill -	1,168	1	18 miles W.N.W. from Hellisö L.H., Norway.	Submarine - -	Captured -	Torpedo -	—
Seatonia - -	3,533	1	80 miles N.W.½ N. from Fastnet.	Submarine - -	Captured -	Torpedo -	—
Spero - -	1,132	2	95 miles W.S.W. from Hellisö L.H., Norway.	Submarine - -	Captured -	Torpedo -	—
Statesman - -	6,153	3	200 miles E. from Malta.	Submarine - -	No warning -	Torpedo -	6
Skerries - -	4,278	4	15 miles N.N.W. from the Sker-ries, Anglesea.	Mine - - -	Mine - -	Mine - -	2 including Master.
†Clan Leslie -	3,937	4	200 miles E. ½ S. from Malta.	Submarine - -	No warning -	Torpedo -	3
†Huntsvale -	5,398	4	200 miles E. from Malta.	Submarine - -	No warning -	Torpedo -	7 including Master.
†Arabia - -	7,933	6	112 miles W. by S. from Cape Matapan.	Submarine - -	No warning -	Torpedo -	2
Suffolk Coast -	780	7	14 miles E.S.E. from Cape Bar-fleur.	Submarine - -	Captured -	Bombs -	—
Killellan - -	1,971	8	17 miles S.W. by S. ¼ S. from Colbart L.V.	Submarine - -	Captured -	Torpedo -	—
Sheldrake - -	2,697	8	20 miles W.S.W. from Marittimo Island.	Submarine - -	Captured -	Gunfire -	Master and Chief Engineer made prisoners.
Sunniside - -	447	9	4 miles E.N.E. from Southwold.	Mine - - -	Mine - -	Mine -	4 including Master.
Bogota - -	4,577	10	120 miles S.W. ½ W. from Ushant.	Submarine - -	No warning	Torpedo -	—
Marga - -	674	10	16 miles N. by W. from Ushant.	Submarine - -	Captured -	Gunfire -	—
H.M.W. (sailing barge).	75	10	1 mile N. by W. from Boulogne L.V.	Mine - - -	Mine - -	Mine -	1
†Morazan - -	3,486	11	145 miles S.W. by W. from Ushant.	Submarine - -	Captured -	Torpedo -	Master made prisoner.
Sarah Radcliffe -	3,333	11	170 miles S.W. from Ushant.	Submarine - -	Captured -	Torpedo -	—
†Kapunda - -	3,383	12	205 miles E.S.E. from Malta.	Submarine - -	No warning -	Torpedo -	—
†Lady Carrington	3,269	12	98 miles N. by W. from Cape Ortegal.	Submarine - -	Captured -	Torpedo -	—
Caterham - -	1,777	13	15 miles S.S.E. from Beachy Head.	Submarine - -	Captured -	Bombs -	—

Name.	Tons.	Date.	Position.	Cause of Loss.	How attacked.	How sunk.	Lives lost.
		1916. Nov.					
Corinth - -	3,669	13	28 miles S. ¾ E. from Flamborough Head.	Submarine - -	Captured -	Bombs -	—
Bernicia - -	957	13	20 miles S.S.E. from Beachy Head.	Submarine - -	Captured -	Bombs -	—
Polpedn - -	1,510	14	20 miles S. from Littlehampton.	Submarine - -	No warning -	Torpedo -	—
†F. Matarazzo --	2,823	15	26 miles E.N.E. from Linosa Island.	Submarine - -	No warning -	Torpedo -	—
Trevarrack -	4,199	16	25 miles W. ½ N. from Les Hanois, Guernsey.	Submarine - -	Captured -	Gunfire -	—
Vanguard (S.V.)	142	16	18 miles N.W. ½ N. from Cape Antifer.	Submarine - -	Captured -	Bombs -	—
†Vasco - -	1,914	16	10 miles W. by S. from Beachy Head.	Mine - - -	Mine - -	Mine - -	17 (including Master).
Britannic (Hospital ship).	48,158	21	Zea Channel -	Mine - - -	Mine - -	Mine - -	21
†Brierton - -	3,255	22	32 miles S.W. from Ushant.	Submarine - -	No warning -	Torpedo -	—
Grenada (S.V.) -	2,268	22	32 miles S.W. by S. from Beachy Head.	Submarine - -	Captured -	Gunfire -	—
Jerseyman - -	358	24	30 miles N.W. ½ W. from Dieppe.	Submarine - -	No warning(?)	Torpedo(?)	—
Emlynverne -	544	25	30 miles N.W. by N. from Cape Antifer.	Submarine - -	Captured -	Gunfire -	—
†City of Birmingham.	7,498	27	90 miles S.E. from Malta.	Submarine - -	No warning -	Torpedo -	4
Maude Larssen -	1,222	27	22 miles W.S.W. from Marittimo.	Submarine - -	Captured -	Bombs -	—
Rhona - -	640	27	19 miles N.W. by N. from Guernsey.	Submarine - -	Captured -	Bombs -	—
†Reapwell --	3,417	27	148 miles N.W. by N. from Alexandria.	Submarine - -	No warning -	Torpedo -	Master made prisoner.
Alison - -	286	28	8 miles E.S.E. from Owers L.V.	Submarine - -	Captured -	Bombs -	—
Alert - -	289	28	6 miles E.S.E. from Owers L.V.	Submarine - -	Captured -	Bombs -	—
Ramsgarth - -	1,553	28	11 miles E. by S. from Owers L.V.	Submarine - -	Captured -	Bomb -	—
Lady of the Lake (S.V.).	79	28	35 miles S.E. from Start Point.	Submarine - -	Captured -	Gunfire -	---
†King Malcolm -	4,351	28	144 miles N.W. by N. from Alexandria.	Submarine - -	No warning -	Torpedo -	Master made prisoner.
†Moresby - -	1,763	28	120 miles N.W. by N. from Alexandria.	Submarine - -	No warning -	Torpedo -	33
†Luciston - -	2,948	29	4 miles E. from Dellamara Point, Malta.	Mine - - --	Mine - -	Mine - -	—
Grace (S.V.) -	135	29	40 miles S.E. by E. from Start Point.	Submarine - -	Captured -	Bomb -	—
†Minnewaska	14,317	29	Suda Bay - -	Mine - - -	Mine - -	Mine - -	—
Christabel (S.V.)	175	30	10 miles N. by W. from St. Ives.	Submarine - -	Captured -	Bomb -	—
Behrend (S.V.) -	141	30	35 miles S.W. from Portland Bill.	Submarine - -	Captured -	Bomb -	—

Name.	Tons.	Date.	Position.	Cause of Loss.	How attacked.	How sunk.	Lives lost.
		1916. Nov.					
Heinrich (S.V.) -	98	30	29 miles S. by E. from Start Point.	Submarine - -	Captured -	Bombs -	—
Roma (S.V.) -	99	30	Off E. Coast of Sardinia.	Submarine - -	Captured -	Gunfire -	—
DECEMBER 1916.		Dec.					
King Bleddyn -	4,387	1	30 miles S. by W. ½ W. from Ushant.	Submarine - -	Captured -	Bombs -	—
†Burcombe -	3,516	1	100 miles S.E. by E. from Malta.	Submarine - -	No warning	Torpedo -	?
Briardene - -	2,701	1	12½ miles S.E. by S. from Bishop Rock.	Submarine - -	Captured -	Bombs -	—
Palacine - -	3,286	2	18 miles E.N.E. from Ushant.	Submarine - -	Captured -	Bombs -	—
Harpalus -	1,445	2	34 miles S.S.W. from Galley Head	Submarine ¬ -	Captured -	Bombs -	—
†Istrar - -	4,582	2	120 miles N.N.W. ½ W. from Alexandria.	Submarine - -	No warning	Torpedo -	1 Chief Engineer made prisoner.
†Voltaire - -	8,618	2	650 miles W. ¼ N. (true) from Fastnet.	Möwe - - -	Captured -	Not known	Crew made prisoners.
Dacia - -	1,856	3	Funchal Roads -	Submarine - -	No warning	Torpedo -	—
Seeker (S.V.) -	74	3	30 miles N.W. from Les Hanois.	Submarine - -	Captured -	Bombs -	—
Mizpah (S.V.) -	57	3	30 miles S.S.E. from Eddystone.	Submarine - -	Captured -	Bombs -	—
†Caledonia - -	9,223	4	125 miles E. by S. from Malta.	Submarine - -	No warning	Torpedo -	1 Master made prisoner.
†Mount Temple -	9,792	6	620 miles W. ½ S. (true) from Fastnet.	Möwe - - -	Captured -	Bombs -	3 Remainder prisoners.
Duchess of Cornwall (S.V.).	152	6	620 miles W. ¾ S. (true) from Fastnet.	Möwe - - -	Captured -	Not known	Crew made prisoners.
Avristan - -	3,818	7	14 miles S. by W. ½ W. from Ushant.	Submarine - -	No warning	Torpedo -	1
†Conch - -	5,620	7	12 miles S. by W. ½ W. from Anvil Point.	Submarine - -	No warning	Torpedo -	28 (including Master).
†Britannia - -	1,814	8	70 miles W. by S. from Cape Sines, Portugal.	Submarine - -	No warning	Torpedo -	2 Master made prisoner.
King George -	3,852	8	700 miles E. ½ N. (true) from C. Race.	Möwe - - -	Captured -	Not known	Crew made prisoners.
Harlington - -	1,089	9	4 miles S.W. from Shipwash L.V.	Mine - - -	Mine - -	Mine -	7
Harlyn - -	1,794	9	4 miles S.W. from Shipwash L.V.	Mine - - -	Mine - -	Mine -	2
Forth - -	1,159	9	4 miles S.W. from Shipwash L.V.	Mine - - -	Mine - -	Mine -	—
Cambrian Range	4,234	9	610 miles E. ½ S. (true) from C. Race.	Möwe - - -	Captured -	Bombs -	Crew made prisoners.
Strathalbyn -	4,331	10	2 miles N.E. by E. from Cherbourg Breakwater.	Mine - - -	Mine - -	Mine -	—

Name.	Gross Tons.	Date.	Position.	Cause of Loss.	How attacked.	How sunk.	Lives lost.
		1916. Dec.					
†Georgic -	10,077	10	590 miles E.S.E. (true) from C. Race.	Möwe - - -	Captured -	Torpedo -	1 Remainder prisoners.
Yarrowdale -	4,652	11	540 miles S.E. ¾ E. (true) from C. Race.	Möwe - - -	Captured -	Taken to Germany.	Crew made prisoners.
Coath - -	975	12	English Channel	Mine (?) - -	Mine (?) -	Mine (?) -	16 including Master.
†St. Ursula -	5,011	12	45 miles S.E. by S. from Malta.	Submarine - -	No warning -	Torpedo -	4
Conrad (S.V.) -	164	12	40 miles S.S.E. from St. Catherines Point.	Submarine - -	Captured -	Bombs -	-—
Saint Theodore -	4,992	12	520 miles W. ½ S. (true) from Flores.	Möwe - - -	Captured -	Not known. Sunk 12th Feb. 1917.	—
†Bretwalda -	4,037	13	220 miles E by S. from Malta.	Submarine - -	No warning -	Torpedo -	—
Glencoe - -	2,560	14	14 miles N.N.W. from Ile d'Yeu.	Submarine - -	Captured -	Torpedo -	—
Burnhope - -	1,941	14	In Hartlepool Bay	Mine - - -	Mine - -	Mine - -	1 (Master).
†Westminster -	4,342	14	196 miles E. by S. from Malta.	Submarine - -	No warning -	Torpedo -	15 (including Master).
†Russian -	8,825	14	210 miles E. by S. from Malta.	Submarine - -	No warning -	Torpedo -	28
Naiad (S.V.) -	1,907	15	25 miles S.E. by S. from Bishop Rock.	Submarine - -	Captured -	Torpedo -	—
Constance Mary (S.V.).	177	15	20 miles N.E. from Cape Barfleur.	Submarine - -	Captured -	Bombs -	—
Bayhall - -	3,898	17	90 miles N. by E. from Cape Ortegal.	Submarine - -	Captured -	Bombs -	Master made prisoner.
Pascal - -	5,587	17	12 miles N. from Casquets.	Submarine - -	Captured -	Torpedo -	2 Master made prisoner.
Flimston - -	5,751	18	21 miles N. by E. ½ E. from Ushant.	Submarine - -	Captured -	Bombs -	Master and Chief Engineer made prisoners.
Opal - - -	599	18	Off Isle of Man -	Mine - - -	Mine - -	Mine - -	12 including Master.
Dramatist - -	5,415	18	490 miles S.W. ½ S. (true) from Flores.	Möwe - - -	Captured -	Bombs -	—
Liverpool - -	686	19	11 miles S.E. by S. from Chicken Rock, Calf of Man.	Mine - - -	Mine - -	Mine - -	3
Hildswell - -	2,494	20	North Sea - -	Mine - - -	Mine - -	Mine - -	22 including Master.
†Itonus - -	5,340	20	60 miles N.W. by W. ½ W, from Malta.	Submarine - -	No warning -	Torpedo -	5 Master made prisoner.
†Murex - -	3,564	21	94 miles N.W. from Port Said.	Submarine - -	No warning -	Torpedo -	1
†Thistleban -	4,117	23	5 miles N.N.W. from Alexandria.	Submarine - -	No warning -	Torpedo -	—
Harry W Adams (S.V.).	127	24	46 miles N.W. by N. from C. Villano.	Submarine - -	Captured -	Gunfire -	—
Bargany - -	872	24?	25 miles N. from Ushant.	Submarine - -	Captured -	Gunfire -	—
Agnes (S.V.) -	99	26	15 miles S.W. by W. from St. Ann's Head.	Submarine - -	Captured -	Bombs -	—

Name.	Gross Tons.	Date.	Position.	Cause of Loss.	How attacked.	How sunk.	Lives lost.
		1916. Dec.					
Spinaway (S.V.)	95	26	About 42 miles N.W. from Cape Villano.	Submarine - -	Captured -	Gunfire -	—
Copsewood -	599	27	34 miles S. by W. ¾ W. from Lizard.	Submarine - -	Captured -	Torpedo -	—
Aislaby - -	2,692	27	10 miles N.E. from Estaca Point.	Submarine - -	Captured -	Bombs -	Master made prisoner.
†Oronsay - -	3,761	28	48 miles S.E. from Malta.	Submarine - -	No warning -	Torpedo -	Master made prisoner.
Pitho (S.V.) -	150	28	30 miles S.E. from Start Point.	Submarine - -	Captured -	Bombs -	—
†Zoroaster -	3,803	29	1¾ miles E.N.E. from Sunk L.V.	Mine - - -	Mine - -	Mine - -	3
Lonada - -	1,286	29	5 miles N. by E. ½ E. from Ship-wash L.V.	Mine - - -	Mine - -	Mine -	6
†Apsleyhall -	3,882	30	28 miles W. by N. from Gozo.	Submarine - -	No warning -	Torpedo -	Master made prisoner.
Jean (S.V.) -	215	30	60 miles E. (true) from St. Paul Rocks.	St. Theodore, after conversion into raider by Möwe.	Captured -	Not known	—
Protector (pilot cutter).	200	31	Off Entrance to River Tyne.	Mine - - -	Mine - -	Mine - -	19 (including Master).

JANUARY 1917.

		1917. Jan.					
†Baycraig - -	3,761	1	84 miles E.S.E. from Malta.	Submarine - -	No warning -	Torpedo -	Master made prisoner.
†Ivernia - -	14,278	1	58 miles S. by E. ¼ E. from Cape Matapan.	Submarine - -	No warning -	Torpedo -	36
Holly Branch -	3,568	1	14 miles N.E. by N. from Ile de Bas.	Submarine - -	Captured -	Bombs -	—
Carlyle - -	466	2	5 miles W.S.W. from Ile de Sein L.H.	Submarine - -	Captured -	Bombs -	—
Wragby - -	3,641	4	45 miles W. by N. from C. Spartel.	Submarine - -	Captured -	Gunfire -	—
Lonclara - -	1,294	4	Off River Wear -	Mine - - -	Mine - -	Mine - -	4
Allie - - -	1,127	5	10 miles W. by N. from Ile de Re.	Submarine - -	Captured -	Bombs -	—
†Lesbian - -	2,555	5	125 miles E. by S. from Malta.	Submarine - -	Captured -	Gunfire -	Master made prisoner.
†Hudworth -	3,966	6	94 miles E.S.E. from Malta.	Submarine - -	No warning -	Torpedo -	—
Beaufront - -	1,720	6	76 miles N.W. by W. from Ushant.	Submarine - -	Captured -	Torpedo -	—
Brenda (S.V.) -	249	7	10 miles S.S.W. from Beachy Head.	Submarine - -	Captured -	Gunfire -	—
†Mohacsfield -	3,678	7	40 miles S.E. by E. ½ E. from Malta.	Submarine - -	Captured -	Not known	3 Master made prisoner.
†Radnorshire -	4,310	7	110 miles E. (true) from Pernambuco.	Möwe - - -	Captured -	Bombs -	—
†Andoni - -	3,188	8	46 miles S.E. from Malta.	Submarine - -	No warning -	Torpedo -	3 Master made prisoner.
†Lynfield - -	3,023	8	32 miles S.E. by S. from Malta.	Submarine - -	Captured -	Not known	1 Master made prisoner.

Name.	Gross Tons.	Date.	Position.	Cause of Loss.	How attacked.	How sunk.	Lives lost.
		1917. Jan.					
†Bayuesk - -	3,286	9	130 miles N. by W. from Alexandria.	Submarine - -	No warning	Torpedo -	7
Excellent - -	1,944	9	40 miles N,W. from Noop Head, Orkneys.	Submarine - -	Captured -	Gunfire -	Master made prisoner.
Minieh - -	3,806	9	170 miles E.N.E. (true) from Pernambuco.	Möwe - - -	Captured -	Bombs -	—
Gladys Royle -	3,268	9	120 miles S. ¼ W. (true) from Sta Maria, Azores.	Seeadler -	Captured -	Bombs -	—
Brookwood -	3,093	10	210 miles N. by W. from C. Finisterre.	Submarine - -	Captured ..	Gunfire -	2
Netherby Hall -	4,461	10	300 miles E. by N. (true) from Pernambuco.	Möwe - - -	Captured -	Bombs -	—
Lundy Island -	3,095	10	190 miles S.E.¼E. true from Sta Maria, Azores.	Seeadler -	Captured -	Gunfire -	Steward made prisoner.
Brentwood - -	1,192	12	4 miles E.N.E. from Whitby.	Mine - - -	Mine - -	Mine - -	2
Auchencrag -	3,916	12	20 miles W. from Ushant.	Submarine - -	Captured -	Torpedo -	4
Toftwood - -	3,082	13	24 miles N. ½ W. from Sept Iles.	Submarine - -	Captured -	Torpedo -	—
Martin - -	1,904	14	8 miles N. by W. from Ushant.	Submarine - -	Captured -	Gunfire -	—
†Port Nicholson -	8,418	15	15 miles W. ½ N. from Dunkirk.	Mine - - -	Mine - -	Mine - -	2
†Garfield - -	3,838	15	60 miles N.E. by N. ½ N. from Alexandria.	Submarine - -	No warning -	Torpedo -	Master made prisoner.
Kinpurney (S.V.)	1,944	15	110 miles W. from Bishop Rock.	Submarine - -	Captured -	Torpedo -	—
Baron Sempill -	1,607	16	180 miles S.W. from Fastnet.	Submarine - -	Captured -	Bombs -	—
Manchester Inventor.	4,247	18	50 miles N.W. by W. ½ W. from Fastnet.	Submarine - -	Captured -	Torpedo -	—
†Nailsea Court -	3,295	19	32 miles W. from the Skelligs.	Submarine - -	No warning -	Torpedo -	—
Tremeadow ·	3,653	19	35 miles N.E. ¾ N. from Ushant.	Submarine - -	Captured -	Gunfire -	—
Lilian H. (S.V.) -	467	19	15 miles S. by E. from Old Head of Kinsale.	Submarine - -	Captured -	Bombs -	—
Neuquen - -	3,583	20	20 miles N.W. by W. from the Skelligs.	Submarine - -	Captured -	Torpedo -	18 including Master.
†Bulgarian -	2,515	20	Atlantic - -	Submarine - -	No warning (probably).	Torpedo -	14 including Master. 9 crew prisoners.
Planudes - -	542	20 (?)	North Sea - -	Mine (?) - -	Mine (?) -	Mine (?) -	11 including Master.
†Trevean - -	3,081	22	240 miles S.W. by W. from Fastnet.	Submarine - -	Captured -	Bombs -	Master and two gunners made prisoners.
†Clan Shaw	3,943	23	Mouth of the Tay.	Mine - - -	Mine - -	Mine - -	2
Jevington - -	2,747	23	52 miles N.W. ½ W. from Cape Ortegal.	Submarine - -	No warning -	Torpedo -	—
Tabasco - -	2,987	26	55 miles W.N.W. from the Skelligs.	Submarine -	Captured -	Torpedo -	—

Name.	Gross Tons.	Date.	Position.	Cause of Loss.	How attacked.	How sunk.	Lives lost
		1917. Jan.					
†Matheran - -	7,654	26	9 miles W. from Dassen Island, Cape of Good Hope.	Mine - - -	Mine - -	Mine - -	1
†Artist -	3,570	27	58 miles W. ½ S. from the Smalls.	Submarine - -	No warning -	Torpedo -	35 including Master.
†Ava - -	5,076	27 (?)	Off S. Ireland (?)	Submarine (?) -	No warning(?)	Torpedo (?)	92 including Master.
Perce (S.V.) -	364	28	150 miles N.E. by N. (true) from St. Paul Rocks.	Seeadler - -	Captured -	Gunfire -	—
†Ravensbourne -	1,226	31	8 miles S.E. from Tyne.	Mine - - -	Mine - -	Mine - -	3
†Dundee - -	2,278	31	10 miles N. by W. from St. Ives Head.	Submarine -	No warning -	Torpedo -	1
Ida Duncan (tug)	139	31	½ mile E. from S. Gare L.H.	Mine - - -	Mine - -	Mine - -	6 including Master.
Lux - -	2,621	(?)	Atlantic - -	Submarine (?) -	No warning(?)	Torpedo (?)	29 including Master.
FEBRUARY 1917.		**Feb.**					
Essonite - -	589	1	3 miles N.N.W. from Trevose Head.	Submarine - -	No warning -	Torpedo -	10
Isle of Arran (S.V.)	1,918	2	100 miles S. from Old Head of Kinsale.	Submarine - -	Captured -	Bombs -	—
Eavestone -	1,858	3	95 miles W. from Fastnet.	Submarine - -	Captured -	Gunfire -	5 including Master.
†Port Adelaide -	8,181	3	180 miles S.W. from Fastnet.	Submarine - -	No warning -	Torpedo -	Master made prisoner.
†Hollinside -	2,682	3	115 miles W.S.W. from Fastnet.	Submarine - -	No warning -	Torpedo -	1
Belford (S.V.) -	1,905	3	110 miles W. from Fastnet.	Submarine - -	Captured -	Bombs -	—
Floridian - -	4,777	4	200 miles W. by N. from Fastnet.	Submarine - -	Captured -	Torpedo -	5 Master, chief engineer, and W/T operator made prisoners.
†Palmleaf - -	5,489	4	230 miles W. from Fastnet.	Submarine - -	No warning -	Torpedo -	Master and chief engineer made prisoners.
†Turino - -	4,241	4	174 miles W. from Fastnet.	Submarine - -	No warning -	Torpedo -	4
†Ghazee - -	5,084	4	2 miles S.S.W. from Galley Head.	Submarine - -	No warning -	Torpedo -	—
†Dauntless -	2,157	4	10 miles from La Coubre Point.	Submarine - -	Captured -	Bombs -	15
Hurstwood -	1,229	5	6 miles N.E. from Whitby.	Submarine - -	No warning -	Torpedo -	4
†Warley Pickering.	4,196	5	46 miles W. by N. from Fastnet.	Submarine - -	No warning -	Torpedo -	—
†Wartenfels -	4,511	5	120 miles S.W. from Fastnet.	Submarine - -	No warning -	Torpedo -	2 Master made prisoner
Azul - -	3,074	5	180 miles W. ½ N. from Fastnet.	Submarine - -	No warning -	Torpedo -	11
†Cliftonian -	4,303	6	4½ miles S. ¾ E. from Galley Head.	Submarine - -	No warning -	Torpedo -	—

Name.	Gross Tons.	Date.	Position.	Cause of Loss.	How attacked.	How sunk.	Lives lost.
		1917. Feb.					
†Saxon Briton -	1,337	6	3 miles N.N.E. from Gurnard Head.	Submarine - -	No warning -	Torpedo -	2
†Vestra - -	1,021	6	5 miles N.E. from Hartlepool.	Submarine - -	No warning -	Torpedo -	2
†Crown Point -	5,218	6	55 miles W. from Scilly Isles.	Submarine - -	No warning -	Torpedo .	7 including Master.
Corsican Prince	2 776	7	3 miles E. from Whitby.	Submarine - -	No warning -	Torpedo -	1
†Saint Ninian -	3,026	7	3 miles E. from Whitby.	Submarine - -	No warning -	Torpedo .	15 including Master.
†California - -	8,669	7	38 miles W. by S. from Fastnet.	Submarine - -	No warning -	Torpedo -	43
Boyne Castle -	245	7	12 miles N. by E. from 'St. Abb's Head.	Submarine - -	Captured -	Gunfire -	—
Saxonian - -	4,855	7	270 miles W. by N. from Fastnet.	Submarine - -	Capture	fire -	1
†Vedamore -	6,330	7	20 miles W. from Fastnet.	Submarine - -	No war -,,-	Torpedo -	23
†Gravine - -	1,242	7	85 miles W. from Fastnet.	Submarine - -	No warning -	Torpedo -	7 Master and 14 made prisoners.
Hanna Larsen -	1,311	8	20 miles E. $\frac{3}{4}$ N. from Spurn Point.	Submarine - -	Captured -	Bombs -	1
Lullington -	2,816	8	3 miles E. from Royal Sove- reign L.V.	Mine - - -	Mine - -	Mine- -	—
†Mantola - -	8,253	8	143 miles W.S.W. from Fastnet.	Submarine - -	No warning -	Torpedo -	7
Beechtree - -	1,277	10	11 miles S.E. from Start Point.	Submarine - -	No warning -	Torpedo -	—
Japanese Prince	4,876	10	24 miles S.W. from Bishop Rock.	Submarine - -	No warning -	Torpedo -	—
Sallagh - -	325	10	Off Bardsey Island	Submarine - -	Captured -	Bombs -	1
Olivia - -	242	11	21 miles S.W. $\frac{1}{2}$ S. from Bardsey Island.	Submarine - -	Captured -	Bombs -	—
Voltaire - -	409	11	25 miles N.E. by N. from S. Bishop.	Submarine - -	Captured -	Bombs -	—
Netherlee - -	4,227	11	92 miles W. $\frac{1}{2}$ S. from Fastnet.	Submarine - -	No warning -	Torpedo -	2
†Lycia - -	2,715	.11	20 miles N.E. by N. from S. Bishop.	Submarine - -	Captured -	Bombs -	—
Ada (S.V.) -	186	11	8 miles S. from Anvil Point.	Submarine - -	Captured -	Gunfire -	—
†Afric	11,999	12	12 miles S.S.W. from Eddystone.	Submarine - -	No warning -	Torpedo -	5
Foreland - -	1,960	12	6 miles S. $\frac{3}{4}$ W. from Shipwash L.V.	Mine - - -	Mine - -	Mine - -	—
Lucent - -	1,409	12	20 miles E. from Lizard.	Submarine - -	Captured -	Gunfire -	—
Cilicia - -	3,750	12	5 miles S. from Dassen Island, Cape of Good Hope.	Mine - - -	Mine - -	Mine -	—
Norwood - -	798	11(?)	North Sea - -	Mine (?) - -	Mine (?) -	Mine (?) -	18 including Master.
Percy Roy (S.V.)	110	13	30 miles S.E. from Cabrera Island.	Submarine - -	Captured -	Bombs -	—
†F. D. Lambert -	2,195	13	1 mile E. from Royal Sovereign L.V.	Submarine - -	No warning -	Torpedo -	—

Name.	Gross Tons.	Date.	Position.	Cause of Loss.	How attacked..	How sunk.	Lives lost.
		1917. Feb.					
†Inishowen Head	3,050	14	1¼ miles S. from ·Skokham Island	Submarine - -	No warning -	Torpedo -	1
Ferga - -	791	14	15 miles S. from Bardsey Island.	Submarine - . -	Captured	Gunfire -	—
Margarita - -	375	14	20 miles S.W. by S. from Bardsey Island.	Submarine - -	Captured -	Bombs -	—
Hopemoor -	3,740	14	20 miles N.W. from the Skelligs.	Submarine - -	No warning -	Torpedo -	—
Marie Leonhardt	1,466	14	2¼ miles E. ½ N. from Sunk L.V.	Mine - - -	Mine - -	Mine - -	5
Greenland -	1,763	14	20 miles S.W. from Bardsey Island.	Submarine - -	Captured -	Bombs -	—
†Longscar - -	2,777	14	15 miles S.W. from River Gironde.	Submarine - -	Captured -	Bombs -	2 gunners made prisoners.
Eudora (S.V.) -	1,991	14	30 miles S.S.W. from Fastnet.	Submarine - -	Captured -	Gunfire -	—
†Marion Dawson	2,300	14	8 miles S.S.W. from Ile d'Oleron.	Submarine - -	Captured -	Bombs -	—
Afton - -	1,156	15	23 miles N. by E. from Strumble Head.	Submarine - -	Captured -	Bombs -	—
Kyanite - -	564	15	27 miles S.S.W. from Bardsey Island.	Submarine - -	Captured -	Bombs -	—
Leven (dredger)	775	15	¾ mile S. by E. ½ E. from Newhaven Breakwater.	Mine - - -	Mine - -	Mine -	—
†Brecknockshire	8,423	15	490 miles E. by N. (true) from Cape Frio, Brazil.	Möwe - - -	Captured -	Not known	Crew made prisoners.
French Prince -	4,766	15	490 miles E.N.E. (true) from Cape Frio, Brazil.	Möwe - - -	Captured -	Not known	Crew made prisoners.
Lady Ann -	1,016	16	3 miles E. by S. from Scarborough.	Submarine - -	No warning -	Torpedo -	11 including Master.
Queenswood -	2,701	16	6 miles S.W. from Hartland Point.	Submarine - -	Captured -	Gunfire -	3
Rose Dorothea (S.V.).	147	16	30 miles S.E. by E. from Cape St. Vincent.	Submarine - -	Captured -	Bombs -	—
Mayola (S.V.) -	146	16	50 miles S.E. by E. from Cape St. Vincent.	Submarine - -	Captured -	Bombs -	—
Eddie - -	2,652	16	550 miles N.E. by E. ¾ E. (true) from Cape Frio, Brazil.	Möwe - - -	Captured -	Not known	Crew made prisoners.
†Iolo - - -	3,840	17	40 miles S. by W. from the Fastnet.	Submarine - -	No warning -	Torpedo -	2 Master, chief engineer, and 2 gunners made prisoners.
†Romsdalen -	2,548	17	10 miles S.W. from Portland Bill.	Submarine - -	No warning -	Torpedo -	—
Valdes - -	2,233	17	7 miles S. from Portland Bill.	Submarine - -	No warning -	Torpedo -	11
†Okement - -	4,349	17	140 miles S.E. by S. from Malta.	Submarine - -	No warning -	Torpedo -	11 including Master.
Worcestershire -	7,175	17	10 miles S.W. from Colombo.	Mine - - -	Mine - -	Mine -	2
Netherton (S.V.)	199	18	16 miles S. from Anvil Point.	Submarine - -	Captured -	Bombs -	—

Name.	Gross Tons.	Date.	Position.	Cause of Loss.	How attacked.	How sunk.	Lives lost.
		1917. Feb.					
Triumph (S.V.)	46	18	45 miles N.N.W. from Roches Douvres.	Submarine - -	Captured -	Gunfire -	—
Brigade - -	425	19	12 miles N.W. ½ W. from Cayeux - sur-Somme.	Submarine - -	Captured -	Gunfire -	—
†Corso - -	3,242	19	110 miles S. by W. from Malta.	Submarine - -	No warning -	Torpedo -	Master, chief engineer, and 2 gunners made prisoners.
Centurion (S.V.)	1,828	19	15 miles S.E. from the Lizard.	Submarine - -	Captured -	Bombs -	—
†Headley - -	4,953	19	35 miles S.S.W. from Bishop Rock.	Submarine - -	No warning -	Torpedo -	—
Pinmore (S.V.) -	2,431	19	540 miles N.W. ½ N. (true) from St. Paul Rocks.	Seeadler - -	Captured -	Bombs -	—
†Rosalie - -	4,237	20	8 miles E. from Jidjelli, Algeria.	Submarine - -	No warning -	Torpedo -	21 including Master.
Perseus - -	6,728	21	11 miles W. from Colombo.	Mine - - -	Mine - -	Mine -	3
†Wathfield -	3,012	21	15 miles N. from C. Carbon.	Submarine - -	No warning -	Torpedo -	18 including Master.
Tecwyn (motor)	132	21	20 miles S. from Portland Bill.	Submarine - -	Captured -	Gunfire -	—
John Miles -	687	22	11 miles S.E. from Hartlepool.	Mine - - -	Mine - -	Mine -	10 including Master.
Invercauld (S.V.)	1,416	22	22 miles S.E. from Mine Head, Ireland.	Submarine - -	Captured -	Torpedo -	—
Nostra Signora del Porto Salvo (S.V.).	136	22	35 miles N.W. from Marittimo.	Submarine - -	Captured -	Bombs -	—
†Trojan Prince -	3,196	23	5 miles N.W. from Point Shershel.	Submarine - -	No warning -	Torpedo -	2
Grenadier -	1,004	23	6 miles E.N.E. from Shipwash L.V..	Submarine - -	No warning -	Torpedo -	8 including Master.
Belgier - -	4,588	23	30 miles W. from Belle Ile.	Submarine - -	Captured -	Gunfire -	—
†Iser - -	2,160	23	14 miles N.W. from Belle Ile.	Submarine - -	No warning -	Torpedo -	1
†Longhirst -	3,053	23	20 miles E. from Cape Bon.	Submarine - -	No warning -	Torpedo -	2
Katherine - -	2,926	23	200 miles N.E. by N. ¾ N. (true) from St. Paul Rocks.	Möwe - - -	Captured -	Not known	Crew made prisoners.
†Beneficent -	1,963	24	Off Mouth of Tees	Mine - - -	Mine - -	Mine -	3
†Falcon - -	2,244	24	190 miles W.N.W. from Fastnet.	Submarine - -	Captured -	Gunfire -	—
†Dorothy - -	3,806	24	25 miles S.E. by S. ½ S. from Pantellaria.	Submarine - -	No warning -	Torpedo -	6
†Laconia - -	18,099	25	160 miles N.W. by W. from Fastnet.	Submarine - -	No warning -	Torpedo -	12
†Aries - -	3,071	25	190 miles N.W. by W. from Fastnet.	Submarine - -	Captured -	Gunfire -	Master made prisoner.
†Huntsman -	7,460	25	180 miles N.W. by W. from the Fastnet.	Submarine - -	No warning -	Torpedo -	2
†Algiers - -	2,361	26	3 miles S. from Owers L.V.	Submarine - -	No warning -	Torpedo -	8

Name.	Gross Tons.	Date.	Position.	Cause of Loss.	How attacked.	How sunk.	Lives lost.
		1917. Feb.					
Sea Gull - -	144	26	4 miles off Folkestone.	Mine - - -	Mine - -	Mine -	2
Hannah Crossdell (S.V.).	151	26	4 miles W. ¾ N. from St. Ann's Head.	Mine (?) - -	Mine (?) -	Mine (?) -	4 including Master.
†Burnby - -	3,665	26	20 miles N. from C. Falcone.	Submarine - -	No warning -	Torpedo -	Master made prisoner.
†Clan Farquhar -	5,858	26	80 miles N. from Ben Ghazi.	Submarine - -	No warning -	Torpedo -	49 including Master, 2nd engineer made prisoner.
British Yeoman (S.V.).	1,953	26	230 miles N.W. by N. ¾ N. (true) from St. Paul Rocks.	Seeadler - -	Captured -		—
†Tritonia - -	4,445	27	20 miles N.W. by W. from Tearagh Is.	Submarine - -	No warning -	Torpedo -	2
Galgorm Castle (S.V.).	1,596	27	90 miles W. from the Fastnet.	Submarine - -	Captured -	Gunfire -	11
†Brodmore - -	4,071	27	70 miles N.W. by N. from Marsa Susa.	Submarine - -	No warning -	Torpedo -	Master made prisoner.
Turritella -	5,528	27	600 miles W. ¾ S. (true) from Minikoi.	Wolf - - -	Captured -	Scuttled, 4 Mar.	—
Harriet Williams (S.V.).	157	28	15 miles N.N.E from C. Antifer.	Submarine - -	Captured -	Bombs -	—

MARCH 1917.

Name.	Gross Tons.	Date.	Position.	Cause of Loss.	How attacked.	How sunk.	Lives lost.
		Mar.					
†Drina - -	11,483	1	2 miles W. from Skokham Island.	Submarine - -	No warning -	Torpedo -	15
Tillycorthie -	382	1	16 miles N. ½ E. from Longstone.	Submarine - -	Captured -	Gunfire -	Master made prisoner.
Chatburn - -	1,942	1	22 miles N.E. ½ E. from Cape Barfleur.	Submarine - -	No warning -	Torpedo -	—
†Munificent -	3,270	1	3½ miles N.N.W. from Cape Gris Nez.	Submarine - -	No warning -	Torpedo -	3
Jumna - -	4,152	1	650 miles W. (true) from Minikoi.	Wolf - - -	Captured -	Bombs -	—
Utopia (S.V.) -	184	2	20 miles S.S.W. from Dungeness.	Submarine - -	Captured -	Gunfire -	—
Gazelle (S.V.) -	119	2	20 miles S.S.W. from Dungeness.	Submarine - -	Captured -	Bomb -	—
Meldon - -	2,514	3	Firth of Lorne -	Mine - - -	Mine - -	Mine - -	—
Connaught - -	2,646	3	29 miles S. by W. ½ W. from Owers L.V.	Submarine - -	No warning -	Torpedo -	3
†River Forth -	4,421	3	60 miles S. by E. from Malta.	Submarine - -	No warning -	Torpedo -	2
†Kincardine -	4,108	3	20 miles N.E. from Tearagh Island.	Submarine - -	No warning -	Torpedo -	—
†Craigendoran -	2,789	3	6 miles E. from Cape Sigli, Algeria.	Submarine - -	No warning -	Torpedo -	3 Master and chief engineer made prisoners.
†Sagamore - -	5,197	3	150 miles W. from the Fastnet.	Submarine - -	No warning -	Torpedo -	52 including Master.

Name.	Gross Tons.	Date.	Position.	Cause of Loss.	How attacked.	How sunk.	Lives lost.
		1917. Mar.					
†Newstead - -	2,836	3	150 miles W.N.W. from the Fastnet.	Submarine - -	No warning -	Torpedo -	15
The Macbain (S.V.).	291	4	20 miles S.S.W. from Portland Bill.	Submarine - -	Captured -	Bomb -	—
†Rhodanthe -	3,061	4	330 miles N.N.W. (true) from St. Vincent (C.V.).	Möwe - - -	Captured -	Not known	Crew made prisoners.
Copenhagen -	2,570	5	8 miles E. ½ N. from N. Hinder L.V.	Submarine - -	No warning -	Torpedo -	6
Cornelia - -	903	6	9 miles W.N.W. from the Skelligs.	Submarine - -	Captured -	Gunfire -	—
†Caldergrove -	4,327	6	200 miles W.N.W. from the Fastnet.	Submarine - -	No warning -	Torpedo -	19 including Master.
Fenay Lodge -	3,223	6	250 miles N.W. by W. ½ W. from the Fastnet.	Submarine - -	No warning -	Torpedo -	4 including Master.
Antonio - -	2,652	7	7 miles from Dartmouth.	Mine (?) - -	Mine (?) -	Mine (?) -	11 including Master.
†Baron Wemyss -	1,605	7	73 miles N.W. by W. from the Fastnet.	Submarine - -	Captured -	Torpedo -	2 including Master.
Westwick -	5,694	7	1 mile S. from Roche Point.	Mine	Mine - -	Mine -	—
†Georgian -	5,088	8	52 miles N. from C. Sidero.	Submarine - -	No warning -	Torpedo -	5
†Dunbarmoor -	3,651	8	180 miles W.N.W. from the Fastnet.	Submarine - -	Captured -	Gunfire -	12 including Master.
Abeja (S.V.) -	174	9	20 miles S.W. ½ S. from Start Point.	Submarine - -	Captured -	Gunfire -	—
†East Point -	5,234	9	9 miles E. by S. ½ S. from the Eddystone.	Submarine - -	No warning -	Torpedo -	—
Inverlogie (S.V.)	2,347	9	15 miles S.W. from the Smalls.	Submarine - -	Captured -	Torpedo -	--
Mediterranean (S.V.).	105	10	13 miles S. from Hook Point, Waterford.	Submarine -	Captured -	Gunfire -	—
T. Crowley (S.V.)	97	10	12 miles S. from Hook Point, Waterford.	Submarine - -	Captured -	Gunfire -	—
James Burton (Cook S.V.).	133	10	25 miles S.S.E. from Malaga.	Submarine - -	Captured -	Gunfire -	—
†Esmeraldas -	4,678	10	420 miles W. by N. (true) from Lisbon.	Möwe - - -	Captured -	Not known	Crew made prisoners.
†Otaki - -	9,575	10	420 miles W. ¾ S. (true) from Lisbon.	Möwe - - -	Captured -	Torpedoes -	6 including Master. Remainder made prisoners.
Wordsworth	3,509	11	680 miles E. (true) from Mahe, Seychelles.	Wolf - - -	Captured -	Bombs -	—
Kwasind - -	2,211	11	Off Southwold -	Mine - - -	Mine - -	Mine -	12
†Folia - -	6,705	11	4 miles E.S.E. from Ram Head, Youghal.	Submarine - -	No warning -	Torpedo -	7
Horngarth -	3,609	11	220 miles E.N.E. (true) from St. Paul Rocks.	Seeadler - -	Captured -	Bombs -	1
G. A. Savage -	357	11 (?)	Bristol Channel -	Submarine (?) -	No warning (?)	Torpedo (?) -	9 including Master.

Name.	Gross Tons.	Date.	Position.	Cause of Loss.	How attacked.	How sunk.	Lives lost.
		1917. Mar.					
Tandil - -	2,897	12	20 miles W. by N. ½ N. from Portland.	Submarine - -	No warning -	Torpedo -	4
Ambient - -	1,517	12	Off Aldeburgh -	Mine - - -	Mine -	Mine - -	—
Pontypridd -	1.556	12	Off Aldeburgh -	Mine - - -	Mine - -	Mine - -	3
Memnon - -	3,203	12	20 miles S.W. from Portland Bill.	Submarine - -	No warning	Torpedo -	6
Glynymel -	1,394	12	23 miles S. by W. from St. Catherine's Pt.	Submarine - -	Captured -	Torpedo -	1
†Bilswood - -	3,097	12	8 miles N.W. from Alexandria.	Mine - - -	Mine - -	Mine - -	—
Lucy Anderson -	1,073	12	55 miles E.S.E. from Noss Head, Wick.	Submarine -	Captured -	Gunfire -	—
Topaz - -	696	12	27 miles E. by N. ½ N. from Cape Barfleur.	Submarine - -	No warning -	Torpedo -	3
†Brika - -	3,549	13	13 miles S.E. by S. from Coningbeg L.V.	Submarine - -	No warning -	Torpedo -	2
†Northwaite -	3,626	13	14 miles W.N.W. from the Blaskets.	Submarine - -	No warning -	Torpedo -	--
†Norwegian -	6,327	13	4 miles S.W. from Seven Heads, Co. Cork.	Submarine - -	No warning -	Torpedo -	5
†Coronda - -	2,733	13	180 miles N.W. from Tory Island.	Submarine - -	No warning -	Torpedo -	9
Elizabeth Eleanor (S.V.).	169	13	77 miles N.W. by W. ½ W. from Trevose Head.	Submarine - -	Captured -	Gunfire -	—
†Demeterton -	6,048	13	730 miles E. by N. (true) from C. Race.	Möwe - - -	Captured -	Bombs -	Crew made prisoners.
†Paignton - -	2,017	14	40 miles N.W. from the Skelligs.	Submarine - -	Captured -	Gunfire -	1
†Rose Lea - -	2,830	14	230 miles W. from Bishop Rock.	Submarine - -	No warning -	Torpedo -	—
†Bray Head -	3,077	14	375 miles N.W. by W. from the Fastnet.	Submarine - -	Captured -	Gunfire -	21 including Master.
†Governor - -	5,524	14	930 miles W. ¼ S. (true) from the Fastnet.	Möwe - - -	Captured -	Torpedo -	4 Remainder made prisoners.
†Frimaire - -	1,778	15	21 miles S.S.E. from Belle Ile.	Submarine - -	No warning -	Torpedo -	12 including Master.
Norma Pratt -	4,416	16	150 miles W. from Bishop Rock.	Submarine -	Captured -	Torpedo	Chief officer and 3rd engineer made prisoners.
William Martin (S.V.).	104	16	9 miles S. by W. ½ W. from Ram Head, Youghal.	Submarine - -	Captured -	Bombs -	—
Sir Joseph (S.V.)	84	16	30 miles S.S.E. from Start Point.	Submarine -	Captured -	Bombs	—
†Narragansett -	9,196	16	Off S.W. Ireland	Submarine - -	No warning -	Torpedo -	46 including Master.
Tasso - -	1,859	17	5 miles S. from Groix Island.	Submarine - -	No warning -	Torpedo -	19 including Master.

Name.	Gross Tons.	Date.	Position.	Cause of Loss.	How attacked.	How sunk.	Lives lost.
		1917. Mar.					
†Antony - -	6,446	17	19 miles W. by N. from Coningbeg L.V.	Submarine - -	No warning -	Torpedo -	55
†Pola - -	3,061	18	280 miles W.N.W. from Ushant.	Submarine - -	No warning -	Torpedo -	5
†Trevose - -	3,112	18	230 miles W. by N. ½ N. from Ushant.	Submarine - -	No warning -	Torpedo -	2
†Joshua Nicholson	1,853	18	Off Wolf Rock -	Submarine - -	No warning -	Torpedo -	26 including Master.
Greypoint -	894	18	2 miles S.E. by E. from Broadstairs Landing.	T.B.D. - -	No warning -	Torpedo -	—
†Ainwick Castle	5,900	19	310 miles W. ½ S. from Bishop Rock.	Submarine - -	No warning -	Torpedo -	40
†Frinton - -	4,194	19	320 miles W. by N. ½ N. from Ushant.	Submarine - -	No warning -	Torpedo -	4
†Hazelpark -	1,964	20	3 miles S. by E. from Start Point.	Submarine -	No warning -	Torpedo -	—
†Stanley - -	3,987	21	230 miles W. by N. from the Fastnet.	Submarine - -	No warning -	Torpedo -	8
Rio Sorocaba -	4,307	21	10 miles S. from Eddystone.	Submarine - -	Captured -	Bombs -	...
Hindustan -	3,692	21	150 miles W.N.W. from the Fastnet.	Submarine - -	No warning -	Torpedo -	2
Rio Colorado -	3,565	22	Entrance to River Tyne.	Mine - - -	Mine - -	Mine -	10 including Master.
†Providence -	2,970	22	1¼ miles S. by W. ½ W. from Barrels L.V.	Submarine - -	No warning	Torpedo -	—
†Rotorua - -	11,140	22	24 miles E. from Start Point.	Submarine - -	No warning -	Torpedo -	1
Chorley - -	3,828	22	25 miles E. by S. from Start Point.	Submarine - -	No warning -	Torpedo -	—
†Stuart Prince -	3,597	22	85 miles N. by W. from Broad Haven.	Submarine - -	No warning -	Torpedo -	20 including Master.
†C'an Macmillan	4,525	23	5 miles S.W. from Newhaven.	Submarine - -	No warning -	Torpedo -	—
†Maine - -	3,616	23	11 miles S.E. by E. from Start Point.	Submarine - -	No warning -	Torpedo -	—
†Eptalofos - -	4,431	23	47 miles N.W. from Malta.	Submarine - -	No warning -	Torpedo -	Master, 2 officers, 4 engineers, 1 gunner made prisoners.
Achille Adam -	460	23	31 miles S.E. by S. from Beachy Head.	Submarine - -	Captured -	Bombs -	6
Exchange -	279	23	30 miles N.W. from Cayeux.	Submarine - -	Captured -	Gunfire -	8
Fairearn - -	592	24	16 miles W.N.W. from S. Stack, Holyhead.	Submarine - -	Captured -	Bombs -	—
Ennistown -	689	24	10 miles S.E. from S. Arklow L.V.	Submarine - -	Captured -	Bombs -	—
Howe (S.V.) -	175	24	4 miles N.E. from N. Arklow L.V.	Submarine - -	Captured -	Bombs -	—

Name.	Gross Tons.	Date.	Position.	Cause of Loss.	How attacked.	How sunk.	Lives lost.
		1917. Mar.					
†Queen Eugenie -	4,358	25	23 miles N.N.E. from Cani Rocks.	Submarine - -	No warning -	Torpedo -	35 (including Master). 1 apprentice and 1 gunner made prisoners.
†Adenwen - -	3,793	25	6 miles S.E. by E. from N. Arklow L.V.	Submarine - -	No warning -	Torpedo -	10
†Vellore - -	4.926	25	21 miles N.W. by N. from Alexandria.	Submarine - -	No warning -	Torpedo -	Master and chief engineer prisoners.
†Berbera - -	4,352	25	60 miles E. from Catania.	Submarine - -	No warning -	Torpedo -	1 2nd officer and 2 cadets made prisoners.
†Baynaen - -	3,227	25	20 miles N.W. by W. from Belle Ile.	Submarine - -	No warning -	Torpedo -	5
Huntleys (S.V.)	186	25	28 miles S.S.W. from Beachy Head.	Submarine - -	Captured -	Bombs -	—
Mary Annie (SV.).	154	25	28 miles S.S.W. from Beachy Head.	Submarine - -	Captured -	Bombs -	—
Brandon (S.V.)	130	25(?)	Not known -	Submarine (reported).	Not known -	Not known	4 including Master.
†Ledbury - -	3,046	26	90 miles N. by E. from Ben Ghazi.	Submarine - -	No warning -	Torpedo -	3
†Holgate - -	2,604	27	10 miles N.W. from the Skelligs.	Submarine - -	No warning -	Torpedo -	Master made prisoner.
†Kelvinhead -	3,063	27	¾ mile W.S.W. from Liverpool Bar L.V.	Mine - - -	Mine - -	Mine - -	—
Neath (auxiliary barque).	5,548	27	28 miles S. by E. from the Fastnet.	Submarine - -	No warning -	Torpedo -	Master made prisoner.
†Thracia - -	2,891	27	12 miles N. from Belle Ile.	Submarine - -	No warning -	Torpedo -	36 including Master.
†Glenogle - -	7,682	27	207 miles S.W. from the Fastnet.	Submarine - -	No warning -	Torpedo -	—
Oakwell - -	248	28	3 miles N.E. from N. Cheek, Robin Hood Bay.	Mine - - -	Mine - -	Mine - -	4
†Snowdon Range	4,662	28	25 miles W. from Bardsey Island.	Submarine - -	No warning -	Torpedo -	4
Hero (tug) -	66	28	Entrance to River Wear.	Mine - - -	Mine - -	Mine - -	1 (Master).
†Gafsa - -	3,974	28	10 miles S.E. ½ S. from Kinsale Head.	Submarine - -	No warning -	Torpedo -	7
Ardglass - -	778	28	4 miles E. from S. Arklow L.V.	Submarine - -	Captured -	Bombs -	—
Wychwood -	1,985	28	4 miles S.S.W. from S. Arklow L.V.	Submarine - -	No warning -	Torpedo -	3
†Cannizaro -	6,133	28	145 miles S.S.W. from the Fastnet.	Submarine - -	No warning -	Torpedo -	--
Harvest Home (S.V.).	103	28	4 miles N.E. from S. Arklow L.V.	Submarine - -	Captured -	Gunfire -	—
Ruby - -	234	28	2½ miles from Auskerry, Orkney Is.	Mine - - -	Mine - -	Mine - -	6 including Master.

Name.	Gross. Tons.	Date.	Position.	Cause of Loss.	How attacked.	How sunk.	Lives lost.
		1917. Mar.					
South Arklow Light Vessel.	—	28	10 miles S.E. by S. ½ S. from Arklow.	Submarine - -	Boarded -	Bombs -	—
†Mascota - -	674	29	8 miles E. from Lowestoft.	T.B.D. - -	Captured -	Not known	7 (seven made prisoners).
Kathleen Lily -	521	29	2 miles E. from N. Cheek, Robin Hood Bay.	Mine - - -	Mine - -	Mine - -	4 including Master.
Lincolnshire -	3,965	29	8 miles S.W. by S. from Hook Point, Waterford.	Submarine - -	No warning -	Torpedo -	—
†Bywell - -	1,522	29	3 miles E. from Scarborough.	Submarine - -	No warning -	Torpedo -	—
†Crispin - -	3,965	29	14 miles S. from Hook Point, Waterford.	Submarine - -	No warning -	Torpedo -	8
Conoid (S.V.) -	165	29	3 miles N. from C. Barfleur.	Submarine - -	Captured -	Gunfire -	—
†Somme - -	1,828	30	20 miles E. by N. from C. Barfleur.	Submarine - -	No warning -	Torpedo -	5
Dee (S.V.) -	1,169	30	410 miles W.by S. (true) from Cape Leeuwin.	Wolf - - -	Captured -	Bombs -	—
Harberton -	1,443	30 (?)	North Sea - -	Submarine (?) -	No warning (?)	Torpedo (?)	15 including Master.
Endymion (S.V.)	67	30	English Channel	Submarine (re-ported).	Not known -	Not known	4 including Master.
†Brodness -	5,736	31	5 miles W.N.W. from Port Anzio.	Submarine - -	No warning -	Torpedo -	—
Boaz (S.V.) -	111	31	15 miles N.E. from C. Barfleur.	Submarine - -	Captured -	Bombs -	—
Primrose (S.V.)	113	31	35 miles S.E. from Start Point.	Submarine - -	Gunfire -	Gunfire -	1
Gippeswic (S.V.)	116	31	15 miles N.E. from C. Barfleur.	Submarine - -	Captured -	Bombs -	—.
Braefield - -	427	31 (?)	Bristol Channel -	Submarine (?) -	No warning (?)	Torpedo (?)	10 including Master.
Coonagh - -	1,412	(?)	English Channel -	Submarine - -	Not known -	Not known	10 including Master.
Acton - -	207	(?)	English Channel -	Submarine - -	Not known -	Not known	6 including Master.
APRIL,	**1917.**						
†Warren - -	3,709	1	20 miles S.W. from Civita Vecchia.	Submarine - -	No warning -	Torpedo -	3 (Master made prisoner).
†Kasenga - -	4,652	1	2 miles from the Hormigas, Cape Palos.	Submarine - -	No warning -	Torpedo -	—
Eastern Belle (S.V.)	97	1	30 miles S.W. from St. Catherine's Point.	Submarine - -	Captured -	Bombs -	—
Silvia (S.V.) -	164	1	15 miles S.S.E. from the Owers L.V.	Submarine - -	Captured -	Bombs -	—
†Zambesi - -	3,759	1	15 miles N. by W. from Alexandria.	Submarine - -	No warning -	Torpedo -	3
†Britannia - -	3,129	2	22 miles W.N.W. from Pantellaria.	Submarine - -	No warning -	Torpedo -	Master and W/T operator made prisoners.
†Ardgask - -	4,542	3	15 miles S.W. from C. Rosello, Sicily.	Submarine - -	No warning -	Torpedo -	1

Name.	Gross Tons.	Date.	Position.	Cause of Loss.	How attacked.	How sunk.	Lives lost.
		1917. Apr.					
Ellen James (S.V.)	165	3	Bay of Biscay -	Submarine - -	Captured -	Gunfire -	5 including Master.
†Parkgate - -	3,232	4	80 miles N.E. from Cap de Fer.	Submarine - -	Captured -	Bombs -	16 Master made prisoner.
†Margit - -	2,490	4	80 miles S.W. ½ W. from C. Matapan.	Submarine - -	No warning -	Torpedo -	—
†Hunstanton -	4,504	4	36 miles W. from Scilly Islands.	Submarine - -	No warning -	Torpedo -	--
‡City of Paris -	9,239	4	46 miles S. by E. from Cap d'Antibes.	Submarine - -	No warning -	Torpedo -	122
†Canadian - -	9,309	5	47 miles N.W. by W. from the Fastnet.	Submarine - -	No warning -	Torpedo -	1 Master.
†Calliope - -	3,829	5	35 miles S.W. from Ustica.	Submarine - -	No warning -	Torpedo -	6 including Master, 1st and 2nd Officers and 3rd Engineer made prisoners.
†Benheather -	4,701	5	110 miles W.N.W. from the Fastnet.	Submarine - -	No warning -	Torpedo -	—
Gower Coast -	804	5 (?)	English Channel	Mine (?) - -	Mine (?) -	Mine (?) -	15 including Master.
†Spithead - -	4,697	6	12 miles N. by W. from Damietta Lt.	Submarine - -	No warning -	Torpedo -	1 Master and Chief Engineer made prisoners.
†Presto - -	1,143	6	4 miles E. from Roker Point, Sunderland.	Mine - - -	Mine - -	Mine -	6
†Powhatan -	6,117	6	25 miles N. by W. from N. Rona.	Submarine - -	No warning -	Torpedo -	36 Master made prisoner.
†Rosalind - -	6,535	6	180 miles W.N.W. from the Fastnet.	Submarine - -	No warning -	Torpedo -	2
†Maplewood -	3,239	7	47 miles S.W. from C. Sperone, Sardinia.	Submarine - -	Captured -	Torpedo -	Master made prisoner.
†Salmo - -	1,721	7	210 miles N.W. from the Fastnet.	Submarine - -	No warning -	Torpedo -	2
†Trefusis - -	2,642	7	30 miles S.E. from C. Pula, Sardinia.	Submarine - -	Captured -	Bombs -	Master, Chief Officer, and Chief Engineer made prisoners.
†Petridge - -	1,712	8	200 miles W.N.W. from Ushant.	Submarine - -	No warning -	Torpedo -	Master and one gunner made prisoners.
Geilan Bahri (S.V.)	19	8	54 miles from Alexandria.	Submarine - -	Captured -	Bomb -	—
†Umvoti - -	2,616	8	200 miles N.W. by W. from Ushant.	Submarine - -	No warning -	Torpedo -	4 Master and gunner made prisoners.

Name.	Gross Tons.	Date.	Position.	Cause of Loss.	How attacked.	How sunk.	Lives lost.
		1917, Apr.					
†T rrington -	5,597	8	Not known -	Submarine - -	No warning -	Torpedo -	34 Master made prisoner.
Kittiwake -	1,866	9	25 miles N.W. from the Maas L.V.	Submarine - -	No warning -	Torpedo -	7
†Dalton - -	3,486	10	25 miles S. by W. from C. Matapan.	Submarine - -	No warning -	Torpedo -	3 Master made prisoner.
Plato - -	1,266	10	32 miles S.E. by E. from Lowestoft.	Submarine - -	No warning -	Torpedo -	—
Salta (Hospital Ship).	7,284	10	½ mile N. from Whistle Buoy, Havre.	Mine - - -	Mine - -	Mine	79
Miss Morris (S.V.)	156	11	20 miles S.E. from Garrucha, Spain.	Submarine - -	Captured -	Bomb -	—
†Vine Branch -	3,442	11 (?)	Not known -	Submarine - -	No warning (probably).	Torpedo -	44 including Master.
†Quaggy - -	993	11	3 miles E. from N. Cheek, Robin Hood Bay.	Mine - - -	Mine - -	Mine	2
†Imperial Transport.	4,648	11	140 miles N.W. by N. ½ N. from Alexandria.	Submarine - -	No warning -	Torpedo -	Master made prisoner.
†Cyfarthfa - -	3,014	11	32 miles W.S.W. from Cerigotto.	Submarine - -	No warning -	Torpedo -	Master made prisoner.
†Tremorvah -	3,654	11	70 miles N.N.W. from C. Bougaroni.	Submarine - -	Captured -	Gunfire -	Master, Chief Engineer, and two gunners made prisoners
†Duchess of Cornwall.	1,706	11	5 miles N. from C. Barfleur.	Submarine - -	No warning -	Torpedo -	23 including Master.
†Glencliffe - -	3,673	12	2¼ miles S.E. from Tabarca Island, Spain.	Submarine - -	No warning -	Torpedo -	1 Chief Engineer and two gunners made prisoners.
†Kildale - -	3,830	12	40 miles E. by S. from Pantellaria.	Submarine - -	No warning -	Torpedo -	1
†Toro - -	3,066	12	200 miles W.N.W. from Ushant.	Submarine - -	No warning -	Torpedo -	14 Master and one gunner made prisoners.
†Lismore - -	1,305	12	22 miles N.W. by N. ½ N. from Havre.	Submarine - -	No warning -	Torpedo -	5
†Argyll - -	3,547	13	110 miles W. from Bishop Rock.	Submarine - -	No warning -	Torpedo -	22
†Bandon - -	1,456	13	2½ miles S.W. from Mine Head, S. Ireland.	Submarine - -	No warning -	Torpedo -	28
Maria (S.V.) ·	175	13	25 miles S. by W. from Portland Bill.	Submarine - -	Captured -	Bombs -	—

Name.	Gross Tons.	Date.	Position.	Cause of Loss.	How attacked.	How sunk.	Lives lost.
		1917. Apr.					
†Zara - -	1,331	13	90 miles W. ¾ W. from Helliso Island.	Submarine - -	No warning -	Torpedo -	27
†Kariba - -	3,697	13	260 miles W.N.W. from Ushant.	Submarine - -	No warning -	Torpedo -	13
Strathcona -	1,881	13	145 miles W.N.W. from Ronaldshay.	Submarine - -	Captured -	Bombs -	9 Master. chief and 3rd engineers made. prisoners.
Spray - -	1,072	14	3½ miles N.E. from Tyne Pier.	Mine - - -	Mine - -	Mine - -	—
†Hermione - -	4,011	14	1½ miles S. from Coningbeg L.V.	Mine - - -	Mine - -	Mine - -	—
Patagonier -	3,832	14	135 miles W. from Gibraltar.	Submarine - -	Captured -	Gunfire .-	Master made prisoner.
†Mashobra - -	8,236	15	140 miles S.W. from C. Matapan.	Submarine - -	No warning -	Torpedo -	8 Master made prisoner.
Alert - -	777	15	Off Dover - -	Mine - - -	Mine - -	Mine - -	11
†Cameronia	10,963	15	150 miles E. from Malta.	Submarine - -	No warning -	Torpedo -	11
†Arcadian - -	8,939	15	26 miles N.E. from Milo.	Submarine - -	No warning -	Torpedo	35
†Cairndhu - -	4,019	15	25 miles W. from Beachy Head.	Submarine - -	No warning -	Torpedo -	11
Victoria (S.V.)-	165	16	30 miles S.W. from Beachy Head.	Submarine - -	Captured -	Bombs -	—
Rochester Castle (S.V.).	102	16	5 miles W.S.W. from C. Grisnez.	Submarine - -	Captured -	Gunfire ·	—
Eduard (S.V.) -	476	16	12 miles S.W. from Beachy Head.	Submarine - -	Captured -	Bombs -	—
Marden - -	297	16	6 miles N.W. from C. Grisnez.	Submarine - -	Gunfire -	Gunfire -	1 (Master).
Towergate -	3,697	16	250 miles N.W. by W. from the Fastnet.	Submarine - -	Captured -	Torpedo -	—
Queen Mary -	5,658	16	180 miles N.W. by W. from the Fastnet.	Submarine - -	No warning -	Torpedo -	9
Charles Goodanew.	791	17	3½ miles E.N.E. from Rattray Head.	Mine - - -	Mine - -	Mine - -	13 including Master.
Brisbane River -	4,989	17	140 miles W. from Gibraltar.	Submarine - -	Captured -	Bombs -	Master made prisoner.
†Aburi - -	3,730	17	125 miles N.W. from Tory Island.	Submarine - -	No warning -	Torpedo -	25
Cairnhill - -	4,981	17	160 miles N.W. from the Fastnet.	Submarine - -	Captured -	Bombs -	Master made prisoner.
†Kish - -	4,928	17	160 miles N.W. by W. from the Fastnet.	Submarine - -	No warning -	Torpedo -	6
Corfu - -	3,695	17	160 miles W. from Gibraltar.	Submarine - -	Captured -	Bombs -	3
William Shepherd (S.V.)	143	17	30 miles S. by W. from St. Anns Head.	Submarine - -	Captured -	Bombs -	—
Dantzic - -	108	17	30 miles S. by W. from St. Ann's Head.	Submarine - -	Captured -	Bombs -	—
Fernmoor - -	3,098	17	150 miles W. from Gibraltar.	Submarine - -	Captured -	Bombs -	—
Lanfranc (Hospital Ship).	6,287	17	42 miles N, ½ E. from Havre.	Submarine - -	No warning -	Torpedo -	5

Name.	Gross Tons.	Date.	Position.	Cause of Loss.	How attacked.	How sunk.	Lives lost.
		1917. Apr.					
†Donegal - -	1,885	17	19 miles S. from Dean L.V.	Submarine - -	No warning -	Torpedo -	11
†Trekieve - -	3,087	18	100 miles W. from Gibraltar.	Submarine - -	No warning	Torpedo -	3 Master made prisoner.
†Rhydwen - -	4,799	18	170 miles N.W. by W. ½ W. from the Fastnet.	Submarine - -	No warning	Torpedo -	6
†Rowena - -	3,017	18	95 miles W. by S. ½ S. from Bishop Rock.	Submarine - -	No warning	Torpedo -	1
†Castillian -	1,923	18	110 miles N.W. by N. from Tory Island.	Submarine - -	No warning .	Torpedo -	10
Thomas (S.V.) -	132	18	40 miles S.E. from C. St. Vincent.	Submarine - -	Captured -	Bombs -	—
†Lena - -	2,463	18 (?)	Not known -	Submarine (reported)	No warning (probably).	Torpedo -	25 including Master.
†Rinaldo - -	4,321	18	18 miles W. by N. from C. Shershel.	Submarine - -	No warning	Torpedo -	—
†Scalpa - -	1,010	18	150 miles N.W. by W. from the Fastnet.	Submarine - -	No warning	Torpedo -	—
†Cragoswald -	3,235	18	60 miles W. by S. from Bishop Rock.	Submarine - -	No warning	Torpedo -	2
†Sculptor - -	3,846	18	120 miles N.W. by W. from the Fastnet.	Submarine - -	No warning	Torpedo -	1
Jewel (S.V.) -	195	19	20 miles S.E. from Coningbeg L.V.	Submarine - -	Captured -	Bombs -	—
†Sowwell - -	3,781	19	170 miles W. ½ S. from Gibraltar.	Submarine - -	No warning -	Torpedo -	21 including Master.
Bethlehem (motor)	379	19	½ mile E. from S. Holm Buoy.	Mine - - -	Mine - -	Mine -	1
†Avocet - -	1,219	19	100 miles W.N.W. from the Fastnet.	Submarine - -	Captured -	Torpedo -	—
†Caithness - -	3,500	19	130 miles N.W. by N. from Cape Ortegal.	Submarine - -	No warning	Torpedo -	47 including Master.
Poltava - -	945	19	3 miles E.N.E. from Souter Point.	Mine - - -	Mine - -	Mine - -	—
†Howth Head -	4,440	19	158 miles N.W. from the Fastnet.	Submarine - -	No warning	Torpedo -	2
Senator Dantziger (S.V.)	164	19	15 miles S. by E. ½ E. from Newhaven.	Submarine - -	Captured -	Gunfire -	—
†Tempus - -	2,981	19	130 miles N.W. by W. ½ W. from the Fastnet.	Submarine - -	No warning	Torpedo -	1
†Annapolis -	4,567	19	74 miles N.W. ½ N. from Eagle Island.	Submarine - -	No warning -	Torpedo -	—
†Gold Coast -	4,255	19	14 miles S. from Mine Head.	Submarine - -	No warning	Torpedo -	—
†Elswick Manor -	3,943	19	180 miles W. from Ushant.	Submarine - -	No warning -	Torpedo -	—
†Cilurnum - -	3,126	19	5 miles S.W. from Penmarch.	Submarine - -	No warning	Torpedo -	1
Lowdale - -	2,660	20	90 miles W. by N. from Gibraltar.	Submarine - -	Captured -	Gunfire -	—
†San Hilario -	10,157	20	270 miles W. by N. from the Fastnet.	Submarine - -	Captured -	Torpedo -	Master made prisoner.
†Portloe - -	3,187	20	160 miles W.N.W. from the Fastnet.	Submarine - -	No warning -	Torpedo -	24 including Master.

Name.	Gross Tons.	Date.	Position.	Cause of Loss.	How attacked.	How sunk.	Lives lost.
		1917. Apr.					
†Malakand - -	7,653	20	145 miles W. ½ N. from Bishop Rock.	Submarine - -	Captured -	Torpedo -	1
†Torr Head -	5,911	20	160 miles N.W. by W. from the Fastnet.	Submarine - -	No warning -	Torpedo -	—
Nentmoor - -	3,535	20	140 miles W. from Gibraltar.	Submarine - -	Captured -	Gunfire -	—
Emma - -	2,520	20	200 miles S.W. by S. from the Fastnet.	Submarine - -	No warning -	Torpedo	2
Ballochbuie -	921	20	7 miles E. from May Island.	Submarine - -	No warning -	Torpedo -	3 including Master.
†Pontiac - -	1,698	21	56 miles S.W. ½ S. from the Fastnet.	Submarine -	No warning -	Torpedo -	2
†Diadem - -	4,307	21	200 miles S.W. by W. from the Fastnet.	Submarine - -	No warning -	Torpedo -	—
†Telena - -	4,778	21	170 miles W.N.W. from the Fastnet.	Submarine - -	No warning -	Torpedo -	—
†Sebek - -	4,601	21	145 miles N.W. from Tory Island.	Submarine - -	No warning -	Torpedo -	1
†Warrior - -	3,674	21	7 miles N. from Fratelli Rocks.	Mine - - -	Mine - -	Mine - -	1
†Neepawah -	1,799	22	120 miles W. from Bishop Rock.	Submarine - -	Captured -	Bombs -	—
†Capenor - -	2,536	22	Entrance to La Pallice Roads.	Mine - - -	Mine - -	Mine - -	—
†Dykland -	4,291	22	200 miles W.N.W. from the Fastnet.	Submarine - -	No warning -	Torpedo -	---
†Imataka - -	1,776	23	15 miles S.S.W. from Daunts Rock.	Submarine - -	No warning -	Torpedo -	—
Auriac - -	871	23	5 miles E.S.E. from St. Abbs Head.	Submarine - -	Captured -	Gunfire -	1
Oswald - -	5,185	23	200 miles S.W. from the Fastnet.	Submarine - -	No warning -	Torpedo -	1
†Eptapyrgion -	4,307	23	150 miles W. by S. from Scilly Islands.	Submarine - -	No warning -	Torpedo -	—
Arethusa (S.V.)	1,279	23	15 miles N.W. from Eagle Island.	Submarine - -	Captured -	Bombs -	—
†Anglesea - . -	4,534	24	160 miles W. from Bishop Rock.	Submarine - -	No warning -	Torpedo -	—
Plutus - -	1,189	24	9 miles N.N.W. from Trevose Head.	Submarine - -	No warning -	Torpedo -	1
†Thistleard -	4,136	24	135 miles WNW. from Tory Island.	Submarine - -	No warning -	Torpedo -	—
†Kenilworth -	2,735	24	3½ miles S.W. by S. from St. Mathieu Point, Brest.	Mine - - -	Mine - -	Mine - -	—
Barnton - -	1,858	24	40 miles W. by S. from Chassiron Light.	Submarine - -	No warning -	Torpedo -	14
Amulree (S.V.)	1,445	24	50 miles N. by E. from Tory Island.	Submarine - -	Captured -	Not known	---
†Ferndene - -	3,770	24	150 miles W. from Bishop Rock.	Submarine - -	No warning -	Torpedo -	9 including Master.
†Abosso - -	7,782	24	180 miles W. by N. from the Fastnet.	Submarine - -	No warning -	Torpedo -	65

Name.	Gross Tons.	Date.	Position.	Cause of Loss.	How attacked.	How sunk.	Lives lost
		1917. Apr.					
Invermay (S.V.)	1,471	25	40 miles N.W. by N. from Eagle Island.	Submarine - -	Captured -	Bombs -	—
†Stephanotis - (ex " Hackensack.")	4,060	25	180 miles N.W. by W. from the Fastnet.	Submarine - -	No warning -	Torpedo -	6
Heathfield (S.V.)	1,643	25	53 miles W. by N. from Eagle Island.	Submarine - -	Captured -	Bombs -	—
†Ballarat - -	11,120	25	24 miles S. by W. from Wolf Rock.	Submarine - -	No warning -	Torpedo -	--
Laura (S.V.) -	335	25	150 miles W.N.W. from the Fastnet.	Submarine - -	Captured -	Bombs -	—
Hesperides -	3,393	25	130 miles N.W. ½ W. from the Fastnet.	Submarine - -	No warning -	Torpedo -	1
†Hirondelle -	1,648	25	13 miles S. by E. from Belle Ile.	Submarine - -	No warning -	Torpedo -	—
†Swanmore -	6,373	25	230 miles W.N.W. from the Fastnet.	Submarine - -	No warning -	Torpedo -	11
†Vauxhall - -	3,629	25	110 miles N.W. by W. from the Fastnet.	Submarine - -	No warning -	Torpedo -	2
†Rio Lages -	3,591	26	155 miles N.W. by W. from the Fastnet.	Submarine - -	No warning -	Torpedo -	3
†Manchester Citizen.	4,251	26	240 miles N.W. from the Fastnet.	Submarine - -	No warning -	Torpedo -	1
†Alhama - -	1,744	26	1½ miles N. from Calais.	Mine - - -	Mine - -	Mine - -	—
Agnes Cairns (S.V.)	146	26	8 miles N.E. from Alderney.	Submarine - -	Captured -	Bombs -	—
†Chertsey - -	3,264	26	4 miles N. from Algiers.	Submarine - -	No warning -	Torpedo -	—
Athole (motor barge).	150	26	20 miles S. from Owers L.V.	Submarine - -	Captured -	Gunfire -	--
†Harflete - -	4,814	26	200 miles N.W. by W. from the Fastnet.	Submarine - -	Gunfire -	Torpedo -	1
Monitor (S.V.) -	120	26	20 miles S. by E. from C. Antibes.	Submarine - -	Captured -	Bombs -	--
†Beemah - -	4,750	27	30 miles S.W. by S. from Bishop Rock.	Submarine - -	No warning -	Torpedo -	3
†Glencluny -	4,812	27	4 miles N.W. from C. Sigli.	Submarine - -	No warning -	Torpedo -	4
†Dromore - -	4,398	27	140 miles N.W. by N. from Tory Island.	Submarine - -	No warning -	Torpedo -	--
†Karuma - -	2,995	27	5 miles N. from C. Sigli.	Submarine - -	No warning -	Torpedo -	2
†Dunmore Head -	2,293	27	135 miles N.W. from Tory Island.	Submarine - -	No warning -	Torpedo -	—
Good Hope(S.V.)	77	27	15 miles N.N.W. from C. Barfleur.	Submarine - -	Gunfire -	Gunfire -	—
Jessie (S.V.) -	108	27	7 miles W. ½ S. from Portland Bill.	Submarine - -	Captured -	Bombs -	—
Burrowa (S.V.)	2,902	27	60 miles W. from Scilly Islands.	Submarine - -	Captured -	Bombs -	--
†Alfalfa - -	2,993	27 (?)	Not known	Submarine - -	No warning (probably).	Torpedo -	30 including Master.
†Bullmouth -	4,018	28	125 miles N.W. by N. from Tory Island.	Submarine - -	No warning -	Torpedo -	

Name.	Gross Tons.	Date.	Position.	Cause of Loss.	How attacked.	How sunk.	Lives lost.
		1917. Apr.					
†Jose de Larrinaga	5,017	28	150 miles W.N.W. from the Fastnet.	Submarine - -	No warning -	Torpedo -	12 including Master.
Port Jackson (S.V.)	2,309	28	180 miles W. by N. from the Fastnet.	Submarine - -	No warning -	Torpedo -	14 including Master.
†Pontiac - -	3,345	28	70 miles N. by E. from Marsa Susa.	Submarine - -	No warning -	Torpedo -	1 Master, chief engineer, and 2 gunners made prisoners.
†Medina - -	12,350	28	3 miles E.N.E. from Start Point.	Submarine - -	No warning -	Torpedo -	6
†Teakwood -	5,315	28	26 miles S.W. by W. from Sapienza Island.	Submarine - -	No warning -	Torpedo -	—
†Terence - -	4,309	28	150 miles N.W. by W. from the Fastnet.	Submarine - -	Gunfire -	Torpedo -	1
†Karonga - -	4,665	29	Strait of Messina	Submarine - -	No warning -	Torpedo -	18 Master prisoner.
Ellen Harrison (S.V.)	103	29	7 miles N.W. from Cherbourg.	Submarine - -	Gunfire -	Gunfire -	—
Mermaid (S.V.)	76	29	18 miles S.S.W. from Anvil Point.	Submarine - -	Captured -	Bombs -	—
†Daleby -	3,628	29	180 miles N.W. from the Fastnet.	Submarine - -	No warning -	Torpedo -	25 including Master.
Victoria - -	1,620	29	5 miles N.E. by N. from Scarborough.	Submarine - -	No warning -	Torpedo -	1
†Comedian - -	4,889	29	200 miles W. by S. from Bishop Rock.	Submarine - -	No warning -	Torpedo -	3 One gunner made prisoner.
†Ikbal - -	5,434	29	200 miles W. by S. from Bishop Rock.	Submarine - -	No warning -	Torpedo -	Master and 2 gunners made prisoners.
Little Mystery (S.V.)	114	30	25 miles S.S.E. from Portland Bill.	Submarine - -	Captured -	Bombs -	—
†Delamere - -	1,525	30	110 miles W. by N. from the Fastnet.	Submarine - -	No warning -	Torpedo -	10
†Horsa - -	2,949	30	195 miles S.W. by W. from the Fastnet.	Submarine - -	No warning -	Torpedo	11 including Master, 1 gunner made prisoner.
†Gretaston -	3,395	(?)	Atlantic - -	Submarine (?) -	Not known -	Not known	29 including Master.
MAY 1917.		May					
†Gena - -	2,784	1	Off Southwold -	Seaplane - -	No warning -	Torpedo	—
C. A. Jaques -	2,105	1	26 miles W.S.W. from Boulogne.	Submarine - -	No warning -	Torpedo -	3
†British Sun -	5,565	1	230 miles E.S.E. from Malta.	Submarine - -	No warning -	Torpedo -	—
Ladywood -	2,314	1	15 miles S.W. from Wolf Rock.	Submarine - -	Captured -	Bombs -	—
†Bagdale - -	3,045	1	13 miles N. by E. ½ E. from Creac'h Point, Ushant.	Submarine - -	No warning -	Torpedo -	23 including Master.

Name.	Gross Tons.	Date.	Position.	Cause of Loss.	How attacked.	How sunk.	Lives lost.
		1917. May					
Firelight - -	1,143	1	1¾ miles East from N. Tyne Pier.	Submarine - -	No warning -	Torpedo -	—
†San Urbano -	6,458	1	180 miles N.W. by W. from the Fastnet.	Submarine - -	No warning -	Torpedo -	4
W. D. Potts (S.V.)	112	1	10 miles S.W. from Portpatrick.	Submarine - -	Captured -	Gunfire -	—
John W. Pearn (S.V.)	75	1	40 miles S.S.E. from Start Point.	Submarine - -	Captured -	Bombs -	—
Helen - -	322	1	11 miles West from the Mull of Galloway.	Submarine - -	Captured -	Bombs -	—
Dora - -	296	1	11 miles West from Mull of Galloway.	Submarine - -	Captured -	Bombs -	—
Juno - -	1,384	2	17 miles E. ¾ S. from Cape Bar-fleur.	Submarine - -	No warning -	Torpedo -	1
†Tela - -	7,226	2	16 miles N.E. ½ E. from Cape Bar-fleur.	Submarine - -	No warning -	Torpedo -	
Warnow - -	1,593	2	6 miles West from Trevose Head.	Submarine - -	No warning -	Torpedo -	14 including Master.
Saint Mungo -	402	2	Ballyhalbert Bay, County Down.	Submarine - -	Captured -	Bombs -	—
Derrymore -	485	2	Ballyhalbert Bay, County Down.	Submarine - -	Captured -	Bombs -	—
Amber - -	401	2	Ballyhalbert Bay, County Down.	Submarine - -	Captured -	Bombs -	—
Ernest (S.V.) -	111	2	6 miles S.E. from Skulmartin L.V.	Submarine - -	Captured -	Bombs -	—
Morion - -	299	2	Ballyhalbert Bay, County Down.	Submarine - -	Captured -	Bombs -	—
†Troilus - -	7,625	2	140 miles W.N.W. from Malin Head.	Submarine - -	No warning -	Torpedo -	—
Beeswing (S.V.)	1,462	2	140 miles W. by N. from the Fastnet.	Submarine - -	Captured -	Gunfire -	—
†Ussa - -	2,066	3	2½ miles N.W. from W. Entrance, Cherbourg.	Mine - - -	Mine - -	Mine -	—
†Frederick Knight	3,604	3	115 miles N.W. by W. from the Fastnet.	Submarine - -	No warning -	Torpedo -	—
Glen Tanar -	817	3	1 mile N.E. from Girdleness.	Mine - - -	Mine - -	Mine -	—
Washington -	5,080	3	Off Rapallo Bay -	Submarine - -	No warning -	Torpedo -	---
†Clodmoor - -	3,753	3	5 miles S.W. from Newhaven.	Submarine - -	No warning -	Torpedo -	—
Herrington -	1,258	4	¾ mile E.S.E. from Red Head, For-far.	Mine - - -	Mine - -	Mine -	—
Joseph (S.V.) -	205	4	20 miles W. by N. from Caen Hr.	Submarine - -	Captured -	Bombs -	—
†Transylvania -	14,315	4	2½ miles South from Cape Vado, Gulf of Genoa.	Submarine - -	No warning -	Torpedo -	12 including Master.
New Design, No. 2 (S.V.).	66	4	15 miles E. by S. from Tuskar Rock.	Submarine - -	Captured -	Bombs -	—
†Pilar de Lar-rinaga.	4,136	4	2 miles S.E. by S. from the Tuskar L.V.	Submarine - -	No warning -	Torpedo -	20 including Master.
†Harmattan -	4,792	5	7 miles N. from Cape Rosa, Al-geria.	Mine - - -	Mine - -	Mine -	36 including Master.
Greta - -	297	5	11 miles S.E. from Mine Head.	Submarine - -	Captured -	Gunfire -	—

Name.	Gross Tons.	Date.	Position.	Cause of Loss.	How attacked.	How sunk.	Lives lost.
		1917. May					
Lodes - -	396	5	4 miles S.E. from Ballycottin.	Mine - - -	Mine - -	Mine - -	7 including Master.
Angela (S.V.) -	122	5	3 miles S.E. from Tyne.	Mine - - -	Mine - -	Mine - -	5
†Feltria - -	5,254	5	8 miles S.E. from Mine Head.	Submarine - -	No warning -	Torpedo -	45 including Master.
†Adansi - -	2,644	6	80 miles W. ½ N. from the Fastnet.	Submarine - -	No warning -	Torpedo -	—
Hebble - -	904	6	1½ miles E. from Roker Pier, Sunderland.	Mine - - -	Mine - -	Mine	5
Maude (S.V.) -	93	7	Near Bardsey Island.	Submarine - -	Captured -	Bombs	—
†Kinross - -	4,120	7	10 miles E. from Wolf Rock.	Submarine - -	No warning -	Torpedo -	—
†Repton - -	2,881	7	45 miles S.S.E. from Cape Matapan.	Submarine - -	No warning -	Torpedo -	3
†Polamhall -	4,010	7	80 miles W.S.W. from Bishop Rock.	Submarine - -	No warning -	Torpedo -	—
Lowmount -	2,070	7	4 miles S.E. from Nab L.V.	Mine - - -	Mine - -	Mine - -	5
Killarney (S.V.)	1,413	8	200 miles W. by N. from the Fastnet.	Submarine - -	Captured -	Gunfire -	—
†Petunia - -	1,749	8	45 miles W. from Bishop Rock.	Submarine - -	No warning -	Torpedo -	2 Master and 2 gunners made prisoners.
Iris (S.V.) - -	75	8 (?)	English Channel	Submarine (?) -	Captured (?)	Bombs (?) -	4 including Master.
†Harpagus -	5,866	9	62 miles S.W. from Planier Island.	Submarine - -	No warning -	Torpedo -	3 Master and Chief Engineer made prisoners.
Broomhill -	1,392	10	9 miles S.W. from Portland Bill.	Submarine - -	Captured -	Bombs -	2
Tarpeia - -	538	11	9 miles N. from Port en Bessin.	Submarine - -	Captured -	Bombs -	—
†Calchas - -	6,748	11	5 miles W. by S. from Tearaght Island.	Submarine - -	No warning -	Torpedo -	--
†Barrister - -	3,679	11	7 miles S.W. from Mine Head, Waterford.	Submarine - -	No warning -	Torpedo -	—
Limasol (S.V.) -	100	11	18 miles S.W. by W. from Monte Cristo.	Submarine - -	Captured -	Bombs -	—
†San Onofre -	9,717	12	64 miles N.W. ½ N. from the Skelligs.	Submarine - -	No warning -	Torpedo -	1
†Galicia - -	5,922	12	3 miles East from Teignmouth.	Mine - - -	Mine - -	Mine - -	—
†Refugio - -	2,642	12	115 miles N.W. ½ W. from Tory Island.	Submarine - -	Captured -	Gunfire -	1
†Egyptian Prince	3,117	12	240 miles S.S.E. from Malta.	Submarine - -	Captured -	Bombs -	—
†Locksley Hall -	3,635	12	30 miles S.E. by S. from Malta.	Submarine - -	No warning -	Torpedo -	6
†Zanoni - -	3,851	12	12 miles N.E. by E. from Cape Oropesa.	Submarine - -	Captured -	Torpedo -	1

Name.	Gross Tons.	Date.	Position.	Cause of Loss.	How attacked.	How sunk.	Lives lost.
		1917 May					
†Wirral - -	4,207	12	23 miles N.W. from Utvaer Island, Norway.	Submarine - -	No warning -	Torpedo -	1
†Jessmore - -	3,911	13	180 miles W.N.W. from the Fastnet.	Submarine - -	No warning -	Torpedo -	—
†Farley - -	3,692	14	70 miles S.W. ½ W. from the Bishop Rock.	Submarine - -	No warning -	Torpedo -	—
Carnmoney(S.V.)	1,299	14	150 miles W. from the Fastnet.	Submarine - -	Captured -	Bombs -	—
Elizabeth Hampton (S.V.)	108	14	25 miles S. by W. from St. Catherine's.	Submarine - -	Captured -	Bombs -	—
†Lewisham -	2,810	14(?)	Atlantic - -	Submarine - -	No warning (probably).	Torpedo -	24 Master and 2 gunners made prisoners.
†Polymnia - -	2,426	15	15 miles W. from the Lizard.	Submarine - -	No warning -	Torpedo -	8
†Tung Shan -	3,999	15	7 miles North from Cape San Antonio.	Submarine - -	Captured -	Bombs -	1 Master, Chief Engineer and one gunner prisoners.
Cuba (S.V.) -	271	15	18 miles E.S.E. from Owers L.V.	Submarine - -	Captured -	Bombs -	—
†Pagenturm -	5,000	16	16 miles W. from Beachy Head.	Submarine - -	No warning -	Torpedo -	4
Dorothy Duff (S.V.)	186	16	14 miles from Cape Cullera.	Submarine - -	Captured -	Bomb -	—
†Highland Corrie	7,583	16	4 miles S. from Owers L.V.	Submarine - -	No warning -	Torpedo -	5
†Middlesex -	8,364	16	150 miles N.W. from Tory Island.	Submarine - -	No warning -	Torpedo -	—
†Kilmaho - -	2,155	16	10 miles W.N.W. from the Lizard.	Submarine - -	No warning -	Torpedo -	21 including Master.
Florence Louisa (S.V.)	115	17	8 miles S. from the Needles.	Submarine - -	Captured -	Bombs -	—
†George Pyman -	3,859	17	130 miles N.W. from Tearaght Island.	Submarine - -	No warning -	Torpedo -	—
Cito - -	819	17	20 miles E. from North Hinder L.V.	T.B.D.'s - -	No warning -	Gunfire -	11 including Master.
Elford - -	1,739	18	2 miles S. from Nab L.V.	Mine - - -	Mine - -	Mine - -	—
†Penhale - -	3,712	18	72 miles N.W. by N. ½ N. from Tearaght Island.	Submarine - -	No warning	Torpedo -	1 Master made prisoner.
†Camberwell -	4,078	18	6 miles S.E. by E. from Dunnose Head.	Mine - - -	Mine - -	Mine - -	7
C.E.C.G. (S.V.)	47	18	30 miles S.S.E. from the Start.	Submarine - -	Captured -	Gunfire -	—
†Millicent Knight	3,563	18	130 miles E. by S. ½ S. from Malta.	Submarine - -	No warning -	Torpedo -	1
†Llandrindod -	3,841	18	165 miles N.W. by W. from the Fastnet.	Submarine - -	No warning -	Torpedo -	Master made prisoner.
Dromore - -	268	18	6 miles South from St. Martin Point, Guernsey.	Submarine - -	Captured -	Gunfire -	—
†Mary Baird -	1,830	18	2½ miles W. ½ N. from Pendeen Cove.	Mine - - -	Mine - -	Mine -	7

Name.	Gross Tons.	Date.	Position.	Cause of Loss.	How attacked.	How sunk.	Lives lost.
		1917. May					
†Mordenwood -	3,125	19	90 miles S.E. by S. ½ S. from Cape Matapan.	Submarine (?) -	No warning	Torpedo (?)	21 including Master.
†Farnham - -	3,102	19	90 miles N.W. from the Fastnet.	Submarine - -	No warning	Torpedo -	17 including Master.
†Mardinian -	3,322	19	4 miles S. by W. from Tabarca Island.	Submarine - -	No warning	Torpedo -	—
†Caspian - -	3,606	20	3½ miles E. from Cape Cervera, Spain.	Submarine - -	Captured -	Torpedo -	25 (including Master). Chief Engineer, 2nd Officer, and 1 gunner made prisoners.
Dana (S.V.) -	182	20	25 miles N. from Les Hanois.	Submarine - -	Captured -	Bombs -	
Mientji (S.V.) -	120	20	25 miles N. from Les Hanois.	Submarine - -	Captured -	Bombs -	—
†Tycho - -	3,216	20	16 miles W. ½ S. from Beachy Head.	Submarine - -	No warning -	Torpedo -	15 including Master.
Porthkerry -	1,920	20	16 miles W. by S. from Beachy Head.	Submarine - -	No warning -	Torpedo -	7 including Master.
†Jupiter - -	2,124	21	15 miles West from Beachy Head.	Submarine - -	No warning	Torpedo -	19 including Master.
†Don Diego -	3,632	21	40 miles E. by S. from Linosa.	Submarine - -	Captured -	Gunfire -	5
†Ampleforth -	3,873	21	15 miles W.S.W. from Gozo.	Submarine - -	No warning -	Torpedo -	4
†City of Corinth	5,870	21	12 miles S.W. from the Lizard.	Submarine - -	No warning -	Torpedo -	
Lanthorn - -	2,299	22	3 miles East from Whitby.	Submarine - -	Captured -	Bombs -	
†England - -	3,798	23	40 miles S. by E. from Cape Bon.	Submarine - -	Captured -	Bombs -	3 including Master.
†Elmmoor - -	3,744	23	36 miles E. by S. from Syracuse.	Submarine - -	No warning -	Torpedo -	Master made prisoner.
†Lesto - -	1,940	23	8 miles West from Ile du Pilier.	Submarine - -	No warning -	Torpedo -	4
†Jersey City -	4,670	24	35 miles N.W. from the Flannan Isles.	Submarine - -	No warning -	Torpedo -	Master made prisoner.
†Belgian - -	3,657	24	50 miles W. ½ S. from the Fastnet.	Submarine - -	No warning -	Torpedo -	2
McClure (S.V.)	220	24	30 miles E. by S. from C. Carbonara.	Submarine - -	Captured -	Bombs -	—
Sjaelland -	1,405	25	18 miles E. by N. from Start Point.	Submarine - -	Captured -	Gunfire -	1 (Master.)
†Kohinur - -	2,265	25	150 miles North from Alexandria.	Submarine - -	No warning -	Torpedo -	37 including Master.
Saint Mirren (S.V.)	1,956	26	45 miles N.W. from Inistrahull.	Submarine - -	Captured -	Gunfire -	—
†Holmesbank -	3,051	26	90 miles N. by W. from Alexandria.	Submarine - -	Captured -	Gunfire -	—

Name.	Gross Tons.	Date.	Position.	Cause of Loss.	How attacked.	How sunk.	Lives lost.
		1917. May					
†Umaria - -	5,317	26	20 miles S.W. by S. from Policastro, Italy.	Submarine - -	Captured -	Torpedo -	5 Chief Engineer, 2nd Officer and 1 Cadet made prisoners.
Dover Castle - (Hospital Ship)	8,271	26	50 miles North from Bona.	Submarine - -	No warning -	Torpedo -	7
†Boldwell - -	3,118	27	35 miles N.E. from Linosa.	Submarine - -	No warning -	Torpedo -	3
†Dartmoor - -	2,870	27	35 miles S.E. from Fastnet.	Submarine - -	No warning -	Torpedo -	25 including Master.
†Antinoe - -	2,396	28	150 miles W.S.W. from Bishop Rock.	Submarine - -	No warning -	Torpedo -	21 including Master.
†Limerick - -	6,827	28	140 miles W. ½ S. from Bishop Rock.	Submarine - -	No warning -	Torpedo -	8
Detlef Wagner (S.V.)	225	28	5 miles W. from Armen Rock.	Submarine - -	Captured -	Bombs -	—
†Clan Murray -	4,835	29	40 miles W. by S. from Fastnet.	Submarine - -	No warning -	Torpedo -	64 (including Master). 3rd Officer and probably 3rd Engineer made prisoners.
†Oswego - -	5,793	29	175 miles W. ½ S. from Bishop Rock.	Submarine - -	No warning -	Torpedo -	—
†Ashleaf - -	5,768	29	150 miles West from Bishop Rock.	Submarine - -	No warning -	Torpedo -	—
†Lisbon - -	1,203	30	5 miles S. from Royal Sovereign L.V.	Mine - - -	Mine - -	Mine - -	1
‡Corbet Woodall	917	30	1½ miles E. from the Nab L.V.	Mine - - -	Mine - -	Mine - -	—
†Hanley - -	3,331	30	95 miles W. from Bishop Rock.	Submarine - -	No warning -	Torpedo -	1
Bathurst - -	2,821	30	90 miles W. from Bishop Rock.	Submarine - -	Captured	Torpedo -	—
†Rosebank - -	3,837	31	120 miles N. from Ben Ghazi.	Submarine - -	No warning -	Torpedo -	2 Master made prisoner.
†Esneh - -	3,247	31	190 miles N.W. by W. from Tory Island.	Submarine - -	No warning -	Torpedo -	—
JUNE 191		June					
†Cavina - -	6,539	1	45 miles W. by S. from the Fastnet.	Submarine - -	No warning -	Torpedo -	---
†Cameronian -	5,861	2	50 miles N.W. by N. ¼ N. from Alexandria.	Submarine - -	No warning -	Torpedo -	11 including Master.
†Hollington -	4,221	2	14 miles S. from Faeroe Islands.	Submarine - -	No warning -	Torpedo -	30 including Master.
Wairuna - -	3,947	2	Off Sunday Island, Kermadec Islands.	Wolf - - -	Captured -	Bombs -	—
†Islandmore -	3,046	3	20 miles N.W. from Cape Falcon, Algeria.	Submarine - -	Captured -	Gunfire -	2 Master made prisoner.

Name.	Gross Tons.	Date.	Position.	Cause of Loss.	How attacked.	How sunk.	Lives lost.
		1917. June					
†Greenbank -	3,881	3 .	12 miles north from Cape Falcon, Algeria.	Submarine - -	Captured -	Torpedo -	1
†Merioneth -	3,004	3	105 miles N. by W. from Tromso.	Submarine - -	Captured -	Gunfire -	—
†Southland -	11,899	4	140 miles N.W. ½ W. from Tory Island.	Submarine - -	No warning -	Torpedo -	4
†City of Baroda -	5,541	4	90 miles N.W. ½ N. from Tory Island.	Submarine - -	No warning -	Torpedo -	6
†Manchester Trader.	3,938	4	8 miles S.E. from Pantellaria.	Submarine - -	Captured -	Gunfire -	1 Second officer made prisoner.
†Phemius - -	6,699	4	80 miles N.W. ½ N. from Eagle Island.	Submarine - -	No warning -	Torpedo -	—
Laura Ann (S.V.)	116	5	20 miles S.S.E. from Beachy Head.	Submarine - -	Captured -	Gunfire -	1 (Master).
†Manchester Miller.	4,234	5	190 miles N.W. ½ N. from the Fastnet.	Submarine - -	No warning -	Torpedo -	8
†Kallundborg -	1,590	5	80 miles S.S.W. from Toulon.	Submarine - -	Captured -	Bombs -	1
†Parthenia - -	5,160	6	140 miles W. by N. from Bishop Rock.	Submarine - -	No warning -	Torpedo -	3
† Sir Francis -	1,991	7	2 miles N.E. from Scarborough.	Submarine - -	No warning -	Torpedo -	10 including Master.
Wilhelm (S.V.)	187	7	20 miles S.E. by S. from the Lizard.	Submarine - -	Captured -	Gunfire -	—
†Ikalis - -	4,329	7	170 miles N.W. ½ W. from the Fastnet.	Submarine - -	No warning -	Torpedo -	—
†Jonathan Holt -	1,522	7	130 miles N.W. by W. ½ W. from the Fastnet.	Submarine - -	No warning -	Torpedo -	—
†Saragossa - -	3,541	8	178 miles N.W. from the Fastnet.	Submarine - -	No warning -	Torpedo -	—
Phantom (S.V.)	251	8	25 miles N.N.W. from Cape La Heve.	Submarine - -	Captured -	Gunfire -	3
Enidwen - -	3,594	8	170 miles N.W. from the Fastnet.	Submarine - -	No warning -	Torpedo -	—
†Orator - -	3,563	8	84 miles W.N.W. from the Fastnet.	Submarine - -	No warning -	Torpedo -	5
†Huntstrick -	8,151	8	80 miles W.N.W. from Cape Spartel.	Submarine - -	No warning -	Torpedo -	15 including Master.
†Cheltonian -	4,426	8	54 miles W. by S. from Planier L. Ho.	Submarine - -	Captured -	Gunfire -	Master and 1 gunner made prisoners.
†Isle of Jura -	3,809	8	15 miles W.S.W. from Cape Spartel.	Submarine - -	Captured -	Bombs -	2
†Harbury - -	4,572	9	170 miles W. ½ N. from Ushant.	Submarine - -	No warning -	Torpedo -	12 including Master.
†Egyptiana -	3,818	9	120 miles W.S.W. from the Scillies.	Submarine - -	No warning -	Torpedo -	—
General Laurie (S.V.).	238	9	70 miles S.W. by S. from Planier L. Ho.	Submarine - -	Captured -	Set on fire -	—

Name.	Gross Tons.	Date.	Position.	Cause of Loss.	How attacked.	How sunk.	Lives lost.
		1917. June					
Marjorie (motor)	119	9	30 miles S.E. by S. from the Lizard.	Submarine - -	Captured -	Bombs -	—
†Appledore -	3,843	9	164 miles S. by W. from the Fastnet.	Submarine - -	No warning -	Torpedo -	—
†Achilles - -	641	9	75 miles W. by S. from the Fastnet.	Submarine - -	Captured -	Gunfire -	Master and 1 gunner made prisoners.
†Clan Alpine -	3,587	9	40 miles N. by E. ½ E. from Muckle Flugga.	Submarine - -	No warning -	Torpedo -	8
†Baron Cawdor -	4,316	9	150 miles S.W. by S. ½ S. from the Fastnet.	Submarine - -	No warning -	Torpedo -	3
†Haulwen - -	4,032	9	250 miles N.W. from the Fastnet.	Submarine - -	No warning -	Torpedo -	4
†Galicia - -	1,400	10	140 miles S.W. by S. ½ S. from the Fastnet.	Submarine - -	No warning -	Torpedo -	4
†Bay State -	6,583	10	250 miles N.W. from the Fastnet.	Submarine - -	No warning -	Torpedo -	—
†Scottish Hero -	2,205	10	440 miles W. by S. ½ S. from the Fastnet.	Submarine - -	Captured -	Gunfire -	1
†Dulwich - -	1,460	10	7 miles N. by E. ½ E. from the Shipwash L.V.	Mine - - -	Mine - -	Mine -	5
†Marie Elsie -	2,615	10	125 miles N. by W. from C. Teriberski, Lapland.	Submarine - -	No warning -	Torpedo -	3
†Perla - -	5,355	10	130 miles N ¾ W. from C. Teriberski, Lapland.	Submarine - -	Captured -	Not known	4
†Ribera - -	3,511	10	70 miles North from C. Wrath.	Submarine - -	No warning -	Torpedo -	—
†Anglian - -	5,532	10	43 miles S.W. by W. ½ W. from the Bishop Rock.	Submarine - -	No warning -	Torpedo -	1
Keeper - -	572	10(?)	Irish Channel -	Submarine (?) -	No warning (?)	Torpedo (?)	12 including Master.
†Teviotdale -	3,847	11	330 miles N.W. by W. from the Fastnet.	Submarine - -	No warning -	Torpedo -	1
†Benha - -	1,878	11	50 miles N. by E. from Marsa Susa.	Submarine - -	Captured -	Bombs -	—
†Polyxena - -	5,737	11	57 miles West from the Fastnet.	Submarine - -	No warning -	Torpedo -	7
†City of Perth -	3,427	11	195 miles S.S.W. from the Fastnet.	Submarine - -	No warning -	Torpedo -	8
†South Point -	4,258	11	30 miles S.W. ½ S. from Bishop Rock.	Submarine - -	No warning -	Torpedo -	—
†Huntsolm -	2,073	11	4 miles E. by S. from the Owers L.V.	Submarine - -	No warning -	Torpedo -	—
†Amakura - -	2,316	12	180 miles N.W. ½ W. from Tory Island.	Submarine - -	No warning -	Torpedo -	2
Alfred (S.V.) -	130	12	15 miles S.W. from Boulogne.	Submarine - -	Captured -	Bombs	—
Alwyn (S.V.) -	73	12	5 miles S.E. from Girdleness.	Submarine - -	Captured -	Bombs -	—

Name.	Gross Tons.	Date.	Position.	Cause of Loss.	How attacked.	How sunk.	Lives lost.
		1917. June					
†St. Andrews -	3,613	13	4 miles West from C. Spartivento, Italy.	Submarine - -	No warning -	Torpedo -	3
Silverburn -	284	13	4 miles S.E. from Cove Bay.	Submarine - -	Captured -	Gunfire -	—
†Darius - -	3,426	13	210 miles S.W. from the Fastnet.	Submarine - -	No warning -	Torpedo -	15
†Kelvinbank -	4,072	13	100 miles North from C. Wrath.	Submarine - -	No warning -	Torpedo -	16 including Master.
†Aysgarth - -	3,118	14	430 miles W.N.W. from C. Finisterre.	Submarine - -	Captured -	Bombs -	3
†New Zealand Transport.	4,481	14	8 miles S.E. from Serpho Pulo, Ægean.	Submarine - -	No warning -	Torpedo -	3
†Dart - -	3,207	14	6 miles S.S.W. from Ballycottin L. Ho.	Submarine - -	No warning -	Torpedo -	4
†Kankakee -	3,718	14	2 miles N.E. from Sunk L.V.	Seaplane - -	No warning -	Torpedo -	2
†Ortolan - -	1,727	14	100 miles W.S.W. from Bishop Rock.	Submarine - -	No warning -	Torpedo -	3
†Carthaginian -	4.444	14	2½ miles N.W. from Innistrahul L. Ho.	Mine - - -	Mine - -	Mine -	—
Wega - -	839	14	20 miles W. by S. from Royal Sovereign L.V.	Submarine - -	No warning -	Torpedo -	5
†Pasha - -	5,930	15	Southern entrance to Straits of Messina.	Submarine - -	No warning -	Torpedo -	3
†Westonby -	3,795	15	195 miles S.W. by S. from the Fastnet.	Submarine - -	No warning -	Torpedo -	—
†Addah - -	4,397	15	35 miles S.W. from Penmarch.	Submarine - -	No warning -	Torpedo -	9
†Wapello - -	5,576	15	14 miles W.S.W. from Owers L.V.	Submarine - -	No warning -	Torpedo -	2
†Jessie - -	2,256	16	260 miles W. ½ S. from Bishop Rock.	Submarine - -	No warning -	Torpedo -	—
Carrie Hervey, (S.V.)	111	16	52 miles S.E. by S. from Armen Rock.	Submarine - -	Captured -	Gunfire -	—
†Stanhope - -	2,854	17	7 miles S.W. by W. from Start Point.	Submarine - -	No warning -	Torpedo -	22
†Fornebo - -	4,259	17	4 miles North from C. Wrath.	Submarine - -	No warning -	Torpedo -	—
†Lizzie Westoll -	2,855	17	120 miles N.W. by W. from the Fastnet.	Submarine - -	No warning -	Torpedo -	—
†Raloo - -	1,012	17	6 miles S.E. by E. from Coningbeg L.V.	Submarine - -	No warning -	Torpedo -	3 including Master.
†Tyne - -	2,909	17	18 miles S.W. from the Lizard.	Submarine - -	No warning -	Torpedo -	
†English Monarch	4,947	18	300 miles N.W. by W. from the Fastnet.	Submarine - -	No warning -	Torpedo -	3
†Thistledhu -	4,032	18	218 miles N.W. ½ W. from the Fastnet.	Submarine - -	No warning -	Torpedo -	4
†Elele - -	6,557	18	300 miles N.W. ¾ W. from the Fastnet.	Submarine - -	No warning -	Torpedo -	—
Queen Adelaide	4,965	18	13 miles N.N.E. from St. Kilda.	Submarine - -	No warning -	Torpedo -	3

Name.	Gross Tons.	Date.	Position.	Cause of Loss.	How attacked.	How sunk.	Lives lost.
		1917. June					
Violet (S.V.) -	158	18	9 miles S.S.E. from Coningbeg L.V.	Submarine - -	Captured -	Gunfire -	—
Kangaroo (S.V.)	76	18	20 miles S. from Tuskar.	Submarine - -	Captured -	Gunfire -	4 including Master.
Gauntlet (S.V.)	58	18	30 miles N.W. from Les Hanois.	Submarine - -	Captured -	Bombs -	—
†Buffalo - -	4,106	18	80 miles N.W. by N. ¼ N. from C. Wrath.	Submarine - -	No warning -	Torpedo -	—
†Batoum - -	4,054	19	6 miles South from the Fastnet.	Submarine - -	No warning -	Torpedo -	1
Kate and Annie (S.V.)	96	19	25 miles N.W. by W. from Les Hanois.	Submarine - -	Captured -	Bombs -	—
†Brookby - -	3,679	19	155 miles S. ½ W. from the Fastnet.	Submarine - -	Captured -	Torpedo -	—
†Kelso - -	1,292	19	33 miles W.S.W. from Bishop Rock.	Submarine - -	No warning -	Torpedo -	—
Penpol - -	2,061	19	Gulf of Bothnia -	Submarine - -	Captured -	Taken to Germany.	—
†Ruperra - -	4,232	20	50 miles E. by S. from Pantellaria.	Submarine - -	No warning -	Torpedo -	—
†Bengore Head -	2,490	20	150 miles N.W. from the Fastnet.	Submarine - -	Captured -	Torpedo -	—
Benita (S.V.) -	130	20	15 miles South from Portland Bill.	Submarine - -	Captured -	Bombs -	—
Black Head -	1,898	21	52 miles E.S.E. from Out Skerries, Shetland.	Submarine - -	No warning -	Torpedo -	—
†Lord Roberts -	4,166	21	270 miles N.W. by N. from the Fastnet.	Submarine - -	Captured -	Gunfire -	—
†Ortona - -	5,524	21	140 miles S.S.W. from the Fastnet.	Submarine - -	No warning -	Torpedo -	1
†Melford Hall -	6,339	22	95 miles N. by W. ¾ W. from Tory Island.	Submarine - -	No warning -	Torpedo -	—·
†Miami - -	3,762	22	11 miles E.S.E. from the Fastnet.	Submarine - -	No warning -	Torpedo -	—
Meggie - -	1,802	24	Gulf of Bothnia -	Submarine - -	Captured -	Taken to Germany.	—
†Clan Davidson -	6,486	24	130 miles S.W. by W. ¼ W. from the Scilly Isles.	Submarine - -	No warning -	Torpedo -	12
†South Wales -	3,668	24	128 miles West from Bishop Rock.	Submarine - -	No warning -	Torpedo -	2
†Sylvanian -	4,858	24	170 miles N.W. from Tory Island.	Submarine - -	No warning -	Torpedo -	2
†Mongolia - -	9,505	24	50 miles S. by W. from Bombay.	Mine - - -	Mine - -	Mine - -	24
†Crown of Arragon	4,500	24	124 miles S.W. ½ W. from Bishop Rock.	Submarine - -	No warning -	Torpedo -	1
†Saxon Monarch	4,828	24	140 miles S.W. by W. from Scilly Isles.	Submarine - -	No warning -	Torpedo -	2
†Cestrian -	8,912	24	4 miles S.E. from Skyro.	Submarine - -	No warning -	Torpedo -	3
†Don Arturo	3,680	25(?)	Atlantic - -	Submarine (reported).	No warning (probably).	Torpedo -	34 including Master.

*Name.	Gross Tons.	Date.	Position.	Cause of Loss.	How attacked.	How sunk.	Lives lost.
		1917. June					
†Guildhall - -	2,609	25	40 miles S.W. by W. ½ W. from Bishop Rock.	Submarine - -	No warning -	Torpedo -	12
†Anatolia - -	3,847	25	1½ miles off Genoa.	Mine - - -	Mine - -	Mine - -	—
Neotsfield (S.V.)	1,875	26	112 miles S.W. by W. from Bishop Rock.	Submarine - -	Captured -	Bombs -	—
†Birdoswald -	4,013	26	25 miles E. ½ S. from Tarragona.	Submarine - -	No warning -	Torpedo -	Master and Chief Engineer prisoners.
†Manistee - -	3,869	26	86 miles W.S.W. from Bishop Rock.	Submarine - -	No warning -	Torpedo -	5
†Cattaro - -	2,908	26	130 miles W.S.W. from Bishop Rock.	Submarine - -	No warning -	Torpedo -	—
Serapis - -	1,932	26	106 miles N.N W. ½ W. from Tory Island.	Submarine - -	No warning -	Torpedo -	19 Master and Chief Officer prisoners.
†Armadale - -	6,153	27	160 miles N.W. from Tory Island.	Submarine - -	No warning -	Torpedo -	3
Solway Prince -	317	27	8 miles North from Alderney.	Submarine - -	Captured -	Bombs -	—
†Tong Hong -	2,184	27	75 miles S.W. from Cape Sicie.	Submarine - -	Captured -	Not known	Master prisoner.
†Ultonia - -	10,402	27	190 miles S.W. from the Fastnet.	Submarine - -	No warning -	Torpedo -	1
Longbenton -	924	27	12 miles S. by W. from Flamborough Head.	Submarine - -	No warning -	Torpedo -	—
†Baron Ogilvy -	4,570	27	172 miles N.W. from Tory Island.	Submarine - -	No warning -	Torpedo -	2
Lizzie Ellen (S.V.).	114	28	46 miles South from Start Point.	Submarine - -	Captured -	Bombs -	—
Haigh Hall -	4,809	30	40 miles East from Malta.	Submarine - -	No warning -	Torpedo -	—
Ilston - -	2,426	30	4 miles S.E. from the Lizard.	Submarine - -	No warning -	Torpedo -	6
Lady of the Lake (S.V.).	51	30	15 miles S.S.W. from Hook Point, Waterford.	Submarine - -	Captured -	Bombs -	—
JULY 1917.		July					
Ariel, (S.V.) -	86	1	25 miles E.N.E. from Rattray Head.	Submarine -	Captured -	Bombs -	—
Don Emilio -	3,651	1	10 miles N.W. by W. from Esha Ness, West Shetland.	Submarine - -	No warning -	Torpedo -	1
†Thirlby - -	2,009	2	122 miles N.W. by W. ¼ W. from the Fastnet.	Submarine - -	No warning -	Torpedo -	2
†City of Cambridge.	3,844	3	10 miles N.W. from Jidjelli.	Submarine - -	No warning -	Torpedo -	—
†Iceland - -	1,501	3	10 miles S.W. from Galley Head.	Submarine - -	No warning -	Torpedo -	2
†Mongara - -	8,205	3	1½ miles from Messina Breakwater.	Submarine - -	No warning -	Torpedo -	—

Name.	Gross Tons.	Date.	Position.	Cause of Loss.	How attacked.	How sunk.	Lives lost.
		1917. July					
†Matador - -	3,642	3	115 miles W. by N. ½ N. from the Fastnet.	Submarine - -	No warning -	Torpedo -	2
†Goathland -	3,044	4	10 miles South from Belle Ile.	Submarine - -	No warning -	Torpedo -	21 including Master.
†Hurstside - -	3,149	4	108 miles N.N.E. ¼ E. from Cape Wrath.	Submarine - -	No warning -	Torpedo -	—
†Cuyahoga -	4,586	5	130 miles W.N.W. from Tory Island.	Submarine - -	No warning -	Torpedo -	—
Ocean Swell (S.V.)	195	5	15 miles S.E. from Start Point.	Submarine - -	Captured -	Gunfire -	—
Cumberland -	9,471	6	16 miles S.W. from Gabo Island, Australia.	Mine - - -	Mine - -	Mine - -	—
Coral Leaf (S.V.)	428	7	18 miles N.W. by N. from Tearaght I.	Submarine - -	Captured -	Gunfire -	—
†Southina - -	3,506	7	6 miles W.N.W. from Cape Sigli, Algeria.	Submarine - -	No warning -	Torpedo -	1
†Turquah - -	3,859	7	10 miles S.W. from Bull Rock.	Submarine - -	No warning -	Torpedo -	—
†Bellucia - -	4,368	7	2 miles S.S.E. from the Lizard.	Submarine - -	No warning -	Torpedo -	4
†Wilberforce -	3,074	7	25 miles South from Cape de Gata.	Submarine - -	No warning -	Torpedo -	1 Master and Chief Engineer prisoners.
†Condesa - -	8,557	7	105 miles West from Bishop Rock.	Submarine - -	No warning -	Torpedo -	—
†Obuasi - -	4,416	8	290 miles N.W. by W. ¼ W. from the Fastnet.	Submarine - -	No warning -	Torpedo -	2 Master made prisoner.
†Vendee - -	1,295	8	Mouth of River Gironde.	Mine - - -	Mine - -	Mine -	3
†Pegu - -	6,348	8	7 miles S.E. from Galley Head.	Mine - - -	Mine - -	Mine -	1
†Valetta - -	5,871	8	118 miles N.W. ¾ W. from the Fastnet.	Submarine - -	No warning -	Torpedo -	—
†Prince Abbas -	2,030	9	29 miles East from Fair Island.	Submarine - -	No warning -	Torpedo -	2
†King David -	3,680	10	360 miles N.W. ½ W. from the Fastnet.	Submarine - -	Captured -	Gunfire -	2
†Seang Choon -	5,807	10	10 miles S.W. from the Fastnet.	Submarine - -	No warning -	Torpedo -	19
†Garmoyle -	1,229	10	14 miles S.E. from Mine Head.	Submarine - -	No warning -	Torpedo -	20 including Master.
†Kioto - -	6,182	11	20 miles S.W. from the Fastnet.	Submarine - -	No warning -	Torpedo -	—
†Anglo-Patagonian.	5,017	11	20 miles W.S.W. from Les Sables d'Olonne.	Submarine - -	No warning -	Torpedo -	4
†Brunhilda -	2,296	11	7 miles E. by S. from Start Point.	Submarine - -	No warning -	Torpedo -	—
†Muirfield -	3,086	11	350 miles N.W. from the Fastnet.	Submarine - -	No warning -	Torpedo -	2 Chief Officer and W/T operator prisoners.

Name.	Gross Tons.	Date.	Position.	Cause of Loss.	How attacked.	How sunk.	Lives lost.
		1917. July					
†Castleton - -	2,395	12	60 miles S.S.W. from Bishop Rock.	Submarine - -	Captured -	Gunfire -	—
Gibel-Yedid -	949	13	150 miles W. ¾ N. from Ushant.	Submarine - -	Captured -	Bombs -	—
†Exford - -	5,886	14	180 miles W. by S. ½ S. from Ushant.	Submarine - -	No warning -	Torpedo -	6
†Calliope - -	2,883	14 (?)	Atlantic - -	Submarine (?) -	No warning(?)	Torpedo (?)	27 including Master.
†Mariston - -	2,903	15	82 miles West from the Fastnet.	Submarine - -	No warning -	Torpedo -	28 including Master.
Dudhope (S.V.)	2,086	15	200 miles West from the Fastnet.	Submarine - -	Captured -	Bombs -	—
Dinorwic (S.V.)	124	15	10 miles S. by E. from Hastings.	Submarine - -	Captured -	Bombs -	—
†Torcello - -	2,929	15	160 miles S.W. by W. from Bishop Rock.	Submarine - -	No warning -	Torpedo -	1
Ebenezer (S.V.)	177	15	25 miles N.W. from Dieppe.	Submarine - -	Captured -	Bombs -	—
†Trelissick - -	4,168	15	80 miles S.W. by W. ¼ W. from Ushant.	Submarine - -	No warning -	Torpedo -	Master and two gunners prisoners.
†Henry R. James	3,146	16	10 miles E. by N. from Ile de Bas.	Mine - - -	Mine - -	Mine -	24
†Ribston - -	3,372	16	85 miles West from the Fastnet.	Submarine - -	No warning -	Torpedo -	25 including Master.
†Valentia - -	3,242	16	70 miles W. ½ S. from Bishop Rock.	Submarine - -	No warning -	Torpedo -	3
†Khephren -	2,774	16	178 miles East from Malta.	Submarine - -	No warning -	Torpedo -	—
Firfield - -	4,029	16	10 miles N.W. from Cape Papas, Nikaria.	Submarine - -	No warning -	Torpedo -	- -
†Tamele - -	3,932	16	65 miles W. by S. from the Fastnet.	Submarine - -	No warning -	Torpedo -	1
†Haworth - -	4,456	17	94 miles West from the Fastnet.	Submarine - -	No warning -	Torpedo -	—
†Bramham - -	1,978	19	10 miles E. by S. from the Lizard.	Mine - - -	Mine - -	Mine -	1
†Eloby - -	6,545	19	75 miles S.E. by E. from Malta.	Submarine - -	No warning -	Torpedo -	56 including Master.
†Beatrice - -	712	20	10 miles E. by S. from the Lizard.	Submarine - -	No warning -	Torpedo -	11
†City of Florence	5,399	20	188 miles W. ¾ N. from Ushant.	Submarine - -	No warning -	Torpedo -	—
†Salsette - -	5,842	20	15 miles S.W. from Portland Bill.	Submarine - -	No warning -	Torpedo -	15
†Nevisbrook -	3,140	20	90 miles W. ½ S. from the Fastnet.	Submarine - -	No warning -	Torpedo -	—
†Fluent - -	3,660	20	16 miles South from Anvil Point.	Mine - - -	Mine - -	Mine -	—
†L. H. Carl -	1,916	20	14 miles W. ½ S. from Portland Bill.	Submarine - -	No warning -	Torpedo -	2
†Ramillies - -	2,935	21	120 miles W.N.W. from Tory Island.	Submarine - -	Captured -	Gunfire -	Master prisoner.
†Coniston Water	3,738	21	70 miles N. by W. from Butt of Lewis.	Submarine - -	No warning -	Torpedo -	1 gunner prisoner.

Name.	Gross Tons.	Date.	Position.	Cause of Loss.	How attacked.	How sunk.	Lives lost.
		1917. July					
Willena Gertrude (S.V.)	317	21	120 miles S. by E. ½ E. from Sta. Maria, Azores.	Submarine - -	Captured -	Bombs -	—
†Paddington -	5,084	21	250 miles West from the Fastnet.	Submarine - -	No warning -	Torpedo -	29 including Master.
Harold (S.V.) -	1,376	21	65 miles N.N.W. ½ W. from Tory Island.	Submarine - -	No warning -	Torpedo -	13 including Master.
†African Prince -	4,916	21	60 miles N.N.W. from Tory Island.	Submarine - -	No warning -	Torpedo -	—
†Dafila - -	1,754	21	85 miles W. by S. ¼ S. from the Fastnet.	Submarine - -	No warning -	Torpedo -	2
†Trelyon - -	3,099	21	3 miles N. from Scarborough.	Mine - - -	Mine - -	Beached, became total wreck.	—
†Cotovia - -	4,020	22	2 miles S.E. by E. from Auskerry.	Mine - - -	Mine - -	Mine -	—
†Rota - -	2,171	22	7 miles S. from Berry Head.	Submarine - -	No warning -	Torpedo -	5 including Master.
†Glow - -	1,141	22	4 miles S.E. by E. from S. Cheek, Robin Hood Bay.	Submarine - -	No warning -	Torpedo -	1
†Ashleigh - -	6 985	23	290 miles S.W. from the Fastnet.	Submarine - -	No warning -	Torpedo -	—
†Huelva - -	4,867	23	270 miles S.W. from the Fastnet.	Submarine - -	No warning -	Torpedo -	—
Sir Walter -	492	24	2½ miles N. from Cape Ortegal.	Submarine - -	Captured -	Bombs -	—
ᵀZermatt - -	3,767	24	355 miles W. by N. from Ushant.	Submarine - -	No warning -	Torpedo -	3
†Blake - -	3,740	24	30 miles N. by W. ½ W. from Cape Wrath.	Submarine - -	No warning -	Torpedo -	5
†Brumaire - -	2,324	24	265 miles W. by N. from Ushant.	Submarine - -	No warning -	Torpedo -	2
†Purley - -	4,500	25	210 miles S.W. ¼ S. from the Fastnet.	Submarine - -	No warning -	Torpedo -	—
†Oakleaf - -	8,106	25	64 miles N.W. ¼ N. from Butt of Lewis.	Submarine - -	No warning -	Torpedo -	—
†Peninsula - -	1,384	25	235 miles S.W. from the Fastnet.	Submarine - -	No warning -	Torpedo -	1
†Monkstone -	3,097	25	240 miles W. from Scilly Islands.	Submarine - -	No warning -	Torpedo -	1
†Rustington -	3,071	25	235 miles W. by S. from Ushant.	Submarine - -	No warning -	Torpedo -	—
†Somerset - -	8,710	26	230 miles W. by S. ½ S. from Ushant.	Submarine - -	No warning -	Torpedo -	—
†Ludgate - -	3,708	26	2 miles S. from Galley Head.	Mine - - -	Mine - -	Mine -	24 including Master.
†Carmarthen -	4,262	26	2 miles S.E. from the Lizard.	Submarine - -	No warning -	Torpedo -	—
†Mooltan - -	9,723	26	53 miles N.N.W. ½ W. from Cape Serrat.	Submarine - -	No warning -	Torpedo -	2
†Candia - -	6,482	27	8 miles S. from Owers L.V.	Submarine - -	No warning -	Torpedo -	1
‡Begona No. 4 -	2,407	27	70 miles W. by N. ½ N. from the Fastnet.	Submarine - -	No warning -	Torpedo -	2
†Belle of England	3,877	27	155 miles W.N.W. from the Fastnet.	Submarine - -	No warning -	Torpedo -	—

Name.	Gross Tons.	Date.	Position.	Cause of Loss.	How attacked.	How sunk.	Lives lost.
		1917. July					
†Whitehall	3,158	28	270 miles W. by N. from the Fastnet.	Submarine - -	No warning -	Torpedo -	1
‡Glenstrae - -	4,718	28	66 miles S.W. by S. ¼ S. from Bishop Rock.	Submarine - -	No warning -	Torpedo -	1
Okhla - -	5,288	29	30 miles W. from Bombay.	Mine - - -	Mine - -	Mine - -	9 including Master.
†Manchester Commerce.	4,144	29	15 miles W. by N. ½ N. from Cape Spartel.	Submarine - -	No warning -	Torpedo -	1
†Adalia - -	3,847	29	53 miles N.E. from Muckle Flugga.	Submarine - -	Captured -	Gunfire -	1
†Manchester Inventor.	4,112	30	80 miles N.N.E. from Muckle Flugga.	Submarine - -	Captured -	Gunfire -	—
†Ganges - -	4,177	30	8 miles S.W. from C. Spartel.	Submarine - -	No warning -	Torpedo -	1
†Shimosa - -	4,221	30	220 miles N.W. ½ W. from Eagle Island.	Submarine - -	No warning -	Torpedo -	17 including Master.
†Fremona -	3,028	31	10 miles N. by W. from Ile de Bas.	Submarine - -	No warning -	Torpedo -	11
†Empress - -	2,914	31	4½ miles E. by S. ½ S. from Withernsea L. Ho.	Mine - - -	Mine - -	Mine - -	5
Ypres - -	305	31	10 miles N.N.W. ½ W. from Cape Trafalgar.	Submarine - -	Captured -	Gunfire -	—-
†Orubian - -	3,876	31	160 miles N.W. ½ W. from Eagle Island.	Submarine - -	No warning -	Torpedo -	1
†Belgian Prince -	4,765	31	175 miles N.W. by W. from Tory Island.	Submarine - -	No warning -	Torpedo -	39 Master made prisoner.
†Snowdonian -	3,870	31	245 miles S. by E. from Sta Maria, Azores.	Submarine - -	Captured -	Bombs ..	—
†Quernmore -	7,302	31	160 miles W. by N. ¾ N. from Tory Island.	Submarine - -	No warning -	Torpedo -	1

AUGUST 1917.

Name.	Gross Tons.	Date.	Position.	Cause of Loss.	How attacked.	How sunk.	Lives lost.
		Aug.					
†Karina - -	4,222	1	17 miles S.S.W. ½ W. from Hook Point, Waterford.	Submarine - -	No warning -	Torpedo -	11
⊺Laertes - -	4,541	1	1¼ miles S.S.W. from Prawle Point.	Submarine - -	No warning -	Torpedo -	14
†Llandudno -	4,187	1	110 miles S. by W. from Porquerolles Island.	Submarine - -	Captured -	Bombs -	1
Alcyone (motor)	149	1	45 miles N.N.W. from Roches Douvres.	Submarine - -	Captured -	Gunfire -	—
†Newlyn - -	4,019	2	2 miles South from Prawle Point.	Submarine - -	No warning -	Torpedo -	4
†Beechpark -	4,763	2	4 miles South from St. Mary's, Scilly.	Submarine - -	No warning -	Torpedo -	—
Hornchurch -	2,159	3	3½ miles E.N.E. from Coquet Island.	Mine - - -	Mine - -	Mine - -	2
†Aube - -	1,837	3	3½ miles N. by W. from Ile d'Yeu.	Submarine - -	No warning -	Torpedo -	1

Name.	Gross Tons.	Date.	Position.	Cause of Loss.	How attacked.	How sunk.	Lives lost.
		1917. Aug.					
†Cairnstrath -	2,128	4	6 miles S.S.W. from Ile du Pilier.	Submarine - -	No warning -	Torpedo -	22 including Master.
†British Monarch	5,749	4	2 miles S.S.W. from Porquerolles Lighthouse.	Mine - - -	Mine - -	Mine - -	—
Azira - -	1,144	4	6 miles S.E. from Seaham Harbour.	Submarine - -	No warning -	Torpedo -	1
†Countess of Mar	2,234	4	55 miles N. ¼ E. from Bayonne.	Submarine - -	No warning -	Torpedo -	20 including Master
†Kathleen - -	3,915	5	90 miles West from Skelligs.	Submarine - -	No warning -	Torpedo -	1 (Master).
Talisman -	153	6	7 miles E.S.E. from Hartlepool.	Submarine - -	Captured -	Bombs -	—
†Rosemount -	3,044	6	45 miles N.E. by N. ½ N. from Muckle Flugga.	Submarine - -	Captured -	Torpedo -	1
†Argalia - -	4,641	6	81 miles N.W. ¾ W. from Tory Island.	Submarine - -	No warning -	Torpedo -	3
Matunga - -	1,608	6	300 miles E. (true) from Riche Island, New Guinea.	Wolf - - -	Captured -	Bombs -	—
†Polanna - -	2,345	6	3 miles East from Whitby.	Submarine - -	No warning -	Torpedo -	2
†Baysoto - -	3,082	6	33 miles S.E. by E. from Girdleness.	Submarine - -	No warning -	Torpedo -	—
‡Port Curtis -	4,710	7	70 miles West from Penmarch.	Submarine - -	Captured -	Bombs -	—
†Iran - -	6,250	7	200 miles E.S.E. from Santa Maria, Azores.	Submarine - -	No warning -	Torpedo -	—
†Llanishen -	3,837	8	8 miles N. by E. from Cape de Creus, Gulf of Lyons.	Submarine - -	No warning -	Torpedo -	2
†Blagdon - -	1,996	9	75 miles E. by S. from Muckle Flugga.	Submarine - -	No warning -	Torpedo -	12 including Master.
†War Patrol -	2,045	10	1 mile West from Penmarch.	Mine - - -	Mine - -	Mine - -	13 including Master.
City of Athens -	5,604	10	20 miles N.W. from Cape Town.	Mine - - -	Mine - -	Mine - -	19
†Sonnie - -	2,642	11	5 miles N.W. from Le Four Lighthouse.	Submarine - -	No warning -	Torpedo -	11
†Lynorta - -	3,684	11	102 miles N.W. by N. from Tory Island.	Submarine - -	No warning -	Torpedo -	2
†Roanoke -	4,803	12	100 miles W.N.W. from the Butt of Lewis.	Submarine - -	Captured -	Bombs -	Master made prisoner.
†Akassa - -	3,919	13	8 miles S.E. from Galley Head.	Submarine - -	No warning -	Torpedo -	7
†Turakina -	9,920	13	120 miles W.S.W. from Bishop Rock.	Submarine - -	No warning -	Torpedo -	2
†Maston - -	3,881	13	35 miles E.N.E. from Cape Spartivento, Italy.	Submarine - -	No warning -	Torpedo -	2
†Wisbech - -	1,282	14	12 miles N.E. from Trevose Head	Submarine - -	No warning -	Torpedo -	2

Name.	Gross Tons.	Date.	Position.	Cause of Loss.	How attacked.	How sunk.	Lives lost.
		1917. Aug.					
†Brodstone -	4,927	15	95 miles W. ¼ S. from Ushant.	Submarine - -	No warning -	Torpedo -	5
†Hylas - -	4,240	15	10 miles East from Butt of Lewis.	Submarine - -	No warning -	Torpedo -	—
†Athenia - -	8,668	16	7 miles North from Inishtrahull.	Submarine - -	No warning -	Torpedo -	15
†Palatine - -	2,110	16	10 miles W.N.W. from Island of Canna.	Submarine - -	No warning -	Torpedo -	Master made prisoner.
†Delphic - -	8,273	16	135 miles S.W. ¾ W. from Bishop Rock.	Submarine - -	No warning -	Torpedo -	5
†Manchester Engineer.	4,465	16	4½ miles S.E. from Flamborough Head.	Submarine - -	No warning -	Torpedo -	—
Edina - -	455	17	30 miles S.E. from Store Dimon, Faroë.	Submarine - -	Captured -	Gunfire -	—
†Rosario - -	1,821	18	Atlantic - -	Submarine - -	No warning -	Torpedo -	20 including Master. 1 fireman prisoner.
†Politania -	3,133	18	10 miles N.W. by W. from Cape Sigli.	Submarine - -	No warning -	Torpedo -	—
†Ardens - -	1,274	18	2 miles East from Filey Brig.	Submarine - -	No warning -	Torpedo -	1
†Monksgarth -	1,928	19	17 miles N. by E. ¼ E. from Ushant N.W. Lighthouse.	Submarine - -	No warning -	Torpedo -	—
†Spectator -	3,808	19	11 miles S.E. from Galley Head.	Submarine - -	No warning -	Torpedo -	—
†Glocliffe · -	2,211	19	9 miles E.N.E. from Berry Head.	Submarine - -	No warning -	Torpedo -	2
Brema - -	1,537	19	7½ miles S. ½ E. from Flamborough Head.	Submarine - -	No warning -	Torpedo -	—
†Gartness - -	2,422	19	180 miles S.E. by E. ¾ E. from Malta.	Submarine - -	No warning -	Torpedo -	13 including Master.
†Claverley -	3,829	20	4 miles S.E. from the Eddystone.	Submarine - -	No warning -	Torpedo -	10
†Elswick Lodge -	3,558	20	260 miles W. by S. from Ushant.	Submarine - -	No warning -	Torpedo -	4
†Incemore - -	3,060	20	52 miles S.E. by E. ½ E. from Pantellaria.	Submarine - -	No warning -	Torpedo -	1
†Edernian -	3,588	20	6 miles S. by E. from Southwold.	Submarine - -	No warning -	Torpedo -	14
†Bulysses -	6,127	20	145 miles W.N.W. from the Butt of Lewis.	Submarine	No warning -	Torpedo -	—
†Volodia -	5,689	21	285 miles W. ¼ S. from Ushant.	Submarine - -	No warning	Torpedo -	10
†Goodwood -	3,086	21	28 miles N.W. by W. from Cape Bon.	Submarine - -	No warning -	Torpedo -	—
†Roscommon -	8,238	21	20 miles N.E. from Tory Island.	Submarine - -	No warning -	Torpedo -	—
‡Devonian -	10,435	21	20 miles N.E. from Tory Island.	Submarine - -	No warning -	Torpedo -	2
†Oslo - -	2,296	21	15 miles E. by N. from Out Skerries, Shetland.	Submarine - -	No warning -	Torpedo -	3
H.S. 4 (tug) and R.B. 6 (barge).	—	21	130 miles W.S.W. from Ushant.	Submarine - -	Captured -	Bombs -	—

Name.	Gross Tons.	Date.	Position.	Cause of Loss.	How attacked.	How sunk.	Lives lost.
		1917. Aug.					
Norhilda - -	1,175	21	5 miles S.E. from Scarborough.	Submarine - -	No warning -	Torpedo -	1
†Verdi - -	7,120	22	115 miles N.W. by N. from Eagle Island.	Submarine - -	No warning -	Torpedo -	6
Winlaton - -	3,270	23	25 miles W. from Cape Spartel.	Submarine - -	No warning -	Torpedo -	2 Master made prisoner.
†Veghtstroom -	1,353	23	7 miles N.W. from Godrevy Lighthouse.	Submarine - -	No warning -	Torpedo -	5
†Boniface - -	3,799	23	7 miles N.E. by N. from Aran Island.	Submarine - -	No warning -	Torpedo -	1
Penelope - -	1,202	24	3 cables from Swalfer Ort Lighthouse, Baltic.	Submarine - -	No warning -	Torpedo -	—
†Springhill -	1,507	24	4 miles N. by E. ¾ E. from Scarborough.	Mine - - -	Mine - -	Mine - -	5
†Kilwinning -	3,071	24	94 miles E.S.E. from Malta.	Submarine - -	No warning -	Torpedo -	—
†Heatherside -	2767	24 (?)	Atlantic - -	Submarine (?) -	No warning(?)	Torpedo (?)	27 including Master.
†Sycamore - -	6,550	25	125 miles N.W. from Tory Island.	Submarine - -	No warning -	Torpedo -	11
†Cymrian - -	1,014	25	13 miles S.E. by S. from Tuskar Rock.	Submarine - -	No warning -	Torpedo -	10
†Malda - -	7,896	25	130 miles W. ¼ S. from Bishop Rock.	Submarine - -	No warning -	Torpedo -	64
†Nascent - -	4,969	25	27 miles S. from Bishop Rock.	Submarine - -	No warning -	Torpedo -	6
†Kenmore - -	3,919	26	30 miles North from Inishtrahull.	Submarine - -	No warning -	Torpedo -	5
†Titian - -	4,170	26	170 miles S.E. ½ E. from Malta.	Submarine - -	No warning -	Torpedo -	—
†W. H. Dwyer -	1,770	26	15 miles E. by N. from Berry Head.	Submarine - -	No warning -	Torpedo -	—
Minas Queen (S.V.).	492	26	350 miles N.W. from C. Finisterre.	Submarine - -	Captured -	Gunfire -	6 including Master.
†Hathor - -	3,823	26	3 miles N.W. from Cape Tedles, Algeria.	Submarine - -	No warning -	Torpedo -	1 Master made prisoner.
†Assyria - -	6,370	26	34 miles N.W. by N. ½ N. from Tory Island.	Submarine - -	No warning -	Torpedo -	—
†Durango - -	3,008	26	50 miles N.W. from Barra Head.	Submarine - -	Captured -	Gunfire -	—
†Marmion - -	4,066	26	300 miles W. ¾ S. from Ushant.	Submarine - -	No warning -	Torpedo -	17
†Nairn - -	3,627	27	125 miles N. by W. ¼ W. from Ben Ghazi.	Submarine - -	No warning -	Torpedo -	—
†Hidalgo - -	4,271	28	120 miles N.E. ½ N. from North Cape.	Submarine - -	No warning -	Torpedo -	15
†Whitecourt -	3,680	28	120 miles N.N.E. from North Cape.	Submarine - -	Captured -	Gunfire -	—
†Vronwen - -	5,714	29	20 miles N.W. by W. from Gozo.	Submarine - -	No warning -	Torpedo -	1
†Treloske - -	3 071	29	145 miles N. by W. ¾ W. from Cape Finisterre.	Submarine - -	No warning -	Torpedo -	1

Name.	Gross Tons.	Date.	Position.	Cause of Loss.	How attacked.	How sunk.	Lives lost.
		1917. Aug.					
†Lynburn - -	587	29	½ mile S.E. from N. Arklow L.V.	Mine - - -	Mine - -	Mine - -	8
Cooroy (S.V.) -	2,470	29	10 miles S. by W. ½ W. from Hook Point, Waterford.	Submarine - -	Captured -	Torpedo -	—
†Noya - -	4,282	30	8 miles W.S.W. from the Lizard.	Submarine - -	No warning -	Torpedo -	1
†Eastern Prince -	2,885	30	30 miles S. ¾ W. from the Eddystone.	Submarine - -	No warning -	Torpedo -	5
†Grelhame - -	3,740	30	4 miles S.W. from Start Point.	Submarine - -	No warning -	Torpedo -	—
†Miniota - -	6,422	31	30 miles S.E. ½ E. from Start Point.	Submarine - -	No warning -	Torpedo -	3
Westbury - -	3,097	31	8 miles S.S.E. from the Fastnet.	Submarine - -	No warning -	Torpedo -	—
†Vernon - -	982	31	22 miles S.E. by S. from Spurn Point.	Submarine - -	No warning -	Torpedo -	1 (Master.)
SEPTEMBER 1917.		Sept.					
†Erato - -	2,041	1	4 miles S.E. from the Lizard.	Mine - - -	Mine - -	Mine - -	—
†Rytonhall -	4,203	2	105 miles W. ½ S. from Ushant.	Submarine - -	Captured -	Torpedo -	—
†Wentworth -	3,828	2	36 miles W. ¼ S. from Belle Ile.	Submarine - -	No warning -	Torpedo -	1 Master and two gunners prisoners.
+Olive Branch -	4,649	2	85 miles N. by E. ½ E. from North Cape.	Submarine - -	No warning -	Torpedo -	1
†Treverbyn -	4,163	3	2 miles E.S.E. from Ushinish Lighthouse, South Uist.	Mine - - -	Mine - -	Mine - -	27 including Master.
†Ragnhild -	1,495	3	14 miles S. by E. ¼ E. from Flamborough Head.	Submarine - -	No warning -	Torpedo -	15 including Master.
†La Negra -	8,312	3	50 miles S.S.W. from Start Point.	Submarine - -	No warning -	Torpedo -	4
†Peerless - -	3,112	4	60 miles S.W. from Bishop Rock.	Submarine - -	No warning -	Torpedo -	2 Master and two gunners prisoners.
†Bishopston -	2,513	4	30 miles S. by E. from St. Catherines.	Submarine - -	No warning -	Torpedo -	2
Glynn, S.V. -	60	5	32 miles N.W. from Les Hanois.	Submarine - -	Captured -	Gunfire -	—
Industry, S.V. -	91	5	20 miles N.N.W. from Les Hanois.	Submarine - -	Captured -	Gunfire -	—
†Echunga - -	6,285	5	40 miles N. by E. from Ushant.	Submarine - -	No warning -	Torpedo	9
Theodor, S.V. -	230	5	13 miles N. by W. ½ W. from Sept Iles.	Submarine - -	Captured -	Bombs -	—
Florence Muspratt, S.V.	79	5	10 miles North from Sept Iles.	Submarine - -	Captured -	Gunfire -	1
Emma, S.V. -	73	5	8 miles N. by W. from Sept Iles.	Submarine - -	Captured -	Gunfire -	—

Name.	Gross Tons.	Date.	Position.	Cause of Loss.	How attacked.	How sunk.	Lives lost.
		1917. Sept.					
Frances, S.V. -	89	5	8 miles N. by W. from Sept Iles.	Submarine - -	Captured -	Bombs -	—
†Tuskar - -	1,159	6	3 miles West from Eagle Island.	Mine - - -	Mine - -	Mine - -	10
†Clan Ferguson -	4,808	6	15 miles N.W. from Cape Spartel.	Submarine - -	No warning -	Torpedo -	10
Hinemoa, S.V. -	2,283	7	35 miles W.S.W. from Bishop Rock.	Submarine - -	Captured -	Gunfire -	—
†Minnehaha -	13,714	7	12 miles S.E. from the Fastnet.	Submarine - -	No warning -	Torpedo -	43
†Hunsbridge -	3,424	7	60 miles S.W. by W. ¾ W. from Cape Spartel.	Submarine - -	No warning -	Torpedo -	2
†Newholm - -	3,399	8	1 mile South from Start Point.	Mine - - -	Mine - -	Mine - -	20
Ezel, S.V. -	163	8	20 miles North from St. Valery (en Caux).	Submarine - -	Captured -	Gunfire -	—
Laura, S.V. -	·86	8	25 miles North from Fecamp.	Submarine - -	Captured -	Bombs -	—
†Harrow - -	1,777	8	4 miles S.E. from Whitby.	Submarine - -	No warning -	Torpedo -	2
Elizabeth, S.V. -	49	8	12 miles E. by S. from Start Point.	Submarine - -	Captured -	Bombs -	—
Storm - -	440	9	1 mile S.E. from Sunk L.V.	Seaplane - -	No warning -	Torpedo -	3
†Swiftsure -	823	9	Shapinsay Sound	Mine - -	Mine - -	Mine - -	1
†Parkmill - -	1,316	10	1¼ miles from Kirkalister Lighthouse, Bressay.	Mine - -	Mine - -	Mine -	
Mary Orr (S.V.)	91	10	8 miles N. by E. from Pendeen Lighthouse.	Submarine - -	Captured -	Bombs -	—
Moss Rose (S.V.)	161	10	7 miles N.N.E. from Pendeen Lighthouse.	Submarine - -	Captured -	Gunfire -	—
Mary Seymour (S.V.)	150	10	7 miles N.N.E. from Pendeen Lighthouse.	Submarine - -	Captured -	Gunfire -	—
Water Lily (S.V.)	111	10	8 miles N. by E. from Pendeen Lighthouse.	Submarine - -	Captured -	Bombs -	—
Jane Williamson (S.V.)	197	10	20 miles N.N.E. from St. Ives.	Submarine - -	Captured -	Gunfire -	4 including Master.
†Luxembourg -	1,417	11	3½ miles N.N.E. from Pendeen Lighthouse.	Mine - - -	Mine - -	Mine - -	—
†Vienna - -	4,170	11	340 miles W. ½ N. from Ushant.	Submarine - -	No warning -	Torpedo -	25 Master prisoner.
†Embleton - -	5,377	11	150 miles W. from Cape Spartel.	Submarine - -	Captured -	Gunfire -	—
William (S.V.) -	60	11	4 miles N.W. by N. from Crackington Haven, Cornwall.	Submarine - -	Captured -	Bombs -	—
†Urd - - -	3,049	11	10 miles N. by E. ½ E. from Cape Palos.	Submarine - -	No warning -	Torpedo -	3
H.S. 3 Tug and R.B. 10 Barge	—	12	18 miles W. by N. from Cape Sines.	Submarine - -	Captured -	Bombs -	—
†Gibraltar -	3,803	12	100 miles S.E. ½ S. from Cape de Creus.	Submarine - -	No warning -	Torpedo -	4
†St. Margaret -	943	12	30 miles S.E. from Lille Dimon Island, Faroe.	Submarine - -	No warning -	Torpedo -	5

Name.	Gross Tons.	Date.	Position.	Cause of Loss.	How attacked.	How sunk.	Lives lost.
		1917. Sept.					
Agricola (S.V.)	49	12	15 miles W.N.W. from Lundy Island.	Submarine - -	Captured -	Bombs -	—
†Chulmleigh -	4,911	14	10 miles S.W. by W. from Cape Salou, Spain.	Submarine - -	No warning -	Torpedo -	—
†Zeta - -	2,269	14	8 miles S. by W. from Mine Head	Submarine - -	No warning -	Torpedo -	—
†Sommeina -	3,317	15	4 miles S.E. from the Manacles.	Mine - - -	Mine - -	Mine - ·	····
Dependence (S.V.)	120	15	6 miles West from the Lizard.	Submarine - -	Captured -	Bombs -	—
†Santaren - -	4,256	15	40 miles N.E. from Muckle Flugga.	Submarine - -	No warning -	Torpedo -	Master and Chief Officer prisoners.
†Rollesby - -	3,955	15	80 miles E.N.E. from Muckle Flugga.	Submarine - -	Captured -	Torpedo -	—
†Arabis - -	3,928	16	210 miles W. by S. from Ushant.	Submarine - -	No warning -	Torpedo -	2C including Master.
†Sandsend - -	3,814	16	6 miles S.E. by E. from Mine Head.	Submarine - -	No warning -	Torpedo -	3
†Queen Amelie -	4,278	17	19 miles N.N.E. from Muckle Flugga.	Submarine - -	Captured -	Torpedo -	—
Port Kembla -	4,700	18	Off Cape Farewell, New Zealand.	Mine - - -	Mine - -	Mine - -	—
†Arendal - -	1,387	18	115 miles W. ½ N. from Cape Spartel.	Submarine - -	Captured -	Gunfire -	—
†Joseph Chamberlain.	3,709	18	50 miles N. by W. from Muckle Flugga.	Submarine - -	No warning -	Torpedo -	18 Master and one gunner prisoners.
†Polar Prince -	3,611	18	8 miles W. by S. from Cape Spartel.	Submarine - -	No warning -	Torpedo -	Master made prisoner.
†Saint Ronald -	4,387	19	95 miles N.N.W. from Tory Island.	Submarine - -	No warning -	Torpedo -	24
Etal Manor -	1,875	19	7 miles S. by W. from Hook Point, Waterford.	Submarine - -	No warning -	Torpedo -	6 including Master.
†Fabian - -	2,246	20	30 miles W. ½ N. from Cape Spartel.	Submarine - -	No warning -	Torpedo -	3
†Kurdistan -	3,720	20	27 miles E.S.E. from Pantellaria.	Submarine - -	No warning -	Torpedo -	—
†Greleen - -	2,286	22	7 miles E. by N. from Berry Head.	Submarine - -	No warning -	Torpedo -	19 including Master.
Trongate - -	2,553	22	5 miles N. from Flamborough Head.	Submarine - -	No warning -	Torpedo -	2
Perseverance (S.V.).	118	23	14 miles N.W. by N. from St. Valery (en Caux).	Submarine - -	Captured -	Gunfire -	—
St. Dunstan (Dredger.)	—	23	12 miles N.W. by N. from Bill of Portland.	Mine - - -	Mine - -	Mine - -	2
†Hornsund - -	3,646	23	2½ miles E.S.E. from Scarborough.	Submarine - -	No warning -	Torpedo -	1

Name.	Gross Tons.	Date.	Position.	Cause of Loss.	How attacked.	How sunk.	Lives lost.
		1917. Sept.					
†Irthington -	2,845	23	3 miles E.N.E. from Cape Vaticano, Italy.	Submarine - -	No warning -	Torpedo -	—
†Rosehill - -	2,788	23	5 miles S.W. by S. from Fowey.	Submarine - -	No warning -	Torpedo -	—
†Iriston - -	3,221	24	7 miles S. by W. from Cape Camerat.	Submarine - -	No warning -	Torpedo -	—
†Boynton - -	2,578	24	5 miles W.N.W. from Cape Cornwall.	Submarine - -	No warning -	Torpedo -	23 including Master.
†City of Swansea	1,375	25	15 miles E.N.E. from Berry Head.	Submarine - -	No warning -	Torpedo -	2
Acorn (S.V.) -	97	26	20 miles S. by E. from Start Point.	Submarine - -	Captured -	Gunfire -	—
†Swan River -	4,724	27	27 miles N.N.W. from Oran.	Submarine - -	No warning -	Torpedo -	—
†Greltoria - -	5,143	27	3 miles N.W. by N. ½ N. from Flamborough Head.	Submarine - -	No warning -	Torpedo -	—
†Sanwen - -	3,689	29	50 miles E. ¾ N. from Cape Bear.	Submarine - -	No warning -	Torpedo -	2
Kildonan - -	2,118	29	2 miles N.N.W. from Pendeen. Lighthouse.	Submarine - -	No warning -	Torpedo -	14 including Master.
†Elmsgarth -	3,503	29	50 miles N.W. ½ W. from Tory Island.	Submarine - -	No warning -	Torpedo -	—
Percy B. (S.V.)	330	29	180 miles N. ¾ W. from Cape Villano.	Submarine - -	Captured -	Gunfire -	—
†Heron - -	885	30	400 miles West from Ushant. (?)	Submarine - -	No warning -	Torpedo -	22 including Master.
†Midlothian -	1,321	30	80 miles South from Cape Greco, Cyprus.	Submarine - -	Captured -	Gunfire -	Master and 2 Gunners prisoners.
†Drake - -	2,267	30	340 miles West from Ushant.	Submarine - -	Captured	Gunfire -	Master prisoner.
OCTOBER 1917.		Oct.					
†Normanton -	3,862	1	115 miles W. ½ N. from Cape Spartel.	Submarine - -	No warning -	Torpedo -	—
Carrabin (S.V.)	2,739	1	10 miles South from Daunts Rock.	Submarine - -	No warning -	Torpedo -	—
†Mersario - -	3,847	1	86 miles W. by N. from Cape Spartel.	Submarine - -	No warning -	Torpedo .	3
Ludovicos (S.V.)	50 apprx.	1	Mediterranean -	Submarine - -	Captured -	Bomb -	—
†Almora - -	4,385	2	100 miles W. ½ N. from Cape Spartel.	Submarine - -	No warning -	Torpedo -	—
†Lugano - -	3,810	2	2 miles S.W. from Bull Point, Rathlin.	Mine - - -	Mine - -	Mine -	—
†Nuceria - -	4,702	2	120 miles W. ½ N. from Cape Spartel.	Submarine - -	No warning -	Torpedo -	2
†Hurst - -	4,718	3	2¼ miles W. by N. from Skokham Id.	Submarine - -	No warning -	Torpedo -	—
†Memling -	7,307	3	Laberildut Channel, near Brest.	Submarine - -	No warning -	Torpedo -	—
†Baron Blantyre	1,844	3	60 miles N.W. ¾ W. from Cape Finisterre.	Submarine - -	No warning -	Torpedo -	1

Name.	Gross Tons.	Date.	Position.	Cause of Loss.	How attacked.	How sunk.	Lives lost.
		1917. Oct.					
†Forestmoor -	2,844	5	54 miles W. by N. ¾ N. from Cape Spartel.	Submarine - -	No warning -	Torpedo -	22 including Master.
†Boutnewydd -	3,296	5	60 miles N.N.E. from Marsa Susa.	Submarine - -	No warning -	Torpedo -	3
Toledo - -	1,159	5 apprx.	Baltic - -	Reported as destroyed to avoid capture.	—	—	—
†Civilian - -	7,871	6	15 miles North from Alexandria.	Submarine - -	No warning -	Torpedo -	2
†Bedale - -	2,116	6	25 miles S.E. by S. from Mine Head.	Submarine - -	No warning -	Torpedo -	3
Alcyone (S.V.)	116	7	12 miles W.N.W. from Boulogne.	Submarine - -	Captured -	Bombs -	—
†Aylevarroo -	908	7 (?)	Off S. Ireland -	Submarine (?) -	No warning(?)	Torpedo (?)	20 including Master.
†Richard de Larrinaga.	5,591	8	15 miles S.E. ½ S. from Ballycottin Id.	Submarine - -	No warning -	Torpedo -	35 including Master.
†Memphian -	6,305	8	7 miles E.N.E. from N. Arklow L.V.	Submarine - -	No warning -	Torpedo -	32
†Greldon - -	3,322	8	7 miles E.N.E. from N. Arklow L.V.	Submarine - -	No warning -	Torpedo -	28 including Master.
†Main - -	715	9	1½ miles East from Drummore, Luce Bay.	Submarine - -	Gunfire -	Gunfire -	12
†Poldown - -	1,370	9	2 miles W.S.W. from Trevose Head.	Mine - - -	Mine - -	Mine -	18 including Master.
†Peshawur - -	7,634	9	7 miles S.E. ¼ E. from Ballyquintin Point, Co. Down.	Submarine - -	No warning -	Torpedo -	11
Gowrie - -	1,031	10	14 miles N.E. from Cherbourg.	Submarine - -	No warning -	Torpedo -	—
†Bostonian -	5,736	10	34 miles S. by E. ½ E. from Start Point.	Submarine - -	No warning -	Torpedo -	4
†Cayo Bonito -	3,427	11	4 miles E.N.E. from Savona.	Submarine - -	No warning -	Torpedo -	6
†Rhodesia - -	4,313	11	7 miles S.E. by S. from Coningbeg L.V.	Submarine - -	No warning -	Torpedo -	4
†Baychattan -	3,758	11	½ a mile S.S.W. from Prawle Point.	Submarine - -	No warning -	Torpedo -	—
†Mira - -	3,700	11	4 miles S.W. ½ W. from Beachy Head.	Mine - - -	Mine - -	Mine -	—
†W. M. Barkley -	569	12	7 miles East from the Kish L.V.	Submarine - -	No warning -	Torpedo -	4 including Master.
Joshua (S.V.) -	60	12(?)	English Channel -	Submarine - -	Not known -	Not known	3 including Master.
†Eskmere -	2,293	13	15 miles W.N.W. from South Stack.	Submarine - -	No warning -	Torpedo -	20 including Master.
†Alavi -	3,627	13	6 miles N.E. from Cape Palos.	Submarine - -	Captured -	Gunfire -	13
†Peebles - -	4,284	13	14 miles S. by E. ½ E. from Flamborough Head.	Submarine - -	No warning -	Torpedo -	—
†East Wales -	4,321	14	8 miles S. by W. ½ W. from Daunts Rock.	Submarine - -	Captured -	Gunfire -	3

Name.	Gross Tons.	Date.	Position.	Cause of Loss.	How attacked.	How sunk.	Lives lost.
		1917. Oct.					
†Semantha -	2,847	14	10 miles N.W. by N. from Cape St. John, Crete.	Submarine -	No warning -	Torpedo -	32 including Master.
†Hartburn -	2,367	15	10 miles South from Anvil Point.	Submarine -	No warning -	Torpedo -	3
†White Head -	1,172	15	40 miles N.N.E. from Suda Bay.	Submarine -	No warning -	Torpedo -	23
†Garthclyde -	2,124	15	12 miles W. ¼ S. from the Lizard.	Submarine -	No warning -	Torpedo -	—
†California -	5,629	17	145 miles N.W. by N. ¾ N. from Cape Villano.	Submarine -	No warning -	Torpedo -	4
†Polvena -	4,750	17	25 miles N. by E. ¼ E. from Ushant.	Submarine -	No warning -	Torpedo -	3
†Manchuria -	2,997	17	60 miles N.W. from Ushant.	Submarine -	No warning -	Torpedo -	26 including Master.
†Adams -	2,223	17	6 miles S.E. by E. from the Lizard.	Submarine -	No warning -	Torpedo -	—
†Madura -	4,484	18	23 miles W.S.W. from Bishop Rock.	Submarine -	No warning -	Torpedo -	3
†Hazelwood -	3,120	18	8 miles S. by E. ½ E. from Anvil Point.	Submarine -	No warning -	Torpedo -	32 including Master.
Sten -	928	18	5 miles North from Godrevy Lighthouse.	Submarine -	No warning -	Torpedo -	9 including Master.
†Amsteldam -	1,233	18	6 miles North from Flamborough Head.	Submarine -	No warning -	Torpedo -	4
†Togston -	1,057	18	20 miles S. by E. ½ E. from Flamborough Head.	Submarine -	No warning -	Torpedo -	5
†Cadmus -	1,879	18	20 miles S. by E. ½ E. from Flamborough Head.	Submarine -	No warning -	Torpedo -	—
†War Clover -	5,174	19	25 miles E. by N. ¾ N. from Pantellaria.	Submarine -	No warning -	Torpedo -	14
Cupica (Motor) -	1,240	19	75 miles W. by S. ½ S. from Bishop Rock.	Submarine -	Captured -	Gunfire -	—
Eldra (S.V.) -	227	19	35 miles N.W. from Treport.	Submarine -	Captured -	Bombs -	—
†Waikawa -	5,666	19	4 miles East from Start Point.	Submarine -	No warning -	Torpedo -	—
†Pera -	7,635	19	105 miles E. ¾ N. from Marsa Susa.	Submarine -	No warning -	Torpedo -	1
†Good Hope -	3,618	19	125 miles E. by S. from Malta.	Submarine -	No warning -	Torpedo -	—
†Australdale -	4,379	19	165 miles N.W. by N. ¾ N. from Cape Villano.	Submarine -	No warning -	Torpedo -	27
†Gemma -	1,385	19	5 miles N. by W. from Flamborough Head.	Submarine -	No warning -	Torpedo -	4
†Elsiston -	2,908	19	150 miles E. by S. ½ S. from Malta.	Submarine -	No warning -	Torpedo -	1
†Britannia -	765	19 (?)	English Channel -	Submarine (?) -	No warning(?)	Torpedo (?)	22 including Master.
†Algarve -	1,274	20	15 miles W.S.W. from Portland Bill.	Submarine -	No warning -	Torpedo -	21 including Master.
†Collegian -	7,520	20	100 miles N.W. by N. ¼ N. from Alexandria.	Submarine -	No warning -	Torpedo -	—
†Colorado -	7,165	20	1½ miles East from Start Point.	Submarine -	No warning	Torpedo -	4

Name.	Gross Tons.	Date.	Position.	Cause of Loss.	How attacked.	How sunk.	Lives lost.
		1917. Oct.					
†Ionian	8,268	20	2 miles West from St. Govan's Head.	Submarine	No warning	Torpedo	7
†Gryfevale	4,437	21	10 miles N. from Cape Blanco.	Submarine	Chased	Ran ashore	—
Tom Roper (S.V.)	120	21	20 miles S.S.E. from Start Point.	Submarine	Captured	Bombs	1
Bunty (tug)	73	21	Off Whitby	Mine	Mine	Mine	5 including Master.
†Zillah	3,788	22	25 miles N.E. from Kildin Island, Murmanski Coast.	Submarine	No warning	Torpedo	18
†Tredegar Hall	3,764	23	4½ miles E.S.E. from Flamborough Head.	Submarine	No warning	Torpedo	3
†Seistan	4,238	23	3½ miles N. by W. ¼ W. from Flamborough Head.	Submarine	No warning	Torpedo	5
†Euston	2,841	24	37 miles S.W. from Cape Matapan.	Submarine	No warning	Torpedo	1
†Ilderton	3,125	24	35 miles N.E. from Kildin Island, Murmanski Coast.	Submarine	No warning	Torpedo	—
†Sheaf Blade	2,378	25	13 miles S.E. by S. from Cape de Gata.	Submarine	No warning	Torpedo	2 including Master.
†Ness	3,050	25	10 miles S.E. from Cape de Gata.	Submarine	Captured	Gunfire	2
†Wearside	3,560	25	3 miles W. by S. from Sunk L.V.	Mine	Mine	Mine	—
Gefion	1,123	25	10 miles N.E. from Berry Head.	Submarine	No warning	Torpedo	2 including Master.
†Sapele	4,366	26	100 miles N.W. from Tory Island.	Submarine	No warning	Torpedo	3
Lady Helen	811	27	½ mile East from S. Cheek, Robin Hood Bay.	Mine	Mine	Mine	7 including Master.
†Redesmere	2,123	28	6 miles W.S.W. from St. Catherines.	Submarine	No warning	Torpedo	19
†Ferrona	4,591	28	7 miles N.E. from Valencia.	Submarine	Captured	Bombs	1
†Baron Garioch	1,831	28	5 miles S.E. from Anvil Point.	Submarine	No warning	Torpedo	2
†Baron Balfour	3,991	28	8 miles North from Sem Island, Murmanski Coast.	Submarine	No warning	Torpedo	—
†Namur	6,701	29	55 miles E. by S. ½ S. from Gibraltar.	Submarine	No warning	Torpedo	1
†Cambric	3,403	31	14 miles West from Cape Shershel.	Submarine	No warning	Torpedo	24 including Master. Four prisoners.
†Estrellano	1,161	31	14 miles W. by N. ½ N. from Pilier Island.	Submarine	No warning	Torpedo	3
North Sea	1,711	31	2½ miles S.W. by S. from Prawle Point.	Submarine	No warning	Torpedo	1
†Phare	1,282	31	2½ miles N. ½ E. from Scarborough.	Submarine	No warning	Torpedo	14

Name.	Gross Tons.	Date.	Position.	Cause of Loss.	How attacked.	How sunk.	Lives lost.
NOVEMBER 1917.		1917. Nov.					
Jessie - -	332	2	3 miles N.E. from Flamborough Head.	Submarine - -	Gunfire -	Beached ; total wreck.	4 including Master.
†Cape Finisterre	4,380	2	1 mile S.S.E. from Manacles Buoy.`	Submarine - -	No warning -	Torpedo -	35 including Master.
†Farraline - -	1,226	2	15 miles N.E. ½ E. from Ushant.	Submarine - -	No warning -	Torpedo -	1
†Antæus -	3,061	4	42 miles N. by W. ½ W. from Cape Bon.	Submarine - -	No warning -	Torpedo -	Master prisoner.
†Border Knight -	3,724	4	1½ miles E.S.E. from the Lizard.	Submarine - -	No warning -	Torpedo -	1
Hilda R. (S.V.)	100	5	20 miles South from Cape St. Mary.	Submarine - -	Captured -	Bombs -	1
†Suntrap - -	1,353	7	2½ miles East from S. Cheek, Robin Hood Bay.	Submarine - -	No warning -	Torpedo -	—
The Marquis -	373	8	16 miles E.S.E. from Rockabill.	Submarine - -	Captured -	Gunfire -	—
†Ardglamis -	4,540	9	125 miles West from Cape Spartel.	Submarine - -	No warning -	Torpedo -	—
†Ballogie - -	1,207	9	1½ miles N.E. from Filey.	Submarine - -	No warning -	Torpedo -	13 including Master.
Lapwing - -	1,192	11	9 miles S.E. from Southwold.	Mine · - -	Mine - -	Mine -	—
Morning Star (motor).	129	12	10 miles S.E. ¾ E. from Cape Barfleur.	Submarine - -	Captured -	Bombs -	—
†Barbary - -	4,185	12	56 miles N.W. by N. from Port Said.	Submarine - -	No warning -	Torpedo -	3 including Master.
†Carlo - -	3,040	13	7 miles S. by W. from Coningbeg L.V.	Submarine - -	No warning -	Torpedo -	2
†Atlas - -	989	13	5 miles S.E. from Owers L.V.	Submarine - -	No warning -	Torpelo -	--
†Axwell - -	1,442	13	3 miles W.S.W. from Owers L.V.	Submarine - -	No warning -	Torpedo -	2
†Axminster -	1,905	13	Off Pakefield Gat	Submarine - -	No warning -	Torpedo -	3
†Australbush -	4,398	13	7 miles E. ½ N. from the Eddystone.	Submarine - -	No warning -	Torpedo -	2
†Ardmore - -	1,304	13	13 miles W.S.W. from Coningbeg L.V.	Submarine - -	No warning -	Torpedo -	19
Dolly Varden (S.V.)	202	14	20 miles N.W. from Treport.	Submarine - -	Captured -	Gunfire -	—
†Prophet - -	3,230	14	3 miles S.E. from Antikithera Island.	Submarine - -	No warning -	Torpedo -	--
†Trowbridge -	3,712	14	12 miles S.E. from Cape de Gata.	Submarine - -	No warning -	Torpedo -	—
†Kyno - -	3,034	16	9 miles N. by E. ¾ E. from Shershel.	Submarine - -	No warning -	Torpedo -	5
†Garron Head -	1,933	16	40 miles N. by E. ½ E. from Bayonne.	Mine - -	Mine - -	Mine - -	28
†Gasconia - -	3,801	16	12 miles N.E. ½ E. from Shershel.	Submarine - -	No warning -	Torpedo -	3
†Western Coast -	1,394	17	10 miles W.S.W. from the Eddystone.	Submarine - -	No warning -	Torpedo -	17
†Victoria - -	974	17	14 miles W. ½ N. from the Eddystone.	Submarine - -	No warning -	Torpedo -	2

Name.	Gross Tons.	Date.	Position.	Cause of Loss.	How attacked.	How sunk.	Lives lost.
		1917. Nov.					
†Clan Maccorquodale.	6,517	17	165 miles N.W. by N. from Alexandria.	Submarine - -	No warning -	Torpedo -	—
†Croxteth Hall -	5,872	17	25 miles West from Bombay.	Mine - - -	Mine - -	Mine -	9
†Gisella - -	2,502	18	2 miles S.W. by S. from Skokham Island.	Submarine - -	No warning -	Torpedo -	2
†Antwerpen -	1,637	18	2 miles S.S.W. from the Runnelstone.	Submarine - -	No warning -	Torpedo -	—
†Aparima - -	5,704	19	6 miles S.W. ¾ W. from Anvil Point.	Submarine - -	No warning -	Torpedo -	56
†Farn - -	4,393	19	5 miles E. by N. from Start Point.	Submarine - -	No warning -	Torpedo -	—
Minnie Coles (S.V.)	116	19	30 miles N.W. by N. from Les Hanois.	Submarine - -	Captured -	Bombs -	—
Robert Brown (S.V.)	119	19	25 miles W.N.W. from Hartland Point.	Submarine - -	Captured -	Bombs -	—
†Jutland - -	2,824	19	18 miles N.E. by N. from Ushant.	Submarine - -	No warning -	Torpedo -	26 including Master.
Clangula - -	1,754	19	4 miles S.W. ¾ W. from Hartland Point.	Submarine - -	No warning -	Torpedo -	15 including Master.
Robert Morris (S.V.)	146	20	155 miles W.S.W. from Bishop Rock.	Submarine - -	Captured -	Bombs -	—
†Aros Castle -	4,460	21	300 miles W. by S. ¼ S. from Bishop Rock.	Submarine - -	No warning -	Torpedo -	2
Elsena - -	335	22	16 miles S.E. ½ S. from S. Arklow L.V.	Submarine - -	Captured -	Gunfire -	—
Conovium (S.V.)	86	22	14 miles S.E. ½ S. from S. Arklow L.V.	Submarine - -	Captured -	Gunfire -	—
†King Idwal -	3,631	22	29 miles S.E. by E. ½ E. from Buchan Ness.	Submarine - -	No warning -	Torpedo -	1
†Kohistan - -	4,732	22	25 miles W. ½ S. from Marittimo.	Submarine - -	No warning -	Torpedo -	—
†Westlands -	3,112	23	10 miles North from Ile de Vierge.	Submarine - -	No warning -	Torpedo -	—
†Ocean - -	1,442	23	4 miles E. by N. from Hartlepool.	Submarine - -	No warning -	Torpedo -	—
†La Blanca -	7,479	23	10 miles S.S.E. from Berry Head.	Submarine - -	No warning -	Torpedo -	2
†Dunrobin -	3,617	24	49 miles S.W. by S. ½ S. from the Lizard.	Submarine - -	No warning -	Torpedo -	31 including Master.
†Sabia - -	2,807	24	6 miles S.S.E. from the Lizard.	Submarine - -	No warning -	Torpedo -	11
†Nyassa - -	2,579	24	3 miles E.S.E. from the Lizard.	Submarine - -	No warning -	Torpedo -	—
French Rose -	465	24	6 miles S. by W. from Shipwash L.V.	Mine - - -	Mine - -	Mine - -	—
†Ostpreussen -	1,779	25	1½ miles East from Shipwash L.V.	Mine - - -	Mine - -	Mine - -	1
†Karema - -	5,285	25	33 miles S.E. by E. from Cape de Gata.	Submarine - -	No warning -	Torpedo -	3
†Ovid - -	4,159	25	65 miles N.E. ½ E. from Suda Bay.	Submarine - -	No warning -	Torpedo -	2

Name.	Gross Tons.	Date.	Position.	Cause of Loss.	How attacked.	How sunk.	Lives lost.
		1917. Nov.					
†Oriflamme -	3,764	25	9 miles South from Nab L.V.	Mine - - -	Mine - -	Mine - -	—
†Groeswen - -	3,570	27	3 miles N.E. ½ E. from Sunk L.V.	Mine - - -	Mine - -	Mine - -	—
Gladys - -	179	27	3 miles S.W. from Cape Gris Nez.	Mine - - -	Mine - -	Mine - -	6
†Almond Branch	3,461	27	2 miles S.E. from Dodman Point.	Submarine - -	No warning -	Torpedo -	1
†Eastfield - -	2,145	27	7 miles E.S.E. from Dodman Point.	Submarine - -	No warning -	Torpedo -	1
†Bleamoor - -	3,755	27	4 miles S.S.E. from Berry Head.	Submarine - -	No warning -	Torpedo -	8
†Apapa - -	7,832	28	3 miles N. by E. from Lynas Point.	Submarine - -	No warning -	Torpedo -	77
†Jane Radcliffe -	4,074	28	2 miles S.W. from Antimilo.	Submarine - -	No warning -	Torpedo -	—
†Georgios Antippa	1,960	28	25 miles S. by E. from Flamborough Head.	Submarine - -	No warning -	Torpedo -	—
†Derbent - -	3,178	30	6 miles N.E. by E. from Lynas Point.	Submarine - -	No warning -	Torpedo -	—
†Kalibia - -	4,930	30	29 miles S.W. from the Lizard.	Submarine - -	No warning -	Torpedo -	25
DECEMBER 1917.		**Dec.**					
†Molesey - -	3,218	1	12 miles S.W. by W. from Brighton L.V.	Submarine - -	No warning -	Torpedo -	—
†Euphorbia -	3,109	1	14 miles E. by S. from Royal Sovereign L.V.	Submarine - -	No warning -	Torpedo -	14
†Rydal Hall -	3,314	1	14 miles E. by S. from Royal Sovereign L.V.	Submarine - -	No warning -	Torpedo -	23
†Birchgrove -	2,821	2	10 miles W. by N. ½ N. from Ile de Groix.	Submarine - -	No warning -	Torpedo -	1
†Kintuck - -	4,639	2	8 miles N.W. by N. ½ N. from Godrevy L.H.	Submarine - -	No warning -	Torpedo -	1
†Berwick Law -	4,680	2	22 miles West from Cape Tenez.	Submarine - -	No warning -	Torpedo -	1 (Master prisoner).
†Copeland - -	1,184	2	15 miles S.S.W. from the Tuskar.	Submarine - -	No warning -	Torpedo -	12
†Wreathier -	852	3	1 mile West from Prawle Point.	Submarine - -	No warning -	Torpedo -	3
†Livonia - -	1,879	3	4 miles E. by N. ½ N. from Start Point.	Submarine - -	No warning -	Torpedo -	23 including Master.
†Dowlais - -	3,016	3	Off Cap de Fer -	Submarine - -	No warning -	Torpedo -	26 including Master.
Eagle - -	182	4	10m iles South from Start Point.	Submarine - -	Captured -	Bombs -	—
†Brigitta - -	2,084	4	6 miles S.W. from the Nab L.V.	Mine - - -	Mine - -	Mine - -	2
†Forfar - -	3,827	4	115 miles S.W. by W. from the Lizard.	Submarine - -	No warning -	Torpedo -	3
†Greenwich -	2,938	5	9 miles South from Planier Island.	Submarine - -	No warning -	Torpedo -	—
†Aigburth - -	824	5	2 miles N.E. by E. from S. Cheek, Robin Hood Bay.	Submarine - -	No warning -	Torpedo -	11 including Master.

Name.	Gross Tons.	Date.	Position.	Cause of Loss.	How attacked.	How sunk.	Lives lost.
		1917. Dec.					
†Ilvington Court	4,217	6	8 miles N.W. by N. from Shershel.	Submarine - -	No warning -	Torpedo -	8
†Asaba - -	972	6	2 miles W.S.W. from the Lizard.	Submarine - -	No warning -	Torpedo -	16 including Master.
†Wyndhurst -	570	6	30 miles South from St. Catherines.	Submarine - -	No warning -	Torpedo -	11 including Master.
†Earl of Elgin -	4,448	7	10 miles W. ½ S. from Carnarvon Bay L.V.	Submarine - -	No warning -	Torpedo -	18 including Master.
Proba (S.V.) -	105	7	3 miles S.E. from the Lizard.	Submarine - -	Captured -	Bombs -	—
†Highgate - -	1,780	7	2½ miles East from S. Cheek, Robin Hood Bay.	Submarine - -	No warning -	Torpedo -	--
†Maindy Bridge	3,653	8	4 miles E.N.E. from Sunderland.	Submarine - -	No warning -	Torpedo -	2
†Lampada - -	2,220	8	3 miles North from Whitby.	Submarine - -	No warning -	Torpedo -	5
†Consols - -	3,756	8	40 miles N.W. ½ N. from Cape Bon.	Submarine - -	No warning -	Torpedo -	3
†War Tune -	2,045	9	1½ miles S.S.E. from Black Head.	Submarine - -	No warning -	Torpedo -	1
†Venetia - -	3,596	9	3 miles N.N.W. fiom Whitby Rock buoy.	Submarine - -	No warning -	Torpedo -	--
†Minorca - -	1,145	11	2 to 3 miles from C. de las Huertas.	Submarine - -	No warning -	Torpedo -	15 including Master.
†Persier - -	3,874	11	50 miles E. from C. Spartivento, Italy.	Submarine - -	No warning -	Torpedo -	1
†D.A. Gordon -	2,301	11	1¼ miles E.S.E. from C. de las Huertas.	Submarine - -	No warning -	Torpedo -	1
†Oldfield Grange	4,653	11	30 miles N.E. from Tory I.	Submarine - -	No warning -	Torpedo -	--
†Leonatus - -	2,099	12	2 miles E. by S. from Kirkabister L.H.	Mine - - -	Mine - -	Mine -	--
†Charleston -	1,866	12	30 miles West from the Smalls.	Submarine -	Captured -	Bombs -	Two gunners prisoners.
†Cordova - -	2,284	12	North Sea - -	T.B.D. - - -	—	--	—
Britannic (S.V.)	92	13	12 miles N.N.W. from Les Hanois.	Submarine - -	Captured -	Bombs -	—
Little Gem - (S.V.).	114	13	Off Channel Islands.	Submarine (reported).	Not known -	Not known	5 including Master.
†Bangarth - -	1,872	13	13 miles N.N.E. from the Tyne.	Submarine - -	No warning -	Torpedo -	2
†Garthwaite -	5,690	13	4 miles East from Whitby.	Submarine - -	No warning -	Torpedo -	14 including Master.
†Arnewood -	2,259	13	4 miles E.S.E. from Sleat Point, Skye.	Mine - - -	Mine -	Mine -	--
†Volnay - -	4,610	14	2 miles E. by S. from Manacles.	Mine - - -	Mine -	Mine -	—
†Coila - -	4,135	14	3 miles S.E. by S. from Canet Point, Valencia.	Submarine - -	No warning -	Torpedo -	3
†Hare - -	774	14	7 miles East from the Kish L.V.	Submarine - -	No warning -	Torpedo -	12
†Bernard - -	3,682	15	180 miles W.S.W. from Bishop Rk.	Submarine - -	No warning -	Torpedo -	1

Name.	Gross Tons.	Date.	Position.	Cause of Loss.	How attacked.	How sunk.	Lives lost.
	1917. Dec.						
†Bristol City -	2,511	16	Atlantic - -	Submarine (reported).	No warning (probably).	Torpedo (probably).	30 including Master.
Formby - -	1,282	16(?)	Irish Sea -	Submarine (?) -	No warning(?)	Torpedo (?)	15 including Master.
†Foylemore -	3,831	16	22 miles E. ½ S. from the Lizard.	Submarine - -	No warning -	Torpedo -	—
†Riversdale -	2,805	18	1 mile South from Prawle Point.	Submarine - -	No warning -	Torpedo -	1
Charles (S.V.) -	56	18	English Channel	Submarine - -	Gunfire -	Gunfire -	1 Master and 2 crew prisoners.
Coningbeg - -	1,279	18(?)	Irish Sea - -	Submarine (?) -	No warning(?)	Torpedo (?)	15 including Master.
†Vinovia - -	7,046	19	8 miles South from Wolf Rock.	Submarine - -	No warning -	Torpedo -	9
†Alice Marie -	2,210	19	6 miles E.N.E. from Start Pt.	Submarine - -	No warning -	Torpedo -	—
†Warsaw - -	608	20	4 miles S.E. by E. from Start Point.	Submarine - -	No warning -	Torpedo -	17 including Master.
†Fiscus - -	4,732	20	10 miles N.N.E. from Cape Ivi.	Submarine - -	No warning -	Torpedo -	1
Eveline - -	2,605	20	9½ miles S. ½ W. from Berry Hd.	Submarine - -	No warning -	Torpedo -	—
†Waverley - -	3,853	20	33 miles N.E. ½ N. from Cape Ivi.	Submarine - -	No warning -	Torpedo -	22
†Polvarth - -	3,146	20	35 miles West from Ushant.	Submarine - -	No warning -	Torpedo -	2
†City of Lucknow	8,293	21	50 miles N.E. by N. ½ N. from Cani Rocks.	Submarine - -	No warning -	Torpedo -	—
†Mabel Baird -	2,500	22	4 miles W.S.W. from the Lizard.	Submarine - -	No warning -	Torpedo -	5
†Colemere - -	2,120	22	35 miles West from the Smalls.	Submarine - -	No warning -	Torpedo -	4
†Clan Cameron -	3,595	22	23 miles S.W. by S. ½ S. from Portland Bill.	Submarine - -	No warning -	Torpedo -	—
†Grantleyhall -	4,008	23	5 miles East from Orfordness.	Mine - - -	Mine - -	Mine - -	--
†Hilda Lea -	1,328	23	24 miles S. by E. from St. Catherines.	Submarine - -	No warning -	Torpedo -	1
†Canova - -	4,637	24	15 miles South from Mine Head.	Submarine - -	No warning -	Torpedo -	7
†Daybreak - -	3,238	24	1 mile East from South Rock L.V.	Submarine - -	No warning -	Torpedo -	21 including Master.
†Turnbridge -	2,874	24	34 miles N.E. by N. from Cape Ivi.	Submarine - -	No warning -	Torpedo -	1
†Argo - -	3,071	24	18 miles N.W. from Cape Tenez.	Submarine - -	No warning	Torpedo -	—
†Cliftondale -	3,811	25	36 miles E. by N. ½ N. from Cape Tenez.	Submarine - -	No warning -	Torpedo -	3 Master prisoner.
†Agberi - -	4,821	25	18 miles N.W. ½ N. from Bardsey Island.	Submarine - -	No warning -	Torpedo -	--
†Umballa - -	5,310	25	8 miles S.W. by W. from Cape Scalca, Gulf of Policastro.	Submarine - -	No warning -	Torpedo -	15
†Tregenna - -	5,772	26	9 miles South from Dodman Point.	Submarine - -	No warning -	Torpedo -	—

Name.	Gross Tons.	Date.	Position.	Cause of Loss.	How attacked.	How sunk.	Lives lost.
		1917. Dec.					
†Benito - -	4,712	26	9 miles South from Dodman Point.	Submarine - -	No warning -	Torpedo -	—
†Adela - -	685	27	12 miles N.W. from the Skerries, Anglesea.	Submarine - -	No warning -	Torpedo -	24
†Santa Amalia -	4,306	28	30 miles N. by E. ½ E. from Malin Head.	Submarine - -	No warning -	Torpedo -	43 including Master.
†Maxton - -	5,094	28	28 miles N. ¼ W. from Malin Head.	Submarine - -	No warning -	Torpedo -	1
†Lord Derby -	3,757	28	7 miles S.W. by S. from St. Ann's Head.	Submarine - -	No warning -	Torpedo -	3
†Chirripo - -	4,050	28	½ mile from Black Head, Belfast.	Mine - - -	Mine - -	Mine - -	—
†Robert Eggleton	2,274	28	10 miles S.W. from Bardsey Island.	Submarine - -	No warning -	Torpedo -	1
†Fallodon - -	3,012	28	12 miles S.S.E. from St. Catherines.	Submarine - -	No warning -	Torpedo -	1
Alfred H. Read	457	28	Entrance to River Mersey.	Mine - - -	Mine - -	Mine - -	39 including Master.
†Clara - -	2,425	28	1½ miles S.S.W. from the Runnelstone.	Submarine - -	No warning -	Torpedo -	—
†Ennismore -	1,499	29	23 miles East from Girdleness.	Submarine - -	No warning -	Torpedo -	10
†Zone - -	3,914	30	4 miles North from St. Ives.	Submarine - -	No warning -	Torpedo -	—
†Hercules - -	1,295	30	3 miles E.N.E. from Whitby.	Submarine - -	No warning -	Torpedo -	12 including Master.
†Aragon - -	9,588	30	Entrance to Alexandria.	Submarine - -	No warning -	Torpedo -	19 including Master.
†Westville - -	3,207	31	5 miles W.S.W. from St. Catherines.	Submarine - -	No warning -	Torpedo -	—
†Osmanieh -	4,041	31	Entrance to Alexandria.	Mine - - -	Mine - -	Mine - -	24 including Master.
JANUARY 1918.		1918. Jan.					
†Sandon Hall -	5,134	1	22 miles N.N.E. from Linosa.	Submarine - -	No warning -	Torpedo -	—
†Boston City -	2,711	2	11 miles W. ½ N. from St. Ann's Head.	Submarine - -	No warning -	Torpedo -	—
†Gallier - -	4,592	2	7 miles E.N.E. from Wolf Rock.	Submarine - -	No warning -	Torpedo -	—
†Gartland - -	2,613	3	5 miles E.S.E. from Owers L.V.	Submarine - -	No warning -	Torpedo -	2
†Birchwood -	2,756	3	25 miles East from Blackwater L.V.	Submarine - -	No warning -	Torpedo -	—
†Steelville - -	3,649	3	20 miles North from Cape Bon.	Submarine - -	No warning -	Torpedo -	—
†Allanton - -	4,253	3	20 miles North from Cape Bon.	Submarine - -	No warning -	Torpedo -	—
Otto S.V. - -	96	4	10 miles S.S.W. from St. John's Point, Co. Down.	Submarine - -	Captured -	Gunfire -	—
Rewa (Hospital Ship)	7,308	4	19 miles W. ¼ S. from Hartland Point.	Submarine - -	No warning -	Torpedo -	4
†Iolanthe - -	3,081	4	10 miles S.E. by E. from Portland Bill.	Submarine - -	No warning -	Torpedo -	—

Name.	Gross Tons.	Date.	Position.	Cause of Loss.	How attacked.	How sunk.	Lives lost.
		1918. Jan.					
†Glenarm Head -	3,908	4	5 miles S.W. by S. from Brighton L.V.	Submarine - -	No warning -	Torpedo -	2 including Master.
†Birtley - -	1,438	4	8 miles N. from Flamboro' Head.	Submarine (?) -	No warning(?)	Torpedo (?)	18 including Master.
†Knightsgarth -	2,889	5	5 miles W.N.W. from Bull Point, Rathlin Island.	Submarine - -	No warning -	Torpedo -	2
†Rio Claro - -	3,687	5	Rapallo Bay -	Submarine - -	No warning -	Torpedo -	—
†War Baron -	5,730	5	8 miles N.E. from Godrevy L.H.	Submarine - -	No warning -	Torpedo -	2
†Rose Marie -	2,220	5	13 miles S.E. from N. Arklow L.V.	Submarine - -	No warning -	Torpedo -	1
†Spenser - -	4,186	6	28 miles S.W. by W. ½ W. from Bardsey Island.	Submarine - -	No warning -	Torpedo -	—
†Halberdier -	1,049	6	27 miles W. by N. from Bardsey Island.	Submarine - -	No warning -	Torpedo -	5
†Gascony - -	3,133	6	10 miles S.S.E. from Owers L.V.	Submarine - -	No warning -	Torpedo -	—
†Arab - -	4,191	7	18 miles N. by E. from Cape Serrat.	Submarine - -	No warning -	Torpedo -	21
Bayvoe - -	2 979	9	10 miles South from Iles de Glenan.	Submarine - -	No warning -	Torpedo -	4
W. C. McKay (S.V.).	145	10(?)	Off the Azores -	Submarine - -	Not known -	Not known	6 including Master.
†Rapallo - -	3,811	13	1¼ miles South from Cape Peloro, Sicily.	Submarine - -	No warning -	Torpedo -	1
†Alster - -	964	14	5 miles E.S.E. from Noss Head, Shetland.	Submarine - -	No warning -	Torpedo -	—
†Spital - -	4,718	15	4 miles S.S.E. from St. Anthony Point.	Submarine - -	No warning -	Torpedo -	—
†War Song -	2,535	15	12 miles West from Ile de Sein.	Submarine - -	Captured -	Gunfire -	16 including Master.
†Kingsdyke -	1,710	17	20 miles N.E. ¾ E. from Cape Barfleur.	Submarine - -	No warning -	Torpedo -	16 including Master.
†Windsor Hall -	3,693	17	45 miles N.W. from Alexandria.	Submarine - -	No warning -	Torpedo -	27 Master prisoner.
Maria P. (S.V.)	263	18	75 miles West from Cape Mannu, Sardinia.	Submarine - -	Captured -	Gunfire -	—
†Trocas - -	4,129	19	10 miles N.E. from Skyros L.H.	Submarine - -	No warning -	Torpedo -	24
†Mechanician -	9,044	20	8 miles West from St. Catherines.	Submarine - -	No warning -	Torpedo -	13
†West Wales -	4,331	21	140 miles S.E. ¾ S. from Malta.	Submarine - -	No warning -	Torpedo -	2
†Teelin Head -	1,718	21	12 miles S.S.W. from Owers L.V.	Submarine - -	No warning -	Torpedo -	13 including Master.
†Serrana - -	3,677	22	10 miles West from St. Catherines.	Submarine - -	No warning -	Torpedo -	5
†Greatham -	2,338	22	3 miles S.E. from Dartmouth.	Submarine - -	No warning -	Torpedo -	7
†Anglo Canadian	4,239	22	33 miles S. ½ E. from Malta.	Submarine - -	No warning -	Torpedo -	3

Name.	Gross Tons.	Date.	Position.	Cause of Loss.	How attacked.	How sunk.	Lives lost.
		1918. Jan.					
†Manchester Spinner.	4,247	22	33 miles S. ½ E. from Malta.	Submarine - -	No warning -	Torpedo -	—
†Birkhall - -	4,541	23	4 miles S.E. from Cape Doro.	Submarine - -	No warning -	Torpedo -	2 including Master.
†Normandy -	618	25	8 miles E. by N. from Cape La Hague.	Submarine - -	No warning -	Torpedo -	14
†Humber - -	280	25	2 miles East from Sunderland.	Submarine - -	No warning -	Torpedo -	7 including Master.
†Eastlands -	3,113	25	13 miles N.W. from Ile de Vierge.	Submarine - -	No warning -	Torpedc -	1
Apostolos Andreas (S.V.)	50 apprx.	25	Mediterranean -	Submarine - -	Captured -	Gunfire -	—
†Cork - -	1,232	26	9 miles N.E. from Lynas Point.	Submarine - -	No warning -	Torpedo -	12
†Hartley - -	1,150	26	2 miles N.E. from Skinningrove.	Submarine - -	No warning -	Torpedo -	—
Rob Roy (S.V.)	112	26	20 miles S.W. from St. Catherines.	Submarine - -	Captured -	Gunfire -	—
Louie Bell (S.V.)	118	26	15 miles North from Cherbourg.	Submarine - -	Captured -	Bombs -	—
†Andania - -	13,405	27	2 miles N.N.E. from Rathlin Island L.H.	Submarine - -	No warning -	Torpedo -	7
W.H.L. (S.V.) -	97	28	8 miles S.S.E. from Portland Bill.	Submarine - -	Captured -	Bombs -	—
†Ethelinda - -	3,257	29	15 miles N.W. from the Skerries, Anglesea.	Submarine - -	No warning -	Torpedo -	26 including Master.
†Geo - - -	3,048	29	6 miles N. by W. from Cape Peloro, Sicily.	Submarine - -	No warning -	Torpedo -	16 including Master.
Taxiarchis (S.V.)	160	29	100 miles S.W. from Cape Gata, Cyprus.	Submarine - -	Captured -	Gunfire -	—
Perriton (S.V.) -	90	29	20 miles E. ½ S. from Berry Head.	Submarine - -	Captured -	Gunfire -	—
†Butetown - -	1,829	29	1½ miles South from Dodman Point.	Submarine - -	No warning -	Torpedo -	2
Ferryhill - -	411	30	15 miles W. ½ N. from Cape Antifer.	Submarine - -	Captured -	Gunfire -	—
†Maizar - -	7,293	30	38 miles N. by W. ½ W. from Cape Ferrat.	Submarine - -	No warning -	Torpedo -	—
†Minnetonka -	13,528	30	40 miles E.N.E. from Malta.	Submarine - -	No warning -	Torpedo -	4 Ten prisoners.
†Towneley -	2,476	31	18 miles N.E. ¼ E. from Trevose Head.	Submarine - -	No warning -	Torpedo -	6 including Master.
FEBRUARY 1918.		1918. Feb.					
Kindly Light (S.V.).	116	1	10 miles E.N.E. from Trevose Head.	Submarine - -	Captured -	Gunfire -	—
†Arrino - -	4,484	1	14 miles N.W. by W. from Ile de Vierge.	Submarine - -	No warning -	Torpedo -	—
†Cavallo - -	2,086	1	6 miles N.W. from Trevose Head.	Submarine - -	No warning -	Torpedo -	3
†Jaffa - -	1,383	2	3 miles E. by S. from Owers L.V.	Submarine - -	No warning -	Torpedo -	10
†Avanti - -	2,128	2	4 miles S.E. by E. from St. Albans Head.	Submarine - -	No warning -	Torpedo -	22 including Master.

Name.	Gross Tons.	Date.	Position.	Cause of Loss	How attacked.	How sunk.	Lives lost.
		1918. Feb.					
†Newminster Abbey.	3,114	2	44 miles E. by N. ½ N. from Cape de Creus.	Submarine - -	No warning -	Torpedo -	—
†Celia· - -	5,004	2	44 miles E. by N. ½ N. from Cape de Creus.	Submarine · -	No warning -	Torpedo -	—
Sofie - ·	354	3 (?)	Bristol Channel -	Submarine - -	Not known -	Not known	8 including Master.
†Aboukir - -	3,660	3	20 miles E. by S. from Cape de Creus.	Submarine - -	Captured -	Gunfire -	Master prisoner.
†Lofoten - -	942	3	7 miles S.E. by E. from Start Pt.	Submarine - -	No warning -	Torpedo -	17
Maid of Harlech (S.V.)	315	4	46 miles N. by W. from Cape Ivi.	Submarine - -	Captured -	Gunfire -	—
⁺Standish Hall -	3,996	4	38 miles W. by N. from Alexandria.	Submarine - -	No warning -	Torpedo -	—
Treveal - -	4,160	4	Off the Skerries, Angle-ey.	Submarine - -	No warning -	Torpedo -	33 including Master.
†Aurania - -	13,936	4	15 miles N. ½ W. from Inishtrahull.	Submarine - -	No warning -	Torpedo -	8
†Cresswell -	2,829	5	18 miles E. by N. ¼ N. from Kish L.V.	Submarine - -	No warning ·	Torpedo -	—
†Tuscania - -	14,348	5	7 miles North from Rathlin Island L.H.	Submarine - -	No warning -	Torpedo -	44
†Mexico City -	5,078	5	15 miles W. by S. ½ S. from S. Stack, Holyhead.	Submarine - -	No warning -	Torpedo -	29 including Master.
†Glenartney -	7,263	5	30 miles N.E. from Cape Bon.	Submarine - -	No warning -	Torpedo -	2
†Beaumaris -	2,372	7	2½ miles N. by W. from the Longships.	Submarine - -	No warning -	Torpedo ·	—
Limesfield ·	427	7	24 miles S.E. by E. from Douglas, Isle of Man.	Submarine - -	Captured -	Gunfire -	—
Ben Rein - -	212	7	35 miles N. ½ W. from Liverpool.	Submarine - -	Captured -	Gunfire -	—
Ardbeg - -	227	7	32 miles N. ½ E. from Mersey Bar L.V.	Submarine - -	Captured -	Gunfire -	—
†Sturton - -	4,406	7	15 miles S.E. by E. ¼ E. from Porquerolles Id.	Submarine - -	No warning -	Torpedo -	—
†Basuta - -	2,876	8	45 miles S.S.W. from the Lizard.	Submarine - -	No warning -	Torpedo -	1
†Artesia - -	2,762	8	190 miles E. by N. from Madeira.	Submarine - -	Captured -	Bombs -	1
Kia Ora (Barge)	77	8	20 miles N. by W. from Dieppe.	Submarine - -	Captured -	Bombs -	—
†Lydie - -	2,559	9	1 mile E. by S. from Manacles buoy.	Submarine - -	No warning ·	Torpedo -	2
†Remford - -	3,035	10	2½ miles East from Cape Carthage.	Submarine - -	No warning -	Torpedo -	28 including Master.
†Merton Hall -	4,327	11	30 miles N. by E. from Ushant.	Submarine - -	No warning -	Torpedo -	57 including Master.
†Baku Standard -	3,708	11	5 miles S. by W. ¼ W. from Tod Head.	Submarine - -	No warning -	Torpedo -	24
†Eleanor - -	1,980	12	9 miles W. by S. ½ S. from St. Catherines.	Submarine - -	No warning -	Torpedo -	34 including Master.

Name.	Gross Tons.	Date.	Position.	Cause of Loss.	How attacked.	How sunk.	Lives lost.
		1918. Feb.					
†St. Magnus -	809	12	3 miles N.N.E. from Peterhead.	Submarine - -	No warning -	Torpedo -	5
†Polo - -	2,915	12	6 miles S.E. by E. from St. Catherines.	Submarine - -	No warning -	Torpedo -	3
†Atlas - -	3,090	14	10 miles E.S.E. from Hartlepool.	Submarine - -	No warning -	Torpedo -	—
Carlisle Castle -	4,325	14	8 miles E. by N. from Royal Sovereign L.V.	Submarine - -	No warning -	Torpedo -	1
†Saga - -	1,143	14	4 miles E.N.E. from Sunderland.	Submarine - -	No warning -	Torpedo -	—
†Ventmoor - -	3,456	14	8 miles S.W. by W. from Skyros L.H.	Submarine - -	No warning -	Torpedo -	21 including Master.
†War Monarch -	7,887	14	11 miles East from Royal Sovereign L.V.	Submarine - -	No warning -	Torpedo -	—
Bessie Stephens (S.V.)	119	14	10 miles W. by S. ½ S. from South L.H., Lundy Island.	Submarine - -	Captured -	Gunfire -	—
†San Rito - -	3,310	15	23 miles S.W by W. ½ W. from Cape Mastiko, Khios.	Submarine - -	No warning -	Torpedo -	3
†Northville -	2,472	17	3½ miles S.E. by E. from Berry Head.	Submarine - -	No warning -	Torpedo -	—
†Pinewood - -	2,219	17	15 miles South from Mine Head.	Submarine - -	Captured -	Gunfire -	2
†Beacon Light -	2,768	19	15 miles S.E. from Butt of Lewis.	Submarine - -	No warning -	Torpedo -	33 including Master.
†Glencarron -	5,117	19	47 miles S. by E. ½ E. from the Lizard.	Submarine - -	No warning -	Torpedo -	—
†Philadelphian -	5,165	19	47 miles S. by E. ½ E. from the Lizard.	Submarine - -	No warning -	Torpedo -	4
Wheatflower -	188	19	10 miles S.E. by S. from Tuskar Rock.	Submarine - -	Captured -	Gunfire -	1
†Barrowmore -	3,832	19	53 miles N.W. by W. ¼ W. from Bishop Rock.	Submarine - -	No warning -	Torpedo -	25 including Master.
†Commonwealth -	3,353	19	5 miles N.E. from Flamborough Head.	Submarine - -	No warning -	Torpedo -	14
†Balgray - -	3,603	20	38 miles S.W. by W. from Dellimara Point, Malta.	Submarine - -	No warning -	Torpedo -	—
†Djerv - -	1,527	20	12 miles N.N.W. from the Skerries, Anglesea.	Submarine - -	No warning -	Torpedo -	2 including Master.
†Zeno - -	2,890	20	48 miles S.W. ½ S. from Dellimara Point Malta.	Submarine - -	No warning -	Torpedo -	—
†Huntsmoor -	4,957	20	23 miles S. ½ W. from Owers L.V.	Submarine - -	No warning -	Torpedo -	20 including Master.
†Rio Verde -	4,025	21	4 miles West from Crammock Head, Mull of Galloway.	Submarine - -	No warning -	Torpedo -	20 including Master.
Cheviot Range -	3,691	21	25 miles South from the Lizard.	Submarine - -	Captured -	Gunfire -	27 including Master.

Name.	Gross Tons.	Date.	Position.	Cause of Loss.	How attacked.	How sunk.	Lives lost.
		1918. Feb.					
†Haileybury -	2,888	22	15 miles S.E. by E. ¾ E. from the Maidens.	Submarine - -	No warning -	Torpedo -	2 including Master.
†British Viscount	3,287	23	12 miles N. by W. ½ W. from the Skerries, Anglesey.	Submarine - -	No warning -	Torpedo -	6
†Remus - -	1,079	23	6 miles S.S.W. from Copinsay, Orkney.	Submarine - -	No warning -	Torpedo -	5
Amsterdam -	806	24.	3 miles S.E. by E. from Coquet Island.	Submarine - -	No warning -	Torpedo -	4
†Renfrew - -	3,830	24	8 miles S.W. from St. Ann's Head.	Submarine - -	No warning -	Torpedo -	40 including Master.
†Rubio - -	2,395	25	4 miles N. ½ E. from Shipwash L.V.	Mine - - -	Mine - -	Mine - -	—
†Eumaeus - -	6,696	26	24 miles N.N.E. from Ile de Vierge.	Submarine - -	No warning -	Torpedo -	—
Glenart Castle (hospital ship).	6,824	26	10 miles West from Lundy Island.	Submarine - -	No warning -	Torpedo -	95 including Master.
†Greavesash -	1,263	26	10 miles N.E. from Cape Barfleur.	Submarine - -	No warning -	Torpedo .	8
†Romny - -	1,024	26	10 miles N.N.E. from Cape Barfleur.	Submarine - -	No warning -	Torpedo -	9
†Maltby - -	3,977	26	10 miles S.W. by S. from Pantellaria.	Submarine - -	No warning -	Torpedo -	5
†Dalewood - -	2,420	26	10 miles S.W. from Isle of Man.	Submarine - -	No warning -	Torpedo -	19 including Master.
†Tiberia - -	4,880	26	1½ miles East from Black Head, Belfast Lough.	Submarine - -	No warning -	Torpedo -	—
†Machaon - -	6,738	27	50 miles N.E. ¾ N. from Cani Rocks.	Submarine - -	No warning -	Torpedo -	—
†Largo - -	1,764	27	12 miles West from Calf of Man.	Submarine - -	No warning -	Torpedo -	—
MARCH 1918.		March.					
†Borga - -	1,046	1	9 miles S.E. by S. from Beer Head.	Submarine - -	No warning -	Torpedo -	5
†Penvearn - -	3,710	1	15 miles N. ½ W. from S. Stack.	Submarine - -	No warning -	Torpedo -	21
Cecil L. Shave (S.V.).	102	1 (?)	Off the Azores -	Submarine (reported).	Not known -	Not known	—
†Carmelite - -	2,583	2	10 miles S.W. by W. from Calf of Man.	Submarine - -	No warning -	Torpedo -	2
†Rockpool - -	4,502	2	12 miles N.E. by N. from Eagle Island.	Submarine - -	No warning -	Torpedo -	Master prisoner.
Bessy (Motor) -	60	2	12 miles N.N.W. from Peel.	Submarine - -	Captured -	Gunfire -	—
†Kenmare - -	1,330	2	25 miles N.W. from the Skerries, Anglesey.	Submarine - -	No warning -	Torpedo -	29 including Master.
†Romeo - -	1,730	3	7 miles South from Mull of Galloway.	Submarine - -	No warning -	Torpedo -	29 including Master.
†Northfield	2,099	3	25 miles S.W. from Lundy Island.	Submarine - -	No warning -	Torpedo -	15 including Master.

Name.	Gross Tons.	Date.	Position.	Cause of Loss.	How attacked.	How sunk.	Lives lost.
		1918. Feb.					
†Castle Eden -	1,949	4	4 miles S.S.E. from Inistrahull L.H.	Submarine - -	No warning -	Torpedo -	1
†Clan Macpherson	4,779	4	24 miles North from C. Serrat.	Submarine - -	No warning -	Torpedo -	18
†Roxburgh -	4,630	4	15 miles E. by N. ½ N. from C. St. John. Crete.	Submarine - -	No warning -	Torpedo -	6
Uskmoor - -	3,189	5	3 miles S.W. from Prawle Point.	Submarine - -	No warning -	Torpedo -	—
†Estrella - -	1,740	5	5 miles S. ½ W. from Shipwash L.V.	Mine - - -	Mine - -	Mine -	20
†Coalgas - -	2,257	5	5 miles S. by W. from Shipwash L.V.	Mine - - -	Mine - -	Mine - -	—
†Kalgan - -	1,862	6	33 miles S.W. ½ W. from Yafa, Syria.	Submarine - -	No warning -	Torpedo -	1
Tarbetness -	3,018	7	12 miles S.W. from Carnarvon L.V.	Submarine - -	No warning -	Torpedo -	—
Erica (S.V.) -	167	8	5 miles S.W. from Bardsey Island.	Submarine - -	Captured -	Gunfire -	—
†Intent - -	1,564	8	4 miles E. by N. from Seaham.	Submarine - -	No warning -	Torpedo -	1
†Madeline -	2,890	8	14 miles E.N.E. from Pendeen L.H.	Submarine - -	No warning -	Torpedo -	3
†Uganda - -	4,315	8	32 miles N.E. ¾ N. from Linosa.	Submarine - -	No warning -	Torpedo -	1
†Corsham -	2,760	8	6 miles E.S.E. from entrance to River Tees.	Submarine - -	No warning -	Torpedo -	9
†Ayr - - -	3,050	8	31 miles N. ½ W. from Linosa.	Submarine - -	No warning -	Torpedo -	—
†Silverdale -	3,835	9	28 miles E. by N. ½ N. from Cani Rocks.	Submarine - -	No warning -	Torpedo -	—
Nanny Wignall (S.V.).	93	9	14 miles S.E. by S. from Tuskar Rock.	Submarine - -	Captured -	Gunfire -	—
†Chagres -	5,288	10	62 miles N. by E. ¾ E. from C. Drepano, Crete.	Submarine - -	No warning -	Torpedo -	1
Stolt-Nielsen -	5,684	11	38 miles S. ½ E. from Dellimara Point, Malta.	Submarine - -	No warning -	Torpedo -	—
†Gaupen - -	622	12	5 miles S.E. by E. ¼ E. from N. Foreland Lt.	Mine - - -	Mine - -	Mine - -	—
Tweed - -	1,025	13	10 miles S. by W. ¼ W. from St. Catherines.	Submarine - -	No warning -	Torpedo -	7
†Lisette - -	895	13	8 miles N.E. by N. from Shipwash L.V.	Submarine - -	No warning -	Torpedo -	1
†Crayford -	1,209	13	110 miles W. by S. from Skudesnes.	Submarine - -	No warning -	Torpedo -	1
Ardandearg -	3,237	14	86 miles E. ¼ N. from Malta.	Submarine - -	No warning -	Torpedo -	2 including Master.
†Castlefort -	1,741	14	2 miles E. by N. from S. Cheek, Robin Hood Bay.	Submarine - -	No warning -	Torpedo -	—
Tweed - -	1,777	14	15 miles S.S.E. from Tuskar Rock.	Submarine - -	No warning -	Torpedo -	—
†Amazon - -	10,037	15	30 miles N. by W. from Malin Head.	Submarine - -	No warning -	Torpedo -	—

Name.	Gross Tons.	Date.	Position.	Cause of Loss.	How attacked.	How sunk.	Lives lost.
		1918. Mar.					
Sparkling Foam (S.V.)	199	15	9 miles S. by E. from Beer Head.	Submarine - -	Captured -	Bombs -	---
†Armonia - -	5,226	15	38 miles S.E. by S. ¼ S. from Porquerolles Id.	Submarine - . -	No warning -	Torpedo -	7
†Clan Macdougall	4,710	15	60 miles S.E. by E. ½ E. from C. Carbonara.	Submarine - -	No warning -	Torpedo -	33 including Master.
†Lightfoot - -	1,875	16	2 miles S. from Owers L.V.	Submarine - -	No warning -	Torpedo -	—
†Ellaston - -	3,192	16	180 miles W. by S. (true) from Palma, Canary Islands.	Submarine - -	Captured -	Bombs -	Master prisoner.
†South Western -	674	16	9 miles S.W. by S. from St. Catherines.	Submarine - -	No warning -	Torpedo -	24
†Oilfield - -	4,000	16	15 miles N.W. from Cape Wrath.	Submarine - -	Torpedoed -	Beached ; refloated ; wreck.	3
Cressida - -	157	17	16 miles W. by N. ½ N. from Skerries, Anglesey.	Submarine - -	No warning -	Torpedo -	3
†Sea Gull - -	976	17	7 miles N.E. from Lynas Point.	Submarine - -	No warning -	Torpedo -	20 including Master.
†Waihemo - -	4,283	17	Gulf of Athens -	Submarine - -	No warning -	Torpedo -	—
Eliza Anne (S.V.)	36	17	33 miles S. by W. ½ W. from the Eddystone.	Submarine - -	Captured -	Bombs -	---
†Ivydene - -	3,541	17	36 miles N.N.E. from C. Bougaroni.	Submarine - -	No warning -	Torpedo -	1
†John H. Barry -	3,083	18	104 miles N. by W. ¾ W. from C. Bougaroni.	Submarine - -	No warning -	Torpedo -	3 including Master.
†Baygitano -	3 073	18	1½ miles S.W. from Lyme Regis.	Submarine - -	No warning -	Torpedo -	2
†Saldanha - -	4,594	18	95 miles N. from Algiers.	Submarine - -	No warning -	Torpedo -	6
†Luxor - -	3,571	19	27 miles S.W. by S. from St. Catherines.	Submarine - -	No warning -	Torpedo -	—
†Burnstone -	2,340	19	44 miles N. from Farn Islands.	Submarine - -	No warning -	Torpedo -	5
†Samoset - -	5,251	20	50 miles N. by E. ¾ E. from Port Said.	Submarine - -	No warning -	Torpedo -	3
†Yochow - -	2,127	20	54 miles N. ¾ E. from Port Said.	Submarine - -	No warning -	Torpedo -	50 including Master.
†St. Dimitrios -	3,359	20	50 miles N. ¾ E. from Port Said.	Submarine - -	No warning ·	Torpedo -	—
Glenford - -	494	20	24 miles E. ½ S. from Rockabill.	Submarine - -	Captured -	Gunfire -	—
†Kassanga -	3,015	20	23 miles S.E. by S. from S. Arklow L.V.	Submarine - -	No warning -	Torpedo -	—
†Begonia - -	3,070	21	44 miles S. by W. from Wolf Rock.	Submarine - -	No warning -	Torpedo -	—
†Ikeda - -	6,311	21	7 miles W. from Brighton L.V.	Submarine - -	No warning -	Torpedo -	—
†Tyrhaug - -	1,483	22	10 miles N.E. from Pendeen L.H.	Submarine - -	No warning -	Torpedo -	2
†Polleon - -	1,155	22	3 miles E.N.E. from entrance to River Tyne.	Submarine - -	No warning -	Torpedo -	4

Name.	Gross Tons.	Date.	Position.	Cause of Loss.	How attacked.	How sunk.	Lives lost.
		1918. Mar.					
†Trinidad - -	2,592	22	12 miles East from Codling L.V.	Submarine - -	No warning -	Torpedo -	39 including Master.
†Etonian - -	6,515	23	34 miles S. by E. ½ E. from Old Head of Kinsale.	Submarine - -	No warning -	Torpedo -	7
†Madame Midas (ex Duva).	1,203	23	38 miles S. by W. ¾ W. from the Lizard.	Submarine - -	No warning -	Torpedo -	—
†Aulton - -	634	23	9 miles S.E. by E. ½ E. from Berwick Harbour.	Submarine - -	No warning -	Torpedo -	2
Jane Gray (S.V.)	124	23	14 miles N. by W. from the Smalls.	Submarine - -	Captured -	Gunfire -	—
†Anteros - -	4,241	24	16 miles W. by N. from South Stack.	Submarine - -	No warning -	Torpedo -	2
John G. Walter (S.V.).	258	24	20 miles S.W. from the Smalls.	Submarine - -	Captured -	Became derelict.	—
Jorgina (S.V.) -	103	24	320 miles N. by W. (true) from Madeira.	Submarine - -	Captured -	—	—
†Hercules -	1,095	25	4 miles N.N.W. from Flamborough Head.	Submarine - -	No warning -	Torpedo -	1
†Destro - -	859	25	5 miles S.W. from Mull of Galloway.	Submarine - -	No warning -	Torpedo -	—
†Lady Cory-Wright.	2,516	26	14 miles S.S.W. from the Lizard.	Submarine - -	No warning -	Torpedo -	39 including Master.
Watauga (S.V.)	127	27	450 miles W. by N. (true) from Lisbon.	Submarine - -	Captured -	Bombs -	5 including Master.
†Allendale - -	2,153	27	52 miles S. by W. from the Lizard.	Submarine - -	No warning -	Torpedo -	1
†Iukosi - -	3,661	28	14 miles S.E. by E. ½ E. from Mull of Galloway.	Submarine - -	No warning -	Torpedo -	3
City of Winchester (S.V.).	83	28	10 miles N.W. by W. from Les Hanois.	Submarine - -	Captured -	Gunfire -	—
†T. R. Thompson	3,538	29	7 miles South from Newhaven.	Submarine - -	No warning -	Torpedo -	33 including Master.
†Lough Fisher -	418	30	12 miles S.S.E. from Helvick Head.	Submarine (?) -	Gunfire (?) -	Gunfire (?)	13 including Master.
†Excellence Pleske	2,059	31	2½ miles S.S.E. from Dungeness.	Submarine - -	No warning -	Torpedo -	13
†Conargo - -	4,312	31	12 miles W. by N. from Calf of Man.	Submarine - -	No warning -	Torpedo -	9
†Vianna - -	401	31	4 miles East from Seaham Harbour.	Submarine - -	No warning -	Torpedo -	4
San Nicola (S.V.)	24	31	18 miles E.NE. from Valetta.	Submarine - -	Captured -	Gunfire -	—

APRIL 1918.

Name.	Gross Tons.	Date.	Position.	Cause of Loss.	How attacked.	How sunk.	Lives lost.
		Apr.					
Ardglass - -	4,617	1	6 miles East from the Maidens.	Submarine - -	No warning -	Torpedo -	6
Solway Queen -	307	2	7 miles West from Black Head, Wigtonshire.	Submarine - -	No warning -	Torpedo -	11 including Master.
†Cyrene - -	2,904	5	15 miles North from Bardsey Island.	Submarine - -	No warning -	Torpedo	24 including Master.

Name.	Gross Tons.	Date.	Position.	Cause of Loss.	How attacked.	How sunk.	Lives lost.
		1918. Apr.					
†Port Campbell	6,230	7	115 miles W.S.W. from Bishop Rock.	Submarine	No warning	Torpedo	—
†Rye	986	7	19 miles N. by W. ½ W. from Cape Antifer.	Submarine	No warning	Torpedo	4
†Highland Brigade	5,669	7	6 miles S. by E. from St. Catherine's.	Submarine	No warning	Torpedo	—
†Boscastle	2,346	7	14 miles N.N.W. from Strumble Head.	Submarine	No warning	Torpedo	18 including Master.
†Bengali	5,684	8	14 miles North from Alexandria.	Submarine	No warning	Torpedo	—
†Henley	3,249	10	25 miles S.W. ½ W. from the Lizard.	Submarine	No warning	Torpedo	6
†Westfield	3,453	10	45 miles S.W. by S. from Bishop Rock.	Submarine	No warning	Torpedo	—
Cicero	1,834	10 apprx.	Baltic	Reported as sunk to avoid capture.	—	—	—
Emilie	1,635	10 apprx.	Baltic	Reported as sunk to avoid capture.	—	—	—
Obsidian	742	10 apprx.	Baltic	Reported as sunk to avoid capture.	—	—	—
†Myrtle Branch	3,741	11	9 miles N.E. by N. from Inishtrahull.	Submarine	No warning	Torpedo	15 including Master.
†Highland Prince	3,390	11	36 miles N.E. ¼ E. from Cape Bon.	Submarine	No warning	Torpedo	3
†Lonhelen	1,281	12	North End of Shipwash.	Mine	Mine	Mine	—
Moyune	4,935	12	32 miles S.E. by E. from Cape Palos.	Submarine	No warning	Torpedo	--
Autolycus	5,806	12	32 miles S.E. by E. from Cape Palos.	Submarine	No warning	Torpedo	---
Wilson (S V.)	110	12	10 miles N.W. from the Smalls.	Submarine	Captured	Bombs	---
†Luis	4,284	12	3½ miles S.S.E. from St. Catherine's.	Submarine	No warning	Torpedo	4
†Harewood	4,150	13	380 miles W. by S. (true) from Lisbon.	Submarine	Captured	Gunfire	2 including Master.
†Marstonmoor	2,744	14	55 miles N.N.E. from Cape Wrath.	Submarine	No warning	Torpedo	—
†Santa Isabel	2,023	14	15 miles West from Cape Verde.	Submarine	Captured	Gunfire	1
†Chelford	2,995	14	10 miles N.W. by W. from Bardsey Island.	Submarine	No warning	Torpedo	—
†Pomeranian	4,241	15	9 miles N.W. by W. ½ W. from Portland Bill.	Submarine	No warning	Torpedo	55 including Master.
†Ailsa Craig	601	15	13 miles W. by N. from Portland Bill.	Submarine	No warning	Torpedo	—
†Hungerford	5,811	16	9 miles S.S.E. from Owers L.V.	Submarine	No warning	Torpedo	8
†Lake Michigan	9,288	16	93 miles N. by W. from Eagle Island.	Submarine	No warning	Torpedo	1 Master.
†Nirpura	7,640	16	110 miles W.N.W. (true) from Cape Roca.	Submarine	No warning	Torpedo	—

Name.	Gross Tons.	Date.	Position.	Cause of Loss.	How attacked.	How sunk.	Lives lost.
		1918. Apr.					
†Ladoga - -	1,917	16	15 miles S.E. from S. Arklow L.V.	Submarine - -	No warning -	Torpedo -	29 including Master.
†Bamse - -	958	17	15 miles W. by N. from Portland Bill.	Submarine - -	No warning -	Torpedo -	4
†Gregynog - -	1,701	18	16 miles S.W. from Hartland Point.	Submarine - -	No warning -	Torpedo -	3
†Runswick -	3,060	18	3 miles North from Trevose Head.	Submarine - -	No warning -	Torpedo -	—
†Dalegarth Force	684	18	12 miles S.W. from Hartland Point.	Submarine - -	No warning -	Torpedo -	5
†Pentyrch - -	3,312	18	5 miles W.N.W. from Brighton L.V.	Submarine - -	No warning -	Torpedo -	1
†Lord Charlemont	3,209	19	22 miles North from Alboran Island.	Submarine - -	No warning -	Torpedo -	8
†War Helmet -	8,184	19	3 miles E. by N. ½ N. from Owers L.V.	Submarine - -	No warning -	Torpedo -	—
†Florrieston -	3,366	20	6 miles E. ½ N. from South Stack.	Submarine - -	No warning -	Torpedo -	19 including Master.
†Lowther Range	3,926	20	20 miles W. by N. ½ N. from S. Stack.	Submarine - -	No warning -	Torpedo -	—
†Bellview - -	3,567	21	16 miles E.N.E. from Cape Bon.	Submarine - -	No warning -	Torpedo -	—
†Westergate -	1,760	21	22 miles E. ½ S. from Start Point.	Submarine - -	No warning -	Torpedo -	24 including Master.
†Normandiet -	1,843	21	34 miles S.W. by W. from Calf of Man.	Submarine - -	No warning -	Torpedo -	19 including Master.
†Landonia - -	2,504	21	27 miles N. by W. ½ W. from Strumble Head.	Submarine - -	No warning -	Torpedo -	21 Master or gunner prisoner.
†Dronning Maud	2,663	22	65 miles N. by E. ¾ E. from Cape Sigli.	Submarine - -	No warning -	Torpedo -	1
Mashalla (Egyptian S.V.).	77	22	50 miles North from Port Said.	Submarine - -	Captured -	Gunfire -	—
†Welbeck Hall -	5,643	22	75 miles N.E. by N. from Port Said.	Submarine - -	No warning -	Torpedo -	4
†Eric Calvert -	1,862	22	4 miles S.S.W. from St. Anthony Point.	Submarine - -	No warning -	Torpedo -	2
†Baron Herries -	1,610	22	43 miles N. by W. ½ W. from Bishop Rock.	Submarine - -	No warning -	Torpedo -	3 2nd officer prisoner.
†Fern - -	444	22	5 miles E. by N. from Kish L.V.	Submarine - -	No warning -	Torpedo -	13
†Laurium - -	582	23	15 miles East from Skegness.	Mine - - -	Mine - -	Mine -	1
Frances (S.V.) -	56	23	6 miles S. from the Lizard.	Submarine - -	Captured -	Bomb -	2
†Agnete - -	1,127	24	4 miles S. by W. from Start Point.	Submarine - -	No warning -	Torpedo -	12 including Master.
Ethel (S.V.) -	100	26	19 miles N. ¾ E. from the Smalls.	Submarine - -	Captured -	Gunfire -	—
†Llwyngwair -	1,304	26	5 miles S.S.E. from Seaham Harbour.	Submarine - -	No warning -	Torpedo -	8 including Master.
†Gresham - -	3.774	26	18 miles N.W. by N. ½ N. from Strumble Head.	Submarine - -	No warning -	Torpedo -	—

Name.	Gross Tons.	Date.	Position.	Cause of Loss.	How attacked.	How sunk.	Lives lost.
		1918. Apr.					
†Romany - -	3,983	27	47 miles S.W. by W. ¾ W. from Cape Sparti-vento, Sardinia.	Submarine - -	No warning -	Torpedo -	—
†Oronsa - -	8,075	28	12 miles W. from Bardsey Island.	Submarine - -	No warning -	Torpedo -	3
†Upcerne - -	2,984	28	4 miles S.E. by S. from Coquet Island.	Submarine - -	No warning -	Torpedo -	16
†Elba - -	1,081	28	6 miles N.W. by N. from Pen-deen.	Submarine - -	No warning -	Torpedo -	10
†Australier -	3,687	29	6 miles S.W. by S. from Dunge-ness.	Submarine - -	No warning -	Torpedo -	5
†Broderick - -	4,321	29	7 miles S.S.E. from Hastings.	Submarine - -	No warning -	Torpedo -	—
Johnny Toole (S.V.)	84	29	Off Carnsore Point.	Submarine - -	Captured -	Gunfire -	—
Christiana Davis (S.V.)	86	29	8 miles S.E. by S. from Tuskar Rock.	Submarine - -	Captured -	Gunfire -	—
†Kut Sang - -	4,895	29	40 miles E.S.E. from Cape Palos.	Submarine - -	No warning -	Torpedo -	59 including Master.
†Kingstonian -	6,564	29	Ashore in Carlo-forte Roadstead.	Submarine - -	Torpedoed -	Total wreck	1
†Ella Sayer -	2,549	29	15 miles E. by N. from Royal Sovereign L.V.	Submarine - -	No warning -	Torpedo -	2
†Conway - -	4,003	30	38 miles S. ½ E. from Cape Palos.	Submarine - -	No warning -	Torpedo -	—
†Kafue - -	6,044	30	11 miles S.W. from Mull of Galloway.	Submarine - -	No warning -	Torpedo	1
†Isleworth - -	2,871	30	3 miles S.W. from Ventnor Pier.	Submarine - -	No warning -	Torpedo -	29
Elsie Birdett (S.V.)	90	(?)	Off Canary Islands	Submarine - -	Not known -	—	6 including Master.
†Kempock - -	255	30	6½ miles S.E. by S. from Cope-land Is. Lt.	Submarine - -	Captured -	Gunfire -	—
†Umba - -	2,042	30	1 mile S. from Royal Sove-reign L.V.	Submarine - -	No warning -	Torpedo -	20 including Master.
MAY 1918.		May					
†Era - - -	2.379	1	18 miles N.E. by E. from Cape Tenez.	Submarine - -	No warning -	Torpedo -	12
†Matiana - -	5,313	1	On Keith Reef -	Submarine - -	No warning -	Torpedo -	—
†Unity - -	1,091	2	3 miles W.S.W. from Varne L.V.	Submarine - -	No warning -	Torpedo -	12
†Franklyn - -	4,919	2	65 miles E. by N. from Port Mahon.	Submarine - -	No warning -	Torpedo -	—
†Medora - -	5,135	2	11 miles W.S.W. from Mull of Galloway.	Submarine - -	No warning -	Torpedo -	Master, W/T operator and gunner prisoners
†Flawyl - -	3,592	2	30 miles E.S.E. from Pantellaria.	Submarine - -	No warning -	Torpedo -	1
†Girdleness -	3,018	2	18 miles N.E. by E. ½ E. from Trevose Head.	Submarine - -	No warning -	Torpedo -	2
†Thorsa - -	1,319	2	3 miles N.N.W. from Pendeen L.H.	Submarine - -	No warning -	Torpedo -	—

Name.	Gross Tons.	Date.	Position.	Cause of Loss.	How attacked.	How sunk.	Lives lost.
		1918. May					
†Polbrae - -	1,087	4	1¼ miles S.W. from Sharpnose, N. Devon.	Submarine - -	No warning -	Torpedo -	2
Tommi (S.V.) -	116	5	Between Chicken Rock and Calf of Man.	Submarine - -	Gunfire .-	Gunfire -	4 including Master.
†Leeds City -	4,298	6	5 miles E. by S. ½ S. from Skulmartin L.V.	Submarine - -	No warning -	Torpedo -	—
†Sandhurst -	3,034	6	6 miles N.W. by W. ¼ W. from Corsewall Point.	Submarine - -	No warning -	Torpedo -	20
†Nantes - -	1,580	7	83 miles E.S.E. from Fair Isle.	Submarine - -	No warning -	Torpedo -	—
Saxon - -	1,595	7	83 miles E.S.E. from Fair Isle.	Submarine - -	No warning -	Torpedo -	22
†Princess Dagmar	913	7 (?)	Bristol Channel -	Submarine (reported).	No warning -	Torpedo -	24 including Master.
†Constantia -	772	8	2 miles E. from S. Cheek, Robin Hood Bay.	Submarine - -	No warning -	Torpedo -	3
†Ingleside - -	3,736	8	80 miles N. by E. from Algiers.	Submarine - -	No warning -	Torpedo -	11
†Dux - -	1,349	8	7 miles N.W. from Godrevy L.H.	Submarine - -	No warning -	Torpedo -	—
†Baron Ailsa -	1,836	9	18 miles N.N.W. from the Smalls.	Submarine - -	No warning -	Torpedo -	10
†Wileysike -	2,501	9	8 miles S.W. from St. Ann's Head.	Submarine - -	No warning -	Torpedo -	4
†Amplegarth -	3,707	10	1 mile W.S.W. from Dover Harbour.	Mine - - -	Mine - -	Mine - -	—
†Itinda - -	5,251	10	40 miles N. from Marsa Susa.	Submarine - -	No warning -	Torpedo -	1
†Szechuen - -	1,862	10	60 miles N. by E. ½ E. from Port Said.	Submarine - -	No warning -	Torpedo -	9
Massouda (S.V.)	240	11	50 miles N. from Marsa Matruh.	Submarine - -	Captured -	Bombs -	—
†Inniscarra -	1,412	12	10 miles S.E. ½ E. from Ballycottin Island.	Submarine - -	No warning-	Torpedo -	28
†Haslingden -	1,934	12	7 miles E. from Seaham Harbour.	Submarine - -	No warning -	Torpedo -	11 including Master.
†Omrah - -	8,130	12	40 miles S.W. ¾ S. from Cape Spartivento, Sardinia.	Submarine - -	No warning -	Torpedo -	1
† Vimeira - -	5,884	12	16 miles W.S.W. from Lampedusa.	Submarine - -	No warning -	Torpedo -	—
† Woolston - -	2,986	14	1½ miles from Syracuse Harbour.	Submarine - -	No warning -	Torpedo -	19 including Master.
†Tartary - -	4,181	16	8 miles E.N.E. from Skulmartin L.V.	Submarine - -	No warning -	Torpedo -	—
†Heron Bridge -	2,420	16	320 miles E. by N. (true) from San Miguel, Azores.	Submarine - -	No warning -	Torpedo -	1
†Tagona - -	2,004	16	5 miles W.S.W. from Trevose Head.	Submarine - -	No warning -	Torpedo -	8 including Master.
†Llancarvan -	4,749	16	370 miles E. ½ N. (true) from San Miguel, Azores.	Submarine - -	No warning -	Torpedo -	- -
†Mavisbrook -	3,152	17	50 miles S.E. by S. ½ S. from Cape de Gata.	Submarine - -	No warning -	Torpedo -	18 including Master.
†Sculptor - -	4,874	17	60 miles N.W. by W. ¼ W. from Oran.	Submarine - -	No warning -	Torpedo ; beached ; wreck.	7 including Master.

Name.	Gross Tons.	Date.	Position.	Cause of Loss.	How attacked.	How sunk.	Lives lost.
		1918. May					
†Hurunui - -	10,644	18	48 miles S. by W. from the Lizard.	Submarine - -	No warning -	Torpedo -	1
†Scholar - -	1,635	18	90 miles W. by S. ¾ S. from Bishop Rock.	Submarine - -	No warning -	Torpedo -	2
†Denbigh Hall -	4,943	18	90 miles W.S.W. from Bishop Rock.	Submarine - -	No warning -	Torpedo -	—
†Chesterfield -	1,013	18	42 miles N.E. by E. ½ E. from Malta.	Submarine - -	No warning -	Torpedo -	4
Ninetta (S.V.) -	7	18	22 miles S.E. by S. from Cape Passero.	Submarine - -	Captured -	Gunfire -	—
†Snowdon - -	3,189	19	84 miles S. ½ W. from Malta.	Submarine - -	No warning -	Torpedo -	2 including Master.
†Chatham - -	3,592	21	80 miles S.W. ¼ S. from Cape Matapan.	Submarine - -	No warning -	Torpedo -	—
†Skaraas - -	1,625	23	1 mile S.W. from Black Head.	Submarine - -	No warning -	Torpedo -	19
†Innisfallen -	1,405	23	16 miles E. ¾ N. from Kish L.V.	Submarine - -	No warning -	Torpedo -	10
Ruth Hickman, S.V.	417	24	60 miles N.N.W. (true) from Graciosa, Azores	Submarine - -	Captured -	Bombs -	—
†Princess Royal -	1,986	26	3 miles W.N.W. from St. Agnes Head.	Submarine - -	No warning -	Torpedo -	19
†Kyarra - -	6,953	26	2 miles S.S.E. from Anvil Point.	Submarine - -	No warning -	Torpedo -	6
†Thames - -	1,327	26	6 miles S.E. by E. from Seaham Harbour.	Submarine - -	No warning -	Torpedo -	4 including Master.
†Leasowe Castle -	9,737	26	104 miles W. by N. ½ N. from Alexandria.	Submarine - -	No warning -	Torpedo -	9 including Master.
†Cairnross - -	4,016	27	110 miles N.N.W. (true) from Flores, Azores.	Submarine - -	No warning -	Torpedo -	—
†Uganda - -	5,431	27	90 miles N.E. by N. ¾ N. from Algiers.	Submarine - -	No warning -	Torpedo -	—
†Merionethshire -	4,308	27	120 miles N. ½ E. (true) from Flores, Azores.	Submarine - -	No warning -	Torpedo -	—
†Begum - -	4,646	29	270 miles W. by S. from Bishop Rock.	Submarine - -	No warning -	Torpedo -	15
Missir - -	786	29	80 miles W. by N. from Alexandria.	Submarine - -	No warning -	Torpedo -	34
†Carlton - -	5,262	29	270 miles W. by S. from Bishop Rock.	Submarine - -	No warning -	Torpedo -	—
†Ausonia - -	8,153	30	620 miles W. by S. ¾ S. (true) from the Fastnet.	Submarine - -	No warning -	Torpedo -	44
†Waneta - -	1,683	30	42 miles S.S.E. from Kinsale Head.	Submarine - -	No warning -	Torpedo -	8
†Asiatic Prince -	2,887	30	190 miles E. by S. ½ S. from Malta.	Submarine - -	No warning -	Torpedo -	—
†Aymeric - -	4,363	30	145 miles S.W. by W. from Cape Matapan.	Submarine - -	No warning -	Torpedo -	—
Alert (S.V.) -	59	31	9 miles N.E. by N. ½ N. from Coquet Island.	Submarine - -	Captured -	Bombs -	—

Name.	Gross Tons.	Date.	Position.	Cause of Loss.	How attacked.	How sunk.	Lives lost.
JUNE 1918.		**1918. June**					
†Nora - -	3,933	3	205 miles S.E. from Malta.	Submarine - -	No warning -	Torpedo -	1
†Glaucus - -	5,295	3	20 miles W. from Cape Granitola, Sicily.	Submarine - -	No warning -	Torpedo -	2
†Polwell - -	2,013	5	6 miles E. by S. ½ S. from Rockabill.	Submarine - -	No warning -	Torpedo -	—
†Harpathian -	4,588	5	Off Cape Henry, Virginia.	Submarine - -	No warning -	Torpedo -	—
†Archbank -	3,767	5	240 miles E.S.E. from Malta.	Submarine - -	No warning -	Torpedo -	1
†Menzaleh - -	1,859	5	230 miles ES. E. from Malta.	Submarine - -	No warning -	Torpedo -	10 Master prisoner.
†Huntsland -	2,871	6	23 miles N. by W. from Havre.	Submarine - -	No warning -	Torpedo -	—
†Diana - -	1,119	7	10 miles S.S.E. from Flamborough Head.	Submarine - -	No warning -	Torpedo -	—
†Hogarth - -	1,231	7	10 miles S. ½ E. from the Longstone.	Submarine - -	No warning -	Torpedo -	26 including Master
†Saima - -	1,147	8	10 miles W. from Trevose Head.	Submarine - -	No warning -	Torpedo -	16 including Master.
†Hunsgrove -	3,063	8	6 miles N.W. from Trevose Head.	Submarine - -	No warning -	Torpedo -	3
†Moidart - -	1,303	9	7 miles S.E. ½ E. from Lyme Regis.	Submarine - -	No warning -	Torpedo -	15
Queen Victoria (S.V.).	92	9	6 miles S.E. from Lundy Island.	Submarine - -	Captured -	Bombs -	—
†Vandalia - -	7,333	9	18 miles W.N.W. from the Smalls.	Submarine - -	No warning -	Torpedo -	—
†Tewfikieh -	2,490	9	115 miles W.N.W. from Alexandria.	Submarine - -	No warning -	Torpedo -	5
†Clan Forbes -	3,946	9	115 miles W.N.W. from Alexandria.	Submarine - -	No warning -	Torpedo -	2
†Pundit -	5,917	9	85 miles W.N.W. from Alexandria.	Submarine - -	No warning -	Torpedo -	6 including Master.
†Mountby -	3,263	10	8 miles E. by S. from the Lizard.	Submarine - -	No warning -	Torpedo -	—
†Stryn - -	2,143	10	5 miles E. from Berry Head.	Submarine - -	No warning -	Torpedo -	8
†Princess Maud -	1,566	10	5 miles N.E. by N. from Blyth.	Submarine - -	No warning -	Torpedo -	3
Lowtyne -	3,231	10	3½ miles E.S.E. from Whitby.	Submarine - -	No warning -	Torpedo -	3
†Borg - -	2,111	10	20 miles S.W. by S. from the Lizard.	Submarine - -	No warning -	Torpedo -	24 including Master.
†Lorle - -	2,686	11	12 miles S.S.W. from the Lizard.	Submarine - -	No warning -	Torpedo -	19 including Master.
†Boma - -	2,694	11	10 miles S.W. ¾ W. from Beer Head.	Submarine - -	No warning -	Torpedo -	—
†Kul - - -	1,095	12	3½ miles N.E. ¼ N. from Wolf Rock.	Submarine - -	No warning -	Torpedo -	4
†Penhallow -	4,318	12	52 miles N. by W. from Cape Caxine.	Submarine - -	No warning -	Torpedo -	1
†Kennington -	1,536	12	15 miles E. from Flamborough Head.	Submarine - -	No warning -	Torpedo -	4

Name.	Gross Tons.	Date.	Position.	Cause of Loss.	How attacked.	How sunk.	Lives lost.
		1918. June					
†Kalo - -	1,957	13	18 miles S. by E. ½ E. from Flamborough Head.	Submarine - -	No warning -	Torpedo -	3
†Kieldrecht -	1,284	15	21 miles E. by S. from Flamborough Head.	Submarine - -	No warning -	Torpedo -	—
†Melanie - -	2,996	16	2 miles East from S. Cheek, Robin Hood Bay.	Submarine - -	No warning -	Torpedo -	5
†Dwinsk - -	8,173	18	400 miles N.E. by N. ¾ N. (true) from Bermuda.	Submarine - -	No warning -	Torpedo -	24
†Norfolk Coast -	782	18	23 miles S.E. from Flamborough Head.	Submarine - -	No warning -	Torpedo -	8
†Montebello -	4,324	21	320 miles W. ½ N. from Ushant.	Submarine - -	No warning -	Torpedo -	41 including Master.
†Rhea - -	1,308	22	Off Etaples -	Mine - - -	Mine - -	Mine - -	—
†London - -	1,706	23	4 miles E. by S. from Whitby.	Submarine - -	No warning -	Torpedo -	—
†Moorlands -	3,602	24	3 miles S.E. by E. from Whitby.	Submarine - -	No warning -	Torpedo -	10
†Atlantian - -	9,399	25	110 miles N. by W. ½ W. from Eagle Island.	Submarine - -	No warning -	Torpedo -	Chief Officer and W/T Operator prisoners.
†Orissa - -	5,358	25	21 miles S.W. by W. ¼ W. from Skerryvore.	Submarine - -	No warning -	Torpedo -	6
†African Transport	4,482	25	3 miles North from Whitby.	Submarine - -	No warning -	Torpedo -	3
Wimmera - -	3,022	26	24 miles N.W. ½ W. from Hooper's Point, N.Z.	Mine - - -	Mine - -	Mine - -	16 including Master.
†Tortuguero -	4,175	26	205 miles N.W. ¼ N. from Eagle Island.	Submarine - -	No warning -	Torpedo -	12
†Keelung - -	6,672	27	110 miles W. ¾ S. from Ushant.	Submarine - -	No warning -	Torpedo -	6
Llandovery Castle (Hospital Ship).	11,423	27	116 miles West from the Fastnet.	Submarine - -	No warning -	Torpedo -	146
Dictator (S.V.) -	99	(?)	Atlantic - -	Submarine (reported)	Not known -	Not known	Crew prisoners.
†Queen - -	4,956	28	130 miles N. ½ W. from Cape Villano.	Submarine - -	No warning -	Torpedo -	20 including Master.
†Sunniva - -	1,913	28	4 miles East from Sunderland.	Submarine - -	No warning -	Torpedo -	2
†Sixty-Six -	214	29	3 miles East from Scarborough.	Submarine - -	No warning -	Torpedo -	6 including Master.
†Florentia - -	3,688	29	2 miles E. by N. from S. Cheek, Robin Hood Bay.	Submarine - -	No warning -	Torpedo -	3
†Herdis - -	1,157	29	7 miles S.E. by S. from S. Cheek, Robin Hood Bay.	Submarine - -	No warning -	Torpedo -	—
W.M.L. (S.V.) -	145	30	400 miles N.N.W. from Cape Finisterre.	Submarine - -	Captured	Gunfire -	4 including Master.
†Origen -	3,545	30	115 miles W. ¼ S. from Ushant.	Submarine - -	No warning	Torpedo -	1

Name.	Gross Tons.	Date.	Position.	Cause of Loss.	How attacked.	How sunk.	Lives lost.
JULY 1918.		1918. July					
†Charing Cross -	2,534	1	4 miles E. by N. from Flamborough Head.	Submarine -	No warning -	Torpedo -	—
†Westmoor -	4,329	1	210 miles N.W. by W. ¾ W. from Casablanca.	Submarine - -	No warning -	Torpedo -	2 Master prisoner.
Admiral (Tug) -	102	2	2 miles N. from Flamborough Head.	Submarine - -	Captured -	Gunfire -	—
Erme (Motor) -	116	2	240 miles N.W by W. from the Fastnet.	Submarine - -	Captured -	Bombs -	—
†Shirala - -	5,306	2	4 miles N.E. by E. ½ E. from Owers L.V.	Submarine - -	No warning -	Torpedo -	8
†Vera Elizabeth (Motor).	179	5	54 miles S. by E. ½ E. from Sydero, Faeroe Islands.	Submarine - -	Captured -	Gunfire -	—
†Bertrand - -	3,613	6	28 miles E.S.E. from Cape Bon.	Submarine - -	No warning -	Torpedo -	—
†Port Hardy -	6,533	6	78 miles W. by N. from Cape Spartel.	Submarine - -	No warning -	Torpedo -	7
†Ben Lomond -	2,814	7	30 miles S.E. from Daunts Rock.	Submarine - -	No warning -	Torpedo -	23 including Master.
†Chicago - -	7,709	8	4 miles N.E. from Flamborough Head.	Submarine - -	No warning -	Torpedo -	3
†War Crocus -	5,296	8	2½ miles E. by N. from Flamborough Head.	Submarine - -	No warning -	Torpedo -	—
†Mars - -	3,550	8	74 miles W. by N. from Bishop Rock.	Submarine - -	No warning -	Torpedo -	—
†Plawsworth -	4,724	13	105 miles W. by N. from Bishop Rock.	Submarine - -	No warning -	Torpedo -	1
†Badagri - -	2,956	13	425 miles W.N.W. from Cape St. Vincent.	Submarine - -.	No warning -	Torpedo -	Chief Officer prisoner.
†Branksome Hall	4,262	14	68 miles N.W. by W. from Marsa Susa.	Submarine - -	No warning -	Torpedo -	—
†Waitemata -	5,432	14	100 miles E. ¾ N. from Marsa Susa.	Submarine - -	No warning -	Torpedo -	—
†Barunga - -	7,484	15	150 miles W. by S. ½ S. from Bishop Rock.	Submarine - -	No warning -	Torpedo -	—
Fisherman (S.V.)	136	16	380 miles N.W. by W. ½ W. from Cape Roca.	Submarine - -	Captured -	Gunfire -	—
†War Swallow -	5,216	16	72 miles S.W. by S. ½ S. from Malta.	Submarine - -	No warning -	Torpedo -	7
†Southborough -	3,709	16	5 miles N. by E. ¼ E. from Scarborough.	Submarine - -	No warning -	Torpedo -	30 including Master.
†Carpathia -	13,603	17	170 miles W. by N. from Bishop Rock.	Submarine - -	No warning -	Torpedo -	5
Ranger (Motor)	79	19	20 miles N.W. from Barra Head.	Submarine - -	Captured -	Bombs -	—
†Justicia - -	32,234	19	20 miles W. by N. ¾ N. from Skerryvore.	Submarine - -	No warning -	Torpedo -	10

Name.	Gross Tons.	Date.	Position.	Cause of Loss.	How attacked.	How sunk.	Lives lost.
		1918. July					
†Gemini - -	2,128	20	7 miles N.W. ½ N. from Godrevy L.H.	Submarine -	- No warning -	Torpedo -	2
†Orfordness -	2,790	20	2½ miles W. by N. from Newquay.	Submarine -	- No warning -	Torpedo -	2
†Kosseir - -	1,855	20	40 miles N.E. by N. ½ N. from Alexandria.	Submarine -	- No warning -	Torpedo -	39 including Master.
†Mongolian -	4,892	21	5 miles S.E. from Filey Brig.	Submarine -	- No warning -	Torpedo -	36
†Anna Sofie -	2,577	23	4 miles W. from Trevose Head.	Submarine -	- No warning -	Torpedo -	1
†Messidor - -	3,883	23	73 miles S.E. by S. ¼ S. from Port Mahon.	Submarine -	- No warning -	Torpedo -	1
†Rutherglen -	4,214	24	50 miles E.S.E. from Port Mahon.	Submarine -	- No warning -	Torpedo -	---
†Magellan - -	3,642	25	53 miles N. ½ E. from Cape Serrat.	Submarine -	- No warning -	Torpedo -	1
†Blairhall - -	2,549	26	3½ miles E.N.E. from Sunderland.	Submarine -	- No warning -	Torpedo -	1
Kirkham Abbey	1,166	27	2 miles N.E. by E. from Winterton.	Submarine -	- No warning -	Torpedo -	8
†Subadar - -	4,911	27	112 miles N. by W. from Cape Roca.	Submarine -	- No warning -	Torpedo -	3
†Chloris - -	984	27	17 miles S. by E. from Flamborough Head.	Submarine -	- No warning -	Torpedo -	3 including Master.
†Hyperia - -	3,908	28	84 miles N.W. by N. from Port Said.	Submarine -	- No warning -	Torpedo -	7 including Master.
†Rio Pallaresa	4,034	29	62 miles E.N.E. from Malta.	Submarine -	- No warning -	Torpedo -	2
AUGUST 1918.		Aug.					
†Malvina - -	1,244	2	1 mile N.N.E. from Flamborough Head.	Submarine -	- No warning -	Torpedo -	14 including Master.
Dornfontein (Motor).	766	2	25 miles W.N.W. from Brier Island, N.S.	Submarine -	- Captured -	Burnt -	—
†Warilda - -	7,713	3	32 miles S.S.W. from Owers L.V.	Submarine -	- No warning -	Torpedo -	7
†Clan Macnab -	4,675	4	14 miles N.N.W. from Pendeen L.H.	Submarine -	- No warning -	Torpedo -	22 including Master.
†Freshfield -	3,445	5	4 miles N.E. by N. from Cape Colonne, Italy.	Submarine -	- No warning -	Torpedo -	3
†Luz Blanca -	4,868	5	35 miles S.W. from Outer Gas Buoy, Halifax, N.S.	Submarine -	- No warning -	Torpedo -	2
†Clan Macneil -	3,939	6	10 miles North from Alexandria.	Submarine -	- No warning -	Torpedo -	—
†Biruta - -	1,733	6	8 miles N.W. ¾ W. from Calais.	Submarine -	- No warning -	Torpedo -	12 including Master.
†Highland Harris	6,032	6	82 miles N. ¾ W. from Eagle Island.	Submarine -	- No warning -	Torpedo -	24

Name.	Gross Tons.	Date.	Position.	Cause of Loss.	How attacked.	How sunk.	Lives lost.
		1918. Aug.					
†Clan Macvey -	5,815	8	½ mile S.E. from Anvil Point.	Submarine - -	No warning -	Torpedo -	7
†Glenlee - -	4,915	9	4 miles E. by N. from Owers L.V.	Submarine - -	No warning -	Torpedo -	1
†Madam Renee -	509	10	1 mile N.N.E. from Scarborough.	Submarine - -	No warning -	Torpedo -	10
†City of Adelaide	8,389	11	60 miles E.N.E. from Malta.	Submarine - -	No warning -	Torpedo -	4
†Penistone -	4,139	11	145 miles S.W. ½ S. from Nantucket Island.	Submarine - -	No warning -	Torpedo -	1
†Anhui - -	2,209	12	2 miles S.E. from Cape Greco, Cyprus.	Submarine - -	No warning -	Torpedo -	4
†City of Brisbane	7,094	13	1½ miles S.S.W. from Newhaven.	Submarine - -	No warning -	Torpedo -	—
†Wallsend - -	2,697	14	1 mile S.E. from S. Cheek, Robin Hood Bay.	Submarine - -	No warning -	Torpedo -	
†Escrick - -	4,151	16	360 miles N.W. by N. from Cape Finisterre.	Submarine - -	No warning -	Torpedo -	1 Master prisoner.
†Mirlo - -	6,978	16	½ mile S. by E. from Wimble Shoal Buoy, Cape Hatteras.	Submarine - -	No warning -	Torpedo -	9
†Eros - -	1,122	17	2 miles N.E. by N. from Filey Brig.	Submarine - -	No warning -	Torpedo -	7 including Master.
†Denebola - -	1,481	17	2 miles N. by W. from Gurnard Head.	Submarine - -	No warning -	Torpedo -	2
†Zinal - -	4,037	17	360 miles N. by E. (true) from Terceira, Azores.	Submarine - -	No warning -	Torpedo -	2
†Idaho - -	3,023	19	120 miles N. by W. ½ W. from Cape Villano.	Submarine - -	No warning -	Torpedo -	11
†Marie Suzanne -	3,106	19	47 miles W. ¾ S. from Mudros Bay.	Submarine - -	No warning -	Torpedo -	—
†Boltonhall -	3,535	20	34 miles S.W. by W. ¼ W. from Bardsey Island.	Submarine - -	No warning -	Torpedo -	5
†Otis Tetrax -	996	20	28 miles S. ¼ E. from Flamborough Head.	Submarine - -	No warning -	Torpedo -	—
†The Stewart's Court.	813	21	4 miles S.S.E. from Seaham Harbour.	Submarine - -	No warning -	Torpedo -	
†Diomed - -	7,523	21	195 miles E.S.E. from Nantucket Island.	Submarine - -	Captured -	Gunfire -	2
†Boscawen - -	1,936	21	23 miles W.N.W. from Bardsey Island.	Submarine - -	No warning -	Torpedo -	1
†Palmella - -	1,352	22	25 miles N.W. ¼ W. from South Stack.	Submarine - -	No warning -	Torpedo -	28 including Master.
Abbasieh (Egyptian S.V.).	140	22	100 miles N.E. from Alexandria.	Submarine - -	Captured -	Gunfire -	—
†Prunelle - -	578	22	2 miles S.E. from Blyth.	Submarine - -	No warning -	Torpedo -	12 including Master.
†Australian Transport.	4,784	23	40 miles W.N.W. from Marittimo.	Submarine - -	No warning -	Torpedo -	1
†Flavia - -	9,291	24	30 miles N.W. by W. from Tory Island.	Submarine - -	No warning -	Torpedo -	1

Name.	Gross Tons.	Date.	Position.	Cause of Loss.	How attacked.	How sunk.	Lives lost.
		1918. Aug.					
†Virent - -	3,771	24	38 miles W. by S. from the Smalls.	Submarine -	- No warning -	Torpedo -	--
†Auckland Castle	1,084	24	5 miles E. by S. ½ S. from Farn Island.	Submarine -	- No warning -	Torpedo -	12 including Master.
†Willingtonia -	3,228	25	13 miles S.W. by W. from Marittimo.	Submarine -	- No warning -	Torpedo -	4
Erik - -	583	25	70 miles N.W. by W. from St. Pierre, N.F.L.	Submarine -	- Captured -	Bombs -	—
†Ant Cassar -	3,544	27	30 miles N.N.W. from Strumble Head.	Submarine -	- No warning -	Torpedo -	—
†Giralda - -	1,100	28	5 miles N.N.W. from Whitby.	Submarine -	- No warning -	Torpedo -	6
†Milwaukee -	7,323	31	260 miles S.W. from the Fastnet.	Submarine - , -	No warning -	Torpedo -	1
SEPTEMBER 1918.		Sept.					
†Mesaba - -	6,833	1	21 miles E. ¼ N. from Tuskar Rock.	Submarine -	- No warning -	Torpedo -	20 including Master.
†City of Glasgow	6,545	1	21 miles E. ¼ N. from Tuskar Rock.	Submarine -	- No warning -	Torpedo -	12
†San Andres -	3,314	2	40 miles N. by W. from Port Said.	Submarine -	- No warning -	Torpedo -	—
†Highcliffe -	3,238	3	13 miles S.E. from Tuskar Rock.	Submarine -	- No warning -	Torpedo -	1
†War Firth -	3,112	4	33 miles S. ¾ W. from the Lizard.	Submarine -	- No warning -	Torpedo -	11
†Arum - -	3,681	4	40 miles E. from Pantellaria.	Submarine -	- No warning -	Torpedo -	—
†Audax - -	975	6	6½ miles E. by N. from N. Cheek, Robin Hood Bay.	Submarine -	- No warning -	Torpedo -	3
†Milly - -	2,964	6	2¼ miles W. ¾ S. from Tintagell Head.	Submarine -	- No warning -	Torpedo -	2
†Bellbank - -	3,250	7	25 miles S.S.W. from Planier Island.	Submarine -	- No warning -	Torpedo -	1
†Ruysdael - -	3,478	7	228 miles W. ¾ S. from Ushant.	Submarine -	- No warning -	Torpedo -	12 including Master.
†Missanabie -	12,469	9	52 miles S. by E. ½ E. from Daunts Rock.	Submarine -	- No warning -	Torpedo -	45
†War Arabis -	5,183	9	88 miles N. by E. ¼ E. from Cape Sigli.	Submarine -	- No warning -	Torpedo -	—
†Galway Castle -	7,988	12	160 miles S.W. ½ S. from the Fastnet.	Submarine -	- No warning -	Torpedo -	143
†Setter - -	956	13	6 miles N.W. by N. from Corsewall Point.	Submarine -	- No warning -	Torpedo -	9 including Master.
†Buffalo - -	286	13	Off Corsewall Point.	Submarine -	- No warning -	Torpedo -	10 including Master.
†M. J. Craig -	691	13	7 miles N.E. ½ E. from Black Head, Belfast.	Submarine -	- No warning -	Torpedo -	4
Aghios Nicolaos (S.V.).	113	14	10 miles S.E. from Paphos.	Submarine -	- Captured -	Bomb -	—

Name.	Gross Tons.	Date.	Position.	Cause of Loss.	How attacked.	How sunk.	Lives lost.
		1918. Sept.					
†Neotsfield -	3,821	14	1½ miles South from Skulmartin L.V.	Submarine - -	No warning -	Torpedo -	—
†Gibel-Hamam -	647	14	Off Abbotsbury, Dorset.	Submarine - -	No warning -	Torpedo -	21 including Master.
†Kendal Castle -	3,885	15	4 miles S.E. from Berry Head.	Submarine - -	No warning -	Torpedo -	18 including Master.
Joseph Fisher (S.V.).	79	15	16 miles E. by N. from Codling L.V.	Submarine - -	Captured -	Gunfire -	—
Energy (S.V.) -	89	15	18 miles E. by N. from Codling L.V.	Submarine - -	Captured -	Gunfire -	—
†Ethel - -	2,336	16	8 miles S.E. from Berry Head.	Submarine - -	No warning -	Torpedo -	—
†Madryn - -	2,244	16	5 miles N.N.E. from Trevose Head.	Submarine - -	No warning -	Torpedo -	—
†Wellington -	5,600	16	175 miles N. by W. from Cape Villano.	Submarine - -	No warning -	Torpedo -	5 including Master.
†Serula - -	1,388	16	13½ miles N.E ½ N. from Strumble Head.	Submarine - -	No warning -	Torpedo -	17 including Master.
†Tasman - -	5,023	16	220 miles N. by W. ¼ W. from Cape Villano.	Submarine - -	No warning -	Torpedo -	14 including Master.
†Philomel - -	3,050	16	12 miles S.E. by E. from Glenan Island.	Submarine - -	No warning -	Torpedo -	—
†Lord Stewart -	1,445	16	6 miles E. ½ N. from Hope's Nose.	Submarine - -	No warning -	Torpedo -	1
†Acadian - -	2,305	16	11 miles S.W. by W. from Trevose Head.	Submarine - -	No warning -	Torpedo -	25 including Master.
†Lavernock -	2,406	17	5 miles S.W. from Trevose Head.	Submarine - -	No warning -	Torpedo -	25 including Master.
†Muriel - -	1,831	17	3½ miles N.E. from Peterhead.	Submarine - -	No warning -	Torpedo -	—
Cairo (Egyptian S.V.).	254	17	110 miles N. by E. from Alexandria.	Submarine - -	Captured -	Gunfire -	—
†John O. Scott -	1,235	18	9 miles W. by N. from Trevose Head.	Submarine - -	No warning -	Torpedo -	18 including Master.
†Primo - -	1,037	18	3½ miles N.N.W. from Godrevy L.H.	Submarine - -	No warning -	Torpedo -	—
†Barrister - -	4,952	19	9 miles W. ½ N. from Chicken Rock.	Submarine - -	No warning -	Torpedo -	30
Staithes - -	336	21	1½ miles S.E. by S. ½ S. from Sunderland.	Submarine - -	No warning -	Torpedo -	4 including Master.
†Downshire -	368	21	8 miles E.S.E. from Rockabill.	Submarine - -	Captured -	Gunfire -	—
†Polesley - -	4,221	21	1 mile North from Pendeen L.H.	Submarine - -	No warning -	Torpedo -	43 including Master.
†Gorsemore -	3,079	22	44 miles S.E. ½ E. from Cape Colonne.	Submarine - -	No warning -	Torpedo -	—
†Edlington -	3,864	23	70 miles E. by S. from Cape Passero.	Submarine - -	No warning -	Torpedo -	—
†Aldershot -	2,177	23	5 miles E.S.E. from Dartmouth.	Submarine - -	No warning -	Torpedo -	1
†Hebburn -	1,938	25	14 miles South from Mine Head.	Submarine - -	No warning -	Torpedo -	6

Name.	Gross Tons.	Date.	Position.	Cause of Loss.	How attacked.	How sunk.	Lives lost.
		1918. Sept.					
†Hatasu	3,193	27	50 miles N. ¾ W. from Oran.	Submarine	No warning	Torpedo	2
†Ealdersby	3,613	28	9 miles E. ½ S. from Codling L.V.	Submarine	No warning	Torpedo	2
Benha (Egyptian S.V.).	95	28	Off Ras el Dabaa	Submarine	Captured	Gunfire	—
†Nyanza	4,053	29	14 miles N.E. by E. from the Maidens.	Submarine	No warning	Torpedo	13 including Master.
†Libourne	1,219	29	10 miles South from the Lizard.	Submarine	No warning	Torpedo	3
OCTOBER 1918.		Oct.					
†Bylands	3,309	1	150 miles N.N.W. from Cape Villano.	Submarine	Captured	Gunfire	—
†Montfort	6,578	1	170 miles W. by S. ¾ S. from Bishop Rock.	Submarine	No warning	Torpedo	5
†Bamse	1,001	2	5½ miles E. ¾ N. from the Lizard.	Submarine	No warning	Torpedo	11
†Poljames	856	2	6 miles South from the Lizard.	Submarine	No warning	Torpedo	13
†Arca	4,839	2	40 miles N.W. by W. from Tory Island.	Submarine	No warning	Torpedo	52 including Master.
†Westwood	1,968	3	5 miles S.W. ½ W. from the Lizard.	Submarine	No warning	Torpedo	1
†Ariel	3,428	3	54 miles North from Cape Tenez.	Submarine	No warning	Torpedo	—
†Eupion	3,575	3	10 miles West from Loop Head.	Submarine	No warning	Torpedo	11
†Oopack	3,883	4	110 miles East from Malta.	Submarine	No warning	Torpedo	—
Kassid Karim (Egyptian S.V.).	103	4	75 miles N. from Alexandria.	Submarine	Captured	Gunfire	—
Industrial (S.V.)	330	4	250 miles S.E. ½ S. (true) from Nantucket Island.	Submarine	Captured	Bombs	—
†Reventazon	4,050	5	14 miles W. by S. from Kassandra Point, Gulf of Salonika.	Submarine	No warning	Torpedo	15 including Master.
†Thalia	1,308	8	4 miles E.S.E. from Filey Brig.	Submarine	No warning	Torpedo	3
Hawanee (S.V.)	124	8	350 miles West (true) from Cape Finisterre.	Submarine	Captured	Bombs	—
†Leinster	2,646	10	7 miles E.S.E. from Kish L.V.	Submarine	No warning	Torpedo	176 including Master.
Hamidieh (Egyptian S.V.).	85	13	50 miles N.W. from Alexandria.	Submarine	Captured	Gunfire	—
†Dundalk	794	14	5 miles N.N.W. from Skerries, Anglesey.	Submarine	No warning	Torpedo	21 including Master.
†Pentwyn	3,587	16	20 miles N.E. by N. ¼ N. from the Smalls.	Submarine	No warning	Torpedo	1
†War Council	5,875	16	85 miles W.S.W. from Cape Matapan.	Submarine	No warning	Torpedo	—
†Bonvilston	2,866	17	9½ miles N.W. by W. from Corsewall Point.	Submarine	No warning	Torpedo	—

Name.	Gross Tons.	Date.	Position.	Cause of Loss.	How attacked.	How sunk.	Lives lost.
		1918. Oct.					
†Hunsdon - -	2,899	18	1 mile S. from Strangford Light Buoy.	Submarine - -	No warning -	Torpedo -	1
†Almerian - -	3,030	19	13 miles W. by S, from Licata, Sicily.	Mine - - -	Mine - -	Mine - -	—
Emily Millington (S.V.).	111	20	13 miles N.N.E. from South Bishop.	Submarine - -	Captured -	Gunfire -	--
†Saint Barchan -	362	21	4 miles from St. John's Point, Co. Down.	Submarine - -	No warning -	Torpedo -	8 including Master.
Moscow - -	1,622	21	Petrograd - -	Bolsheviks - -	—	Scuttled -	--
NOVEMBER 1918.							
†Surada - -	5,324	2	Port Said swept channel.	Submarine - -	No warning -	Torpedo -	—
†Murcia - -	4,871	2	12 miles North from Port Said.	Submarine - -	No warning -	Torpedo -	1

II.—BRITISH FISHING VESSELS CAPTURED OR DESTROYED BY THE ENEMY.

Name.	Tons.	Date.	Position.	Cause of Loss.	How attacked.	How sunk.	Lives lost.
AUGUST 1914.		1914. Aug.					
Tubal Cain -	227	7	50 miles W.N.W. from Stalberg, Iceland.	Kaiser Wilhelm der Grosse.	Captured -	Gunfire -	—
Marnay - -	153	22	85 miles E. by N. from Spurn.	Torpedo Boat -	Captured -	Bomb -	Crew made prisoners.
Capricornus -	194	22	85 miles E. by N. from Spurn.	Torpedo Boat -	Captured -	Not known	Crew made prisoners.
Skirbeck - -	171	22	North Sea - -	Cruiser - -	Captured -	Gunfire -	Crew made prisoners.
Wigtoft - -	155	22	North Sea - -	Cruiser - -	Captured -	Gunfire -	Crew made prisoners.
Walrus - -	159	22	North Sea - -	Cruiser - -	Captured -	Gunfire -	Crew made prisoners.
Flavian - -	186	22	North Sea - -	Torpedo Boat -	Captured -	Not known	Crew made prisoners.
Julian - -	185	22	North Sea - -	Torpedo Boat -	Captured -	Not known	Crew made prisoners.
Indian - -	185	22	North Sea - -	Torpedo Boat -	Captured -	Not known	Crew made prisoners.
Pegasus - -	155	24–26	North Sea - -	Torpedo Boat -	Captured -	Not known	Crew made prisoners.
Chameleon -	132	24–26	North Sea - -	Torpedo Boat -	Captured -	Not known	Crew made prisoners.
Rideo - -	230	24–26	North Sea - -	Torpedo Boat -	Captured -	Not known	Crew made prisoners.

Name.	Tons.	Date.	Position.	Cause of Loss.	How attacked.	How sunk.	Lives lost.
		1914. Aug.					
Argonaut	225	24–26	North Sea -	Torpedo Boat	Captured	Not known	Crew made prisoners.
Lobelia	147	24–26	North Sea -	Torpedo Boat	Captured	Not known	Crew made prisoners.
Harrier	208	24–26	North Sea -	Torpedo Boat	Captured	Not known	Crew made prisoners.
Pollux	182	24–26	North Sea -	Torpedo Boat	Captured	Not known	Crew made prisoners.
Porpoise	159	25	70 miles E.N.E. from Inner Dowsing L.V.	Torpedo Boat	Captured	Bomb	Crew made prisoners.
Lindsey	144	25	70 miles E.N.E. from Inner Dowsing L.V.	Torpedo Boat	Captured	Bomb	Crew made prisoners.
Kesteven	150	25	69 miles E. by N. from Inner Dowsing L.V.	Torpedo Boat	Captured	Bomb	Crew made prisoners.
Rhine	117	25	North Sea -	Torpedo Boat	Captured	Not known	Crew made prisoners.
Zenobia	152	25	North Sea -	Torpedo Boat	Captured	Not known	Crew made prisoners.
Valiant	198	25	Off Whitby	Torpedo Boat	Captured	Not known	Crew made prisoners.
Mersey	196	25	North Sea -	Torpedo Boat	Captured	Not known	Crew made prisoners.
Seti	169	26	North Sea -	Torpedo Boat	Captured	Not known	Crew made prisoners.
St. Cuthbert	189	24–26	70 miles E.N.E. from Spurn.	Torpedo Boat	Captured	Not known	Crew made prisoners.
Barley Rig	70	27	Off Tyne -	Mine -	Mine -	Mine -	5
SEPTEMBER 1914.		Sept.					
Ajax	120	2	Off the mouth of the Humber.	Mine -	Mine -	Mine -	9 including Skipper.
Fittonia	146	2	27 miles E. by S. from Spurn.	Mine -	Mine -	Mine -	7
Imperialist	195	6	40 miles E.N.E. from Tyne	Mine -	Mine -	Mine -	2
Revigo	230	7	25 miles E. ½ N. from Spurn.	Mine -	Mine -	Mine -	—
Kilmarnock	165	22	31 miles E. from Spurn.	Mine -	Mine -	Mine -	6
Rebono	176	23	25 miles E. by N. from Spurn L.V.	Mine -	Mine -	Mine -	1
OCTOBER 1914.		Oct.					
Rosella	243	29	25 miles S.E. from Tyne.	Mine -	Mine -	Mine -	2
Our Tom	40	29	45 miles S.E. from Southwold.	Mine -	Mine -	Mine -	3
NOVEMBER 1914.		Nov.					
Fraternal	100	3	16 miles N.E. by N from Lowestoft.	Mine -	Mine -	Mine -	3
Will and Maggie	100	3	17 miles E. by N. from Lowestoft.	Mine -	Mine -	Mine -	6

Name.	Tons.	Date.	Position.	Cause of Loss.	How attacked.	How sunk.	Lives lost.
		1914. Nov.					
Copious - -	100	3	15 miles E. by S. from Yarmouth.	Mine - - -	Mine - -	Mine - -	9 including Skipper.
Speculator - - (Smack).	60	10	Near Smith's Knoll	Mine - - -	Mine - -	Mine - -	5
Seymolicus -	50	18	12 miles E. by N. ½ N. from Smith's Knoll.	Mine - - -	Mine - -	Mine -	9 including Skipper.
Lord Carnarvon -	50	20	Off Yarmouth -	Mine - - -	Mine - -	Mine -	10 including Skipper.

DECEMBER 1914.

Name.	Tons.	Date.	Position.	Cause of Loss.	How attacked.	How sunk.	Lives lost.
		Dec.					
Earl Howard -	226	11	90 miles N.E. by N. from Spurn L.V.	Mine (?) - -	Mine (?) -	Mine (?) -	9 including Skipper.
Wayside Flower (Motor).	35	16	Off Hartlepool -	German bombarding squadron.	Gunfire -	Gunfire -	
Constance (Motor)	40	16	Off Hartlepool -	German bombarding squadron.	Gunfire -	Gunfire -	
Manx Queen -	219	16	North Sea - -	Torpedo boat -	Captured -	Not known	Crew made prisoners.
Ocana - -	260	23	75 miles N.E. by E. from Flamborough Head.	Mine - - -	Mine - -	Mine - -	9

JANUARY 1915.

Name.	Tons.	Date.	Position.	Cause of Loss.	How attacked.	How sunk.	Lives lost.
		1915. Jan.					
Windsor - -	172	22	55 miles E. from Spurn Point.	Mine - - -	Mine - -	Mine - -	—
Golden Oriole -	50	22	37 miles E. by N. from Lowestoft.	Mine - - -	Mine - -	Mine - -	.—

MARCH 1915.

Name.	Tons.	Date.	Position.	Cause of Loss.	How attacked.	How sunk.	Lives lost.
		Mar.					
Sapphire - -	289	1	Off Filey - -	Mine - - -	Mine - -	Mine - -	1

APRIL 1915.

Name.	Tons.	Date.	Position.	Cause of Loss.	How attacked.	How sunk.	Lives lost.
		April					
Jason - -	176	1	40 miles N.E. by E. from Tyne.	Submarine - -	Captured -	Bomb -	.—
Gloxinia - -	145	1	40 miles N.E. by E. from Tyne.	Submarine - -	Captured -	Bomb -	—
Nellie - -	109	1	35 miles N.E. by E. from Tyne.	Submarine - -	Captured -	Bomb -	—
Acantha - -	322	5	25 miles E. by N. from Longstone.	Submarine - -	Captured -	Torpedo -	—
Zarina - -	154	7	72 miles E. by N. from Spurn L.V.	Submarine - -	No warning -	Torpedo -	9 including Skipper.
Vanilla - -	158	18	53 miles E. by S. from Inner Dowsing L.V.	Submarine - -	No warning -	Torpedo -	9 including Skipper.
Glencarse - -	188	18-20	Between Shetlands and Aberdeen.	Submarine - -	Captured -	Reported taken to Germany.	Crew made prisoners.
St. Lawrence -	196	22	88 miles E. ½ N. from Spurn L.V.	Submarine - -	Captured -	Bomb -	2
Cancer - -	183	22	North Sea - -	Probably T.B. -	Captured -	Not known	Crew made prisoners.
Recolo - -	170	26	60 miles E. by N. from Spurn Point.	Mine - - -	Mine - -	Mine - -	2
Lilydale - -	129	28	37 miles E. from St. Abbs Head.	Submarine - -	Captured -	Bomb -	.—

Name.	Tons.	Date.	Position.	Cause of Loss.	How attacked.	How sunk.	Lives lost.
MAY 1915.		1915. May					
St. George - -	215	2	65 miles E. ½ N. from Aberdeen.	Submarine - -	Gunfire -	Gunfire -	Crew made prisoners.
Martaban - -	148	2	22 miles E. ½ N. from Aberdeen.	Submarine - -	Captured -	Gunfire -	—
Cruiser - -	146	2	50 miles S.E. from Aberdeen.	Submarine - -	Gunfire -	Gunfire -	4 including Skipper.
Sunray - -	167	2	56 miles N.N.E. from Longstone.	Submarine - -	Captured -	Gunfire -	—
Mercury - -	222	2	14 miles E. ½ N. from Aberdeen.	Submarine - -	Captured -	Gunfire -	—
St. Louis No. 1 -	211	2	60 miles E. by N. ½ N. from May Is.	Submarine - -	Captured -	Gunfire -	—
Iolanthe - -	179	3	140 miles E.N.E. from Hornsea.	Submarine - -	Captured -	Bomb -	—
Hero - - -	173	3	150 miles E.N.E. from Hornsea.	Submarine - -	Captured -	Bomb -	—
Northward Ho ! -	180	3	145 miles E.N.E. from Hornsea.	Submarine - -	Captured -	Bomb -	—
Scottish Queen -	125	3	50 miles E.S.E. from Aberdeen.	Submarine - -	Captured -	Gunfire -	—
Coquet - -	176	3	160 miles E.N.E. from Spurn.	Submarine - -	Captured -	Bomb -	—
Progress - -	273	3	160 miles E.N.E. from Spurn.	Submarine - -	Captured -	Bomb -	—
Hector - -	179	3	160 miles E.N.E. from Spurn.	Submarine - -	Captured -	Gunfire -	—
Bob White - -	192	3	155 miles N.E. by E. ½ E. from Spurn.	Submarine - -	Captured -	Gunfire -	—
Uxbridge - -	164	3	North Sea - -	Mine - - -	Mine - -	Mine - -	—
Rugby - -	205	4	100 miles N.E. from Spurn.	Submarine - -	Captured -	Bomb -	—
Sceptre - -	166	5	40 miles S.E. by S. from Peterhead.	Submarine - -	Captured -	Gunfire -	—
Straton - -	198	5	40 miles E. from Hartlepool.	Submarine - -	Captured -	Gunfire -	—
Merrie Islington -	147	6	6 miles N.N.E. from Whitby Rock Buoy.	Submarine - -	Captured -	Bomb -	—
Don - - -	151	6	100 miles E. by S. from Spurn.	Mine - - -	Mine - -	Mine - -	7
Benington - -	131	7	10 miles S.E. from Peterhead.	Submarine - -	Captured -	Gunfire -	—
Hellenic - -	159	8	98 miles E. by S. from Spurn.	Mine - - -	Mine - -	Mine - -	3
King Charles -	163	17	N.W. corner of Dogger Bank.	Torpedo boat	Captured -	Not known	Crew made prisoners.
Euclid - -	165	18	N.W. corner of Dogger Bank.	Torpedo boat	Captured -	Not known	Crew made prisoners.
Duke of Wellington.	182	18	N.W. corner of Dogger Bank.	Torpedo boat	Captured -	Not known	Crew made prisoners.
Titania - -	179	18	N.W. corner of Dogger Bank.	Torpedo boat	Captured -	Not known	Crew made prisoners.
Crimond - -	173	19	60 miles E. from Wick.	Submarine - -	Captured -	Bomb -	—
Lucerne - -	154	19	50 miles N.E. by N. from Rattray Hd.	Submarine - -	Captured -	Bomb -	—
Chrysolite - -	222	19	25 miles S.W. by S. from Lerwick.	Submarine - -	Captured -	Bomb -	—
Angelo - -	173	21	Dogger Bank -	Mine - - -	Mine - -	Mine - -	—

Name.	Tons.	Date.	Position.	Cause of Loss.	How attacked.	How sunk.	Lives lost.
		1915. May					
Sabrina - -	179	21	160 miles E.N.E. from Spurn L.V.	Mine - - -	Mine - -	Mine - -	9 including Skipper.
Condor - -	151	29	30 miles N.E. from Scarborough.	Mine - - -	Mine - -	Mine - -	9 including Skipper.
JUNE 1915.		June					
Victoria - -	155	1	145 miles W. by S. from St. Ann's Head.	Submarine - -	Captured -	Bomb -	6 including Skipper.
Hirose - -	274	2	130 miles W. by S. ½ S. from Lundy Island.	Submarine - -	Captured -	Bomb -	—
Ena May - -	90	3	60 miles S.W. by S. ½ S. from Sumburgh Head.	Submarine - -	Captured -	Gunfire -	—
Chrysoprasus -	119	3	45 miles E. by S. from Papa, Stronsay.	Submarine - -	Captured -	Gunfire -	—
Dogberry - -	214	3	120 miles N.N.E. from Aberdeen.	Submarine - -	Captured -	Bomb -	—
Kathleen - -	92	3	40 miles E.S.E. from Start Point, Orkney.	Submarine - -	Captured -	Bomb -	—
E. & C. (Smack) -	60	3	40 miles S.E. by E. from Lowestoft.	Submarine - -	Captured -	Bomb -	—
Boy Horace (Smack).	69	3	50 miles S.E. from Lowestoft.	Submarine - -	Captured -	Bomb -	—
Strathbran -	163	3	35 miles E.S.E. from Pentland Skerries.	Submarine - -	Captured -	Gunfire -	—
Economy (Smack)	69	4	50 miles S.E. from Lowestoft.	Submarine - -	Captured -	Bomb -	—
Petrel - -	187	4	55 miles N.N.E. ½ E. from Buchanness.	Submarine - -	Captured -	Gunfire -	—
Cortes - -	174	4	50 miles E.S.E. from Copinsay.	Submarine - -	Captured -	Bomb -	—
Evening Star -	120	4	50 miles E.S.E. from Copinsay.	Submarine - -	Captured -	Gunfire -	—
Ebenezer - -	113	4	117 miles S.W. by S. ½ S. from Out Skerries.	Submarine - -	Captured -	Gunfire -	—
Explorer - -	156	4	73 miles N.E. by N. from Buchanness.	Submarine - -	Captured -	Gunfire -	—
Persimon -	255	5	50 miles N.E. from Buchanness.	Submarine - -	Captured -	Gunfire -	—
Gazehound -	138	5	50 miles E. by N. from Aberdeen.	Submarine - -	Captured -	Gunfire -	—
Curlew - -	134	5	50 miles E. by N. from Aberdeen.	Submarine - -	Captured -	Gunfire -	—
Bardolph - -	215	5	115 miles S. by W. from Sumburgh Head.	Submarine - -	Captured -	Gunfire -	—
Star of the West -	197	5	55 miles N.E. ½ N. from Buchanness.	Submarine - -	Captured -	Gunfire -	—
Japonica - -	145	5	45 miles E. from Kinnaird Head.	Submarine - -	Captured -	Gunfire -	—
Arctic - -	169	5	65 miles E.S.E. from Spurn.	Submarine - -	Gunfire -	Gunfire -	4 including Skipper.
Dromio - -	208	6	35 miles N.E. by E. from Buchanness.	Submarine - -	Captured -	Scuttled -	—
Pentland - -	204	7	75 miles E.N.E. from Hornsea.	Submarine - -	Captured -	Gunfire -	—
Nottingham -	165	7	70 miles N.E. from Spurn.	Submarine - -	Captured -	Gunfire -	—

Name.	Tons.	Date.	Position.	Cause of Loss.	How attacked.	How sunk.	Lives lost.
		1915. June					
Velocity - -	186	7	75 miles N.E. from Spurn.	Submarine - -	Captured -	Gunfire -	—
Saturn - -	183	7	86 miles N.E. from Spurn.	Submarine - · -	Captured -	Gunfire -	—
Castor - -	182	9	85 miles N.E. by E. from Spurn.	Submarine - -	Captured -	Gunfire -	—
Tunisian - -	211	9	95 miles N.E. by N. from Spurn.	Submarine - -	Captured -	Gunfire -	—
J. Leyman -	197	9	100 miles E. by N. from Spurn.	Submarine - -	Captured -	Gunfire -	—
Cardiff - -	163	9	90 miles N.E. by E. from Spurn.	Submarine - -	Captured -	Gunfire -	—
Edward (Smack)	52	9	48 miles E. by S. from Lowestoft.	Submarine - -	Captured -	Bomb -	—
Qui Vive (Smack)	50	9	48 miles E. by S. from Lowestoft.	Submarine - -	Captured -	Bomb -	—
Britannia (Smack)	43	9	55 miles E. from Lowestoft.	Submarine - -	Captured -	Bomb -	—
Welfare (Smack) -	45	9	50 miles E.S.E. from Lowestoft.	Submarine - -	Captured -	Bomb -	—
Laurestina (Smack).	48	9	30 miles N.N.W. from Maas L.V.	Submarine - -	Captured -	Bomb -	—
Intrepid (Smack)	59	10	60 miles S.E. from Lowestoft.	Submarine - -	Captured -	Bomb -	—
Waago - -	154	11	80 miles N.E. by N. from Spurn.	Submarine - -	Captured -	Bomb -	—
Plymouth - -	165	11	67 miles N.E. ½ N. from Spurn.	Submarine - -	Captured -	Gunfire -	—
Dovey - -	160	11	50 miles E. by S. from Spurn.	Mine - - -	Mine - -	Mine -	9 including Skipper.
Queen Alexandra	208	13	8 miles E. by S. ½ S. from Tod Head.	Mine - - -	Mine - -	Mine -	—
Argyll - -	280	15	¼ mile from Sunk L.V.	Submarine - -	No warning -	Torpedo -	7 including Skipper.
Premier - -	169	20	75 miles N. by W. from Troup Head.	Submarine - -	Captured -	Gunfire -	—
Ugiebrae - -	79	23	35 miles E.N.E. from Out Skerries.	Submarine - -	Captured -	Gunfire -	—
Elizabeth - -	94	23	40 miles E.N.E. from Out Skerries.	Submarine - -	Captured -	Gunfire -	—
Lebanon - -	111	23	30 miles E. ½ N. from Muckle Flugga.	Submarine - -	Captured -	Gunfire -	—
Quiet Waters -	63	23	35 miles E. by N. from Balta Sound.	Submarine - -	Captured -	Gunfire -	—
Josephine - -	85	23	40 miles N.E. by E. ½ E. from Out Skerries.	Submarine - -	Captured -	Gunfire -	—
Uffa - - -	79	23	45 miles E.N.E. from Out Skerries.	Submarine - -	Captured -	Gunfire -	—
Viceroy - -	150	23	50 miles E.N.E. from Out Skerries.	Submarine - -	Captured -	Gunfire -	—
Research - -	89	23	42 miles N.E. from Out Skerries.	Submarine - -	Captured -	Gunfire -	—
Primrose - -	91	23	40 miles N.E. by E. from Out Skerries.	Submarine - -	Captured -	Gunfire -	—
Piscatorial - -	84	23	41 miles E.N.E. from Out Skerries.	Submarine - -	Captured -	Gunfire -	—

Name.	Tons.	Date.	Position.	Cause of Loss.	How attacked.	How sunk.	Lives lost.
		1915. June					
Four - - -	84	23	45 miles N.E. by E. ¼E. from Out Skerries.	Submarine - -	Captured -	Gunfire -	—
J. M. & S. - -	78	23	42 miles E.N.E. from Out Skerries.	Submarine - -	Captured -	Gunfire -	—
Star of Bethlehem	77	23	40 miles E.N.E. from Out Skerries.	Submarine - -	Captured -	Gunfire -	—
Vine - - -	110	24	30 miles N.E. by E. from Out Skerries.	Submarine - -	Captured -	Gunfire -	—
Monarda - -	87	24	41 miles E.N.E. from Out Skerries.	Submarine - -	Captured -	Gunfire -	—
Commander -	149	24	49 miles E. from Balta Sound.	Submarine - -	Captured -	Gunfire -	—
Campania - -	167	26	60 miles N. by W. from Hoy Head.	Submarine - -	Captured -	Gunfire -	—

JULY 1915.

Name.	Tons.	Date.	Position.	Cause of Loss.	How attacked.	How sunk.	Lives lost.
		July					
Cheshire - -	148	7	50 miles E. by S. from Spurn.	Mine - - -	Mine - -	Mine - -	8
Syrian - -	176	11	45 miles E.N.E. from Hornsea.	Submarine - -	Captured -	Gunfire -	—
Hainton - -	156	11	45 miles N.E. by E. from Hornsea.	Submarine - -	Captured -	Gunfire -	—
Purple Heather (Smack).	42	12	23 miles S.E. by S. from Lowestoft.	Submarine - -	Captured -	Bomb -	—
Merlin (Smack) -	47	12	20 miles E.S.E. from Lowestoft.	Submarine - -	Captured -	Bomb -	—
Speedwell (Smack)	38	12	19 miles S.E. by E. from Lowestoft.	Submarine - -	Captured -	Bomb -	—
Woodbine (Smack)	29	12	18 miles S.E. from Lowestoft.	Submarine - -	Captured -	Burnt -	—
Star of Peace -	180	22	114 miles N. ½ W. from Hoy Head.	Submarine - -	Captured -	Gunfire -	—
King Athelstan -	159	22	100 miles N. by W. from Hoy Head.	Submarine - -	Captured -	Bomb -	—
Sutton - -	332	23	130 miles N.N.W. from Cape Wrath.	Submarine - -	Captured -	Gunfire -	—
Hermione - -	210	23	135 miles N.N.W. from Cape Wrath.	Submarine - -	Captured -	Gunfire -	—
Honoria - -	207	23	35 miles N.N.W. from Cape Wrath.	Submarine - -	Captured -	Gunfire -	—
Roslin - -	128	24	60 miles N. by W. from Butt of Lewis.	Submarine - -	Captured -	Gunfire -	—
Strathmore - -	163	24	60 miles N. by W. from Butt of Lewis.	Submarine - -	Captured -	Gunfire -	—
Anglia - -	107	24	25 miles N.W. from Sulisker.	Submarine - -	Captured -	Gunfire -	—
Cassio - -	172	24	123 miles N.W. by W. from Hoy Head.	Submarine - -	Captured -	Gunfire -	—
Perseus - -	155	24	60 miles E. from Spurn.	Mine - - -	Mine - -	Mine - -	10 including Skipper.
Henry Charles (Smack).	41	24	30 miles E.N.E. from Lowestoft.	Submarine - -	Captured -	Bomb -	—
Kathleen (Smack)	46	24	30 miles E.N.E. from Lowestoft.	Submarine - -	Captured -	Bomb -	—

Name.	Tons.	Date.	Position.	Cause of Loss.	How attacked.	How sunk.	Lives lost.
		1915. July					
Activity (Smack)	56	24	30 miles E.N.E. from Lowestoft.	Submarine - -	Captured -	Bomb -	—
Prosper (Smack)	45	24	30 miles E.N.E. from Lowestoft.	Submarine - -	Captured -	Bomb -	--
Emblem - -	157	25	60 miles N. by W. from Hoy Head.	Submarine - -	Captured -	Gunfire -	—
Honoria - -	179	25	100 miles W.N.W. from N. Ronaldshay.	Submarine - -	Captured -	Gunfire .	—
Cydonia - -	259	25	70 miles N. by W. from Hoy Head.	Submarine - -	Captured -	Gunfire -	—
Gadwall - -	192	25	70 miles N. by W. from Hoy Head.	Submarine - -	Captured -	Gunfire -	—
Celtic - -	264	25	70 miles N. by W. from Hoy Head.	Submarine - -	Captured -	Gunfire -	—
Westward Ho! (Smack).	47	27	25 miles S.E. from Lowestoft.	Submarine - -	Captured -	Bomb -	—
Salacia (Smack) -	48	27	15 miles E. from Lowestoft.	Submarine - -	Captured -	Bomb -	--
Iceni (Smack) -	44	27	15 miles E. from Lowestoft.	Submarine - -	Captured .	Bomb -	--
Young Percy (Smack).	45	28	30 miles E. by N. from Lowestoft.	Submarine - -	Captured -	Bomb -	—
Coriander (Smack).	46	30	20 miles E.S.E. from Lowestoft.	Submarine - -	Captured -	Bomb -	—
Fitzgerald (Smack).	51	30	30 miles E.S.E from Lowestoft.	Submarine - -	Captured -	Bomb -	—
Achieve (Smack)	43	30	35 miles E. by N. from Lowestoft.	Submarine - -	Captured -	Bomb -	—
Quest (Smack) -	46	30	35 miles E. by N. from Lowestoft.	Submarine - -	Captured -	Bomb -	—
Prospector (Smack).	59	30	28 miles E.N.E. from Lowestoft.	Submarine - -	Captured -	Bomb -	—
Strive (Smack) -	63	30	35 miles E. by N. from Lowestoft.	Submarine - -	Captured -	Bomb -	—
Athena (Smack) -	45	30	35 miles E. by N. from Lowestoft.	Submarine - -	Captured -	Bomb -	—
Venture (Smack)	44	30	27 miles E.N.E. from Lowestoft.	Submarine - -	Captured -	Bomb -	—
Tors - - -	158	30	43 miles E. from Spurn.	Mine - - -	Mine - -	Mine - -	8
AUGUST 1915.		Aug.					
Alert (Smack) -	59	1	18 miles N.E. from Lowestoft.	Submarine - -	Captured -	Burnt -	—
Lark (Fishing Boat).	—	1	Off Lowestoft -	Submarine - -	— .	—	—
Grimbarian -	146	4	56 miles E. by N. from Spurn.	Mine - -	Mine - -	Mine - -	6
Challenger (Smack).	50	4	23 miles E. by N. from Lowestoft.	Submarine - -	Captured -	Bomb -	—
Heliotrope (Smack).	28	4	23 miles E. by N. from Lowestoft.	Submarine - -	Captured -	Bomb -	—
Hesperus (Smack)	57	6	37 miles E.N.E. from Lowestoft.	Submarine - -	Captured -	Bomb -	—
Fisherman (Smack).	24	6	37 miles E.N.E. from Lowestoft.	Submarine - -	Captured -	Bomb -	—
C. E. S. (Smack)	47	6	42 miles E.N.E. from Lowestoft.	Submarine - -	Captured -	Bomb -	—
Ivan (Smack) -	44	6	42 miles E.N.E. from Lowestoft.	Submarine - -	Captured -	Bomb -	—
Ocean Queen -	185	6	23 miles N. by W. from Muckle Flugga.	Submarine - -	Captured -	Bomb -	—
Westminster -	252	6	20 miles E.S.E. from Muckle Flugga.	Submarine - -	Captured -	Bomb -	—
Xmas Rose (Smack).	27	6	Off Lowestoft -	Submarine - -	Captured -	Bomb -	—
Arbor Vitæ (Smack)	26	8	35 miles N.E. by N. from Lowestoft.	Submarine - -	Captured -	Bomb -	—

Name.	Tons.	Date.	Position.	Cause of Loss.	How attacked.	How sunk.	Lives lost.
		1915. **Aug.**					
Thrush - -	264	9	50 miles W. from Eagle Island.	Submarine - -	Captured -	Bomb -	—
Esperance (Smack).	46	10	17 miles N.E. by E. from Cromer.	Submarine - -	Captured -	Gunfire -	—
Young Admiral (Smack).	60	11	17 miles E. by N. from Cromer.	Submarine - -	Captured -	Bomb -	—
Trevear (Smack)	47	11	17 miles E. by N. from Cromer.	Submarine - -	Captured -	Bomb -	—
Welcome (Smack)	56	11	17 miles E. by N. from Cromer.	Submarine - -	Captured -	Bomb -	—
Palm (Smack) -	47	11	17 miles E. by N. from Cromer.	Submarine - -	Captured -	Bomb -	—
Illustrious (Smack).	59	11	17 miles E. by N. from Cromer.	Submarine - -	Captured -	Bomb -	—
George Crabbe (Smack).	42	11	16 miles E. by N. from Cromer.	Submarine - -	Captured -	Bomb -	—
George Borrow (Smack).	62	11	15 miles E.N.E. from Cromer.	Submarine - -	Captured -	Bomb -	—
Ocean's Gift (Smack).	60	11	36 miles E. from Cromer.	Submarine - -	Captured -	Bomb -	—
Humphrey (Smack).	41	11	48 miles E. $\frac{3}{4}$ S. from Cromer.	Submarine - -	Captured -	Bomb -	—.
Leader (Smack) -	57	11	20 miles E. by N. from Lowestoft.	Submarine - -	Captured -	Bomb -	—
Sunflower (Smack)	60	12	30 miles E. by N. from Lowestoft.	Submarine - -	Captured -	Bomb -	—
Amethyst (Smack)	57	13	7 miles E.S.E. from Lowestoft.	Submarine - -	Captured -	Bomb -	—
E. M. W. (Smack)	47	13	29 miles N.E. by N. from Cromer.	Submarine - -	Captured -	Bomb -	—
J. W. F. T. (Smack).	60	13	29 miles N.E. by N. from Cromer.	Submarine - -	Captured -	Bomb -	—
Gloria - -	130	14	55 miles E. by N. from Aberdeen.	Submarine - -	Captured -	Gunfire -	--
White City (Smack).	45	14	At Cromer Knoll	Submarine - -	Captured -	Bomb -	—
Bona Fide (Smack)	59	14	35 miles E.N.E. from Lowestoft.	Submarine - -	Captured -	Bomb -	—
Repeat - -	107	17	18 miles W. by S. from Bardsey Island.	Submarine - -	Captured -	Gunfire -	--
George Baker -	91	17	45 miles N. from Bishop Rock.	Submarine - -	Captured -	Gunfire -	—
Commander Boyle	290	23	40 miles N. by W. from Rattray Head.	Mine - - -	Mine - -	Mine - -	3
Boy Bert (Smack)	57	23	50 miles E. from Lowestoft.	Submarine - -	Captured -	Bomb -	—
Integrity (Smack)	52	23	24 miles E.S.E. from Cromer.	Submarine - -	Captured -	Bomb -	—
Young Frank (Smack).	49	23	58 miles N.E. by E. $\frac{1}{2}$ E. from Lowestoft.	Submarine - -	Captured -	Bomb -	—
SEPTEMBER 1915.		**Sept.**					
Emblem (Smack)	50	7	44 miles E.S.E. from Lowestoft.	Submarine - -	Captured -	Bomb -	--
Victorious (Smack)	43	7	44 miles· from Lowestoft.	Submarine - -	Captured -	Bomb -	—
Constance (Smack)	57	7	44 miles E.S.E. from Lowestoft.	Submarine - -	Captured -	Bomb -	—
Emmanuel (Smack).	44	7	44 miles E.S.E. from Lowestoft.	Submarine - -	Captured -	Bomb -	—
Devonian - -	128	9	30 miles N.E. $\frac{1}{2}$ N. from Spurn L.V.	Mine (?) -	Mine (?) -	Mine (?) -	9 including Skipper.
Boy Ernie (Smack)	47	10	58 miles E. from Cromer.	Submarine - -	Captured -	Bomb -	—
Nimrod (Smack) ·	51	10	45 miles E. by S. from Lowestoft.	Submarine - -	Captured -	Bomb -	—
Albion (Smack) -	25	30	8 miles S. by W. from Berry Head.	Mine - - -	Mine - -	Mine -	3 including Skipper.

Name.	Tons.	Date.	Position.	Cause of Loss.	How attacked.	How sunk.	Lives lost.
NOVEMBER 1915.		**1915.** Nov.					
King William -	162	5	125 miles E. by N. from Spurn L.V.	Mine - - -	Mine - -	Mine - -	2 including Skipper.
JANUARY 1916.		**1916.** Jan.					
Foam Crest (Smack).	46	18	25 miles S.E. by E. from Lowestoft.	Submarine - -	Captured -	Bomb -	—
Evelyn (Smack) -	55	18	35 miles S.E. by E. from Lowestoft.	Submarine - -	Captured -	Bomb -	—
Sunshine (Smack)	52	18	28 miles S.E. from Lowestoft.	Submarine - -	Captured -	Bomb -	—
Crystal (Smack) -	57	27	25 miles E.S.E. from Southwold.	Submarine - -	Captured -	Bomb -	—
Radium (Smack)	59	31	25 miles S.E. by E. from Lowestoft.	Submarine - -	Captured -	Bomb -	—
Arthur William (Smack).	44	31	24 miles S.E. from Lowestoft.	Submarine - -	Captured -	Bomb -	—
Hilda (Smack) -	44	31	25 miles E.S.E. from Southwold.	Submarine - -	Captured -	Bomb -	—
FEBRUARY 1916.		Feb.					
W. E. Brown (Smack).	34	21	20 miles S.E. from Lowestoft.	Submarine - -	Captured -	Bomb -	—
Oleander (Smack)	34	21	28 miles S.E. from Lowestoft.	Submarine - -	Captured -	Bomb -	—
MARCH 1916.		Mar.					
Reliance (Smack)	54	1	25 miles E. by S. from Lowestoft.	Submarine - -	Captured -	Bomb -	—
Try On (Smack)	46	1	26 miles E. by S. from Lowestoft.	Submarine - -	Captured -	Bomb -	—
Harold (Smack)	56	1	18 miles E. from Lowestoft.	Submarine - -	Captured -	Bomb -	—
Trevose (Smack)	46	1	18 miles E. by N. from Lowestoft.	Submarine - -	Captured -	Bomb -	—
Springflower (Smack)	59	6	28 miles East from Lowestoft.	Submarine - -	Captured -	Bomb -	—
Young Harry (Smack).	43	6	35 miles E. from Lowestoft.	Submarine - -	Captured -	Bomb -	—
Khartoum - -	303	26	6 miles N.E. from Longstone L.V.	Mine - - -	Mine - -	Mine - -	9
APRIL 1916.		April					
Alfred (Smack) -	24	25	27 miles E. by S. from Lowestoft.	Submarine - -	Captured -	Bomb -	—
Horus - -	173	25	North Sea - -	Enemy Squadron -	Captured -	Not known	Crew prisoners.
Blessing (Motor)	19	28	16 miles E. by N. from Tyne.	Submarine - -	Captured -	Bomb -	—
MAY 1916.		May					
Research (Smack)	44	17	35 miles East from Cromer.	Submarine - -	Captured -	Bomb -	1
Wanderer (Smack).	47	17	North Sea -	Submarine - -	Captured -	Bomb -	—
Boy Percy (Smack).	46	17	North Sea - -	Submarine - -	Captured -	Bomb -	—
Boy Sam (Smack).	46	17	North Sea - -	Submarine - -	Captured -	Bomb -	—
Osprey (Motor) -	18	18	13 miles E.N.E. from Spurn L.V.	Submarine - -	Captured -	Bomb -	—

Name.	Tons.	Date.	Position.	Cause of Loss.	How attacked.	How sunk.	Lives lost.
JULY 1916.		1916. July					
Queen Bee (Smack).	34	4	28 miles N.E. from Scarborough.	Submarine - -	Captured -	Bomb -	1 (Skipper)
Annie Anderson - (Motor).	77	5	16 miles E. by S. from the Tyne.	Submarine - -	Captured -	Bomb -	—
Peep o' Day -	52	5	25 miles E.N.E. from the Tyne.	Submarine - -	Captured -	Bomb -	—
Petunia - -	58	6	18 miles E.S.E. from the Tyne.	Submarine - -	Captured -	Bomb -	1
Nancy Hunnam -	58	6	24 miles E. by S. from the Tyne.	Submarine - -	Captured -	Bomb -	—
Watchful (Motor)	52	6	23 miles S.E. by S. from the Tyne.	Submarine - -	Captured -	Bomb -	—
Newark Castle -	85	6	23 miles S.E. from the Tyne.	Submarine - -	Captured -	Bomb -	—
Girl Bessie -	62	6	23 miles S.E. by E. from the Tyne.	Submarine - -	Captured -	Bomb -	—
Staffa - -	176	10	45 miles E. by N. from the Tyne.	Submarine - -	Captured -	Bomb -	—
Florence - -	149	13	10 miles N.E. from Scarborough.	Submarine - -	Captured -	Bomb -	—
Dalhousie - -	89	13	10 miles N.N.E. from Whitby.	Submarine - -	Captured -	Bomb -	—
Mary Ann (Fishing Boat).	5	13	13 miles N. by F. from Whitby.	Submarine - -	Captured -	Scuttled -	—
Success (Fishing Boat).	6	13	13 miles N. by E. from Whitby.	Submarine - -	Captured -	Scuttled -	—
Recorder - -	149	14	16 miles N.E. by E. from the Tyne.	Submarine - -	Captured -	Bomb -	—
Langley Castle -	93	14	18 miles N.E. by E. from the Tyne.	Submarine - -	Captured -	Bomb -	—
Bute - - -	176	14	25 miles S.E. from the Tyne.	Submarine - -	Captured -	Bomb -	—
Ben Aden - -	176	14	15 miles E. from Hartlepool.	Submarine - -	Captured -	Bomb -	—
Girl's Friend -	55	14	21 miles E. from Hartlepool.	Submarine - -	Captured -	Bomb -	—
Loch Tay (Smack)	44	17	10 miles N.N.E. from N. Haisboro L.V.	Submarine - -	Captured -	Bomb -	—
Waverley (Smack)	59	17	10 miles N.N.E. from N. Haisboro L.V.	Submarine - -	Captured -	Bomb -	—
V. M. G. (Smack)	59	17	6 miles N.E. from N. Haisboro L.V.	Submarine - -	Captured -	Bomb -	—
Glance (Smack) -	60	17	10 miles E.N.E. from N. Haisboro L.V.	Submarine - -	Captured -	Bomb -	—
Gertrude (Smack)	57	17	10 miles E.N.E. from N. Haisboro L.V.	Submarine - -	Captured -	Bomb -	—
Loch Nevis (Smack).	58	17	Near Smith's Knoll.	Submarine - -	Captured -	Bomb -	—
Volunteer (Motor)	15	27	15 miles N.E. from the Tyne.	Submarine - -	Captured -	Bomb -	—
Jane Stewart (Motor).	15	27	15 miles N.E. from the Tyne.	Submarine - -	Captured -	Bomb -	—
Speedwell (Motor)	11	27	12 miles N.E. from the Tyne.	Submarine - -	Captured -	Bomb -	—
Renown - -	61	28	15 miles N.E. from the Tyne.	Submarine - -	Captured -	Bomb -	—
Andrewina (Motor)	50	28	12 miles N.E. from the Tyne.	Submarine - -	Captured -	Bomb -	—
Good Design (Motor).	40	28	15 miles N.E. by E. from the Tyne.	Submarine - -	Captured -	Bomb -	—
Spero Meliora (Motor).	11	28	15 miles N.E. from the Tyne.	Submarine - -	Captured -	Bomb -	—
Johan (Motor) -	49	28	15 miles N.E. by E. from the Tyne.	Submarine - -	Captured -	Bomb -	—

Name.	Tons.	Date.	Position.	Cause of Loss.	How attacked.	How sunk.	Lives lost.
		1916. July					
Janet Ovenstone (Motor).	15	28	13 miles E.N.E. from the Tyne.	Submarine - -	Rammed -	Rammed -	—
King James -	163	31	15 miles S.E. from the Tyne.	Submarine - -	Captured -	Bomb -	—
Braconash - -	192	31	18 miles S.E. from the Tyne.	Submarine - -	Captured -	Bomb -	—
Tatiana - -	285	31	19 miles S.E. from the Tyne.	Submarine - -	Captured -	Bomb -	—
AUGUST 1916.							
		Aug.					
Helvetia - -	167	1	5 miles E. from Seaham.	Submarine - -	Captured -	Bomb -	—
Rhodesia - -	110	1	14 miles E.S.E. from Tyne.	Submarine - -	Captured -	Bomb -	—
Smiling Morn -	126	2	10 miles E. from Coquet Island.	Submarine - -	Captured -	Bomb -	—
Twiddler - -	99	2	8 miles E. from Coquet Island.	Submarine - -	Captured -	Bomb -	—
Olympia - -	221	3	3 miles E. from Coquet Island.	Submarine - -	Captured -	Gunfire -	—
Lucania - -	92	3	7½ miles E.N.E. from Coquet Island.	Submarine - -	Captured -	Bomb -	—
Trawler Prince -	126	3	12 miles S.S.E. from Longstone Light.	Submarine - -	Captured -	Bomb -	—
Merchant Prince	130	3	14 miles S.E. by E. from Farne Islands.	Submarine - -	Captured -	Bomb -	—
Egyptian Prince -	129	5	12 miles S S.E. from Longstone Light.	Submarine - -	Captured -	Bomb -	—
St. Olive - -	202	5	11 miles E. from Coquet Island.	Submarine - -	Captured -	Bomb -	—
Loch Lomond (Smack).	42	6	18 miles E. from Yarmouth.	Submarine - -	Captured -	Gunfire -	—
Dragoon (smack)	30	20	36 miles N.E. by N. from Cromer.	Submarine - -	Captured -	Bomb -	—
Equinox - -	198	25	39 miles S.E. by E. from Humber L.V.	Mine - - -	Mine - -	Mine - -	9 including Skipper.
SEPTEMBER 1916.		1916. Sept.					
Dorado (Smack) -	36	9	20 miles S.S.E. from Start Point.	Submarine - -	Captured -	Bomb -	—
Muriel Franklin (Smack).	29	9	20 miles S.E. from Start Point.	Submarine - -	Captured -	Gunfire -	—
Consolation (Smack).	47	9	15 miles S.E. from Start Point.	Submarine - -	Captured -	Gunfire -	—
Favourite (Smack)	38	9	20 miles S.E. from Start Point.	Submarine - -	Captured -	Gunfire -	—
Mercury - -	183	23	65 miles S.E. by E. ½ E. from Spurn L.V.	Submarine - -	Captured -	Bomb -	—
Viella - -	144	23	38 miles S.E. by E. from Spurn L.V.	Submarine - -	Captured -	Bomb -	—
Restless - -	125	23	40 miles S.E. by E. from Spurn L.V.	Submarine - -	Captured -	Gunfire -	—
Beechwold - -	129	23	40 miles S.E. by E. from Spurn L.V.	Submarine - -	Gunfire -	Gunfire -	—
Weelsby - -	112	23	40 miles S.E. by E. from Spurn L.V.	Submarine - -	Captured -	Bomb -	—

Name.	Tons.	Date.	Position.	Cause of Loss.	How attacked.	How sunk.	Lives lost.
		1916. Sept					
Britannia III. -	138	23	40 miles S.E. by E. from Spurn L.V.	Submarine - -	Captured -	Gunfire -	—
Refino - -	182	23	39 miles S.E. by E. from Spurn L.V.	Submarine - -	Captured -	Gunfire -	—
Andromeda -	149	23	39 miles S.E. by E. from Spurn L.V.	Submarine - -	Captured -	Gunfire -	—
Rego - - -	176	23	40 miles S.E. by E. from Spurn L.V.	Submarine - -	Captured -	Gunfire -	—
Cockatrice - -	115	23	40 miles S.E. by E. from Spurn L.V.	Submarine - -	Captured -	Gunfire -	—
Phœnix - -	117	23	45 miles E.S.E. from Spurn L.V.	Submarine - -	Captured -	Gunfire -	—
Devonshire -	148	24	33 miles N.E. ½ N. from Spurn L.V.	Submarine -	Captured -	Gunfire -	—
Briton - -	134	24	18 miles S.E. by S. from Flamborough Head.	Submarine - -	Captured -	Gunfire -	—
Albatross - -	158	24	20 miles E. from Flamborough Head.	Submarine - -	Captured -	Gunfire -	—
Aphelion - -	197	24	20 miles E. from Flamborough Head.	Submarine - -	Captured -	Gunfire -	—
Fisher Prince -	125	24	20 miles N.E. from Scarborough.	Submarine - -	Captured -	Gunfire -	—
Otterhound -	150	24	20 miles N.E. from Scarborough.	Submarine - -	Captured -	Gunfire -	—
Otter - -	123	24	20 miles N.E. from Scarborough.	Submarine - -	Captured -	Gunfire -	—
Harrier - -	162	24	20 miles N.E. from Scarborough.	Submarine - -	Captured ·	Gunfire -	—
Tarantula - -	155	24	20 miles N.E. from Scarborough.	Submarine - -	Captured -	Gunfire -	·—
Marguerite - -	151	24	20 miles N.E. from Scarborough.	Submarine - -	Captured -	Gunfire -	—
Sunshine - -	74	24	20 miles N.E. from Scarborough.	Submarine - -	Captured -	Gunfire -	—
Loch Ness - -	176	25	20 miles N.E. from Scarborough.	Submarine - -	Captured -	Gunfire -	—
Gamecock - -	151	25	20 miles N.E. from Scarborough.	Submarine - -	Captured -	Gunfire -	—
Nil Desperandum	148	25	20 miles N.E. from Scarborough.	Submarine - -	Captured -	Bomb -	—
Quebec - -	133	25	16 miles E. by N. from Whitby.	Submarine - -	Captured -	Gunfire -	—
St. Hilda - -	94	25	20 miles N.E. from Scarborough.	Submarine - -	Captured -	Gunfire -	—
Trinidad - -	147	25	23 miles N.E. from Whitby.	Submarine - -	Captured -	Gunfire -	—
Seal - - -	135	25	33 miles E. by S. from Hartlepool.	Submarine - -	Captured -	Gunfire -	—
Cynthia - -	133	25	23 miles E. by S. ½ S. from Flamborough Head.	Submarine - -	Captured -	Gunfire -	—
Bella (Motor) -	11	25	Off Tod Head -	Submarine - -	Captured -	Not known	Crew made prisone s.

Name.	Tons.	Date.	Position.	Cause of Loss.	How attacked.	How sunk.	Lives lost.
		1916. **Sept.**					
Marjorie (Smack)	55	28	Off Smith's Knoll	Submarine - -	Captured -	Bomb -	—
Loch Ryan -	186	28	North Sea - -	Submarine - -	Reported captured.	Taken to Germany.	Crew made prisoners.
Fuchsia - -	145	—	North Sea - -	Submarine -	Captured -	Not known	Crew made prisoners.
OCTOBER 1916.		**Oct.**					
Rado - -	182	4	15 miles N.E. by E. from Spurn L.V.	Submarine - -	Captured -	Bomb -	—
Jersey - -	162	4	16 miles N.E. by E. from Spurn L.V.	Submarine - -	Captured -	Bomb -	—
Jennie Bullas (Motor).	26	4	14 miles E.N.E. from Spurn L.V.	Submarine - -	Captured -	Bomb -	—
Rover - -	42	5	10 miles E.N.E. from Spurn L.V.	Submarine - -	Captured -	Bomb -	—
Magnus - -	154	8	40 miles E.N.E. from Longstone.	Submarine - -	Captured -	Bomb -	—
Effort - -	159	22	30 miles E.N.E. from Buchanness.	Submarine - -	Captured -	Gunfire -	—
Titan - -	171	26	56 miles S.E. from Girdleness.	Submarine - -	Captured -	Gunfire -	—
Nellie Bruce -	79	30	Off Beru Fiord, Iceland.	Submarine - -	Gunfire -	Gunfire -	—
Floreal - -	163	30	20 miles N. by W. from Flannan Islands.	Submarine - -	Captured -	Bomb -	—
NOVEMBER 1916.		**Nov.**					
Kyoto - -	282	2	90 miles S.W. by W. from Fastnet.	Submarine - -	Captured -	Gunfire -	—
Caswell - -	245	2	90 miles S.W. by W. from Fastnet.	Submarine - -	Captured -	Bombs -	—
Harfat Castle -	274	2	90 miles S.W. by W. from Fastnet.	Submarine - -	Captured -	Bombs -	—
Vineyard - -	126	8	13 miles S. by E. $\frac{3}{4}$ E. from Aberdeen.	Mine - - -	Mine - -	Mine - -	8 including Skipper.
Veronica (Smack)	27	11	9 miles from Start Point.	Submarine - -	Captured -	Bombs -	—
Superb (Smack) -	50	13	5 miles N.E. by E. from Smith's Knoll Spar Buoy.	Submarine - -	Captured -	Gunfire -	—
Our Boys (Smack)	63	13	4 miles N. by E. from Smith's Knoll Spar Buoy	Submarine - -	Captured -	Gunfire -	—
Hatsuse - -	282	14	86 miles S.W. by W. from Fastnet.	Submarine - -	Captured -	Gunfire -	—
Clematis (Smack)	22	28	35 miles S.E. from Start Point.	Submarine - -	Captured -	Bombs -	—
Vulcan (Smack) -	27	28	28 miles S.E. by E. from Berry Head.	Submarine - -	Captured -	Bombs -	—
Provident (Smack)	38	28	24 miles W. by S. from Portland Bill.	Submarine - -	Captured -	Bombs -	—
Amphitrite (Smack).	44	28	24 miles W. by S. from Portland Bill.	Submarine - -	Captured -	Gunfire -	—
Catena (Smack) -	36	28	25 miles S.W. by S. from Berry Head.	Submarine - -	Captured -	Gunfire -	—

Name.	Tons.	Date.	Position.	Cause of Loss.	How attacked.	How sunk.	Lives lost.
		1916. Nov.					
Sea Lark (Smack)	42	28	24 miles S.E. by S. from Berry Head.	Submarine - -	Captured -	Gunfire -	—
Concord (Smack)	42	30	28 miles S.E. by S. from Start Point.	Submarine - -	Captured	Bombs -	—
DECEMBER 1916.		Dec.					
E.L.G. (Smack) -	25	1	25 miles N.W. from Trevose Head.	Submarine - -	Captured -	Bombs -	—
T. and A. C. (Smack).	23	1	20 miles N.N.W. from Trevose Head.	Submarine - -	Captured -	Bombs -	—
Camellia (Smack)	46	1	Off Eddystone -	Mine - - -	Mine - -	Mine -	3 (including Skipper).
Margaret - -	54	17	Between Hastings and Dungeness.	Mine - - -	Mine - -	Mine - -	6 (including Skipper).
Athole - -	112	17	8 miles E. by S. from Tod Head.	Mine - - -	Mine - -	Mine -	—
Arran - -	176	18	110 miles E. from Longstone.	Submarine - -	Captured -	Gunfire -	—
JANUARY 1917.		Jan.					
Gladys - -	275	21	40 miles N.W. by N. from Inishtrahull.	Submarine - -	Captured -	Gunfire -	—
Star of the Sea -	197	21	43 miles N.W. by N. ½ N. from Inishtrahull.	Submarine - -	Captured -	Gunfire -	—
Lucy - - -	280	21	42 miles N.W. by N. from Inishtrahull.	Submarine - -	Captured -	Gunfire -	—
Ethel (smack) -	23	22	30 miles S.S.E. from Start Point.	Submarine - -	Captured -	Gunfire -	—
George E. Benson.	155	—	North Sea - -	Submarine - -	Captured -	- - -	Crew made prisoners.
Alexandra - -	179	28	60 miles E. from Longstone.	Submarine - -	Captured -	Bombs -	Skipper made prisoner
Shamrock -	173	29	115 miles N.N.E. from Longstone.	Submarine - -	Captured -	Gunfire -	—
Wetherill (smack)	46	30	25 miles N.N.W. from Trevose Head.	Submarine - -	Captured -	Gunfire -	—
Merit (smack) -	39	30	20 miles N. by E. from Trevose Head.	Submarine - -	Captured -	Gunfire -	—
W. A. H. (smack)	47	30	32 miles N.W. from Trevose Head.	Submarine - -	Captured -	Gunfire -	—
Trevone (smack)	46	30	30 miles N.W. by N. from Trevose Head.	Submarine - -	Captured -	Gunfire -	2 including Skipper.
Helena and Samuel (smack).	59	30	30 miles N.N.W. from Trevose Head.	Submarine - -	Captured -	Gunfire -	—
Thistle - -	167	29	140 miles N.E. by E. ½ E. from the Tyne.	Submarine - -	Captured -	Gunfire -	—
Euonymous (smack).	59	30	34 miles N.W. from Trevose Head.	Submarine - -	Captured -	Gunfire -	—

Name.	Tons.	Date.	Position.	Cause of Loss.	How attacked.	How sunk.	Lives lost.
		1917. Jan.					
Vera - -	150	—	North Sea - -	Submarine (?) -	Reported captured.	Not known	Crew prisoners.
Agnes - -	125	—	North Sea - -	Submarine (?) -	Reported captured.	Not known	Crew prisoners.
FEBRUARY 1917.		Feb.					
Inverlyon (smack).	59	1	15 miles N. by W. from Trevose Head.	Submarine - -	Captured -	Gunfire -	—
Ada (smack) -	24	1	40 miles N.N.W. from Trevose Head.	Submarine - -	Captured -	Bombs -	—
Primrose - -	136	5	17 miles S.S.W. from Tod Head.	Mine - - -	Mine - -	Mine -	9 including Skipper.
Resolute - -	125	5	64 miles E. by S. from St. Abb's Head.	Submarine - -	Captured -	Gunfire -	—
Emerald (smack)	57	5	32 miles N.E. ¾ E. from Lowestoft.	Submarine - -	Captured -	Gunfire -	—
Adelaide - -	133	6	30 miles E.N.E. from the Tyne.	Submarine - -	Captured -	Bombs -	—
Romeo - -	114	6	70 miles E. from Berwick.	Submarine - -	Captured -	Scuttled -	—
Rupert - -	114	6	42 miles E.N.E. from the Tyne.	Submarine - -	Captured -	Bombs -	—
Mary Ann (smack).	17	8	18 miles N.N.E. from St. Ives Head.	Submarine - -	Captured -	Bombs -	—
Duke of York -	150	9	34 miles E. by S. from Girdleness.	Submarine - -	Captured -	Bombs -	—
Benbow - -	172	9	25 miles E. by S. from Bell Rock.	Submarine - -	Captured -	Bombs -	—
Ostrich - -	148	10	135 miles N.E. from Longstone.	Submarine - -	Captured -	Gunfire -	—
Athenian - -	171	10	105 miles E. by S. ¼ S. from Aberdeen.	Submarine - -	Captured -	Scuttled -	—
Ireland, - -	152	10	105 miles E.S.E. from Girdleness.	Submarine - ,	Captured -	Gunfire -	—
Ashwold - -	129	11	130 miles N.E. by N. from Shields.	Submarine - -	Captured -	Gunfire -	Skipper made prisoner.
Brissons (smack)	60	12	9 miles W. from Trevose Head.	Submarine - -	Captured -	Bomb -	—
Dale - ,	198	12	42 miles S. by E. ¼ E. from N. Ronaldshay.	Submarine - -	Captured -	Bombs -	Skipper made prisoner.
Barnsley - -	144	13	13 miles N. from Inishtrahull.	Submarine - -	Captured -	Bombs -	Skipper and chief engineer made prisoners.
King Alfred -	159	13	75 miles S. from Fair Isle.	Submarine - -	Captured -	Bomb -	Skipper made prisoner.
Friendship (smack).	37	13	Off Smalls - -	Submarine - -	Captured -	Not known	4 including Skipper.
Zircon (smack) -	48	13	26 miles S.W. from Smalls.	Submarine - -	Captured -	Bombs -	—
Belvoir Castle -	221	14	15 miles S.E. ½ E. from Buchan Ness.	Submarine - -	Captured -	Bomb -	Skipper made prisoner.
Mary Bell -	144	14	50 miles E. by N. from Aberdeen.	Submarine - -	Captured -	Bomb -	Skipper made prisoner.
Excel - -	157	17	53 miles N.E. from the Tyne.	Submarine - -	Captured -	Gunfire -	—
Halcyon - -	190	19	Off Butt of Lewis	Mine - - -	Mine - -	Mine -	10 including Skipper.

Name.	Tons.	Date.	Position.	Cause of Loss.	How attacked.	How sunk.	Lives lost.
K. L. M. (smack)	28	1917. Feb. 21	8 miles N.W. by W. from Eddystone.	Submarine - -	Captured -	Gunfire -	—
Monarch (smack)	35	21	14 miles S.E. by S. from Eddystone.	Submarine - -	Captured -	Bomb -	—
Energy (smack)	25	21	11 miles S.S.E. ½ S. from Eddystone.	Submarine - -	Captured -	Gunfire -	—
Frolic - -	183	22	90 miles E. by S. from Aberdeen.	Submarine - -	Captured -	Gunfire -	—
Lord Collingwood.	148	22	129 miles N.E. ¼ E. from Longstone.	Submarine - -	Captured -	Not known	—

MARCH 1917.

Name.	Tons.	Date.	Position.	Cause of Loss.	How attacked.	How sunk.	Lives lost.
Herbert Ingram	142	Mar. 1	70 miles E. from Longstone.	Submarine - -	Captured -	Bomb -	—
Redcap - -	199	1	97 miles E. from Longstone.	Submarine - -	Gunfire -	Gunfire -	1
Vulcana - -	219	7	40 miles E.S.E. from Auskerry L.H.	Submarine - -	Gunfire -	Gunfire -	2 including Skipper.
Naamah - -	269	7	35 miles S. by E. from N. Ronaldshay.	Submarine - -	Captured -	Gunfire -	—
Thrift (smack) -	40	11	15 miles W. from Trevose Head.	Submarine - -	Gunfire -	Gunfire -	—
Inter-nos (smack).	59	12	12 miles N.N.W. from Trevose Head.	Submarine - -	Captured -	Bomb -	—
Rivina (smack)	22	12	15 miles N.N.W. from Trevose Head.	Submarine - -	Captured -	Bomb -	—
Lent Lily (smack).	23	12	13 miles N.N.W. from Trevose Head.	Submarine - -	Captured -	Bomb -	—
Gracia (smack) -	25	12	12 miles N. by W. from Trevose Head.	Submarine - -	Captured -	Bomb -	—
Nellie (smack) -	60	12	13 miles N. by W. from Trevose Head.	Submarine - -	Captured -	Bomb -	—
C.A.S. (smack)	56	12	12 miles N.N.W. from Trevose Head.	Submarine - -	Captured -	Bomb -	—
Jessamine (smack).	56	12	14 miles N.N.W. from Trevose Head.	Submarine - -	Captured -	Bomb -	—
Hyacinth (smack).	61	12	15 miles N. by W. from Trevose Head.	Submarine - -	Captured -	Bomb -	—
Reindeer (smack).	52	12	15 miles S.E. from Berry Head.	Submarine - -	Captured -	Not known	—
Forget-me-not (smack).	40	12	12 miles S.W. by W. from Portland Bill.	Submarine - -	Captured -	Not known	—
Ena (smack) -	56	12	10 miles N. by W. from Trevose Head.	Submarine - -	Captured -	Bomb -	—
Provero (smack)	24	12	25 miles N.W. from Trevose Head.	Submarine - -	Captured -	Bomb -	—
Try (smack) -	34	13	10 miles S. from Wolf Rock.	Submarine - -	Captured -	Gunfire -	—
Gold Seeker (smack).	62	13	4 miles from Smith's Knoll Spar Buoy.	Submarine - -	Captured -	Gunfire -	—
Comrades (smack).	58	13	2½ miles N.W. from Smith's Knoll Middle Buoy.	Submarine - -	Captured -	Gunfire -	—

Name.	Tons.	Date.	Position.	Cause of Loss.	How attacked.	How sunk.	Lives lost.
		1917. Mar.					
Navenby - -	167	13	85 miles E. by S. ½ S. from Rattray Head.	Submarine - -	Captured -	Bomb -	—
Pencaer (smack)	46	16	8 miles S.E. from Mine Head L.H.	Submarine - -	Captured -	Bomb -	—
Gowan (motor) -	25	17	15 miles E.S.E. from Longstone.	Submarine - -	Captured -	Gunfire -	—
Kestrel - -	181	17	20 miles E. by S. from Longstone.	Submarine - -	Captured -	Gunfire -	—
Guard (smack) -	38	17	8 miles S.W. from Coningbeg L.V.	Submarine - -	Captured -	Gunfire -	—
Avance (smack)	60	21	25 miles W.S.W. from Portland Bill.	Submarine - -	Captured -	Gunfire -	—
Curlew (smack)	51	22	14 miles S. from Berry Head.	Submarine - -	Captured -	Bomb -	—
Qui Vive (smack).	22	24	15 miles S.E. from Eddystone.	Submarine - -	Captured -	Bomb -	—
Boy Walter (smack).	43	24	15 miles S.E. from Eddystone.	Submarine - -	Captured -	Bomb -	—
Mayflower (smack).	38	24	15 miles S.E. from Eddystone.	Submarine - -	Captured -	Bomb -	—
Endeavour (smack).	25	24	15 miles S.E. from Eddystone.	Submarine - -	Captured -	Bomb -	—
H.C.G. (smack)	24	24	15 miles S.E. from Eddystone.	Submarine - -	Captured -	Bomb -	—
Enigma (smack)	24	24	15 miles S.E. from Eddystone.	Submarine - -	Captured -	Bomb -	—
Reindeer (smack)	28	24	15 miles S. from Eddystone.	Submarine - -	Captured -	Bomb -	—
Alice (smack) -	61	24	12 miles S.S.W. from Eddystone.	Submarine - -	Captured -	Bomb -	—
Satanita (smack)	30	24	12 miles S.S.W. from Eddystone.	Submarine - -	Captured -	Bomb -	—
Median - -	214	25	30 miles E. by S. from Aberdeen.	Submarine - -	Captured -	Bomb -	—
Prince of Wales	158	25	17 miles E. by S. from Girdleness.	Submarine - -	Captured -	Bomb -	—.
Rosslyn - -	113	25	54 miles E. ¼ S. from Girdleness.	Submarine - -	Captured -	Bomb -	—
Galatia - -	150	28	30 miles S.S.W. from Buchan Ness.	Submarine - -	Captured -	Bomb -	—
Moulmein -	151	28	25 miles N.E. from Longstone.	Submarine - -	Captured -	Scuttled -	—
Petrel - -	151	30	120 miles E. from Aberdeen.	Submarine - -	Captured -	Gunfire -	—
Nuttalia - -	229	—	North Sea - -	Submarine (?)	Captured -	Reported taken to Germany.	—
APRIL	**1917.**	April					
Lord Scarborough	158	2	100 miles E. from May Island.	Submarine - -	Captured -	Scuttled -	—
Maggie Ross -	183	4	70 miles N.E. from Aberdeen.	Submarine - -	Captured -	Gunfire -	—
Gibraltar - -	188	4	20 miles E.N.E. from Rattray Head.	Submarine - -	Captured -	Bomb -	—
Lord Kitchener -	158	6	45 miles N. by E. from Kinnaird Head.	Submarine - -	Captured -	Bomb -	—
Recto - -	177	6	45 miles N. by E. from Kinnaird Head.	Submarine - -	Captured -	Bomb -	—
Narberth Castle	168	6	30 miles N.N.W. from Dennis Head.	Submarine - -	Captured -	Gunfire -	—
Nestor - -	176	6	20 miles N.W. by N. ½ N. from N. Ronaldshay.	Submarine - -	Captured -	Gunfire -	—

Name.	Tons.	Date.	Position.	Cause of Loss.	How attacked.	How sunk.	Lives lost
		1917. April					
Precedent (smack)	36	11	12 miles E.S.E. from Berry Head.	Submarine - -	Captured -	Bombs -	—
Equerry - -	168	12	35 miles N.E. from Kinnaird Head.	Submarine - -	Captured ·	Gunfire -	—
Chinkiang - -	125	12	30 miles N.E. from Buchan Ness.	Submarine - -	Captured -	Gunfire -	—
Caliban - -	215	12	45 miles N.E. by N. from Rattray Head.	Submarine - -	Captured -	Gunfire -	—
Crown Prince -	103	12	45 miles N.E. by E. from Girdleness.	Submarine - -	Captured -	Gunfire -	—
Lillian - -	120	12	45 miles N.E. by E. from Girdleness.	Submarine - -	Captured -	Gunfire -	—
Fife Ness - -	123	12	23 miles E.N.E. from Fraserburgh.	Submarine - -	Captured -	Gunfire -	—
Largo Bay - -	125	12	30 miles N.E. by E. from Buchan Ness.	Submarine - -	Captured -	Gunfire -	—
Osprey - -	106	12	45 miles N.E. by E. from Girdleness.	Submarine - -	Captured -	Gunfire -	—
Stork - - -	152	13	20 miles E. ½ S. from St. Abb's Head.	Submarine - -	Captured ·	Bombs -	—
Sutterton - -	160	15	65 miles E.S.E. from St. Abb's Head.	Submarine - -	Captured -	Bomb -	1
Dalmatian - -	186	15	North Sea - -	Submarine - -	Captured -	Bombs -	9 including Skipper.
Lord Chancellor -	135	16	50 miles N.E. from Longstone.	Submarine - -	Captured -	Bombs -	—
U.S.A. - -	182	17	16 miles E.N.E. from Longstone.	Submarine - -	Captured -	Bombs -	—
John S. Boyle -	143	18	25 miles E. by S. from St. Abb's Head.	Submarine - -	Captured -	Bombs -	—
Rameses - -	155	18	60 miles N.E. from Blyth.	Submarine - -	Captured -	Bombs -	—
Witham - -	144	18	125 miles E. by S. ½ S. from St. Abb's Head.	Submarine - -	Captured -	Gunfire -	—
Erith - - -	168	20	40 miles S. ½ W. from Girdleness.	Submarine - -	Captured -	Bombs -	—
Grecian - -	119	20	22 miles N.E. by E. from Longstone.	Submarine - -	Captured -	Bomb -	—
Jedburgh - -	165	21	35 miles N.N.W. from Foula Island.	Submarine - -	Captured -	Bomb -	—
Yeovil - -	164	21	35 miles N.N.W. from Foula Island.	Submarine - -	Captured -	Bomb -	1
Nightingale -	91	22	26 miles S. from Aberdeen.	Submarine - -	Captured -	Bomb -	- —
Mayfly - -	191	24	70 miles N.E. by N. from Spurn L.V.	Submarine - -	Gunfire -	Gunfire -	2 including Skipper.
Heather - -	58	24	14 miles W. by N. from Bishop Rock.	Submarine - -	Captured -	Bombs -	—
Upton Castle -	145	24	60 miles E. from Longstone.	Submarine - -	Captured -	Bomb -	—
Boy Denis (smack).	41	26	12 miles S.S.W. from Start Point.	Submarine - -	Captured -	Bomb -	—
Active - -	149	26	80 miles E.S.E. from St. Abb's Head.	Submarine - -	Captured -	Bomb -	—

Name.	Tons.	Date.	Position.	Cause of Loss.	How attacked.	How sunk.	Lives lost.
		1917. Apr.					
Pursue (smack) -	37	28	12 miles S.W. from Bolt Head.	Submarine - -	Captured -	Bomb -	—
Dilston Castle -	129	29	16 miles E. by S. from Aberdeen.	Submarine - -	Captured -	Bombs -	—
Argo - · -	131	30	15 miles E. ½ S. from Buchan Ness.	Submarine - -	Captured -	Gunfire -	—
Andromache -	313	—	North Sea - -	Submarine - -	Captured -	Not known	Skipper made prisoner.
Brothertoft -	155	—	North Sea - -	Submarine (re-ported).	Captured -	Not known	
Expedient - -	145	—	North Sea - -	Submarine (re-ported).	Captured -	Not known	
Industria -	133	—	North Sea - -	Submarine (re-ported).	Captured -	Not known	

MAY 1917.

Name.	Tons.	Date.	Position.	Cause of Loss.	How attacked.	How sunk.	Lives lost.
		May					
United (smack) -	61	2	5 miles N.W. from Godrevy L.H.	Submarine - -	Captured -	Bomb -	—
Sir Edward Birkbeck (smack).	23	3	16 miles S.E. from Stags.	Submarine - -	Captured -	Bomb -	—
Hibernia (smack)	21	3	14 miles S.E. from Baltimore Harbour.	Submarine - -	Captured -	Bomb -	—
Eleanor (smack) -	31	3	13 miles S. from Stags.	Submarine - -	Captured -	Bomb -	—
Fastnet (smack)	31	3	13 miles S. from Stags.	Submarine - -	Captured -	Bomb -	—
Lucky Lass (smack).	10	3	15 miles S. from Stags.	Sumbarine - -	Captured -	Scuttled -	—
North Star (smack).	15	3	13 miles S. from Stags.	Submarine - -	Captured -	Bomb -	—
Carbery King (smack).	21	3	14 miles S. from Stags.	Submarine - -	Captured -	Bomb -	—
Strumble (smack)	45	4	10 miles N.N.E. from Strumble Head.	Submarine - -	Captured -	Bomb -	—
Victorious (smack)	39	4	10 miles N.N.E. from Strumble Head.	Submarine - -	Captured -	Bomb -	—
Edith Cavell (motor).	20	5	7½ miles E. from Robin Hood Bay.	Submarine - -	Captured -	Bomb -	—
Kitty - - -	181	9	25 miles E.N.E. from St. Abb's Head.	Submarine - -	Captured -	Bomb -	Skipper and Chief Engineer made prisoners.
Windward Ho ! -	226	9	3 miles S. from Peterhead.	Mine - - -	Mine - -	Mine - -	8 including Skipper.
G. L. C. (smack)	24	12	6 miles S.E. from Eddystone.	Submarine - -	Captured -	Bomb -	—
Bel Lily - -	168	14	1½ miles E. by N. from Peterhead.	Mine - - -	Mine - -	Mine - -	10 including Skipper.
Primrose - -	62	18	22 miles W. by S. ½ S. from Bishop Rock.	Submarine - -	Captured -	Gunfire -	—
Adventure - -	50	18	49 miles W. by S. from Wolf.	Submarine - -	Captured -	Gunfire -	—
Sisapon - -	211	23	Faroe Banks -	Submarine - -	Captured -		—
Olearia - -	209	23	Faroe Banks -	Submarine - -	Captured -	Bombs -	—

Name.	Tons.	Date.	Position.	Cause of Loss.	How attacked.	How sunk.	Lives lost.
JUNE 1917.		June					
Teal - - -	141	1	57 miles N.W. by N. from Sule Skerry Light.	Submarine - -	Captured -	Gunfire -	—
Shamrock - -	170	2	66 miles N.N.E. from Sule Skerry.	Submarine - -	Captured -	Gunfire -	—
St. Bernard -	186	2	65 miles N. by W. from Noup Head.	Submarine - -	Captured -	Gunfire -	—
Prudence (smack)	25	3	15 miles W.S.W. from Eddystone.	Submarine - -	Captured -	Gunfire -	—
Geralda (smack)	46	3	22 miles N.E. ½ E. from Cromer.	Mine - - -	Mine - -	Mine -	—
Virgilia - -	209	3	5 miles E. from Girdleness.	Submarine - -	Captured -	Bombs -	Skipper made prisoner.
Golden Hope -	22	7	30 miles E. from Kinnaird Head.	Submarine - -	Captured -	Bombs -	—
Cariad (smack) -	38	8	6 miles E. by S. from Start Point.	Submarine - -	Captured -	Bombs -	—
Torbay Lass (smack).	38	8	9 miles E. by S. from Start Point.	Submarine - -	Captured -	Bombs -	—
Onward (smack)-	39	8	9 miles E. by S. from Start Point.	Submarine - -	Captured -	Bombs -	—
Ocean's Pride (smack).	42	8	9 miles E. by S. from Start Point.	Submarine - -	Captured -	Bombs -	—
Frances (motor) -	20	28	10 miles N.E. from Spurn Point.	Submarine - -	Captured -	Bombs -	—
Rose of June (motor).	20	28	10 miles N.E. from Spurn Point.	Submarine - -	Captured -	Bombs -	—
William and Betty (motor).	21	28	10 miles N.E. from Spurn Point.	Submarine - -	Captured -	Bombs -	—
Elsie (motor) -	20	28	10 miles N.E. from Spurn Point.	Submarine - -	Captured -	Bombs -	—
Glenelg - -	32	28	10 miles N.E. from Spurn Point.	Submarine - -	Captured -	Bombs -	—
Harbinger - -	39	28	10 miles N.E. from Spurn Point.	Submarine - -	Captured -	Bombs -	—
Corona - -	48	28	65 miles E. from Sumburgh Head.	Submarine - -	Captured -	Gunfire -	—
Frigate Bird (motor).	20	28	North Sea - -	Submarine (?) -	Captured (?)	Not known	
Gem - -	79	29	18 miles E. by S. from Rattray Head.	Submarine - -	Captured -	Gunfire -	—
Manx Princess -	87	29	18 miles E. by S. from Rattray Head.	Submarine - -	Captured -	Gunfire -	—
JULY 1917.		1917. July					
Gleam (Smack)	54	1	½ mile E.N.E. from S. Owers Buoy.	Submarine - -	Captured -	Gunfire -	—
Advance (Smack)	44	1	5 miles S.E. from S. Owers Buoy.	Submarine - -	Captured -	Gunfire -	—
Radiance (Smack)	57	1	3 miles N. by E. from North Leman Buoy.	Submarine - -	Captured -	Bombs -	—

Name.	Tons.	Date.	Position.	Cause of Loss.	How attacked.	How sunk.	Lives lost.
		1917. July					
Eclipse - -	185	1	100 miles N. by W. from Brough of Birsa,Orkney.	Submarine - -	Captured -	Gunfire -	—
General Buller -	72	2	26 miles E.S.E. from Sumburgh Head.	Submarine - -	Captured -	Gunfire -	—
Hamnavoe -	57	2	26 miles E.S.E. from Sumburgh Head.	Submarine - -	Captured -	Gunfire -	—
Chrysolite (Smack)	57	4	4 miles North from Haisbro L.V.	Mine - - -	Mine - -	Mine -	5
Loch Katrine -	151	4	85 miles S.S.E from Sando, Faeroe Islands.	Submarine - -	Captured -	Gunfire -	—
†Stoic - -	200	10	60 miles S. by E. from Sydero.	Submarine - -	Captured -	Gunfire -	—
†Pretoria - -	283	10	60 miles S. by E. from Sydero.	Submarine - -	Captured -	Gunfire -	—
Romantic - -	197	10	60 miles S. by E. from Sydero.	Submarine - -	Captured -	Gunfire -	—
Mabel - -	205	10	60 miles S. by E. from Sydero.	Submarine - -	Captured -	Bombs -	—
Pacific - -	235	10	60 miles S. by E. from Sydero.	Submarine - -	Captured -	Gunfire -	—
Cedric - -	197	10	60 miles S. by E. from Sydero.	Submarine - -	Captured -	Bombs -	—
Sea King - -	185	10	60 miles S. by E. from Sydero.	Submarine - -	Captured -	Bombs -	—
Peridot - -	214	10	60 miles S. by E. from Sydero.	Submarine - -	Captured -	Bombs -	—
†Asama - -	284	16	160 miles S.W. by S. from the Fastnet.	Submarine - -	Captured -	Gunfire -	1
Young Bert (smack).	59	31 (?)	North Sea - -	Submarine (reported).	Captured -	Not known	
AUGUST 1917.		Aug.					
Narcissus - -	58	6	12 miles S.E. from the Tyne.	Submarine - -	Captured -	Bombs -	—
Gloriosa (smack)	23	11	12 miles S. by W. from Caldy Island.	Submarine - -	Captured -	Bombs -	—
Eleazar - -	111	12	25 miles S.W. by W. from St. Ann's Head.	Submarine - -	Captured -	Gunfire -	—
Jane S. (motor)	12	14	11 miles S.E. from St. Abb's Head.	Mine - - -	Mine - -	Mine - -	5
Susie (smack) -	38	17	10 miles N.E. by E. from Scarborough.	Submarine - -	Captured -	Gunfire -	1
SEPTEMBER 1917.		Sept.					
Unity (smack) -	56	5	8 miles East from Cross Sand L.V.	Submarine - -	Captured -	Bombs -	—
Margaret (motor)	12	5	Near Wick -	Mine - - -	Mine - -	Mine - -	5
Rosary (smack)	37	6	6 miles W. by N. from Smith's Knoll Spar Buoy.	Submarine - -	Captured -	Bombs -	—
Family's Pride (motor).	39	8	28 miles E. by S. from Peterhead.	Submarine - -	Captured -	Bombs -	—
Rosy Cross (smack).	25	11	4 miles N W. by W. from Crackington Haven, Cornwall.	Submarine - -	Captured -	Bombs -	—
Ronald (smack)	38	17	25 miles S.W. from Coningbeg L.V.	Submarine - -	Captured -	Gunfire -	—
Our Bairns (smack).	38	17	25 miles S.W. from Coningbeg L.V.	Submarine - -	Captured -	Gunfire -	—

Name.	Tons.	Date.	Position.	Cause of Loss.	How attacked.	How sunk.	Lives lost.
OCTOBER 1917.		1917. Oct.					
Willing Boys (smack).	51	2	10 miles N.W. from Smith's Knoll Spar Buoy.	Mine - - -	Mine - -	Mine - -	5
Perseverance (smack).	30	4	15 miles S. by W. from the Eddystone.	Submarine - -	Captured -	Gunfire -	—
Rupee (smack)	39	4	12 miles North from Lundy Island.	Submarine - -	Captured -	Gunfire -	4 including Skipper.
Young Clifford (smack).	47	4	12 miles North from Lundy Island.	Submarine - -	Captured -	Gunfire -	—
Reliance - -	60	7 (?)	North Sea - -	Mine (?) - -	Mine (?) -	Mine (?) -	10 including Skipper.
NOVEMBER 1917.		Nov.					
Bremier (smack)	23	27	16 miles S.E. from Start Point.	Submarine - -	Captured -	Gunfire -	—.
Courage (smack)	39	30	6 miles W. by N. from Lundy, North Lighthouse.	Submarine - -	Captured -	Gunfire -	—
Gazelle (smack)	41	30	6 miles W. by N. from Lundy, North Lighthouse.	Submarine - -	Captured -	Gunfire -	—
DECEMBER 1917.		Dec.					
Rion (smack) -	39	1	8 miles N.E. from Start Point.	Submarine - -	Captured -	Bombs -	—
Forward (smack)	40	10	Off Aldeburgh -	Submarine - -	Captured -	Bombs -	—
John M. Smart -	113	12	10 miles East from the Tyne.	T.B.D. - -	Gunfire -	Gunfire -	4
Amadavat -	171	12	East Coast of Shetlands.	Mine (?) - -	Mine (?) -	Mine (?) -	9 including Skipper.
Neptune (smack).	50	17	Galway Bay -	Mine - - -	Mine - -	Mine - -	4
JANUARY 1918.		1918. Jan.					
Veda (smack) -	25	2	30 miles S.S.W. from Eddystone.	Submarine - -	Captured -	Gunfire -	—
Gratitude (smack).	40	4	8 miles S.E. by E. from Berry Head.	Submarine - -	Captured -	Bombs -	—
Day Spring (smack).	39	4	8 miles S.E. from Berry Head.	Submarine - -	Captured -	Bombs -	—
Varuna (smack)	40	4	15 miles S.E. by E. from Berry Head.	Submarine - -	Captured -	Bombs -	—
Premier - -	89	7	3 miles West from L. Eynort, Skye.	Submarine - -	Captured -	Gunfire -	1
May (smack) -	24	26	18 miles S.E. $\frac{1}{2}$ E. from Berry Head.	Submarine - -	Captured -	Bombs -	—
Ibex (smack) -	42	29	14 miles S.E. by E. from Berry Head.	Submarine - -	Captured -	Gunfire -	—
Addax (smack) -	40	29	14 miles S.E. by E. from Berry Head.	Submarine - -	Captured -	Gunfire -	—
General Leman (smack).	45	29	14 miles S.E. by E. from Berry Head.	Submarine - -	Captured -	Gunfire -	—
Perseverance (smack).	40	29	14 miles S.E. by E. from Berry Head.	Submarine - -	Captured -	Gunfire -	—

Name.	Tons.	Date.	Position.	Cause of Loss.	How attacked.	How sunk.	Lives lost.
FEBRUARY	**1918.**	1918. Feb.					
Holkar (smack)	48	6	8 miles North from Trevose Head.	Submarine - -	Captured -	Gunfire -	—
Straton - -	197	8	26 miles East from Humber L.V.	Mine - - -	Mine - -	Mine - -	—
Maggie Smith (motor).	24	9	3 miles North from Bell Rock.	Submarine - -	Captured -	Bomb (?) -	3
Commander (smack).	47	16	8 miles S.W. from Beer Head.	Submarine - -	Captured -	Bombs -	—
Snowdrop (smack).	40	20	8 miles S.W. ½ S. from the Eddystone.	Submarine - -	Captured -	Gunfire -	—
Irex (smack) -	16	21	10 miles E. by S. from Hopes Nose.	Submarine - -	Captured -	Bomb -	—
Leonora (smack)	26	21	11 miles East from Hopes Nose.	Submarine - -	Captured -	Gunfire -	—
Rosebud (smack)	44	21	10 miles S.S.E. from Hopes Nose.	Submarine - -	Captured -	Bomb -	—
Idalia (smack)	23	21	10 miles S.E. by S. from Berry Head.	Submarine - -	Captured -	Bomb -	—
Oryx (smack) -	38	21	10 miles S.E. by S. from Berry Head.	Submarine - -	Captured -	Gunfire -	—
Reaper - -	91	21	2 miles N.E. from Tynemouth.	Mine - - -	Mine - -	Mine - -	8 including Skipper.
†Rambler - -	92	26	4 miles E. from Blyth.	Mine - - -	Mine - -	Mine - -	9 including Skipper.
MARCH 1918.		Mar.					
Marguerite (smack).	10	9	25 miles N. ¼ E. from Beaumaris Point.	Submarine - -	Captured -	Bombs -	—
Sunrise (smack)	24	10	18 miles S.E. from Maughold Head, I. of Man.	Submarine - -	Captured -	Bombs -	—
Wave (smack) -	23	10	10 miles S.W. by W. from St. Bees Head.	Submarine - -	Captured -	Bombs -	—
W. A. Massey -	84	11	4 miles W. by N. from Handa Id., Minch.	Mine - - -	Mine - -	Mine - -	10 including Skipper.
Honora (motor)	29	28	6 miles E.N.E. from Whitby.	Submarine - -	Captured -	Gunfire -	—
Botha (motor) -	17	28	3 miles East from Whitby.	Submarine - -	Captured -	Bombs -	—
Noel (motor) -	21	28	6 miles N.E. by E. from Whitby.	Submarine - -	Captured -	Gunfire -	—
Brotherly Love (motor).	19	28	6 miles N.E. by E. from Whitby.	Submarine - -	Captured -	Gunfire -	—
St. Michan -	43	30	10 miles E. from Lambay Island.	Submarine - -	Captured -	Gunfire -	—
Geraldine - (Smack.)	23	30	10 miles E. from Lambay Island.	Submarine - -	Not known -	Not known	5 including Skipper.
APRIL 191 .		Apr.					
Ruth (Smack) -	44	13	1½ miles E.S.E. from S. Cross Sand buoy.	Submarine - -	Captured -	Bombs -	—
Tyne Wave -	121	23	20 miles W.N.W. from Ramna Stacks, Shetland.	Submarine - -	Captured -	Gunfire -	—

Name.	Tons.	Date.	Position.	Cause of Loss.	How attacked.	How sunk.	Lives lost.
Peregrine - -	76	1918. Apr. 23	15 miles N.N.W. from Ramna Stacks, Shetland.	Submarine - -	Captured -	Gunfire -	—
MAY 1918.							
Eclipse (smack)	47	May 26	10 miles N.E. by N. from Smith's Knoll Spar Buoy.	Submarine - -	Captured -	Gunfire -	—
Dayspring (smack).	57	26	10 miles N.E. by N. from Smith's Knoll Spar Buoy.	Submarine - -	Captured -	Gunfire -	—
Fortuna (smack)	61	26	10 miles N.E. by N. from Smith's Knoll Spar Buoy.	Submarine - -	Captured -	Bombs -	---
Wayside Flower (motor).	21	27	20 miles N.E. by N. from the Humber.	Submarine - -	Captured -	Bombs -	- -
Coronation (motor).	19	28	13 miles E.S.E. from Flamborough Head.	Submarine - -	Captured -	Gunfire	—
Seabird (motor)	15	30	26 miles W.N.W. from Calf of Man.	Submarine - -	Captured -	Bombs -	—.
Glad Tidings (smack).	15	30	26 miles W.N.W. from Calf of Man.	Submarine - -	Captured -	Bombs -	—
Never Can Tell (smack).	31	30	26 miles W.N.W. from Calf of Man.	Submarine - -	Captured -	Bombs -	—
Sparkling Wave (smack).	29	30	26 miles W.N.W. from Calf of Man.	Submarine - -	Captured -	Bombs -	—
St. Mary (smack)	29	30	26 miles W.N.W. from Calf of Man.	Submarine - -	Captured -	Bombs -	—
Cyprus (smack)	35	30	26 miles W.N.W. from Calf of Man.	Submarine - -	Captured -	Bombs -	—
Honey Bee (motor).	34	30	26 miles W.N.W. from Calf of Man.	Submarine - -	Captured -	Bombs -	—
Jane Gordon (smack).	27	30	26 miles W.N.W. from Calf of Man.	Submarine - -	Captured -	Bombs -	—
Lloyd (smack) -	35	30	26 miles W.N.W. from Calf of Man.	Submarine - -	Captured -	Bombs -	—
Marianne McCrum (smack).	30	30	26 miles W.N.W. from Calf of Man.	Submarine - -	Captured -	Bombs -	—
Pretty Polly (smack).	19	31	Off Roundstone Bay, W. of Ireland.	Submarine - -	Gunfire -	Gunfire -	7
JUNE 1918.							
†Egret - -	169	June 1	2 miles E. by N. from Humber L.V.	Submarine - -	No warning -	Torpedo -	11 including Skipper.
Dianthus (smack)	40	6	5 miles N. ½ E. from Smith's Knoll Spar Buoy.	Submarine - -	Captured -	Bombs -	—
Active (smack) -	46	6	5 miles N. ½ E. from Smith's Knoll Spar Buoy.	Submarine - -	Captured -	Gunfire -	—

Name.	Tons.	Date.	Position.	Cause of Loss.	How attacked.	How sunk.	Lives lost.
Beryl (smack) -	57	1918. June 6	5 miles N. ½ E. from Smith's Knoll Spar Buoy.	Submarine - -	Captured -	Bombs -	—
Eros - -	181	8	North Sea - -	Mine - - -	Mine -	Mine - -	6 including Skipper.
Pochard - -	146	28	North Sea - -	Mine - - -	Mine -	Mine -	—
JULY 1918.		July					
Aby (Motor) -	25	7	25 miles E. ¾ N. from Spurn Point.	Submarine - -	Captured -	Bombs -	—
Albion (Motor)	22	7	25 miles E. ¾ N. from Spurn Point.	Submarine - -	Captured -	Bombs -	—
Boy Jack (Smack).	57	26	4 miles East from Cross Sand L.V.	Submarine - -	Captured -	Bombs -	3
Fear Not (Smack).	59	27	14 miles N.N.E. from Haisborough L.V.	Submarine - -	Captured -	Bombs -	—
Passion Flower (Smack).	46	27	14 miles N.N.E. from Haisborough L.V.	Submarine - -	Captured -	Bombs -	—
I'll Try (Smack)	51	27	14 miles N.N.E. from Haisborough L.V.	Submarine - -	Captured -	Bombs -	—
Valour (Smack)	39	27	14 miles N.N.E. from Haisborough L.V.	Submarine - -	Captured -	Bombs -	—
Paragon (Smack)	56	27	8 miles N.E. by E. from Haisborough L.V.	Submarine - -	Captured -	Bombs -	—
Le Bijou (Smack).	46	27	9 miles N.E. from Haisborough L.V.	Submarine - -	Captured -	Bombs -	—
Success (Smack)	54	27	7 miles N.E. by E. from Haisborough L.V.	Submarine - -	Captured -	Gunfire -	—
Counsellor (Smack).	56	27	2½ miles North from Haisborough L.V.	Submarine - -	Captured -	Bombs -	—
Francis Robert (Smack).	44	28	8 miles N.E. from Haisborough L.V.	Submarine - -	Captured -	Gunfire -	—
AUGUST 1918.		Aug.					
Nelson A. (S.V.).	72	4	25 miles from Shelburne, N.S.	Submarine - -	Captured -	Bomb -	—
Triumph - -	239	20	60 miles S.W. by S. from Cape Canso, N.S.	Submarine - -	Captured -	Converted into a raider.	—
Uda A. Saunders (S.V.).	125	20	52 miles South from Cape Canso, N.S.	Submarine - - (Triumph.)	Captured -	Bombs -	—
Lucille M. Schnare (S.V.).	121	20	52 miles South from Cape Canso, N.S.	Submarine - - (Triumph.)	Captured -	Bombs -	—
Pasadena (S.V.).	91	21	70 miles S.S.E. from Cape Canso, N.S.	Submarine - -	Captured -	Bomb -	—
E. B. Walters (S.V.).	98	25	35 miles W. by S. from Little Miquelon, N.F.L.	Submarine - -	Captured -	Bombs -	—
C. M. Walters (S.V.).	107	25	35 miles W. by S. from Little Miquelon, N.F.L.	Submarine - -	Captured -	Bombs -	—
Verna D. Adams (S.V.).	132	25	35 miles W. by S. from Little Miquelon, N.F.L.	Submarine - - (Triumph.)	Captured -	Bombs -	—

Name.	Tons.	Date.	Position.	Cause of Loss.	How attacked.	How sunk.	Lives lost.
		1918. Aug.					
Clayton W. Walters (S.V.)	80	25	Off St. Pierre, N.F.L.	Submarine - -	Captured -	Bombs .	—
Marion Adams (S.V.).	99	25	Off St. Pierre, N.F.L.	Submarine - -	Captured -	Bombs .	—
Gloaming (S.V.)	100	26	70 miles S.S.W. from St. Pierre, N.F.L.	Submarine - -	Captured -	Bombs .	—
Elsie Porter - (S.V.).	136	30	290 miles E. ½ N. from St. John's, N.F.L.	Submarine - -	Captured -	Bombs .	—
Potentate (S.V.).	136	30	290 miles E. ½ N. from St. John's, N.F.L.	Submarine - -	Captured -	Bombs .	—
SEPTEMBER 1918.							
		Sept. 22					
†Euthamia - -	142	22	65 miles E. by N. ½ N. from Humber L.V.	Mine - - -	Mine - -	Mine - -	—
NOVEMBER 1918.							
		Nov. 7					
Conster (Smack)	25.	7	Off Rye - -	Mine - -	Mine - -	Mine - -	—

III.—BRITISH MERCHANT VESSELS DAMAGED OR MOLESTED BY THE ENEMY BUT NOT SUNK.

Name.	Tons.	Date.	Position.	Attacked by	How attacked.	How saved.	Lives lost.
AUGUST 1914.		1914. Aug.					
Craigforth - -	2,900	5	In Bosphorus -	Mine - - -	Mine - -	Beached -	—
Lynton Grange -	4,252	6	N. Atlantic -	Dresden - -	Captured -	Released -	—
Drumcliffe -	4,072	6	N. Atlantic -	Dresden - -	Captured -	Released -	—
Hostilius -	3,325	6	N. Atlantic -	Dresden - -	Captured -	Released -	—
Galician ' -	6,762	15	N. Atlantic -	Kaiser Wilhelm der Grosse.	Captured -	Released -	—
Arlanza - -	15,044	16	N. Atlantic -	Kaiser Wilhelm der Grosse.	Captured -	Released -	—
Siamese Prince -	4,847	16	S. Atlantic -	Dresden - -	Captured -	Released -	—
Isle of Hastings -	1,575	20	Philippeville -	Goeben and Breslau	Gunfire -	Damaged -	—
Katharine Park -	4,854	26	S. Atlantic -	Dresden - -	Captured -	Released -	—
Holtby -	3,675	30	2½ miles from Seaham.	Mine - - -	Mine - -	Arrived Tyne.	—
SEPTEMBER 1914.		Sept.					
Southport - -	3,588	4	Caroline Is. -	Geier - - -	Captured -	Escaped -	—
Kabinga - -	4,657	12	Bay of Bengal -	Emden - -	Captured -	Released -	—
Ortega - -	8,075	19	S. Atlantic -	Dresden - -	Chased -	Speed -	—
Chupra - -	6,175	22	Madras - -	Emden - -	Gunfire -	Damaged -	1
Gryfevale - -	4,437	26	Indian Ocean -	Emden - -	Captured -	Released -	—
OCTOBER 1914.		Oct.					
Farn - - -	4,393	5	140 miles S.W. ¾ S. (true) from St. Paul Rocks.	Karlsruhe - -	Captured -	Interned at San Juan P.R. Released Feb. 1917.	—
St. Egbert -	5,596	18	Indian Ocean -	Emden - -	Captured -	Released -	—
Exford - -	4,542	19	Indian Ocean -	Emden - -	Captured -	Recaptured	—

Name.	Tons.	Date.	Position.	Attacked by	How attacked.	How saved.	Lives lost.
		1915. Oct.					
Royal Sceptre -	3,838	27	530 miles W. (true) from St. Paul Rocks.	Karlsruhe - -	Captured -	Released -	—
Glenturret - -	4,696	28	Malacca Strait -	Emden - -	Captured -	Released -	—
Friederike - -	3,574	30	Novorossisk -	Turkish warships -	Gunfire -	Damaged -	—
Newburn - -	3,554	30	Indian Ocean -	Emden - -	Captured -	Released -	—
NOVEMBER 1914.							
Colusa - -	5,732	1	Pacific - -	Prinz Eitel Friedrich.	Chased -	Escaped -	—
DECEMBER 1914.		Dec.					
Colchester -	1,209	11	North Sea - -	Submarine - -	Chased -	Speed -	—
Munificent - -	3,270	16	West Hartlepool	German warships -	Gunfire -	Damaged -	1
Phœbe - -	2,754	16	East Hartlepool -	German warships -	Gunfire -	Damaged -	1
Gallier - -	4,592	25	Off Scarborough -	Mine - - -	Mine - -	Arrived Scarborough.	—
JANUARY 1915.		1915. Jan.					
Westergate -	1,742	1	North Sea - -	Mine - - -	Mine - -	Towed in -	—
Graphic - -	1,871	30	22 miles N.W. from Liverpool Bar L.V.	Submarine - -	Chased -	Speed -	—
FEBRUARY 1915.		Feb.					
Asturias (Hospital Ship).	12,002	1	15 miles N.N.E. from Havre L.V.	Submarine - -	Torpedo -	Missed -	—
Laertes - -	4,541	10	12 miles N.E. by E. from Schowen L.V.	Submarine - -	Gunfire and torpedo.	Speed -	—
Torquay - -	870	12	Off Filey - -	Mine - - -	Mine - -	Towed in -	1
Wavelet - -	2,992	13	11 miles N.E. by N. from N. Goodwin.	Mine - - -	Mine - -	Beached -	12
Kirkham Abbey -	1,166	14	North Sea - -	Submarine - -	Chased -	Speed -	—
Colchester - -	1,209	17	North Sea - -	Submarine - -	Chased -	Speed -	—
Penhale - -	3,712	21	3 miles W. from Holyhead.	Submarine - -	Chased -	Speed -	—
Victoria - -	1,689	22	6 miles from Boulogne.	Submarine - -	Torpedo -	Missed -	—
Chasehill - -	4,583	22	S. Atlantic -	Kronprinz Wilhelm	Captured -	Released -	—
Kalibia - -	4,930	23	Off Dungeness -	Submarine - -	Chased -	Speed -	—
Hungarian Prince	4,765	24	Off Beachy Head	Submarine - -	Chased -	Speed -	—
Surrey - -	5,987	25	Off Calais - -	Mine - - -	Mine - -	Towed in -	—
St. Andrew (Hospital Ship).	2,528	25	10 miles N.W. by W. from Boulogne.	Submarine - -	Chased -	Speed -	—
Thordis - -	501	28	English Channel -	Submarine - -	Torpedo -	Missed -	—
MARCH 1915.		1915. Mar.					
Wrexham - -	1,414	2	North Sea - -	Submarine - -	Chased -	Speed -	—
Ningchow - -	9,021	4	Bristol Channel -	Submarine - -	Chased -	Speed -	—
Lydia - -	1,133	5	English Channel -	Submarine - -	Torpedo -	Missed -	—
Clan Macrae -	5,058	9	Off Liverpool Bar L.V.	Submarine - -	Chased -	Speed -	—
Adenwen - -	3,798	11	20 miles N.W. from Casquets.	Submarine - -	Bombs after capture.	Towed in -	—
Helen - -	322	11	8 miles N.N.W. from Liverpool Bar L.V.	Submarine - -	Torpedo -	Missed -	—
Atlantic City -	4,707	12	6 miles E. from South Rock.	Submarine - -	Chased -	Speed -	—
Umtata - -	2,655	14	English Channel -	Submarine - -	Torpedo -	Missed -	—

Name.	Tons.	Date.	Position.	Attacked by	How attacked.	How saved.	Lives lost.
		1915. Mar.					
Sutton Hall (Belgian Relief).	4,460	14	English Channel -	Submarine - -	Torpedo -	Missed -	—
Quentin - -	1,274	14	5 miles N.N.W. from Maas L.V.	Submarine - -	Chased -	Speed -	—
†Atalanta - -	519	14	12 miles W.S.W. from Inishturk Island.	Submarine - -	Set on fire after capture.	Towed in -	—
Blonde - -	613	15	3 miles off N. Foreland.	Aircraft - -	Bomb - -	Missed -	—
Hyndford - -	4,286	15	12 miles S. from Beachy Head.	Submarine - -	Torpedoed -	Beached -	1
Highland Scot -	7,604	16	English Channel -	Submarine - -	Chased -	Speed -	—
Wolverton - -	3,868	16	5 miles E. by S. from Fontana L.H., Odessa.	Mine - - -	Mine - -	Towed in -	1
Blue Jacket -	3,515	18	15 miles E. from Owers L.V.	Submarine - -	Torpedoed -	Arrived Southampton Water.	—
Strathfillan (Belgian Relief).	4,353	18	Off Beachy Head	Submarine - -	Chased -	Speed -	—
Colchester - -	1,209	18	Off Hook of Holland.	Submarine - -	Chased -	Speed -	—
San Dunstano -	6,220	19	English Channel	Submarine - -	Chased -	Speed -	—
John Duncan -	1,832	20	Near Royal Sovereign L.V.	Submarine - -	Chased -	Speed -	—
Dorset Coast -	672	20	English Channel -	Submarine - -	Chased -	Speed -	—
Elfland (Belgian Relief).	4,190	21	Off North Hinder L.V.	Aircraft - -	Bomb - -	Missed -	—
Ennismore - -	1,499	21	10 miles N.E. by N. from Coquet Island.	Submarine - -	Torpedo -	Missed -	—
Lestris - -	1,384	21	14 miles E. from Galloper.	Aircraft - -	Bombs -	Missed -	—
Tycho - -	3,216	21	In the Downs -	Submarine - -	Torpedo -	Missed -	—
Pandion - -	1,279	21	Between N. Hinder and Galloper.	Aircraft - -	Bombs -	Missed -	—
Osceola - -	393	22	North Sea - -	Aircraft - -	Bombs -	Missed -	—
Teal - - -	764	23	North Sea	Aircraft - -	Bombs and darts.	Missed -	—
Delmira - -	3,459	25	23 miles N.N.E. from Cape Antifer.	Submarine - -	Bomb after capture.	Beached -	—
Tewfikieh - -	2,490	25	Off Ailsa Craig -	Submarine - -	Chased -	Speed -	—
Lizzie - -	802	25	English Channel	Submarine - -	Chased -	Speed -	—
Groningen - -	988	25	North Sea - -	Submarine - -	Chased -	Speed -	—
Ousel - -	1,284	27	Between N. Hinder and Galloper.	Aircraft - -	Bombs -	Missed -	—
Dunedin - -	4,796	28	St. George's Channel.	Submarine - -	Chased -	Speed -	—
Brussels - -	1,380	28	8 miles W. from Maas L.V.	Submarine - -	Chased -	Speed -	—
City of Cambridge	3,844	28	25 miles N.W. by N. from Bishop Rock.	Submarine - -	Gunfire -	Speed -	—
Theseus - -	6,724	29	40 miles S.W. from Scilly Islands.	Submarine - -	Gunfire -	Speed -	—
Staffa - -	1,008	30	Off N. Galloper Buoy.	Aircraft - -	Bombs -	Missed -	—
APRIL 1915.		1915 April					
San Silvestre -	6,233	2	21 miles S. from Eddystone.	Submarine - -	Chased -	Speed -	—
Homer (tug) -	150	8	25 miles S.W. from Owers L.V.	Submarine - -	Gunfire and torpedo.	Speed -	—
Denaby - -	2,987	8	Off St. Catherine's Point.	Submarine - -	Torpedo -	Missed -	—
Wayfarer - -	9,599	11	60 miles W.N.W. from Scilly Isles.	Submarine - -	Torpedoed -	Towed in -	2

Name.	Tons.	Date.	Position.	Attacked by.	How attacked.	How saved.	Lives lost.
		1915. April.					
Serula - -	1,388	11	Off N. Hinder L.V.	Aircraft - -	Bombs -	Missed -	—
Imber - -	2,154	12	3 miles W. from N. Hinder L.V.	Aircraft - - -	Bombs -	Missed -	—
Manitou - -	6,849	16	Mediterranean -	Turkish T.B.	3 torpedoes -	Missed -	8
†La Rosarina -	8,332	17	Off S. of Ireland -	Submarine - -	Chased -	By gun -	—
Lestris - -	1,384	19	2 miles E. from N. Hinder L.V.	Submarine - -	Chased -	Speed -	—
Arvonian - -	2,794	22	English Channel -	Submarine - -	Torpedo -	Missed -	—
MAY 1915.							
		May					
Cayo Romano -	3,675	4	Off the Fastnet -	Submarine - -	Torpedo -	Missed -	—
Etonian - -	6,438	7	Off Queenstown -	Submarine - -	Chased -	Speed -	—
Narragansett -	9,196	7	Off S. Ireland -	Submarine - -	Torpedo -	Missed -	—
City of Exeter -	9,300	7	Off Queenstown -	Submarine - -	Chased -	Speed -	—
†Arabia - -	7,933	9	English Channel -	Submarine - -	Chased -	Speed -	—
City of Dortmund (Belgian Relief).	803	10	8 miles E. ½ N. from N. Hinder L.V.	Submarine - -	Torpedo -	Missed -	—
Poona - -	7,626	10	40 miles S.W. from Portland.	Submarine - -	Chased -	Speed -	—
Comeric (Belgian Relief).	3,980	20	Near N. Hinder L.V.	Submarine - -	Torpedo -	Missed -	.—
Marquette - -	7,057	25	English Channel -	Submarine - -	Chased -	Speed -	—
Ousel - -	1,284	27	2 miles E. from Elbow Buoy.	Submarine - -	Chased -	Speed -	—
†Argyllshire -	12,097	27	Off Havre - -	Submarine - -	Two torpedoes	Missed -	—
†Ping Suey -	6,458	29	English Channel -	Submarine - -	Gunfire -	By gun -	—
Megantic -	14,878	30	Off S. of Ireland -	Submarine - -	Chased -	Speed -	—
Colchester - -	1,209	30	North Sea - -	Submarine - -	Chased -	Speed -	—
†Demerara - -	11,484	31	Off S. of Ireland -	Submarine - -	Chased -	By gun -	—
Kelvinia - -	5,039	31	Bristol Channel -	Submarine - -	Chased -	Rescued -	—
Highland Laird -	4,223	31	St. George's Channel.	Submarine - -	Chased -	Speed -	—
†Garmoyle - -	1,229	31	Bristol Channel -	Submarine - -	Chased -	By gun -	—
Hambleton Range	3,682	31	English Channel -	Submarine - -	Chased -	Speed -	—
JUNE 1915.							
†Pontypridd -	1,556	1	40 miles S. ½ W. from Wolf Rock.	Submarine - -	Chased -	By gun -	—
Ballycotton -	1,273	6	30 miles S. from Waterford.	Submarine - -	Torpedo -	Missed -	—
Llandovery Castle	11,423	8	Off Cape Finisterre.	Submarine - -	Chased -	Speed -	—
Teespool - -	1,577	9	Bristol Channel -	Submarine - -	Gunfire -	Speed -	—
Tenasserim -	5,089	9	Off S. of Ireland -	Submarine - -	Chased -	Speed -	—
Orthia - -	4,225	10	Bristol Channel -	Submarine - -	Chased -	Speed -	—
Brussels - -	1,380	11	North Sea - -	Submarine - -	Chased -	Speed -	—
Alt - - -	1,004	15	St. George's Channel.	Submarine - -	Torpedo -	Missed -	—
Cromer - -	812	15	Near Galloper -	Submarine - -	Chased -	Speed -	—
Brussels - -	1,380	15	Near Sunk L.V. -	Submarine - -	Chased -	Speed -	—
Turnwell - -	4,264	16	35 miles S.W. from Tuskar.	Submarine - -	Bombs after capture.	Arrived Milford Haven.	—
Cameronia - -	10,963	20	23 miles W. from Skerries, Anglesey.	Submarine - -	Chased -	Speed -	—
Clan Robertson -	4,826	20	St. George's Chan.	Submarine - -	Chased -	Speed -	—
Twilight - -	3,100	20	White Sea - -	Mine - - -	Mine -	Arrived Archangel.	—
Sachem - -	5,354	21	23 miles W. from Liverpool Bar L.V.	Submarine - -	Chased -	Speed -	—
Herbert Fischer -	938	22	2 miles S.E. from Southwold.	Submarine - -	Torpedo -	Missed -	—
Kenmare - -	1,330	27	Between Ardmore and Capel Island.	Submarine - -	Gunfire -	Speed -	—
Orduna - -	15,499	28	20 miles S.W. from Smalls.	Submarine - -	Chased -	Speed -	—

Name.	Tons.	Date.	Position.	Attacked by	How attacked.	How saved.	Lives lost.
		1915. June					
Brussels - -	1,380	29	56 miles E. from Sunk L.V.	Submarine - -	Chased -	Speed -	—.
Teiresias - -	7,606	30	Small Bitter Lake	Mine - - -	Mine - -	Towed in -	--

JULY 1915.

Name.	Tons.	Date.	Position.	Attacked by	How attacked.	How saved.	Lives lost.
		July					
City of Edinburgh	6,255	2	English Channel -	Submarine - -	Torpedo ; gunfire.	Torpedo missed.	4
†Zealandic - -	8,090	2	English Channel -	Submarine - -	Chased -	Speed -	—
†Arabia - -	7,933	3	English Channel -	Submarine - -	Chased -	Speed -	—
Guido - -	2,093	3	North Sea - -	Submarine - -	Gunfire -	Speed -	—
Anglo Californian	7,333	4	90 miles S. from Queenstown.	Submarine - -	Gunfire -	Rescued -	21 including Master.
Groningen - -	988	6	4 miles from Galloper.	Aircraft - -	Bombs -	Missed -	--
Traquair - -	1,067	8	Knock Deep -	Submarine - -	Chased -	Speed -	---
Orduna - -	15,499	9	30 miles S. from Queenstown.	Submarine - -	Torpedo ; gunfire.	Torpedo missed.	--
Etonian - -	6,438	9	Off S. of Ireland -	Submarine - -	Chased -	Speed -	—
Panama - -	5,981	10	11 miles S. from Lizard.	Submarine - -	Chased -	Speed -	—
Warri - -	2,493	14	3 miles S.W. from Shipwash.	Submarine - -	Torpedo -	Missed -	—
†Corso - -	1.178	15	English Channel -	Submarine - -	Chased -	By gun -	—.
Batonm - -	4,054	18	North Sea - -	Submarine - -	Torpedoed -	Beached -	6
Brussels - -	1,380	20	20 miles E. ½ S. from S. Inner Gabbard Buoy.	Submarine - -	Torpedo -	Missed -	—
†Sheerness -	1,274	20	North Sea - -	Submarine - -	Chased -	By gun -	—
Madura - -	4,484	26	Entrance to White Sea.	Mine - - -	Mine - -	Arrived Archangel.	—
Canto - -	1,202	28	North Sea -	Submarine - -	Torpedo -	Missed -	—
Chinkoa - -	5,222	31	Off the Tagus -	Submarine - -	Chased -	Speed -	—
Galicia - -	5,922	31	In the Downs -	Mine - - -	Mine - -	Beached -	—

AUGUST 1915.

Name.	Tons.	Date.	Position.	Attacked by	How attacked.	How saved.	Lives lost.
		Aug.					
Como - -	1,246	4	Near N. Ronaldshay.	Submarine - -	Chased -	Rescued -	—
Cito - - -	819	5	2½ miles E. by S. from Aldborough Napes.	Submarine - -	Chased -	Speed -	—
Highland Harris -	6,023	6	North from Scilly Is.	Submarine - -	Chased -	Speed -	—
Edenside - -	322	8	Off Rattray Head	Submarine - -	Chased -	Speed -	—
Moto - - -	1,941	10	Bristol Channel -	Submarine - -	Torpedo -	Missed -	—
†Woodfield - -	3,584	12	Bristol Channel -	Submarine - -	Torpedo -	Missed -	—
Start Point -	3,840	14	10 miles S.E. from Tuskar.	Submarine - -	Chased -	Speed -	—
Highland Corrie -	7,583	14	3 miles E.N.E. from N. Foreland.	Mine - - -	Mine - -	Arrived Tilbury.	—
Eimstad - -	689	17	1 mile N. of Cross Sand L.V.	Submarines - -	Gunfire -	Darkness -	—
Matje - -	278	17	43 miles N. by E. from S. Bishops.	Submarine - -	Gunfire -	Rescued -	—
Cromer - -	812	17	North Sea - -	Submarine - -	Torpedo -	Missed -	—
City of Liverpool	1,101	18	40 miles S.S.W. from Smalls.	Submarine - -	Gunfire -	Rescued -	—
†Lady Wolseley -	1,424	18	55 miles N.E. ¼ E. from Longships.	Submarine - -	Gunfire -	By gun -	—
Nicosian - -	6,369	19	73 miles S. by W. from Old Head of Kinsale.	Submarine - -	Gunfire after capture.	Rescued -	—
Bovic - -	6,583	19	Off S. of Ireland -	Submarine - -	Chased -	Speed -	—

Name.	Tons.	Date.	Position.	Attacked by	How attacked.	How saved.	Lives lost.
		1915. Aug.					
San Melito - -	10,160	21	70 miles S.W. from Lizard.	Submarine - -	Gunfire -	Rescued -	—
Westbury - -	3,097	21	50 miles S. from Wolf.	Submarine - -	Gunfire -	Rescued -	—
Avocet -	1,219	22	Off S. of Ireland -	Submarine - -	Gunfire -	Speed -	—
Avocet - -	1,219	22	Off S. of Ireland -	Submarine - -	Chased -	Speed -	—
Baron Polwarth -	4,913	30	West from Scilly Is.	Submarine - -	Chased -	Speed -	—
Bretwalda - -	4,037	30	3 miles E. from Longsand L.V.	Mine - - -	Mine - -	Towed in -	—

SEPTEMBER 1915.

		Sept.					
†Southland - -	11,899	2	Ægean Sea -	Submarine - -	Torpedoed -	Since arrived.	—
W. T. Lewis (S.V.)	2,166	2	95 miles W. by N. from Fastnet.	Submarine - -	Gunfire after capture.	Towed in -	—
Crossby - -	3,893	4	200 miles W. from Bishop.	Submarine - -	Chased -	Speed -	—
Fulmar - -	1,270	6	9 miles W. from N. Hinder.	Aircraft - -	Bombs -	Missed -	—
Leicestershire -	8,059	7	Bay of Biscay -	Submarine - -	Chased -	Speed -	—
†Antilochus -	9,039	10	Mediterranean -	Submarine - -	Gunfire -	By gun -	—
San Zeferino -	6,430	18	2 miles N.N.W. from S. Goodwin L.V.	Mine - - -	Mine - -	Beached -	2
Nigretia - -	3,187	18	Off S. Foreland -	Mine - - -	Mine - -	Beached -	—

OCTOBER 1915.

		Oct.					
†Olympic - -	46,359	1	40 miles W. from C. Matapan.	Submarine - -	Chased -	Speed -	—
Enfield - -	2,124	4	4 miles S.S.W. from Folkestone Pier.	Mine - - -	Mine - -	Beached -	—
Ajax - - -	7,040	10	Mediterranean -	Submarine - -	Gunfire -	Rescued -	—
Oslo - - -	2,296	11	5 miles E. by N. ½ N. from Holy Island.	Submarine - -	Chased -	Speed -	—
Volscian - -	570	16	2½ miles S. by E. ½ E. from Longsand L.V.	Mine - - -	Mine - -	Beached -	—
Aleppo - -	3,870	18	1½ miles E. from Sunk Head Buoy.	Mine - - -	Mine - -	Beached -	—
Glenroy - -	2,755	29	20 miles E.N.E. from Peterhead.	Submarine - -	Chased -	Speed -	—
Avocet - -	1,408	30	8 miles W. from N. Hinder.	Aircraft - -	Bombs and machine gun.	Bombs missed.	—

NOVEMBER 1915.

		Nov.					
Japanese Prince -	4,876	3	Mediterranean -	Submarine - -	Chased -	Speed -	—
Dotterel - -	1,596	4	14 miles W. ½ N. from N. Hinder.	Aircraft - -	Bombs and machine guns.	Bombs missed.	—.
Mercian - -	6,305	4	Mediterranean -	Submarine - -	Gunfire -	Speed -	—
†City of York -	7,834	5	Mediterranean -	Submarine - -	Chased -	By gun -	—
†Huntsman -	7,460	5	Mediterranean -	Submarine - -	Chased -	By gun -	—
Lady Plymouth -	3,521	5	Off Algiers -	Submarine - -	Chased -	Speed -	—
Lady Plymouth -	3,521	6	Off Algiers -	Submarine - -	Gunfire -	Speed -	—
Pola - - -	3,061	6	Off Tukush Is., Algeria.	Submarine - -	Chased -	Speed -	—
City of Cambridge	3,844	8	Mediterranean -	Submarine - -	Chased -	Speed -	—
†Kashgar - -	8,840	9	Mediterranean -	Submarine - -	Chased -	By gun -	—
Ballater - -	2,286	21	In S. Edinburgh Channel.	Mine - - -	Mine - -	Towed in -	—
†City of Marseilles	8,250	23	Mediterranean -	Submarine - -	Gunfire -	By gun -	—

Name.	Tons.	Date.	Position.	Attacked by	How attacked.	How saved.	Lives lost.
		1915. Nov.					
†City of Lahore -	6,948	24	10 miles E. from Cape de Gata.	Submarine - -	Chased -	By gun -	—
Balgownie - -	1,061	27	Near N. Hinder -	Aircraft - -	Bombs and machine guns.	Bombs missed.	—
DECEMBER 1915.		Dec.					
†Benalla - -	11,118	3	Mediterranean -	Submarine - -	Gunfire -	By gun -	—
†Torilla - -	5,205	3	Mediterranean -	Submarine - -	Gunfire -	Rescued -	—
Andania - -	13,405	3	Mediterranean -	Submarine - -	Chased -	Rescued -	-—
†Tintoretto -	4,181	8	70 miles N.W. from Alexandria.	Submarine - -	Torpedo ; gunfire.	Missed ; gun	—
Southgarth -	2.414	12	Off La Panne, Belgium.	Aircraft - -	Bombs -	Missed -	—
†Cawdor Castle -	6,243	13	Mediterranean -	Submarine - -	Gunfire -	By gun -	—
Teucer - -	9,045	16	Mediterranean -	Submarine - -	Chased -	Speed -	-—
Levenpool - -	4,844	16	North Sea - -	Mine - - -	Mine - -	Beached -	—
Huronian - -	8,766	28	8 miles S. by E. from Fastnet.	Submarine - -	Torpedoed -	Arrived Bantry Bay.	—
†Ionic - -	12,332	31	Mediterranean -	Submarine - -	Torpedo -	Missed -	—
JANUARY 1916.		1916. Jan.					
San Tirso - -	6,236	1	Mediterranean -	Submarine - -	Chased -	Speed -	—
Glociiffe - -	2,211	2	North Sea - -	Mine - - -	Mine - -	Beached -	-—
Breslau - -	1,339	14	6 miles N.W. from Boulogne.	Mine - - -	Mine - -	Beached -	—
†Appam - -	7,781	15	135 miles E. ½ N. (true) from Madeira.	Möwe - -	Captured -	Released by order of U.S. Court.	2 gunners made prisoners.
†Baron Napier -	4,943	17	Mediterranean -	Submarine - -	Gunfire -	By gun -	—
†Esneh - -	3,247	17	Mediterranean -	Submarine - -	Gunfire -	By gun -	—
Gemma - -	1,385	22	Off Deal - -	Aircraft - -	Bombs -	Missed -	—
†Norseman -	9,542	22	Gulf of Salonica -	Submarine - -	Torpedoed -	Beached -	—
Falls City - -	4,729	22	South from Kentish Knock.	Mine - - -	Mine - -	Beached -	—
Carlo - - -	1,987	23	North Sea - -	Aircraft - -	Bombs -	Missed -	—
Esneh - -	3,247	23	Mediterranean -	Submarine - -	Torpedo -	Missed -	—
Astræa - -	3,229	26	Mediterranean -	Submarine - -	Captured -	Rescued -	—
†Trewellard -	4,202	27	Mediterranean -	Submarine - -	Chased -	By gun -	—
†Malta - -	6,064	28	Mediterranean -	Submarine - -	Gunfire -	By gun -	—
†Ingoma - -	5,686	30	Mediterranean -	Submarine - -	Gunfire -	By gun -	—
†Sebek - -	4,601	30	Mediterranean -	Submarine - -	Chased -	By gun -	—
FEBRUARY 1916.		Feb.					
†Professor - -	3,580	8	Mediterranean -	Submarine - -	Chased -	By gun -	—
Elswick Manor -	3,943	8	North Sea - -	Mine - - -	Mine - -	Towed in -	—
†Demerara - -	11,484	17	N. Atlantic -	Möwe - -	Chased -	Escaped -	—
Glenfoyle - -	1,680	20	North Sea - -	Aircraft - -	Bombs -	Missed -	—
†Olympic - -	46,359	23	Mediterranean -	Submarine - -	Torpedo -	Missed -	—
†Hunsworth -	3,038	28	Mediterranean -	Submarine - -	Gunfire -	By gun -	—
†Olympic - -	46,359	28	Mediterranean -	Submarine - -	Torpedo -	Missed -	—
†Benedict - -	3,378	28	Mediterranean -	Submarine - -	Gunfire -	By gun -	—
Malvina - -	1,244	29	North Sea - -	Mine - - -	Mine - -	Towed in -	—
Den of Ogil -	5,689	29	North Sea - -	Mine - - -	Mine - -	Towed in -	—
†Nyanza - -	6,695	29	Mediterranean -	Submarine - -	Chased -	By gun -	—
†Sebek - -	4,601	29	Mediterranean -	Submarine - -	Torpedo -	Missed -	—
MARCH 1916.		March					
†Turbo - -	4,782	1	Mediterranean -	Submarine - -	Gunfire -	By gun -	—
Arracan - -	5,520	5	Entrance to English Channel.	Submarine - -	Gunfire -	Speed -	—
Foreland - -	1,960	8	Off Islay - -	Submarine - -	Torpedo -	Missed -	—

Name.	Tons	Date.	Position.	Attacked by	How attacked.	How saved.	Lives lost.
		1916. March					
Falcon - -	675	16	10 miles N.W. by W. ½ W. from N. Hinder.	Submarine - -	Torpedo -	Missed -	—
Berwindvale -	5,242	16	30 miles W. from Fastnet.	Submarine - -	Torpedoed and captured.	Rescued -	—
Lutterworth -	994	18	21 miles N. from C. Antifer.	Submarine - -	Torpedo -	Missed -	—
†Kaisar-i-Hind -	11,430	23	Mediterranean -	Submarine - -	Torpedo -	Missed -	—
Eveline - -	2,605	23	85 miles S.W. by S. from Tuskar.	Submarine - -	Torpedo -	Missed -	—
†Phrygia - -	3,353	24	110 miles West from Fastnet.	Submarine - -	Gunfire -	By gun -	—
Duendes - -	4,602	25	70 miles West from Scilly Islands.	Submarine - -	Gunfire -	Speed -	—
†Inkonka - -	3,430	25	160 miles West from Scilly Islands.	Submarine - -	Torpedo -	Missed -	—
Musician - -	4,764	26	St. George's Channel.	Submarine - -	Chased -	Speed -	—
Mallard - -	1,300	30	15 miles E. ¾ S. from Inner Gabbard Buoy.	Submarine - -	Chased -	Speed -	—
Clinton - -	3,381	31	1½ miles S. by E. from Pakefield Gat Buoy.	Mine - - -	Mine - -	Beached -	—

APRIL 1916.

Name.	Tons	Date.	Position.	Attacked by	How attacked.	How saved.	Lives lost.
		April					
†Megantic - -	14,878	2	Mediterranean -	Submarine - -	Gunfire -	By gun -	—
†Laomedon -	6,693	2	Mediterranean -	Submarine - -	Gunfire -	By gun -	—
Brema - -	1,537	3	Between Shipwash and Longsand L.V.	Submarine - -	Torpedo -	Missed -	—
Ganges - -	4,177	5	Mediterranean -	Submarine - -	Gunfire -	Speed -	—
Vennacher - -	4,700	6	28 miles W.N.W. from Skerryvore.	Submarine - -	Torpedoed -	Arrived Lough Swilly.	—
Danubian - -	5,064	7	West of Scotland	Submarine - -	Gunfire -	Speed -	—
†Polyxena - -	5,737	9	Mediterranean -	Submarine - -	Gunfire -	By gun -	—
†Sydney Reid -	2,852	19	30 miles off Ushant	Submarine - -	Gunfire -	By gun -	—
†Norman Prince -	3,464	22	90 miles South from the Fastnet.	Submarine - -	Gunfire -	By gun -	—
†Bonvilston -	2,866	23	Mediterranean -	Submarine - -	Torpedo -	Missed -	—
F. D. Lambert -	2,195	25	5 miles E.S.E. from Gorleston Pier.	German warship -	Gunfire -	Damaged -	—
†Wandle - -	889	29	15 miles S.S.E. from Souter Point, Durham.	Submarine - -	Gunfire -	By gun -	—
Sussex - -	5,686	29	100 miles West from Ushant.	Submarine - -	Gunfire -	Speed -	—

MAY 1916.

Name.	Tons	Date.	Position.	Attacked by	How attacked.	How saved.	Lives lost.
		May					
†Phrygia - -	3,353	1	Bay of Biscay -	Submarine - -	Chased -	By gun -	—
†Clan MacFadyen	2,816	2	Bay of Biscay -	Submarine - -	Gunfire -	By gun -	—
†Port Augusta -	4,063	2	Bay of Biscay -	Submarine - -	Gunfire -	By gun -	—
†Clan Lindsay -	3,937	3	Bay of Biscay -	Submarine - -	Gunfire -	By gun -	—
Lestris - -	1,384	6	8 miles E. from N. Hinder.	Submarine - -	Chased -	Speed -	—
†Ramore Head -	4,444	9	Mediterranean -	Submarine - -	Chased -	By gun -	—
†Pagenturm -	5,000	12	Bay of Biscay -	Submarine - -	Chased -	Speed -	—
East Wales -	4,331	13	Off Cape Finisterre.	Submarine - -	Gunfire -	Speed -	—
†Rooke - -	3,391	17	Mediterranean -	Submarine - -	Gunfire -	By gun -	—
Seattle - -	5,133	19	Dunkirk Dock -	Aircraft - -	Bombs -	Damaged -	1
Ernst - -	653	19	Dunkirk Dock -	Aircraft - -	Machine gun	Slight damage.	—
Lord Strathcona -	7,335	20	Dunkirk Dock -	Aircraft - -	Bomb - -	Slight damage.	1

Name.	Tons.	Date.	Position.	Attacked by	How attacked.	How saved.	Lives lost.
		1916. May					
Valentia - -	3,242	21	Dunkirk Dock -	Aircraft - -	Bomb - -	Slight damage.	—
Ernst - -	653	21	Dunkirk Dock -	Aircraft - -	Bomb - -	Slight damage.	—
†Media - -	5,437	27	Mediterranean -	Submarine - -	Chased -	By gun -	—
JUNE 1916.		June					
†Maryland - -	4,731	1	Mediterranean -	Submarine - -	Torpedo -	Missed -	—
Parkgate - -	3,232	1	2 miles E.N.E. from Sunk Buoy.	Mine - - -	Mine - -	Beached -	—
†Cypria - -	2,950	2	Mediterranean -	Submarine - -	Gunfire -	By gun -	—
†Malakand -	7,653	9	Mediterranean -	Submarine - -	Torpedo -	Missed -	—
†Clodmoor -	3,753	16	Mediterranean -	Submarine - -	Gunfire -	By gun -	—
†Uganda - -	5,431	17	Mediterranean -	Submarine - -	Gunfire -	By gun -	—
Thurso - -	1,244	18	3 miles N.N.W. from Longstone.	Submarine - -	Chased -	Speed -	—
¡Le Coq - -	3,419	18	Mediterranean -	Submarine - -	Gunfire -	By gun -	—
†Malda - -	7,884	20	Mediterranean -	Submarine - -	Chased -	By gun -	—
†Ashby - -	1,947	24	Mediterranean -	Submarine - -	Gunfire -	Rescued -	—
†Mexico City -	5,078	25	Mediterranean -	Submarine - -	Gunfire -	By gun -	—
†Eloby - -	6,545	26	Mediterranean -	Submarine - -	Torpedo -	Missed	—
JULY 1916.		July					
†Reynolds - -	3,264	5	Mediterranean -	Submarine - -	Chased -	By gun -	—
†Strathness -	4,353	15	Mediterranean -	Submarine - -	Gunfire -	By gun -	—
†Kingsmere -	5,476	17	Mediterranean -	Submarine - -	Gunfire -	By gun -	—
†Anglesea - -	4,534	18	Mediterranean -	Submarine - -	Gunfire -	By gun -	—
Rubio - -	2,395	24	Mediterranean -	Submarine - -	Gunfire -	Rescued -	—
Frodingham -	1,081	29	Off Bridlington -	Aircraft - -	Bombs -	Missed -	—
†Bosnian - -	2,506	30	Mediterranean -	Submarine - -	Gunfire -	By gun -	—
AUGUST 1916.		Aug.					
†Kalimba - -	4,982	1	Mediterranean -	Submarine - -	Gunfire -	By gun -	—
Destro - -	859	3	10 miles N.E. by E. from Coquet Island.	Submarine - -	Gunfire -	Speed -	—
Galway Castle -	7,988	3	Near Gull L.V. -	Aircraft - -	Bombs -	Missed -	—
Ivo (S.V.) -	56	3	19 miles S.S.W. from Portland Bill.	Submarine - -	Bomb after capture.	Towed in -	—
Oruro - -	1,919	8	East Coast of Scotland.	Submarine - -	Chased -	Speed -	—
Hessle - -	952	10	Off Cape Barfleur	Submarine - -	Chased -	Rescued -	—
†Pacuare - -	3,891	18	Mediterranean -	Submarine - -	Gunfire -	By gun -	—
†Kincardine -	4,108	25	Mediterranean -	Submarine - -	Torpedo -	Missed -	—
Rio Tinto - -	2,165	26	Mediterranean -	Submarine - -	Chased -	Speed -	—
†Devian - -	3,689	26	Mediterranean -	Submarine - -	Gunfire -	By gun -	—
Katharine Park -	4,854	26	Bay of Biscay -	Mine - - -	Mine - -	Beached -	—
†Italiana - -	2,663	27	Mediterranean -	Submarine - -	Gunfire -	By gun -	—
†Strathness -	4,354	29	Mediterranean -	Submarine - -	Gunfire -	By gun -	—
†Polo - -	1,906	31	Mediterranean -	Submarine - -	Gunfire -	By gun -	—
†Regent - -	3,281	31	Mediterranean -	Submarine - -	Gunfire -	By gun -	—
SEPTEMBER 1916.		Sept.					
†Antinous - -	3,682	1	Mediterranean -	Submarine - -	Gunfire -	By gun -	—
†Glenogle - -	7,682	2	Mediterranean -	Submarine - -	Gunfire -	By gun -	—
Spen - -	900	3	English Channel -	Submarine - -	Gunfire -	Speed -	—
†Hunstanton -	4,504	5	Mediterranean -	Submarine - -	Gunfire -	By gun -	—
†San Dunstano -	6,220	6	English Channel -	Submarine - -	Gunfire -	By gun -	—
Ancona - -	1,168	6	English Channel -	Submarine - -	Gunfire -	Rescued -	—
†Bengali - -	5,684	6	English Channel -	Submarine - -	Gunfire -	By gun -	—
†Atalanta - -	519	11	English Channel -	Submarine - -	Gunfire -	By gun -	—
†Kyarra - -	6,953	11	Mediterranean -	Submarine - -	Chased -	Speed -	—
†Avocet - -	1,219	12	Off Ushant -	Submarine - -	Chased -	By gun -	—

Name.	Tons.	Date.	Position.	Attacked by	How attacked.	How saved.	Lives lost.
		1916. Sept.					
†Tahiti -	7,586	12	Mediterranean -	Submarine - -	Torpedo -	Missed -	—
†Irthington -	3,845	12	Mediterranean -	Submarine - -	Torpedo -	Missed -	—
†Cilurnum -	3,126	13	Mediterranean -	Submarine - -	Torpedo -	Failed to explode.	—
†Eptalofos - -	4,431	14	Mediterranean -	Submarine - -	Gunfire -	Rescued -	—
†Aysgarth -	3,118	14	Mediterranean -	Submarine - -	Torpedo -	Missed -	—
†Highcliffe-	3,238	14	Mediterranean -	Submarine - -	Gunfire -	By gun	—
Bellview -	3,567	17	Mediterranean -	Submarine - -	Gunfire -	By gun	—
†Dunbar -	3,672	17	Mediterranean -	Submarine - -	Torpedo -	Missed -	—
†Martaban -	5,106	18	Mediterranean -	Submarine - -	Gunfire -	By gun	—
†Katuna -	4,641	18	Mediterranean -	Submarine - -	Chased -	By gun	—
†Clan Chisholm -	2,647	18	Mediterranean -	Submarine - -	Gunfire -	By gun	—
†Persic - -	12,042	20	Mediterranean -	Submarine - -	Torpedo -	Missed -	—
Pembroke -	918	24	22 miles N. from Casquets.	Submarine - -	Gunfire -	Speed -	—
†Strathness -	4,354	24	Mediterranean -	Submarine - -	Gunfire -	By gun	—
†Dunrobin - -	3,617	26	Mediterranean -	Submarine - -	Gunfire -	By gun	—
Princess Victoria	1,687	28	English Channel	Submarine - -	Torpedo -	Missed -	—
†Nellore - -	6,853	29	Mediterranean -	Submarine - -	Gunfire -	By gun	—
†Pentyrch - -	3,382	30	Mediterranean -	Submarine - -	Torpedo ; gunfire.	Torpedo missed. By gun -	—
†Califol - -	6,572	30	West of Shetland	Submarine - -	Chased -	Rescued -	—
OCTOBER 1916.		Oct.					
†Carlo -	1,987	1	Mediterranean -	Submarine - -	Gunfire -	By gun -	—
†Jutland -	2,824	2	Mediterranean -	Submarine - -	Gunfire -	By gun -	—
†Melania -	5,824	2	Mediterranean -	Submarine - -	Torpedo -	Missed -	—
Camlake -	3,230	5	Mediterranean -	Submarine - -	Gunfire -	Rescued -	—
†Hyndford -	4,286	6	Arctic Sea -	Submarine - -	Gunfire -	By gun -	—
Coronilla -	1,312	7	English Channel	Submarine - -	Chased -	Weather -	—
Jupiter -	2,124	7	40 miles N.E. by E. from Longstone.	Submarine - -	Damaged by bomb after capture.	Towed in -	—
†Somali -	6,712	8	Mediterranean -	Submarine - -	Torpedo -	Missed -	—
†Sebek -	4,601	12	Mediterranean -	Submarine - -	Torpedoed -	Beached -	—
†Malda -	7,884	16	Mediterranean -	Submarine - -	Chased -	By gun -	—
†Royal Sceptre -	3,838	19	Mediterranean -	Submarine - -	Gunfire -	By gun -	—
†Glenmay -	2,485	20	English Channel	Submarine - -	Gunfire -	By gun -	—
Glenmorag -	3,535	20	English Channel	Submarine - -	Gunfire -	Speed -	—
†Matiana -	5,313	21	English Channel	Submarine - -	Gunfire -	By gun -	—
†Stork -	2,029	21	English Channel	Submarine - -	Gunfire -	By gun -	—
†Australia -	7,526	21	English Channel	Submarine - -	Chased -	By gun -	—
†Cyrene -	2,904	22	Off Ushant -	Submarine - -	Gunfire -	By gun -	—
†Lady Plymouth	3,521	22	Mediterranean -	Submarine - -	Torpedo -	Missed -	—
†Russian -	8,825	22	Mediterranean -	Submarine - -	Torpedo -	Missed -	—
Trevorian -	4,144	22	Black Sea -	Submarine - -	Torpedo -	Missed -	—
†Kandy -	4,921	23	Off South of Ireland.	Submarine - -	Chased -	By gun -	—
Alexandrian -	4,467	23	Off S.W. of Ireland.	Submarine - -	Torpedo -	Missed -	—
†Izaston -	3,060	24	English Channel	Submarine - -	Chased -	By gun -	—
Bagdale -	3,045	24	English Channel	Submarine - -	Captured -	Rescued -	—
†Venetia -	3,596	24	English Channel	Submarine - -	Gunfire -	By gun -	—
Joseph Davis -	2,243	24	English Channel	Submarine - -	Gunfire -	Rescued -	—
†Queen -	4,956	25	Mediterranean -	Submarine - -	Torpedo -	Missed -	—
†City of Edinburgh	6,255	26	English Channel	Submarine - -	Gunfire -	By gun -	—
†Fabian -	2,246	26	St. George's Channel.	Submarine - -	Gunfire -	By gun -	1
Morlais -	950	26	English Channel	Submarine - -	Gunfire -	Rescued -	—
Princess Thyra -	781	29	English Channel	Submarine - -	Gunfire -	Speed -	—
†Mantola -	8,253	30	North Sea -	Mine - - -	Mine -	Arrived London.	—
†Arlington Court	4,346	30	50 miles S.W. from Cape St. Vincent.	Submarine - -	Chased -	By gun -	—
NOVEMBER 1916.		Nov.					
†Lindenhall -	4,003	1	Mediterranean -	Submarine - -	Gunfire -	By gun -	—
†Daybreak -	3,238	1	Arctic Sea -	Submarine - -	Gunfire -	By gun -	—
†Huntspill -	5,440	1	Arctic Sea -	Submarine - -	Torpedoes -	Missed -	—

Name.	Tons.	Date.	Position.	Attacked by	How attacked.	How saved.	Lives lost.
		1916. Nov.					
†Polo -	1,906	2	Mediterranean -	Submarine - -	Torpedo -	Missed -	—
Siamese Prince -	4,847	4	210 miles S.W. from Scilly Isles.	Submarine - -	Gunfire -	Speed -	—
Ryhope - -	1,334	7	English Channel	Submarine - -	Gunfire -	Speed -	—
†Carlo - -	1,987	9	Bay of Biscay -	Submarine - -	Gunfire -	By gun -	—
†City of Cairo -	7,672	11	Off Cape Ortegal	Submarine - -	Gunfire -	By gun -	—
†Malda - -	7,884	11	English Channel	Submarine - -	Gunfire	Weather -	—
†Clan Buchanan -	5,212	12	Off Cape Ortegal	Submarine - -	Gunfire -	By gun -	—
†Islandia - -	2,069	13	Mediterranean -	Submarine - -	Gunfire -	By gun -	—
†Clan Chisholm -	2,647	13	Off Cape Finisterre.	Submarine - -	Gunfire -	By gun -	—
Idaho - -	4,887	14	190 miles W. by N. from Ushant.	Submarine - -	Torpedoes --	Missed ; rescued.	—
Bayhowel - -	4,343	14	Off Ushant -	Submarine - -	Chased -	Rescued -	—
Serbistan -	2,934	14	Off Ushant -	Submarine - -	Chased -	Rescued -	—
†Esneh - -	3,247	14	English Channel	Submarine - -	Gunfire -	By gun -	—
†Lake Michigan -	9,288	15	9 miles from Brest	Mine - - -	Mine - -	Reached Brest.	—
Saint Leonards -	4,574	15	Off Havre - -	Mine - - -	Mine - -	Reached Havre.	—
†Kintail - -	3,537	15	Off Ushant -	Submarine - -	Gunfire -	By gun -	—
†Monmouth -	4,078	17	Off Cherbourg -	Mine - - -	Mine - -	Towed in -	—
†Kintail - -	3,537	17	English Channel	Submarine - -	Chased -	By gun -	—
†Tanfield - -	4,300	18	English Channel	Submarine - -	Chased -	Weather -	—
Palm Branch -	3,891	21	English Channel	Submarine - -	Gunfire -	Speed -	—
Errington Court -	4,461	21	Off S.W. Ireland	Submarine - -	Gunfire -	Speed -	—
†Peshawur -	7,634	22	Off Ushant -	Submarine - -	Chased -	By gun -	—
Braemar Castle (hospital ship).	6,318	23	Mykoni Channel	Mine (?) - -	Mine (?) -	Beached -	4
†Egyptiana -	3,818	24	Off Cape Finisterre	Submarine - -	Gunfire -	By gun -	—
†Clan Colquhoun	5,856	25	Mediterranean -	Submarine - -	Gunfire -	By gun -	--
†Arum - -	3,681	25	Mediterranean -	Submarine - -	Gunfire -	By gun -	—
†Highland Heather	6,036	26	Mediterranean -	Submarine - -	Torpedoed -	Arrived -	—
†Huntscape -	2,933	27	English Channel	Submarine - -	Gunfire -	By gun -	—
†Ballater -	2,286	28	English Channel	Submarine - -	Gunfire -	By gun -	—
†Pikepool -	3,683	28	Mediterranean -	Submarine - -	Torpedo -	Missed -	—
†Megantic -	14,878	28	Mediterranean -	Submarine - -	Chased -	Speed -	—
†Polanna -	2,345	29	English Channel	Submarine - -	Gunfire -	By gun -	—
Swazi -	4,941	29	Entrance to English Channel.	Submarine - -	Chased -	Rescued -	—
†Kandy -	4,921	29	English Channel	Submarine - -	Gunfire	By gun -	—
†Ibex -	951	30	English Channel	Submarine - -	Chased -	Speed -	—
Verdala -	5,880	30	Off Ushant -	Submarine - -	Gunfire -	Rescued -	—
Eggesford -	4,414	30	30 miles N. from Ushant.	Submarine - -	Damaged after capture.	Towed in -	—
DECEMBER 1916.		1916. Dec.					
†Dykland -	4,291	1	Off Ushant -	Submarine - -	Gunfire -	By gun -	—
†Dunachton -	5,201	1	Mediterranean -	Submarine - -	Gunfire -	By gun -	—
†Kintuck -	4,616	2	Off S.W. Ireland	Submarine - -	Gunfire -	By gun -	—
†Nagoya -	6,854	2	Mediterranean -	Submarine - -	Gunfire -	By gun -	—
†Umona -	3,753	2	Arctic Sea -	Submarine - -	Gunfire -	By gun -	—
†Reims -	3,717	2	Mediterranean -	Submarine - -	Chased -	Speed -	—
†Tapton -	3,569	3	Off Ushant -	Submarine - -	Gunfire -	By gun -	—
†Lucellum -	5,184	3	Mediterranean -	Submarine - -	Torpedoed -	Arrived Villefranche.	—
†Sutherland Grange.	6,852	4	Off Ushant -	Submarine - -	Gunfire -	Speed -	—
Taxandrier -	4,231	4	Off Ushant -	Submarine - -	Gunfire -	Rescued -	—
Rossia -	4,576	4	Off Ushant -	Submarine - -	Chased -	Speed -	—
†Castalia -	6,396	5	Mediterranean -	Submarine - -	Gunfire -	By gun -	—
†Camberwell -	4,078	5	Mediterranean -	Submarine - -	Gunfire -	By gun -	—
†Poona -	7,626	6	English Channel -	Mine - - -	Mine - -	Towed in -	—
†John Sanderson	3,274	6	Entrance to English Channel.	Submarine - - ?	Gunfire -	By gun -	—
†Usher -	3,594	7	Off Scilly Is. -	Submarine - -	Chased -	By gun -	—
†Usher -	3,594	8	W. from Ushant -	Submarine - -	Chased -	By gun -	—
†Antar -	3,580	8	Off Coast of Portugal.	Submarine - -	Chased -	By gun -	—

Name.	Tons.	Date.	Position.	Attacked by	How attacked.	How saved.	Lives lost.
		1916. Dec.					
†Astyanax - -	4,872	9	Off S. Ireland -	Submarine - -	Chased -	Speed -	—
†Rosefield - -	3,089	10	Mediterranean -	Submarine - -	2 torpedoes -	Missed -	—
†Caledonia - -	7,572	14	3 miles E. from Planier Island Light.	Mine - - . -	Mine - -	Arrived Marseilles.	1
Hildawell - -	2,494	14	Off Usbant -	Submarine - -	Chased -	Rescued -	—
†Queen - -	4,956	15	Off S. Ireland -	Submarine - -	Gunfire -	By gun -	—
Vancouver -	4,419	15	Bay of Biscay -	Submarine - -	Gunfire -	Rescued -	—
†Rio Tinto - -	2,165	15	150 miles S.W. by S. from Fastnet.	Submarine - -	Gunfire -	By gun -	—
†Maryland - -	4,731	16	W. from Gibraltar	Submarine - -	Gunfire -	By gun -	—
Red Rose -	401	16	English Channel -	Submarine - -	Captured -	Rescued -	—
Englishman (S.V.).	144	16	N. from Scillies -	Submarine - -	Gunfire -	Rescued -	—
†Petrograd -	1,713	17	Mediterranean -	Submarine - -	Chased -	By gun -	—
†Dartmoor - -	2,870	19	Mediterranean -	Submarine - -	Gunfire -	By gun -	—.-
†Griqua - -	3,344	20	Mediterranean -	Submarine - -	Gunfire -	By gun -	—
Arracan - -	5,520	21	Off S.W. Ireland -	Submarine - -	Chased -	Speed -	—
†Clan Stuart -	5,775	22	Mediterranean -	Submarine - -	Torpedo -	Missed -	—
William Middleton.	2,543	23	Bristol Channel -	Submarine - -	Captured -	Rescued -	—
Bertrand - -	3,613	23	Bristol Channel -	Submarine - -	Gunfire -	Rescued -	—
†Benalder - -	3,044	23	Mediterranean -	Submarine - -	Torpedoed -	Arrived Alexandria.	—
†Wisbech - -	1,282	23	Bay of Biscay -	Submarine - -	Gunfire -	By gun -	—
†Paul Paix -	4,196	24	Bristol Channel -	Mine - - -	Mine - -	Towed in -	—
†Newstead -	2,836	24	W. from Gibraltar	Submarine - -	Chased -	Speed -	—
†Cameronian -	5,861	24	Mediterranean -	Submarine - -	Torpedo -	Missed -	—
†Suffolk - -	7,573	28	English Channel -	Mine - -	Mine - -	Arrived Portsmouth.	—
†Polesley - -	4,221	28	Mediterranean -	Submarine - -	Chased -	By gun -	—
†Oxonian - -	6,306	28	Mediterranean -	Submarine - -	Torpedo -	Missed -	—
†Malda - -	7,884	30	Mediterranean -	Submarine - -	Torpedo -	Missed -	—
†Aspenleaf -	7,535	30	English Channel -	Mine - - -	Mine - -	Towed in -	—
†City of Oran -	7,395	31	English Channel -	Submarine - -	Gunfire -	By gun -	—

JANUARY 1917.

		1917. Jan.					
†Sussex - -	5,686	1	Off Calais - -	Mine - - -	Mine - -	Beached -	—
†Bengali - -	5,684	2	Mediterranean -	Submarine - -	Gunfire -	By gun -	—
Luga - -	1,988	2	Bay of Biscay -	Submarine - -	Gunfire -	Speed -	—
†Cromarty -	2,742	2	Bay of Biscay -	Submarine - -	Chased -	By gun -	—
†Huntsend -	8,826	3	Mediterranean -	Submarine - -	Torpedoed -	Towed in -	1
Eastgate -	4,277	5	Bay of Biscay -	Submarine - -	Captured -	Brought in -	—
†La Rosarina -	8,332	6	Off Ushant -	Submarine - -	Gunfire -	By gun -	—
†Bampton - -	4,496	7	Off Coast of Portugal.	Submarine - -	Chased -	Speed -	—
Alexandrian -	4,467	9	20 miles S.W. from Fastnet.	Submarine - -	Gunfire and torpedo.	Beached Berehaven.	—
†Inventor - -	7,679	10	W. from Scillies -	Submarine - -	Gunfire -	By gun -	—
†Knight Companion.	7,241	10	Off C. Finisterre -	Submarine - -	Gunfire -	By gun -	—
†Amazon - -	10,037	13	Off C. Finisterre -	Submarine - -	Torpedo -	Missed -	—
Fernley - -	3,820	13	English Channel -	Submarine - -	Gunfire -	Rescued -	—
Ussa - -	2,066	14	English Channel -	Submarine - -	Gunfire -	Speed -	—
†Cardiganshire -	9,426	14	Mediterranean -	Submarine - -	Chased -	Speed -	—
†Comeric - -	3,980	15	Mediterranean -	Submarine - -	Torpedo -	Missed -	—
†Caithness -	3,500	18	Bay of Biscay -	Submarine - -	Gunfire -	By gun -	—
†Deseado - -	11,477	19	Off S.W. Ireland -	Submarine - -	Gunfire -	By gun -	—
†Trevaylor -	4,249	19	Off S.W. Ireland -	Submarine - -	Gunfire -	By gun -	—
†Bendoran -	4,074	22	225 miles S.W. by W. from Fastnet.	Submarine - -	Gunfire -	Rescued -	—
Argo - -	1,102	22	North Sea - -	Submarine - -	Gunfire -	Speed -	—
†Messina - -	4,271	23	Entrance to English Channel.	Submarine - -	Chased -	Speed -	—
†Clumberhall -	3,599	25	Off S.W. Ireland -	Submarine - -	Chased -	Speed -	—
Valentia - -	3,242	26	114 miles N.W. by W. from the Skelligs.	Submarine - -	Gunfire -	Speed -	—

Name.	Gross Tons.	Date.	Position.	Attacked by	How attacked.	How saved.	Lives lost.
		1917. Jan.					
†Liddesdale -	4,403	26	65 miles W. by N. from the Skelligs.	Submarine - -	Gunfire -	By gun -	—
†Ingleby - -	3,815	27	Mediterranean -	Submarine - -	Torpedo -	Missed -	—
†Miniota - -	4,928	31	Off S. Ireland -	Submarine - -	Gunfire -	By gun -	—
Baron Garioch -	1,831	31	North Sea - -	Submarine - -	Torpedo -	Missed -	—
†Foyle - -	4,703	31	Entrance to English Channel.	Submarine - -	Gunfire -	By gun -	—

FEBRUARY 1917.

Name.	Gross Tons.	Date.	Position.	Attacked by	How attacked.	How saved.	Lives lost.
		Feb.					
Wellholme (S.V.)	89	1	English Channel -	Submarine - -	Gunfire -	Rescued -	—
†Malta - -	2,236	2	Off S. Ireland -	Submarine - -	Gunfire -	Speed -	—
†Saturnia - -	8,611	3	Off S.W. Ireland -	Submarine - -	Torpedo ; gunfire.	Missed ; by gun.	—
†Tiverton - -	3,825	3	Mediterranean -	Submarine - -	Torpedo -	Missed -	—
†Tresillian - -	3,585	4	Off S.W. Ireland -	Submarine - -	Torpedo ; gunfire.	Missed ; by gun.	—
Manchester Hero	5,738	5	Off S.W. Ireland -	Submarine - -	Gunfire -	Rescued -	—
Ambassador -	2,578	5	Off S.W. Ireland -	Submarine - -	Gunfire -	Rescued -	—
Ainsdale (S.V.)	1,825	5	Off S.W. Ireland -	Submarine - -	Gunfire -	Towed in -	—
†Kaffir Prince -	2,228	5	Off S.W. Ireland -	Submarine - -	Gunfire -	By gun -	—
†Argyllshire -	12,097	5	3 miles S.W. from Start Point.	Submarine - -	Torpedoed -	Arrived -	—
Dorothy - -	3,806	6	Mediterranean -	Submarine - -	Torpedo -	Missed -	—
Mona's Queen -	1,559	6	English Channel -	Submarine - -	Torpedo -	Missed -	—
†Explorer - -	7,608	6	Off S. Ireland -	Submarine - -	Torpedoed -	Arrived -	—
Tyndareus -	11,000	6	10 miles off Cape Agulhas.	Mine - -	Mine - -	Towed in -	—
Wallace - -	3,930	7	Off S. Ireland -	Submarine - -	Gunfire -	Rescued -	1 Chief Officer made prisoner.
†Cranley - -	4,644	7	Off S. Ireland -	Submarine - -	Chased -	Speed -	—
Etal Manor -	1,875	7	North Sea - -	Submarine - -	Torpedo -	Missed -	—
Hotham Newton	2,648	8	Entrance to English Channel. -	Submarine - -	Gunfire -	Rescued -	—
Peregrine - -	1,681	8	English Channel -	Submarine - -	Gunfire -	Speed -	—
Hornsey - -	1,803	8	North Sea - -	Submarine - -	Gunfire -	Rescued -	—
†Jumna - -	4,152	8	Mediterranean -	Submarine - -	Chased -	Speed -	—
†San Fraterno -	9,587	10	Entrance to Firth of Forth.	Mine - -	Mine - -	Beached -	—
†Roanoke - -	3,755	11	4 miles S.E. from Girdleness.	Submarine - -	Torpedoed -	Towed in -	1
†Woodfield -	4,300	11	6 miles S.S.E. from Beachy Head.	Submarine - -	Torpedoed -	Beached -	—
†Ariadne Christine.	3,550	11	Off Scilly Isles -	Submarine - -	Gunfire -	By gun -	—
†Cyclops - -	9,033	11	Off S.W. Ireland -	Submarine - -	Chased -	Speed -	—
†Geddington Court.	3,989	11	Mediterranean -	Submarine - -	Two torpedoes	Missed -	—
Portuguese Prince	4,981	11	Bay of Biscay -	Submarine - -	Gunfire -	Speed -	—
Pinna - -	6,288	12	7½ miles S.S.E. from S. Bishop.	Submarine - -	Torpedoed -	Beached -	—
†Gleneden -	4,735	12	St. George's Channel.	Submarine - -	Gunfire -	By gun -	—
Kamouraska -	4,903	12	Off S.W. Ireland	Submarine - -	Torpedo -	Missed -	—
†Chenab - -	3,549	12	Mediterranean -	Submarine - -	Gunfire -	Speed -	—
†Sequoya - -	5,263	13	Bristol Channel -	Submarine - -	Gunfire -	By gun -	1
†Auteros - -	4,241	13	Off S. Ireland -	Submarine - -	Torpedo -	Missed -	—
†Trowbridge -	3,712	14	Mediterranean -	Submarine - -	Torpedoed -	Towed in -	1
Millicent Knight	3,563	14	In the Downs -	Aircraft -	Bombs -	Missed -	—
Harrow - -	1,777	15	North Sea - -	Submarine - -	Torpedo -	Missed -	—
Kittiwake -	1,866	15	St. George's Channel.	Submarine - -	Torpedo -	Missed -	—
†Celtic - -	20,904	15	Irish Sea - -	Mine - -	Mine - -	Arrived Liverpool.	—
Pollerea - -	1,209	16	Bay of Biscay -	Submarine - -	Gunfire -	Arrived Bayonne.	—
†The Princess -	623	16	Bristol Channel -	Submarine - -	Gunfire -	By gun -	—
†Delphic - -	8,273	16	Off S.W. Ireland	Submarine - -	Torpedo -	Missed -	—

Name.	Gross Tons.	Date.	Position.	Attacked by	How attacked.	How saved.	Lives lost.
		1917. Feb.					
†Grelford - -	2,823	16	Bay of Biscay -	Submarine - -	Gunfire -	By gun -	—
†Sheerness - -	1,274	16	Bristol Channel -	Submarine - -	Gunfire -	By gun -	—
Buranda - -	3,651	16	Mediterranean -	Submarine - -	Gunfire -	Arrived Alicante.	—
†Grelford - -	2,823	17	Off Ushant -	Submarine - -	Gunfire -	By gun -	—
Gwent - -	5,754	17	Entrance to English Channel.	Submarine - -	Chased -	Speed -	—
†Cambrian -	5,626	18	English Channel -	Submarine - -	Chased -	Gunfire ↲	—
†Hunsworth -	2,991	18	English Channel -	Submarine - -	Torpedoed -	Towed in -	2
†Asturian -	3,193	18	Mediterranean -	Submarine - -	Gunfire -	Rescued -	2
†Berrima -	11,137	18	English Channel -	Submarine - -	Torpedoed -	Towed in -	4
†Janeta -	4,271	18	Mediterranean -	Submarine - -	Gunfire -	By gun -	—
†Kovno -	1,985	18	North Sea - -	Submarine - -	Chased -	Speed -	—
†Araguaya -	10,537	19	Off S.W. Ireland -	Submarine - -	Chased -	Speed -	—
†Northwaite -	3,626	19	Mediterranean -	Submarine - -	Gunfire -	By gun -	—
†Carperby -	2,104	20	Off St. Ives -	Submarine - -	Torpedo -	Missed -	—
†Tahiti -	7,585	20	English Channel -	Submarine - -	Chased -	Gunfire -	—
†Nascent -	3,720	21	Off S. Ireland -	Submarine - -	Gunfire -	By gun -	—
†Cameronian	5,861	21	Mediterranean -	Submarine - -	Torpedo -	Missed -	—
†Canadian -	9,309	22	Off S.W. Ireland -	Submarine - -	Chased -	Speed -	—
†Gambia -	3,296	22	English Channel -	Submarine - -	Chased -	Speed -	—
†Ashtabula	7,025	22	North Sea - -	Mine - - -	Mine - -	Arrived London.	—
Largo Law	3,974	24	English Channel -	Submarine - -	Torpedo ; gunfire.	Missed ; fog	—
†Somme -	1,828	24	English Channel -	Submarine - -	Gunfire -	By gun -	—
†Megantic -	14,878	24	Mediterranean -	Submarine - -	Torpedo -	Missed -	—
†Silverdale	3,835	24	Off S.W. Ireland	Submarine - -	Torpedo -	Missed -	—
†Gleneden -	4,735	24	Mediterranean -	Submarine - -	Torpedo -	Missed -	—
†Hooton -	1,892	25	Bristol Channel -	Submarines - -	Chased . -	By gun -	—
†Novington	3,442	25	Mediterranean -	Submarine - -	Torpedo -	Missed -	—
†Venus -	3,152	25	Mediterranean -	Submarine - -	Gunfire -	By gun -	—
†Cameron -	3,044	26	Off W. Ireland -	Submarine - -	Gunfire -	Rescued -	—
Lydia -	1,133	27	English Channel -	Submarine - -	Gunfire -	Rescued -	—
†San Patricio -	9,712	27	Off Orkney Islands.	Submarine - -	Chased -	By gun -	—
†Polzeath -	882	27	English Channel -	Submarine - -	Gunfire -	By gun -	—
†Bellorado -	4,649	27	Mediterranean -	Submarine - -	Gunfire -	By gun -	3 including Master.
†Ayr - -	3,050	27	Off S.W. Ireland	Submarine - -	Gunfire -	By gun -	—
†Huntscape	2,933	28	English Channel -	Submarine - -	Gunfire -	By gun -	—
†Lynorta -	3,684	28	Mediterranean -	Submarine - -	Chased -	Speed -	—
†Rowena -	3,017	28	Mediterranean -	Submarine - -	Gunfire -	By gun -	—

MARCH 1917.

Name.	Gross Tons.	Date.	Position.	Attacked by	How attacked.	How saved.	Lives lost.
		March					
Glenart Castle (hospital ship).	6,807	1	English Channel -	Mine (?) - -	Mine (?) -	Towed in -	--
†Euterpe -	3,540	1	Mediterranean -	Submarine - -	Torpedoed -	Arrived -	2
†Tabarka -	3,933	1	Mediterranean -	Submarine - -	Torpedo -	Missed -	—
†Birchgrove	2,821	1	North Sea - -	Submarine - -	Gunfire -	By gun -	—
Sarus (crane barge).	819	1	Off Boulogne -	Submarine - -	Gunfire -	Rescued -	—
Donegal -	1,885	1	English Channel -	Submarine - -	Chased -	Speed -	—
Trojan -	4,017	2	Off S.W. Ireland	Submarine - -	Torpedo -	Missed -	—
†Argyll -	3,547	3	Off S.W. Ireland	Submarine - -	Gunfire -	By gun -	—
Adelaide (S.V.)	180	4	English Channel -	Submarine - -	Gunfire after capture.	Towed in -	—
†Princess Melita -	1,094	5	North Sea - -	Submarine - -	Torpedo -	Missed -	—
†Syndic -	2,727	6	Off S.W. Ireland -	Submarine - -	Gunfire -	By gun -	—
†Zambesi -	3,759	7	English Channel -	Submarine - -	Chased -	Speed -	—
†Pagenturm	5,000	7	Mediterranean -	Submarine - -	Torpedo -	Failed to explode.	—
Salvus -	2,259	10	Off S. Ireland -	Submarine - -	Two torpedoes.	Missed -	—
†Aracataca -	4,154	10	250 miles W.N.W. from Fastnet.	Submarine - -	Gunfire -	By gun -	1

Name.	Gross Tons.	Date.	Position.	Attacked by	How attacked.	How saved.	Lives lost.
		1917. March					
†Boonah - -	5,926	10	Off W. Ireland -	Submarine - -	Chased -	Gun - -	—
Pylades - -	681	10	North Sea - -	Submarine - -	Torpedo -	Missed -	—
†San Eduardo -	6,225	10	8 miles S.S.E. from Stornoway.	Submarine - -	Torpedoed -	Arrived -	—
†Ambassador -	2,578	10	Entrance to English Channel.	Submarine - -	Gunfire -	By gun -	—
†Spectator - -	3,808	11	Off S.W. Ireland	Submarine - -	Gunfire -	By gun -	—
†Eddystone -	853	11	Bristol Channel -	Submarine - -	Gunfire -	By gun -	—
†Semantha -	2,847	12	Off S. Ireland -	Submarine - -	Gunfire -	By smoke -	—
†Port Chalmers -	6,534	12	Off S.W. Ireland	Submarine - -	Chased -	By gun -	—
†Winnebago -	4,666	12	Off Scilly Islands	Submarine - -	Torpedoed -	Towed in -	—
Ravelston -	2,085	12	North Sea - -	Submarine - -	Torpedo -	Missed -	-
†Raphael - -	4,699	12	Off S. Ireland -	Submarine - -	Chased -	Speed -	—
Luciline - -	3,765	13	40 miles W.N.W. from Tearaght Island.	Submarine - -	Torpedoed -	Beached -	15
†Glencliffe -	3,673	13	St. George's Channel.	Submarine - -	Gunfire -	By gun -	—
†Trecarne - -	4,196	13	W. from Scilly Islands.	Submarine - -	Gunfire -	By gun -	—
†Burgundy -	3,364	13	Off S.W. Ireland	Submarine - -	Gunfire -	By gun -	—
†Orsova - -	12,036	14	3 miles E. by S. ½ S. from Eddystone.	Submarine - -	Torpedoed -	Reached port.	8
†Ranella - -	5,583	14	Off S. Ireland -	Submarine - -	Torpedo -	Missed -	—
†Tortuguero -	4,175	14	Off N.W. Ireland	Submarine - -	Gunfire -	Speed -	—
†Fallodon -	3,012	14	English Channel -	Submarine - -	Gunfire -	By gun -	—·
†Polescar - -	5,832	14	Off N.W. Ireland	Submarine - -	Chased -	Speed -	—
†Lepanto - -	6,389	15	English Channel -	Submarine - -	Gunfire -	By gun -	—
†Willaston - -	5,658	15	Entrance to English Channel.	Submarine - -	Gunfire -	By gun -	—
Raymond (S.V.)	200	16	Off Ushant - -	Submarine - -	Gunfire -	Rescued -	—
†Ruahine - -	10,758	17	167 miles S.W. by S. from Fastnet.	Submarine - -	Torpedo -	Missed -	—
†Anglo-Egyptian	7,379	17	Mediterranean -	Submarine - -	Chased -	Speed -	—
†Karmala - -	8,983	17	Mediterranean -	Submarine - -	Torpedo; gunfire.	Missed ; by gun.	—
†Laurel Leaf -	5,631	17	Off S. Ireland -	Submarine - -	Torpedo -	Missed -	—
†Baygitano -	3,073	17	W. from Ushant -	Submarine - -	Torpedo -	Missed -	—
Danubian - -	5,064	20	11 miles S. by W. from Asses Ears, Aden.	Mine - - -	Mine - -	Arrived -	—
†Huntscape -	2,933	21	English Channel -	Submarine - -	Torpedoed -	Arrived -	—
Asturias (hospital ship).	12,002	21	5 miles S. from Start Point.	Submarine - -	Torpedoed -	Beached -	35
†South Pacific -	3,661	22	Mediterranean -	Submarine - -	Chased -	By gun -	—
†Mexico - -	5,549	23	English Channel	Submarine - -	Torpedoed -	Arrived -	—
Genesee - -	2,892	23	North Sea - -	Submarine - -	Torpedo -	Missed -	—
Sagenite - -	712	23	North Sea - -	Submarine - -	Torpedo -	Missed -	—
†Crown of Granada.	2,746	23	Atlantic - -	Submarine - -	Gunfire -	By gun -	—
†Coronado - -	6,539	24	Off S.W. Ireland	Submarine - -	Gunfire -	By gun -	—
†Shimosa - -	4,221	24	Atlantic - -	Submarine - -	Gunfire -	By gun -	—
†Ionian - -	8,268	24	English Channel -	Submarine - -	Torpedo -	Missed -	—
†Manhattan -	8,004	25	W. from Scilly Islands.	Submarine - -	Gunfire -	By gun -	—
†Thessalia -	3,691	25	Mediterranean -	Submarine - -	Torpedo -	Missed -	—
†Tremorvah -	3,654	26	Mediterranean -	Submarine - -	Torpedo -	Missed -	—
†Loos - -	2,787	26	Mediterranean -	Submarine - -	Gunfire -	By gun and smoke.	—
Kelsomoor -	3,174	26	Off S.W. Ireland -	Submarine - -	Torpedo -	Missed -	—
†Trecarne - -	4,196	26	Mediterranean -	Submarine - -	Chased -	Speed -	—
†Ventura de Larrinaga.	4,618	27	Off S.W. Ireland	Submarine - -	Gunfire -	Speed -	—
†Baron Napier -	4,943	27	Off S.W. Ireland	Submarine - -	Torpedo -	Missed -	—
Andree - -	3,689	27	Off Ushant -	Submarine - -	Torpedo -	Missed ·-	—
†Kurmark - -	5,137	27	Mediterranean -	Submarine - -	Torpedo -	Missed -	—
Le Coq - -	3,419	27	Bay of Biscay -	Submarine - -	Torpedo -	Missed -	—
†Borderer - -	4,372	28	St. George's Channel.	Submarine - -	Gunfire -	Nightfall -	—
†Kurdistan -	3,720	28	Off S. Ireland -	Submarine - -	Two torpedoes	Missed -	—

Name.	Gross Tons.	Date.	Position.	Attacked by	How attacked.	How saved.	Lives lost.
		1917. March					
†Geo - - -	3,048	29	Mediterranean -	Submarine - -	Torpedo -	Missed -	—
†Khiva - -	8,947	29	Mediterranean -	Submarine - -	Torpedo -	Missed -	—
Amsterdam -	1,777	30	North Sea - -	Submarine - -	Torpedo -	Missed -	—
†Edernian - -	3,588	30	English Channel	Mine - - -	Mine - -	Reached Dieppe.	—
†Parklands -	1,607	30	English Channel	Submarine - -	Chased -	By gun -	—
Penmorvah -	4,323	31	English Channel	Submarine - -	Torpedo -	Missed -	—
Amulet - -	1,018	31	North Sea - -	Aircraft - -	Bombs -	Missed -	—
Quentin - -	1,274	31	North Sea - -	Aircraft - -	Bombs -	Missed -	—
Gloucester Castle (Hospital Ship).	7,999	31	English Channel	Submarine - -	Torpedoed -	Towed in -	3
†Valacia - -	6,526	31	English Channel	Submarine - -	Torpedoed -	Towed in -	—
†Queen Louise -	4,879	31	English Channel	Submarine - -	Torpedoed	Reached Havre.	—
Sofie - -	354	31	English Channel	Submarine - -	Gunfire -	Weather -	—·
†Ocean Monarch	4,511	31	Off S. Ireland -	Submarine - -	Torpedo -	Failed to explode.	—
†Parklands -	1,607	31	English Channel	Submarine - -	Gunfire -	By gun -	—
†Ariosto - -	4,313	31	Mediterranean -	Submarine - -	Torpedo -	Missed -	—
APRIL 1917.		April					
†Wandby - -	3,981	2	Bay of Biscay -	Submarine - -	Gunfire -	By gun -	—
†Brodliffe - -	5,893	3	Mediterranean -	Submarine - -	Torpedo -	Missed -	—
†Oberon - -	5,142	3	Mediterranean -	Submarine - -	Torpedoed -	Arrived -	—
†Cloughton -	4,221	3	Mediterranean -	Mine - - -	Mine - -	Towed in -	—
†Queensland Transport.	4,663	4	Mediterranean -	Submarine - -	Torpedo -	Missed -	—
Southerndown -	4,431	4	Atlantic - -	Submarine - -	Chased -	Speed -	—
†Dundrennan -	4,248	4	Mediterranean -	Submarine - -	Gunfire -	By gun -	—
†Kanawha - -	3,884	4	Off Ushant -	Submarine - -	Gunfire -	Speed -	—
†Hyacinthus -	5,756	4	Off N.W. Ireland	Submarine - -	Torpedo -	Missed -	—
†Kangaroo - -	4,348	5	Mediterranean -	Submarine - -	Gunfire -	By gun -	—
†Ethelaric - -	3,232	6	Off S.W. Ireland	Submarine - -	Torpedo -	Missed -	—
Lime Branch -	5,379	6	Off Canary Islands	Submarine - -	Chased -	Speed -	—
†Hillhouse - -	3,049	6	Off S.W. Ireland	Submarine - -	Torpedo ; gunfire.	Missed ; by gun.	—
†Lapland - -	18,565	7	Off Liverpool Bar L.V.	Mine - - -	Mine - -	Arrived -	2
†Carmarthenshire	7,823	8	Off entrance to English Channel.	Submarine - -	Gunfire -	By gun -	—··
†Lord Derby -	3,757	9	Mediterranean -	Submarine - -	Torpedo -	Missed -	—
†Neto - -	1,696	9	English Channel -	Submarine - -	Torpedo -	Missed -	—··
†Cyclops - -	9,033	11	W. from Scilly Islands.	Submarine - -	Torpedo -	Missed -	—··
†Troilus - -	7,625	11	North Sea - -	Submarine - -	Chased -	Speed -	—
†Monsaldale -	2,805	11	Mediterranean -	Submarine - -	Gunfire -	By gun and smoke.	—
†Branksome Hall	4,262	11	English Channel -	Submarine - -	Torpedoed -	Towed in	—
†Echunga - -	4,589	13	Off N.W. Scotland.	Submarine - -	Gunfire -	Rescued -	—
Lime Branch -	5,379	13	W. from Ushant -	Submarine - -	Torpedoed -	Arrived -	—
†Ajana - -	7,759	14	English Channel -	Submarine - -	Torpedo -	Missed -	—
†Tarantia - -	4,754	14	W. from Ushant -	Submarine - -	Torpedo -	Missed -	—
†Boveric - -	4,445	14	Mediterranean -	Submarine - -	Torpedo -	Missed -	—
†Adala - -	3,847	15	North Sea - -	Submarine - -	Gunfire -	Weather	—
†Highcliffe -	3,238	16	English Channel	Submarine - -	Gunfire -	By gun -	—
†City - -	2,893	16	English Channel	Submarine - -	Torpedo -	Missed -	—
†Benguela - -	5,520	17	Off W. Ireland -	Submarine - -	Torpedo -	Missed -	—
†Khephren -	2,774	17	Mediterranean -	Submarine - -	Torpedo -	Missed -	—
†Ryton - -	3,991	17	Mediterranean -	Submarine - -	Torpedo -	Missed -	—
†Nirvana - -	6,021	17	English Channel	Mine - - -	Mine - -	Arrived -	—
†Gisella - -	2,502	17	Off Island of Lewis.	Mine - - -	Mine - -	Arrived -	1
†Winifredian -	10,422	17	North Sea - -	Mine - - -	Mine - -	Arrived -	—
†Clan Sutherland	2,820	17	English Channel	Submarine - -	Torpedoed -	Beached -	12
†Lanuvium -	4,417	17	Mediterranean -	Submarine - -	Chased -	By gun -	—

Name.	Gross Tons.	Date.	Position.	Attacked by	How attacked.	How saved	Lives lost.
		1917. April					
†Nigaristan -	4,345	18	Bristol Channel -	Submarine - -	Gunfire -	By gun -	—
†Hurst - -	4,718	18	W. from Gibraltar	Submarine - -	Gunfire -	By gun -	—
†Clan Sinclair -	5,215	18	Atlantic - -	Submarine - -	Torpedo ; gunfire.	Missed ; by gun.	—
†Frankier - -	3,836	18	Entrance to English Channel.	Submarine - -	Torpedo -	Missed -	—
†Thermidor -	3,788	19	Off W. Ireland -	Submarine - -	Chased -	Speed -	—
Old Head (S.V.)	105	19	Off Coningbeg L.V.	Submarine - -	Gunfire after capture.	Towed in -	—
†Bristol City -	2,511	19	Off S.W. Ireland	Submarine - -	Torpedo -	Missed -	—
†Limeleaf - -	7,339	19	English Channel -	Submarine - -	Torpedoed -	Towed in -	7
†Lumina - -	5,856	19	North Sea - -	Mine - - -	Mine - -	Towed in -	—
†Suwanee - -	2,748	20	Atlantic - -	Submarine - -	Gunfire -	By gun -	—
†Terek - -	3,710	20	Off W. Ireland -	Submarine - -	Torpedo -	Missed -	—
†Oriflamme -	3,764	20	Off W. Ireland -	Submarine - -	Torpedo -	Missed -	—
†Ikalis - -	4,329	20	Mediterranean -	Submarine - -	Torpedo -	Missed -	—
†Inverness - -	3,734	20	W. from Gibraltar	Submarine - -	Gunfire -	By gun -	—
†Leasowe Castle	9,737	20	W. from Gibraltar	Submarine -	Torpedoed -	Arrived -	—
†Roumanian Prince	4,147	21	Off S.W. Ireland	Submarine - -	Gunfire -	Speed -	—
†Crown of Toledo	5,806	21	Off S.W. Ireland	Submarine - -	Chased -	Speed -	—
†Elysia -	6,368	21	Off S.W. Ireland	Submarine - -	Torpedo -	Missed -	—
†Wapello - -	5,576	21	Off S.W. Ireland	Submarine - -	Gunfire -	By gun -	—
†Valeria - -	5,865	22	Off S.W. Ireland	Submarine - -	Chased -	By gun -	—
†Austrian - -	3,127	22	Off S.W. Ireland	Submarine - -	Chased -	Rescued -	—
†Karroo - -	6,127	22	W. from Scilly Islands.	Submarine - -	2 torpedoes ; gunfire.	Missed ; rescued.	—
†Izaston - -	3,060	22	Bay of Biscay -	Submarine - -	Torpedo -	Missed -	—
Tommi (S.V.) -	138	23	Off St. Ives -	Submarine - -	Gunfire after capture.	Towed in -	—
†Normanby -	4,219	23	W. from Gibraltar	Submarine - -	Gunfire -	By smoke -	—
†Nephrite - -	673	23	Bristol Channel -	Submarine - -	Gunfire -	By gun -	—
†Drumcliffe -	4,073	24	Atlantic - -	Submarine - -	Chased -	Rescued -	—
†Thirlby - -	2,009	24	Atlantic - -	Submarine - -	Torpedo -	Missed -	—
Huntsholm -	2,073	24	English Channel	Submarine - -	Torpedo -	Missed -	—
†Martaban - -	5,106	25	Off S.W. Ireland	Submarine - -	Gunfire -	By gun -	—
†Baltic -	23,876	25	Off W. Ireland -	Submarine - -	Torpedo -	Missed -	—
†Bideford - -	3,562	25	Off Dunkirk -	T.B.D.'s - -	Gunfire -	Slightly damaged.	—
‡Lynorta - -	3,684	25	Off entrance to English Channel.	Submarine - -	Gunfire -	By gun -	—
†Flaxmere - -	1,525	25	Off S.W. Ireland	Submarine - -	Chased -	By gun -	—
†Florrieston -	3,366	25	Mediterranean -	Submarine - -	Torpedo -	Missed -	—
†Ascania - -	9,121	26	W. from Scilly Islands.	Submarine - -	Chased -	Gunfire -	—
†Pontwen -	4,796	26	Off W. Ireland -	Submarine - -	Gunfire -	By gun and smoke.	—
†Knight of the Thistle.	6,675	26	Off S.W. Ireland	Submarine - -	Chased -	Speed -	—
†Baltic -	23,876	26	Off S. Ireland -	Submarine - -	Torpedo -	Missed -	—
Karnak - -	3,171	26	English-Channel -	Submarine - -	Gunfire -	Speed -	—
†Polzeath - -	882	26	English Channel	Submarine - -	Gunfire -	By gun -	—
Quantock - -	4,470	26	Off Fastnet -	Submarine - -	Torpedoed -	Towed in -	2
†Roseleaf - -	6,572	27	Off N.W. Ireland	Submarine - -	Gunfire -	By gun -	—
†Headcliffe -	3,654	27	Off S. Ireland -	Submarine - -	Gunfire -	By gun -	—
Amelia and Jane (S.V.).	62	27	English Channel	Submarine - -	Gunfire after capture.	Towed in -	—
†Clan Macarthur	7,382	27	Off Scilly Isles -	Submarine - -	Chased -	Speed -	—
†Bernard - -	3,682	28	Entrance to English Channel.	Submarine - -	Chased -	By gun -	—
†Sheaf Blade -	2,378	28	Entrance to English Channel.	Submarine - -	Gunfire -	By gun -	—
Rob Roy (S.V.)	93	28	St. George's Channel.	Submarine - -	Captured -	Rescued -	—
Freighter -	297	28	English Channel -	Submarine - -	Torpedo -	Missed -	—
Highgate - -	1,780	29	North Sea - -	Aeroplane -	Bombs -	Missed -	—
†Palma - -	7,632	29	W. from Scilly Islands.	Submarine - -	Gunfire -	By gun -	—
†Gena - -	2,784	29	North Sea - -	Submarine - -	Gunfire -	By gun -	—
†Princess Helena	677	29	North Sea - -	Submarine - -	Gunfire -	By gun -	—
†Nantes - -	1,640	29	North Sea - -	Submarine - -	Chased -	By gun -	—
†Lord Downshire	4,808	29	W. from Ushant -	Submarine - -	Chased -	Speed -	—

Name.	Gross Tons.	Date.	Position.	Attacked by	How attacked.	How saved.	Lives lost.
		1917. **April**					
†Pretorian - -	6,948	30	Off S.W. Ireland	Submarine - -	Chased -	Speed -	—
†Arranmoor -	4,008	30	Bristol Channel -	Submarine - -	Gunfire -	Speed -	—
†Sutlej - -	3,549	30	Off S.W. Ireland	Submarines - -	Torpedo -	Missed -	—
†Huntsmoor -	4,957	30	W. from Scilly Islands.	Submarine - -	Gunfire -	By gun -	—
Oilfield - -	4,005	30	English Channel -	Submarine - -.	Gunfire -	Rescued -	—
†Kamouraska -	4,903	30	Off Ushant -	Submarine - -	Gunfire .	By gun -	—
†Vestalia -. -	5,528	30	English Channel -	Submarine - -	Chased -	By gun -	—
MAY 1917.		**May**					
†Haslingden -	1,934	1	English Channel -	Submarine - -	Torpedo -	Missed -	—
‡Querida - -	1,175	1	English Channel -	Submarine - -	Chased -	Gunfire -	—
†Cordova - -	2,284	1	Off Entrance to English Channel.	Submarine - -	Torpedo -	Missed -	—
†Quarrydene -	2,883	1	Off W. Ireland -	Submarine - -	Gunfire -	By gun -	—
†Nellore - -	6,853	1	Mediterranean -	Submarine - -	Chased -	Speed -	—
†Devonshire -	500	1	Irish Sea - -	Submarine - -	Gunfire -	By gun -	—
†Dorie - -	3,264	1	Off S.W. Ireland	Submarine - -	Torpedoed -	Towed in -	—
†Camerata - -	3,723	2	Mediterranean -	Submarine - -	Torpedoed -	Beached -	
†Hambleton Range.	3,682	2	North Sea - -	Submarine - -	Chased -	Speed -	—
†San Melito -	10,160	2	Off Orkney Islands.	Submarine - -	Chased -	By gun -	—
†Gorsemore -	3,079	2	Bristol Channel -	Submarine - -	Torpedo -	Missed -	—
†Isla - -	222	2	Irish Sea - -	Submarine - -	Gunfire -	By escort -	—
†Archbank -	3,767	2	English Channel	Submarine - -	Gunfire -	Rescued -	—
City of London -	225	3	North Sea - -	Submarine - -	Gunfire -	Missed -	—
†Palm Branch -	3,891	3	Arctic Sea - -	Submarines - -	Torpedo ; gunfire.	Missed ; by gun.	—
Yorkshire -	394	4	St. George's Channel.	Submarine - -	Gunfire -	Rescued -	—
†Ben Lomond	2,814	4	Mediterranean -	Submarine - -	Torpedo -	Missed -	—
†Maidan -	8,205	4	St. George's Channel.	Submarine - -	Chased -	By gun -	—
†Monmouthshire -	5,097	4	Atlantic - -	Submarine - -	Chased -	By gun -	—
†Talawa - -	3,834	5	Mediterranean -	Submarine - -	Torpedoed -	Beached -	—
†Mahanada -	7,196	5	Off Scilly Islands	Submarine - -	Chased -	By gun -	—
†Bengore Head -	2,490	5	Off S. Ireland -	Submarine - -.	Gunfire -	By gun -	. .
†Photinia - -	4,583	5	W. from Ushant -	Submarine - -	Torpedo -	Missed -	—
†Norton - -	1,825	5	Off S. Ireland -	Submarine - -	Chased -	Speed -	—
Katie Cluett (S.V.).	136	6	English Channel	Submarine - -	Gunfire -	Towed in -	. .
†New Abbotshall	783	7	North Sea - -	Submarine - -	Gunfire -	By gun -	—
†Griqua - -	3,344	7	Mediterranean -	Submarine - -	Gunfire -	By gun -	—
†Southwaite -	3,618	7	Off entrance to English Channel.	Submarine - -	Torpedo -	Missed -	. .
†Crown of Leon -	3,391	7	Mediterranean -	Submarine - -	Torpedoed -	Beached -	1
†San Patricio -	9,712	8	Bristol Channel -	Submarine - -	Torpedoed -	Arrived -	—
†Astyanax - -	4,872	9	Off S.W. Ireland	Submarine - -	Chased -	Speed -	—
‡Malda - -	7,884	9	North Sea - -	Submarine - -	Torpedo -	Missed -	—
†Kassanga - -	3,015	10	Mediterranean -	Submarine - -	Gunfire -	By gun and smoke.	—
‡Treverbyn -	4,163	10	English Channel	Submarine - -	Gunfire -	By gun -	—
†Hessle - -	952	10	North Sea - -	Submarine - -	Torpedo -	Missed -	—
†Putney - -	3,232	10	Mediterranean -	Submarine - -	Torpedo -	Missed -	—
†Clan MacNab -	4,675	10	Mediterranean -	Submarine - -	Torpedo -	Missed -	—
†Hindoo - -	4,915	11	Mediterranean -	Submarine - -	Torpedoed -	Beached -	—
Waterville -	1,968	12	Off Elbow Light Buoy.	Mine - - -	Mine - -	Beached -	—
†Cuthbert - -	3,834	12	Off S.W. Ireland	Submarine - -	Torpedo -	Missed -	—
‡Calabria - -	4,376	12	Mediterranean -	Submarine - -	Chased -	Speed -	—
†Rio Claro - -	3,687	12	Mediterranean -	Submarine - -	Torpedo -	Missed -	—
†Cliffside - -	4,850	12	Mediterranean -	Submarine - -	Torpedo -	Missed -	—
†Ismailia - -	3,704	12	Mediterranean -	Submarine - -	Torpedo -	Missed -	—
†Anglo Chilean -	6,900	13	Mediterranean -	Submarine - -	Gunfire -	By gun -	—
†Neilrose - -	3,568	13	Off S.W. Ireland	Submarine - -	Torpedo -	Missed -	—
Galtee - -	565	13	English Channel	Submarine - -	Torpedo -	Missed -	—
Trevaylor - -	4,249	13	Mediterranean -	Submarine - -	Gunfire -	Rescued -	—
†Fiscus - -	4,170	13	North Sea - -	Submarine - -	Torpedo -	Missed -	—
†Canara - -	6,012	14	Mediterranean -	Submarine - -	Torpedo -	Missed -	—

Name.	Gross Tons.	Date.	Position.	Attacked by	How attacked.	How saved.	Lives lost.
		1917. May					
†Volga - -	4,404	14	Mediterranean -	Submarine - -	Torpedoed -	Beached -	—
†Arlington Court	4,346	14	Off S.W. Ireland	Submarine - -	Torpedoed -	Towed in -	—
†Grelhame - -	3,740	14	Off Entrance to English Channel.	Submarine - -	Chased -	Gun - -	—
†Upcerne - -	2,984	14	Off Entrance to English Channel.	Submarine - -	Chased -	Weather -	—
†Baychattan -	3,758	15	English Channel	Submarine - -	Gunfire -	By gun -	—
†Ibex -	951	15	English Channel	Submarine - -	Torpedo -	Missed -	—
†Nellore - -	6,853	15	Mediterranean -	Submarines - -	Gunfire -	By gun -	—
†Pancras - -	4,436	15	Mediterranean -	Submarine - -	Gunfire -	Beached ; refloated.	—
†Huntsholm -	2,073	17	English Channel	Submarine - -	Torpedo -	Missed -	—
†Chiswick - -	3,246	17	North Sea -	Submarine - -	Chased -	Gun - -	—
†Denetown- -	653	18	English Channel	Submarine - -	Gunfire -	Rescued -	—
†Celtic - -	20,904	19	Off S.W. Ireland	Submarine - -	Torpedo -	Missed -	—
†Karagola - -	7,000	19	W. from Gibraltar	Submarine - -	Chased -	Gunfire and smoke.	—
†Kwarra - -	4,441	19	Atlantic - -	Submarine - -	Chased -	Gunfire -	—
†Southwestern Miller.	6,514	20	English Channel	Submarines - -	Chased -	Escort -	—
†Birchgrove -	2,821	20	North Sea - -	Seaplanes - -	Torpedoes ; machine gun.	Missed ; by gun.	—
†Karroo - -	6,127	21	English Channel	Submarine - -	Gunfire -	By gun -	—
†Medora - -	5,135	21	Off the Lizard -	Submarine - -	Torpedo -	Missed -	—
†Austrian - -	3,127	21	Off N.W. Ireland	Submarine - -	Torpedo -	Missed -	—
Highgate - -	1,780	21	North Sea - -	Submarine - -	Torpedo -	Missed -	—
†Ioanna - -	3,459	22	English Channel	Submarine - -	Chased -	Rescued -	—
†Myrtle Branch -	3,741	22	Atlantic - -	Submarine - -	Torpedo -	Missed -	—
†Marie Suzanne -	3,106	22	Mediterranean -	Submarine - -	Torpedo -	Missed -	—
†Chicago City -	2,324	23	Off S. Ireland -	Submarine - -	Torpedoed -	Towed in ; beached.	2
†Nellore - -	6,853	23	Entrance to English Channel.	Submarine - -	Torpedo -	Missed -	—
†Carperby - -	2,104	23	English Channel	Submarine - -	Torpedo -	Missed -	—
†Madura - -	4,484	24	Entrance to English Channel.	Submarine - -	2 torpedoes -	One missed ; one failed to explode.	—
New Pioneer -	722	25	English Channel	Submarine - -	Chased -	Speed -	—
†Rabymere -	1,776	25	Off S. Ireland -	Submarine - -	Torpedo -	Missed -	—
†Myrtle Branch -	3,741	25	Off W. Ireland -	Submarine - -	Torpedo -	Missed -	—
†Atlas - -	3,090	25	Mediterranean -	Submarine - -	Torpedo -	Missed -	—
Manchester Inventor.	4,112	25	Off W. Ireland -	Submarine - -	Chased -	Speed -	—
†Clan Graham -	5,213	26	Mediterranean -	Submarine - -	Gunfire -	By gun -	—
†Inca - -	3,593	26	Off S.W. Ireland	Submarine - -	Torpedo -	Missed -	—
†Inverness - -	3,734	26	Off Scilly Isles -	Submarine - -	Torpepo -	Missed -	—
Baku Standard -	3,708	26	North Sea - -	Submarine - -	Chased -	By escort -	—
†Indian Transport	4,111	27	English Channel	Submarine - -	Gunfire -	By gun -	—
†Meaford - -	1,889	27	Off entrance to English Channel.	Submarine - -	Chased -	By gun -	—
†Cymric Vale -	3,580	27	Bay of Biscay -	Submarine - -	Gunfire -	By gun -	—
†Cresswell - -	2,829	28	Off S.W. Ireland -	Submarine - -	Gunfire -	By gun -	—
†Peebles - -	4,284	29	English Channel -	Submarine - -	Gunfire -	By gun -	—
†Hyson - -	6,608	29	English Channel -	Submarine - -	Chased -	By gun -	—
†Pavia - -	2,945	29	Off S.W. Ireland -	Submarine - -	Torpedo -	Missed -	—
†Grangetown -	1,640	29	North Sea - -	Submarine - -	Torpedo -	Missed -	—
†Cairnross - -	4,016	30	Mediterranean -	Submarine - -	Torpedo -	Missed -	—
†San Ricardo -	6,465	30	Off N.W. Ireland	Submarine - -	Gunfire -	By escort -	—
†El Uruguayo -	8,361	30	Off N.W. Ireland	Submarine - -	Chased -	Speed -	—
†Fernley - -	3,820	30	Off S.W. Ireland -	Submarine - -	Torpedoed -	Arrived -	—
†Ozarda - -	4,791	31	Mediterranean -	Submarine - -	Torpedoed -	Beached -	—
JUNE 1917.		June					
†Turnbridge -	2,874	1	Off S.W. Ireland -	Submarine - -	Gunfire -	Speed -	—
†Antinous - -	3,682	1	Off the Lizard -	Submarine - -	Torpedo -	Missed -	—
†Cymric Vale -	3,580	1	Atlantic - -	Submarine - -	Chased -	Speed -	—
†Kingstonian -	6,564	1	Ashore near Cape Granitola, Sicily.	Submarine - -	Torpedo -	Missed -	—

Name.	Gross Tons.	Date.	Position.	Attacked by	How attacked.	How saved.	Lives lost.
		1917. June					
†Cotovia - -	4,020	1	Arctic - -	Submarine - -	Gunfire -	By gun -	—
†Waiwera - -	6,237	2	Off the Lizard -	Submarine - -	Torpedo -	Missed -	—
†Hypatia - -	5,663	2	Atlantic - -	Submarine - -	Torpedo -	Missed -	—
†Snowdonian -	3,870	2	Mediterranean -	Submarine - -	Gunfire -	Smoke -	—
†Tonawanda -	3,421	2	English Channel -	Submarine - -	Torpedoed -	Reached port.	—
†Dockleaf - -	5,311	3	Mediterranean -	Mine - - -	Mine - -	Reached port.	—
†San Lorenzo -	9,607	3	Off N.W. Ireland	Submarine - -	Torpedoed -	Reached port.	—
Cornhill - -	900	4	Off Cape Wrath -	Submarine - -	Gunfire -	Rescued -	—
†Manchester Port	4,093	4	Atlantic - -	Submarine - -	Gunfire -	By gun -	—
†Miniota - -	4,928	4	Atlantic - -	Submarine - -	Gunfire -	By gun -	—
†Graciana - -	3,536	5	Off N.W. Ireland	Submarine - -	Gunfire -	By gun -	—
†Tuskar - -	1,159	6	Off N.W. Ireland	Submarine - -	Gunfire -	By gun -	—
†Mitra - -	5,592	6	Mediterranean -	Submarine - -	Torpedoed -	Reached port	—
†Imani - -	4,590	7	W. from Ushant -	Submarine - -	Gunfire -	By gun -	—
†Cape Transport	4,109	7	Bay of Biscay -	Submarine - -	Gunfire -	Gun - -	—
†Jerseymoor -	5,662	7	Bay of Biscay -	Submarine - -	Gunfire -	By gun -	—
†Oldfield Grange	4,653	7	English Channel -	Submarine - -	Torpedoed -	Beached -	—
†Mahopac - -	2,216	7	English Channel -	Submarine - -	Torpedoed -	Beached -	—
†Cranmore - -	3,157	7	Off W. Ireland -	Submarine - -	Torpedoed -	Beached -	—
†Errington Court	4,461	7	Mediterranean -	Mine - - -	Mine - -	Beached -	—
†Chevington -	3,876	8	English Channel -	Submarine - -	Chased -	Speed -	—
†Addington -	1,613	8	English Channel -	Submarine - -	Gunfire -	By gun and smoke.	—
†Manchester Engineer.	4,465	8	Arctic - -	Submarine - -	Chased -	Rescued -	—
†Freshfield -	3,445	8	Mediterranean -	Submarine - -	Gunfire -	By gun -	—
†Russian Prince -	4,158	8	Off S.W. Ireland -	Submarine - -	Torpedoed -	Reached port	—
†Gaboon - -	3,297	9	Atlantic - -	Submarine - -	Gunfire -	By gun -	—
†Akabo - -	3,814	9	Off S.W. Ireland -	Submarine - -	3 torpedoes -	Missed -	—
†Sapele - -	3,152	9	Off S.W. Ireland -	Submarine - -	Chased -	Speed -	—
†Itola - -	5,257	9	Mediterranean -	Submarine - -	Torpedo -	Missed -	—
†Ceramic - -	18,481	9	Entrance to English Channel.	Submarine - -	Torpedo -	Missed -	—
†Fernleaf - -	5,838	10	Off S.W. Ireland -	Submarine - -	Chased -	By gun -	—
†Loch Lomond -	2,619	10	W. from Gibraltar	Submarine - -	Gunfire -	By gun and smoke.	—
†Lautaro - -	3,476	10	Mediterranean -	Submarine - -	Chased -	By gun -	—
†Harpathian -	4,588	10	English Channel -	Submarine - -	Torpedo -	Missed -	—
†Acadian - -	2,305	10	West from Gibraltar.	Submarine - -	Gunfire -	Gun - -	—
†Athenia - -	8,668	11	N.W. Ireland -	Submarine - -	Chased -	Speed -	—
†Pathan - -	4,956	11	Off S.W. Ireland -	Submarine - -	Chased -	Rescued -	—
†Kerry Range -	5,856	11	Off N.W. Ireland	Submarine - -	Torpedo -	Missed -	—
†Mackinaw -	3,204	11	W. from Scilly Isles.	Submarine - -	Torpedo -	Missed -	—
†Minnie de Larrinaga.	5,046	11	Atlantic - -	Submarine - -	Gunfire -	Gun - -	—
†Leafield - -	2,539	11	Entrance to English Channel.	Submarine - -	Torpedo -	Missed -	—
†Pentwyn - -	3,587	11	Atlantic - -	Submarine - -	Torpedo ; gunfire.	Missed ; by gun.	—
†Thessaly - -	3,128	11	Atlantic - -	Submarine - -	Gunfire -	By gun -	1
†Metagama -	12,420	11	Off S.W. Ireland	Submarine - -	Torpedo -	Missed -	—
†Holywell - -	4,867	11	Off S.W. Ireland	Submarine - -	Gunfire -	Rescued -	—
†Eurymachus -	4,995	11	Atlantic - -	Submarine - -	Chased -	Speed -	—
†Dominic - -	2,966	11	Off N.W. Ireland	Submarine - -	Chased -	By gun and smoke.	—
†Ausonia - -	8,153	11	Off S. Ireland -	Submarine - -	Torpedoed -	Reached port	1
†City of Exeter -	9,373	11	Off Bombay -	Mine - - -	Mine - -	Reached port	—
†Knight Companion.	7,241	11	Atlantic - -	Submarine - -	Torpedoed -	Towed in -	—
†Margarita -	2,788	11	English Channel -	Submarine - -	Torpedoed -	Reached port	—
†Eustace - -	3,995	11	English Channel -	Submarine - -	Torpedoed -	Reached port	—
†Coronado - -	6,539	12	Off S. Ireland -	Submarine - -	Torpedoed -	Reached port	—
†Haverford -	11,635	12	Off S. Ireland -	Submarine - -	Torpedo -	Missed -	—
†Indian - -	9,121	12	Off S.W. Ireland -	Submarine - -	Torpedo -	Missed -	—
†Quillota - -	3,692	12	Atlantic - -	Submarine - -	Gunfire -	By gun -	—
†Bouvilston -	2,866	12	W. from Gibraltar	Submarine - -	Gunfire -	By gun -	—
†Paris - -	599	13	Entrance to English Channel.	Submarine - -	Torpedo -	Missed -	—

Name.	Gross Tons.	Date.	Position.	Attacked by	How attacked.	How saved.	Lives lost.
		1917. June					
†Kintuck - -	4,639	13	Atlantic - -	Submarine - -	Gunfire -	Gun - -	—
†Lorle - -	2,686	13	Off Ushant -	Submarine - -	Torpedo -	Missed -	—
†Collegian - -	7,237	14	Off S. Ireland -	Submarine - -	Torpedo -	Missed -	—
†Ramore Head -	4,444	14	Atlantic - -	Submarine - -	Torpedo -	Missed -	—
†Canto - -	1,243	14	North Sea - -	Seaplanes - -	3 torpedoes ; machine gun.	Missed -	—
†Lowther Castle -	4,439	14	Mediterranean -	Mine - - -	Mine - -	Reached port.	—
†Nascopie - -	1,870	14	Arctic Sea - -	Submarine - -	Gunfire -	Gun - -	—
†Winamac - -	5,767	15	Off S. Ireland -	Submarine - -	Torpedo -	Missed -	—
Scartho - -	569	15	North Sea - -	Submarine - -	Torpedo -	Missed -	—
†Branksome Hall	4,262	15	English Channel -	Submarine - -	Torpedo -	Missed -	—
†Crane - -	2,033	15	Off entrance to English Channel.	Submarine - -	Torpedo -	Missed -	—
†Queen Alexandra	785	15	English Channel -	Submarine - -	Chased -	By gun -	—
†Camito - -	6,611	15	Off entrance to English Channel.	Submarine - -	Gunfire -	Gun - -	—
†Teesdale - -	2,470	15	English Channel -	Submarine - -	Torpedoed -	Beached -	—
†Elvaston - -	4,130	15	Mediterranean -	Submarine - -	Torpedoed -	Reached port.	3
†Deddington -	2,827	15	Bay of Biscay -	Submarine - -	Chased -	Gun - -	—
†Fallodon - -	3,012	16	Off S. Ireland -	Submarine - -	Torpedoed -	Towed in -	—
†Bayford - *	4,113	16	Atlantic - -	Submarine - -	Torpedo -	Missed -	—
†Rutherglen -	4,214	16	Atlantic - -	Submarine - -	Gunfire -	Gun - -	—
†Elysia - -	6,397	16	Off S. Ireland -	Submarine - -	Torpedo -	Missed -	—
Ardmore - -	1,304	16	Off S. Ireland -	Submarine - -	Chased -	Rescued -	—
†Claveresk - -	3,829	17	Off Casablanca -	Submarine - -	Torpedo -	Missed -	—
†Kaiser-i-Hind -	11,430	17	W. from Gibraltar	Submarine - -	Torpedo -	Missed -	—
†Alban - -	5,223	17	Off W. Ireland -	Submarine - -	Torpedo -	Missed -	—
†Kathlamba -	6,382	18	Off entrance to English Channel.	Submarine - -	Torpedoed -	Reached port.	—
†Marie Suzanne -	3,106	18	Atlantic - -	Submarine - -	Gunfire -	Rescued -	—
†Palma - -	7,632	18	Atlantic - -	Submarine - -	3 torpedoes -	Missed -	—
†Trevanion -	4,267	18	Mediterranean -	Submarine - -	2 torpedoes -	Missed -	—
†Whateley Hall -	3,712	18	W. from Gibraltar	Submarine - -	Gunfire -	By gun and smoke.	—
†Minnie Coles (S.V.)	116	18	Irish Channel -	Submarine - -	Gunfire -	Towed in -	—
†Hazelwood -	3,120	18	Mediterranean -	Submarine - -	Torpedo -	Missed -	—
†Hurst - -	4,718	19	Mediterranean -	Submarine - -	Torpedo -	Missed -	—
†Ganges - -	3,497	19	Atlantic - -	Submarine - -	Torpedo -	Missed -	—
†Morinier - -	3,804	19	Bay of Biscay -	Submarine - -	Gunfire -	By gun -	—
†Wonganella -	3,998	19	Atlantic - -	Submarine - -	Gunfire -	Gun - -	—
†Great City -	5,525	19	Off Scilly Isles -	Submarine - -	Torpedoed -	Towed in -	4
Mary Ann (S.V.)	164	19	English Channel -	Submarine - -	Set on fire after capture.	Towed in -	—
†Aylestone -	3,400	19	Atlantic - -	Submarine - -	Gunfire -	Gun - -	—
†Devona - -	3,779	20	Bay of Biscay -	Submarine - -	Gunfire -	By gun -	—
†Valeria - -	5,865	20	Off S.W. Ireland	Submarine - -	Chased -	By gun -	—
†Lancastrian -	5,120	20	Off entrance to English Channel.	Submarine - -	Chased -	Speed -	—
†Nitonian - -	6,381	20	Off W. Ireland -	Submarine - -	Gunfire -	By gun -	—
†Buranda - -	3,651	20	Off Ushant -	Submarine - -	Gunfire -	Gun - -	—
†Charing Cross -	2,534	22	Off N.W. Ireland	Submarine - -	Gunfire -	Gun - -	—
†Osmanieh -	4,041	23	Mediterranean -	Submarine - -	2 torpedoes -	Missed -	—
†Celia - -	5,004	24	Atlantic - -	Submarine - -	Chased -	Gun - -	—
†Lackenby -	2,108	25	Bristol Channel -	Submarine - -	Torpedo -	Missed -	—
†Fernleaf - -	5,838	25	Atlantic - -	Submarine - -	Gunfire -	Gun - -	—
†Southern - -	5,694	25	Mediterranean -	Mine - - -	Mine - -	Beached -	—
†Gorsemore -	3,079	26	Entrance to English Channel.	Submarine - -	Gunfire -	Gun - -	1
†Swindon - -	5,084	26	Off N.W. Ireland	Submarine - -	2 torpedoes -	Missed -	—
†Haverford -	11,635	26	Off W. Scotland -	Submarine - -	Torpedoed -	Beached -	8
†Aurania - -	13,936	26	N.W. Ireland -	Submarine - -	Chased -	Gun - -	—
†Elysia - -	6,397	26	N.W. Ireland -	Submarine - -	Gunfire -	Gun - -	—
†Skipton Castle -	3,823	26	Mediterranean -	Submarine - -	Gunfire -	Gun - -	—
†City of Hankow	7,369	27	N.W. Scotland -	Submarine - -	Torpedo -	Missed -	—
†Claveresk -	3,829	27	W. Ireland - -	Submarine - -	Gunfire -	Gun - -	—
†Elsie (S.V.) -	165	28	English Channel -	Submarine - -	Gunfire -	Weather -	—

Name.	Gross Tons.	Date.	Position.	Attacked by	How attacked.	How saved.	Lives lost.
		1917. June					
Northfield -	2,099	28	English Channel	Submarine - -	Torpedoed -	Reached port	—
†Cheyenne - -	4,987	29	English Channel	Submarine - -	Torpedo· -	Missed -	—
†Morocco - -	3,783	29	Off Cape Wrath -	Submarine - -	Gunfire -	Gun - -	—
Fairmuir - -	593	30	Arctic Sea - -	Submarine - -	Chased -	Speed -	—
†Purley - -	4,500	30	Atlantic - -	Submarine - -	Torpedo -	Missed -	—
†Ardens - -	1,274	30	North Sea - -	Submarine - -	Torpedo -	Missed -	—
†Normandiet -	1,843	30	English Channel	Submarine - -	Torpedo -	Missed -	—
†Poldennis - -	3,539	30	Mediterranean -	Submarine - -	Chased -	Speed -	—
JULY 1917.							
		July					
†Tintoretto -	4,181	1	Atlantic - -	Submarine - -	Torpedo -	Missed -	—
†Demerara - -	11,484	1	Bay of Biscay -	Submarine - -	Torpedoed -	Beached -	1
†Bayvoe - -	2,979	3	English Channel -	Submarine - -	Torpedo -	Missed -	—
†Lingneld - -	4.065	4	English Channel -	Submarine - -	Gunfire -	Gun and weather.	—
†Miniota - -	4,928	4	N.W. Ireland -	Submarine - -	Gunfire -	Gun - -	—
†Gladstone (Tug)	214	4	N.W. of Ireland -	Submarine - -	Chased -	Gun - -	—
†Cowrie - -	4,893	4	S.W. Ireland -	Submarine - -	Torpedo -	Missed -	—
†Clan Macintosh	4.774	5	Entrance to English Channel.	Submarine - -	Gunfire -	Gun - -	—
†Eburna - -	4,735	5	Mediterranean -	Submarine - -	Torpedoed -	Arrived -	—
†Karroo - -	6,127	6	English Channel -	Submarine - -	Torpedo -	Missed -	—
†Ariadne Christine	3,550	6	English Channel -	Submarine - -	Torpedoed -	Beached -	—
†Wabasha - -	5,864	6	English Channel -	Submarine - -	Torpedoed -	Arrived -	2
†Glenturret -	4,696	6	Atlantic - -	Submarine - -	Gunfire -	Gun - -	—
†Siamese Prince -	4,847	6	Atlantic - -	Submarine - -	Chased -	Gun - -	—
†Hero - -	1,812	7	W. Ireland -	Submarine - -	Chased -	Gun - -	—
†Coblenz - -	1,338	7	Atlantic - -	Submarine - -	Torpedo; Gunfire.	Missed ; gun	1
Onitsha - -	3,921	8	West of Ireland -	Submarine - -	Torpedo -	Missed -	—
†Plutarch - -	5,613	8	N.W.'Ireland -	Submarine - -	Torpedo -	Missed -	—
†Clifftower -	3,509	8	English Channel -	Submarine - -	Torpedo -	Missed -	—
†Cuthbert - -	3,834	8	S.W. Ireland -	Submarine - -	Chased -	Gun - -	—
†Manitou - -	6,849	8	Mediterranean -	Submarine - -	Torpedo -	Missed -	—
†Clan Chisholm -	2,647	8	Atlantic - -	Submarine - -	Chased -	Gun - -	—
†Peebles - -	4,284	8	Off Ushant -	Submarine - -	Gunfire -	Gun - -	—
Jarrix - -	429	9	North Sea - -	Seaplanes - -	Torpedo -	Missed -	--
Largo - -	1,764	9	N. Scotland -	Submarine - -	Chased -	Smoke apparatus.	—
†Haslingden -	1,934	9	North Sea - -	Seaplane - -	Torpedo -	Missed -	--
†Battersea - -	860	9	North Sea - -	Seaplane - -	Torpedo -	Missed -	--
†Hartley - -	1,150	9	North Sea - -	Seaplane - -	Torpedo -	Missed -	—
†Flamma - -	1,920	10	North Sea - -	Mine - -	Mine · -	Beached -	—
Grosvenor -	267	11	Dunkirk Harbour	Aircraft - -	Bombs -	Missed -	—
†Mercian - -	6,305	12	S. Ireland - -	Submarine - -	Torpedo -	Missed -	- -
†Tredegar Hall -	3,764	12	Off Ushant -	Submarine - -	Torpedo ; Gunfire.	Missed ; Gun.	—
†Mile End - ' -	859	12	North Sea - -	Submarine - -	Chased -	Gunfire -	---
†Dunrobin - -	3,617	12	Channel - -	Submarine - -	Torpedo ; Gunfire.	Missed ; gun.	—.-
†Nellore - -	6,853	13	Mediterranean -	Submarine - -	Torpedo -	Missed -	—
†Elstree Grange -	3,930	13	Atlantic - -	Submarine - -	Chased " -	Gun - -	—
†Pentwyn - -	3,587	13	S. Ireland - -	Submarine - -	Torpedo -	Missed -	—
†Rhesus - -	6,704	14	S.W. Ireland -	Submarine - -	Torpedo -	Missed -	—
†Kelbergen -	4,751	14	Atlantic - -	Submarine - -	Gunfire -	Gun - -	—
†Westmeath -	9,179	15	English Channel	Submarine - -	Torpedoed -	Arrived -	—
†Incemore - -	3,060	15	Mediterranean -	Submarine - -	Torpedoed -	Arrived -	—
†Abinsi - -	6,365	15	S.W. Ireland -	Submarine - -	Torpedo -	Missed -	—
†Leeds City -	4,298	15	Off Ushant -	Submarine - -	Torpedo -	Missed -	—
†Agamemnon -	7,011	16	S.W. Ireland -	Submarine - -	Chased -	Gun - -	—
†Benguela - -	5,520	16	N.W. Ireland -	Submarine - -	Torpedo ; gunfire.	Missed ; gun.	—
†Saturnia - -	8,611	16	S.W. Ireland -	Submarine - -	Torpedo -	Missed -	—
†Khiva - -	8,947	16	Mediterranean -	Submarine - -	Torpedo -	Missed -	—
†Vireut - -	3,771	17	Mediterranean -	Submarine - -	Torpedoed -	Beached -	—.
†Kaiser-i-Hind -	11,430	17	S.W. Scilly -	Submarine - -	Torpedo -	Missed -	—
†City of Canton -	6,692	18	N.W. Scotland -	Submarine - -	Gunfire -	Gun - -	—
†Blakemoor -	3,752	19	S.W. Ireland -	Submarine - -	Torpedo -	Missed -	—
†Loch Lomond -	2,619	19	Mediterranean -	Submarine - -	Torpedoes -	Missed -	—
†Polyphemus -	4,968	20	W. Scotland -	Submarine - -	Torpedo -	Missed -	—
†Hurtsend - -	8,826	20	Entrance to English Channel.	Submarine - -	Chased -	Speed -	—
†Ceramic - -	18,481	21	Bristol Channel -	Submarine - -	Chased -	Rescued -	--

Name.	Gross Tons.	Date.	Position.	Attacked by	How attacked.	How saved.	Lives lost.
		1917. July.					
†Polyphemus -	4,968	21	W. Scotland -	Submarine - -	Torpedo -	Missed -	—
†Volodia - -	5,689	21	W. Scilly Is. -	Submarine - -	Chased -	Gun - -	—
†Highland Monarch.	3,931	22	Mediterranean -	Submarine - -	Torpedo -	Missed -	—
†Yearby - -	2,639	22	English Channel	Submarine - -	Torpedo -	Missed -	—
†Corinthic - -	12,343	22	English Channel	Submarine - -	Chased -	Speed -	—
†Waipara - -	6,393	23	S.W. Ireland -	Submarine - -	Torpedo -	Missed -	—
†Paul Paix -	4,196	25	Off S. Ireland -	Submarine - -	Torpedo -	Missed -	—
†Effra - -	1,325	25	North Sea - -	Submarine - -	Torpedo -	Missed -	—
Stettin - -	876	25	North Sea - -	Submarine - -	Torpedo -	Missed -	—
†Baynyassa -	4,937	25	Atlantic - -	Submarine - -	Gunfire -	Gun -	—
†Ryde - -	3,556	26	Atlantic - -	Submarine - -	Gunfire -	Gun - -	—
†Ethelwynne -	3,230	26	North Sea - -	Mine - - -	Mine - -	Towed in -	—
†Khiva - -	8,947	27	Atlantic - -	Submarine - -	Chased -	Speed -	—
†Bellagio - -	3,919	27	English Channel	Submarine - -	Torpedoed -	Beached -	1
†Ocamo - -	1,910	27	Atlantic - -	Submarine - -	Torpedo -	Missed -	—
†Ardgryfe - -	4,897	27	Atlantic - -	Submarine - -	Gunfire -	Gun - -	—
†Comanchee -	5,588	28	N.W. Ireland -	Submarine - -	Torpedoed -	Arrived -	—
†Tabchee - -	6,508	28	N.W. Ireland -	Submarine - -	Torpedo -	Missed -	—
†Alexandra -	3,865	28	W. from Ushant -	Submarine - -	Gunfire -	Gun - -	—
†Livonia - -	1,879	28	W. from Ushant -	Submarine - -	Gunfire -	Gun - -	—
†Saturnia - -	8,611	29	Atlantic - -	Submarine - -	Torpedo -	Missed -	—
†Ajana - -	7,759	29	N.W. Ireland -	Submarine - -	Chased -	Speed -	—
†Devona - -	3,779	30	Atlantic - -	Submarine - -	Gunfire -	Gun - -	—
†Karina - -	4,222	30	W. Ireland - -	Submarine - -	Torpedo -	Missed -	—
†Excellence Pleske.	2,059	30	Mediterranean -	Submarine - -	Torpedo -	Missed -	—
†Beacon Grange	4,237	31	W. Ireland - -	Submarine - -	Gunfire -	Gun - -	1
†Hunsbrook -	4,463	31	W. Ireland - -	Submarine - -	Torpedo - Gunfire -	Missed - Gun.	—
†Worsley Hall -	3,489	31	Atlantic - -	Submarine - -	Torpedo ; Gunfire.	Missed ; gun and smoke.	—
†Hannah - -	3,697	31	Dunkirk Harbour	Aircraft - -	Bomb - -	Slightly damaged.	—
AUGUST 1917.		Aug.					
†Rokeby - -	3,786	1	Mediterranean -	Mine - - -	Mine - -	Towed in -	—
†Glamorgan -	3,539	1	West from Gibraltar.	Submarine - -	Torpedo -	Missed -	—
†City of Colombo	6,000	1	Atlantic - -	Submarine - -	Gunfire -	Gun - -	—
†Tarantia -	4,754	2	Off Ushant -	Submarine - -	Gunfire -	Gun - -	—
†El Cordobes -	5,683	2	Atlantic - -	Submarine - -	Chased -	Speed -	—
†Newby Hall -	4,391	3	West Ireland -	Submarine - -	Chased -	Rescued -	—
†City of Colombo	6,000	4	Atlantic - -	Submarine - -	Chased -	Gun - -	—
†Mahronda -	7,630	4	Atlantic - -	Submarine - -	Gunfire -	Gun - -	—
†Eda - - -	2,525	5	North Sea - -	Submarine - -	Chased -	Gun - -	—
†Welshman -	5,730	6	Off Ushant -	Submarine - -	Torpedo -	Missed -	—
†Zamora -	3,639	6	North Sea - -	Submarine - -	Torpedoed -	Towed in -	1
†Scarlet Tower -	3,187	6	Atlantic - -	2 Submarines -	Gunfire -	Gun - -	—
†Inveric - -	4,789	6	Atlantic - -	Submarine - -	Gunfire -	Gun - -	—
†Naukin - -	6,853	7	English Channel -	Submarine - -	Torpedo -	Missed -	—
Emlyn - -	370	7	North Sea - -	Submarine - -	Gunfire -	Attack abandoned.	—
†Morinier - -	3,804	8	Mediterranean -	Submarine - -	Torpedo -	Failed to explode.	—
†Alster - -	964	8	North Sea - -	Submarine - -	Torpedo -	Missed -	—
†Canara - -	6,012	9	Mediterranean -	Submarine - -	Torpedoed -	Towed in -	9
†Oakfield - -	3,618	9	South of Ireland -	Submarine - -	Torpedoed -	Reached port	—
†Belgic - -	24,540	11	South of Ireland -	Submarine - -	Torpedo -	Missed -	—
†Lowther Range -	3,926	11	N.W. Scotland -	Submarine - -	Torpedo -	Missed -	—
†Parattah - -	4,196	11	Atlantic - -	Submarine - -	Chased -	Attack abandoned.	—
†Camito - -	6,611	13	N.W. Ireland -	Mine - - -	Mine - -	Reached port	—
†Leafield - -	2,539	14	English Channel	Submarine - -	Torpedo -	Missed -	—
†Ardeola - -	3,140	14	West of Ireland -	Submarine - -	Torpedo -	Missed -	—
†Normandiet -	1,858	14	Bristol Channel -	Submarine - -	Gunfire -	Gun - -	—
†Natica - -	5,579	14	Bristol Channel -	Submarine - -	Torpedo -	Missed -	—
†Induna - -	4,426	14	Off N.W. Ireland	Submarine - -	Torpedo -	Missed -	—
†Manchuria -	2,997	15	S.W. from Scilly	Submarine - -	Chased -	Speed and weather.	—
†Rapallo - -	3,810	15	Atlantic - -	Submarine - -	Chased -	Attack abandoned.	—
†Flaminian -	3,227	15	Mediterranean -	Submarine - -	Torpedo -	Missed -	—
†Blakemoor -	3,752	15	Atlantic -	Submarine - -	Torpedo -	Missed -	—

Name.	Gross Tons.	Date.	Position.	Attacked by	How attacked.	How saved.	Lives lost.
		1917. Aug.					
†Eastgate - -	4,277	16	Atlantic - -	Submarine - -	Torpedoed -	Reached port	—
†Horseferry -	1,812	17	North Sea - -	Submarine - -	Chased -	Gun - -	—
†Ricardo A. Mestres.	4,468	17	Atlantic - -	Submarine - -	Torpedo -	Missed -	—
†Ovid - -	4,159	18	S.W. from Cape Spartel.	Submarine - -	Torpedo -	Missed -	—
†Cliftonhall -	3,900	19	Atlantic - -	Submarine - -	Torpedo ; gunfire.	Missed ; gun	—
†Waimana - -	7,852	19	Atlantic - -	Submarine - -	Chased -	Gun - -	—
†Winifredian -	10,422	19	North of Ireland	Submarine - -	Torpedo -	Missed -	—
†Canopic - -	12,097	19	Mediterranean -	Submarine - -	Chased -	Gun - -	—
†Vasari - -	10,117	21	N.W. Ireland -	Submarine - -	Torpedo -	Missed -	—
†Trongate - -	2,553	22	Atlantic - -	Submarine - -	Torpedo -	Missed -	—
†Lundy - -	2,857	23	Mediterranean -	Submarine - -	Torpedo -	Missed -	—
†Manxman -	4,827	23	W. from Gibraltar	Submarine - -	Torpedo -	Missed -	—
†Baron Fairlie -	3,593	25	Atlantic - -	Submarine - -	Chased -	Gun - -	—
†Glenturret -	4,696	25	Atlantic - -	Submarine - -	2 Torpedoes	Missed -	—
†Polwell - -	2,013	25	Atlantic - -	Submarine - -	Torpedo -	Missed -	—
†Cherryleaf -	5,896	25	English Channel	Submarine - -	Torpedo -	Missed -	—
†Hercules - -	1,095	26	North Sea - -	Submarine - -	Torpedo -	Missed -	—
Bhamo - -	5,244	26	Off Cape Agulhas	Mine - - -	Mine - -	Reached port.	—
†Luga - -	1,988	26	North Sea - -	Submarine - -	Chased -	Rescued -	—
†Kurdistan -	3,720	27	North Sea - -	Submarine - -	Torpedo -	Missed -	—
†Devon City -	4,316	29	English Channel	Submarine - -	2 torpedoes -	Missed -	—
†Clifftower -	3,509	29	Mediterranean -	Submarine - -	Torpedoed -	Towed in -	—
†Ardendearg -	3,237	29	Atlantic - -	Submarine - -	Gunfire -	Gun - -	—
†Novington -	3,442	29	E. from Shetlands	Submarine - -	Torpedo -	Failed to explode.	—
†Haslemere -	2,180	31	Mediterranean -	Submarine - -	Chased -	Gun - -	—
SEPTEMBER 1917.		Sept.					
†Arrino -	4,484	1	Atlantic - -	Submarine - -	Gunfire -	Gun - -	—
†Orangemoor -	4,134	2	Dunkirk Harbour	Aircraft - -	Bombs -	Damaged -	—
†Umgeni - -	2,622	3	North of Shetland	2 Submarines -	Gunfire -	Gun - -	—
†Datchet - -	3,076	3	Mediterranean -	Submarine - -	Chased -	Gun - -	—
†Siamese Prince -	4,847	4	Bay of Biscay -	Submarine - -	Torpedo -	Missed -	—
†Lady Cloe -	1,581	4	English Channel -	Submarine - -	Chased -	Speed -	—
†San Dunstano -	6,220	5	English Channel -	Submarine - -	Torpedoed -	Reached port.	1
†Colin Stuart -	659	6	English Channel -	Submarine - -	Torpedo -	Missed -	—
†Aldershot -	2,177	6	Bay of Biscay -	Submarine - -	Torpedo -	Missed -	—
†Pearleaf - -	5,919	6	N.W. Scotland -	Submarine - -	Chased -	Gun - -	—
†Brodmead -	5,646	7	West from Gibraltar.	Submarine - -	Torpedoed -	Reached port.	12 including Master.
†St. Edmund -	1,223	7	Off Scilly Islands	Submarine - -	Chased -	Gun - -	—
†Grelfryda - -	5,136	7	North Sea - -	Submarine - -	Torpedoed -	Beached -	—
†Scottish Prince -	2,897	7	English Channel -	Submarine - - *	Torpedoed -	Reached port.	—
Brunla - -	750	7	English Channel -	Submarine - -	Torpedo -	Missed -	—
†Myrmidon -	4,965	7	Mediterranean -	Submarine - -	Torpedoed -	Beached -	2
†Tropic - -	8,230	7	English Channel -	Submarine - -	Torpedo -	Missed -	—
†Huntsclyde -	2,705	8	English Channel -	Submarine - -	Chased -	Gun - -	—
†Nina - -	1,082	8	North Sea - -	Submarine - -	Gunfire -	Gun - -	—
†Tuscarora -	7,106	9	Atlantic - -	Submarine - -	Torpedoed -	Reached port.	3
†Knowsley Hall -	4,190	10	West from Gibraltar.	Submarine - -	Gunfire -	Rescued -	—
†Parana - -	4,182	10	Atlantic - -	Submarine - -	Torpedo ; Gunfire.	Missed ; Rescued.	—
†Ioanna - -	3,459	10	Bristol Channel -	Submarine - -	Torpedoed -	Reached port.	—
†Margarita -	2,788	10	East Shetland -	Mine - - -	Mine - -	Towed in -	—
†Cento - -	3,708	11	South Ireland -	Submarine - -	Torpedoed -	Reached port.	2
†British Transport.	4,143	11	Atlantic - -	Submarine - -	2 torpedoes ; gunfire.	Missed ; gun	—
†Johan Siem -	1,660	12	Bristol Channel -	Submarine - -	Gunfire -	Gun - -	—
†Glenelg - -	4,160	12	East Shetland -	Mine - - -	Mine - -	Towed in -	1
†Usher - -	3,594	12	Mediterranean -	Submarine - -	Gunfire -	Gun - -	—
†Hyndford - -	4,286	13	West from Gibraltar.	Submarine - -	Gunfire -	Speed and darkness.	—

Name.	Gross Tons.	Date.	Position.	Attacked by	How attacked.	How saved.	Lives lost.
		1917. Sept.					
†Rossia - -	4,576	13	North Scotland -	Submarine - -	Gunfire -	Gun - - -	—
†Bengali - -	5,684	13	Mediterranean -	Submarine - -	Torpedoed -	Reached port.	1
†Thetis - -	649	13	English Channel -	Submarine - -	Chased -	Gun - - -	—
†Ada - -	3,821	13	Mediterranean -	Submarine -	Chased -	Gun - - -	—
†Iolanthe - -	3,081	14	North Shetlands -	Submarine -	Torpedo ; Chased.	Missed ; Gun.	—
†Idomeneus -	6,692	15	West Scotland -	Submarine -	Torpedoed -	Beached -	4
†Orangemoor -	4,134	17	South Ireland -	Submarine -	Torpedo -	Missed -	—
†City of Lincoln -	5,867	18	S.W. Scilly -	Submarine -	Torpedoed -	Towed in -	9
†Admiral Cochrane.	6,600	18	North Sea - -	Submarine -	Torpedo -	Missed -	—
†Isleworth - -	2,871	18	North Scotland -	Submarine -	Chased -	Weather and darkness.	—
†Monkshaven -	3,357	19	North Sea - -	Submarine -	Torpedo -	Missed -	—
†Roumanian Prince.	4,147	19	N.W. Ireland -	Submarine -	Torpedo -	Missed -	—
†Greldon - -	3,322	20	English Channel -	Submarine -	Torpedo -	Missed -	—
†Taywood -	505	21	South Ireland -	Submarine -	Gunfire -	Gun - - -	—
†Aldworth - -	3,369	22	Atlantic - -	Submarine -	Torpedo -	Missed -	—
†North Britain -	3,679	22	Atlantic - -	Submarine -	Gunfire -	Gun - - -	—
†Empire - -	4,496	23	Mediterranean -	Submarine -	Chased -	Gun - - -	—
†Mary Maud (S.V.).	85	23	St. George's Channel.	Submarine -	Gunfire -	Attack abandoned.	—
†Petersham -	3,381	24	N. Ireland - -	Submarine -	Gunfire -	Gun - - -	—
†Auricula - -	815	24	Bay of Biscay -	Submarine -	Torpedo -	Missed -	—
Mary Grace (S.V.).	58	24	South Ireland -	Submarine -	Gunfire -	Towed in -	—
†Paliki - -	1,578	24	North Sea - -	Submarine -	Torpedo -	Missed -	—
†Elve - -	899	24	Atlantic - -	Submarine -	Chased -	Attack abandoned.	—
†Elve - -	899	25	Atlantic - -	Submarine -	Chased -	Attack abandoned.	—
†Polescar - -	5,832	25	Dunkirk Harbour	Aircraft - -	Bombs -	Damaged -	2
†Craonne - -	4,264	25	Atlantic - -	Submarine -	Gunfire -	Gun and smoke.	—
†San Zeferino -	6 430	26	St. George's Channel.	Submarine -	Torpedoed -	Reached port.	3
†Port Victor -	7,280	26	English Channel -	Submarine -	Torpedoed -	Reached port	—
†Barima - -	1,498	26	S.W. Scilly Ids. -	Submarine -	Chased -	Speed -	—
Portaferry	236	26	North Sea - -	Submarine -	Torpedo -	Missed -	—
†Chao Chow Fu -	1,909	27	Mediterranean -	Submarine -	Torpedo -	Missed -	—
†Genesee - -	2,892	27	North Sea - -	Submarine -	Torpedo -	Missed -	—
†William Middleton.	2,543	28	St. George's Channel.	Mine - -	Mine - -	Reached port.	2
†North Britain -	3,679	29	West from Gibraltar.	Submarine -	Torpedo -	Missed -	—
†Benavon - -	3,996	30	Atlantic - -	Submarine -	Gunfire -	Gun - - -	—
†Cronstadt -	1,674	30	Atlantic - -	Submarine -	Gunfire -	Gun - - -	—
†Vigo - -	4,224	30	Atlantic - -	Submarine -	Gunfire -	Gun - - -	—
OCTOBER 1917.		Oct.					
†Copenhagen -	4,540	1	Atlantic - -	Submarine -	Gunfire -	Gun - - -	—
†Clydebrae -	502	2	North Sea - -	Submarine -	Torpedoed -	Beached -	5 including Master.
†Devereux - -	1,371	2	North Sea - -	Submarine -	Chased -	Gun - -	—
†Verdun - -	5,691	4	English Channel	Submarine -	Torpedo -	Missed -	—
†Kaffir Prince -	2,228	4	Atlantic - -	Submarine -	Chased -	Darkness -	—
†Le Coq - -	3,419	6	Bay of Biscay -	Mine - -	Mine - -	Towed in -	—
Harborne - -	1,278	7	English Channel	Submarine -	Torpedo -	Missed -	—
H.S. 48 (Tug) -	—	9	West from Gibraltar.	Submarine -	Torpedo -	Missed -	—
†Boston City -	2,711	11	Off N. Ireland -	Submarine -	Torpedo -	Missed -	—
†Cape Corso -	3,890	12	Bristol Channel -	Submarine -	Torpedoed -	Towed in -	13
†Fleswick - -	648	13	St. George's Channel.	Submarine -	Torpedo -	Missed -	—
†Newquay - -	4,191	13	North Sea - -	Submarine -	Torpedoed -	Towed in -	—
Woodburn -	2,360	13	English Channel	Submarine -	Torpedoed -	Arrived in port.	—
†Andorinha -	2,548	13	South Ireland -	Submarine -	Torpedo -	Failed to explode.	—
†Daghild - -	8,000	14	English Channel	Submarine -	Torpedo -	Missed -	—
†Ethyl - -	3,082	14	Atlantic - -	Submarine -	Gunfire -	Gun - - -	—

Name.	Gross Tons.	Date.	Position.	Attacked by	How attacked.	How saved.	Lives lost.
		1917. Oct.					
†Carmelite - -	2,583	15	Off Land's End -	Submarine - -	Torpedo -	Missed -	—.
†San Nazario -	10,064	15	S.W. from Scilly	Submarine - -	Torpedoed -	Reached port.	—
†Sealda - -	5,382	15	W. from Ushant-	Submarine - -	Torpedo -	Missed -	—
†Leander - -	2,793	15	English Channel	Submarine - -	Torpedoed -	Towed in -	—
†Netherpark -	4,362	15	W. from Ushant -	Submarine - -	Torpedo -	Missed -	—
†Sealda - -	5,382	16	Atlantic - -	Submarine - -	Torpedo ; Gunfire.	Missed ; Gun.	—
Goorkha (hospital ship).	6,335	17	Mediterranean -	Mine - - -	Mine - -	Arrived in port.	—
†Domino - -	1,120	17	North Sea -	Submarine - -	Torpedo -	Missed -	—
†Dallington -	2,534	18	English Channel	Submarine - -	Torpedo -	Missed -	—
†Wellington -	5,600	19	English Channel	Submarine - -	Torpedoed -	Arrived in port.	—
†Orna - -	4,783	19	Atlantic - -	Submarine - -	Torpedo ; gunfire.	Missed -	—
†Teespool -	4,577	19	English Channel	Submarine - -	Torpedoed -	Beached -	4
†Wearside - -	3,560	19	North Sea -	Submarine - -	Torpedo -	Missed -	—
†Frank Parish -	2,893	20	North Sea -	Submarine - -	Torpedo -	Failed to explode.	—
†Maidan - -	8,205	20	Mediterranean -	Submarine - -	Torpedo -	Missed -	—
†Domino - -	1,120	20	North Sea -	Submarine - -	Torpedo -	Missed -	—
†Burma - -	7,470	20	Mediterranean -	Submarine - -	Torpedo -	Missed -	—
†St. Fillans -	4,622	21	English Channel -	Submarine - -	Torpedo -	Missed -	—
†Sportsman -	572	21	North Sea -	Submarine - -	Torpedo -	Missed -	—
†Silverlip -	9,718	21	N W. Scotland -	Submarine - -	Torpedo -	Missed -	—
†Mapleleaf -	8,039	21	Atlantic - -	Submarine - -	Torpedo -	Missed -	—
Comeric -	3,979	22	Atlantic - -	Submarine - -	Torpedo -	Missed -	—
†Lepanto - -	6,389	23	English Channel -	Submarine - -	Torpedoed -	Arrived in port.	2
†Novington -	3,442	24	East Shetlands -	Submarine - -	Torpedoed -	Beached -	—
†Kalo - -	1,957	25	Mediterranean -	Submarine - -	Torpedo - Gunfire -	Missed - Gun.	—
†Clermiston -	1,282	26	Mediterranean -	Submarine - -	Torpedo -	Missed -	—
†Lightfoot -	1,875	26	North Sea -	Submarine - -	Chased -	Weather -	—
†Canadian - -	2,214	27	Mediterranean -	Submarine - -	Torpedo -	Missed -	—
†Denebola -	1,481	28	North Sea -	Submarine - -	Torpedo -	Missed -	—
Elwick - -	1,717	28	English Channel -	Submarine - -	Torpedo -	Missed -	—

NOVEMBER 1917.

Name.	Gross Tons.	Date.	Position.	Attacked by	How attacked.	How saved.	Lives lost.
		Nov.					
†Margam Abbey	4,367	1	Mediterranean -	Submarine - -	Torpedoed -	Beached -	2
†Branksome Hall	4,262	2	English Channel	Submarine - -	Torpedoed -	Beached -	—
†St. Agnes -	1,195	2	North Sea -	Submarine - -	Chased -	Fog - -	—
†Atlantian -	9,399	3	Irish Channel -	Submarine - -	Torpedoed -	Reached port	—
†Rodskjaer -	2,724	3	English Channel -	Submarine - -	Gunfire -	Gun - -	—
†Lucida -	1,477	4	North Sea -	Submarine - -	Torpedoed -	Beached -	4
†Clan Cumming -	4,808	5	English Channel	Submarine - -	Torpedoed -	Towed in -	13
†Amberton -	4,556	5	Mediterranean -	Submarine - -	Torpedoed -	Beached -	—
†Eider -	1,236	5	North Sea -	Submarine - -	Torpedo -	Missed -	—
†Benledi -	3,931	8	W. from Gibraltar	Submarine - -	Torpedo ; gunfire.	Missed ; gun	1
†Derwent River -	4,724	8	W. from Gibraltar	Submarine - -	Chased -	Gun - -	—
†Clan Macneil -	3,939	9	W. from Gibraltar	Submarine - -	Torpedo -	Missed -	—
†Appleleaf -	5,891	10	North Sea -	Mine - -	Mine -	Towed in -	—
†Inniscarra -	1,412	11	St. George's Chan.	Submarine - -	Torpedo -	Missed -	—
†Southgate -	3,661	11	Mediterranean -	Mine - -	Mine -	Reached port	—
†Cavallo -	2,086	12	English Channel -	Submarine - -	Chased -	Gun - -	—
†Southgare -	818	12	North Sea -	Submarine - -	Chased -	Gun - -	—
†Baysarua -	4,986	15	Mediterranean -	Submarine - -	Torpedo -	Missed -	—
†Glenfruin -	3,097	16	Mediterranean -	Submarine - -	Torpedo -	Missed -	—
†Abaris -	2,892	17	English Channel -	Submarine - -	Torpedoed -	Towed in -	3
†David Lloyd George	4,764	17	English Channel -	Submarine - -	Torpedoed -	Reached port	—
†Huntsgulf -	3,185	18	Mediterranean -	Submarine - -	Torpedoed -	Reached port	—
†Marie Suzanne -	3,106	19	Atlantic - -	Submarine - -	Gunfire -	Gun - -	—
†City of Chester -	5,413	19	English Channel -	Submarine - -	Torpedo - Torpedo -	Missed - Failed to explode.	—
†Carpentaria -	7,755	19	English Channel -	Submarine - -	Torpedo -	Missed -	—
†Rathlin -	1,321	19	St. George's Chan.	Submarine - -	Chased -	Speed -	—
†Breynton -	4,240	21	St. George's Chan.	Submarine - -	Torpedoed -	Reached port	—

Name.	Gross Tons.	Date.	Position.	Attacked by	How attacked.	How saved.	Lives lost.
		1917. Nov.					
†Kenmare - -	1,330	21	Irish Channel -	Submarine - -	Torpedo -	Missed -	—
†Ubbergen - -	1,877	21	Mediterranean -	Submarine - -	Torpedo -	Missed -	---
†Sardinia - -	6,580	21	Mediterranean -	Submarine - -	Torpedo -	Missed -	---
†Redbridge -	3,834	22	St. George's Chan.	Submarine - -	Torpedoed -	Reached port	---
†Hartland - -	4,785	22	St. George's Chan.	Submarine - -	Torpedoed -	Reached port	2
†Canonesa - -	5,583	22	English Channel -	Submarine - -	Torpedo -	Missed -	---
†Boma - -	2,694	23	English Channel -	Submarine - -	Chased -	Speed -	—
†Benue - -	4,408	23	Irish Channel -	Submarine - -	Torpedo -	Missed -	—
†Rutherglen -	4,214	24	Atlantic - -	Submarine - -	Chased -	Speed -	—
†Quaysider - -	595	26	English Channel -	Submarines - -	Gunfire -	Gun - -	—
†Crenella - -	7,035	26	S.W. Ireland -	Submarine - -	Torpedoed -	Reached port	—
†Flavia - -	9,291	26	S.W. Ireland -	Submarine - -	Torpedo -	Missed -	—
†Thornhill - -	3,848	27	Mediterranean -	Submarine - -	Torpedoed -	Beached -	1
†Glenbridge -	3,845	27	Mediterranean -	Submarine - -	Torpedoed -	Beached -	—
†Upcerne - -	2,984	27	Irish Sea - -	Submarine - -	Torpedo -	Missed -	—
†Herschel - -	6,293	27	Mediterranean -	Submarine - -	Torpedo -	Missed -	—
†Glenrazan -	4,044	27	English Channel -	Submarine - -	Torpedo -	Missed -	—
†Kirkholm - -	4,753	28	English Channel -	Submarine - -	Torpedo -	Missed -	—
†Agenoria - -	2,977	28	Irish Channel -	Submarine - -	Torpedoed -	Beached -	1
†Madeline - -	2,890	29	Bay of Biscay -	Submarine - -	Torpedo -	Missed -	--
†Exmouth - -	3,923	29	Mediterranean -	Submarine - -	Torpedo -	Failed to explode.	—
†Linhope - -	1,339	29	North Sea - -	Submarine - -	Chased -	Gun - -	—
†Carrigan Head -	4,201	29	English Channel -	Submarine - -	Torpedo -	Missed -	—
†Somersby - -	3,647	30	Bristol Channel -	Submarine - -	Gunfire -	Gun - -	—
†Nunima - -	2,938	30	Bristol Channel -	Submarine - -	Torpedo -	Missed -	—
DECEMBER 1917.		**Dec.**					
†Helenus - -	7,555	1	English Channel -	Submarine - -	Torpedoed -	Towed in -	—
†Cretic -	13,518	1	West from Gibraltar.	Submarine - -	Chased -	Speed -	—
†Bonvilston -	2,866	1	English Channel	Submarine - -	Torpedo -	Missed -	—
†El Uruguayo -	8,361	2	English Channel -	Submarine - -	Torpedo -	Missed -	—
†The Countess -	624	3	South Ireland -	Submarine - -	Torpedo -	Missed -	—
†Leafield - -	2,539	3	Irish Channel -	Submarine - -	Chased -	Speed -	---
†Lord Dufferin -	4,664	3	Mediterranean -	Submarine - -	Torpedo ; Gunfire.	Missed - Gun.	—
†Milton -	3,267	4	St. George's Channel.	Submarine - -	Torpedo -	Reached port	1
†Manchester Mariner.	4,106	4	English Channel -	Mine - - -	Mine - -	Mine defence.	—
Dolphin - -	353	5	Calais - -	Aircraft - -	Bomb - -	Slightly damaged.	—
†Earlswood -	2,353	5	English Channel -	Submarine - -	Torpedoed -	Reached port	2
†Oneida - -	698	5	English Channel -	Submarine - -	Torpedo -	Missed -	—
†Excellence Pleske.	2,059	5	Mediterranean -	Submarine - -	Torpedo -	Missed -	---
†Llangorse - -	4,703	5	Mediterranean -	Submarine - -	Torpedo -	Missed -	—
†Dundalk - -	794	6	Irish Channel -	Submarine - -	Gunfire -	Gun - -	—
†Linhope - -	1,339	7	North Sea -	Submarine - -	Torpedo -	Missed -	—
†Benlawers - -	3,949	7	North Sea -	Submarine - -	Torpedo -	Missed -	—
†Chyebassa -	6,249	8	Mediterranean -	Submarine - -	Torpedoed -	Reached port	—
†Sedbergh - -	4,230	9	English Channel -	Submarine - -	Torpedoed -	Towed in -	1
†Nyanza - -	6,695	9	English Channel	Submarine - -	Torpedoed -	Reached port	49
†Eros - -	1,843	9	English Channel	Submarine - -	Torpedo -	Failed to explode.	—
†Darino - -	1,359	9	North Sea -	Submarine - -	2 torpedoes -	Missed -	—
†Aureole - -	3.998	10	West Scotland -	Mine - -	Mine - -	Reached port	—
†Bayusona - -	986	10	English Channel	Submarine - -	Gunfire -	Gun - -	—
†Penmount -	2,314	10	English Channel	Submarine - -	Torpedo -	Missed -	—
†Gwynwood -	1,084	10	North Sea -	Submarine - -	Torpedo -	Missed -	—
†Eastern City -	5,992	11	Mediterranean -	Submarine - -	Gunfire -	Gun - -	—
†Occident -	813	13	North Sea -	Submarine - -	Torpedo -	Failed to explode.	—
†Torquay - -	870	14	North Sea -	Submarine - -	Torpedo -	Missed -	—
†Newhailes -	1,423	14	North Sea -	Submarine - -	Torpedo -	Missed -	---
†Sachem - -	5,354	15	English Channel	Submarine - -	Torpedoed -	Reached port	---
†Ninian - -	6,385	15	English Channel	Submarine - -	Torpedo -	Missed -	—
†Australpeak -	4,432	15	Atlantic - -	Submarine - -	Torpedo -	Missed -	—
†North Britain -	3,679	15	Atlantic - -	Submarine - -	Torpedo -	Missed -	—
†Hungerford -	5,811	16	Mediterranean -	Submarine - -	2 torpedoes -	Missed -	—
†Novian - -	6,368	17	Atlantic - -	Submarine - -	Torpedo -	Missed -	—
†Kenmare - -	1,330	18	Irish Channel -	Submarine - -	Chased -	Gun - -	—
†Kaisar-i-Hind -	11,430	18	W. from Gibraltar	Submarine - -	Torpedo -	Missed -	—

Name.	Gross Tons.	Date.	Position.	Attacked by	How attacked.	How saved.	Lives lost.
		1917. Dec.					
†Trevelyan -	3,066	19	English Channel	Submarine - -	Torpedoed -	Beached -	—
†Baron Cathcart -	1,860	19	Irish Channel -	Submarine - -	Torpedo -	Missed -	—
†Teesbridge -	3,898	19	Atlantic - -	Submarine - -	Gunfire -	Gun - -	—
†Seattle - -	5,133	20	Mediterranean -	Submarine - -	Gunfire - Torpedo -	Gun - - Missed.	—
†Polaria -	3,546	20	Mediterranean -	Submarine - -	Gunfire -	Gun - -	—
†Sorrento -	2,892	20	Mediterranean -	Submarine - -	Gunfire -	Gun - -	—
†Yang-Tsze -	6,457	21	Irish Channel -	Submarine - -	Torpedo -	Missed -	—
†Relillio -	2,398	21	English Channel	Submarine - -	Torpedo -	Missed -	—
†Mabel Baird -	2,500	21	Bristol Channel -	Submarine - -	Torpedo -	Missed -	—
†Hunsbrook -	4,463	22	Bristol Channel -	Submarine - -	Torpedoed -	Beached -	3
†Cypria -	2,950	22	Irish Channel -	Submarine - -	Torpedo -	Missed -	—
Elwick -	1,717	23	Bristol Channel -	Submarine - -	2 torpedoes -	Missed -	—
†Dunedin -	4,796	23	Mediterranean -	Mine - - -	Mine - -	Towed in -	—
†Dorie - -	3,264	23	Irish Channel -	Submarine - -	Chased -	Attack abandoned.	—
†Elmleaf -	5,948	24	N.W. Scotland -	Submarine - -	Torpedoed -	Reached port	—
†Luciston -	2,877	24	English Channel	Submarine - -	Torpedoed -	Beached -	—
†Hyacinthus -	5,756	25	English Channel	Submarine - -	Torpedoed -	Reached port	—
†Modesta -	3,832	25	English Channel	Submarine - -	Torpedo -	Missed -	—
†Asiatic Prince -	2,887	26	English Channel	Submarine - -	Torpedo -	Missed -	—
Leinster -	2,646	27	Irish Channel -	Submarine - -	Torpedo -	Missed -	—
†Battersea -	860	28	North Sea -	Submarine - -	Chased -	Gun - -	—
†Inverness -	3,734	29	North Sea -	Submarine - -	Torpedoed -	Reached port	—
†Broompark -	2,126	30	English Channel	Submarine - -	Torpedo -	Missed -	—
†Baron Inchcape	7,005	30	Mediterranean -	Submarine - -	Torpedo -	Missed -	—
†Bathampton -	3,282	31	English Channel	Submarine - -	Torpedo -	Missed -	—
†Devonshire -	500	31	St. George's Channel.	Submarine - -	Torpedo -	Missed -	—

JANUARY 1918.

Name.	Gross Tons.	Date.	Position.	Attacked by	How attacked.	How saved.	Lives lost.
		Jan.					
†Genesee -	2,892	i	North Sea -	Submarine - -	Torpedoed -	Reached port	—
†Egyptian Transport.	4,648	1	Mediterranean -	Submarine - -	Torpedoed -	Beached -	5
†Fleswick -	648	1	Irish Channel -	Submarine - -	Gunfire -	Gun - -	...
†Kingsley -	633	2	English Channel	Submarine - -	Gunfire -	Gun - -	5
†El Paraguayo -	8,508	2	Bristol Channel -	Submarine - -	Torpedo -	Missed -	—
†Enda - -	842	2	Irish Channel -	Submarine - -	Torpedo ; Gunfire.	Missed ; Gun.	—
†Deneb -	1,230	2	Bristol Channel -	Submarine - -	Torpedo -	Missed -	—
†Beechleaf -	5,861	3	Mediterranean -	Submarine - -	Torpedo -	Missed -	—
Victor (S.V.) -	163	4	Bristol Channel -	Submarine - -	Gunfire -	Rescued -	—
†Newlands -	3,012	5	Irish Channel -	Submarine - -	Torpedo -	Missed -	—
Hong Moh -	3,910	5	S.E. Arabia -	Mine - - -	Mine - -	Slight damage.	—
†Arca -	4,839	6	English Channel	Submarine - -	Torpedoed -	Reached port	—
†Portwood -	2,241	9	English Channel	Submarine - -	Torpedo -	Missed -	—
†Cardiff -	2,808	10	Bay of Biscay -	Submarine - -	Torpedoed -	Beached -	8
†Gregynog -	1,701	11	English Channel	Submarine - -	Torpedo -	Missed -	—
†Ramore Head -	4,585	11	St. George's Channel.	Submarine - -	Chased -	Gun - -	—
†Horsham -	401	14	Great Yarmouth -	T.B.D. - -	Gunfire -	Damaged -	1
†Hova -	4,264	15	Mediterranean -	Submarine - -	Torpedo -	Missed -	—
†Messidor -	3,883	17	Bay of Biscay -	Submarine - -	Torpedoed -	Reached port	—
†War Thistle -	5,166	17	English Channel	Submarine - -	Torpedoed -	Reached port	—
†Izaston -	3,060	17	North Sea -	Submarine - -	Gunfire -	Gun - -	—
†Hampstead -	3,447	18	Mediterranean -	Submarine - -	Gunfire -	Gun - -	—
†War Anemone -	5,214	18	English Channel -	Submarine - -	Chased -	Speed -	...
†Dux -	1,349	19	English Channel	Submarine - -	Torpedo -	Missed -	—
†Hunsgrove -	3,063	19	English Channel	Submarine - -	Chased -	Speed -	—
†Saint Clair -	621	19	North Sea -	Submarine - -	Gunfire -	Smoke and gun.	2
†Cumbrian -	1,131	19	English Channel -	Submarine - -	2 torpedoes -	Failed to explode.	—
†Highland Loch -	7,493	20	English Channel	Submarine - -	Torpedo -	Missed -	—
†Harmonides -	3,521	20	English Channel	Submarine - -	Torpedoed -	Reached port	...
†Isleworth -	2,871	20	Bristol Channel -	Submarine - -	Torpedo -	Missed -	—
†Queen Margaret	4,972	20	English Channel -	Mine - - -	Mine - -	Reached port	—
†Admiral Cochrane.	6,565	22	English Channel -	Submarine - -	Torpedoed -	Towed in -	—
†Corton -	3,405	22	English Channel -	Submarine - -	Torpedoed -	Towed in -	3
†Chinkoa -	5,222	22	English Channel -	Submarine - -	Torpedo -	Missed -	...

Name.	Gross Tons.	Date.	Position.	Attacked by	How attacked.	How saved.	Lives lost.
		1918. Jan.					
†Knight of the Garter.	6,689	22	Mediterranean -	Submarine - -	Torpedo -	Missed -	—
†Nembe - -	3,855	23	Off Scilly Isles -	Submarine - -	Chased -	Weather -	—
†Justicia - -	32,234	23	Irish Channel -	Submarine - -	Torpedo -	Missed -	—
†Lackenby -	2,108	25	English Channel	Submarine - -	Torpedo -	Missed -	—
†Alice M. Craig -	916	25	North Sea - -	Submarine - -	Torpedo -	Missed -	—
†Manhattan -	8,115	26	English Channel -	Submarine - -	Torpedoed -	Reached port	—
†Vestris - -	10,494	26	English Channel-	Submarine - -	Torpedo -	Missed -	—
†Remus - -	1,079	26	North Sea - -	Submarine - -	Torpedo -	Missed -	—
†Sea Gull -	976	27	Irish Channel -	Submarine - -	Torpedo -	Missed ⤚	—
†Dublin - -	711	28	Irish Channel -	Submarine - -	Chased -	Weather -	—
†Ravonia - -	703	29	North Sea - -	Submarine - -	Torpedo -	Missed -	—
†Normannia -	1,567	29	English Channel-	Submarine - -	Torpedo -	Missed -	—
†Slieve Bawn -	1,061	30	Irish Channel -	Submarine - -	Torpedo -	Missed -	—
†Findhorn - -	1,122	30	Irish Channel -	Submarine - -	Gunfire -	Gun - -	—
†Brighton - -	3,463	30	Mediterranean -	Submarine - -	2 Torpedoes	Missed -	—
†Eggesford -	4,414	31	Mediterranean -	Submarine - -	Torpedoed -	Reached port	—
†Starling - -	804	31	English Channel-	Submarine - -	Chased -	Gun - -	—
†Commonwealth	3,353	31	Mediterranean -	Submarine - -	Torpedo -	Missed -	—

FEBRUARY 1918.

Name.	Gross Tons.	Date.	Position.	Attacked by	How attacked.	How saved.	Lives lost.
		Feb.					
†Glenamoy -	7,269	1	Mediterranean -	Submarine - -	Torpedoed -	Reached port	—
†Chertsey - -	3,264	1	English Channel	Submarine - -	Torpedo -	Missed -	—
†Mourino - -	1,819	1	Bristol Cnannel -	Submarine - -	Torpedo -	Missed -	—
†Levensau - -	2,155	3	North Sea - -	Submarine - -	Gunfire -	Weather -	—
†Petrograd -	1,713	3	Bristol Channel -	Submarine - -	2 Torpedoes	Failed to explode.	—
†Longertie - -	1,126	3	North Sea - -	Submarine - -	Torpedo -	Missed -	—
†Holmpark -	1,468	3	North Sea - -	Submarine - -	Torpedo ˙ -	Missed -	—
†Ravenshoe -	3,592	4	Mediterranean -	Submarine - -	Torpedoed -	Reached port.	—
†Euryades - -	5,713	4	Irish Channel -	Submarine - -	Torpedo -	Missed -	—
Sardinia - -	6,580	4	Mediterranean -	Submarine - -	Torpedoed -	Reached port.	—
†General Church	6,600	4	Mediterranean -	Submarine - -	Torpedoed -	Reached port.	2
†Herefordshire -	7,198	4	Mediterranean -	Submarine - -	Torpedo -	Missed -	—
†Franklyn -	4,919	5	Mediterranean -	Submarine - -	Torpedo -	Missed -	—
†Westmoreland -	9,512	6	Irish Channel -	Submarine - -	Torpedoed -	Beached -	1
†Eda - -	2.525	7	Irish Channel -	Submarine - -	Chased -	Gun - -	—
†Sandhurst -	3,034	8	Mediterranean -	Submarine - -	Torpedo -	Missed -	—
Scotsman - -	181	8	Irish Channel -	Submarine - -	Chased -	Speed -	—
†Oakdale - -	1,340	8	Irish Channel -	Submarine - -	Gunfire -	Gun - .	—
†Cimbrier - -	3,905	8	Mediterranean -	Submarine - -	Torpedoed -	Reached port.	—
†Sphynx - -	1,569	8	English Channel	Submarine - -	Torpedo -	Missed -	—
†Antenor - -	5,319	9	Mediterranean -	Submarine - -	Torpedoed -	Reached port.	—
†Pomaron -	1,809	9	Irish Channel -	Submarine - -	Torpedo -	Missed -	—
†Knight of the Garter.	6,689	11	English Channel	Submarine - -	2 Torpedoes	Missed -	—
†Helenes - -	3,332	11	W. from Gibraltar	Submarine - -	Gunfire -	Gun - -	—
†Swansea Vale -	1,310	12	North Sea - -	Submarine - -	2 Torpedoes	1 missed ; 1 failed to explode.	—
†Syndic - -	2,727	12	North Sea - -	Submarine - -	2 torpedoes -	Missed -	—.
†Farnworth -	5,896	12	Atlantic -	Submarine - -	Gunfire -	Gun - -	—
†Sarpen - -	1,864	13	Bristol Channel -	Submarine - -	Torpedo -	Missed -	—
†Lackawanna -	4,125	13	North Sea - -	Submarine - -	Torpedoed -	Reached port.	—
Clarecastle -	627	14	St. George's Chan.	Submarine - -	Torpedo -	Missed -	—
†Skaraas - -	1,625	14	English Channel	Submarine - -	Torpedo -	Missed -	—
†Skegness - -	2,801	15	North Sea - -	Submarine - -	2 torpedoes -	Missed -	—
†Thames - -	1,327	15	North Sea - -	Submarine - -	Torpedo -	Missed -	—
†Pikepool - -	3,683	16	English Channel	Submarine - -	Torpedoed -	Reached port.	—
†Mountby - -	3,263	16	W. from Gibraltar	Submarine - -	Chased -	Smoke -	—
†Craonne - -	4,264	16	W. from Gibraltar	Submarine - -	Gunfire -	Gun - -	—
†Lady Tennant -	452	19	Bristol Channel -	Submarine - -	Torpedo -	Missed -	—
†Athenic - -	4,078	19	North Sea - -	Submarine - -	Torpedoed -	Towed in -	—
†Elleric - -	3.559	20	Mediterranean -	Submarine - -	Chased -	Gun - -	—

Name.	Gross Tons.	Date.	Position.	Attacked by	How attacked.	How saved.	Lives lost.
		1918. Feb.					
†Largo - -	1,764	22	English Channel	Submarine - -	Torpedo -	Missed -	—
†Birchleaf - -	5,873	23	Irish Channel -	Submarine - -	Torpedoed -	Beached -	3 Master prisoner.
†Bellerby - -	3,089	23	English Channel	Submarine - -	Torpedo -	Missed -	—
†Courtfield -	4,592	23	English Channel	Submarine - -	Torpedo -	Missed -	—
†Mirita - -	5,830	23	Atlantic - -	Submarine - -	Gunfire -	Gun - -	—
†Nyanza - -	6,695	24	English Channel	Submarine - -	Torpedoed -	Towed in -	4
†Duke of Cumberland.	2,036	24	Irish Channel -	Submarine - -	Torpedo -	Missed -	—
†Slieve Bawn -	1,061	25	Irish Channel -	Submarine - -	2 torpedoes -	Missed -	—
†Appalachee -	3,767	25	North Ireland -	Submarine - -	Torpedoed -	Towed in -	—
†Berwen - -	3,752	26	North Sea - -	Mine - - -	Mine - -	Towed in -	—
†Kerman - -	4,397	27	Mediterranean -	Submarine - -	Torpedoed -	Reached port.	—
†Marconi - -	7,402	27	Mediterranean -	Submarine - -	Torpedoed -	Reached port.	2
†Aulton - -	634	27	North Sea - -	Submarine - -	Torpedo -	Missed -	—
†Sheaf Field -	1,533	27	Irish Channel -	Submarine - -	2 torpedoes -	Missed - -	—
†Benedict - -	3,378	27	Irish Channel -	Submarine - -	Gunfire -	Gun - -	—
Princess Irma -	1,520	27	Off Hook of Holland.	Aircraft - -	Bomb - -	Missed -	—
Kirkham Abbey	1,166	27	Off Hook of Holland.	Aircraft - -	Bomb - -	Missed -	—
Lady Carmichael (tug).	—	27	Off Hook of Holland.	Aircraft - -	Bomb ; machine gun.	Missed : slightly damaged.	—

MARCH 1918.

Name.	Gross Tons.	Date.	Position.	Attacked by	How attacked.	How saved.	Lives lost.
		Mar.					
†Petroleine -	4 217	2	Atlantic - -	Submarine - -	Gunfire -	Gun - -	—
†Spey - -	470	2	Mediterranean -	Submarine - -	Gunfire -	Gun - -	—
†Dundarg (S.V.)	145	2	Irish Sea - -	Submarine - -	Gunfire -	Gun - -	—
†Clan Graham -	5,213	4	Mediterranean -	Submarine - -	Torpedoed -	Reached port	3
†British Princess	7,034	4	North Ireland -	Submarine - -	Torpedoed -	Reached port	1
†Silvia - -	2,035	4	North Sea - -	Submarine - -	2 torpedoes -	Missed -	—
†Clan Mackenzie	6,544	5	English Channel -	Submarine - -	Torpedoed -	Reached port	6
Blush Rose -	645	5	North Sea - -	Submarine - -	2 torpedoes -	Missed -	—
†Kosseir - -	1,855	5	Mediterranean -	Aircraft - -			—
†Gibel-Derif -	804	5	English Channel -	Submarine - -	Chased -	Gun - -	—
Favorita Clara -	512	6	Bay of Biscay -	Submarine - -	Torpedo -	Missed -	—
†Bruse - -	1,711	6	North Sea - -	Submarine - -	Torpedo -	Missed -	—
†Lord Charlemont	3,209	6	English Channel -	Submarine - -	Torpedo -	Missed -	—
†Cliffside - -	4,969	7	English Channel -	Submarine - -	Torpedoed -	Beached -	—
†Volpone - -	531	7	English Channel -	Submarine - -	Torpedo -	Missed -	—
†Saba - -	4,257	8	English Channel -	Mine - - -	Mine - -	Reached port	—
†Mitra - -	5,592	8	Mediterranean -	Submarine - -	Torpedoed -	Reached port	—
†Flixton - -	4,286	10	English Channel -	Submarine - -	Torpedo -	Missed -	—
Guildford Castle (hospital ship).	8,036	10	Bristol Channel -	Submarine - -	2 torpedoes -	1 failed to explode, 1 missed.	—
†Nellore - -	6,853	11	W. from Gibraltar	Submarine - -	Gunfire -	Speed -	—
†Atlantic - -	3,016	11	Mediterranean -	Submarine - -	Chased -	Gun - -	—
†Clarissa Radcliffe	5,754	12	English Channel -	Submarine - -	Torpedoed -	Reached port	—
†Kerry - -	1,199	12	Irish Channel -	Submarine - -	Torpedo -	Missed -	—
†Savan - -	4,264	12	English Channel -	Submarine - -	Torpedoed -	Reached port	1
†Herbert Fischer	938	13	North Sea - -	Submarine - -	Torpedo -	Missed -	—
†Umta - -	5,422	14	Mediterranean -	Submarine - -	Torpedoed -	Reached port	8
†Comrie Castle -	5,173	14	English Channel -	Submarine - -	Torpedoed -	Beached -	9
†Silvia - -	2,035	15	North Sea - -	Submarine - -	Gunfire -	Gun - -	—
†Portsea - -	3,283	15	S.W. from Madeira	Submarine - -	Chased -	Speed -	—
†Sheaf Brook -	3,514	15	Mediterranean -	Submarine - -	Torpedo -	Missed -	—
†Meissonier -	7,206	16	W. from Gibraltar	Submarine - -	Gunfire -	Speed -	—
†Author - -	5,596	16	English Channel -	Submarine - -	Torpedo -	Slight damage.	—
Corbiere (motor)	22	17	English Channel -	Submarine - -	Torpedo -	Missed -	—
†Lady Charlotte -	3,593	17	Irish Channel -	Submarine - -	Chased -	Attack abandoned.	—
†Garryvale -	3,917	17	Mediterranean -	Submarine - -	2 torpedoes -	Missed -	—
†Navigator -	3,803	18	English Channel -	Submarine - -	Torpedo -	Slight damage.	—
†Ibex - -	951	18	English Channel -	Submarine - -	Chased -	Gun - -	—
†Grainton - -	6,042	18	Irish Sea - -	Submarine - -	Torpedoed -	Reached port	—

Name.	Gross Tons.	Date.	Position.	Attacked by	How attacked.	How saved.	Lives lost.
		1918. Mar.					
†Longnewton -	1,878	19	English Channel -	Submarine - -	Torpedo -	Missed -	---
†Elysia - -	6,397	19	Mediterranean -	Submarine - -	Torpedo -	Missed -	—
†Boorara - -	6,570	20	English Channel -	Submarine - -	Torpedoed -	Reached port	5
†Dunaff Head -	5,877	20	Irish Chan..el -	Submarine - -	Chased -	Gun - -	—
†Custodian -	9,214	20	Irish Channel -	Submarine - -	Torpedoed -	Reached port	3
†Lord Ormonde -	3,914	20	Mediterranean -	Submarine - -	Torpedoed -	Reached port	—
†Western Australia.	2,937	20	English Channel	Submarine - -	Torpedo -	Missed -	—
†Hunsdon - -	2,899	21	English Channel -	Submarine - -	Chased -	Gun - -	.—
†Morocco - -	3,783	21	English Channel -	Submarine - -	Gunfire -	Gun - -	—
†Stanja - -	1,845	21	English Channel -	Submarine - -	Torpedo -	Missed -	—
†Ulster - -	2,641	22	Irish Channel -	Submarine - -	Torpedo -	Missed -	—
†Lady Tennant -	452	22	Irish Channel -	Submarine - -	Gunfire -	Gun - -	—
†Llanelly - -	369	22	St. George's Chan.	Submarine - -	Torpedo -	Missed -	—
†Chupra - -	6,175	22	East of the Azores	Submarine - -	Gunfire -	Gun - -	—
†Demodocus -	6,689	23	Mediterranean -	Submarine - -	Torpedoed -	Reached port	6
†Meline - -	6,970	23	North Sea - -	Submarine - -	Torpedoed -	Reached port	—
†Mary Ann Mandal (S.V.).	112	23	English Channel -	2 Submarines	Gunfire -	Gun - -	---
†Mary Sinclair (S.V.).	118	23	English Channel -	2 Submarines	Gunfire -	Gun - -	—
†Sequoya -	5,263	23	English Channel -	Submarine - -	Torpedoed -	Reached port	—
†Lucerna - -	3,247	23	Irish Channel -	Submarine - -	Torpedo -	Missed -	—
†Morvada - -	8,193	23	Mediterranean -	Submarine - -	Torpedo -	Missed -	—
†Shadwell - -	4,091	23	Mediterranean -	Submarine - -	Torpedoed -	Reached port	13
† War Knight -	7,951	24	English Channel -	Mine after collision.	Fire and Mine.	Beached -	32 including Master.
†Anchoria - -	5,430	24	North Ireland -	Submarine - -	Torpedoed -	Reached port	—
†Mirlo - -	6,978	24	English Channel -	Submarine - -	Torpedo -	Missed -	—
†Austrian - -	3,127	24	Irish Channel -	Submarine - -	Chased -	Gun - -	—
†Emma Minlos -	1,286	25	North Sea - -	Submarine - -	Torpedo -	Missed -	—
†Norseman -	352	25	Little Minch -	Submarine - -	Gunfire -	Gun - -	—
† Warturm - -	4,965	25	Mediterranean -	Submarine - -	Torpedoed -	Reached port	2
†British Star -	6,888	26	North Sea - -	Submarine - -	Torpedoed -	Reached port	—
†Patriotic - -	2,254	27	Irish Channel -	Submarine - -	Torpedo -	Missed -	—
†Glenbrook -	251	27	North Sea - -	Submarine - -	Rifle fire -	Gun - -	—
†Bovic - -	6,583	27	Irish Channel -	Submarine - -	Torpedo -	Missed -	—
†Poplar Branch -	5,391	28	Irish Channel -	Submarine - -	Torpedo -	Missed -	—
*Dryden - -	5,839	28	River Mersey -	Mine - -	Mine - -	Reached port	—
†Nairung - -	4,478	28	Mediterranean -	Submarine - -	Torpedo -	Missed -	—
†Leafield - -	2,539	28	Irish Channel -	Submarine - -	Gunfire -	Gun - -	—
†Henry Fürst -	1,500	29	North Sea - -	Submarine - -	Torpedo -	Missed -	—
†Kul - - -	1,095	29	English Channel -	Submarine - -	Torpedo -	Missed -	—
†Kentucky - -	7,169	29	English Channel -	Submarine - -	Torpedo -	Missed -	—
†Linmere - -	1,579	29	Irish Channel -	Submarine - -	Chased -	Attack abandoned.	—
†Oranian - -	3,942	29	Irish Sea - -	Submarine - -	Torpedo -	Missed -	—
†Gracefield -	2,733	30	English Channel -	·Submarine - -	Torpedo -	Missed -	—
† Westerham -	531	30	North Sea - -	Submarine - -	Torpedo -	Missed -	—
†Milwaukee -	7,323	31	Irish Channel -	Submarine - -	Torpedo -	Missed -	—
† Alcinous - -	6,743	31	English Channel -	Submarine - -	Torpedoed -	Reached port	—
†Celtic - -	20,904	31	Irish Channel -	Submarine - -	Torpedoed -	Reached port	6

APRIL 1918.

Name.	Gross Tons.	Date.	Position.	Attacked by	How attacked.	How saved.	Lives lost.
		Apr.					
†Mongolian -	4,892	1	English Channel -	Submarine - -	Chased -	Speed -	—
†Sunik - -	5,017	1	Mediterranean -	Submarine - -	Torpedo -	Missed -	—
†Clapham - -	763	4	English Channel -	Submarine - -	Torpedo -	Missed -	—.-
†Zingara - -	3,463	5	St. George's Chan.	Submarine - -	Torpedo -	Missed -	—
†Clam - -	3,552	5	Irish Channel -	Submarine - -	Torpedoed -	Reached port	-.-
Saint Barchan -	362	5	Irish Channel -	Submarine - -	Gunfire -	Missed -	—
†Ulster - -	2,641	6	Irish Channel -	Submarine - -	Torpedo -	Missed -	—
† Fagerton - -	851	6	North Sea - -	Submarine - -	3 Torpedoes -	Missed -	—
†Headcliffe -	3,654	6	Off Gambia River	Submarine - -	Gunfire -	Gun - -	—
Galacum - -	585	6	English Channel -	Submarine - -	2 Torpedoes -	Missed -	—
†Cadillac - -	11,106	7	W. from Scilly Is.	Submarine - -	Torpedoed -	Reached port	—
†Knight Templar	7,175	7	S.W.from Scilly Is.	Submarine - -	Torpedoed -	Reached port	-—
†Kumara - -	6,063	7	Atlantic - -	Submarine - -	Torpedo -	Missed; gun -	—
Eboe - -	4,866	7	Off Sierra Leone	Submarine - -	Gunfire -	Speed -	—
†Ormiston -	4,843	7	Atlantic - -	Submarine - -	3 torpedoes -	Missed -	—
†Tainui - -	9,965	8	English Channel -	Submarine - -	Torpedoed -	Reached port	—
Genesee (Tug) -	—	8	W. from Scilly Is.	Submarine - -	Gunfire -	Speed -	—
†Northland -	11,905	8	English Channel -	Submarine - -	Torpedo -	Missed -	—

Name.	Gross Tons.	Date.	Position.	Attacked by	How attacked.	How saved.	Lives lost.
		1918. Apr.					
†Asian - -	5,614	8	English Channel -	Submarine - -	Torpedo -	Missed -	---
†Uskside - -	2,209	8	North Sea - -	Submarine - -	Torpedo -	Missed -	—
†Sunik - -	5,017	9	Mediterranean -	Submarine - -	Torpedoed -	Beached -	—
†Warwickshire -	8,012	10	Mediterranean -	Submarine - -	Torpedoed -	Reached port	—
†Airedale - -	3,044	10	Mediterranean -	Submarine - -	Torpedoed -	Beached -	—
†Hunsworth -	2,991	10	English Channel -	Submarine - -	Torpedo -	Missed -	—
†Burutu - -	3,902	10	Off Monrovia -	Submarine - -	Torpedo ; Gunfire.	Missed ; gun.	2
†Paul Paix -	4,196	10	English Channel -	Submarine - -	Torpedoed -	Reached port	—
†Kingstonian -	6,564	11	Mediterranean -	Submarine - -	Torpedoed -	Beached -	1
†Eupion - -	3,575	12	St. George's Chan.	Submarine - -	2 Torpedoes	Missed -	—
Munster - -	2,646	13	Irish Channel -	Submarine - -	Torpedo -	Missed -	—
Bassam - -	3,040	13	Off Sierra Leone	Submarine - -	Chased -	Speed -	---
†Norton - -	1,825	13	Off Ailsa Craig -	Submarine - -	Torpedo -	Missed -	—
†Boma - -	2,694	14	Bristol Channel -	Submarine - -	Torpedo -	Undamaged -	—
†Kathlamba -	6,382	14	Irish Channel -	Submarine - -	Torpedo -	Missed -	---
†Ausonia - -	8,153	14	Atlantic - -	Submarine - -	Torpedo -	Missed -	—
†Erivan - -	2,419	15	North Sea - -	Submarine - -	2 Torpedoes	Missed -	—
†Tanfield - -	4,538	15	English Channel -	Submarine - -	Torpedoed -	Reached port	—
†City of Win-chester.	7,981	15	English Channel -	Submarine - -	Torpedoed -	Reached port	—
†Vulture - -	1,168	15	North Sea - -	Submarine - -	Torpedo -	Missed -	—
George Harper -	1,613	16	English Channel -	Submarine - -	Torpedoed -	Reached port	2
†Kursk - -	7,869	17	Mediterranean -	Submarine - -	Torpedo -	Missed -	—
†Haverford -	11,635	17	Atlantic - -	Submarine - -	2 Torpedoes	Missed -	—
†Eupion - -	3,575	18	English Channel -	Submarine - -	Torpedo -	Failed to explode.	—
†Malpas Belle (S.V.).	179	18	English Channel	Submarine - -	Gunfire -	Weather -	—
†Southern Coast -	1,872	18	Irish Channel -	Submarine - -	Torpedo -	Missed -	—
†Thomas Holt -	1,521	20	Irish Channel -	Submarine - -	Gunfire -	—	—
†Cumbria - -	627	20	Irish Channel -	Submarine - -	Gunfire -	Gun - -	—
†Coya - -	3,040	20	Irish Channel -	Submarine - -	Torpedo -	Missed -	—
†Priestfield -	4,033	20	Irish Channel -	Submarine - -	Torpedo -	Failed to explode.	---
†Megantic - -	14,878	20	St. George's Chan.	Submarine - -	Torpedo -	Missed -	—
†Lompoc - -	7,270	21	North Sea - -	Submarine - -	Torpedoed -	Reached port	—
†Drammenseren -	3,188	21	St. George's Chan.	Submarine - -	Torpedo -	Missed -	---
†Kaisar-I-Hind -	11,430	22	Mediterranean -	Submarine - -	Torpedo -	Missed -	—
†Hitchin - -	1,933	25	English Channel	Submarine - -	Torpedo -	Missed -	—
†Yang-Tsze -	6,457	25	W. from Gibraltar	Submarine - -	Torpedo -	Missed -	—
*Traveller - -	3,042	26	N.W. Ireland -	Submarine - -	Torpedo -	Missed -	—
†Broom - -	576	26	Irish Channel -	Submarine - -	Torpedo -	Missed -	—
Mango - -	341	26	Irish Channel -	Submarine - -	Torpedo -	Missed -	—
†Upada - -	5,257	27	Mediterranean -	Submarine - -	Torpedoed -	Reached port	1
†Ramsay - -	4,318	27	Off S. Cape Blanco	Submarine - -	2 Torpedoes ; Gunfire.	Missed ; gun.	---
†Orion - -	851	28	Bristol Channel -	Submarine - -	Torpedo -	Missed -	—
†Libourne - -	1,219	28	Bristol Channel -	Submarine - -	Torpedo -	Missed -	---
†Comic - -	878	28	Irish Channel -	Submarine - -	Chased -	Speed -	—
†Alert (S.V.) -	163	28	Bristol Channel -	Submarine - -	Gunfire -	Gun - -	—
†Oxonian - -	6,383	29	Irish Channel -	Submarine - -	2 Torpedoes	Missed -	—
†Nidd - -	996	30	English Channel	Submarine - -	Torpedo -	Missed -	—
†Hollyleaf - -	5,167	30	Mediterranean -	Submarine - -	Torpedo -	Missed -	—

MAY 1918.

Name.	Gross Tons.	Date.	Position.	Attacked by	How attacked.	How saved.	Lives lost.
		May					
†Toromeo - -	4,149	1	English Channel -	Submarine - -	Torpedo -	Missed -	—
†Canonesa - -	5,583	1	English Channel -	Submarine - -	Torpedoed -	Reached port	8
†Ravenstone -	3,049	1	Mediterranean -	Submarine - -	3 Torpedoes	Missed -	—
†Lexington -	5,287	2	W. from Gibraltar	Submarine - -	Gunfire -	Speed -	—
†Magdeburg -	1,451	2	North Sea - -	Submarine - -	Torpedo -	Missed -	—
†Lady Plymouth	3,521	2	Mediterranean -	Submarine - -	Torpedo -	Missed -	—
Prosper - -	1,075	2	English Channel -	Submarine - -	Torpedo -	Missed -	—
†Highland Watch	6,031	2	W. from Gibraltar	Submarine - -	2 torpedoes -	Missed -	—
†Chiverstone -	2,946	3	Atlantic - -	Submarine - -	Torpedo -	Missed -	—
†Rosstrevor -	805	3	Irish Channel -	Submarine - -	Torpedo -	Missed -	—
†Pancras - -	4,436	3	Mediterranean -	Submarine - -	Torpedoed -	Reached port	2
†Sphynx - -	1,569	4	Irish Channel -	Submarine - -	2 torpedoes -	Missed -	—
†M. J. Hedley -	419	4	Irish Channel -	Submarine - -	Gunfire -	Rescued -	1

Name.	Gross Tons.	Date.	Position.	Attacked by	How attacked.	How saved.	Lives lost.
		1918. May					
†Sunniva -	1,913	4	North Sea - -	Submarine - -	Torpedo -	Missed -	—
†Pensilva - -	4,316	4	Irish Channel -	Submarine - -	Gunfire -	Gun - -	—
†Clan Ross -	5,971	5	Mediterranean -	Submarine - -	Torpedoed -	Reached port	9
Pandora (S.V.) -	86	5	Irish Channel -	Submarine - -	Gunfire	Towed in -	—
†Wheatear -	383	5	Irish Channel -	Submarine - -	Gunfire -	Gun - -	—
†Claddagh - -	640	5	St. George's Chan.	Submarine - -	Torpedo -	Missed -	—
†Lowther Castle -	4,439	7	Mediterranean -	Submarine - -	Torpedo -	Missed -	—
†Southern Coast -	1,872	7	English Channel -	Submarine - -	Torpedo -	Missed -	—
†Quito - -	3,358	8	Irish Channel -	Submarine - -	Torpedoed -	Reached port	—
†Southern Coast -	1,872	8	St. George's Channel.	Submarine - -	Gunfire -	Smoke ; rescued.	—
†Elizabetta -	335	8	Irish Channel -	Submarine - -	Gunfire -	Gun and smoke.	5 Crew prisoners.
†Camborne (S.V.)	118	8	Bristol Channel -	Submarine - -	Gunfire -	Gun - -	—
Cairnvalona (in tow).	4,840	8	North Sea - -	Submarine - -	Torpedo -	Missed -	—
†Venus -	3,152	8	Mediterranean -	Submarine - -	Torpedo -	Missed -	—
†Blackheath -	4,868	9	Mediterranean -	Submarine - -	Torpedo -	Missed -	—
†Alban - -	5,223	11	Irish Channel -	Submarine - -	Torpedo -	Missed -	—
†Ainsdale - -	1,905	12	North Sea - -	Submarine - -	Torpedo -	Missed -	—
†Benlawers -	3,949	12	Irish Channel -	Mine - - -	Mine - -	Reached port	5
†Esperanza de Larrinaga.	4,981	13	N. Ireland - -	Submarine - -	Torpedoed -	Reached port	1
†Huntress -	4,997	13	Atlantic - -	Submarine - -	Torpedo -	Missed -	—
†Inverness -	3,734	14	Mediterranean -	Submarine - -	Torpedo -	Missed -	—
†Egret -	1,394	14	English Channel -	Submarine - -	Torpedo -	Missed -	—
†Clifftower -	3,509	14	S. Ireland - -	Submarine - -	Torpedo -	Missed -	—
†Pennyworth -	5,388	15	English Channel -	Submarine - -	Torpedoed -	Reached port	1
†War Grange -	3,100	15	Bristol Channel -	Submarine - -	Torpedoed -	Beached -	5
†Priestfield -	4,033	15	Irish Channel -	Submarine - -	Torpedo -	Missed -	—
†Cremyil (S.V.) -	141	15	English Channel -	Submarine - -	Chased -	Gun - -	—
†Elswick Grange	3,926	17	Mediterranean -	Submarine - -	Torpedoed -	Reached port	1
†Media - -	5,437	18	Mediterranean -	Submarine - -	Torpedoed -	Reached port	—
†Thomas Holt -	1,521	18	St. George's Chan.	Submarine - -	Torpedo -	Missed -	—
†Courtfield -	4,592	19	English Channel	Submarine - -	Torpedo -	Failed to explode.	—
†Cambrian King -	3,601	19	Mediterranean -	Submarine - -	Chased -	Attack abandoned.	—
†Saxilby - -	3,630	19	Mediterranean -	Submarine - -	Torpedoed -	Reached port	—
†Manchester Importer.	4,028	20	English Channel -	Submarine - -	Torpedoed -	Reached port	—
†Cressington Court.	4,396	21	English Channel -	Submarine - -	Torpedo -	Missed -	—
†Grebe - -	761	21	English Channel -	Submarine - -	Torpedo -	Missed -	—
†Trelawny -	3,877	22	Bristol Channel -	Submarine - -	Torpedo -	Missed -	—
†Crosshands	716	22	Bristol Channel -	Submarine - -	Gunfire -	Gun - -	—
†Arzila -	2,737	23	English Channel -	Submarine - -	Torpedo -	Missed -	—
†Olive -	1,047	23	Irish Channel -	Submarine - -	Torpedo -	Missed -	—
†Parana -	4,182	23	S.W. from Scilly Islands.	Submarine - -	2 torpedoes -	Missed -	—
†Hubert - -	3,930	24	Irish Channel -	Submarine - -	Torpedo -	Missed -	—
†Elysia -	6,397	24	Mediterranean -	Submarine - -	Torpedoed -	Reached port	13
†Anne - -	4,083	25	English Channel -	Submarine - -	Torpedoed -	Reached port	1
†Rathlin Head -	7,378	25	S.W. Ireland -	Submarine - -	Torpedoed -	Reached port	3
†Jabiru -	1,703	26	English Channel -	Submarine - -	Torpedo -	Failed to explode.	—
†Wyncote -	4,937	26	English Channel -	Submarine - -	Torpedo -	Missed -	—
†Pembroke Coast	809	27	Bristol Channel -	Submarine - -	Torpedo -	Missed -	—
†Grinkle -	322	27	North Sea - -	Submarine - -	Chased -	Gun - -	—
†Walton Hall -	4,932	27	Atlantic - -	Submarine - -	Torpedo -	Missed -	—
†War Angler -	5,210	28	S.W. Ireland -	Submarine - -	2 torpedoes -	Missed -	—
†Ewell -	1,036	28	North Sea - -	Submarine - -	Torpedo -	Missed -	—
†Antinous -	3,682	29	Mediterranean -	Submarine - -	Torpedoed -	Reached port	—
†Teviot -	3,271	29	English Channel -	Submarine - -	Torpedo -	Missed -	—
†Nirvana -	6,021	29	English Channel -	Submarine - -	Torpedo -	Missed -	—
†Elswick Hall -	3,797	29	Mediterranean -	Submarine - -	Torpedo -	Missed -	—
†War Panther -	5,260	30	English Channel -	Submarine - -	Torpedoed -	Reached port	—
†Dungeness -	2,748	30	North Sea - -	Submarine - -	Torpedoed -	Reached port	4
†Squadron -	362	30	Irish Channel -	Submarine - -	Torpedo -	Missed -	—
†Denbighshire -	3,844	30	Mediterranean -	Submarine - -	Torpedo -	Missed -	—
†Galileo -	6,287	31	English Channel -	Submarine - -	Torpedoed -	Beached -	—
Verbena (S.V.) -	41	31	English Channel	Submarine - -	Gunfire -	Rescued -	—

Name.	Gross Tons.	Date.	Position.	Attacked by	How attacked.	How saved	Lives lost.
		1918. June					
JUNE 1918.							
†Busk - -	367	1	Irish Channel -	Submarine - -	Gunfire -	Gun - -	—
†Dunaff Head -	5,877	2	Entrance to Clyde	Submarine - -	Torpedo -	Missed -	—
†Antiope - -	3,004	3	North Sea - -	Submarine - -	Torpedoed -	Reached port	—
†Roquelle - -	4,364	3	Irish Channel -	Submarine - -	2 Torpedoes	Missed -	—
†Cento - -	3,708	4	North Sea - -	Submarine - -	Torpedoed -	Reached port	3
†Strombus - -	6,163	4	Mediterranean -	Submarine - -	Torpedoed -	Reached port	2
†Kansas - -	6,074	4	Irish Channel -	Submarine - -	2 Torpedoes	Missed -	—
†Southville -	3,518	4	Mediterranean -	Submarine - -	Torpedo -	Missed -	—
†Clematis - -	3,406	5	Mediterranean -	Submarine - -	2 torpedoes -	Missed -	—
†Mantilla - . -	5,660	6	Atlantic - -	Submarine - -	Chased -	Speed -	—
Highlander -	975	8	North Sea - -	Submarine - -	Torpedo -	Missed -	—
†Eastern Coast -	1,607	9	St. George's Chan.	Submarine - -	Torpedo -	Missed -	—
†Henzada - -	5,829	9	St. George's Chan.	Submarine - -	Torpedo -	Missed -	—
†Essex - -	8,722	9	St. George's Chan.	Submarine - -	Torpedo -	Missed -	—
†Brodholme -	5,747	10	Mediterranean -	Submarine - -	Torpedoed -	Beached -	4
†Gala - -	1,015	12	North Sea - -	Submarine - -	Torpedo -	Failed to explode.	—
†Herbert Fischer	938	13	North Sea - -	Submarine - -	Torpedo -	Missed -	—
†Hans Jost -	934	13	North Sea - -	Submarine - -	Torpedo -	Missed -	—
†Keemun - -	9,074	13	Atlantic - -	Submarine - -	Gunfire -	Gun - -	—
†Rugbeian - -	4,042	13	Mediterranean -	Submarine - -	Torpedo -	Missed -	—
†Gregory - -	2,030	13	North Sea - -	Submarine - -	Torpedo -	Missed -	—
†Cairnmona -	4,666	15	North Sea - -	Submarine - -	Torpedoed -	Reached port	3
‡Sikh - -	5,150	16	Mediterranean -	Submarine - -	Torpedo -	Missed -	—
†Rossia - -	4,576	16	Mediterranean -	Submarine - -	Torpedo -	Missed -	—
‡Kandy - -	4,921	17	Mediterranean -	Submarine - -	Torpedoed -	Reached port	—
‡City of Manchester.	5,556	17	Mediterranean -	Submarine - -	Torpedo -	Missed -	—
†Sea Serpent -	2,424	20	English Channel -	Submarine - -	Torpedo -	Missed -	—
†Clan Maclaren -	2,832	20	Atlantic - -	Submarine - -	Torpedo -	Missed -	—
†Malancha - -	10,572	21	Atlantic - -	Submarine - -	Chased -	Speed -	—
†Malwa - -	10,883	21	Mediterranean -	Submarine - -	Torpedo -	Missed -	—
†Glenlee - -	4,915	25	Atlantic - -	Submarine - -	Gunfire -	Gun - -	—
†Khiva - -	9,017	25	Atlantic - -	Submarine - -	Chased -	Gun - -	—
†Raranga - -	10,040	26	English Channel	Submarine - -	Torpedoed -	Reached port	—
†Exmoor - -	4,329	28	English Channel	Submarine - -	2 Torpedoes	Missed -	—
†Noord-Holland -	1,006	28	North Sea - -	Submarine - -	Torpedo -	Missed -	—
Poltolia - -	1,831	29	English Channel -	Submarine - -	Torpedo -	Missed -	—
†Kwang-ping -	1,999	29	Mediterranean -	Submarine - -	Torpedo -	Missed -	—
†Helenus - -	7,555	30	North Sea - -	Submarine - -	Torpedo -	Missed -	—
†Clumberhall -	3,599	30	Bay of Biscay -	Submarine - -	Torpedo -	Missed -	—
†Wilton - -	4,281	30	English Channel	Submarine - -	Torpedoed -	Reached port	—
JULY 1918.		July					
†Thames - -	1,079	1	English Channel -	Submarine - -	Torpedo -	Missed -	—
†Tregarthen -	4,263	1	Mediterranean -	Submarine - -	Torpedo -	Missed -	—
†Magdala - -	4,814	1	Mediterranean -	Submarine - -	2 torpedoes -	Missed -	—
†Royal Sceptre -	3,838	2	English Channel -	Submarine - -	Torpedoed -	Reached port	—
†Copenhagen -	4,540	2	W. from Gibraltar	Submarine - -	Torpedo -	Missed -	—
†Hornby Grange	2,356	3	English Channel -	Submarine - -	Torpedo -	Missed -	—
†Hosanger - -	1,620	3	North Sea - -	Submarine - -	Torpedo -	Missed -	—
†Baron Inchcape	7,005	4	English Channel -	Submarine - -	Torpedo -	Missed -	—
†Merida - -	5,951	4	Mediterranean -	Submarine - -	Torpedoed -	Reached port	1
†Huntscraft -	5,113	6	English Channel -	Submarine - -	Torpedoed -	Reached port	6
†Nevasa - -	9,071	6	Atlantic - -	Submarine - -	Gunfire -	Gun - -	—
†Salieut - -	3,879	7	W. from Scilly I.	Submarine - -	Torpedo -	Missed -	—
†Barunga - -	7,484	7	English Channel -	Submarine - -	Torpedo -	Missed -	—
†Stockwell - -	5,643	8	North Sea - -	Submarine - -	Torpedo -	Missed -	—
†Baysarnia - -	3,458	8	W. from Gibraltar	Submarine - -	Torpedo -	Missed -	—
†Luga - -	1,988	9	North Sea - -	Submarine - -	Chased -	Gun - -	—
†Charles Theriault (S.V.).	339	10	Atlantic - -	Submarine - -	Set on fire -	Towed in -	—
Katherine Ellen (S.V.).	111	11	St. George's Chan.	Submarine - -	Gunfire -	Towed in -	—
†Rion - -	2,186	13	North Sea - -	Submarine - -	Torpedo -	Failed to explode.	—
Trebiskin (S.V.)	59	13	St. George's Chan.	Submarine - -	Gunfire -	Towed in -	—
†Imber - -	2,154	13	Mediterranean -	Submarine - -	Torpedoed -	Reached port	—
†Trevisa - -	1,813	14	Bristol Channel -	Submarine - -	2 torpedoes -	Missed -	—
†San Tirso -	6,236	14	N. Ireland - -	Submarine - -	Torpedo -	Missed -	—
Medway - -	929	15	Irish Channel -	Submarine - -	Torpedo -	Missed -	—

Name.	Gross Tons.	Date.	Position.	Attacked by	How attacked.	How saved.	Lives lost.
		1918. July					
†Niceto de Larrinaga.	5,591	15	Irish Channel -	Submarine - -	Torpedo -	Missed -	—
†Tudor Prince -	4,292	16	English Channel -	Submarine - -	Torpedo -	Missed -	—
†Patriotic -	2,254	17	Irish Channel -	Submarine - -	Torpedo -	Missed -	—
†Harlseywood -	2,701	17	Bristol Channel -	Submarine - -	Torpedoed -	Beached -	1
†War Spray -	3,100	17	Bay of Biscay -	Submarine - -	2 torpedoes -	Missed -	—
†Polperro - -	3,365	19	Mediterranean -	Submarine - -	Torpedoed -	Reached port	3
*Genesee - -	2,830	21	North Sea - -	Submarine - -	Torpedoed -	Reached port	—
†Upada - -	5,257	21	Mediterranean -	Submarine - -	Torpedoed -	Reached port	3
†Athena - -	250	21	North Sea - -	Submarine - -	Torpedo ; gunfire.	Missed ; by gun.	—
†Eurylochus -	5,723	22	Off Madeira -	Submarine - -	Chased -	Speed -	—
†City of Cork -	1,301	23	Bristol Channel -	Submarine - -	2 torpedoes -	Missed -	—
Boorara - -	6,570	23	North Sea - -	Submarine - -	Torpedoed -	Reached port	—
†Defender - -	8,520	24	S. Ireland - -	Submarine - -	Torpedoed -	Reached port	—
†Indore - -	7,300	25	N. Ireland - -	Submarine - -	Torpedoed -	Beached -	2
†British Major -	4,147	26	Atlantic - -	Submarine - -	Gunfire -	Gun - -	—
†Melita - -	13,967	26	Atlantic - -	Submarine - -	Gunfire -	Gun - -	—
†City of Bombay	5,186	26	Atlantic - -	Submarine - -	Gunfire -	Gun - -	—
†Baron Napier -	4,943	26	Atlantic - -	Submarine - -	Gunfire -	Gun - -	—
†Lombok - -	5,934	26	English Channel	Submarine - -	Torpedo -	Missed -	—
†Zamora - -	3,639	26	Atlantic - -	Submarine - -	Gunfire -	Gun - -	—
†Olive - -	1,047	27	Irish Channel -	Submarine - -	Torpedo -	Missed -	—
†Lady Gwendolen	2,163	29	North Sea - -	Submarine - -	Torpedo -	Missed -	—
†Savan - -	4,264	29	North Sea - -	Submarine - -	Torpedo -	Missed -	—
†Mary Annie (S.V.).	196	29	North Sea - -	Submarine - -	Gunfire -	Slightly damaged.	—
Englishman (Tug).	62	29	North Sea - -	Submarine - -	Gunfire -	Speed -	—
†Plover - -	187	29	North Ireland -	Submarine - -	Gunfire -	Gun - -	—
†Bayronto - -	6,045	30	English Channel	Submarine - -	Torpedoed -	Reached port	2
†War Deer - -	5,323	30	North Sea - -	Submarine - -	Torpedoed -	Reached port	—
†Wallsend - -	2,697	31	North Sea - -	Submarine - -	Torpedo -	Missed -	—
†Freshfield -	3,445	31	Mediterranean -	Submarine - -	2 torpedoes -	Missed -	—

AUGUST 1918.

Name.	Gross Tons.	Date.	Position.	Attacked by	How attacked.	How saved.	Lives lost.
		Aug.					
†Crenella - -	7,082	1	S.W. of Ireland -	Submarine - -	Torpedo -	Missed -	—
†Neto - -	1,696	1	Bristol Channel -	Submarine - -	Torpedo -	Missed -	—
†Kirkwood - -	1,674	1	Bristol Channel -	Submarine - -	Torpedo -	Missed -	—
†War Rambler -	5,495	2	Bristol Channel -	Submarine - -	2 torpedoes -	Missed -	—
†Spermina - -	3,355	2	Mediterranean -	Submarine - -	Torpedo -	Missed -	—
†Wyvisbrook -	3,158	2	North Sea - -	Submarine - -	Torpedo -	Missed -	—
†Everilda - -	3,080	3	Bay of Biscay -	Submarine - -	Torpedo -	Missed -	—
†Mendocino - -	6,973	3	Atlantic - -	Submarine - -	Chased -	Gun - -	—
†Waipara - -	6,994	4	English Channel -	Submarine - -	Torpedoed -	Reached port	1
†Thrift - -	506	4	North Sea - -	Submarine - -	Torpedo -	Missed -	—
†Dallington -	2,542	5	English Channel -	Submarine - -	Torpedo -	Missed -	—
†Fernley - -	3,820	5	Atlantic - -	Submarine - -	Torpedo -	Missed -	—
†Polescar - -	5,832	5	English Channel -	Submarine - -	Torpedoed -	Reached port	—
*Tuscan Prince -	5,275	5	English Channel -	Submarine - -	Torpedoed -	Reached port	2
†Rhodesian Transport.	4,986	5	Atlantic - -	Submarine - -	Chased -	Gun - -	—
Gladys M. Hoilett (S.V.).	203	5	W. Atlantic -	Submarine - -	Bombs -	Towed in -	—
†Bencleuch -	4,159	6	Off Cape Hatteras	Submarine - -			—
†Tasmanian Transport.	4,491	7	English Channel -	Submarine - -	Torpedo -	Missed -	—
†Clan Macvey -	5,815	7	English Channel	Submarine - -	Torpedo -	Missed -	—
†Portwood - -	2,241	8	English Channel	Submarine - -	Torpedoed -	Reached port	3
†Anselma de Larrinaga.	4,090	9	English Channel	Submarine - -	Torpedoed -	Reached port	—
†Kent - -	8,678	12	North Sea - -	Submarine - -	Torpedo -	Missed -	—
†Wad Lukkus -	206	12	English Channel	Submarine - -	Torpedo -	Missed -	—
†Scottish Prince	2,897	12	Mediterranean -	Submarine - -	Torpedo -	Missed -	—
†Exmouth - -	3,923	12	Mediterranean -	Submarine - -	Torpedo -	Missed -	—
†Yarrow - -	908	12	Irish Sea - -	Submarine - -	Torpedo -	Missed -	—
†Desna - -	11,483	14	W. from Ushant -	Submarine - -	2 torpedoes -	Missed -	—
†Slieve Gallion -	1,071	15	Irish Channel -	Submarine - -	Torpedo -	Missed -	—
†Snowdon - -	1,021	15	Irish Channel -	Submarine - -	Torpedo -	Missed -	—
†Islandia - -	2,069	16	Bristol Channel -	Submarine - -	Torpedo -	Missed -	—
†Lackawanna -	4,125	16	East from New York.	Submarine - -	2 torpedoes ; gunfire.	Missed ; gun	—
†Australpeak -	4,432	16	Irish Sea - -	Submarine - -	Torpedo -	Missed -	—

Name.	Gross Tons.	Date.	Position.	Attacked by	How attacked.	How saved.	Lives lost.
		1918. Aug.					
†Fylde (tug, towing 4 S.V.)	256	16	St. George's Chan.	Submarine	Gunfire	Gun	—
†Liddesdale	4,403	18	Mediterranean	Submarine	Torpedo	Failed to explode.	—
†Charity	1,735	19	Bristol Channel	Submarine	Torpedoed	Reached port	—
Umvolosi	2,980	19	Indian Ocean	Mine	Mine	Reached port	—
†Indian	9,121	21	West of Ireland	Submarine	Torpedo	Missed	—
†Thespis	4,343	21	E. from New York	Submarine	Torpedo	Missed	—
†Greenore	1,488	22	Irish Channel	Submarine	2 Torpedoes	Missed	—
†Sheerness	1,274	22	Irish Channel	Submarine	Torpedo	Missed	—
†Helenus	7,555	22	Atlantic	Submarine	Gunfire	Speed	—
†Brandenburg	1,578	24	North Sea	Submarine	Torpedo	Missed	—
†Delphinula	5,238	24	Mediterranean	Submarine	Torpedoed	Reached port	—
Bianca (Aux.)	408	24	W. Atlantic	Submarine	Gunfire; bombs.	Towed in	—
†Vane Tempest	687	25	North Sea	Submarine	Torpedo	Missed	—
†Highlander	975	25	North Sea	Submarine	Torpedo	Missed	—
†Grace	354	25	North Sea	Submarine	Torpedo	Missed	—
†Pelican	638	26	S.W. Ireland	Submarine	Gunfire	Gun	—
†Archimedes	5,364	27	English Channel	Submarine	Torpedo	Missed	—
†Lompoc	7,270	28	North Sea	Submarine	Torpedoed	Reached port	1
†Henzada	5,820	29	Mediterranean	Submarine	Torpedo	Missed	—
†Andree	3,689	29	St. George's Chan.	Submarine	Torpedo	Missed	—
†Tambov	4,361	31	Atlantic	Submarine			—
†Baron Polwarth	4,913	31	Atlantic	Submarine	Torpedo	Missed	—
†Largo Law	4,005	31	Atlantic	Submarine	Torpedo	Missed	—

SEPTEMBER 1918.

Name.	Gross Tons.	Date.	Position.	Attacked by	How attacked.	How saved.	Lives lost.
		Sept.					
†Actor	6,082	1	Irish Channel	Submarine	Torpedoed	Reached port	—
†Rose	1,098	1	Mediterranean	Submarine	Chased	Speed	—
†British Star	6,976	1	W. Atlantic	Submarine	Chased	Speed	—
†Baron Minto	4,537	1	Mediterranean	Submarine	Torpedoed	Reached port	—
†Ariadne Christine	3,550	2	Arctic Ocean	Mine	Mine	Towed in	—
†Alcinous	6,743	2	W. Atlantic	Submarine	Gunfire	Gun	—
†Huntsend	8,826	3	N.W. Ireland	Submarine	Torpedo	Missed	—
†Bechuana	4,148	4	Atlantic	Submarine	2 torpedoes	Missed	—
†Islandia	2,069	4	English Channel	Submarine	Torpedo	Missed	—
†War Ranee	5,500	5	Atlantic	Submarine	Torpedo	Missed	—
†Persic	12,042	7	N.W. Scilly Isles	Submarine	Torpedoed	Reached port	—
†Monmouth	4,078	7	W. Atlantic	Submarine	Gunfire	Gun	—
†P.L.A. 17	1,126	8	North Sea	Submarine	Torpedo	Missed	—
†Juliston	2,459	9	Mediterranean	Submarine	Torpedo	Missed	—
†Policastra	4,594	9	Mediterranean	Submarine	Torpedoed	Reached port	—
†Pearleaf	5,911	11	North Sea	Submarine	Torpedo	Missed	—
†Chao Chow Fu	1,909	12	Mediterranean	Submarine	Torpedoed	Reached port	—
†Newby Hall	4,391	13	W. Atlantic	Submarine	Torpedo: Gunfire.	Missed; gun.	—
†Bondicar	1,441	15	Bristol Channel	Submarine	Torpedo	Missed	—
†Huntscliffe	5,442	15	W. Atlantic	Submarine	Chased	Gun	—
†Dipton	3,811	16	Atlantic	Submarine	2 torpedoes	Missed	—
†Holmpark	1,468	18	Bristol Channel	Submarine	Torpedo	Missed	—
†Cognac	814	19	Bristol Channel	Submarine	Torpedo	Missed	—
†Lackawanna	4,125	20	Irish Channel	Submarine	Torpedo	Missed	—
†Orient	739	20	North Sea	Submarine	Torpedo	Failed to explode.	—
†Lancastrian	5,134	20	English Channel	Submarine	Torpedo	Missed	—
†Henry Furst	1,500	20	North Sea	Submarine	Torpedo	Missed	—
†Minia	2,061	21	Atlantic	Submarine	Torpedo	Missed	—
†Islandia	2,069	21	Irish Channel	Submarine	Torpedo	Missed	—
†Anchises	10,046	23	Atlantic	Submarine	Gunfire	Gun	—
†Alban	5,223	24	Atlantic	Submarine	Gunfire	Gun	—
†Roselands	4,383	25	Bristol Channel	Submarine	Chased	Gun	—
†Malwa	10,883	26	Mediterranean	Submarine	Torpedo	Failed to explode.	—
†Algores	342	28	Irish Channel	Submarine	Torpedo	Missed	—
†Reginolite	2,631	29	W. Atlantic	Submarine	Gunfire	Gun	—

OCTOBER 1918.

Name.	Gross Tons.	Date.	Position.	Attacked by	How attacked.	How saved.	Lives lost.
		Oct.					
†Karmala	8,983	1	N.W. Ireland	Submarine	Torpedo	Missed	—
†Magdala	4,814	2	Atlantic	Submarine	Chased	Gun	—

Name.	Gross Tons.	Date.	Position.	Attacked by	How attacked.	How saved.	Lives lost.
		1918. Oct.					
†A. E. McKinstry	1,964	2	English Channel	Submarine - -	Torpedo -	Missed -	—
†Nevasa - -	9,071	2	W. Atlantic -	Submarine - -	Gunfire -	Speed -	—
†Chindwara -	5,192	2	Atlantic - -	Submarine - -	Torpedo ; gunfire.	Missed ; gun	—
†Nizam - -	5,322	2	Atlantic - -	Submarine - -	Chased -	Speed -	—
†Benrinnes -	4,798	2	Atlantic - -	Submarine - -	2 torpedoes -	Missed -	—
†Kingfield - -	3,028	8	Mediterranean -	Submarine - -	Torpedo -	Missed -	—
†Waimarino -	4,204	9	Mediterranean -	Submarine - -	Torpedo -	Missed -	—
†Sheerness -	1,274	10	Irish Channel -	Submarine - -	Torpedo -	Missed -	—
†War Crag - -	3,120	12	Mediterranean -	Submarine - -	Torpedo -	Missed -	—
†Darro - -	11,484	13	Irish Channel -	Submarine - -	Torpedo -	Missed -	—
†Chimu - -	4,259	14	Mediterranean -	Submarine - -	2 torpedoes -	Missed -	—
†Messina - -	4,271	15	Atlantic - -	Submarine - -	Gunfire -	Gun - -	—
†Harperley -	3,990	17	Atlantic - -	Submarine - -	Torpedo -	Missed -	—
†Briarleaf - -	5,822	17	Atlantic - -	Submarine - -	Torpedo ; gunfire.	Exploded prematurely ; gun.	—
†Duke of Cumberland.	2,036	22	Irish Channel -	Submarine - -	Torpedo -	Missed -	—
†Duke of Connaught.	1,564	22	Irish Channel -	Submarine - -	Chased -	Speed -	—

NOVEMBER 1918.

Name.	Gross Tons.	Date.	Position.	Attacked by	How attacked.	How saved.	Lives lost.
†War Roach -	5,215	2	Port Said swept channel.	Submarine - -	Torpedo -	Reached port	—
†Sarpedon - -	4,393	7	Mediterranean -	Submarine - -	Torpedo -	Missed -	—

162

TABLE "A."

Showing Number and Gross Tonnage of BRITISH MERCHANT VESSELS Lost through Enemy Action during each Month since the Outbreak of War; and Number of Lives Lost.

Month.	By Cruisers, T.B.'s, &c.			By Submarines.			By Mines.			By Aircraft.			Total.		
	No.	Gross Tonnage.	Lives lost.	No.	Gross Tonnage.	Lives lost.	No.	Gross Tonnage.	Lives lost.	No.	Gross Tonnage.	Lives lost.	No.	Gross Tonnage.	Lives lost.
1914.															
August -	8	33,796	–	–	–	–	1	6,458	–	–	–	–	9	40,254	–
September	19	84,403	–	–	–	–	2	3,816	29	–	–	–	21	88,219	29
October -	14	65,161	–	1	866	–	4	11,778	24	–	–	–	19	77,805	24
November	2	3,784	–	2	2,084	–	1	3,020	–	–	–	–	5	8,888	–
December	5	15,995	–	–	–	–	5	10,040	16	–	–	–	10	26,035	16
1915.															
January -	3	12,304	–	7	17,126	21	1	2,624	–	–	–	–	11	32,054	21
February	4	10,350	–	8	21,787	9	2	4,235	21	–	–	–	14	36,372	30
March -	2	7,031	–	21	64,448	161	–	–	–	–	–	–	23	71,479	161
April -	–	–	–	11	22,453	38	–	–	–	–	–	–	11	22,453	38
May -	–	–	–	19	84,025	1,208	–	–	–	–	–	–	19	84,025	1,208
June -	–	–	–	29	76,497	78	2	6,701	3	–	–	–	31	83,198	81
July -	–	–	–	19	48,844	26	1	4,003	2	–	–	–	20	52,847	28
August -	–	–	–	42	135,153	205	7	13,311	43	–	–	–	49	148,464	248
September	–	–	–	22	89,693	44	8	11,997	33	–	–	–	30	101,690	77
October -	–	–	–	10	39,061	35	7	15,095	7	–	–	–	17	54,156	42
November	–	–	–	23	84,816	25	9	9,677	93	–	–	–	32	94,493	118
December	–	–	–	16	65,011	416	5	9,479	3	–	–	–	21	74,490	419
1916.															
January -	8	27,888	17	5	27,974	28	3	6,426	19	–	–	–	16	62,288	64
February	4	14,735	1	7	24,059	34	14	36,096	243	1	970	13	26	75,860	291
March -	–	–	–	19	83,492	44	7	15,597	29	–	–	–	26	99,089	73
April -	–	–	–	37	126,540	119	6	14,653	12	–	–	–	43	141,193	131
May -	–	–	–	12	42,165	6	8	22,356	8	–	–	–	20	64,521	14
June -	1	1,380	1	11	33,849	34	4	1,747	29	–	–	–	16	36,976	64
July -	2	4,710	–	21	69,962	58	5	7,760	11	–	–	–	28	82,432	69
August -	–	–	–	22	42,553	4	1	801	4	–	–	–	23	43,354	8
September	1	964	–	34	84,596	16	7	19,012	4	–	–	–	42	104,572	20
October -	1	1,676	–	41	146,891	182	7	27,681	15	–	–	–	49	176,248	197
November	–	–	–	42	96,672	55	7	72,137	45	–	–	–	49	168,809	100
December	10	51,999	4	36	109,936	91	12	20,357	91	–	–	–	58	182,292	186
1917.															
January -	6	19,304	–	35	109,954	245	8	24,408	31	–	–	–	49	153,666	276
February -	7	28,679	–	86	256,394	355	12	28,413	47	–	–	–	105	313,486	402
March -	11	42,893	18	103	283,647	630	13	26,938	51	–	–	–	127	353,478	699
April -	–	–	–	155	516,394	997	14	28,888	128	–	–	–	169	545,282	1,125
May -	1	819	11	106	320,572	507	14	28,114	73	1	2,784	–	122	352,289	591
June -	1	3,947	–	116	391,004	384	4	19,256	29	1	3,718	3	122	417,925	416
July -	–	–	–	88	319,931	401	11	44,927	67	–	–	–	99	364,858	468
August -	1	1,608	–	84	310,551	415	6	17,651	47	–	–	–	91	329,810	462
September -	–	–	–	68	173,437	293	9	22,335	60	1	440	3	78	196,212	356
October -	1	1,159	–	79	261,649	578	6	13,324	30	–	–	–	86	276,132	608
November -	–	–	–	56	154,806	376	8	18,754	44	–	–	–	64	173,560	420
December	1	2,284	–	76	227,195	520	8	23,608	65	–	–	–	85	253,087	585
1918.															
January -	–	–	–	57	179,973	291	–	–	–	–	–	–	57	179,973	291
February	–	–	–	68	224,501	697	1	2,395	–	–	–	–	69	226,896	697
March -	–	–	–	79	194,839	490	3	4,619	20	–	–	–	82	199,458	510
April -	3	4,211	–	67	209,469	488	2	1,863	1	–	–	–	72	215,543	489
May -	–	–	–	59	188,729	407	1	3,707	–	–	–	–	60	192,436	407
June -	–	–	–	49	158,660	453	2	4,330	16	–	–	–	51	162,990	469
July -	–	–	–	37	165,449	202	–	–	–	–	–	–	37	165,449	202
August -	–	–	–	41	145,721	217	–	–	–	–	–	–	41	145,721	217
September	–	–	–	48	136,859	521	–	–	–	–	–	–	48	136,859	521
October -	1	1,622	–	23	54,577	318	1	3,030	–	–	–	–	25	59,229	318
To November 11	–	–	–	2	10,195	1	–	–	–	–	–	–	2	10,195	1
TOTAL to 11th November 1918 -	117	442,702	52	2099	6,635,059	12723	259	673,417	1493	4	7,912	19	2479	7,759,090	14287

TABLE "B."

Showing Number and Gross Tonnage of BRITISH FISHING VESSELS Lost through Enemy Action during each Month since the Outbreak of War; and Number of Lives Lost.

Month.	By Cruisers, T.B.'s, &c.			By Submarines.			By Mines.			Total.		
	No.	Gross Tonnage.	Lives lost.	No.	Gross Tonnage.	Lives lost.	No.	Gross Tonnage.	Lives lost.	No.	Gross Tonnage.	Lives lost.
1914.												
August	25	4,368	–	–	–	–	1	70	5	26	4,438	5
September	–	–	–	–	–	–	6	1,032	25	6	1,032	25
October	–	–	–	–	–	–	2	283	5	2	283	5
November	–	–	–	–	–	–	6	460	42	6	460	42
December	3	294	–	–	–	–	2	486	18	5	780	18
1915.												
January	–	–	–	–	–	–	2	222	–	2	222	–
February	–	–	–	–	–	–	–	–	–	–	–	–
March	–	–	–	–	–	–	1	289	1	1	289	1
April	–	–	–	10	1,760	20	1	170	2	11	1,930	22
May	4	689	–	22	3,982	4	6	977	28	32	5,648	32
June	–	–	–	58	7,749	17	2	368	9	60	8,117	26
July	–	–	–	36	3,966	–	3	461	26	39	4,427	26
August	–	–	–	36	2,454	–	2	436	9	38	2,890	9
September	–	–	–	6	292	–	2	153	12	8	445	12
October	–	–	–	–	–	–	–	–	–	–	–	–
November	–	–	–	–	–	–	1	162	2	1	162	2
December	–	–	–	–	–	–	–	–	–	–	–	–
1916.												
January	–	–	–	7	357	–	–	–	–	7	357	–
February	–	–	–	2	68	–	–	–	–	2	68	–
March	–	–	–	6	304	–	1	303	9	7	607	9
April	1	173	–	2	43	–	–	–	–	3	216	–
May	–	–	–	5	201	1	–	–	–	5	201	1
June	–	–	–	–	–	–	–	–	–	–	–	–
July	–	–	–	36	2,796	2	–	–	–	36	2,796	2
August	–	–	–	12	1,474	–	1	198	9	13	1,672	9
September	–	–	–	38	4,811	–	–	–	–	38	4,811	–
October	–	–	–	9	1,138	–	–	–	–	9	1,138	–
November	–	–	–	14	1,474	–	1	126	8	15	1,600	8
December	–	–	–	3	224	–	3	212	9	6	436	9
1917.												
January	–	–	–	16	2,020	2	–	–	–	16	2,020	2
February	–	–	–	28	3,152	4	2	326	19	30	3,478	23
March	–	–	–	43	3,586	3	–	–	–	43	3,586	3
April	–	–	–	41	5,920	14	–	–	–	41	5,920	14
May	–	–	–	17	1,054	–	2	394	18	19	1,448	18
June	–	–	–	20	1,296	–	1	46	–	21	1,342	–
July	–	–	–	17	2,679	1	1	57	5	18	2,736	6
August	–	–	–	4	230	1	1	12	5	5	242	6
September	–	–	–	6	233	–	1	12	5	7	245	5
October	–	–	–	3	116	4	2	111	15	5	227	19
November	–	–	–	3	87	–	–	–	–	3	87	–
December	1	113	4	2	79	–	2	221	13	5	413	17
1918.												
January	–	–	–	10	375	1	–	–	–	10	375	1
February	–	–	–	9	306	3	3	380	17	12	686	20
March	–	–	–	9	209	–	1	84	10	10	293	10
April	–	–	–	3	241	–	–	–	–	3	241	–
May	–	–	–	16	504	7	–	–	–	16	504	7
June	–	–	–	4	312	11	2	327	6	6	639	17
July	–	–	–	12	555	3	–	–	–	12	555	3
August	–	–	–	13	1,536	–	–	–	–	13	1,536	–
September	–	–	–	–	–	–	1	142	–	1	142	–
October	–	–	–	–	–	–	–	–	–	–	–	–
To November 11	–	–	–	–	–	–	1	25	–	1	25	–
TOTAL to 11th November 1918 -	34	5,637	4	578	57,583	98	63	8,545	332	675	71,765	434

TABLE " C."

Showing Number and Gross Tonnage of BRITISH MERCHANT VESSELS DAMAGED or MOLESTED (but not Sunk) by the Enemy during each Month since the Outbreak of War; and Number of Lives Lost.

Month.	By Cruisers. No.	Gross Tonnage	Lives lost.	By Submarines. No.	Gross Tonnage.	Lives lost.	By Mines. No.	Gross Tonnage.	Lives lost.	By Aircraft. No.	Gross Tonnage.	Lives lost.	Total. No.	Gross Tonnage.	Lives lost.
1914.															
August	8	44,731	–	–	–	–	2	6,575	–	–	–	–	10	51,306	–
September	5	26,932	1	–	–	–	–	–	–	–	–	–	5	26,932	1
October	7	30,193	–	–	–	–	–	–	–	–	–	–	7	30,193	–
November	1	5,732	–	–	–	–	–	–	–	–	–	–	1	5,732	–
December	2	6,024	2	1	1,209	–	1	4,592	–	–	–	–	4	11,825	2
1915.															
January	–	–	–	1	1,871	–	1	1,742	–	–	–	–	2	3,613	–
February	1	4,583	–	10	37,043	–	3	9,849	13	–	–	–	14	51,475	13
March	–	–	–	29	93,250	1	1	3,868	1	8	10,915	–	38	108,033	2
April	1	6,849	8	7	31,479	2	–	–	–	2	3,542	–	10	41,870	10
May	–	–	–	19	117,591	–	–	–	–	–	–	–	19	117,591	–
June	–	–	–	18	77,273	–	2	10,706	–	–	–	–	20	87,979	–
July	–	–	–	16	77,492	31	2	10,406	–	1	988	–	19	88,886	31
August	–	–	–	19	55,639	–	2	11,620	–	–	–	–	21	67,259	–
September	–	–	–	5	35,056	–	2	9,617	2	1	1,270	–	8	45,943	2
October	–	–	–	4	58,450	–	3	6,564	–	1	1,408	–	8	66,422	–
November	–	–	–	11	64,460	–	1	2,286	–	2	2,657	–	14	69,403	–
December	–	–	–	8	70,295	–	1	4,844	–	1	2,414	–	10	77,553	–
1916.															
January	1	7,781	–	10	50,997	–	3	8,279	–	2	3,372	–	16	70,429	–
February	1	11,484	–	7	114,010	–	3	10,876	–	1	1,680	–	12	138,050	–
March	–	–	–	13	50,657	–	1	3,381	–	–	–	–	14	54,038	–
April	1	2,195	–	12	58,543	–	–	–	–	–	–	–	13	60,738	–
May	–	–	–	10	38,156	–	–	–	–	5	17,016	2	15	55,172	2
June	–	–	–	11	50,635	–	1	3,232	–	–	–	–	12	53,867	–
July	–	–	–	6	22,528	–	–	–	–	1	1,081	–	7	23,609	–
August	–	–	–	13	34,825	–	1	4,854	–	1	7,988	–	15	47,667	–
September	–	–	–	29	122,933	–	–	–	–	–	–	–	29	122,933	–
October	–	–	–	32	125,770	1	1	8,253	–	–	–	–	33	134,023	1
November	–	–	–	36	157,633	–	4	24,258	4	–	–	–	40	181,891	4
December	–	–	–	41	168,838	–	5	34,502	1	–	–	–	46	203,340	1
1917.															
January	–	–	–	29	140,722	1	1	5,686	–	–	–	–	30	146,408	1
February	–	–	–	74	313,971	15	4	48,516	–	1	3,563	–	79	366,050	15
March	–	–	–	77	329,192	64	3	15,459	–	2	2,292	–	82	346,943	64
April	1	3,562	–	92	426,680	21	6	47,587	3	1	1,780	–	100	479,609	24
May	–	–	–	97	388,258	3	1	1,968	–	1	2,821	–	99	393,047	3
June	–	–	–	122	549,907	18	5	29,278	–	1	1,243	–	128	580,428	18
July	–	–	–	76	383,793	6	2	5,150	–	6	8,337	–	84	397,280	6
August	–	–	–	54	252,504	10	3	15,641	–	–	–	–	57	268,145	10
September	–	–	–	61	213,199	37	3	9,491	3	2	9,966	2	66	232,656	42
October	–	–	–	43	162,755	24	2	9,754	–	–	–	–	45	172,509	24
November	–	–	–	50	191,601	27	2	9,552	–	–	–	–	52	201,153	27
December	–	–	–	60	223,533	56	3	12,900	–	1	353	–	64	236,786	56
1918.															
January	1	401	1	49	188,550	23	2	8,882	–	–	–	–	52	197,833	24
February	–	–	–	53	186,283	12	1	3,752	–	2	2,686	–	56	192,721	12
March	–	–	–	81	322,239	63	3	18,047	32	1	1,855	–	85	342,141	95
April	–	–	–	65	277,984	6	–	–	–	–	–	–	65	277,984	6
May	–	–	–	74	237,420	54	1	3,949	5	–	–	–	75	241,369	59
June	–	–	–	40	183,206	12	–	–	–	–	–	–	40	183,206	12
July	–	–	–	54	208,228	18	–	–	–	–	–	–	54	208,228	18
August	–	–	–	54	199,764	7	1	2,980	–	–	–	–	55	202,744	7
September	–	–	–	34	144,601	–	1	3,550	–	–	–	–	35	148,151	–
October	–	–	–	18	85,196	–	–	–	–	–	–	–	18	85,196	–
To November 11	–	–	–	2	9,608	–	–	–	–	–	–	–	2	9,608	–
TOTAL to 11th November 1918 -	30	150467	12	1,727	7,335,827	512	84	432,446	64	44	89,227	4	1,885	8,007,967	592

INDEX.

184

Section III
SHIPS OF THE ROYAL NAVY: STATEMENT OF LOSSES DURING THE SECOND WORLD WAR

SHIPS OF THE ROYAL NAVY
STATEMENT OF LOSSES
DURING THE
SECOND WORLD WAR

3rd September, 1939 to 2nd September, 1945

CONTENTS

PART I

WARSHIPS AND AUXILIARY VESSELS

List of Losses
Arranged according to Year and Class

(This return excludes Ships of the Dominion and Royal Indian Navies)

NOTES

(i) (R) Signifies that the vessel was requisitioned for Naval Service.

(ii) Tonnage is Standard displacement unless otherwise stated.

(iii) Gross Registered Tonnage is shown in italics.

(iv) The list excludes Steam and Motor boats and small requisitioned and acquired Craft when the known tonnage is below 10 tons.

LIST OF ABBREVIATIONS

A/C	Aircraft.
A/S	Anti-Submarine
D/C	Depth Charge.
(E)	Estimated.
E/B	E-Boat
E.M.B.	Explosive Motor Boat.
S.C.	Surface Craft.
S/M	Submarine.
T/B	Torpedo Boat.
U/B	U-Boat.

Class	Name	Tonnage	Date of Completion	Date of Loss	How Lost and Where
				1939	
BATTLESHIP ...	ROYAL OAK	29,150	1. 5.16	14 Oct.	Sunk by U/B, torpedo in Scapa Flow, Orkneys.
AIRCRAFT CARRIER (ex CRUISER).	COURAGEOUS	22,500	1.17 As A/C Carrier 5. 5.28	17 Sept.	Sunk by U/B, torpedo, West of Ireland.
DESTROYERS ...	BLANCHE	1,360	14. 2.31	13 Nov.	Sunk by mine, Thames Estuary.
	GIPSY	1,335	22. 2.36	21 Nov.	Sunk by mine off Harwich.
	DUCHESS...	1,375	27. 1.33	12 Dec.	Sunk in collision, W. Scotland.
SUBMARINE ...	OXLEY	1,354	22. 7.27	10 Sept.	Sunk by accident off Norway.
ARMED MERCHANT CRUISER.	RAWALPINDI (R) ...	16,697	1925 As AMC 10.39	23 Nov.	Sunk by SCHARNHORST S.E. of Iceland.
MOTOR TORPEDO BOAT.	No. 6	18	17.11.36	16 Nov.	Foundered in bad weather off Sardinia.
TRAWLERS ...	NORTHERN ROVER (R) ...	655	1936	31 Oct.– 5 Nov.	Overdue at Kirkwall, Orkneys.
	MASTIFF	520	16. 5.38	20 Nov.	Sunk by mine, Thames Estuary.
	ARAGONITE (R)	315	1934	22 Nov.	Mined off Deal.
	WASHINGTON (R) ...	209	1909	6 Dec.	Sunk by mine en route for Yarmouth.
	WILLIAM HALLETT (R)...	202	1919	13 Dec.	Mined, Tyne area.
	JAMES LUDFORD ...	506	30. 4.19	14 Dec.	Sunk by mine off Tyne.
	EVELINA (R)	202	1919 }	16 Dec.	Sunk, probably by mine, Tyne area.
	SEDGEFLY (R)	520	1939 }		
	DROMIO (R)	380	1929	22 Dec.	Sunk in collision, North of Whitby.
	BARBARA ROBERTSON (R)	325	1919	23 Dec.	Sunk by U/B, gunfire, North of Hebrides, W. Scotland.
	LOCH DOON (R) ...	534	1937	25 Dec.	Sunk, probably by mine, off Blyth.
BOOM DEFENCE VESSEL.	BAYONET	605	16. 3.39	21 Dec.	Sunk by mine, Firth of Forth.
TUG	NAPIA (R)	155	1914	20 Dec.	Sunk as result of explosion, probably caused by mine, off Ramsgate.

Class	Name	Tonnage	Date of Completion	Date of Loss	How Lost and Where
				1939	
DRIFTERS ...	RAY OF HOPE (R) ...	*98*	1925	10 Dec.	Mined, Thames Estuary.
	GLEN ALBYN (R) ...	*82*	1909 ⎫	23 Dec.	Mined, Loch Ewe, W. Scotland.
	PROMOTIVE (R)	*78*	1908 ⎭		
OILER	BIRCHOL	*1,115*(E)	12. 9.17	29 Nov.	Wrecked, Hebrides.
AMMUNITION	LUCY BORCHARDT ...	*1,850*	1905	14 Sept. ⎫	
HULKS	CARLO	*1,737*	1911	15 Sept.	
	MOURINO	*2,165*	1906	15 Sept. ⎬	Cause and place unknown.
	STANLARD	*1,737*	1912	15 Sept.	
	DUNMORE HEAD ...	*1,682*	1898	29 Sept. ⎭	
				1940	
AIRCRAFT CARRIER (ex CRUISER).	GLORIOUS	22,500	1.17 As A/C Carrier 10. 3.30	8 June	Sunk by gunfire, SCHARNHORST and GNEISENAU, lat. of Narvik, Norway.
CRUISERS ...	EFFINGHAM	9,550	9. 7.25	18 May	Struck submerged rock, wrecked Vestfiold, Norway.
	CALYPSO	4,180	8. 6.17	12 June	Sunk by U/B, torpedo, South of Crete.
DESTROYERS ...	GRENVILLE (Leader) ...	1,485	1. 7.36	19 Jan.	Sunk by mine, North Sea.
	EXMOUTH (Leader) ...	1,475	9.11.34	21 Jan.	Sunk, probably U/B, torpedo, Moray Firth.
	DARING	1,375	25.11.32	18 Feb.	Sunk by U/B, torpedo, off Duncansby Head, N. Scotland.
	GLOWWORM	1,345	22. 1.36	8 Apr.	Sunk by ADMIRAL HIPPER, gunfire, off Norway.
	GURKHA	1,870	21.10.38	9 Apr.	Sunk by A/C, bombs, off Stavanger, Norway.
	HUNTER	1,340	30. 9.46	10 Apr.	Sunk by S.C., gunfire, in battle of Narvik.
	HARDY (Leader) ...	1,505	11.12.36	10 Apr.	Driven ashore, gunfire, Narvik.
	AFRIDI (Leader) ...	1,870	29. 4.38	3 May	Sunk by A/C, bombs, off Norway.
	VALENTINE (Leader) ...	1,090	27. 6.17	15 May	Bombed, grounded and abandoned in River Schelde.
	WHITLEY	1,100	14.10.18	19 May	Damaged by bombs, beached, between Nieuport & Ostend.
	WESSEX	1,100	11. 5.18	24 May	Sunk by A/C, bombs, off Calais.
	GRAFTON	1,335	20. 3.36	29 May	Sunk by E/B, torpedo, off Dunkirk.
	GRENADE	1,335	28. 3.36	29 May	Sunk by A/C, bombs, in Dunkirk Harbour.
	WAKEFUL	1,100	20.11.17	29 May	Sunk by E/B, torpedo, off Dunkirk.
	BASILISK	1,360	4. 3.31 ⎫	June	Sunk by A/C, bombs, off Dunkirk.
	HAVANT	1,400	19.12.39 ⎬		
	KEITH (Leader) ...	1,400	20. 3.31 ⎭		
	ACASTA	1,350	11. 2.30 ⎫	June	Sunk by SCHARNHORST and GNEISENAU, gunfire, when returning from Norway.
	ARDENT	1,350	14. 4.30 ⎭		
	KHARTOUM	1,710	6.11.39	23 June	Beached after damage by internal explosion caused by burst torpedo air vessel off Perim Harbour.
	WHIRLWIND	1,100	28. 3.18	5 July	Sunk by U/B, torpedo, S.W. of Ireland.
	ESCORT	1,375	30.10.34	11 July	Sunk by U/B, torpedo, W. Mediterranean.
	IMOGEN	1,370	2. 6,37	16 July	Damaged in collision, caught fire and abandoned off Duncansby Head, N. Scotland.
	BRAZEN	1,360	8. 4.31	20 July	Sunk by A/C off Dover.
	CODRINGTON (Leader) ...	1,540	4. 6.30	27 July	Bombed and sunk in Dover Harbour.
	WREN	1,120	27. 1.23	27 July	Bombed and sunk off Aldeburgh, Suffolk.
	DELIGHT	1,375	31. 1.33	29 July	Bombed and sunk off Portland.
	HOSTILE	1,340	10. 9.36	23 Aug.	Mined and sunk off Cape Bon, Mediterranean.
	ESK	1,375	28. 9.34 ⎫	1 Sept.	Sunk by mine, North Sea.
	IVANHOE	1,370	24. 8.37 ⎭		
	VENETIA	1,090	27.12.17	19 Oct.	Sunk by mine, Thames Estuary.
	STURDY	905	15.10.19	30 Oct.	Wrecked, Tiree Is. W. Scotland.
	ACHERON	1,350	13.10.31	17 Dec.	Sunk by mine off Isle of Wight.
	HYPERION	1,340	3.12.36	22 Dec.	Sunk by mine off Pantellaria, Mediterranean.

Class	Name	Tonnage	Date of Completion	Date of Loss	How Lost and Where
SUBMARINES	SEAHORSE	640	2.10.33	1940 10 Jan.	Lost in Heligoland Bight.
	UNDINE	540	21. 8.38	15 Jan.	Lost in Heligoland Bight D/C., S.C. Formally paid off.
	STARFISH	640	27.10.33	20 Jan.	Lost in Heligoland Bight D/C., S.C. Formally paid off.
	THISTLE	1,090	4. 7.39	14 Apr.	Lost off Skudesnes, Norway, probably torpedoed, U/B.
	TARPON	1,090	8. 2.40	22 Apr.	Lost North Sea, probably mine.
	STERLET	670	6. 4.38	27 Apr.	Lost, Skagerrak, cause unknown.
	UNITY	540	15.10.38	29 Apr.	Lost, in collision, Tyne area.
	GRAMPUS	1,520	10. 3.37	24 June	Lost in Mediterranean off Augusta, Sicily, cause unknown.
	ODIN	1,475	21.12.29	27 June	Lost in Gulf of Taranto, Mediterranean, cause unknown.
	ORPHEUS...	1,475	23. 9.30	27 June	Lost, probably torpedoed by Italian S/M, between Malta and Alexandria.
	SHARK	670	31.12.34	6 July	Lost, A/C, off Skudesnes, Norway.
	SALMON	670	8. 3.35	14 July	Lost, probably mined, S.W. Norway.
	PHOENIX	1,475	3. 2.31	17 July	Lost, off Sicily, cause unknown.
	NARWHAL	1,520	28. 2.36	1 Aug.	Lost, probably off Trondheim, Norway, cause unknown. Formally paid off.
	OSWALD	1,475	1. 5.29	1 Aug.	Rammed and sunk, 10 miles S.E. Spartevento Bay, by Italian destroyer.
	SPEARFISH	670	11.12.36	2 Aug.	Lost, probably by U/B, torpedo, off Norway. Formally paid off.
	THAMES	1,805	14. 9.32	3 Aug.	Lost, off Norway, probably mined.
	RAINBOW	1,475	18. 1.32	19 Oct.	Sunk off Calabria, S. Italy, by gunfire, Italian S/M. Formally paid off.
	TRIAD	1,090	16. 9.39	20 Oct.	Lost off Calabria, S. Italy, cause unknown.
	H. 49	410	25.10.19	27 Oct.	Lost, D/C, off Dutch Coast, German A/S, S.C. Formally paid off.
	SWORDFISH	640	28.11.32	16 Nov.	Lost, off Ushant, cause unknown.
	REGULUS	1,475	7.12.30	6 Dec.	Lost, Otranto Strait, S. Italy, cause unknown. Formally paid off.
	TRITON	1,095	9.11.38	18 Dec.	Lost in S. Adriatic, probably mined.
ARMED MERCHANT CRUISERS.	CARINTHIA (R)	20,277	1925 As A.M.C. 1.40	7 June	Sunk by U/B, torpedo, West of Ireland.
	SCOTSTOUN (R) ...	17,046	1925 As A.M.C. 9.39	13 June	Sunk by U/B, torpedo, N.W. Approaches.
	ANDANIA (R)	13,950	1922 As A.M.C. 11.39	16 June	Sunk by U/B, torpedo, S.E. of Iceland.
	TRANSYLVANIA (R) ...	16,923	1925 As A.M.C. 10.39	10 Aug.	Sunk by U/B, torpedo, North of Ireland.
	DUNVEGAN CASTLE (R)...	15,007	1936 As A.M.C. 12.39	28 Aug.	Sunk by U/B, torpedo, West of Ireland.
	LAURENTIC (R)	18,724	1927 As A.M.C. 10.39	3 Nov.	Sunk by U/B, torpedo, N.W. Approaches.
	PATROCLUS (R)	11,314	1923 As A.M.C. 1.40	4 Nov.	Attacked by U/B (3rd). Sank West of Ireland.
	JERVIS BAY (R)... ...	14,164	1922 As A.M.C. 10.39	5 Nov.	Sunk by ADMIRAL SHEER, N. Atlantic.

Class	Name	Tonnage	Date of Completion	Date of Loss	How Lost and Where
ARMED MERCHANT CRUISERS (cont).	FORFAR (R)	16,402	1922 As A.M.C. 11.39	1940 2 Dec.	Sunk by U/B, torpedo, West of Ireland.
ARMED BOARDING VESSELS ...	KING ORRY (R) VAN DYCK (R)	1,877 13,241	1913 1921	30 May 10 June	Sunk by A/C at Dunkirk. Lost in convoy, probably by air attack, Narvik area.
ANTI-AIRCRAFT SHIP	CURLEW	4,290	20.12.17	26 May	Sunk by A/C, bombs, off Ofot Fiord, Norway.
AUXILIARY ANTI-AIRCRAFT SHIPS SLOOPS	CRESTED EAGLE (R) ... FOYLE BANK (R) ... BITTERN	1,110 5,582 1,190	1925 1930 15. 3.38	29 May 4 July 30 Apr.	Sunk by A/C off Dunkirk. Sunk by A/C at Portland. Sunk by A/C, bombs, off Namsos, Norway.
CORVETTE ...	PENZANCE ... ... DUNDEE ... ... GODETIA	1,025 1,060 940	15. 1.31 31. 3.33 15. 7.40	24 Aug. ⎱ 15 Sept. ⎰ 6 Sept.	Sunk by U/B, torpedo, N. Atlantic. Sunk in collision off N. Ireland.
RIVER GUN BOAT	MOSQUITO	585	19. 4.40	1 June	Sunk by A/C during withdrawal from Dunkirk.
MINELAYERS ...	PRINCESS VICTORIA (R) PORT NAPIER (R) ...	2,197 9,600	1939 1940	18–19 May 27 Nov.	Mined, entrance to Humber. Lost by fire, Loch Alsh, W. Scotland.
NETLAYER ...	KYLEMORE (R) ...	319	1897	21 Aug.	Sunk by A/C, Harwich.
MINE DESTRUCTOR VESSEL.	CORBURN	3,060	1936	21 May	Sunk by mine off Le Havre.
MINESWEEPERS ...	SPHINX	875	27. 7.39	3 Feb.	Sunk by A/C, bombs, off N.E. Scotland.
	DUNOON	710	19. 6.19	30 Apr.	Sunk by mine off Great Yarmouth.
	BRIGHTON BELLE (R) ...	396	1900	28 May	Sunk in collision with submerged wreck in Downs.
	GRACIE FIELDS (R) ... WAVERLEY (R) ... ... DEVONIA (R)	393 537 622	1936 ⎱ 1899 ⎰ 1905	29 May 31 May	Sunk by A/C, bombs, off Dunkirk. Beached and abandoned after damage by A/C, bombs, off Dunkirk.
	BRIGHTON QUEEN (R)... SKIPJACK	807 815	1905 3. 5.34	1 June 1 June	Lost by gunfire off Dunkirk. Sunk by A/C, bombs, off Dunkirk.
	DUNDALK ... ... MERCURY (R)	710 621	2. 5.19 1934	16 Oct. 25 Dec.	Sunk by mine off Harwich. Sank after damage by own mine, South of Ireland.
DEGAUSSING SHIP	BALMORE (R)	1,925	1920	11 Nov.	War Cause.
MOTOR TORPEDO BOATS.	No. 15 ... ... 106	18 —	17. 2.39 6.40	24 Sept. ⎱ 16 Oct. ⎰	Sunk by mine, Thames Estuary
	17	18	13. 3.39	21 Oct.	Sunk by explosion, probably mine, off Ostend.
	16	18	3. 3.39	31 Oct.	Sunk by mine, Thames Estuary
MOTOR ATTENDANT CRAFT.	No. 5	—	12.10.36	26 Dec.	Presumed sunk by mine off N.E. Gunfleet.
MOTOR LAUNCHES	No. 109 ... ... 127 ... ... 111	57 65 57	1. 8.40 7.11.40 27. 7.40	30 Oct. 22 Nov. 25 Nov.	Sunk by mine off Humber. Sunk by mine, Thames Estuary Sunk, presumed mined, off Humber.
TRAWLERS ...	KINGSTON CORNELIAN ...	550	1934	5 Jan.	Sunk in collision, East of Gibraltar Straits.
	VALDORA (R)	251	1916	12 Jan.	Believed sunk by A/C, Cromer area.
	FORT ROYAL ... ... ROBERT BOWEN (R) ... FIFESHIRE (R)	550 290 540	1931 ⎱ 1918 ⎰ 1938	9 Feb. 20 Feb.	Sunk by A/C, off Aberdeen. Sunk by A/C, East of Copinsay Orkneys.
	BENVOLIO (R) ... ... PERIDOT ... ... LOCH ASSATER (R) ...	352 550 210	1930 1933 1910	23 Feb. 15 Mar. 22 Mar.	Sunk by mine off Humber. Sunk by mine off Dover. Sunk by British mine, East Coast of Scotland.
	RUTLANDSHIRE (R) ...	458	1936	20 Apr.	Attacked by A/C, grounded, Namsos, Norway.

Class	Name	Tonnage	Date of Completion	Date of Loss	How Lost and Where
TRAWLERS (cont.)	BRADMAN (R)	452	1937	1940 25 Apr.	Sunk by A/C, West Coast of Norway.
	HAMMOND (R)	452	1936	25 Apr.*	Sunk by A/C, Aandalsnes, Norway.
	LARWOOD (R)	452	1936	25 Apr.* }	Sunk by A/C, West Coast of Norway.
	CAPE SIRETOKO (R) ...	590	1939	28 Apr. }	Norway.
	CAPE CHELYUSKIN ...	550	1936	29 Apr.	Sunk by A/C, bombs, off Norway.
	JARDINE (R)	452	1936	30 Apr.	Sunk by own forces after damage by A/C, West Coast of Norway.
	WARWICKSHIRE (R) ...	466	1936	30 Apr.	Sunk by A/C, Trondheim area, Norway.
	ASTON VILLA (R) ...	546	1937 }	3 May	Sunk by A/C off Norway.
	GAUL	550	1936 }		
	ST. GORAN (R) ...	565	1936	3 May	Sunk by A/C, Namsos, Norway.
	LOCH NAVER (R) ...	278	1919	6 May	Sunk in collision off Hartlepool.
	RIFSNES (R)	431	1932	20 May	Sunk by A/C off Ostend.
	CAPE PASSARO (R) ...	590	1939	21 May }	Sunk by A/C, Narvik area,
	MELBOURNE (R) ...	466	1936	22 May }	Norway.
	CHARLES BOYES (R) ...	290	1918	25 May	Sunk by mine, East Coast of England.
	THOMAS BARTLETT (R)	290	1918	28 May	Sunk by British mine off Calais.
	THURINGIA	550	1933	28 May	Sunk by mine, North Sea.
	CALVI (R)	363	1930 }	29 May	Sunk by A/C, bombs, off
	POLLY JOHNSON (R) ...	290	1918 }		Dunkirk.
	ST. ACHILLEUS (R) ...	484	1934	31 May	Sunk by mine, Dunkirk area.
	ARGYLLSHIRE (R) ...	540	1938 }	1 June	Sunk by E/B, during evacuation from Dunkirk.
	STELLA DORADO ...	550	1935 }		
	BLACKBURN ROVERS (R)	422	1934	2 June	Sunk by U/B or mine, North Sea.
	WESTELLA	550	1934	2 June	Torpedoed or mined off Dunkirk.
	JUNIPER	505	9.3.40	8 June	Sunk by ADMIRAL HIPPER, gunfire, off Norway.
	SISAPON (R)	326	1928	12 June	Mined off Harwich.
	MYRTLE	550	1928	14 June	Sunk by mine, Thames Estuary.
	MURMANSK (R) ...	348	1929	17 June	Grounded at Brest and abandoned.
	CAYTON WYKE	550	1932	8 July	Sunk by S.C., torpedo, off Dover.
	CRESTFLOWER	550	1930	19 July	Foundered after damage by A/C off Portsmouth.
	CAMPINA (R)	289	1913	22 July	Mined off Holyhead.
	FLEMING (R)	356	1929	24 July	Sunk by A/C, Thames Estuary.
	KINGSTON GALENA ...	550	1934 }	24 July	Sunk by A/C off Dover.
	RODINO (R)	230	1913 }		
	STAUNTON (R)	283	1908	28 July	Presumed blown up by magnetic mine, Thames Estuary.
	CAPE FINISTERRE (R) ...	590	1939	2 Aug.	Sunk by A/C off Harwich.
	DRUMMER (R)	297	1915	4 Aug.	Mined off Brightlingsea, Essex.
	MARSONA (R)	276	1918	4 Aug.	Sunk by mine off Cromarty.
	OSWALDIAN (R) ...	260	1917	4 Aug.	Mined, Bristol Channel.
	RIVER CLYDE (R) ...	276	1919	5 Aug.	Sunk by mine off Aldeburgh, Suffolk.
	PYROPE (R)	295	1932	12 Aug.	Sunk by A/C, Thames Estuary.
	TAMARISK	545	1925	12 Aug.	Sunk by A/C, bombs, Thames Estuary.
	ELIZABETH ANGELA (R)	253	1928	13 Aug.	Sunk by A/C in Downs.
	RESPARKO (R)	248	1916	20 Aug.	Sunk by A/C at Falmouth.
	ROYALO (R)	248	1916	1 Sept.	Sunk by mine off S. Cornwall.
	DERVISH (R)	346	1911	9 Sept.	Mined off Humber.
	HARVEST MOON ...	72	1904	9 Sept.	Sunk as blockship.
	LOCH INVER (R) ...	356	1930	24 Sept.	Probably mined, Harwich area.
	STELLA SIRIUS	550	1934	25 Sept.	Sunk by bombs during air raid on Gibraltar.
	RECOIL (R)	344	1938	28 Sept.	Lost on patrol, presumed mined, English Channel.
	COMET (R)	301	1924	30 Sept.	Sunk by mine off Falmouth.
	KINGSTON SAPPHIRE (R)	356	1929	5 Oct.	Sunk by U/B, torpedo, Straits of Dover.
	SEA KING (R)	321	1916	9 Oct.	Sunk by underwater explosion in Grimsby Roads.
	RESOLVO (R)	231	1913	12 Oct.	Sunk by mine, Thames Estuary.
	WARWICK DEEPING ...	550	1934	12 Oct.	Sunk by S.C., torpedo, English Channel.
	LORD STAMP (R) ...	448	1935	14 Oct.	Sunk by mine, English Channel.
	KINGSTON CAIRNGORM(R)	448	1935	18 Oct.	Sunk by mine, English Channel.

* Subsequently salved.

Class	Name	Tonnage	Date of Completion	Date of Loss	How Lost and Where
				1940	
TRAWLERS (cont.)	VELIA (R)	290	1914	19 Oct.	Sunk, presumed mined, Harwich Area.
	WAVEFLOWER	550	1929	21 Oct.	Sunk by mine off Aldeburgh, Suffolk.
	HICKORY...	505	19. 4.40	22 Oct.	Sunk by mine, English Channel.
	JOSEPH BUTTON (R) ...	290	1918	22 Oct.	Sunk by mine off Aldeburgh. Suffolk.
	LORD INCHCAPE (R) ...	338	1924	25 Oct.*	Sunk by mine off Plymouth.
	TILBURY NESS (R) ...	279	1918	1 Nov.	Sunk by A/C, Thames Estuary.
	RINOVA (R)	429	1931	2 Nov.	Sunk by mine off Falmouth.
	WILLIAM WESNEY (R) ...	364	1930	7 Nov.	Sunk by mine off Orfordness.
	KINGSTON ALALITE ...	550	1933	10 Nov.	Sunk by mine off Plymouth.
	STELLA ORION (R) ...	417	1935	11 Nov.	Mined, Thames Estuary.
	DUNGENESS (R) ...	263	1914	15 Nov.	Bombed and total loss off Haisborough, Norfolk.
	ARSENAL	550	1933	16 Nov.	Sunk in collision off Clyde.
	FONTENOY (R)	276	1918	19 Nov.	Sunk by A/C off Lowestoft.
	ETHEL TAYLOR (R) ...	276	1917	22 Nov.	Mined off Tyne.
	AMETHYST	627	1934	24 Nov.	Sunk by mine, Thames Estuary
	CONQUISTADOR (R) ...	224	1915	25 Nov.	Sunk in collision, Thames Estuary.
	KENNYMORE (R) ...	225	1914	25 Nov.	Mined, Thames Estuary.
	ELK (R)	181	1902	27 Nov.	Mined at Plymouth.
	MANX PRINCE (R) ...	221	1910	28 Nov. }	Mined, entrance to Humber.
	CALVERTON (R) ...	214	1913	29 Nov. }	
	CHESTNUT	505	21. 5.40	30 Nov.	Sunk by mine off N. Foreland, Kent.
	CAPRICORNUS (R) ...	219	1917	7 Dec.	Sunk by mine off S.E. England.
	CORTINA (R)	213	1913	7 Dec.	Sunk in collision off Humber.
	REFUNDO (R)	258	1917	18 Dec.	Sunk by mine off Harwich.
	PELTON (R)	358	1925	24 Dec.	Sunk by E/B off Yarmouth.
	BANDOLERO	913	1935	30 Dec.	Sunk in collision, Gulf of Sollum, Egypt.
WHALERS ...	SEVRA (R)	253	1929	6 Nov. }	Mined off Falmouth.
	A.N. 2 (R)	221	1926	8 Nov. }	
YACHTS	PRINCESS (R) ...	730	1924	11 Jan.	Sunk in collision, Bristol Channel.
	AMULREE (R)	89	1938	1 June	Sunk in collision, Dover Straits.
	GRIVE (R)	687	1905	1 June	Sunk by A/C during withdrawal from Dunkirk.
	BOOMERANG VI (R) ...	19	1938	8 June	Lost by fire.
	PELLAG II (R)	44	1937	10 June	Presumed lost at Dunkirk.
	CAMPEADOR V (R) ...	195	1938	22 June	Sunk by mine off Portsmouth
	WARRIOR II (R) ...	1,124	1904	11 July	Sunk by A/C off Portland.
	GULZAR (R)	197	1934	29 July	Sunk in air attack, Dover Harbour.
	WHITE FOX II (R) ...	23	1933	27 Aug.	Lost by fire.
	EMELLE (R)	43	1916	31 Aug.	Cause and place not known.
	RHODORA (R)	687	1929	7 Sept.	Lost in collision, Bristol Channel.
	SHASHI III (R) ...	155	—	7 Sept.	Lost by fire.
	SAPPHO (R)	387	—.	30 Sept.	Presumed torpedoed, Falmouth area.
	AISHA (R)	117	1934	11 Oct.	Sunk, believed mined, Thames Approaches.
	GAEL (R)	101	1904	24 Nov.	Mined, entrance to Humber.
BOOM DEFENCE VESSELS	LOCH SHIN (R) ...	255	1930	26 May	Capsized at Harstad, Norway, after being damaged by A/C and beached.
	CAMBRIAN (R)	338	1924	30 May	Mined in Spithead.
	MARCELLE (R)	64	1925	10 Nov.	Mined, Bristol Channel.
	RISTANGO (R)	178	1913	14 Nov.	Fouled Medway boom, Sheerness.
	THOMAS CONNOLLY (R)	290	1918	17 Dec.	Sunk by mine, Sheerness.
GATE VESSEL ...	PLACIDAS FAROULT (R)	136	1927	30–31 Oct.	Cause and place unknown.
GUARDSHIP	LORMONT (R)	1,561	1927	7 Dec.	Sunk in collision off Humber.
TUGS	FAIRPLAY TWO (R) ...	282	1921	2 Mar.	Wrecked on Yorkshire Coast.
	ST. ABBS	550	5. 3.19 }	1 June	Sunk by A/C, at Dunkirk.
	ST. FAGAN	550	7. 7.19 }		
	TWENTE (R)	239	1937	12 June	Lost through enemy action.
	CORINGA (R)	294	1914	23 June	Lost in Atlantic, cause unknown.
	SAUCY (R)	597	1918	4 Sept.	Mined, Firth of Forth.
	SALVAGE KING (R) ...	1164	1925	12 Sept.	Grounded West of Duncansby Head, N.E. Scotland.
	DANUBE III (R) ...	234	1924	13 Oct.	Mined off Sheerness.

* Subsequently salved.

Class	Name	Tonnage	Date of Completion	Date of Loss	How Lost and Where
TUGS *(cont.)*	SEAGEM (R)	92	1939	1940 30 Oct. (approx.)	Missing, presumed lost.
	MURIA (R)	192	1914	8 Nov.	Sunk by mine off N. Foreland.
	GUARDSMAN (R) ...	102	1905	15 Nov.	Sunk by mine off N. Foreland.
MOORING VESSEL	STEADY	758 (deep)	18. 4.16	17 July	Sunk by mine off Newhaven.
DRIFTERS ...	RIANT (R)	95	1919	25 Jan.	Lost in bad weather off West Coast, Scotland.
	MAIDA (R)	107	1914	16 Mar.	Sunk by mine off East Coast, England.
	GOLDEN DAWN (R) ...	80	1913	4 Apr.	Sunk at Ardrossan, W. Scotland.
	BOY ROY (R)	95	1911	28 May	Bombed, beached and abandoned in Dunkirk Harbour.
	OCEAN REWARD (R) ...	95	1912	28 May	Sunk in collision off Dover.
	PAXTON (R)	92	1911	28 May	Damaged by A/C, and beached at Dunkirk.
	COMFORT (R)	60 (Net)	—	29 May	Rammed and sunk by accident off Dover.
	GIRL PAMELA (R) ...	93	1912	29 May	Sunk in collision off Dunkirk.
	NAUTILUS (R) ...	64 (Net)	1929	29 May	Sunk at Dunkirk.
	FAIR BREEZE (R) ...	92	1925	1 June	Struck wreck off Dunkirk.
	LORD CAVAN (R) ...	96	1915	1-2 June	Sunk by gunfire off Dunkirk.
	OCEAN LASSIE (R) ...	96	1919	4 June	Sunk by mine off Harwich.
	DEWEY EVE (R) ...	109	1916	9 June	Sunk in collision, Scapa, Orkneys.
	OCEAN SUNLIGHT (R) ...	131	1929	13 June	Mined off Newhaven.
	CHARDE (R)	99	1919	21 June	Sunk in collision at Portsmouth.
	EMBRACE (R)	94	1907	2 Aug.	Grounded, total loss, at Loch Alsh, W. Scotland.
	YOUNG SID (R) ...	100	1912	10 Aug.	Sunk in collision, Moray Firth, E. Scotland.
	MANX LAD (R) ...	24	1937	16 Aug.	Sunk by mine off Holyhead.
	ALFRED COLEBROOK ...	56	1912	9 Sept.	Sunk as blockship, Richborough Channel, S.E. England.
	WHITE DAISY (R) ...	79	1910	25 Sept.	Sunk.
	SCOTCH THISTLE (R) ...	84	1913	6-7 Oct.	Grounded, total loss, Thames Estuary.
	SUMMER ROSE (R) ...	96	1919	13 Oct.	Sunk by mine off Sunderland.
	APPLE TREE (R) ...	84	1907	15 Oct.	Sunk in collision, Oban Harbour.
	DUTHIES (R)	89	1914	25 Oct.	Sunk by A/C, at Montrose.
	PERSEVERE (R) ...	19·8	1937	27 Oct.	Mined, Firth of Forth.
	HARVEST GLEANER (R)...	96	1918	28 Oct.	Sunk by A/C, East Coast, England.
	TORBAY II (R) ...	83	1910	1 Nov	Sunk by A/C off Dover.
	GOODWILL (R) ...	28 (Net)	—	2 Nov.	Sunk.
	REED (R)	99	1911	7 Nov.	Mined, Thames Estuary.
	SHIPMATES (R) ...	82	1911	14 Nov.	Sunk by A/C, Dover Harbour.
	THE BOYS (R) ...	92	1914	14 Nov.	Sunk in heavy weather in Downs, S.E. England.
	GO AHEAD (R) ...	100	1919	18 Nov.	Sunk in collision, Sheerness.
	XMAS ROSE (R) ...	96	1918	21 Nov.	Sunk by mine, Thames Estuary.
	YOUNG FISHERMAN (R)	95	1914	29 Nov.	Grounded, total loss, Oban, W. Scotland.
	CARRY ON (R) ...	93	1919	17 Dec.	Sunk by mine, Sheerness.
	PROFICIENT (R)	57	—	19 Dec.	Grounded, total loss, Whitby, Yorkshire.
	LORD HOWARD (R) ...	98	1917	24 Dec.	Sunk in collision, Dover Harbour.
	TRUE ACCORD (R) ...	92	1921	26 Dec.	Sunk in collision, Yarmouth Area.
TANKERS & OILERS	BOARDALE	8,406(E)	7. 7.37	30 Apr.	Sunk after grounding Narvik, Norway.
	OLEANDER	7,048	—	8 June	Sunk in Harstead Bay, Norway, after being damaged and beached (26th May).
	WAR SEPOY	5,574	6. 2.19	19 July	Damaged beyond repair by A/C, off Dover.
FREIGHTERS ...	CAPE HOWE (R) ...	4,443	1930	21 June }	Sunk by U/B, S.W. Approaches
	WILLAMETTE VALLEY (R)	4,702	1928	29 June }	
COLLIERS	MAINDY HILL (R) ...	1,918	1911	9 Mar.	Sunk in collision off Hartlepool.
	KING CITY (R) ...	4,744	1928	15 Aug. (approx.)	Sunk by German Raider, Indian Ocean.
	GLYNWEN (R)	1,076	1923	14 Oct.	Sunk by enemy action.

Class	Name	Tonnage	Date of Completion	Date of Loss	How Lost and Where
				1940	
MOTOR CANAL BOATS.	AMBLEVE	—	—	30 May	Ran aground Dunkirk.
	YSER	—	—	}	
	ESCAUT	—	—		} Lost at Dunkirk.
	SEMOIS	—	—		
EXAMINATION VESSEL.	LADY SLATER (R) ...	273	1934	30 July	Caught fire and became total loss.
BALLOON BARRAGE VESSEL.	BOREALIS (R)	451	1930	10 Aug.	Sunk.
SPECIAL SERVICE VESSELS.	DURHAM CASTLE ...	8,240	1904	26 Jan.	Sunk by mine off Cromarty on way to Scapa.
	BRANKSEA	214	1890	10 Feb.	Sunk off Girdleness on way to Scapa. Cause unknown.
	ILSENSTEIN	8,216	1904	18 Feb.	Sunk as blockship at Scapa.
	BUSK	367	1906	19 Feb.	Sunk as blockship.
	CARRON	1,017	1894	3 Mar.	Sunk as blockship at Scapa.
	GONDOLIER	250	1886	18–25 Mar.	Sunk as blockship.
	REDSTONE	3,110	1918	2 May	Sunk as blockship at Scapa.
	FLORENTINO ...	1,822	1921	25 May	Sunk as blockship at Zeebrugge, Belgium.
	MASHOBRA (R)	8,324	1920	25 May	Damaged by A/C, and beached at Narvik.
	TRANSEAS	1,499	1924	25 May }	Sunk as blockships at Zeebrugge, Belgium.
	ATLANTIC GUIDE ...	1,943	1924	27 May	
	BORODINO ...	2,004	1911	27 May }	
	EDV. NISSEN (R) ...	2,062	1921 }	3 June	Sunk as blockships.
	HOLLAND (R)	1,251	1919 }		
	WESTCOVE	2,735	1912	3 June	Sunk as blockship at Dunkirk.
	GOURKO	1,975	1911	4 June	Mined off Dunkirk.
	PACIFICO	687	1905	4 June	Sunk as blockship at Dunkirk.
	JACOBUS	1,262	1920	10 June	Sunk as blockship at Dieppe.
	KAUPO (R)	2,420	1888	10 June	Sunk as blockship.
	RIVER TYNE ...	1,525	1920	10 June	Sunk as blockship at Dieppe.
	TWEEDLEDEE ...	163	1925 }	1 July	Sunk as blockships.
	TWEEDLEDUM ...	163	1925 }		
	JAMES 83 ...	397	1926	3 July*	Sunk as blockship.
	EMERALD WINGS ...	2,139	1920	5 July (date of arrival)	Sunk as blockship at Scapa.
	JAMES 9	85	1924	8 July }	Sunk as blockships.
	UMVOTI (R)	5,183	1903	29 July	
	MOREA	1,968	–	16 Aug. }	
	MINNIE DE LARINAGA ...	5,046	1914	7–9 Sept.*	Total loss from A/C, London Docks.
	EMPIRE SEAMAN ...	1,927	1922	4 Dec.	Sunk, cause unknown.
	GAMBHIRA ...	5,257	1919		
	JUNIATA	1,139	1918		
	LAKE NEUCHATEL ...	3,859	1907	}	Sunk as blockships, presumed during 1940.
	LYCEA	2,338	1924		
	MARTIS	2,483	1894		
	MOYLE	1,761	1907	}	
				1941	
BATTLESHIPS ...	BARHAM	31,100	4.10.15	25 Nov.	Sunk by U/B, torpedoes, off Sollum, Egypt.
	PRINCE OF WALES ...	35,000	31. 3.41	10 Dec.	Sunk by Japanese torpedo-carrying A/C, E. Coast of Malaya.
BATTLE CRUISERS	HOOD	42,100	15. 5.20	24 May	Sunk in action with BISMARCK, N. Atlantic.
	REPULSE	33,250	7. 8.16	10 Dec.	Sunk by Japanese torpedo-carrying A/C, E. Coast of Malaya.
MONITOR	TERROR	7,200	2. 8.16	23 Feb.	Bombed (22nd) and sunk off Derna, Libya.
AIRCRAFT CARRIER	ARK ROYAL	22,000	16.11.38	14 Nov.	Torpedoed (13th) by U/B and sunk, W. Mediterranean.
AUXILIARY AIR-CRAFT CARRIER.	AUDACITY (ex HANN-OVER) (German prize Vessel).	11,000 (deep)	1939 As A/C Carrier 9.41	21 Dec.	Sunk by U/B, torpedo, N. Atlantic.
CRUISERS	SOUTHAMPTON	9,100	6. 3.37	11 Jan.	Sunk by dive bombers, East of Malta.

* Subsequently salved.

Class	Name	Tonnage	Date of Completion	Date of Loss	How Lost and Where
CRUISERS (contd)...	BONAVENTURE	5,450	24. 5.40	1941 31 Mar.	Sunk by U/B, torpedoes, South of Crete.
	FIJI	8,000	17. 5.40	22 May	Sunk by A/C, bombs, during evacuation of Crete.
	GLOUCESTER	9,600	31. 1.39	22 May	Sunk by A/C, bombs, during evacuation of Crete.
	YORK	8,250	1. 5.30	22 May	Lost at Suda Bay, Crete after damage on various dates by E.M.B. and A/C.
	DUNEDIN	4,850	10.19	24 Nov.	Sunk by U/B, torpedo, between W. Africa and Brazil.
	GALATEA	5,220	14. 8.35	14 Dec.	Sunk by U/B, torpedo, off Alexandria.
	NEPTUNE	7,175	23. 2.34	19 Dec.	Sunk by mine off Tripoli, Libya.
DESTROYERS ...	GALLANT	1,335	25. 2.36	20 Jan.	Damaged by mine (10th) and taken in tow. Later bombed and sunk in Malta Harbour.
	DAINTY	1,375	22.12.32	24 Feb.	Sunk by A/C, off Tobruk, Libya.
	EXMOOR	1,000	1.11.40	25 Feb.	Sunk by explosion presumed E/B, torpedo, off Lowestoft.
	MOHAWK	1,870	7. 9.38	16 Apr.	Torpedoed by destroyer, East of Tunisia. Sunk by own Forces.
	DIAMOND	1,375	3.11.32	27 Apr.	Sunk by A/C, bombs, during evacuation of Greece.
	WRYNECK	1,100	9.11.18		
	JERSEY	1,760	28. 4.39	2 May	Mined in entrance to Grand Harbour, Malta.
	JUNO	1,760	25. 8.39	21 May	Sunk by A/C, bombs, during battle of Crete.
	GREYHOUND	1,335	1. 2.36	22 May	
	KASHMIR	1,760	26.10.39	22 May	
	KELLY (Leader) ...	1,760	23. 8.39	23 May	
	MASHONA	1,870	30. 3.39	28 May	Sunk by A/C, bombs, N. Atlantic.
	HEREWARD	1,340	9.12.36	29 May	Sunk by A/C, bombs, off Crete.
	IMPERIAL	1,370	30. 6.37	29 May	Sunk by own forces after being bombed, off Crete.
	WATERHEN (On loan to R.A.N.).	1,100	17. 7.18	29 June	Sunk by A/C, bombs, off Sollum, Egypt.
	DEFENDER	1,375	31.10.32	11 July	Sunk by A/C, bombs, off Sidi Barrani, Egypt.
	FEARLESS	1,375	19.12.34	23 July	Sunk during air attack on convoy, Central Mediterranean.
	BATH (On loan to R.NOR. N.).	1,060	21. 3.19	19 Aug.	Sunk by U/B, torpedo, S.W. of Ireland.
	BROADWATER	1,190	28. 2.20	18 Oct.	Sunk by U/B, torpedo, N. Atlantic.
	COSSACK	1,870	10. 6.38	27 Oct.	Foundered after being torpedoed by U/B (23rd), West of Gibraltar.
	KANDAHAR	1,760	10.10.39	19 Dec.	Mined off Tripoli, Libya, and subsequently sunk by own forces.
	STANLEY	1,190	19. 5.19	19 Dec.	Sunk by U/B, torpedo, N Atlantic.
SUBMARINES ...	SNAPPER	670	14. 6.35	12 Feb.	Lost, Bay of Biscay. Formally paid off.
	USK	540	11.10.40	3 May	Presumed mined, off Cape Bon, Tunisia.
	UNDAUNTED	540	30.12.40	13 May	Presumed Sunk by D/C, S.C. off Tripoli, Libya.
	UMPIRE	540	10. 7.41	19 July	Rammed and sunk by trawler North Sea, off the Wash.
	UNION	540	22. 2.41	22 July	Presumed lost between Tunisia and Pantellaria.
	CACHALOT	1,520	15. 8.38	4 Aug.	Rammed by Italian destroyer off Cyrenaica. Formally Paid off.
	P. 33	540	30. 5.41	20 Aug.	Presumed mined off Tripoli, Libya.
	P. 32	540	3. 5.41	23 Aug.	Formally paid off.
	TETRARCH	1,093	15. 2.40	2 Nov.	Lost W. Mediterranean, on passage Malta to Gibraltar.
	PERSEUS	1,475	15. 4.30	1 Dec.	Mined off Zante, W. Greece.
	H. 31	410	21. 2.19	24 Dec.	Presumed mined, Bay of Biscay.
ARMED MERCHANT CRUISERS.	VOLTAIRE (R)	13,301	1923 As AMC 1.40	4 Apr. (Approx.)	Sunk by surface raider, mid-Atlantic.

Class	Name	Tonnage	Date of Completion	Date of Loss	How Lost and Where
				1941	
ARMED MERCHANT CRUISERS (*cont.*)	COMORIN (R)	*15,241*	1925 As AMC 1.40	6 Apr.	Destroyed by fire, N. Atlantic.
	RAJPUTANA (R) ...	*16,644*	1926 As AMC 12.39	13 Apr.	Sunk by U/B, torpedo, West of Iceland.
	SALOPIAN (R)	*10,549*	1926 As AMC 10·39	13 May	Sunk by U/B, torpedo, N. Atlantic.
ARMED BOARDING VESSELS	ROSAURA (R)	*1,552*	1905	18 Mar.	Sunk by mine off Tobruk, Libya.
	CHAKDINA (R)	*3,033*	1914	5 Dec.	Sunk by A/C, E. Mediterranean
	CHANTALA (R)	*3,129*	1920	7 Dec.	Sunk by mine, Tobruk Harbour
OCEAN BOARDING VESSELS.	CRISPIN (R)	*5,051*	1935	3 Feb.	Sunk by U/B, torpedo, N. Atlantic.
	MANISTEE (R)	*5,368*	1920	24 Feb.	
	CAMITO (R)	*6,833*	1915	6 May	Sunk by U/B, torpedo, N. Atlantic.
	LADY SOMERS (R) ...	*8,194*	1929	15 July	
	MALVERNIAN (R)	*3,133*	1937	19 July	Abandoned after being bombed
AUXILIARY FIGHTER CATAPULT SHIPS.	PATIA (R)	*5,355*	1922	27 Apr.	Sunk by A/C, off Northumberland.
	SPRINGBANK (R) ...	*5,155*	1926	27 Sept.	Sunk by U/B, torpedo, N. Atlantic.
ANTI-AIRCRAFT SHIP.	CALCUTTA	4,200	21. 8.19	1 June	Sunk by A/C, bombs, during evacuation of Crete.
AUXILIARY ANTI-AIRCRAFT SHIP.	HELVELLYN (R) ...	*642*	1937	20 Mar.	Sunk by A/C, London Docks,
SLOOPS	GRIMSBY	990	17. 5.34	25 May	Sunk by A/C, off Tobruk Libya.
	AUCKLAND	1,250	16.11.38	24 June	Sunk by A/C, bombs, off Tobruk, Libya.
CORVETTES ...	PINTAIL	580	28.11.39	10 June	Sunk by mines off Humber.
	PICOTEE	900	5. 9.40	12 Aug.	Presumed lost, probably torpedoed by U/B, off Iceland.
	ZINNIA	900	30. 3.41	23 Aug.	Sunk by U/B, torpedo, N. Atlantic.
	FLEUR DE LYS	900	26. 8.40	14 Oct.	Sunk by U/B, torpedo, West of Gibraltar.
	GLADIOLUS	965	6. 4.40	16 Oct.	Presumed torpedoed by U/B, N. Atlantic.
	WINDFLOWER (On loan to R.C.N.).	900	4. 2.41	7 Dec.	Sunk by collision in fog, W. Atlantic.
	SALVIA	955	20. 9.40	24 Dec.	Sunk by U/B, torpedo, off Egypt.
AUXILIARY A / S VESSEL.	KAMPAR (R)	*971*	1915	13 Dec.	Destroyed by A/C at Penang after damage (12th.)
RIVER GUN BOATS	LADYBIRD	625	5.16	12 May	Dive bombed and sunk, Tobruk Libya.
	GNAT	625	12.15	21 Oct.	Torpedoed by U/B off Bardia, Libya. Total loss.
	PETEREL	310	29.11.27	8 Dec.	Sunk by Japanese Forces at Shanghai.
	MOTH	625	1.16	12 Dec.	Scuttled at Hong Kong.
	TERN	262	15.11.27	19 Dec.	
	CICALA	625	2.16	21 Dec.	Sunk by A/C, bombs, Hong Kong.
	ROBIN	226	23. 7.34	25 Dec.	Scuttled at Hong Kong.
CONVOY SERVICE SHIPS.	FIONA (R)	*2,190*	1927	18 Apr.	Sunk by A/C off Sidi Barrani, Egypt.
	CHAKLA (R)	*3,081*	1914	29 Apr.	Sunk by A/C, Tobruk Harbour Libya.
MINELAYERS ...	LATONA	2,650	4. 5.41	25 Oct.	Attacked by A/C, E. Mediterranean.
	REDSTART	498	28.10.38	19 Dec.	Scuttled at Hong Kong.
NETLAYER ...	TONBRIDGE (R) ...	*683*	1924	22 Aug.	Sunk by A/C off Yarmouth, Norfolk.
MINE DESTRUCTOR VESSELS.	QUEENWORTH	3,010	1925	9 May	Sunk by A/C, North Sea.
	CORFIELD	3,000	1937	8 Sept.	Sunk by mine explosion off Humber.

Class	Name	Tonnage	Date of Completion	Date of Loss	How Lost and Where
				1941	
MINESWEEPERS ...	HUNTLEY	710	22. 5.19	31 Jan.	Sunk by A/C, E. Mediterranean
	SOUTHSEA (R)	825	1930	16 Feb.	Mined and beached off Tyne. Constructive total loss.
	MARMION (R)	409	1906	9 Apr.	Sunk by A/C at Harwich. Salved but constructive total loss.
	FERMOY	710	23. 7.19	4 May	Sunk by A/C, bombs, in dock at Malta.
	STOKE	710	30.10.18	7 May	Sunk by A/C at Tobruk.
	CITY OF ROCHESTER ...	194	1904	19 May	Sunk by aerial mine.
	WIDNES	710	17. 9.18	20 May	Bombed and beached in Suda Bay, Crete.
	SNAEFELL (R)	466	1907	5 July	Sunk by A/C, Tyne Area.
	BANKA (R)	623	1914	10 Dec.	Sunk by mine or A/C, E. Coast of Malaya.
MOTOR MINESWEEPER.	No. 39	226	26. 4.41	7 Aug.	Mined and sunk, Thames Estuary.
MOTOR TORPEDO BOATS.	No. 41	33	7.11.40	14 Feb.	Sunk by mine, North Sea.
	28	37	10. 7.40	7 March	Lost by fire.
	67	17	19. 4.40		
	213	17	24.10.40	23 May–	Sunk by A/C, destroyed or
	214	17	10.40	2 June	beached, in Suda Bay, Crete.
	216	17	3. 1.41		
	217	17	7. 1.41		
	68	17	19. 4.40	14 Dec.	Sunk in collision off Libya.
	8	18	3. 9.37	16 Dec.	Destroyed by fire during raid on Hong-Kong.
	12	18	3. 8.38	20 Dec.	Sunk in action with Japanese Landing Craft, Hong-Kong.
	26	13·8	10. 9.38		
	7	18	31. 8.38	26 Dec.	Scuttled at Hong-Kong.
	9	18	8.10.37		
	10	18	11. 7.38		
	11	18	26. 7.38	26 Dec.	Scuttled at Hong-Kong.
	27	13·8	10. 9.38		
MOTOR A/S BOATS	No. 3	19	13. 6.39	28 Feb.	Beached after damage by mine, Suez Canal.
	30	23	18. 8.41	14 Dec.	Fouled boom and sank, Humber.
MOTOR GUN BOATS	No. 12	31	10. 8.40	3 Feb. (approx.)	Sunk by mine, Milford Haven.
	98	—	—	June (approx.)	Lost in air raid on HORNET.
	90	33	—	16 July	Destroyed by fire, Portland Harbour.
	92	33	—		
	62	28	31.12.40	9 Aug.	Lost in collision, North Sea.
MOTOR LAUNCHES	No. 1003...	40	3. 1.41	20 Apr.	Lost in torpedoed ship in Atlantic.
	1037...	40	3. 1.41		
	1011...	40	16.11.40	10 May	Bombed and sunk on passage from Suda Bay to Sphakia, Crete.
	1030...	40	11.11.40	28 May	Lost on passage from Suda Bay, Crete.
	144...	73	12.11.40	22 Sept.	Sunk by mine, English Channel.
	288...	73	19. 8.41	11 Oct.	Lost through stress of weather, off Hartlepool.
	219...	73	17. 5.41	21 Nov.	Grounded off Stornoway, N.W. Scotland. Constructive total loss.
TRAWLERS ...	DESIREE (R)	213	1912	16 Jan.	Mined, Thames Estuary.
	RELONZO (R)	245	1914	20 Jan.	Mined, Crosby Channel, Liverpool.
	LUDA LADY (R) ...	234	1914	22 Jan.	Mined, Humber area.
	DAROGAH (R)	221	1914	27 Jan.	Mined, Thames Estuary.
	ALMOND	505	20. 8.40	2 Feb.	Sunk by mine off Falmouth.
	ARCTIC TRAPPER (R) ...	352	1928	3 Feb.	Sunk by A/C off Ramsgate.
	TOURMALINE	641	1935	5 Feb.	Sunk by A/C, off N. Foreland, Kent.
	RUBENS (R)	320	1937	13 Feb.	Sunk by A/C, Western Approaches.
	ORMONDE (R)	250	1906	16 Feb.	Sunk by A/C off E. Coast of Scotland.
	OUSE	462	8.17	20 Feb.	Sunk by mine, Tobruk, Libya.
	LINCOLN CITY (R) ...	398	1933	21 Feb.	Sunk by A/C, Faroe Islands.
	REMILLO (R)	266	1917	27 Feb.	Sunk by mine, Humber.
	ST. DONATS (R) ...	349	1924	1 Mar.	Sunk in collision off Humber.
	COBBERS (R)	275	1919	3 Mar.	Sunk by A/C, North Sea.

Class	Name	Tonnage	Date of Completion	Date of Loss	How Lost and Where
TRAWLERS (cont.) ...	KERVADO (R)	252	1920	1941 6 Mar. ⎫	Sunk by mine, English Channel.
	GULLFOSS	730	1929	9 Mar. ⎬	
	LADY LILIAN (R) ...	581	1939	16 Mar. ⎭	Sunk by A/C, West of Ireland.
	DOX (R)	35	1931	20 Mar.	Sunk by enemy action.
	ASAMA (R)	303	1929	21 Mar.	Sunk by A/C in attack on Plymouth.
	LORD SELBORNE (R) ...	247	1917	31 Mar.	Sunk by mine, Humber.
	CRAMOND ISLAND (R) ...	180	1910	2 Apr. ⎫	Sunk by A/C off St. Abb's Head
	FORTUNA (R)	259	1906	2–3 Apr. ⎬	E. Scotland.
	ROCHE BONNE (R) ...	258	1913	7 Apr.	Sunk by A/C off the Lizard, Cornwall.
	KOPANES (R)	351	1915	19 Apr.	Sunk by A/C off Tyne.
	TOPAZE	608	1935	20 Apr.	Lost in collision off Clyde.
	CAROLINE (R) ...	253	1930	28 Apr.	Sunk by mine off Milford Haven.
	JEAN FREDERIC (R) ...	329	1919	1 May	Sunk by A/C off Start Point, English Channel.
	ALBERIC (R) ...	286	1910	3 May	Sunk in collision off Scapa, Orkneys.
	BEN GAIRN (R) ...	234	1916	4 May	Sunk by parachute mine, Lowestoft.
	SUSARION (R)	260	1917	7 May	Sunk by A/C off Humber.
	SILICIA (R)	250	1913	8 May	Mined off Humber.
	VAN ORLEY (R) ...	352	1927	May	Declared a constructive total loss.
	EVESHAM (R)	239	1915	27 May	Sunk by A/C off Yarmouth, Norfolk.
	SINDONIS	913 (deep)	1934	29 May	Sunk by A/C at Tobruk.
	ASH	505	6. 5.40	5 June	Sunk by mine, Thames Estuary.
	RESMILO (R)	258	1917	20 June	Sunk by A/C at Peterhead, E. Scotland.
	BEECH	540	1929	22 June	Sunk by A/C in Scrabster, N. Scotland.
	NOGI (R)	299	1923	23 June	Sunk by A/C off Norfolk.
	TRANIO (R)	275	1918	26 June	Sunk by A/C bombs, whilst in tow, North Sea.
	FORCE (R)	324	1917	27 June	Sunk by A/C off Yarmouth, Norfolk.
	AKRANES (R)	358	1929	4 July	Sunk by A/C, Bridlington Bay, Yorkshire.
	AGATE	627	1934	6 Aug.	Grounded, total loss, off Cromer Norfolk.
	LORINDA (R)	348	1928	20 Aug.	Sank through engine trouble and fires off Freetown, W. Africa.
	BRORA	530	4. 6.41	6 Sept.	Grounded, total loss, Hebrides, W. Scotland.
	STRATHBORVE (R) ...	216	1930	6 Sept.	Mined off Humber.
	MARCONI (R)	322	1916	20 Sept.	Lost in collision off Harwich.
	EILEEN DUNCAN (R) ...	223	1910 ⎫	30 Sept.	Sunk by A/C, N. Shields.
	STAR OF DEVERON (R)	220	1915 ⎭		
	ALDER	560	1929	22 Oct.	Grounded, total loss, E. Scotland.
	EMILION (R)	201	1914	24 Oct.	Mined, Thames Estuary.
	FLOTTA	530	11. 6.41	6 Nov.	Foundered after grounding (29 Oct.) off Buchan Ness, E. Scotland.
	FRANCOLIN (R) ...	322	1916	12 Nov.	Sunk by A/C off Cromer, Norfolk.
	ST. APOLLO (R) ...	580	1940	22 Nov.	Sunk in collision off Hebrides, W. Scotland.
	MILFORD EARL (R) ...	290	1919 ⎫	8 Dec.	Sunk by A/C off East Coast Scotland.
	PHINEAS BEARD (R) ...	278	1918 ⎭		
	LADY SHIRLEY (R) ...	477	1937	11 Dec.	Sunk by U/B, Gibraltar Straits.
	HENRIETTE (R)	261	1906	26 Dec.	Sunk by mine off Humber.
WHALERS ...	SOUTHERN FLOE (R) ...	344	1936	11 Feb.	Sunk by mine off Tobruk, Libya.
	SARNA (R)	268	1930	25 Feb.	Sunk by mine, Suez Canal.
	KOS XXIII (R) ...	353	1937	23 May (approx.)	Total loss in Suda Bay, Crete.
	SYVERN (R)	307	1937	27 May	Sunk by enemy action on passage from Crete area.
	KOS XXII (R) ...	353	1937	2 June (date reported)	Sunk on passage from Crete area.
	THORBRYN (R)	305	1936	19 Aug.	Sunk by A/C off Tobruk, Libya.
	KOS XVI (R)	258	1932	24 Aug.	Sunk in collision, North Sea.
	SKUDD 3 (R)	245	1929	27 Aug.	Sunk by A/C, Tobruk, Libya.
	WHIPPET (R)	353	1937	4 Oct.	Bombed and sunk.
	EGELAND (R)	153	1912	29 Nov.	Grounded, Palestine Coast, total loss.

Class	Name	Tonnage	Date of Completion	Date of Loss	How Lost and Where
				1941	
YACHTS	MOLLUSC (R)	597	1906	17 Mar.	Sunk by A/C off Blyth, Northumberland.
	WILNA (R)	461	1939	24 Mar.	Abandoned after A/C attack, Portsmouth.
	SURF (R)	496	1902	6 Apr.	Sunk by A/C at Piraeus.
	TORRENT (R)	336	1930	6 Apr.	Mined and sunk off Falmouth.
	YORKSHIRE BELLE (R)	56	1938	11 Apr.	Sunk by mine, Humber entrance.
	CALANTHE (R)	370	1898	24 Apr.	Sunk by A/C off Milos, Greece.
	NYULA (R)	48	1936	2 May	Sunk in collision off Tyne.
	VIVA II (R)	521	1929	8 May	Sunk by A/C off N. Coast of Cornwall.
	SEA ANGLER (R) ...	23	—	19 May	Destroyed by fire.
	HANYARDS (R)	16.5	1931	21 May	Cause and place unknown.
	ROSABELLE	525	1901	11 Dec.	Sunk by explosion, probably torpedoed by U/B, Straits of Gibraltar.
BOOM DEFENCE VESSELS.	OTHELLO (R)	201	1907	11 Apr.	Sunk by mine, Humber.
	ALDGATE	290	23. 6.34 ⎫		
	BARLIGHT	730	12.12.38 ⎬	19 Dec.	Scuttled at Hong Kong.
	WATERGATE	290	23. 6.34 ⎭		
GATE VESSEL ...	KING HENRY (R) ...	162	1900	13 June	Sunk by A/C off Lowestoft.
ACCOMMODATION SHIP.	GYPSY (R)	261	—	11 May	Sunk at Tower Pier during air raid on London.
TUGS	ST. CYRUS	810	5. 4.19	22 Jan.	Sunk by mine off Humber.
	PEUPLIER (R)	—	—	29–30 Apr.	Sunk.
	IRENE VERNICOS (R) ...	250	—	June (approx.)	Constructive total loss.
	ASSURANCE	675	28. 9.40	18 Oct.	Grounded, total loss, Lough Foyle, N. Ireland.
	HELEN BARBARA ...	—	—	21 Oct.	Abandoned in sinking condition, due to heavy weather.
	LETTIE (R)	89	1914	9 Nov.	Sunk, cause unknown, off St. Abb's Head, E. Scotland.
	INDIRA (R)	637	1918	15 Dec.	Sunk during air attack on Hong Kong.
SALVAGE VESSEL...	VIKING (R)	—	—	6 Apr.	Sunk by A/C, Piraeus, Greece.
SCHOONERS ...	KEPHALLINIA (R) ...	1,267	1893	13 Aug.	Foundered off Alexandria.
	KANTARA (R)	—	—	26 Sept.	Cause and place unknown.
	MARIA DI GIOVANNI (R)	—	—	22 Nov.	Grounded, West of Tobruk, Libya.
DRIFTERS ...	NEW SPRAY (R) ...	70	1912	3 Jan.	Lost in gale off Sheerness.
	DUSKY QUEEN (R) ...	40	1920	9 Jan.	Grounded, constructive total loss, Dover Straits.
	UBEROUS (R)	92	1918	11 Jan.	Grounded off Londonderry.
	MIDAS (R)	89	1910	3 Feb.	Sunk in collision off Dungeness.
	IMBAT (R)	92	1918	4 Feb.	Sunk in collision, Scapa, Orkneys.
	BOY ALAN (R)	109	1914	10 Feb.	Sunk in collision, Thames Estuary.
	GLOAMING (R)	21 (Net)	1928	20 Mar.	Mined off Humber.
	SOIZIK (R)	—	—	20 Mar.	Lost by enemy action.
	BAHRAM (R)	72	1924	3 Apr.	Mined in Humber Estuary.
	D'ARCY COOPER (R) ...	126	1928	9 Apr.	Sunk by A/C, Harwich.
	RYPA (R)	31	—	12 Apr.	
	YOUNG ERNIE (R) ...	88	1924	18 Apr.	Sunk in collision off Tyne.
	GOWAN HILL (R) ...	96	1920	7 May	Sunk by A/C, Greenock.
	THISTLE (R)	79	1904	8 May	Mined off Lowestoft.
	UBERTY (R)	93	1912	8 May	Sunk by A/C off Lowestoft.
	M.A. WEST (R) ...	96	1919	14 May	Sunk by A/C off Norfolk Coast.
	JEWEL (R)	84	1908	18 May	Sunk by mine off Belfast Lough.
	AURORA II (R) ...	—	—	24 May	Sunk by A/C at Tobruk, Libya.
	COR JESU (R)	97	1931	8 June	Sunk in air attack off Alnmouth, Northumberland.
	DEVON COUNTY (R) ...	86	1910	1 July ⎫	
	RECEPTIVE (R)	86	1913	3 July ⎬	Sunk by mine, Thames Estuary.
	LORD ST. VINCENT (R)	115	1929	7 July ⎭	
	FERTILE VALE (R) ...	91	1917	17 July	Sunk in collision off River Tay, E. Scotland.
	CHRISTINE ROSE (R) ...	—	—	10 Sept.	Grounded, Knap Rock, Argyll, W. Scotland.
	FORERUNNER (R) ...	92	1911	14 Oct.	Sunk in collision, Thames Estuary. Constructive total loss.
	MONARDA (R)	109	1916	8 Nov.	Foundered, Thames Estuary.

Class	Name	Tonnage	Date of Completion	Date of Loss	How Lost and Where
DRIFTERS (*cont.*)	BOY ANDREW (R) ...	97	1918	1941 9 Nov.	Lost in collision, Firth of Forth, E. Scotland.
	BLIA (R)	—	1936	11 Nov.	Presumed lost.
	HARMONY (R)	24 (Net)	—	15 Nov.	Lost in collision off Invergordon, N.E. Scotland.
	ROWAN TREE (R) ...	91	1917	21 Nov.	Grounded and capsized, entrance to Lowestoft Harbour
	FISHER GIRL (R) ...	85	1914	25 Nov.	Sunk by A/C, Falmouth Harbour.
	FISKAREN (R)	—	—	23 Dec.	Sunk in collision, Belfast, N. Ireland.
	TOKEN (R)	89	1914	23 Dec.	Grounded, broke up in gale, Skerry Sound, Orkneys.
TENDER	CHABOOK (R) ... ... (Tender to SHEBA)	—	—	22 Mar.	Formally paid off.
TANKERS & OILERS.	PERICLES (R)	8,324	1936	14 Apr.	Lost in heavy weather on passage to Alexandria.
	OLNA	12,667	20.10.21	18 May	Bombed and set on fire, Crete.
	JOHN P. PEDERSEN (R)	6,128	1930	20 May	Sunk by U/B, N. Atlantic.
	CAIRNDALE	8,129	26. 1.39	30 May	Sunk by U/B, torpedo, West of Gibraltar Straits.
	SILDRA (R)	7,313	1927	19 Aug.	Sunk by U/B off W. Africa.
	DARKDALE	8,145	15.11.40	22 Oct.	Sunk by explosion, believed torpedoed by U/B, St. Helena.
	WAR MEHTAR	5,502	2. 3.20	20 Nov.	Torpedoed and sunk off Yarmouth.
STORE CARRIERS	ULSTER PRINCE (R) ...	3,791	1930	25 Apr.	Grounded off Nauplia and attacked by A/C during evacuation from Greece.
	TUNA (R)	662	1907	Sept. date (reported)	Constructive total loss after fire at Aden.
	TIBERIO (R)	237	1902	23 Dec.	Foundered off Mersa Matruh, Egypt.
ARMAMENT STORE CARRIER.	ESCAUT (R)	1,087	1938	3–4 Aug.	Sunk by A/C off Suez.
COLLIERS	BOTUSK (R)	3,092	1919	31 Jan.	War Cause.
	BELHAVEN (R) ...	1,498	1921	13–14 Mar.*	Sunk by bombs during air raid on Clyde.
EXAMINATION VESSELS.	No. 4 (R)	—	—	Feb. (approx.)	Sunk by enemy action.
	10 (R)	281	—	7 June	Mined off entrance to Milford Haven.
	TUNG WO (R)	1,337	1914	13 Dec.	Abandoned as result of enemy action.
BALLOON BARRAGE VESSEL.	SATURNUS (R)	200	1935	1 May	Constructive total loss.
SPECIAL SERVICE VESSELS.	MINNIE DE LARINAGA ...	5,046	1914	5 Feb.	Sunk as blockship at Dover.
	FIDELIA	147	1891	5 May	Sunk by A/C, Lowestoft Harbour.
	VITA (R)	—	—	22 Sept.	Cause and place unknown.
	NORSJOEN (R)	—	—	19 Nov.	Wrecked on enemy coast.
	KANTUNG (R)	—	—	} 9 Dec.	Sunk as blockships in Anking Harbour.
	MACAO (R)	—	—		
	NORSEMANN (R) ...	—	—	Dec.	Cause and place unknown.
SMALL MISCELLANEOUS CRAFT.	AGHIOS PANTALEIMON (R)	105	—	30 May	Presumed lost.
	DANEHILL	14	1933	1 Dec.	Formally paid off.
ARMED TRADER ...	KUDAT (R)	1,725	1914	30 Dec.	Sunk by A/C at Port Swettenham, Malaya.
AIRCRAFT CARRIERS	HERMES	10,850	18. 2.24	1942 9 Apr.	Sunk by Japanese A/C off Ceylon.
	EAGLE	22,600	20. 2.24	11 Aug.	Sunk by U/B, torpedo, W. Mediterranean.
(AUXILIARY AIRCRAFT CARRIER).	AVENGER	13,785 (deep)	2. 3.42	15 Nov.	Sunk by U/B, torpedo, West of Gibraltar Straits.
CRUISERS	EXETER	8,390	23. 7.31	1 Mar.	Sunk in action with Japanese S.C., Java Seas.
	NAIAD	5,450	24. 7.40	11 Mar.	Sunk by U/B, torpedo, E. Mediterranean.

* Subsequently Salved.

Class	Name	Tonnage	Date of Completion	Date of Loss	How Lost and Where
				1942.	
CRUISERS—(*cont.*)	CORNWALL	10,000	8. 5.28 ⎱	5 Apr.	Sunk by Japanese dive bombers, Indian Ocean.
	DORSETSHIRE	9,975	30 9.30 ⎰		
	EDINBURGH	10,000	6. 7.39	2 May	Sunk by destroyer, torpedoes, after U/B damage (30th Apr.), Barent's Sea, Arctic.
	TRINIDAD	8,000	14.10.41	15 May	Sunk by own forces after damage by torpedo carrying A/C, Barent's Sea, Arctic.
	HERMIONE	5,450	25. 3.41	16 June	Sunk by U/B, torpedo, E. Mediterranean.
	MANCHESTER	9,400	4. 8.38	13 Aug.	Sunk by E/B, torpedo, off Kelibia Roads, Tunisia.
DESTROYERS	VIMIERA	1,090	19. 9.17	9 Jan.	Sunk by mine, Thames Estuary.
	GURKHA (ex LARNE) ...	1,920	18. 2.41	17 Jan.	Sunk by U/B, torpedo, E. Mediterranean.
	MATABELE	1,870	25. 1.39	17 Jan.	Sunk by U/B, torpedo, Barent's Sea, Arctic.
	THANET	1,000	30. 8.19	27 Jan.	Sunk in action with Japanese S.C., off Malaya.
	BELMONT	1,190	22.12.19	31 Jan.	Sunk by U/B, torpedo, W. Atlantic.
	MAORI	1,870	30.11.38	11/12 Feb.	Sunk during air raid on Grand Harbour, Malta.
	ELECTRA	1,375	13. 9.34	27 Feb.	Sunk by S.C., gunfire, Java Sea.
	JUPITER	1,760	25. 6.39	27 Feb.	Sunk by torpedo, Java Sea.
	ENCOUNTER	1,375	2.11.34	1 Mar.	Sunk in action, S.C., Java Sea.
	STRONGHOLD	905	2. 7.19	2 Mar.	Sunk in action, S.C., South of Java.
	VORTIGERN	1,090	25. 1.18	15 Mar.	Sunk by E/B, torpedo, off Cromer.
	HEYTHROP	1,050	21. 6.41	20 Mar.	Sunk by U/B, torpedo, E. Mediterranean.
	SOUTHWOLD	1,050	9.10.41	24 Mar.	Sunk by mine off Malta.
	JAGUAR	1,760	12. 9.39	26 Mar.	Sunk by U/B, torpedo, E. Mediterranean.
	LEGION	1,920	19.12.40	26 Mar.	Sunk by A/C, Malta Harbour.
	CAMPELTOWN ...	1,090	20. 1.19	28 Mar.	Sunk as explosion vessel at St. Nazaire.
	TENEDOS	1,000	11. 6.19	5 Apr.	Sunk by A/C, during attack on Colombo.
	HAVOCK	1,340	16. 1.37	6 Apr.	Grounded, total loss, off Kelibia, Tunisia.
	LANCE	1,920	13. 5.41	9 Apr.*	Sunk by A/C, bombs, at Malta.
	VAMPIRE (On loan to R.A.N.).	1,090	22. 9.17	9 Apr.	Sunk by A/C, bombs, East of Ceylon.
	KINGSTON	1,760	14. 9.39	11 Apr.	Sunk by A/C, bombs, at Malta.
	PUNJABI	1,870	29. 3.39	1 May	Sunk after collision, N. Atlantic.
	KIPLING	1,760	22.12.39	11 May	⎫
	LIVELY	1,920	20. 7.41	11 May	⎬ Sunk by A/C, E. Mediterranean.
	JACKAL	1,760	13. 4.39	12 May	⎭
	GROVE	1,050	5. 2.42	12 June	Sunk by U/B, torpedo, E. Mediterranean.
	AIREDALE	1,050	8. 1.42	15 June	Sunk by A/C, during attack on convoy, E. Mediterranean.
	BEDOUIN	1,870	15. 3.39	15 June	Sunk by A/C, torpedo, Central Mediterranean.
	HASTY	1,340	11.11.36	15 June	Sunk by U/B, torpedo, E. Mediterranean.
	NESTOR (on loan to R.A.N.).	1,760	12. 2.41	15 June	Sunk by A/C, bombs, E. Mediterranean.
	KUJAWIAK (ex OAKLEY) (on loan to Polish Navy).	1,050	17. 6.41	16 June	Sunk by mine off Malta.
	WILD SWAN ...	1,120	14.11.19	17 June	Sunk by A/C, bombs, Western Approaches.
	FORESIGHT	1,350	15. 5.35	13 Aug.	Sunk by A/C, torpedo, Central Mediterranean.
	BERKELEY	1,000	6. 6.40	19 Aug.	Sunk by A/C during operations at Dieppe.
	SIKH	1,870	12.10.38	14 Sept.	Sunk by gunfire, shore batteries, Tobruk.
	ZULU	1,870	6. 9.38	14 Sept.	Sunk by A/C, bombs, E. Mediterranean.
	SOMALI (Leader) ...	1,870	7.12.38	24 Sept.	Sunk in tow, after U/B, torpedo (20th), off Iceland.
	VETERAN	1,120	13.11.19	26 Sept.	Sunk by U/B, torpedo, N. Atlantic.
	BROKE (Leader)... ...	1,480	20. 1.25	8 Nov.	Sunk by gunfire, shore batteries, Algiers.

* Subsequently Salved.

Class	Name	Tonnage	Date of Completion	Date of Loss	How Lost and Where
DESTROYERS (*cont.*)	MARTIN	1,920	4. 4.42	1942 10 Nov.	Sunk by U/B, torpedo, W. Mediterranean.
	QUENTIN	1,705	15. 4.42	2 Dec.	Sunk by A.C, torpedo, W. Mediterranean.
	PENYLAN	1,050	31. 8.42	3 Dec.	Sunk by E/B, torpedo, English Channel.
	BLEAN	1,050	23.8.42	11 Dec.	Sunk by U/B, torpedo, West of Oran, Algeria.
	FIREDRAKE	1,350	30. 5.35	16 Dec.	Sunk by U/B, torpedo, N. Atlantic.
	PARTRIDGE	1,540	22. 2.42	18 Dec.	Sunk by U/B, torpedo, W. Mediterranean.
	ACHATES	1,350	27. 3.30	31 Dec.	Sunk by S.C. gunfire, when escorting convoy, Barent's Sea, Arctic.
SUBMARINES ...	TRIUMPH	1,090	2. 5.39	20 Jan.	Lost, possibly mined, Aegean Sea. Formally Paid Off.
	TEMPEST	1,090	6.12.41	13 Feb. Approx.	Sunk by D/C, Italian S.C., Gulf of Taranto.
	P.38	540	17.10.41	25 Feb.	Lost, possibly mined, Gulf of Hammamet, Tunisia.
	P.39	540	16.11.41	26 Mar.	Sunk by A/C, bombs, at Malta.
	P.36	540	24. 9.41 ⎫	1 Apr.	Sunk by A/C during raid on Malta Harbour.
	PANDORA	1,475	30. 6.30 ⎬		
	UPHOLDER	540	31.10.40 ⎭	14 Apr.	Lost, Probably S.C., D/C, off Tripoli.
	JASTRZAB (*ex* P.551) (on loan to Polish Navy).	800	9. 7.23	2 May	Sunk by gunfire, own forces, N. Norway, Arctic Ocean, after accidental damage.
	URGE	540	12.12.40	6 May	Lost, possibly mined, E. Mediterranean.
	OLYMPUS	1,475	14. 6.30	8 May	Sunk by mine off Grand Harbour, Malta.
	P.514	530	7.10.18	21 June	Rammed and Sunk by own Forces, W. Atlantic.
	THORN	1,090	26. 8.41	11 Aug.	Lost, probably mined, Libya, E. Mediterranean. Formally Paid Off.
	TALISMAN	1,093	29. 6.40	18 Sept.	Lost, in Sicilian Channel. Formally Paid Off.
	UNIQUE	540	27. 9.40	24 Oct.	Lost, cause unknown, West of Gibraltar Straits.
	UNBEATEN	540	20.11.40	11 Nov.	Lost, possibly by own forces, Bay of Biscay.
	UTMOST	540	17. 8.40	24 Nov.	Lost, probably by S.C., D/C, off Cape Marittimo, West of Sicily.
	P.222	715	4. 5.42	12 Dec.	Lost, probably by S.C, D/C, off Naples.
	TRAVELLER	1,090	10. 4.42	12 Dec.	Lost, probably by D/C from Italian T.B., Gulf of Taranto. Formally paid off.
CHARIOTS ...	No. VI	1·2*	8. 9.42 ⎫	31 Oct.	Lost in Operation TITLE (projected attack on TIRPITZ in Ofot Fiord, Norway).
	No. VIII	1·2*	11. 9.42 ⎭		
ARMED MERCHANT CRUISER.	HECTOR (R)	*11,198*	1924	5 Apr.	Bombed and set on fire during air raid on Colombo.
ANTI-AIRCRAFT SHIPS.	CAIRO	4,200	14.10.19	12 Aug.	Sunk by U/B, torpedo, off Bizerta, Tunisia.
	COVENTRY	4,290	21. 2.18	14 Sept.	Sunk by dive bombers, E. Mediterranean.
	CURAÇOA	4,290	18. 2.18	2 Oct.	Lost in collision, N.W. Approaches.
AUXILIARY ANTI-AIRCRAFT SHIP.	TYNWALD	3,650 (deep)	1.10.41	12 Nov.	Sunk by mine, off Bougie, Algeria.
SLOOP	IBIS	1,300	30. 8.41	10 Nov.	Sunk by A/C, W. Mediterranean
CORVETTES ...	ARBUTUS	900	12.10.40	5 Feb.	Sunk by U/B, torpedo, N. Atlantic.
	ALYSSE (*ex* ALYSSUM) (On loan to Free French Force).	950	17. 6.41	8 Feb.	Sunk by U/B, torpedo, W. Atlantic.
	SPIKENARD (On loan R.C.N.).	900	7. 4.41	11 Feb.	Sunk by U/B, torpedo, N. Atlantic.

* Submerged.

Class	Name	Tonnage	Date of Completion	Date of Loss	How Lost and Where
CORVETTES (cont.)	HOLLYHOCK	1,010	19.11.40	1942 9 Apr.	Sunk by A/C, bombs, East of Ceylon.
	AURICULA	915	5. 3.41	5 May	Mined in Courrier Bay, Madagascar.
	MIMOSA (On loan to Free French Force).	1,015	11. 5.41	9 June	Sunk by U/B, torpedo, W. Atlantic.
	GARDENIA	1,015	24. 5.40	9 Nov.	Sunk in collision with own Forces, off Oran, Algeria.
	MONTBRETIA (On loan to R. Nor. N.).	1,015	29. 9.41	18 Nov.	Sunk by U/B, torpedo, N. Atlantic.
	MARIGOLD	1,015	28. 2.41	9 Dec.	Sunk by A/C, torpedo, West of Gibraltar Straits.
	SNAPDRAGON	955	28.10.40	19 Dec.	Sunk by A/C, bombs, Central Mediterranean.
CUTTERS	CULVER	1,546	1929	31 Jan.	Sunk by U/B, torpedo, N. Atlantic.
	HARTLAND	1,546	1928 }	8 Nov.	Sunk by gunfire, Oran Harbour.
	WALNEY	1,546	1930 }		
AUXILIARY A/S VESSELS.	SHU KWANG (R) ...	788	1924	13 Feb.	Sunk by A/C, Dutch East Indies.
	SIANG WO (R)	2,595	1926	13 Feb.	Bombed and beached, Dutch East Indies.
	KUALA (R)	954	1911	14 Feb.	Sunk by A/C, Dutch East Indies.
	TIEN KWANG (R) ...	787	1925	Feb.	Lost or destroyed to prevent falling into enemy hands, Singapore Area.
	MATA HARI (R) ...	1,020	1915	28 Feb.	Sunk by A/C in Sunda Strait, Java Sea.
PATROL VESSEL ...	GIANG BEE (R) ...	1,646	1908	Feb.	Lost or destroyed to prevent falling into enemy hands, Singapore Area.
RIVER GUN BOATS	SCORPION	700	14.12.38	13 Feb.	Sunk by gunfire from Japanese S.C., Banka Straits, Sumatra, after attack by A/C (9th).
	DRAGONFLY	625	5. 6.39	14 Feb. }	Sunk by A/C, bombs, after leaving Singapore.
	GRASSHOPPER ...	625	13. 6.39	14 Feb. }	
MINELAYER ...	KUNG WO (R)	4,636	1921	14 Feb.	Sunk by A/C, bombs, near Lingga Archipelago, Singapore Area.
MINESWEEPERS ...	HUA TONG (R) ...	280	1927	13 Feb. (approx.)	Sunk by A/C in Palembang River, Sumatra.
	CHANGTEH (R)	244	—	14 Feb.	Sunk by A/C, bombs, Singapore Area.
	KLIAS (R)	207	1927	15 Feb.	Scuttled at Palembang, Sumatra.
	JARAK (R)	208	—	17 Feb.	Sunk by A/C, bombs, Singapore Area.
	MALACCA (R)	210	1927	18 Feb.	Scuttled in Tjemako River, Sumatra.
	FUH WO (R)	953	1922 }		Lost by enemy action or destroyed to prevent falling into enemy hands at Singapore.
	LI WO (R)	707	1938 }	Feb.-Mar.	
	SIN AIK LEE (R) ...	198	1928 }		
	TAPAH (R)	208	1926 }		
	SCOTT HARLEY (R) ...	620	1913	3 Mar.	Sunk, probably by S.C., Indian Ocean.
	ABINGDON	710	6.11.18	5 Apr.	Sunk by A/C, bombs, during raid on Malta.
	FITZROY	800	1. 7.19	27 May	Sunk by mine off Great Yarmouth.
	GOSSAMER	815	31. 3.38	24 June	Sunk by A/C, bombs, in Kola Inlet, N. Russia.
	NIGER	815	4. 6.36	6 July	Sunk by mine off Iceland.
	LEDA	815	19. 5.38	20 Sept.	Sunk by U/B, torpedo, Greenland Sea.
	CROMER	656	4. 4.41	9 Nov.	Sunk by mine, E. Mediterranean.
	ALGERINE	940	23. 3.42	15 Nov.	Sunk by U/B, torpedo, off Bougie, Algeria.
	BRAMBLE	815	22. 6.39	31 Dec.	Sunk by S.C, gunfire, Barents Sea, Arctic.
MOTOR MINE-SWEEPERS.	No. 180	226	29. 1.42	13 Feb.	Rammed in convoy, sank off Tyne.
	51	226	29.11.41	4 Mar.	Scuttled, South of Java, to prevent falling into enemy hands.

Class	Name	Tonnage	Date of Completion	Date of Loss	How Lost and Where
				1942	
MOTOR MINE-SWEEPERS (cont.)	No. 174	226	6. 7.42	12 July* ·	Sunk in A/C. attack, Brixham, Devon.
DEGAUSSING SHIP	DAISY (R)	50	1902	25 Apr.	Lost through heavy weather at Greenock.
STEAM GUN BOAT	No. 7	135	11. 3.42	19 June	Sunk in action with S.C. English Channel.
MOTOR TORPEDO BOATS.	No. 47	33	8. 7.41	17 Jan.	Sunk in action by S.C., off Gris Nez, N.E. France.
	74	33	17.12.41	28 Mar. (approx.)	Lost after leaving St. Nazaire.
	215	17	6.12.40	29 Mar.	Paid off, presumed lost.
	220	35	30. 7.41	13 May	Sunk in action with E/B. off Ambleteuse, N.E. France.
	338	—	—	16 May	Wrecked by fire and explosion, Trinidad.
	259	32	—	June	Lost in tow in Mediterranean.
	201	38·6	27.11.41	15 June ⎫	Sank after action with S.C.
	44	33	1. 4.41	7 Aug. ⎬	Dover Straits.
	237	38·6	18. 6.42	7 Aug.	Sank after action with S.C., off Barfleur, France.
	43	33	13. 1.41	18 Aug.	Sunk by S.C. off Gravelines, N.E. France.
	218	35	9. 6.41	18 Aug.	Sunk by S.C. and mine, Dover Straits.
	308	34·4	31. 1.42 ⎫		
	310	38	10. 2.42 ⎪	14 Sept.	Lost probably by A/C. attack, Tobruk.
	312	34·4	21. 2.42 ⎬		
	314	34·4	2. 3.42 ⎭		
	29	34	2. 6.40	6 Oct.	Sank after collision when in action with E/B's. North Sea.
	87	38·6	12. 6.42	31 Oct. ⎫	Sunk by mine, North Sea.
	30	34	11. 7.40	18 Dec. ⎬	
MOTOR GUN BOATS	No. 314	67	26. 6.41	28 Mar.	Sunk by own forces at St. Nazaire, as no longer serviceable.
	328	67	13.10.41	21 July	Lost during attack on enemy convoy, Dover Straits.
	601	85	9. 3.42	24 July	Sunk by enemy action, Dover Straits.
	501	—	19. 5.42	27 July	Sunk after internal explosion, off Lands End, Cornwall.
	335	67	3.10.41	10/11 Sept.	Seriously damaged, set on fire in action with S.C., North Sea.
	18	30	22. 5.41	30 Sept.	Sunk by gunfire, S.C., off Terschelling, Holland.
	78	33	8. 6.42	2/3 Oct.	Attacked by S.C., gunfire, off Holland, beached and abandoned.
	76	33	14. 5.42	6 Oct.	Sunk by E/B, North Sea.
	19	30	28. 7.41	6 Nov.	Bombed and wrecked on slipway.
MOTOR LAUNCHES	KELANA (R)	88	—	16 Jan.	Sunk by A/C. Malaya.
	PENGHAMBAT	—	— ⎫	Feb.	Lost or destroyed to prevent falling into enemy hands at Singapore.
	PENINGAT (R)	—	— ⎬		
	No. 311	73	29.11.41	14 Feb.	Sunk by Japanese gunfire, Banka Straits, Sumatra.
	169	73	27.11.40	15 Feb.	Destroyed by fire and explosion, Gibraltar Harbour.
	310	73	29.11.41	15 Feb.	Lost by enemy action, S.C., Tjebia Island.
	1062	40	1.42	16 Feb.	Sunk by gunfire, Banka Straits, Sumatra.
	1063	40	1.42	1 Mar.	Sunk in action, Tanjong Priok, Java.
	129	73	14.10.40	22 Mar.	Sunk by A.C. bombs, off Algeria.
	457	73	21.11.41	28 Mar.	Sunk in action, St. Nazaire.
	156	73	18.12.40 ⎫		Sunk by own forces at St. Nazaire as no longer serviceable.
	270	73	26. 6.41 ⎬	28 Mar.	
	446	73	21.11.41 ⎭		
	177	73	12.40 ⎫		
	No. 192 (On loan to Free French Force).	73	1. 8.41		
			⎬	28 Mar.	Missing, presumed sunk, at St. Nazaire.
	No. 262 (On loan to Free French Force).	73	18. 6.41 ⎭		

* Subsequently salved.

Class	Name	Tonnage	Date of Completion	Date of Loss	How Lost and Where
				1942	
MOTOR LAUNCHES (cont.)	No. 267 (On loan to Free French Force).	73	25. 7.41		
	No. 268 (On loan to Free French Force).	73	17. 7.41	28 Mar.	Missing, presumed sunk, at St Nazaire.
	No. 298	73	21.11.41		
	306	73	18.12.41		
	447	73	8. 1.42	28 Mar.	Sunk in action, St. Nazaire.
	160	73	27.12.40	6 May	Sunk by A/C. bombs, Brixham, S. Devon.
	130	73	9.10.40	7 May	Sunk by gunfire during engagement off Malta.
	301	73	2.12.41	9 Aug.	Sunk by explosion, Freetown Area.
	103	57	28. 6.40	24 Aug.	Sunk by mine, Dover Straits.
	352	73	9. 6.42	14 Sept.	Sunk by A/C, Tobruk, Libya.
	353	73	26. 5.42		
	1153	40	18. 8.42	Sept.	Destroyed by enemy action en route for Turkey.
	339	73	16.10.41	7 Oct.	Sunk by S.C., torpedo, North Sea.
	242	73	28. 5.41	29 Nov.	Gutted by fire.
TRAWLERS ...	IRVANA (R)	276	1917	16 Jan.	Sunk by A/C off Yarmouth, Norfolk.
	ERIN (R)	394	1933	18 Jan.	Sunk by explosion, Gibraltar Harbour.
	HONJO (R)	308	1928		
	ROSEMONDE (R) ...	364	1910	22 Jan.	Probably torpedoed by U/B, Atlantic.
	LOCH ALSH (R) ...	358	1926	30 Jan.	Sunk by A/C, Humber Area.
	CAPE SPARTEL (R) ...	346	1929	2 Feb.	
	CLOUGHTON WYKE (R)	324	1918	2 Feb.	
	BOTANIC	670 (deep)	1928	18 Feb.	Sunk by A/C, bombs, North Sea.
	WARLAND	406 (deep)	—		
	NORTHERN PRINCESS (R) (On loan to U.S.N.).	655	1936	7 Mar.	Sunk, cause unknown, W. Atlantic.
	NOTTS COUNTY (R) ...	541	1937	8 Mar.	Sunk by mine or U/B, South of Iceland.
	STELLA CAPELLA ...	815 (deep)	1937	19 Mar.	Missing, Iceland Area.
	SOLOMON (R)	357	1928	1 Apr.	Mined and sunk, North of Cromer.
	ST. CATHAN (R) (On loan to U.S.N.).	565	1936	11 Apr.	Sunk in collision off S. Carolina, U.S.A.
	LORD SNOWDON (R) ...	444	1934	13 Apr.	Sunk in collision off Falmouth.
	CORAL	705	1935	Apr.	Sunk by A/C during raid on Malta.
	JADE	630	1933	21 Apr.	
	SENATEUR DUHAMEL (On loan to U.S.N.) (R) ...	913	1927	6 May	Sunk in collision off Wilmington, U.S.A.
	BEDFORDSHIRE (On loan to U.S.N.).	913 (deep)	1935	11 May	Sunk by U/B off Cape Lookout, N. Carolina.
	BEN ARDNA (R) ...	226	1917	12 May	Sunk in collision, Tyne Area.
	AGHIOS GEORGIOS IV (R)	164	—	8 June	Sunk in Mozambique Channel.
	KINGSTON CEYLONITE (On loan to U.S.N.).	940	1935	15 June	Sunk by mine off Chesapeake Bay, U.S.A.
	TRANQUIL (R)	294	1912	16 June	Sunk in collision off Deal.
	SWORD DANCE	530	20. 1.41	5 July	Sunk in collision, Moray Firth, E. Scotland.
	MANOR (R)	314	1913	9 July	Sunk during E/B attack, English Channel.
	LAERTES	530	9. 4.41	25 July	Sunk by U/B, torpedo, Freetown Area.
	PIERRE DESCELLIERS (R)	153	1933	13 Aug.	Sunk by A/C, bombs, off Salcombe.
	WATERFLY (R)	387	1931	17 Sept.	Sunk by A/C off Dungeness.
	ALOUETTE (R)	520	1939	19 Sept.	Sunk by U/B, torpedo, off Portugal.
	PENTLAND FIRTH (On loan to U.S.N.).	900 (deep)	1934	19 Sept.	Sunk in collision off New York.
	LORD STONEHAVEN (R)	444	1934	2 Oct.	Sunk during E/B attack off Eddystone, English Channel.
	INVERCLYDE (R) ...	215	1914	16 Oct.	Sank in tow off Beachy Head.
	ULLSWATER	555	15.11.39	19 Nov.	Sunk by E/B, probably torpedoed, English Channel.
	LEYLAND	857 (deep)	1936	25 Nov.	Sunk in collision, Gibraltar Bay.
	BEN ROSSAL (R) ...	260	1929	29 Nov.*	Sank at moorings.

* Subsequently salved.

Class	Name	Tonnage	Date of Completion	Date of Loss	How Lost and Where
				1942	
TRAWLERS (cont.)	JASPER	596	1932	1 Dec.	Sunk by E/B., torpedo, English Channel.
	BENGALI	880 (deep)	1937		
	CANNA	545	7. 4.41	5 Dec.	Sunk by explosion at Lagos, Nigeria.
	SPANIARD	880 (deep)	1937		
WHALERS ...	SOTRA (R)	313	1925	29 Jan.	Sunk by A/C., off Bardia, Libya.
	TRANG (R)	205	1912	14 Feb.	Set on fire and abandoned Cooper Channel, Singapore.
	RAHMAN (R)	209	1926	1 Mar.	Lost or destroyed, Batavia.
	GEMAS (R)	207	1925	2 Mar.	Scuttled, Tjilatjap, Java.
	JERANTUT (R) ...	217	1927	8 Mar.	Scuttled, Palembang, Sumatra.
	SHERA (R)	253	1929	9 Mar.	Capsized in heavy swell and pack ice, Barents Sea.
	JERAM (R)	210	1927	Mar.	Presumed lost, Singapore Area.
	SULLA (R)	251	1928	25 Mar.	Sunk, probably by S.C., Barents Sea. Formally paid off.
	SVANA (R)	268	1930	8 Apr.	Sunk by A/C.. at Alexandria.
	THORGRIM (R) ...	305	1936		
	SAMBHUR (R) ...	223	1926	5 May	Stranded off Colombo.
	COCKER (R) ...	305	1936	3 June	Sunk by U/B. off Bardia, Libya.
	PARKTOWN (R) ...	250	1929	21 June	Sunk by E/B.'s off Tobruk, Libya.
YACHTS ...	SILVIA (R)	—	—	15 Feb.	Constructive total loss.
	SURPRISE	1,144	1896	28 Feb.	Caught fire and capsized at Lagos, West Africa.
	SONA	519	1922	4 Jan.	Sunk by A/C. during attack on Poole, Dorset.
	THALIA	161	1904	11 Oct.	Sunk in collision Lymn of Lorne, West Scotland.
BOOM DEFENCE VESSELS.	DOWGATE	290	18.11.35	Feb.	Lost or destroyed to prevent falling into enemy hands at Singapore.
	LUDGATE	290	18.11.35		
	CHORLEY (R) ...	284	1914	25 Apr.	Foundered off Start Point, Devon.
	TUNISIAN (R) ...	238	1930	9 July	Mined and sunk, Harwich Area.
	PANORAMA	548	1919	30 Oct.*	Overdue at Bathurst, W. Africa. Formally paid off.
NAVAL SERVICING BOAT.	No. 9 (On loan to U.S. Authorities).	20	–.12.40	14 Sept.	Sunk.
DESTROYER DEPÔT SHIP.	HECLA	10,850	6. 1.41	12 Nov.	Sunk by U/B., Torpedo, West of Gibraltar Straits.
SUBMARINE DEPÔT SHIP	MEDWAY	14,650	6. 7.29	30 June	Sunk by U/B., torpedo, off Alexandria.
BOOM ACCOMMODATION SHIP.	SUI WO (R)	2,672	1896	Feb.	Lost or destroyed to prevent falling into enemy hands at Singapore.
BASE SHIP ...	ANKING (R)	3,472	1925	3 Mar.	Sunk by gunfire from Japanese S.C., South of Java, Indian Ocean.
TUGS	DAISY (R)	—	—	2 Jan.	Foundered on passage from Alexandria to Tobruk.
	PENGAWAL	—	—	14 Feb.	Sunk by A/C., Durian Straits, Singapore.
	ST. BREOCK	810	—	14 Feb.	Sunk by A/C., bombs, off Sumatra.
	ST. JUST	810	1919	14 Feb.	Sunk by A/C., Durian Straits, Singapore.
	WO KWANG (R) ...	350	1927	Feb.	Assumed lost at Singapore.
	VAILLANT (R) ...	58	—	15 Feb.	Formally paid off.
	YIN PING (R) ...	—	1914	15 Feb.	Sunk by gunfire.
	ST. SAMPSON (R) ...	451	1919	7 Mar.	Foundered in Red Sea.
	ADEPT	700	–.3.42	17 Mar.	Grounded, total loss, Hebrides, W. Scotland.
	WEST COCKER ...	229	30.8.19	6 Apr.	Sunk by A/C. during raid on Malta.
	EMILY (R)	—	—	7 Apr.	
	HELLESPONT	690	—	Apr.	
	J.T.A. 6 (R)	—	—	Apr.*	Constructive total loss.

* Subsequently salved.

Class	Name	Tonnage	Date of Completion	Date of Loss	How Lost and Where
Tugs (cont.)	Andromeda (R) ...	—	—	1942 18 Apr.	Sunk by A/C during raid on Malta.
	C. 308	154	—	11 May ⎫	Sunk by mine off Malta
	St. Angelo	150 (deep)	1935	30 May ⎭	
	Vision	—	—	18 Jun.	Sunk at Mersa Matruh, Egypt.
	Alaisia (R)	72	1929	20 Jun.	Lost by enemy action at Tobruk, Libya.
	J.T.A. 1 (R)	—	— ⎫		
	J.T.A. 7 (R)	—	— ⎬ 20 Jun.		Lost at Tobruk, Libya.
	J.T.A. 14 (R)	—	— ⎭		
	St. Olaves (R)	468	1919	21 Sept.	Grounded, total loss, off Duncansby Head, N.E. Scotland.
	Caroline Moller (R)	444	1919	7 Oct.	Torpedoed and sunk by E/B's, North Sea.
	Baia (R)	—	—	3 Nov.	Lost in tow between Mogadishu and Mombasa.
	St. Issey	810	28.12.18	28 Dec.	Sunk, probably by U/B, off Benghazi, Libya.
Mooring Vessel	Moor	767	15.8.19	Apr.	Blown up and Sunk by enemy action at Malta.
Drifters ...	Unicity (R)	96	1919	31 Jan.	Capsized and sank while on sweeping duties of Blyth.
	Boy Roy (R)	20	—	11 Feb.	Cause and place unknown.
	Victoria I (R)	—	—	25 Mar.	Sunk by enemy action.
	Catherine (R)	78	1914	8 Jun.	Foundered in Scapa area, Orkneys.
	Trusty Star	96	1920	10 June ⎫	Mined off Malta.
	Justified	93	1925	16 June ⎭	
	Highland Queen (R)	—	—	20–21 June	Scuttled during fall of Tobruk, Libya.
	Intrepede (R)	—	—	13 Aug.	Sunk by A/C off Salcombe.
	Golden Sunbeam (R)	84	1920	19 Aug.	Sunk in Collision off Dungeness, English Channel.
	Winsome (R)	46	1902	18 Nov.	Sunk at Fairlie, total loss.
	Legend (R)	—	—	28 Dec.	Cause and place unknown.
Tankers and Oilers.	Nyholt (R)	8,087	1931	17 Jan.	Sunk by U/B, W. Atlantic.
	Circe Shell (R) ...	8,207	1931	21 Feb.	Sunk by U/B off Venezuela.
	Finnanger (R) ...	9,551	1928	24 Feb.	Sunk by U/B, N. Atlantic.
	War Sirdar	5,518	−. 2.20	1 Mar.	Lost on reef, N.W. Batavia.
	Francol	2,623 (E)	18.12.17	3 Mar.	Sunk by gunfire, Japanese S.C., South of Java.
	Slavol	2,623	1.11.17	26 Mar.	Sunk by U/B, torpedo, en route for Tobruk, Libya.
	Svenor (R)	7,616	1931	27 Mar.	Sunk by U/B, W. Atlantic.
	Plumleaf	5,916	11. 3.17	4 Apr.	Sunk by A/C, bombs, at Malta.
	Sandar (R)	7,624	1928	2 May	Sunk by U/B off Tobago, W. Indies.
	Beth (R)	6,852	1930	18 May	Sunk by U/B, off Barbados, W. Indies.
	Montenol	2,646	20.11.17	21 May	Torpedoed by U/B, N. Atlantic. Sunk by own forces.
	Aldersdale	8,402	17. 9.37	26 May	Sunk, Cause unknown, Barents Sea, Arctic.
	Dinsdale	8,250	11. 4.42	31 May	Sunk by U/B, torpedo, S. Atlantic.
	Slemdal (R)	7,374	1931	15 Jun.	Sunk by U/B, N. Atlantic.
	Andrea Brovig (R) ...	10,173	1940	23 Jun. ⎫	Sunk by U/B, W. Indies.
	Leiv Eiriksson (R) ...	9,952	1936	27 Jun. ⎭	
	Tankexpress (R) ...	10,095	1937	25 Jul.	Sunk by U/B, off W. Africa.
	Havsten (R)	6,161	1930	3 Aug.	Sunk by U/B, W. Atlantic.
	Malmanger (R) ...	7,078	1920	9 Aug.	Sunk by U/B. off W. Africa.
	Mirlo (R)	7,455	1922	11 Aug.	Sunk by U/B, off W. Africa.
	Thelma (R)	8,297	1937	26 Aug.	Cause and place unknown.
	Vardaas (R)	8,176	1931	30 Aug.	Sunk by U/B, off Tobago, W. Indies.
	Sveve (R)	6,313	1930	10 Sept.	Sunk by U/B, N. Atlantic.
	Thorshavet (R) ...	11,015	1938	3 Nov.	Sunk by U/B, Caribbean Sea.
	Belita (R)	6,323	1933	3 Dec.	Sunk by U/B, off Socotra, Arabian Sea.
Distilling Ship	Staghound (R) ...	468	1894	27 Mar.*	Sunk by A/C, bombs, at Torquay.
Water Carrier	Kalgah (R)	—	—	24 Sept.	Cause and place unknown.
Colliers ...	Zannis L. Cambanis (R)	5,317	1920	21 Jan.	Mined off Singapore.
	Fernwood (R) ...	1,892	1923	18 Sept.*	Sunk by A/C, at Dartmouth.

* Subsequently salved.

Class	Name	Tonnage	Date of Completion	Date of Loss	How Lost and Where
				1942	
FLEET AIR ARM TARGET VESSEL.	ST. BRIAC (R)	2,312	1924	12 Mar.	Sunk by mine off Aberdeen, E. Scotland.
EXAMINATION VESSEL.	SOLEN (R)	—	—	Feb.	Presumed lost at Singapore.
BALLOON BARRAGE VESSEL.	REIDAR (R)	—	1915	28 Dec.	Constructive total loss.
SPECIAL SERVICE VESSELS.	COLLINGDOC	1,780	1925	Mar.	Sunk as Blockship.
	MARS (R)	—	1938	May (date reported)	}Cause and place unknown.
	FREYA I (R)	—	1934	2 May	
	JOKER (R)	—	—	16 July	Lost in tow in heavy weather.
	SJO (R)	—	1938	Dec. (Date reported)	
	ARTHUR (R)	—	—	1 Dec.	}Cause and place unknown.
	ASEL I (R)	10	1919	11 Dec.	
	FIDELITY (R)	2,456	—	30 Dec.	Probably torpedoed by U/B, N. Atlantic.
SMALL MISCELLANEOUS CRAFT.	BOY PETER	14	—	5 Feb.	Lost by fire·
	SHUN AN (R) ...	—	—	Feb.	Lost or destroyed to prevent falling into enemy hands at Singapore.
	MATCHLOCK	70	—	—	Sunk by mine at Canton. Date unknown.
TRANSPORT VESSELS.	ZOODOCHOS PIGHI (R) ...	170	—	13 March.	Sunk by enemy action, E. Mediterranean.
	TERPSITHEA (R) ...	157	1919	29 Apr.	Mined at Famagusta, Cyprus
	FAROUK (R)	91	—	13 June	Cause and place unknown.
ARMED TRADERS	LARUT (R)	894	1927	} 22 Jan.	Sunk by A/C off East Coast, Sumatra.
	RAUB (R)	1,161	1926		
	VYNER BROOKE (R) ...	1,670	1928	14 Feb.	Sunk by A/C off Banka Straits, Sumatra.
	LIPIS (R)	845	1927	Feb.	Believed lost off Singapore by enemy action.
HARBOUR DUTY VESSELS.	NYKEN (R)	111	—	Jan. (date reported)	Constructive total loss.
	CHRYSOLITE (R)	—	1934	15 July	Cause and place unknown.
	VASSILIKI (R)	—	—	23 July	Sunk by U/B on passage from Beirut to Famagusta.
	RUBY (R)	46 Net.	1902	9 Oct.	Wrecked in gale, Scapa Flow, Orkneys.
	BRODRENE (R) ...	—	1922	26 Dec.	Sunk in collision, Hvalfiord, Iceland.
FERRY SERVICE VESSEL.	SANDOY (R)	49	1940	11 Dec.	Cause and place unknown.
DUMB BARGES ...	CELT				
	COOLIE				
	COSSACK				
	DERVISH				
	MAORI				
	MATABELE				Sunk for boom defence purposes, presumed in 1942.
	ODESSA				
	PARTISAN				
	PHILISTINE				
	REDRESS				
	RESPITE				
	REVENGE				
	VALENCIA				
	DARTMOUTH (R) ...	226 (deep) (E)	1923	2 Oct.	Sunk as blockship.
				1943	
AIRCRAFT CARRIER (ESCORT CARRIER).	DASHER	13,785 (deep)	2.7.42	27 Mar.	Sunk, probably due to petrol explosion, South of Cumbrae Island, W. Scotland.
CRUISER	CHARYBDIS	5,450	3.12.41	23 Oct.	Sunk by E/B, torpedoes, English Channel.
DESTROYERS ...	HARVESTER	1,400	25.3.40	11 Mar.	Sunk by U/B, torpedo, N. Atlantic.
	LIGHTNING	1,920	28.5.41	12 Mar.	Sunk by E/B, torpedo, Central Mediterranean.

Class	Name	Tonnage	Date of Completion	Date of Loss	How Lost and Where
DESTROYERS (cont.)	BEVERLEY	1,190	3. 4.20	1943 11 Apr.	Sunk by U/B, torpedo, N. Atlantic.
	ESKDALE (on loan to R. Nor. N.).	1,050	31. 7.42	14 Apr.	Sunk by E/B, torpedo, off Lizard Head, Cornwall.
	PAKENHAM (Leader) ...	1,550	4. 2.42	16 Apr.	Sunk by own forces after damage in action with destroyers off Sicily.
	PUCKERIDGE	1,050	30. 7.41	6 Sept.	Sunk by U/B, torpedo, W. Mediterranean.
	INTREPID	1,370	29. 7.37	27 Sept.	Sunk by A/C, in Leros Harbour Dodecanese.
	ORKAN (ex MYRMIDON) (On loan to Polish Navy).	1,920	5.12.42	8 Oct.	Sunk by U/B, torpedo, N. Atlantic.
	PANTHER	1,540	12.12.41	9 Oct.	Sunk by A/C, bombs, Scarpanto Strait, Dodecanese.
	HURWORTH	1,050	5.10.41	22 Oct.	Sunk by mine off Kalimno, Dodecanese.
	LIMBOURNE	1,050	24.10.42	23 Oct.	Sunk by own forces after damage by E/B, torpedoes, English Channel.
	ECLIPSE	1,375	29.11.34	24 Oct.	Sunk by mine off Kalimno, Dodecanese.
	DULVERTON	1,050	27. 9.41	13 Nov.	Sunk by A/C, glider bomb, off Kos, Dodecanese.
	HOLCOMBE	1,050	16. 9.42	} 12 Dec.	Sunk by U/B., torpedo, West Mediterranean.
	TYNEDALE	1,000	2.12.40		
	HURRICANE	1,400	21.6.40	24 Dec.	Sunk by U/B., torpedo, N. Atlantic.
SUBMARINES ...	P. 48	540	18. 6.42	4 Jan.	Lost, possibly mined, Gulf of Tunis.
	P. 311	1,090	7. 8.42	8 Jan.	Lost, possibly mined, off Maddalena, Sardinia.
	VANDAL	540	20. 2.43	24 Feb.	Lost by accident, Firth of Clyde, W. Scotland.
	UREDD (ex P.·41) (On loan to R. Nor. N.).	540	12.12.41	24 Feb. (approx.)	Lost, probably mined, Bodo area, Norway.
	TIGRIS	1,093	20. 6.40	10 Mar.	Lost, cause unknown, Gulf of Naples.
	THUNDERBOLT	1,090	1.11.40	13 Mar.	Sunk by S.C., D/C, off Cape Milazzo, Sicily.
	TURBULENT	1,090	2.12.41	23 Mar. (approx.)	Lost, probably mined, off Sardinia.
	REGENT	1,475	11.11.30	16 Apr.	Sunk by S.C., Straits of Otranto.
	SPLENDID	715	8. 8.42	21 Apr.	Scuttled after D/C attack, W. Coast of Corsica.
	SAHIB	715	13. 5.42	24 Apr.	Scuttled after D/C attack off Cape Milazzo, Sicily.
	UNTAMED	540	14. 4.43	30 May†	Failed to surface during exercises off Campbeltown.
	PARTHIAN	1,475	13. 1.31	11 Aug.	Lost, possibly mined, S. Adriatic.
	SARACEN	715	27. 6.42	18 Aug.	Sunk by S.C., D/C, off Bastia, Corsica.
	USURPER...	540	2. 2.43	11 Oct. (approx.)	Lost, probably mined, Gulf of Genoa.
	TROOPER	1,090	29. 8.42	17 Oct.	Lost, possibly mined, Aegean Sea.
	SIMOOM	715	30.12.42	19 Nov. (approx.)	Lost, Dardanelles Approach.
X CRAFT	X 8	29·8*	21. 1.43	17 Sept.	} Lost in attack on Tirpitz, Kaa Fiord, Alten Fiord, Norway.
	X 5	29·8*	29.12.42	} 22 Sept.	
	X 6	29·8*	21. 1.43		
	X 7	29·8*	14. 1.43		
	X 10	29·8*	8. 2.43	3 Oct.	
	X 9	29·8*	29. 1.43	15 Oct.	
CHARIOTS	No. XV	1·2*	6.10.42	} 2 Jan.	Lost in Operation PRINCIPAL (Palermo, Italy).
	XVI...	1·2*	10.10.42		
	XIX	1·2*	16.10.42		
	XXII	1·2*	29.10.42		
	XXIII	1·2*	23.10.42		
	X	1·2*	15. 9.42	} 8 Jan.	Lost in Operation PRINCIPAL (Maddalena, Sardinia).
	XVIII	1·2*	14.10.42		
	XII	1·2*	30. 9.42	} 19 Jan.	Lost in Operation WELCOME (Tripoli).
	XIII	1·2*	30. 9.42		

* Submerged.
† Subsequently salved and renamed VITALITY.

Class	Name	Tonnage	Date of Completion	Date of Loss	How Lost and Where
CHARIOTS (cont.).	No. LII ... LVII	1·2* 1·2*	14. 5.43 ⎱ 29. 6.43 ⎰	1943 22 Nov.	Jettisoned in heavy weather in attack on German shipping in Norwegian Fiords.
WELMAN CRAFT ...	No. 10 ...	2·4*	12. 5.43	9 Sept.	Accidently lost during exer-. cises.
	45 ... 46 ... 47 ... 48 ...	2·4* 2·4* 2·4* 2·4*	2. 9.43 ⎫ 7. 9.43 ⎬ 2. 9.43 ⎪ 13. 9.43 ⎭	22 Nov.	Lost during attack on Bergen Harbour, Norway.
AUXILIARY ANTI-AIRCRAFT SHIP.	POZARICA ...	4,540 ·	7. 3.41	13 Feb.	Capsized after torpedo attack by A/C off Bougie, Algeria (29 Jan.).
SLOOP	EGRET ...	1,250	10.11.38	27 Aug.	Sunk by A/C, glider bomb, off N.W. Spain.
FRIGATE	ITCHEN ...	1,325	28.12.42	23 Sept.	Sunk by U/B, torpedo, N. Atlantic.
CORVETTES ...	SAMPHIRE ...	1,015	30. 6.41	30 Jan.	Sunk by U/B, torpedo, W. Mediterranean.
	ERICA ...	955	7. 8.40	9 Feb.	Sunk by mine, N.E. of Benghazi, Libya.
	POLYANTHUS ...	1,015	23. 4.41	20 Sept.	Sunk by U/B, torpedo, N. Atlantic.
MINELAYERS ...	CORNCRAKE ...	700	7.12.42	25 Jan.	Foundered in bad weather, N. Atlantic.
	WELSHMAN ...	2,650	25. 8.41	·1 Feb.	Sunk by U/B, torpedo, off Libya.
	ABDIEL ...	2,650	15. 4.41	10 Sept.	Sunk by mine in Taranto Bay, S. Italy.
MINESWEEPERS ...	HYTHE ...	605	5. 3.42	11 Oct.	Sunk by U/B, torpedo, off Bougie, Algeria.
	CROMARTY ...	605	13.12.41	23 Oct.	Sunk by mine, Western Approaches to Straits of Bonifacio, Mediterranean.
	HEBE ...	815	23.10.37	22 Nov.	Sunk by mine off Bari, E. Italy.
	FELIXSTOWE ...	656	11. 7.41	18 Dec.	Sunk by mine off Sardinia.
	CLACTON ...	605	4. 6.42	31 Dec.	Sunk by mine off Corsica.
B.Y.M.S. MINE-SWEEPER.	No. 2019...	290	15. 8.42	19 Sept.	Mined and beached off Cotrone, Italy.
MOTOR MINESWEEPERS.	No. 89 ...	240	5. 1.42	12 May	Sunk by mine off Bizerta, Tunisia.
	70 ...	240	18. 5.42	24 Sept.	Sunk, believed by mine, in Gulf of Taranto, S. Italy.
MOTOR TORPEDO BOATS.	No. 105 ...	9	– 8.40	1 Jan.	Taken in tow and sunk by own forces.
	262 ...	32	—	24 Feb.	Formally paid off.
	622 ...	95	–.10.42	10 March	Sunk by S.C. when attacking convoy off Terschelling, Holland.
	631 ... (On loan to R.Nor.N.)	95	–. 8.42	14 March	Grounded during attack on ships in Norwegian Fiords.
	63 ... 64 ...	35 35	18. 2.42 ⎱ 23. 2.42 ⎰	2 April	Sunk in collision off Benghazi.
	267 ...	32	—	2 April	Damaged in rough weather on passage, Benghazi to Malta. Sunk by own forces.
	639 ...	95	22. 1.43	28 April	Sunk by A/C, Central Mediterranean.
	311 ...	34·4	17. 2.42	2 May	Sunk by mine, Central Mediterranean.
	61 ...	35	9. 1.42	9 May	Lost by stranding in attack on Motor Barges at Kelibia, Tunisia.
	264 ...	32	—	10 May	Sunk by mine off Sousse, Tunisia.
	316 ...	34·4	12. 3.42	17 July	Sunk by torpedo from Italian cruiser off Reggio, S. Italy.
	288 ...	40	26. 3.43	21/22 July	Sunk by A/C, Augusta, Sicily.
	665 ...	95	5.43	15 Aug.	Sunk by gunfire, shore batteries, Messina, Sicily.
	77 ...	38·6	28. 5.42	8 Sept.	Sunk by A/C off Vibo Valencia, S.W. Italy.

* Submerged.

Class	Name	Tonnage	Date of Completion	Date of Loss	How Lost and Where
MOTOR TORPEDO BOATS (cont.).	No. 636	95	1.43	1943 15 Oct.	Sunk by S.C. off Elba,W. Italy.
	356	37	1. 7.43	16 Oct.	Sunk by S.C. off Holland.
	669	95	29. 4.43	26 Oct.	Sunk by S.C. off Norwegian coast.
	606	90	7. 7.42	3/4 Nov.	Sunk by S.C. off Hook of Holland.
	222 ... ... (On loan to R. Neth. N.).	38·6	15. 2.42	9/10 Nov.	Sunk by mine, North Sea.
	230	38·6	5. 5.42	9/10 Nov.	Rammed by M.T.B.222 in action, North Sea.
	626 ... ... (On loan to R. Nor. N.).	95	8.42⎫	22 Nov.	Lost by fire, Lerwick, Shetland.
	686	95	9. 6.43⎬		
	73	38·6	3.10.41⎭	24 Nov.	Sunk by A/C, Maddalena, Sardinia.
	357	37	25. 8.43	24 Dec.	Sunk by accident after damage by S.C. (23rd).
MOTOR GUN BOATS	No. 109	37	30. 9.42	25 Feb.	Mined and severely damaged (7th). Formally paid off.
	79	37	24. 7.42	28 Feb.	Sunk in action with S.C., Hook of Holland area.
	110	37	14.11.42	29 May	Sunk in action with S.C. in vicinity of Dunkirk.
	648	90	1.43	14 June	Sunk by A/C, Pantellaria, Central Mediterranean.
	644	90	12.42	26 June	Mined between Marsala and Mazzara, Sicily. Sunk by own forces.
	641	90	29.12.42	14/15 July	Sunk by gunfire from battery on Italian mainland, Straits of Messina.
	64	28	11. 2.41	8 Aug.*	Foundered on patrol in heavy weather between Ostend and U.K.
MOTOR LAUNCHES	No. 251	75·5	7.41	6 Mar.	Rammed and sunk by accident, Atlantic.
	1157	40	30.12.42⎫	Apr.	Lost in shipment.
	1212	40	11.12.42⎭		
	133	75·5	12.12.40	11 May	Destroyed by fire and explosion W. Scotland.
	1154	40	30. 1.43	14 May	Sunk by mine at Bizerta, Tunisia.
	108	66	4. 7.40	5 Sept.	Sunk by mine, English Channel
	1015	40	24. 2.41	Oct.	Lost due to heavy gales, E. Mediterranean.
	835	75·5	8. 8.43	12 Oct. ⎫	Sunk by A/C, Leros, Dodecanese.
	579	75·5	3. 6.43	26 Oct. ⎭	
	1054	40	6.11.41	Nov.	Total loss.
	1244	40	20. 8.43	Nov. ⎫	Lost on passage.
	1289	40	2. 7.43	Nov. ⎭	
	358	75·5	9.42	12 Nov.	Lost off Leros, Dodecanese.
	126	75·5	19. 9.40	27 Nov.	Lost after damage by U/B, torpedo, W. Italy.
	1388	40	25.11.43	24 Dec.	Grounded off Hartlepool.
	1121	40	10. 7.42	31 Dec.	Formally paid off.
TRAWLERS ...	HORATIO	545	27. 1.41	7 Jan.	Sunk by E/B, torpedo, W. Mediterranean.
	JURA	545	12. 6.42	7 Jan.	Sunk by torpedo, U/B, or A/C, W. Mediterranean.
	KINGSTON JACINTH (R)	356	1929	12 Jan.	Mined off Portsmouth.
	STRONSAY	545	24. 4.42	5 Feb.	Sunk by explosion, probably mine, off Philippeville, W. Mediterranean.
	TERVANI (R)	409	1930	7 Feb.	Probably sunk by U/B off Cape Bougaroni, Algeria.
	BREDON	750	29. 4.42	8 Feb.	Sunk by U/B, torpedo, N. Atlantic.
	LORD HAILSHAM ...	891 (deep)	1934	27 Feb.	Attacked by E/Bs, probably torpedoed, English Channel.
	MORAVIA (R)	306	1917	14 Mar.	Sunk by mine, North Sea.
	CAMPOBELLO	545	21.10.42	16 Mar.	Foundered on passage to U.K. after being badly damaged at Quebec.
	CAULONIA (R)	296	1912	31 Mar.	Ran aground and foundered, Rye Bay, Sussex.
	ADONIS	1,004	1915	15 Apr.	Sunk by E/B, torpedo, off Lowestoft.

* Subsequently salved.

Class	Name	Tonnage	Date of Completion	Date of Loss	How Lost and Where
TRAWLERS (cont.)	HERRING...	590	15. 4.43	1943 22 Apr.	Sunk in collision, North Sea.
	DANEMAN	1,050 (deep)	1937	8 May	Believed to have struck submerged ice. Abandoned after being taken in tow, N. Atlantic.
	HONG LAM (R)... ...	104	—	26 May	Foundered off Adam's Bridge, between India and Ceylon. Formally paid off.
	RED GAUNTLET (R) ...	338	1930	5 Aug.	Sunk by E/Bs, North Sea.
	ZEE MEEUW (R) ...	—	—	21 Sept.	Sunk in collision, Gravesend Reach, Thames.
	DONNA NOOK (R) ...	307	1916	25 Sept.	Sunk in collision, North Sea.
	FRANC TIREUR (R) ...	314	1916	25 Sept.	Sunk by E/B off Harwich.
	ARACARI (R)	245	1908	3 Oct.	Grounded, total loss, Filicudi Island, North of Sicily.
	MEROR (R)	250	1905	3 Oct.	Mined, Humber area.
	ORFASY	545	14. 7.42	22 Oct.	Lost, probably by U/B torpedo, off W. Africa.
	WILLIAM STEPHEN (R)...	235	1917	25 Oct.	Sunk by E/B off Cromer.
	AVANTURINE (R) ...	296	1930	1 Dec.	Sunk by E/Bs off Beachy Head.
	RYSA	545	13. 8.41	8 Dec.	Sunk by mine off Maddalena, Sardinia.
	KINGSTON BERYL (R)...	356	1928	25 Dec.	Mined, N.W. Approaches.
WHALERS... ...	BODO (R)	351	—	4 Jan.	Mined off E. Coast of Scotland.
	HARSTAD (R)	258	—	27 Feb.	Sunk by E/B, English Channel.
	SANTA (R)	355	1936	23 Nov.	Mined, West of Maddalena, Sardinia.
YACHTS	SARGASSO (R)	223	1926	6 June	Mined off Isle of Wight.
	ATTENDANT (R) ...	357	1913	Nov. (date reported)	Cause and place unknown.
BOOM DEFENCE VESSELS.	FABIOUS (R)	230 (deep)	—	16 Jan.	Sunk.
	BARFLAKE	750	23. 9.42	22 Nov.	Sunk by mine, Naples.
BARRAGE VESSELS	B.V.42	270	9.12.18	22 Dec.	Lost by explosion, Leith Docks, E. Scotland.
NAVAL SERVICING BOAT.	No. 30	8	5. 3.41	8 Nov.	Sunk.
NAVAL AUXILIARY BOAT.	LILY	—	—	24–25 Dec.	Sunk in collision off Portland.
TUGS	HORSA	700	21.12.42	16 Mar.	Grounded, total loss, Osfles Rock, E. Iceland.
	CORY BROS (R)... ...	38	—	9 Aug.	Constructive, total loss.
	TIENTSIN (R)	—	—	26 Oct.	Foundered, Red Sea, on passage to Massawa.
RESCUE SHIP ...	ST. SUNNIVA (R) ...	1,368	1931	22 Jan.	Marine cause.
DRIFTERS ...	PREMIER (R)	14	1918	3 Feb.	Collided with No. 10 Holme Hook Buoy, Humber, and sank.
	UT PROSIM (R)	91	1925	2 Mar.	Sunk by gunfire in Dover Harbour.
	GOLDEN GIFT (R) ...	89	1910	6 Apr.	Sunk in collision in Oban Bay, W. Scotland.
	THORA (R)	37	1930	26 Apr.	Fouled boom in bad weather, Grimsby.
	NORNES (R)	—	1902	14 Aug.	
	NOSS HEAD	22 Net	—	9 Sept.	
	ROSA (R)	83	1908	11 Sept.	Cause and place unknown.
	NISR (R)	—	—	16 Sept.	
	BRAE FLETT (R) ...	54 Net	1902	22 Sept.	
	OCEAN RETRIEVER (R) ...	95	1912	22 Sept.	Mined, Thames Estuary.
	GOLDEN EFFORT (R) ...	86	1914	23 Sept.	Sunk, cause unknown, off Greenock.
	CHANCELLOR (R) ...	24	1916	30 Oct.	Sunk in tow.
	ROSE VALLEY (R) ...	100	1918	16 Dec.	Sunk in collision.
TANKERS AND OILERS.	ALBERT L. ELLSWORTH (R).	8,309	1937	8 Jan. (approx.)	Sunk by U/B off W. Africa.
	MINISTER WEDEL (R) ...	6,833	1930	9 Jan.	
	ROSEWOOD (R)	5,989	1931	9 Mar.	Torpedoed and presumed sunk.
	HALLANGER (R)... ...	9,551	1928	30 Mar.	Sunk by U/B, W. Mediterranean.
	ALCIDES (R)	7,634	1930	2 Aug. (approx.)	Sunk by Japanese Raider, Indian Ocean.

Class	Name	Tonnage	Date of Completion	Date of Loss	How Lost and Where
				1943	
TANKERS AND OILERS (*cont.*)	THORSHOVDI (R) ...	9,944	1937	4 Aug.	War cause.
	MARIT (R)	5,542	1918	4 Oct.	Sunk by U/B, off Benghazi, Libya.
	LITIOPA (R)	5,356	1917	22 Oct.	Sunk by U/B off W. Africa.
VICTUALLING STORE SHIP.	MORAY (R)	206	1918	13 Mar.	Foundered off Milford Haven.
WATER CARRIER	EMPIRE ARTHUR (R) ...	760	1942	22 Nov.	Capsized and sank, Freetown, W. Africa.
COLLIER	NEVA (R)	1,456	1928	22 Jan.	Presumed sunk by U/B, N. Atlantic.
WATER BOATS ...	ISBJORN (R)	—	—	13 May	Sunk.
	CECIL (R)	—	—	18 Dec.	Constructive total loss.
SPECIAL SERVICE VESSELS.	FEIOY (R)	—	—	Jan.	} Cause and place unknown.
	GULDBORG (R)	—	—	22 Jan.	
	BERGHOLM (R)	50	1935	23 Mar.	
	BRATTHOLM (R) ...	50	1937	30 Mar.	
	DAH PU (R)	1,974	1922	28 June	Torpedoed by U/B, Muscat Harbour, E. Coast of Arabia.
	EVANGELISTRIA (CHIOS 345) (R).	—	—	23 Sept.	Sunk by enemy action.
	BILLDORA (R)	—	—	} 11 Nov.	Sunk by enemy action.
	SQUALLY (R)	—	—		
	WESTWICK (R) ...	18	1935		
SMALL MISCELLANEOUS CRAFT.	NAIEM	—	—	Jan.	Sunk at Tobruk.
	FOLIOT	33	1905	17 Nov.	Sunk in Collision.
HARBOUR DUTY VESSEL.	ST. ANNE (R)	37	—	Dec.	Cause and place unknown.
DUMB BARGES ...	NELL JESS	96	1902	May	Wrecked, English Channel.
	CLACTON	196 (deep) (E).	—	Nov.* (approx.)	} Cause and place unknown.
	FOUR	204 (deep) (E).		Nov. (approx.)	
	GREENFINCH	218 (deep) (E).	—	Nov.* (approx.)	
	MONICA	233 (deep) (E).	—	Nov.* (approx.)	
	SAN FRANCISCO ...	241 (deep) (E).	—	Nov. (approx.)	
	UTOPIA	226 (deep) (E).	—	Nov. (approx.)	
				1944	
CRUISERS	SPARTAN	5,770	10. 8.43	29 Jan.	Sunk by A/C, Glider Bomb, off Anzio, W. Italy.
	PENELOPE	5,270	13.11.36	18 Feb.	Sunk by U/B, torpedo, Anzio area, W. Italy.
	DURBAN	4,850	31.10.21	9 June	Sunk as blockship for Mulberry Harbour, Normandy.
	DRAGON ... ... (on loan to Polish Navy)	4,850	16. 8.18	8 July	Damaged by human torpedo off Normandy. Constructive total loss.
DESTROYERS ...	JANUS	1,760	5. 8.39	23 Jan.	Sunk by A/C, torpedo, off Anzio, W. Italy.
	HARDY (Leader) ...	1,730	14. 8.43	30 Jan.	Sunk by U/B, torpedo, Barents Sea, Arctic.
	WARWICK	1,100	20. 3.18	20 Feb.	Sunk by U/B, torpedo, off N. Cornwall.
	INGLEFIELD (Leader) ...	1,530	25. 6.37	25 Feb.	Sunk by A/C, glider bomb, off Anzio, W. Italy.
	MAHRATTA	1,920	8. 4.43	25 Feb.	Sunk by U/B, torpedo, Barents Sea, Arctic.
	LAFOREY (Leader) ...	1,935	26. 8.41	30 Mar.	Sunk by U/B, torpedo, North of Sicily.
	SVENNER (ex SHARK) ... (On loan to R. Nor. N.)	1,710	18. 3.44	6 June	Sunk by S.C., torpedo, off Normandy.

* Subsequently Salved.

Class	Name	Tonnage	Date of Completion	Date of Loss	How Lost and Where
				1944	
DESTROYERS (cont.)	WRESTLER	1,100	15. 5.18	6 June	Damaged beyond repair by mine off Normandy.
	BOADICEA	1,360	7. 4.31	13 June	Sunk by A/C, torpedo, off Portland, English Channel.
	QUAIL	1,705	7. 1.43	18 June	Sank in tow, Bari to Taranto, after damage by mine (15th Nov. 1943).
	FURY	1,350	18. 5.35	21 June	Damaged beyond repair by mine off Normandy.
	SWIFT	1,710	6.12.43	24 June	Sunk by mine off Normandy.
	ISIS	1,370	2. 6.37	20 July ⎫	Sunk by human torpedo, or
	QUORN	1,000	21. 9.40	3 Aug. ⎭	mine off Normandy.
	ROCKINGHAM	1,190	31. 7.19	27 Sept.	Sunk by mine, E. Scotland.
	ALDENHAM	1,050	5. 2.42	14 Dec.	Sunk by mine, N.E. Adriatic.
SUBMARINES ...	P. 715 (ex GRAPH) ... (German Prize vessel)	880 (submerged)	—	20 Mar.	Dismantled, broke adrift and lost on West Coast of Islay, W. Scotland.
	STONEHENGE	715	15. 6.43	22 Mar. (approx.)	Lost on patrol, probably off Nicobar Islands, Indian Oc.
	SYRTIS	715	23. 4.43	28 Mar.	Sunk by mine off Bodo, Norway.
	SICKLE	715	1.12.42	18 June (approx.)	Sunk, probably mined, Anti-Kithera Channel, Greece.
	B.1 (ex SUNFISH) ... (On loan to Soviet Navy)	670	2. 7.37	27 July	Lost on passage to U.S.S.R. with Soviet crew.
	STRATAGEM	715	9.10.43	22 Nov.	Sunk by S.C., D/C, off Malacca, East Indies.
X CRAFT	X. 22	29·8*	31.10.43	7 Feb.	Lost in collision, Pentland Firth, N. Scotland.
CHARIOTS ...	No. LVIII	1·2*	11. 6.43 ⎫	22 June	Lost in attack on Spezia.
	LX	1·2*	17. 8.43 ⎭		
	LXXIX	1·94*	17. 4.44 ⎫	28 Oct.	Lost in operation, Puket Harbour.
	LXXX	1·94*	15. 5.44 ⎭		
AUXILIARY ANTI-AIRCRAFT SHIP.	GLEN AVON (R) ...	678 (deep)	1912	2 Sept.	Foundered in gale, Seine Bay, Normandy.
SLOOPS	WOODPECKER	1,350	14.12.42	27 Feb.	Stern blown off (20th) by torpedo. Capsized and sank in tow, N. Atlantic.
	KITE	1,350	1. 3.43	21 Aug.	Sunk by U/B, torpedo, Greenland Sea.
FRIGATES ...	TWEED	1.375	28. 4.43	7 Jan. ⎫	Sunk by U/B, torpedo, N.
	GOULD	1,600	18. 9.43	1 Mar. ⎭	Atlantic.
	LAWFORD	1,150	3.11.43	8 June	Bombed and sunk on service as H.Q. ship, Normandy.
	BLACKWOOD	1,150	29. 3.43 ⎫	15 June	Sunk by U/B, torpedo, English
	MOURNE	1,365	30. 4.43 ⎭		Channel.
	BICKERTON	1,300	17.10.43	22 Aug.	Sunk by U/B, torpedo, Barents Sea, Arctic.
	BULLEN	1,300	25.10.43	6 Dec.	Sunk by U/B, torpedo, N.W. Scotland.
	CAPEL	1,150	16. 8.43	26 Dec.	Sunk by U/B, torpedo, off Cherbourg.
CORVETTES ...	ASPHODEL	1,015	11. 9.40	9 Mar.	Sunk by U/B, torpedo, N. Atlantic.
	HURST CASTLE	1,060	9. 6.44	1 Sept.	Sunk by U/B, torpedo, off N.W. Ireland.
	ROSE ... ... (On loan to R. Nor. N.)	1,060	31.10.41	26 Oct.	Sunk in collision, W. Atlantic.
	TUNSBERG CASTLE ... (ex SHREWSBURY CASTLE) (On loan to R. Nor. N.)	1,060	29. 4.44	12 Dec.	Sunk by mine off N. Russia.
NETLAYER ...	MINSTER (R)	707	1924	8 June	Sunk by mine, Seine Bay, Normandy.
MINESWEEPERS ...	CATO	1,110	29. 7.43	6 July ⎫	Sunk by human torpedo, off
	MAGIC	1,110	28.10.43	6 July ⎭	Normandy.
	PYLADES	1,110	27.11.43	8 July	
	LOYALTY	940	22.4.43	22 Aug.	Sunk by mine, or U/B, torpedo, English Channel.
	BRITOMART	815	24. 8.39 ⎫	27 Aug.	Sunk by accident in attack by
	HUSSAR	815	16. 1.35 ⎭		friendly aircraft off Normandy

* **Submerged.**

Class	Name	Tonnage	Date of Completion	Date of Loss	How Lost and Where
B.Y.M.S. MINE-SWEEPERS.	No. 2022	290	12. 9.42	1944 16 Aug.	Lost, after damage by mine, Frejus Gulf, S. France.
	2255	290	30.11.43	5 Oct.	Sunk by mine, Boulogne.
	2030	290	30. 7.42	8 Oct.	Sunk by mine off Le Havre.
	2077	290	7. 7.43	25 Oct.	Sunk by mine, Gulf of Corinth, Greece.
MOTOR MINE-SWEEPERS.	No. 229	255	25.10.42	13 June }	} Sunk by mine off Normandy.
	8	255	8. 1.41	24 June }	
	1019	360	23. 8.43	2 July	Sunk by mine off Cherbourg.
	55	255	3. 9.41	10 July	Sunk by mine off Normandy.
	117	255	7. 4.42	1 Sept.	Sunk by mine, Civita Vecchia, W. Italy.
	278	255	8. 3.43	14 Sept.	Stranded on rocks in Le Rance River, St. Malo, N. France.
	170	255	7. 9.42	12 Oct.	Sunk by mine off Gorgona Island, W. Italy.
	101	255	6. 2.43	29 Nov.	Sunk by mine off Salonika, Greece.
	257	255	9.10.43	11 Dec.	Sunk by mine, River Schelde, Holland.
MOTOR TORPEDO BOATS.	No. 417	37	8. 9.42	15/16 Mar.	Sunk by S.C., whilst attacking convoy between Calais and Boulogne.
	352	37	31. 5.43	25/26 Mar.	Sunk in collision, North Sea.
	241	38·6	30. 3.42	31 Mar.	Sunk by enemy action off Ijmuiden and Helder.
	707	95	11.43	18 Apr.	Cut in two in collision off N. Ireland.
	671	95	16. 5.43	24 Apr.	Sunk in torpedo attack on destroyers off Barfleur, N. France.
	708	95	11.43	5 May	Damaged by friendly A/C English Channel, and subsequently sunk by own forces.
	732	97	17. 4.44	28 May	Sunk by accident, English Channel.
	248	41	4. 3.43	6 June	Sunk in collision, English Channel.
	681	95	7.43	9/10 June	Sunk when attacking convoy off Holland.
	448	37	23. 9.43	11 June	Sunk by accident in torpedo attack by friendly aircraft off Normandy.
	734	97	30. 5.44	26 June	Damaged by Beaufighters and eventually sunk by own forces, North Sea.
	640	85	1.11.42	26/27 June	Sunk by mine, Leghorn-Spezia area.
	460 (On loan to R.C.N.).	41	22. 3.44	3 July	Sunk by mine off Normandy.
	666	95	10. 6.43	4/5 July	Sunk by S.C. off Holland.
	463 (On loan to R.C.N.).	41	25. 3.44	8 July	Sunk by mine off Normandy.
	434	37	25. 1.43	9 July	Sunk by S.C. off Normandy.
	372	47	7.10.43	23/24 July	Sunk by S.C., gunfire, when patrolling off Cape Loviste, Adriatic.
	412	37	14. 2.42	26/27 July	Sunk in collision off Normandy.
	430	37	16.11.42	26/27 July	Rammed by E/B off Normandy.
	93	38·6	10. 9.42	18 Aug.	Lost in collision off Harwich.
	360	37	30. 6.43 }	1 Oct.	Sunk by S.C. off Ymuiden, Holland.
	347	37	18. 3.43 }		
	287	36·5	12. 3.43 }	24 Nov.	Grounded on Levron Island, Adriatic, and subsequently destroyed by own forces.
	371	—	4.10.43 }		
	782	108	25.10.44	29 Dec.	Sunk by mine off River Schelde, Holland.
MOTOR GUN BOATS	No. 17	30	19.12.40	11 June	Sunk, possibly mined, off Normandy.
	326	67	18. 8.41	28 June	Sunk by mine off Normandy.
	313	67	12. 6.41	16 Aug.	Sunk by mine or torpedo off Normandy.
	663	90	8. 3.43	10 Oct.	Sunk by mine off Maestra Point, N.E. Adriatic.
MOTOR LAUNCHES	No. 210 (On loan to R. Nor. N.).	75·5	7. 4.41	15 Feb.	Sunk by mine off Dieppe.

Class	Name	Tonnage	Date of Completion	Date of Loss	How Lost and Where
MOTOR LAUNCHES (cont.).	1083	40	23.10.41	1944 20 Feb.	Lost through grounding in Gulf of Kos, Aegean.
	387	75·5	1. 6.43	5 Mar.	Destroyed by internal explosion, Beirut Harbour, Syria.
	1380	40	16. 9.43	May	Missing in Aegean.
	265	75·5	30. 5.41 ⎫	1 July	Destroyed by petrol fire and explosion, Freetown, W. Africa.
	287	75·5	23. 8.41 ⎭		
	443	75·5	11.41	12 July	Mined off Vada, W. Italy. Fore part blown off.
	563	75·5	3. 3.43	16 Aug.	Sunk by mine off Frejus, S. France.
	1179	40	4. 3.43	21 Aug.	Sunk off Rio Bueno, Jamaica, in hurricane.
	216	75·5	28. 5.41	28 Sept.	Foundered in heavy weather after being mined (19th), North Sea.
	1227	44	24.11.42	5 Oct.	Sunk by S.C., off Piraeus, Greece.
	1057	40	30. 9.41	13 Oct.	Lost through detonation of demolition charges off Kilindini, E. Africa.
	870	75·5	2. 8.44	15 Oct.	Sunk by mine off Piraeus, Greece.
	916	75·5	16. 9.44	8 Nov.	Sunk by mine at Walsoorden, Holland.
TRAWLERS ...	WALLASEA	545	31. 7.43	6 Jan.	Sunk by S.C., torpedo, off Mounts Bay, Cornwall.
	PINE	545	3. 7.40	31 Jan.	Sunk by E/B, torpedo, off Selsey Bill, Sussex.
	CAP D'ANTIFER (R) ...	—	—	13 Feb.	Sunk by E/Bs off Humber.
	WYOMING (R)	302	1915	20 May	Mined and sunk off Harwich.
	BIRDLIP	750	23.12.41	13 June	Sunk by U/B, torpedo, off W. Africa.
	LORD AUSTIN (R) ...	473	1937	24 June	Mined and sunk, Seine Bay, Normandy.
	GANILLY	545	3. 9.43	5 July	Sunk by mine, English Channel.
	TEXAS	301	—	19 July	Sunk in collision, Jamaica Area.
	LORD WAKEFIELD ...	825 (deep)	1933	29 July	Sunk by A/C off Normandy.
	GAIRSAY	545	30. 4.43	3 Aug.	Sunk by human torpedo off Normandy.
	CHOICE (R)	197	—	25 Aug.	Foundered, total wreck, Arromanches, Normandy.
	MIRABELLE (R)	203	1918	17 Sept.	Rammed and sunk by accident.
	VIDONIA (R)	276	—	6 Oct.	Sunk in collision, English Channel.
	COLSAY	554	4. 3.44	2 Nov.	Sunk by human torpedo off Ostend.
	TRANSVAAL (R)	250	—	18 Nov.	Foundered in gale, English Channel.
	NORTHCOATES (R) ...	277	—	2 Dec.	Sank in tow, through stress of weather, English Channel.
MOTOR FISHING VESSELS.	No. 70	43·5	1. 5.43	27 Feb.	Lost after striking submerged object en route for Casteloriso, Dodecanese.
	1032	93	—. 2.44	13 Sept.	Sunk in tow.
	117	50	30.12.43	14 Oct.	Sunk by explosion, probably mine, off Pasha Island, N. Aegean.
WHALERS	MAALØY (R)	249	—	27 Mar.	Sunk by U/B off Ceylon.
	FIRMAMENT (R)	248	1930	30 May	Grounded, total loss, off Alexandria.
	SOUTHERN PRIDE (R) ...	582	1936	16 June	Stranded, total loss, off Sierra Leone.
	BEVER (R)	252	1930	30 Nov.	Sunk by mine off Pireaus, Greece.
YACHTS	ORACLE	745	—	29 Jan.	Destroyed by fire off Liverpool.
	BREDA	1,207	—	18 Feb.	Sank after collision, Campbeltown Loch.
NAVAL AUXILIARY BOAT.	SPIDER BOY	14	—	14 Jan.	Cause and place unknown.
TRAINING SHIP (Ex BATTLESHIP)	CENTURION.	25,500	—. 5.13	9 June	Sunk as blockship for Mulberry Harbour, Normandy.

Class	Name	Tonnage	Date of Completion	Date of Loss	How Lost and Where
				1944	
TUGS	ADHERENT	700	30. 3.42	14 Jan.	Foundered, N. Atlantic.
	ROODE ZEE (R) ...	468	—	24 Apl.	Sunk by E/B, torpedo, off Dungeness.
	SESAME	700	18. 1.44	11 June	Sunk by E/B, torpedo, off Normandy.
	SOLITAIRE	91	1904	20 June	Capsized and sank off Normandy.
SALVAGE VESSEL	SÀLVIKING	1,490	27. 1.43	14 Feb.	Sunk by U/B, torpedo, Indian Ocean.
DRIFTERS... ...	NOT MANN (R)... ...	—	—	11 Jan. ⎫	Cause and place unknown.
	LE DUE PAOLE (R) ...	—	—	21 Feb. ⎭	
	FORECAST (R)	96	1925	10 Apr.	Sunk at Greenock.
	GLEAM (R)	57	1922	15 June	Sunk in collision.
	FAIRHAVEN (R)... ...	96	1919	5 Sept.	Foundered, N.E. Atlantic.
	SUPPORTER (R)... ...	88	1914	4–5 Nov.	Grounded off Newhaven. Total loss.
HARBOUR TENDER	SENGA (R)	—	—	21 Jan.*	Sunk in collision off Londonderry.
OILER	WAR DIWAN	5,551	22. 8.19	16 Dec.	Sunk by mine, River Schelde, Holland.
WATER CARRIER...	GENERAAL VAN DER HEIJDEN (R).	1,213	1929	14 Apr.	Marine cause.
COLLIERS	OLGA E. EMBIRICOS (R)	4,677	1922	29 Jan.	Sunk by U/B, Gulf of Aden.
	IOANNIS FAFALIOS (R)...	5,670	1919	5 Sept.	War cause.
	YEWDALE (R)	823	1929	3 Oct.	Marine cause.
	P.L.M. 21 (R)	5,400	1921	3 Dec.	Grounded off Milford Haven. Subsequently sank.
WATER BOATS ...	GENERAAL VAN SWIETEN	1,300	1928	14 Apr.	Marine cause.
	CHANT 69 (R)	400	1944	14 June	Capsized off Normandy.
	PETRONELLA (R) ...	2,770	1927	15 Oct.	Mined off Pireaus, Greece.
EXAMINATION VESSEL.	FRATTON (R)	757	1925	18 Aug.	Sunk at anchor by underwater explosion, probably torpedoed by S.C., Seine Bay, Normandy.
SPECIAL SERVICE VESSELS.	DOVER HILL	5,815	1918	7 Feb. ⎫	
	FLOWERGATE	5,200	1911	7 Feb.	
	BECHEVILLE	4,200	1924	8 Feb.	
	PANOS	4,900	1920	8 Feb.	
	ELSWICK PARK	4,200	1920	10 Feb.	
	SALTERSGATE	3,900	1924	11 Feb.	
	ALYNBANK (R)	5,157	1925	Feb.	
	EMPIRE BUNTING ...	6,448	1919	Feb.	
	EMPIRE DEFIANCE ...	4,632	1909	Feb.	
	EMPIRE FLAMINGO ...	5,200	1920	Feb.	
	EMPIRE MOORHEN ...	5,617	1919	Feb.	
	EMPIRE TAMAR	6,581	1907	Feb.	
	EMPIRE WATERHEN ...	6,004	1920	Feb.	
	INGMAN (R)	3,169	1907	Feb.	
	MODLIN	3,569	1906	Feb.	
	VINLAKE...	3,938	1913	21 Feb.	
	LYNGHAUG	2,839	1919	26 Feb.	
	SIREHEI	3,888	1907	26 Feb.	⎬ Sunk as blockships.
	EMPIRE TANA	6,148	1923	Mar.	
	GEORGIOS P.	4,052	1903	Mar.	
	NJEGOS (R)	4,393	1908	Mar.	
	WINHA	3,391	1904	Mar.	
	MANCHESTER SPINNER...	4,767	1918	25 Mar.	
	MARIPOSA	3,800	1914	27 Mar.	
	BENDORAN	5,600	1919	28 Mar.	
	VERA RADCLIFFE ...	5,600	1925	30 Mar.	
	FORBIN (R)	7,291	1922	Apr.	
	INNERTON	5,300	1919	16 Apr.	
	BELGIQUE	4,606	1902	June	
	EMPIRE BITTERN ...	8,500	1902	June	
	PARKHAVEN	4,803	1920	June	
	PARKLAAN	3,807	1911	June	
	NORFALK...	5,672	1919	24 June	
	NORJERV...	5,600	1919	26 June	
	STANWELL	5,800	1914	29 June	
	MAYCREST	5,900	1913	30 June	
	BOSWORTH	6,672	1919	4 Sept. ⎭	

* Subsequently salved.

Class	Name	Tonnage	Date of Completion	Date of Loss	How Lost and Where
SPECIAL SERVICE VESSELS (cont.)	SYLVIA (R)	—	—	1944 20 Sept.	Lost by enemy action.
	DUPLEX (R)	—	—	4 Oct.	Cause and place unknown.
	GRETHE MORTENSEN (R)	35	1943	7 Nov.	Abandoned in sinking condition off N. Foreland, Kent.
SMALL MISCELLANEOUS CRAFT.	AYIOS IOANNIS (CHIOS 466) (R).	—	—	15 Dec.	Cause and place unknown.
	EUSTATHIOS GHIOKIS (R)	—	—	16 Dec.	Constructive total loss.
TRANSPORT VESSELS.	EVANGELISTRIA (SAMOS 82) (R).	—	—	25 Jan.	Constructive total loss.
	TRIUMPH VI (R) ...	46	1903	15 Dec.	Sunk in collision, Rosyth area.
HARBOUR DEFENCE VESSEL.	MANORA (R)	—	1936	17 Dec.	Lost through fouling boom.
HARBOUR DUTY VESSEL.	ISMINI (R)	—	—	16 Oct.	Cause and place unknown.
FERRY SERVICE VESSEL.	SANDVIKHORN (R) ...	78 (Net)	1917	Jan.	Sunk in collision, Londonderry.
SAILING BARGES...	DELTA	—	1898	Nov.	Sank at Harty Point, Sheppey.
	DUNDONALD	50	1897	29 Nov.	Foundered when moored off Chatham.
	E.F.Q.	32	1900	Dec.	Sank at Sheerness.
DESTROYERS ...	DEIATELNYI (ex CHURCHILL) (On loan to Soviet Navy).	1,190	17. 4.20	1945 16 Jan.	Sunk by U/B, torpedo, Arctic Ocean.
	LA COMBATTANTE (ex HALDON) (On loan to French Navy).	1,050	30.12.42	23 Feb.	Sunk by mine, North Sea.
SUBMARINE ...	PORPOISE	1,500	11. 3.33	19 Jan. (Approx.)	Sunk, probably by A/C, Malacca Strait, E. Indies.
CHARIOTS ...	No. V	1·2*	1. 9.42	June (date reported)	Lost, W. Scotland.
	XI	1·2*	19. 9.42		
	XIV	1·2*	5.10.42		
	XVII	1·2*	3.10.42	June	
	XX	1·2*	16.10.42	(date	Lost at Malta.
	XXI	1·2*	19.10.42	reported)	
	XXIV	1·2*	17.11.42		
	XXV	1·2*	23.11.42		
	XXIX	1·2*	18. 1.43	June	
	XXXI	1·2*	19. 1.43	(date	Lost, W. Scotland.
	XXXIV	1·2*	8. 2.43	reported)	
SLOOPS	LARK	1,350	10. 4.44	17 Feb.	Damaged beyond repair by torpedo.
	LAPWING	1,460	21. 3.44	20 Mar.	Sunk by U/B, torpedo, off Kola Inlet, N. Russia.
FRIGATE	GOODALL	1,150	4.10.43	29 Apr.	Torpedoed by U/B, off Kola Inlet, N. Russia. Sunk by own forces.
CORVETTES ...	DENBIGH CASTLE ...	1,060	30.12.44	13 Feb.	Damaged by mine or U/B torpedo, grounded, total loss, N. Russia.
	BLUEBELL	1,060	19. 7.40	17 Feb.	Sunk by U/B, torpedo, Barents Sea, Arctic.
	VERVAIN	1,020	9. 6.41	20 Feb.	Sunk by U/B, torpedo, off S. Ireland.
MINESWEEPERS ...	REGULUS	1,010	20. 5.44	12 Jan.	Sunk by mine, Corfu Channel, Greece.
	GUYSBOROUGH (On loan to R.C.N.).	672	22. 4.42	17 Mar.	Sunk by U/B, torpedo, Bay of Biscay.
	SQUIRREL	940	16. 8.44	24 July	Damaged by mine off Puket, Siam, sunk by own forces.
	VESTAL	940	10. 9.43	26 July	Sunk by A/C, off Puket, Siam.
B.Y.M.S. MINESWEEPER.	No. 2053	290	11. 6.43	28 Apr.	Sunk by mine off Porto Corsini, N.E. Italy.
MOTOR MINESWEEPERS.	No. 248	255	11. 9.43	30 Jan.	Sunk by mine off River Schelde, Holland.

* Submerged.

Class	Name	Tonnage	Date of Completion	Date of Loss	How Lost and Where
MOTOR MINE-SWEEPERS (*cont.*)	No. 68	255	28.12.41	1945 4 Feb.	Sunk by mine off Cephalonia, Greece.
	168	255	5. 7.42	25 June	Sunk by mine in Genoa Harbour, Italy.
MOTOR TORPEDO BOATS.	No. 690	102	15. 9.43	18 Jan.	Lost after striking wreck.
	255	36	30. 7.43		
	438	37	31. 3.43		
	444	37	21. 7.43		
	459 (On loan to R.C.N.).	41	. 2. 3.44		
	461 (On loan to R.C.N.).	41	15. 3.44		
	462 (On loan to R.C.N.).	41	25. 3.44	14 Feb.	Lost by fire and explosion, Ostend Harbour.
	465 (On loan to R.C.N.).	41	31. 3.44		
	466 (On loan to R.C.N.).	41	18. 4.44		
	776	108	8.44		
	789	108	17.10.44		
	791	108	4.11.44		
	798	.108	16.10.44		
	605	102	16. 6.42	17 Feb.	Foundered after striking submerged obstruction on passage Ostend to Dover.
	655	102	− 1.43	21 Mar.	Sunk by mine, Quarnero Gulf, N.E. Adriatic.
	705	102	7. 8.43	23 Mar.	Sunk by mine, Maknare Channel, N.E. Adriatic.
	494	44	9.11.44	7 Apr.	Rammed and sunk by E/Bs, North Sea.
	5001...	108	18.12.44	7 Apr.	Sunk by E/Bs, North Sea.
	710	102	18. 9.43	10 Apr.	Sunk by mine near Zara, N.E. Adriatic.,
	697	102	−. 7.43	17 Apr.	Sunk by mine off Krk Island, N.E. Adriatic.
	715 ... ... (On loan to R. Nor. N.)	102	9.12.43	19 May	Sunk by explosion at Fosnavaag, Norway.
	243	40	18.11.42	July (date reported)	Sunk as targets.
	635	102	−.11.42		
	242	40.	23.10.42	July	Sunk whilst being towed to Malta.
	712	102	10. 2.44	19 July	Formally paid off.
	261	32·4	—	26 Aug.	Sunk at Alexandria.
MOTOR GUN BOATS	No. 99	—	—	Apr.	Constructive total loss.
	2002...	93	5. 7.43	12 May	Sunk by mine on passage Aberdeen to Gothenburg, Sweden.
	2007...	93	28. 8.43	24 May	Broke in two off Aberdeen after grounding (22nd).
MOTOR LAUNCHES	No. 1163...	46	31.12.42	5 Jan.	Sunk by torpedo, probably S.C., Mulat Island, N.E. Adriatic.
	891	75·5	28. 3.44	24 Jan.	Sunk by mine, Kyauk Pyu, North of Ramree Island, Burma.
	183	75·5	10. 2.41	11 Feb.	Sunk after collision with East Pier, Dieppe, N. France.
	1417...	46	28. 3.44	15 Feb.	Sunk by mine, in tow, off Flushing.
	466	75·5	31. 3.42	25 Mar.	Sunk by mine off Walcheren, Holland.
	558	75·5	12. 2.43	5 May	Mined, N. Adriatic, total loss.
	591	75·5	18. 4.44	9 May	Foundered in tidal wave, Sittang River estuary, Burma.
	905	75·5	10. 5.44		
	230	75·5	28. 3.41	17 Aug.	Sunk in collision.
TRAWLERS ...	HAYBURN WYKE (R) ...	324	1917	2 Jan.	Torpedoed by U/B at anchor off Ostend, Belgium.
	NORTHERN ISLES (R) ...	655	1936	19 Jan.	Ran aground while on loop patrol off Durban, S. Africa. Total loss.
	COMPUTATOR (R) ...	286	1919	21 Jan.	Sunk in collision, Seine Bay, Normandy.
	ARLEY (R)	304	1914	3 Feb.	Damaged by mine. Sank in tow, North Sea.
	ELLESMERE	580	12.10.39	24 Feb.	Sunk by U/B, torpedo, English Channel.

Class	Name	Tonnage	Date of Completion	Date of Loss	How Lost and Where
				1945	
TRAWLERS (cont.)	EBOR WYKE (R) ...	348	1929	2 May	Presumed torpedoed by U/B off E. Coast of Iceland.
	CORIOLANUS	545	6. 2.41	5 May	Sunk by mine, N. Adriatic.
	HILDASAY	545	30. 9.41	21 June	Grounded on reef near Kilindini, total loss.
	ELIZABETH THERESE (R)	156	1934	4 July	Sunk.
	LA NANTAISE (R) ...	359	—	8 July	Sunk in collision off S.E. England.
	KURD (R)	352	1930	10 July	Sunk by mine off Lizard Head, Cornwall.
WHALERS... ...	TREERN (R) ... ... (On loan to S.A.N.F.)	247	1929	12 Jan.	Sunk by mine off E. Coast of Greece.
	SOUTHERN FLOWER (R)	328	1928	3 Mar.	Torpedoed by U/B off Reykjavik, Iceland.
	SPERCHEIOS (ex NOBLE NORA) (R). (On loan to R.H.N.)	160	—	3 Apr.	Capsized and sank off Greece.
NAVAL SERVICING BOAT.	No. 38	20	—	9 Feb.	Capsized and sank after damage.
NAVAL AUXILIARY BOATS.	No. 47	—	—	Jan. (date reported)	Cause and place unknown.
	48	—	—		
	49	—	—		
	58	—	—		
	59	—	—		
TUGS	HESPERIA	1,118	21. 5.43	9 Feb.	Grounded off Libya.
	ALLIGATOR	395	6. 2.41	Mar. (date reported)	Cause and place unknown.
	ATHLETE...	570	15.11.43	17 July	Sunk by mine off Leghorn, Italy.
DRIFTERS... ...	GOLDEN WEST (R) ...	—	—	15 Jan.	Foundered in Aberdeen Harbour, E. Scotland.
	HIGH TIDE (R)... ...	106	1919	30 Mar.	Foundered off N. Wales.
	BROADLAND (R) ...	76	1913	6 June	Lost in heavy weather, N. Atlantic.
FUELLING SHIP ...	ILTON CASTLE (R) ...	—	—	1 Aug.	Cause and place unknown.
COLLIER	ROLFSBORG (R)... ...	1,831	1915	13 July	Sunk in collision, Firth of Forth, E. Scotland.
BALLOON BARRAGE VESSELS.	SVERRE (R)	—	1938	2 Jan.	Foundered off E. Coast, England.
	TANEVIK (R)	—	—	19 Jan.	Foundered in tow from Methil to Buckie, E. Scotland.
SPECIAL SERVICE VESSEL.	ARMENIER (R)	914	—	Apr.	Scuttled.
TRANSPORT VESSEL	MARY VI (R)	13	—	2 Mar.	Destroyed by fire.
HARBOUR DUTY VESSEL.	AYIOS IOANNIS (CHIOS 116) (R).	—	—	13 Apr.	Cause and place unknown.
TRAIN FERRY ...	DAFFODIL	2,500	—	18 Mar.	Sank after being mined off Dieppe (17th).

II. SUMMARY OF LOSSES—BY YEAR AND CLASS

Class	3rd Sept., 1939 to 31st Dec., 1939	1940	1941	1942	1943	1944	1st Jan., 1945 to 15th Aug., 1945	Total Number Lost	Total Displacement Tonnage lost (Tons)
Battleships	1	—	2	—	—	—	—	3	95,250
Battle Cruisers	—	—	2	—	—	—	—	2	75,350
Monitor	—	—	1	—	—	—	—	1	7,200
Aircraft Carriers	1	1	1	2	—	—	—	5	100,450 (deep)
Auxiliary Aircraft Carriers	—	—	1	1	1	—	—	3	38,570
Cruisers	—	3	8	8	1	1	2	23	164,230
Destroyers	3	34	22	46	16	16	2	139	195,130
Submarines	1	23	11	18	16	6	1	76	67,673
X Craft	—	—	—	—	6	—	1	7	880 (Sub.)
Chariots	—	—	—	2	11	4	11	28	208·6 (Sub.)
Welman Craft	—	—	—	—	5	—	—	5	35·08 (Sub.) / 12 (Sub.)
Armed Merchant Cruisers	1	9	4	1	—	—	—	15	227,437
Armed Boarding Vessels	—	2	3	—	—	—	—	5	22,832
Ocean Boarding Vessels	—	—	5	—	—	—	—	5	28,579
Auxiliary Fighter Catapult Ships	—	—	2	—	—	—	—	2	10,570
Anti-Aircraft Ships	—	1	1	3	—	—	—	5	21,270
Auxiliary Anti-Aircraft Ships	—	2	—	1	1	1	1	6	4,540 (deep) / 4,328 / 7,334
Sloops	—	3	2	1	1	2	2	11	13,575
Frigates	—	—	—	—	1	8	1	10	12,865
Corvettes	—	1	7	10	3	4	3	28	27,050
Cutters	—	—	—	3	—	—	—	3	4,638
Aux. A/S Vessels	—	1	—	5	—	—	—	6	7,115
Patrol Vessel	—	1	—	—	—	—	—	1	1,646
River Gunboats	—	1	7	3	—	—	—	11	5,833
Convoy Service Ships	—	—	2	—	—	—	—	2	5,271
Minelayers	—	2	2	1	3	—	—	8	9,148 / 16,433
Netlayers	—	1	1	1	—	—	—	3	1,709
Mine Destructor Vessel	—	1	2	—	—	—	—	3	9,070
Minesweepers	—	10	9	18	5	6	4	52	25,064
B.Y.M.S. Minesweepers	—	—	—	—	1	4	1	6	9,728
Motor Minesweepers	—	—	1	3	2	9	3	18	1,740
Degaussing Ships	—	1	—	1	—	—	—	2	4,549
Steam Gun Boat	—	—	—	1	—	—	—	1	1,975
Motor Torpedo Boats	1	4	16	18	25	25	26	115	135
Motor Attendant Craft	—	—	—	—	—	—	—	—	5,723·9 (a)
Motor A/S Boats	—	1	2	—	—	—	—	2	42 (b)
Motor Gun Boats	—	—	5	9	7	4	3	28	1,386 (c)

II. SUMMARY OF LOSSES—BY YEAR AND CLASS—continued

CLASS	3rd Sept., 1939 to 31st Dec., 1939 (No.)	1940 (No.)	1941 (No.)	1942 (No.)	1943 (No.)	1944 (No.)	1st Jan., 1945 to 15th Aug., 1945 (No.)	Total Numbers Lost (No.)	Total Displacement Tonnage lost (Tons)
MOTOR LAUNCHES	—	3	7	30	16	14	9	79	4,819·4 / 88 (d)
TRAWLERS	11	92	57	39	25	16	11	251	36,314 / 10,000 (deep) / 57,435 / 186·5
MOTOR FISHING VESSELS	—	—	—	—	—	3	—	3	9,659
WHALERS	—	2	10	13	3	4	3	35	12,403·5 (c)
YACHTS	—	15	11	4	2	2	—	34	3,793
BOOM DEFENCE VESSELS	1	5	4	5	2	—	—	17	230 / 1,848 (deep)
BARRAGE VESSELS	—	—	1	—	—	—	—	1	270
GATE VESSELS	—	1	—	—	1	—	—	2	298
NAVAL SERVICING BOATS	—	—	—	1	1	1	—	3	48
NAVAL AUXILIARY BOATS	—	—	—	1	1	—	5	7	14 (e)
DESTROYER DEPÔT SHIP	—	—	—	—	1	—	—	1	10,850
SUBMARINE DEPÔT SHIP	—	—	—	1	—	—	—	1	14,650
ACCOMMODATION SHIP	—	—	1	—	—	—	—	1	261
BOOM ACCOMMODATION SHIP	—	—	—	—	—	1	—	1	2,672
TRAINING SHIP	—	—	—	1	—	—	—	1	25,500
BASE SHIP	—	—	—	—	1	—	—	1	3,472
GUARDSHIP	—	1	—	—	—	—	—	1	1,561
TUGS	1	11	7	25	3	4	3	54	6,658 / 150 (deep) / 11,080 (f)
SALVAGE VESSELS	—	—	1	—	—	1	—	2	1,490 (c)
RESCUE SHIP	—	—	—	1	—	—	—	1	1,368
MOORING VESSELS	—	1	—	1	—	—	—	2	767 / 758 (deep)
SCHOONERS	—	3	—	—	—	—	—	3	1,267 (d)
DRIFTERS	3	38	33	11	13	6	3	107	7292·9 / 273 (net) (g)
TENDERS	—	—	—	—	1	1	—	2	—
TANKERS AND OILERS	1	3	7	25	8	1	—	45	331,496 (b)
FUELLING SHIP	—	—	—	1	—	—	—	1	468 (b)
OIL DISTILLING SHIP	—	—	—	—	—	1	—	1	4,690 (b)
STORE CARRIERS	—	—	3	—	—	—	—	3	206
VICTUALLING STORE SHIP	—	—	1	—	—	—	—	1	1,973 (c)
WATER CARRIERS	—	—	1	1	—	1	—	3	1,087
ARMAMENT STORE CARRIER	—	—	1	1	—	1	—	3	9,171
AMMUNITION HULKS	5	—	—	—	—	—	—	5	9,145
FREIGHTERS	—	2	—	—	—	—	—	2	—
COLLIERS	—	3	2	2	1	4	1	13	39,394

	30	317 (e)	284 (h)	359 (l)	205 (k)	208 (m)	100 (m)	Total
WATER BOATS								5 — 4,470 (d)
FLEET AIR ARM TARGET SHIP								1 — 2,312 (b)
MOTOR CANAL BOATS			3					4 — — (d)
EXAMINATION VESSELS	1	1	1	1		1		6 — 2,648 (a)
BALLOON BARRAGE VESSELS	35	7	8	9			2	5 — 651 (h)
SPECIAL SERVICE VESSELS			2	2	2	40	1	100 — 280,444 (i)
SMALL MISC. CRAFT			3			2		9 — 866 (c)
TRANSPORT VESSELS			3			2		6 — 477
ARMED TRADERS		1	4		1	1	1	5 — 6,295 (b)
HARBOUR DEFENCE VESSELS								1 — —
HARBOUR DUTY VESSELS			5		1	1		8 — 148 / 46 (net) (j)
TRAIN FERRY							1	1 — 2,500
FERRY SERVICE VESSELS			1			1		2 — 49 / 78 (net)
SAILING BARGES						1		3 — 123
DUMB BARGES				7		3		21 — 1,544 / 96 (deep) (h)
TOTAL NOS.	30	317	284	359	205	208	100	1,503
TOTAL TONNAGE		(e)	(h)	(l)	(k)	(m)	(m)	(n)
STANDARD DISPLACEMENT	58,723	135,828	305,771·6	254,910	70,561·2	109,475·7	24,488·3	959,757·8
DEEP DISPLACEMENT		758	11,913	24,132	17,274	1,503	—	55,580
SUBMERGED DISPLACEMENT		—	—	2·4	204	916·08	13·2	1,135·68
GROSS REGISTERED TONNAGE	30,738	344,331·8	209,630·5	239,756	87,871	228,711	6,459	1,147,497·3
NET REGISTERED TONNAGE		152	45	46	76	78	—	397

(a) Excludes tonnage of 3 vessels which is unknown.
(b) Tonnage unknown.
(c) Excludes tonnage of 1 vessel which is unknown.
(d) Excludes tonnage of 2 vessels which is unknown.
(e) Excludes tonnage of 6 vessels which is unknown.
(f) Excludes tonnage of 14 vessels which is unknown.
(g) Excludes tonnage of 15 vessels which is unknown.
(h) Excludes tonnage of 17 vessels which is unknown.
(i) Excludes tonnage of 4 vessels which is unknown.
(j) Excludes tonnage of 5 vessels which is unknown.
(k) Excludes tonnage of 13 vessels which is unknown.
(l) Excludes tonnage of 46 vessels which is unknown.
(m) Excludes tonnage of 12 vessels which is unknown.
(n) Excludes tonnage of 106 vessels which is unknown.

III. ANALYSIS OF CAUSES OF LOSS BY CLASSES

Class	Cause of Loss (Enemy)							Cause of Loss (other)							Total
	Mine	Aircraft	Submarine	Surface Craft	Rammed	Shore Batteries	Action with the Enemy. Cause unknown	Wrecked	Used as Blockship	Collision	Accident	Fire	Own Forces	Unknown	
Battleships		1	2												3
Battle Cruisers		1		1											2
Monitor		1													1
Aircraft Carriers		1	3	1											5
Auxiliary Aircraft Carriers			2											1	3
Cruisers	1	7	8 (a)	5 (b)			2								23
Destroyers	23	50	35 (c)	20 (d)	2		2	2	1	3	1				139
Submarines	23 (e)	5 (d)	4 (f)	13 (g)				1		3	5		2	20	76
X Craft							6				1				7
Chariots							15	2						11	28
Welman Craft							4							1	5
Armed Merchant Cruisers	2	1	10					2							15
Armed Boarding Vessels		3 (d)	1							1					5
Ocean Boarding Vessels		1	4												5
Aux. Fighter Catapult Ships		1	1												2
Anti-Aircraft Ships	1	3								1					5
Auxiliary Anti-Aircraft Ships		3					2	1							6
Sloops		4	4 (d)				2	1							11
Frigates		1	9												10
Corvettes	5 (h)	3	16 (i)							4					28
Cutters		1	1				1								3
Auxiliary A/S Vessels		5					1								6
Patrol Vessel			1												1
River Gun Boats		5	1	1			1						3		11
Convoy Service Ships		2													2
Minelayers	2	2	1					1		1			1		8
Netlayers	1	2													3
Mine Destructor Vessels	2	1													3
Minesweepers	15 (j)	17	7 (k)	2 (d)			5	1			3		2		52
B.Y.M.S. Minesweepers	6														6
Motor Minesweepers	14 (d)	1					1	1					1		18
Degaussing Ship	1						1								2
Steam Gun Boat						1									1
Motor Torpedo Boats	18 (d)	9 (l)		21 (m)	2	1	11	8		8	7	16	8	6	115
Motor Attendant Craft	1 (m)														1
Motor A/S Boats	1											1			2
Motor Gun Boats	8 (o)	8		6							1	5			28
Motor Launches	16 (d)	21	7	4 (d)			3	2		1	8	5	3	9	79
Trawlers	79 (p)	71 (d)	18 (q)	20				14	1	27	8		3	10	251
Motor Fishing Vessels	1 (m)						1							1	3
Whalers	8	6	3	3 (d)			4	6		1		1	2	1	35
Yachts	5 (d)	9	1 (m)				2			6		6		5	34
Boom Defence Vessels	7	1								6			3		17

Type															Total
Barrage Vessel											1				1
Gate Vessels		1						1						1	2
Naval Servicing Boats							1		1						3
Naval Auxiliary Boats			1							1				2	7
Destroyer Depot Ship			1												1
Submarine Depot Ship	1						1								1
Accommodation Ship										1					1
Boom Accommodation Ship															1
Training Ship				1											1
Base Ship									1						1
Guardship		10	1	3										10	1
Tugs	9 (d)	1	1 (n)				8	13						18 (d)	54
Salvage Vessels			1					1							2
Rescue Ships	1						1	1						1	1
Mooring Vessels															2
Schooners							5	2		22					3
Drifters	22	14		2			3	21	1	1	3			18 (d)	107
Tenders	1	3	29 (d)					5		1				1	2
Tankers and Oilers		1												2	45
Fuelling Ship	1													1	1
Oil and Distilling Ship								2							1
Store Carriers		1		1				1				1			3
Victualling Store Ship								2			3			1	3
Water Carriers															1
Armament Store Carrier														1	5
Ammunition Hulks							3							5	2
Freighters	1	2	2 (d)	1			2	2		2					13
Colliers	1						2	2						2	5
Water Boats	1						3								4
F.A.A. Target Ship															6
Motor Canal Boats	1			1 (n)											5
Examination Vessels								2				1			4
Balloon Barrage Vessels	2	3	2 (d)				5	3			1	1		3	6
Special Service Vessels	1						2							14	5
Small Miscellaneous Craft	1	4					1	1	70			1		4	100
Transport Vessels							1			1				2	9
Armed Traders								1							6
Harbour Defence Vessels															5
Harbour Duty Vessels	1		1				1			1	1			5	8
Train Ferry															1
Ferry Service Vessels										1				1	2
Sailing Barges								1		1				2	3
Dumb Barges														6	21
Total	**281**	**271**	**172**	**109**	**5**	**4**	**116**	**114**	**89**	**85**	**38**	**37**	**28**	**154**	**1,503**

(a) Includes 1 sunk by human torpedo.
(b) Includes 1 partly caused by aircraft.
(c) Includes 1 unconfirmed and 2 sunk by human torpedoes or mine.
(d) Includes 1 unconfirmed.
(e) Includes 20 unconfirmed.
(f) Includes 3 unconfirmed.
(g) Includes 5 unconfirmed.

(h) Includes 1 sunk by human torpedo.
(i) Includes 2 unconfirmed.
(j) Includes 1 sunk by aerial mine, 2 unconfirmed, 1 possibly sunk by aircraft and 1 by submarine.
(k) Includes 3 sunk by human torpedoes.
(l) Includes 4 unconfirmed.
(m) Includes 1 also mined.

(n) Unconfirmed.
(o) Includes 2 unconfirmed, 1 possibly torpedoed.
(p) Includes 6 unconfirmed, 1 possibly sunk by submarine.
(q) Includes 2 sunk by human torpedoes, and 6 unconfirmed as torpedoed ; 1 possibly mined and 1 possibly sunk by aircraft.
(r) Includes 13 sunk for boom defence purposes.

IV. SUMMARY OF LOSSES BY YEAR AND CAUSE

Year	Cause of Loss (Enemy)							Cause of Loss (other)							Total
	Mine	Aircraft	Sub-marine	Surface Craft	Rammed	Shore Batteries	Action with the Enemy Cause unknown	Wrecked	Used as Blockship	Collision	Accident	Fire	Own Forces	Unknown	
1939	15	—	3	1	—	—	—	2	—	2	1	—	—	6	30
1940	86	75	23	18	1	—	12	17	31	23	6	5	—	20	317
1941	50	95	29	6	1	—	18	22	3	19	2	7	12	20	284
1942	28	81	56	42	1	2	48	14	16	14	9	6	10	32	359
1943	36	12	24	25	—	2	27	19	—	9	8	3	3	37	205
1944	43	6	27	15	1	—	10	25	39	14	10	3	—	15	208
1945	23	2	10	2	1	—	1	15	—	4	2	13	3	24	100
TOTAL	281	271	172	109	5	4	116	114	89	85	38	37	28	154	1,503

V. CLASSIFIED NOMINAL LIST OF LOSSES

BATTLESHIPS

BARHAM
PRINCE OF WALES
ROYAL OAK

Total 3

BATTLE CRUISERS

HOOD
REPULSE

Total 2

MONITOR

TERROR

Total 1

AIRCRAFT CARRIERS

ARK ROYAL
COURAGEOUS
EAGLE
GLORIOUS
HERMES

Total 5

**AUXILIARY AIR-
CRAFT CARRIERS**

AUDACITY
AVENGER
DASHER

Total 3

CRUISERS

BONAVENTURE
CALYPSO
CHARYBDIS
CORNWALL
DORSETSHIRE
DRAGON
DUNEDIN
DURBAN
EDINBURGH
EFFINGHAM
EXETER
FIJI
GALATEA
GLOUCESTER
HERMIONE
MANCHESTER
NAIAD
NEPTUNE
PENELOPE
SOUTHAMPTON
SPARTAN
TRINIDAD
YORK

Total 23

DESTROYERS

ACASTA
ACHATES
ACHERON
AFRIDI
AIREDALE
ALDENHAM
ARDENT
BASILISK
BATH

DESTROYERS (*cont.*)

BEDOUIN
BELMONT
BERKELEY
BEVERLEY
BLANCHE
BLEAN
BOADICEA
BRAZEN
BROADWATER
BROKE
CAMPBELTOWN
CODRINGTON
COSSACK
DAINTY
DARING
DEFENDER
DEITELNYI
  (*ex* CHURCHILL)
DELIGHT
DIAMOND
DUCHESS
DULVERTON
ECLIPSE
ELECTRA
ENCOUNTER
ESCORT
ESK
ESKDALE
EXMOOR
EXMOUTH
FEARLESS
FIREDRAKE
FORESIGHT
FURY
GALLANT
GIPSY
GLOWWORM
GRAFTON
GRENADE
GRENVILLE
GREYHOUND
GROVE
GURKHA (1)
GURKHA (*ex* LARNE)
HARDY (1)
HARDY (2)
HARVESTER
HASTY
HAVANT
HAVOCK
HEREWARD
HEYTHROP
HOLCOMBE
HOSTILE
HUNTER
HURRICANE
HURWORTH
HYPERION
IMOGEN
IMPERIAL
INGLEFIELD
INTREPID
ISIS
IVANHOE
JACKAL
JAGUAR
JANUS
JERSEY
JUNO
JUPITER
KANDAHAR
KASHMIR
KEITH
KELLY
KHARTOUM
KINGSTON
KIPLING
KUJAWIAK
  (*ex* OAKLEY)
LA COMBATTANTE
  (*ex* HALDON)
LAFOREY
LANCE
LEGION

DESTROYERS (*cont.*)

LIGHTNING
LIMBOURNE
LIVELY
MAHRATTA
MAORI
MARTIN
MASHONA
MATABELE
MOHAWK
NESTOR
ORKAN (*ex* MYRMIDON)
PAKENHAM
PANTHER
PARTRIDGE
PENYLAN
PUCKERIDGE
PUNJABI
QUAIL
QUENTIN
QUORN
ROCKINGHAM
SIKH
SOMALI
SOUTHWOLD
STANLEY
STRONGHOLD
STURDY
SVENNER (*ex* SHARK)
SWIFT
TENEDOS
THANET
TYNEDALE
VALENTINE
VAMPIRE
VENETIA
VETERAN
VIMIERA
VORTIGERN
WAKEFUL
WARWICK
WATERHEN
WESSEX
WHIRLWIND
WHITLEY
WILD SWAN
WREN
WRESTLER
WRYNECK
ZULU

Total 139

SUBMARINES

B. 1 (*ex* SUNFISH)
CACHALOT
GRAMPUS
H. 31
H. 49
JASTRZAB
  (*ex* P. 551)
NARWHAL
ODIN
OLYMPUS
ORPHEUS
OSWALD
OXLEY
P. 32
P. 33
P. 36
P. 38
P. 39
P. 48
P. 222
P. 311
P. 514
P. 715 (*ex* GRAPH)
PANDORA
PARTHIAN
PERSEUS
PHOENIX
PORPOISE

SUBMARINES (*cont.*)

RAINBOW
REGENT
REGULUS
SAHIB
SALMON
SARACEN
SEA HORSE
SHARK
SICKLE
SIMOOM
SNAPPER
SPEARFISH
SPLENDID
STARFISH
STERLET
STONEHENGE
STRATAGEM
SWORDFISH
SYRTIS
TALISMAN
TARPON
TEMPEST
TETRARCH
THAMES
THISTLE
THORN
THUNDERBOLT
TIGRIS
TRAVELLER
TRIAD
TRITON
TRIUMPH
TROOPER
TURBULENT
UMPIRE
UNBEATEN
UNDAUNTED
UNDINE
UNION
UNIQUE
UNITY
*UNTAMED
UPHOLDER
UREDD (*ex* P. 41)
URGE
USK
USURPER
UTMOST
VANDAL

Total 76

X CRAFT

X 5
X 6
X 7
X 8
X 9
X 10
X 22

Total 7

CHARIOTS

No. V
VI
VIII
X
XI
XII
XIII
XIV
XV
XVI
XVII
XVIII
XIX
XX
XXI

* Subsequently salved and renamed VITALITY

CHARIOTS (cont.)	ANTI-AIRCRAFT SHIPS	CUTTERS	MINESWEEPERS

CHARIOTS (cont.)

No. XXII
XXIII
XXIV
XXV
XXIX
XXXI
XXXIV
LII
LVII
LVIII
LX
LXXIX
LXXX

Total 28

WELMAN CRAFT

No. 10
45
46
47
48

Total 5

ARMED MERCHANT CRUISERS

ANDANIA (R)
CARINTHIA (R)
COMORIN (R)
DUNVEGAN CASTLE (R)
FORFAR (R)
HECTOR (R)
JERVIS BAY (R)
LAURENTIC (R)
PATROCLUS (R)
RAJPUTANA (R)
RAWALPINDI (R)
SALOPIAN (R)
SCOTSTOUN (R)
TRANSYLVANIA (R)
VOLTAIRE (R)

Total 15

ARMED BOARDING VESSELS

CHAKDINA (R)
CHANTALA (R)
KING ORRY (R)
ROSAURA (R)
VAN DYCK (R)

Total 5

OCEAN BOARDING VESSELS

CAMITO (R)
CRISPIN (R)
LADY SOMERS (R)
MALVERNIAN (R)
MANISTEE (R)

Total 5

AUXILIARY FIGHTER CATAPULT SHIPS

PATIA (R)
SPRINGBANK (R)

Total 2

ANTI-AIRCRAFT SHIPS

CAIRO
CALCUTTA
COVENTRY
CURACOA
CURLEW

Total 5

AUXILIARY ANTI-AIRCRAFT SHIPS

CRESTED EAGLE (R)
FOYLEBANK (R)
GLEN AVON (R)
HELVELLYN (R)
POZARICA
TYNWALD

Total 6

SLOOPS

AUCKLAND
BITTERN
DUNDEE
EGRET
GRIMSBY
IBIS
KITE
LAPWING
LARK
PENZANCE
WOODPECKER

Total 11

FRIGATES

BICKERTON
BLACKWOOD
BULLEN
CAPEL
GOODALL
GOULD
ITCHEN
LAWFORD
MOURNE
TWEED

Total 10

CORVETTES

ALYSSE (ex ALYSSUM)
ARBUTUS
ASPHODEL
AURICULA
BLUEBELL
DENBIGH CASTLE
ERICA
FLEUR DE LYS
GARDENIA
GLADIOLUS
GODETIA
HOLLYHOCK
HURST CASTLE
MARIGOLD
MIMOSA
MONTBRETIA
PICOTEE
PINTAIL
POLYANTHUS
ROSE
SALVIA
SAMPHIRE
SNAPDRAGON
SPIKENARD
TUNSBERG CASTLE (ex SHREWSBURY CASTLE)
VERVAIN
WINDFLOWER
ZINNIA

Total 28

CUTTERS

CULVER
HARTLAND
WALNEY

Total 3

AUXILIARY A/S VESSELS

KAMPAR (R)
KUALA (R)
MATA HARI (R)
SHU KWANG (R)
SIANG WO (R)
TIEN KWANG (R)

Total 6

PATROL VESSEL

GIANG BEE (R)

Total 1

RIVER GUNBOATS

CICALA
DRAGONFLY
GNAT
GRASSHOPPER
LADYBIRD
MOSQUITO
MOTH
PETEREL
ROBIN
SCORPION
TERN

Total 11

CONVOY SERVICE SHIPS

CHAKLA (R)
FIONA (R)

Total 2

MINELAYERS

ABDIEL
CORNCRAKE
KUNG WO (R)
LATONA
PORT NAPIER (R)
PRINCESS VICTORIA (R)
REDSTART
WELSHMAN

Total 8

NETLAYERS

KYLEMORE (R)
MINSTER (R)
TONBRIDGE (R)

Total 3

MINE DESTRUCTOR VESSELS

CORBURN
CORFIELD
QUEENWORTH

Total 3

MINESWEEPERS

ABINGDON
ALGERINE
BANKA (R)
BRAMBLE
BRIGHTON BELLE (R)
BRIGHTON QUEEN (R)
BRITOMART
CATO
CHANGTEH (R)
CITY OF ROCHESTER
CLACTON
CROMARTY
CROMER
DEVONIA (R)
DUNDALK
DUNOON
FELIXSTOWE
FERMOY
FITZROY
FUHWO (R)
GOSSAMER
GRACIE FIELDS
GUYSBOROUGH
HEBE
HUA TONG (R)
HUNTLEY
HUSSAR
HYTHE
JARAK (R)
KLIAS (R)
LEDA
LI WO (R)
LOYALTY
MAGIC
MALACCA (R)
MARMION (R)
MERCURY (R)
NIGER
PYLADES
REGULUS
SCOTT HARLEY (R)
SIN AIK LEE (R)
SKIPJACK
SNAEFELL (R)
SOUTHSEA (R)
SPHINX
SQUIRREL
STOKE
TAPAH (R)
VESTAL
WAVERLEY (R)
WIDNES

Total 52

B.Y.M.S. MINE-SWEEPERS

No. 2019
2022
2030
2053
2077
2255

Total 6

MOTOR MINESWEEPERS

No. 8
39
51
55
68
70
89
101
117
168
170
174*
180
229
248

* Subsequently Salved.

MOTOR MINESWEEPERS (cont.)	MOTOR TORPEDO BOATS (cont.)	MOTOR GUN BOATS (cont.)	MOTOR LAUNCHES (cont.)
No. 257	No. 316	No. 76	No. 1015
278	338	78	1030
1019	347	79	1037
	352	90	1054
Total 18	356	92	1057
	357	98	1062
	360	99	1063
DEGAUSSING SHIPS	371	109	1083
	372	110	1121
Balmore (R)	412	313	1153
Daisy (R)	417	314	1154
	430	326	1157
Total 2	434	328	1163
	438	335	1179
	444	501	1212
STEAM GUN BOAT	448	601	1227
	459	641	1244
No. 7	460	644	1289
	461	648	1380
Total 1	462	663	1388
	463	2002	1417
	465	2007	
	466		Total 79
	494	Total 28	
MOTOR TORPEDO BOATS	605		
	606		
No. 6	622	MOTOR LAUNCHES	TRAWLERS
7	626		
8	631	Kelana (R)	Adonis
9	635	Penghambat	Agate
10	636	Peningat (R)	Aghios Georgios (IV) (R)
11	639	No. 103	Akranes (R)
12	640	108	Alberic (R)
15	655	109	Alder
16	665	111	Almond
17	666	126	Alouette (R)
26	669	127	Amethyst
27	671	129	Aracari (R)
28	681	130	Aragonite (R)
29	686	133	Arctic Trapper (R)
30	690	144	Argyllshire (R)
41	697	156	Arley (R)
43	705	160	Arsenal
44	707	169	Asama (R)
47	708	177	Ash
61	710	183	Aston Villa (R)
63	712	192	Avanturine (R)
64	715	210	Bandolero
67	732	216	Barbara Robertson (R)
68	734	219	Bedfordshire
73	776	230	Beech
74	782	242	Ben Ardna (R)
77	789	251	Ben Gairn (R)
87	791	262	Bengali
93	798	265	*Ben Rossal (R)
105	5001	267	Benvolio (R)
106		268	Birdlip
201	Total 115	270	Blackburn Rovers (R)
213		287	Botanic
214		288	Bradman (R)
215	MOTOR ATTENDANT CRAFT	298	Bredon
216		301	Brora
217	No. 5	306	Calverton (R)
218		310	Calvi (R)
220	Total 1	311	Campina (R)
222		339	Campobello
230		352	Canna
237	MOTOR A/S BOATS	353	Cap D'Antifer (R)
241		358	Cape Chelyuskin
242	No. 3	387	Cape Finisterre (R)
243	30	443	Cape Passaro (R)
248		446	Cape Siretoko (R)
255	Total 2	447	Cape Spartel (R)
259		457	Capricornus (R)
261		466	Caroline (R)
262	MOTOR GUN BOATS	558	Caulonia (R)
264		563	Cayton Wyke
267	No. 12	579	Charles Boyes (R)
287	17	591	Chestnut
288	18	835	Choice (R)
308	19	870	Cloughton Wyke (R)
310	62	891	Cobbers (R)
311	64	905	Colsay
312		916	
314		1003	
		1011	

* Subsequently Salved.

TRAWLERS (cont.)

Comet (R)
Computator (R)
Conquistador (R)
Coral
Coriolanus
Cortina (R)
Cramond Island (R)
Crestflower
Daneman
Darogah (R)
Dervish (R)
Desirée (R)
Donna Nook (R)
Dox (R)
Dromio (R)
Drummer (R)
Dungeness (R)
Ebor Wyke (R)
Eileen Duncan (R)
Elizabeth
  Angela (R)
Elizabeth Therese (R)
Elk (R)
Ellesmere
Emilion (R)
Erin
Ethel Taylor
Evelina (R)
Evesham (R)
Fifeshire (R)
Fleming (R)
Flotta
Fontenoy (R)
Force (R)
Fort Royal
Fortuna (R)
Francolin (R)
Franc Tireur (R)
Gairsay
Ganilly
Gaul
Gullfoss
*Hammond (R)
Harvest Moon
Hayburn Wyke (R)
Henriette (R)
Herring
Hickory
Hildasay
Hong Lam (R)
Honjo (R)
Horatio
Inverclyde (R)
Irvana (R)
Jade
James Ludford
Jardine (R)
Jasper
Jean Frederick (R)
Joseph Button (R)
Juniper
Jura
Kennymore (R)
Keryado (R)
Kingston Alalite
Kingston Beryl (R)
Kingston Cairngorm (R)
Kingston Ceylonite
Kingston Cornelian
Kingston Galena
Kingston Jacinth (R)
Kingston Sapphire (R)
Kopanes (R)
Kurd (R)
Lady Lilian (R)
Lady Shirley (R)
Laertes
La Nantaise (R)
*Larwood (R)
Leyland
Lincoln City (R)
Loch Alsh (R)
Loch Assater (R)
Loch Doon (R)
Loch Inver (R)
Loch Naver (R)

TRAWLERS (cont.)

Lord Austin (R)
Lord Hailsham
*Lord Inchcape (R)
Lord Selborne (R)
Lord Snowden (R)
Lord Stamp (R)
Lord Stonehaven (R)
Lord Wakefield
Lorinda (R)
Luda Lady (R)
Manor (R)
Manx Prince (R)
Marconi (R)
Marsona (R)
Mastiff
Melbourne (R)
Meror (R)
Milford Earl (R)
Mirabelle (R)
Moravia (R)
Murmansk (R)
Myrtle
Nogi (R)
Northcoates (R)
Northern Isles (R)
Northern Princess (R)
Northern Rover (R)
Notts County (R)
Orfasy
Ormonde (R)
Oswaldian (R)
Ouse
Pelton (R)
Pentland Firth
Peridot
Phineas Beard (R)
Pierre Descelliers (R)
Pine
Polly Johnson (R)
Pyrope (R)
Recoil (R)
Red Gauntlet (R)
Refundo (R)
Relonzo (R)
Remillo (R)
Resmilo (R)
Resolvo (R)
Resparko (R)
Rifsnes (R)
Rinova (R)
River Clyde (R)
Robert Bowen (R)
Roche Bonne (R)
Rodino (R)
Rosemonde (R)
Royalo
Rubens (R)
Rutlandshire (R)
Rysa
St. Achilleus (R)
St. Apollo (R)
St. Cathan (R)
St. Donats (R)
St. Goran (R)
Sea King (R)
Sedgefly (R)
Senateur Duhamel (R)
Silicia (R)
Sindonis
Sisapon (R)
Solomon (R)
Spaniard
Star of Deveron (R)
Staunton (R)
Stella Capella
Stella Dorada
Stella Orion (R)
Stella Sirius
Strathborve (R)
Stronsay
Susarion (R)
Sword Dance
Tamarisk
Tervani (R)
Texas
Thomas Bartlett (R)
Thuringia

TRAWLERS (cont.)

Tilbury Ness (R)
Topaze
Tourmaline
Tranio (R)
Tranquil (R)
Transvaal (R)
Ullswater
Valdora (R)
Van Orley (R)
Velia (R)
Vidonia (R)
Wallasea
Warland
Warwick Deeping
Warwickshire (R)
Washington (R)
Waterfly (R)
Wave Flower
Westella
William Hallett (R)
William Stephen (R)
William Wesney (R)
Wyoming (R)
Zee Meeuw (R)

Total 251

MOTOR FISHING VESSELS

No. 70
117
1032

Total 3

WHALERS

A.N. 2 (R)
Bever (R)
Bodö (R)
Cocker (R)
Egeland (R)
Firmament (R)
Gemas (R)
Harstad (R)
Jeram (R)
Jerantut (R)
Kos XVI (R)
Kos XXII (R)
Kos XXIII (R)
Maaløy (R)
Parktown (R)
Rahman (R)
Sambhur (R)
Santa (R)
Sarna (R)
Sevra (R)
Shera (R)
Skudd 3 (R)
Sotra (R)
Southern Floe (R)
Southern Flower (R)
Southern Pride (R)
Spercheios (ex Noble Nora) (R)
Sulla (R)
Svana (R)
Syvern (R)
Thorbryn (R)
Thorgrim (R)
Trang (R)
Treern (R)
Whippet (R)

Total 35

YACHTS

Aisha (R)
Amulree (R)
Attendant (R)
Boomerang VI (R)
Breda

YACHTS (cont.)

Calanthe (R)
Campeador V (R)
Emelle (R)
Gael (R)
Grive (R)
Gulzar (R)
Hanyards (R)
Mollusc (R)
Nyula (R)
Oracle
Pellag II (R)
Princess (R)
Rhodora (R)
Rosabelle
Sappho (R)
Sargasso (R)
Sea Angler (R)
Shashi III (R)
Silvia (R)
Sona
Surf (R)
Surprise
Thalia
Torrent (R)
Viva II (R)
Warrior II (R)
White Fox II (R)
Wilna (R)
Yorkshire Belle (R)

Total 34

BOOM DEFENCE VESSELS

Aldgate
Barflake
Barlight
Bayonet
Cambrian (R)
Chorley (R)
Dowgate
Fabious (R)
Loch Shin (R)
Ludgate
Marcelle (R)
Othello (R)
*Panorama
Ristango (R)
Thomas Connolly (R)
Tunisian (R)
Watergate

Total 17

BARRAGE VESSEL

No. 42

Total 1

GATE VESSELS

King Henry (R)
Placidas Faroult (R)

Total 2

NAVAL SERVICING BOATS

No. 9
30
38

Total 3

* Subsequently salved.

NAVAL AUXILIARY BOATS

LILY
SPIDER BOY
No. 47
48
49
58
59

Total 7

DESTROYER DEPÔT SHIP

HECLA

Total 1

SUBMARINE DEPÔT SHIP

MEDWAY

Total 1

ACCOMMODATION SHIP

GYPSY (R)

Total 1

BOOM ACCOMMODATION SHIP

SUI WO (R)

Total 1

TRAINING SHIP (ex BATTLESHIP)

CENTURION

Total 1

BASE SHIP

ANKING (R)

Total 1

GUARDSHIP

LORMONT (R)

Total 1

TUGS

ADEPT
ADHERENT
ALAISIA (R)
ALLIGATOR
ANDROMEDA (R)
ASSURANCE
ATHLETE
BAIA (R)
C. 308
CAROLINE MOLLER (R)
CORINGA (R)
CORY BROS (R)
DAISY (R)
DANUBE III (R)
EMILY (R)
FAIRPLAY TWO (R)
GUARDSMAN (R)
HELEN BARBARA
HELLESPONT
HESPERIA
HORSA
INDIRA (R)

TUGS (cont.)

IRENE VERNICOS (R)
J.T.A. 1 (R)
*J.T.A. 6 (R)
J.T.A. 7 (R)
J.T.A. 14 (R)
LETTIE (R)
MURIA (R)
NAPIA (R)
PENGAWAL
PEUPLIER (R)
ROODE ZEE (R)
ST. ABBS
ST. ANGELO
ST. BREOCK
ST. CYRUS
ST. FAGAN
ST. ISSEY
ST. JUST
ST. OLAVES (R)
ST. SAMPSON (R)
SALVAGE KING (R)
SAUCY (R)
SEAGEM (R)
SESAME
SOLITAIRE
TIENTSIN (R)
TWENTE (R)
VAILLANT (R)
VISION
WEST COCKER
WO KWANG (R)
YIN PING (R)

Total 54

SALVAGE VESSELS

SALVIKING
VIKING (R)

Total 2

RESCUE SHIP

ST. SUNNIVA (R)

Total 1

MOORING VESSELS

MOOR
STEADY

Total 2

SCHOONERS

KANTARA (R)
KEPHALLINIA (R)
MARIA D. GIOVANNI (R)

Total 3

DRIFTERS

ALFRED COLEBROOK
APPLE TREE (R)
AURORA II (R)
BAHRAM (R)
BLIA (R)
BOY ALAN (R)
BOY ANDREW (R)
BOY ROY (R) (1)
BOY ROY (R) (2)
BRAE FLETT (R)
BROADLAND (R)
CARRY ON (R)
CATHERINE (R)
CHANCELLOR (R)
CHARDE (R)
CHRISTINE ROSE (R)
COMFORT (R)
COR JESU (R)
D'ARCY COOPER (R)
DEVON COUNTY (R)

DRIFTERS (cont.)

DEWEY EVE (R)
DUSKY QUEEN (R)
DUTHIES (R)
EMBRACE (R)
FAIR BREEZE (R)
FAIRHAVEN (R)
FERTILE VALE (R)
FISHERGIRL (R)
FISKAREN (R)
FORECAST (R)
FORERUNNER (R)
GIRL PAMELA (R)
GLEAM
GLEN ALBYN (R)
GLOAMING (R)
GO AHEAD (R)
GOLDEN DAWN (R)
GOLDEN EFFORT (R)
GOLDEN GIFT
GOLDEN SUNBEAM (R)
GOLDEN WEST (R)
GOODWILL (R)
GOWAN HILL (R)
HARMONY (R)
HARVEST GLEANER (R)
HIGHLAND QUEEN (R)
HIGHTIDE (R)
IMBAT (R)
INTREPEDE (R)
JEWEL (R)
JUSTIFIED
LE DUE PAOLE (R)
LEGEND (R)
LORD CAVAN (R)
LORD HOWARD (R)
LORD ST. VINCENT (R)
MAIDA (R)
MANX LAD (R)
M. A. WEST (R)
MIDAS (R)
MONARDA (R)
NAUTILUS (R)
NEW SPRAY (R)
NISR (R)
NORNES (R)
NOSS HEAD
NOT MANN (R)
OCEAN LASSIE (R)
OCEAN RETRIEVER (R)
OCEAN REWARD (R)
OCEAN SUNLIGHT (R)
PAXTON (R)
PERSEVERE (R)
PREMIER
PROFICIENT (R)
PROMOTIVE (R)
RAY OF HOPE (R)
RECEPTIVE (R)
REED (R)
RIANT (R)
ROSA (R)
ROSE VALLEY (R)
ROWAN TREE (R)
RYPA (R)
SCOTCH THISTLE (R)
SHIPMATES (R)
SOIZIK (R)
SUMMER ROSE (R)
SUPPORTER (R)
THE BOYS (R)
THISTLE (R)
THORA
TOKEN (R)
TORBAY II (R)
TRUE ACCORD (R)
TRUSTY STAR
UBEROUS (R)
UBERTY (R)
UNICITY (R)
UT PROSIM (R)
VICTORIA I (R)
WHITE DAISY (R)
WINSOME (R)
XMAS ROSE (R)
YOUNG ERNIE (R)
YOUNG FISHERMAN (R)
YOUNG SID (R)

Total 107

TENDERS

CHABOOK (R)
*SENGA (R)

Total 2

TANKERS AND OILERS

ALBERT L. ELLSWORTH (R)
ALCIDES (R)
ALDERSDALE
ANDREA BROVIG (R)
BELITA (R)
BETH (R)
BIRCHOL
BOARDALE
CAIRNDALE
CIRCE SHELL (R)
DARKDALE
DINSDALE
FINNANGER (R)
FRANCOL
HALLANGER (R)
HAVSTEN (R)
JOHN P. PEDERSON (R)
LEIV EIRIKSSON (R)
LITIOPA (R)
MALMANGER (R)
MARIT (R)
MINISTER WEDEL (R)
MIRLO (R)
MONTENOL
NYHOLT (R)
OLEANDER
OLNA
PERICLES (R)
PLUMLEAF
ROSEWOOD (R)
SANDAR (R)
SILDRA (R)
SLAVOL
SLEMDAL (R)
SVENOR (R)
SVEVE (R)
TANK EXPRESS (R)
THELMA (R)
THORSHAVET (R)
THORSHOVDI (R)
VARDAAS (R)
WAR DIWAN
WAR MEHTAR
WAR SEPOY
WAR SIRDAR

Total 45

FUELLING SHIP

ILTON CASTLE (R)

Total 1

DISTILLING SHIP

*STAGHOUND (R)

Total 1

STORE CARRIERS

TIBERIO (R)
TUNA (R)
ULSTER PRINCE (R)

Total 3

VICTUALLING STORE SHIP

MORAY (R)

Total 1

* Subsequently salved.

WATER CARRIERS

EMPIRE ARTHUR (R)
GENERAL VAN DER
HEIJDEN (R)
KALGAH (R)

Total 3

ARMANENT STORE CARRIER

ESCAUT (R)

Total 1

AMMUNITION HULKS

CARLO
DUNMORE
LUCY BORCHARDT
MOURINO
STANLARD

Total 5

FREIGHTERS

CAPE HOWE (R)
WILL AMETTE VALLEY (R)

Total 2

COLLIERS

*BELHAVEN (R)
BOTUSK (R)
FERNWOOD (R)
GLYNWEN (R)
IOANNIS FAFALIOS (R)
KING CITY (R)
MAINDY HILL (R)
NEVA (R)
OLGA E.
EMBIRICOS (R)
P.L.M. 21 (R)
ROLFSBORG (R)
YEWDALE (R)
ZANNIS L.
CAMBANIS (R)

Total 13

WATER BOATS

CECIL (R)
CHANT. 69 (R)
GENERAL VAN
SWIETEN (R)
ISBJORN (R)
PETRONELLA (R)

Total 5

FLEET AIR ARM TARGET SHIP

ST. BRIAC (R)

Total 1

MOTOR CANAL BOATS

AMBLEVE
ESCAUT
SEMOIS
YSER

Total 4

EXAMINATION VESSELS

No. 4 (R)
No. 10 (R)
FRATTON (R)
LADY SLATER (R)
SOLEN (R)
TUNG WO (R)

Total 6

BALLOON BARRAGE VESSELS

BOREALIS (R)
REIDAR (R)
SATURNUS (R)
SVERRE (R)
TANEVIK (R)

Total 5

SPECIAL SERVICE VESSELS

AKSEL I (R)
ALYNBANK (R)
ARMENIER (R)
ARTHUR (R)
ATLANTIC GUIDE
BECHEVILLE
BELGIQUE
BENDORAN
BERGHOLM (R)
BILLDORA (R)
BORODINO (R)
BOSWORTH
BRANKSEA
BRATTHOLM (R)
BUSK
CARRON
COLLINGDOC
DAH PU (R)
DOVER HILL
DUPLEX (R)
DURHAM CASTLE
EDV. NISSEN (R)
ELSWICK PARK
EMERALD WINGS
EMPIRE BITTERN
EMPIRE BUNTING
EMPIRE DEFIANCE
EMPIRE FLAMINGO
EMPIRE MOORHEN
EMPIRE SEAMAN
EMPIRE TAMAR
EMPIRE TANA
EMPIRE WATERHEN
EVANGELISTRIA
(CHIOS 345) (R)
FEIOY (R)
FIDELIA
FIDELITY (R)
FLORENTINO
FLOWERGATE
FORBIN (R)
FREYA I (R)
GAMBHIRA
GEORGIOS P.
GONDOLIER
GOURKO
GRETHE MORTENSEN (R)
GULDBORG (R)
HOLLAND (R)
ILSENSTEIN
INGMAN (R)
INNERTON
JACOBUS
JAMES 9
JAMES 83

SPECIAL SERVICE VESSELS (cont.)

JOKER (R)
JUNIATA
KANTUNG (R)
KAUPO (R)
LAKE NEUCHATEL
LYCEA
LYN CHAUG
MACAO
MANCHESTER SPINNER
MARIPOSA
MARS (R)
MARTIS
MASHOBRA (R)
MAYCREST
†MINNIE DE LARINAGA
MODLIN
MOREA
MOYLE
NJEGOS (R)
NORFALK
NORJERV
NORSEMAN (R)
NORSJOEN (R)
PACIFICO
PANOS
PARKHAVEN
PARKLAAN
REDSTONE
RIVER TYNE
SALTERSGATE
SIREHEI
SJO (R)
SQUALLY (R)
STANWELL
SYLVIA (R)
TRANSEAS
TWEEDLE DEE
TWEEDLE DUM
UMVOTI
VERA RADCLIFFE
VINLAKE
VITA (R)
WESTCOVE
WESTWICK (R)
WINHA

Total 99‡

SMALL MISCELLANE-OUS CRAFT

AGHIOS PANTALEIMON (R)
AYIOS IOANNIS
(CHIOS 466) (R)
BOY PETER
DANEHILL
EUSTATHIOS GHIOKIS (R)
FOLIOT
MATCHLOCK
NAIEM
SHUN AN (R)

Total 9

TRANSPORT VESSELS

EVANGELISTRIA
(SAMOS 82) (R)
FAROUK (R)
MARY VI (R)
TERPSITHEA (R)
TRIUMPH VI (R)
ZOODOCHOS PIGHI (R)

Total 6

ARMED TRADERS

KUDAT (R)
LARUT (R)
LIPIS (R)
RAUB (R)
VYNER BROOKE (R)

Total 5

HARBOUR DEFENCE VESSEL

MANORA (R)

Total 1

HARBOUR DUTY VESSELS

AYIOS IOANNIS
(CHIOS 116) (R)
BRODRENE (R)
CHRYSOLITE (R)
ISMINI (R)
NYKEN (R)
RUBY (R)
ST. ANNE (R)
VASSILIKI (R)

Total 8

TRAIN FERRY

DAFFODIL

Total 1

FERRY SERVICE VESSELS

SANDOY (R)
SANDVIKHORN (R)

Total 2

SAILING BARGES

DELTA
DUNDONALD
E.F.Q.

Total 3

DUMB BARGES

CELT
*CLACTON
COOLIE
COSSACK
DARTMOUTH (R)
DERVISH
FOUR
*GREENFINCH
MAORI
MATABELE
*MONICA
NELL JESS
ODESSA
PARTISAN
PHILISTINE
REDRESS
RESPITE
REVENGE
SAN FRANCISCO
UTOPIA
VALENCIA

Total 21

* Subsequently salved.
‡ Includes 1 ship to be counted twice.
† Reported sunk and salved 1940. Finally sunk 1941.

PART II

LANDING SHIPS, CRAFT AND BARGES

I—LIST OF LOSSES
ARRANGED ACCORDING TO YEAR AND CLASS

NOTES

(i) (R) Signifies that the vessel was requisitioned for Naval Service.

(ii) Tonnage for Landing Ships is Standard Displacement unless otherwise stated.

(iii) Gross Registered Tonnage is shewn in italics.

(iv) W.L. signifies War Load Displacement.

LIST OF ABBREVIATIONS

A/C Aircraft.
E/B E-Boat.
U/B U/Boat.

Class and Nos.	Date of Loss	How Lost and Where
LANDING CRAFT ASSAULT	1940.	
(W.L. 11–13·5 tons)		
Nos. 4, 18 (total 2)	29 May	Lost in CLAN MACALISTER, sunk by A/C at Dunkirk.
16	29 May	Sunk by A/C at Dunkirk.
8, 15 (total 2)	31 May	Lost at Dunkirk.
11, 14 (total 2)	9 June ⎫	Lost in home waters.
1, 2 (total 2)	14 June ⎬	
6	July (date reported)	Cause and place unknown.
LANDING CRAFT MECHANISED		
(Mark I) (W.L. 30–37 tons)		
Nos. 10, 11, 14, 15, 18–20 (total 7)	6–27 May	Presumed lost during operations at Narvik, Norway.
12, 22 (total 2)	2 June ⎫	Abandoned at Dunkirk.
17	3 June ⎬	
LANDING CRAFT PERSONNEL (Large)		
(W.L. 8–11 tons)		
No. 30	20–21 Dec.	Lost in air raid on Liverpool.

Class	Name	Tonnage	Date of Completion	Date of Loss	How Lost and Where
RAIDING CRAFT CARRIER.*	PRINCE PHILIPPE (R) ...	*2,938*	1939	1941 15 July	Sunk in collision off W. Scotland.

Class and Nos.	Date of Loss	How Lost and Where
LANDING CRAFT ASSAULT	1941	
(W.L. 11–13·5 tons)		
Nos. 28	May	Lost during evacuation of Crete.
119	July (date reported).	Sunk in home waters.
31, 32, 38, 39, 45, 48, 49, 51, 60, 63, 64, 75, 79–81, 87, 105, 113 (total 18) ⎫⎬	Aug. (date reported).	Lost in Middle East.
121	24 Dec.	Cause and place unknown.
70	—	Lost in Middle East.
LANDING CRAFT MECHANISED		
(Mark I) (W.L. 30–37 tons)		
Nos. 106	May	Lost at Crete.
32, 55, 67, 95, 96, 103, 107, 108 (total 8) ...	Aug. (date reported). ⎫	Lost in Middle East.
82, 97 (total 2)	Aug.–Sept. ⎬	
1	—	Sunk in home waters.

* Raiding Craft were subsequently redesignated Landing Craft Personnel (Large).

Class and Nos.	Date of Loss	How Lost and Where
	1941	
LANDING CRAFT PERSONNEL (Large) (W.L. 8–11 tons)		
Nos. 107–109 (total 3)	May	Lost in home waters in transit from U.S.A.
63	Aug. (date reported).	Lost in Middle East.
59, 71 (total 2)	2 Sept.	Lost through heavy weather while at anchor, Middle East.
193, 194 (total 2)	Dec.	Lost overboard through heavy weather in Home waters.
24–27, 38, 82 (total 6)	—	Lost in Home waters.
LANDING CRAFT SUPPORT (Medium) (Mark I) (W.L. 9–10·7 tons)		
No. 1	—	Unknown.
LANDING CRAFT TANK (Mark I) (W.L. 372 tons)		
Nos. 16	2 June	Lost in Suda Bay, Crete.
6, 20 (total 2)	June	Lost in Middle East.
10	17 July	Lost by enemy action, Middle East.
8	29 July	
1, 12, 15, 19 (total 4)	Aug. (date reported).	Lost in Middle East.
5	Aug. (date reported).	Lost in Home waters.
14	12 Aug.	
2, 7 (total 2)	12–13 Oct.	Lost after leaving Tobruk.
11	16 Dec.	Lost in Middle East.
LANDING CRAFT TANK (Mark II) (W.L. 450–453 tons)		
Nos. 102, 103 (total 2)	10 Oct.	
105, 109 (total 2)	4 Nov.	Lost in Home Waters.
110, 143 (total 2)	Nov.	

Class	Name	Tonnage	Date of Completion	Date of Loss	How Lost and Where
				1942	
LANDING SHIP INFANTRY (LARGE).	KARANJA (R)	9,890	1931	12 Nov.	Sunk by A/C, Bougie, Algeria.

Class and Nos.	Date of Loss	How Lost and Where
	1942.	
LANDING CRAFT ASSAULT (W.L. 11–13·5 tons)		
Nos. 166	19 Apr.	
211	Apr.	Lost in Home Waters.
138	June	
193	20 June	Lost during fall of Tobruk.
196	July	Lost by enemy action.
37, 52, 92, 94, 97, 102, 192, 209, 214, 215, 237, 247, 251, 262, 284, 314, 317 (total 17)	19 Aug.	Lost in operation JUBILEE (Dieppe).
35, 55, 128, 135, 153, 167, 169, 176, 187–189, 218, 219, 221, 227, 235, 239, 244, 245, 259–261, 266, 269, 271, 286, 287, 301, 307, 309, 310, 321, 375, 423, 436, 447, 451 (total 37).	Nov. (approx.)	Lost in operation TORCH (N. Africa).
LANDING CRAFT FLAK (Mark II) (W.L. 500–540 tons)		
No. 2	19 Aug.	Lost in operation JUBILEE (Dieppe).
LANDING CRAFT MECHANISED (Mark I) (W.L. 30–37 tons)		
Nos. 51, 53 (total 2)	Mar.	Lost in Middle East.
38	Apr. (date reported).	Lost in Mediterranean.
46	5 May	Capsized and sank, E. Indies.
84, 90, 93, 119, 122, 135, 137 (total 7) ...	June	Lost in Middle East.
110, 113, 145, 146, 148 (total 5)	20 June	Lost during fall of Tobruk.
140	July	
23–25, 34, 45 (total 5)	Aug.	Lost in Middle East.
56	19 Aug.	Lost in operation JUBILEE (Dieppe).
31	Oct. (date reported).	Lost in Home Waters.
89	22 Oct.	Believed lost in tow en route to Colombo.
63–65, 69, 72, 73, 120, 147, 153, 161, 169, 186 (total 12).	Nov.	Lost in operation TORCH (N. Africa).
139	20 Nov.	Lost through heavy weather in Middle East.
98	6 Dec.	Lost by enemy action in Benghazi area.

Class and Nos.	Date of Loss	How Lost and Where
LANDING CRAFT MECHANISED	1942	
(Mark III) (W.L. 52 tons)		
Nos. 501, 510, 516 (total 3)	Aug.	Lost in Middle East.
508, 509, 519, 522, 523, 532, 537, 547, 620 (total 9).	13 Oct.	Lost in SOUTHERN EMPRESS, torpedoed in convoy, N. Atlantic.
611, 613, 632–634, 636 (total 6)	14 Oct.	Lost in EMPIRE TARPON, off N.W. Scotland.
518, 520, 528, 539, 543, 551, 555, 556, 558, 564, 567, 569, 571, 572, 574, 581, 584, 590, 592, 593, 595, 596, 606, 609, 624, 635 (total 26).	Nov.	Lost in operation TORCH (N. Africa).
LANDING CRAFT PERSONNEL (Large)		
(W.L. 8–11 tons)		
Nos. 180–185 (total 6)	Feb.	Lost at Singapore.
57	Mar.	Bombed at Tobruk.
117	Mar.	Lost in Home Waters.
64	20 June	Lost during fall of Tobruk.
65	30 June	Lost in bad weather off Alexandria.
93	10 July	Destroyed by fire at Shoreham.
42, 45, 81, 157, 164, 174, 210, 212 (total 8)	19 Aug.	Lost in operation JUBILEE (Dieppe).
83	2 Sept.	Lost by fire at Newhaven.
29	15 Sept.	Lost by fire in Middle East.
209	6 Nov.	Lost in Seaford Bay.
138, 507, 543, 544, 550, 560, 562, 565, 566, 568, 573, 575, 576, 759 (total 14).	Nov.	Lost in operation TORCH (N. Africa).
36	24–25 Dec.	Lost by fire at Chittagong, India.
LANDING CRAFT PERSONNEL (Ramped)		
(W.L. 9–11 tons)		
Nos. 1008	Aug.	Damaged and sunk in heavy weather in Home Waters.
1012	Aug.	Sunk in collision in Home Waters.
617	15 Sept.	Sunk in Home Waters.
622	24 Sept.	
603, 620, 629, 721, 783, 794, 837, 850, 858, 901, 909, 1009, 1029, 1036 (total 14).	Nov. (approx.)	Lost in operation TORCH (N. Africa).
578 ... ...·	13 Dec.	Lost at Inveraray, W. Scotland.
LANDING CRAFT SUPPORT (Medium)		
(Mark I) (W.L. 9–10·7 tons)		
Nos. 4, 6, 15, 18, 19, 22 (total 6)	20 June	Lost during fall of Tobruk.
9	19 Aug.	Lost in operation JUBILEE (Dieppe).
11, 14 (total 2)	Nov.	Lost in operation TORCH (N. Africa).
LANDING CRAFT SUPPORT (Medium)		
(Mark II) (W.L. 12·5 tons)		
No. 28	Nov.	Lost in operation TORCH (N. Africa).
LANDING CRAFT TANK		
(Mark II) (W.L. 450–453 tons)		
Nos. 155	Mar.	Lost on passage to Gibraltar.
119, 150 (total 2)	20 June	Lost at Tobruk.
121, 124, 126, 145, 159 (total 5)	19 Aug.	Lost in operation JUBILEE (Dieppe).
120	20 Nov.	Lost in heavy weather.
LANDING CRAFT TANK		
(Mark V) (W.L. 291–311 tons)		
Nos. 2006	13 Oct.	
2281	27 Oct.	
2190, 2192, 2284 (total 3)	28 Oct.	Lost in transit from U.S.A
2187	Nov.	
2054, 2312 (total 2)...	Dec.	
LANDING CRAFT VEHICLE		
(W.L. 10–11 tons)		
Nos. 597	12 Sept.	Lost in Home Waters.
798	25 Sept.	
579	13 Dec.	Lost at Inveraray, W. Scotland.
752, 754 (total 2)	30 Dec.	Lost in FIDELITY, sunk N. Atlantic.
LANDING BARGES		
(B.B.) (150 ton type)		
Nos. 332, 362 (total 2)	19 Sept.	Sunk by A/C near Salcombe.
(C.C.) (200 ton type)		
No. 382 ... ... · ...	Sept.	Cause and place unknown.

Class	Number	Tonnage	Date of Completion	Date of Loss	How Lost and Where
Landing Ships Tank (Class II).	429	2,750	21. 2.43	1943 3 July	Lost by fire, Mediterranean.
	414	2,750	20. 1.43	15 Aug.	Torpedoed by A/C. off Cani Rocks, Tunisia. Beached off Bizerta.
	79	2,750	17. 7.43	30 Sept.	Sunk by A/C. off Corsica.

Class and Nos.	Date of Loss	How Lost and Where
LANDING CRAFT ASSAULT (W.L. 11–13·5 tons)	1943	
Nos. 272	Apr.	Lost in Mediterranean.
78	June (date reported).	Lost in tow from Algiers to Djedjelli.
222, 312 (total 2)	June (date reported).	Lost in Mediterranean.
446	29 Aug.	Lost in heavy weather in Mediterranean.
675	24 Sept.	Lost during gale at Salerno.
212, 316, 505, 545 (total 4)	Nov. (date reported).	Lost in Mediterranean.
813	29 Nov.	Lost during exercises in Home Waters.
553	2 Dec.	Sunk in collision off Southampton.
645, 646 (total 2)	21 Dec.	Lost in heavy weather, English Channel.
723	Dec. (approx.)	Broke adrift from Hopetoun II, Port Edgar.
LANDING CRAFT EMERGENCY REPAIR (W.L. 10 tons)		
Nos. 1, 9 (total 2)	Oct.	Lost in Mediterranean.
LANDING CRAFT FLAK (Mark III) (W.L. 550 tons)		
No. 13	12 June	Bombed off Pantellaria, Central Mediterranean. Total wreck.
LANDING CRAFT GUN (Large) (Mark III) (W.L. 627 tons)		
Nos. 15	25 Apr.	⎫ Lost off Milford Haven in heavy weather.
16	26 Apr.	⎭
LANDING CRAFT INFANTRY (Large) (W.L. 380–384 tons)		
Nos. 162	7 Feb.	Exploded and sank en route for Algiers.
7	21 Apr.	Sunk by A/C. off Algiers.
107	2 Sept.	Wrecked off Reggio, Italy.
309	23 Oct.	Sunk by A/C. in Biscay area.
LANDING CRAFT MECHANISED (Mark I) (W.L. 30–37 tons)		
Nos. 26	2 Jan.	⎫ Sunk in Mediterranean, off Libya.
58	25 Jan.	⎭
80	6 Feb.	Standed off Benghazi. Total loss.
61	8 Feb.	Sunk in Benghazi Harbour through heavy weather.
232	Oct. (approx.)	Lost in Mediterranean.
181	Nov. (date reported).	Lost in Azores.
33	20 Dec.	Damaged beyond repair in Home Waters.
LANDING CRAFT MECHANISED (Mark III) (W.L. 52 tons)		
Nos. 545, 938, 1044 (total 3)	Oct. (approx.).	Lost in Mediterranean.
1165, 1182 (total 2)	Oct. (approx.).	Lost in Home Waters.
583	Nov. (date reported).	Lost in Mediterranean.

Class and Nos.	Date of Loss	How Lost and Where
	1943	
LANDING CRAFT PERSONNEL (Large) (W.L. 8–11 tons)		
Nos. 17	3 Jan.	Lost by fire at Chittagong, India.
80	15 Jan.	Broke adrift during gale in Home Waters.
203–206 (total 4)	Jan.	Lost at Sourabaya, Java.
87	25 Feb.	Lost in Home Waters.
106	4 Mar.	Wrecked off Tobruk.
276, 277 (total 2)	Mar.	Lost in transit.
126	Aug.	Burnt out.
325	4 Sept.	} Sunk at Bombay.
316	12 Sept.	
136	8 Dec.	Caught fire and blew up during exercises off Southampton.
LANDING CRAFT PERSONNEL (Ramped) (W.L. 9–11 tons)		
Nos. 673, 680, 684, 685, 689, 692, 693, 727 (total 8).	4 Mar.	Lost in MARIETTA E., sunk by U/B. in Convoy, Indian Ocean.
780, 782 (total 2)	17 April	Lost in SEMBILAN. Sunk by U/B, Indian Ocean.
769	June (date reported).	Lost in Mediterranean.
879	12 Sept.	Wrecked at Bombay.
1019	28 Sept.	Sunk during heavy weather in Salerno Bay, Italy.
753, 771, 795 (total 3)	19 Dec.	Lost during beaching exercises in Home Waters.
613, 661, 1035 (total 3)	22 Dec.	Lost overboard from HILARY.
LANDING CRAFT PERSONNEL (Medium) (W.L. 7·5 tons)		
Nos. 17	5 Jan.	Lost off Isle of Wight.
14	Nov. (date reported).	—
LANDING CRAFT PERSONNEL (Small) (W.L. 6 tons)		
No. 116	22 Dec.	Lost during exercises in Home Waters.
LANDING CRAFT SUPPORT (Large) (Mark I) (W.L. 23 tons)		
No. 201	Sept.	Lost in collision, English Channel.
LANDING CRAFT SUPPORT (Medium) (Mark I) (W.L. 9–13·5 tons)		
Nos. 23	Mar.	Lost on patrol, Mayu River, Burma.
17	25 Apr.	Sunk by enemy action, Mayu River, Burma.
16	29 Aug.	Lost in India.
LANDING CRAFT TANK (Mark I) (W.L. 372 tons)		
No. 3	11 Oct.*	Presumed lost in attack on Kos, Dodecanese. Formally paid off.
LANDING CRAFT TANK (Mark II) (W.L. 450–453 tons)		
Nos. 106, 107 (total 2)	6 Jan.	Sunk in Benghazi Harbour as result of heavy weather.
115	28 Oct.	Sunk by A/C. off Casteloriso, Aegean.
LANDING CRAFT TANK (Mark III) (W.L. 625–640 tons)		
Nos. 326	2 Feb.	Lost by weather or mine off Isle of Man.
403	24 Feb.	Lost through stress of weather off Barra Head, outer Hebrides.
381	27 Feb.	Missing from Convoy after attack by E/Bs, English Channel.
358	18 June	Lost in Mediterranean.
395	18 June	Mined and grounded in Mediterranean.
353	27 July	Sunk by A/C. at Syracuse, Sicily.
391	1 Oct. (approx.).	Formally paid off.

* Later recovered and redesignated N.S.C.(L) 94.

Class and Nos.	Date of Loss	How Lost and Where
	1943	
LANDING CRAFT TANK		
(Mark III) (W.L. 625–640 tons)—*cont.*		
Nos. 333, 343, 385 (total 3)	14 Nov.	Sunk in gale off Land's End.
332	16 Nov.	Lost off Gijon, Spain, after engine failure.
418	16 Nov.	Lost in gale off N.W. France.
329	23 Nov.	Damaged beyond economical repair.
LANDING CRAFT TANK		
(Mark IV) (W.L. 611–640 tons)		
Nos. 547	8 July	Foundered off Malta.
624	8 Sept.	Formally paid off.
572, 626 (total 2)	9 Sept.	
553	1 Oct.	
618	2 Oct.	Lost in Mediterranean.
621	7 Oct.	
583	4 Nov.	
LANDING CRAFT TANK		
(Mark V) (W.L. 291–311 tons)		
Nos. 2239, 2267, 2344 (total 3)	17 Jan.	Lost in VESTFOLD, torpedoed in convoy, N. Atlantic.
2335	7 Feb.	Lost in DAGHILD, torpedoed in convoy, N. Atlantic.
2480	8 Mar.	Lost in FORT LAMY, torpedoed in convoy, N. Atlantic.
2341	10 Mar.	Lost in BONNEVILLE, torpedoed in convoy, N. Atlantic.
2398	Mar.	Lost in GORGAS.
2231	30 Sept.	Lost in L.S.T. 79, sunk off Corsica.
LANDING CRAFT VEHICLE		
(W.L. 10–11 tons)		
Nos. 584	15 Mar.	Sunk off Inellan, W. Scotland.
825	21–22 May	Blew up during exercises off W. Scotland.
LANDING CRAFT VEHICLE (Personnel)		
(W.L. 10·5–13·5 tons)		
No. 1040	1 Nov.	Capsized off Newhaven after engine room flooding.

Class	Name or Number	Tonnage	Date of Completion	Date of Loss	How Lost and Where
				1944	
LANDING SHIPS INFANTRY (LARGE).	EL HIND (R)	5,319	—	14 Apr.	Destroyed by fire in Bombay Docks.
	EMPIRE BROADSWORD ...	4,285 (Light)	—	2 July	Sunk by mine off Normandy.
	EMPIRE JAVELIN ...	4,285 (Light)	—	28 Dec.	Lost on passage from Portsmouth to Le Havre, believed torpedoed by U/B.
LANDING SHIP INFANTRY (SMALL).	PRINCE LEOPOLD (R) ...	2,938	1930	29 July	Torpedoed by U/B, capsized and sank, English Channel.
LANDING SHIPS TANK (CLASS II).	No. 411	2,750	8. 1.43	1 Jan.	Mined or torpedoed (31 Dec., 1943) on passage from Maddalena to Bastia. Abandoned owing to heavy weather.
	No. 422	2,750	5. 2.43	26 Jan.	Mined and sunk in Operation SHINGLE (Anzio).
	No. 418	2,750	1. 2.43	16 Feb.	Sunk after 2 underwater explosions, Operation SHINGLE (Anzio).
	No. 305	2,750	7.12.42	20 Feb.	Sunk by U/B, torpedo, during Operation SHINGLE (Anzio).
	No. 362	2,750	23.11.42	2 Mar.	Sunk by U/B, torpedo, Biscay area.
	No. 407	2,750	31.12.42	24 Apr.	Damaged beyond repair by weather in Mediterranean.
	No. 420	2,750	16. 2.43	7 Nov.	Sunk by mine off Ostend.
FIGHTER DIRECTION TENDER.	No. 216	2,750	4. 8.43	7 July	Sunk by A/C, torpedo, off Barfleur, N. France.

Class and Nos.	Date of Loss	How Lost and Where
LANDING CRAFT ASSAULT	1944	
(W.L. 11—13·5 tons)		
Nos. 783, 790, 865 (total 3)	19 Jan. (date reported)	Lost in Home Waters off E. Scotland.
845	29 Jan.	Became waterlogged and sank during exercises off Leith, E. Scotland.
323, 394, 428, 697 (total 4)	Jan. (approx.)	Lost in Operation SHINGLE (Anzio).
552	9 Feb.	Wrecked during exercises off E. Scotland.
726, 908 (total 2)	1 March	Lost in Home Waters.
130	May (date reported)	Destroyed by fire at Marve.
364, 382, 398, 417, 433, 459, 492, 526, 573, 761 (total 10)	May (date reported)	Cause and place unknown.
33, 56, 146 (total 3)	June (date reported)	Lost in E. Indies.
182	June (date reported)	Cause and place unknown.
107	6 June	Sunk.
59, 69 (total 2)	15 June	Lost, Bombay area.
171, 208, 279, 289, 303, 320, 337, 339, 341, 349, 350, 352, 360, 367, 383, 387, 401, 409, 418, 424, 431, 434, 442, 458, 462, 463, 476, 485, 494, 496, 503, 509, 518–520, 522, 525, 530, 535, 540, 566, 579, 581, 584, 586, 588–590, 592–594, 611, 613, 623, 637, 642, 649–652, 655, 661, 664, 665, 673, 683, 691, 692, 704, 705, 710, 717, 721, 722, 729, 731, 738, 748, 750, 768, 775, 779, 780, 788, 791, 792, 795–797, 803, 808–810, 812, 814, 815, 821, 825, 827, 835, 849, 853, 857, 859, 860, 867, 869–871, 879, 881, 886, 900, 903, 911, 913, 914, 918–920, 929, 933, 946, 949, 958, 978, 984, 998–1000, 1005, 1008, 1013, 1016, 1021, 1024, 1026–1028, 1034, 1050, 1057–1059, 1063, 1068, 1069, 1074, 1082, 1086, 1088, 1091, 1093, 1096, 1129, 1131, 1132, 1137, 1138, 1143, 1144, 1146, 1149–1151, 1155, 1156, 1213, 1215, 1216, 1251–1253, 1256, 1338–1341, 1343, 1372, 1379, 1381–1383 (total 184).	June-July	Lost in Operation NEPTUNE (Normandy).
54	July (date reported)	Lost in E. Indies.
248, 400 (total 2)	1 July	Lost in Mediterranean.
1393	3 July	Lost in Operation OVERLORD (Normandy).
1304	14 July	Lost in heavy weather in Home Waters.
577, 625 (total 2)	Sept. (date reported)	Lost in Mediterranean.
848, 1378 (total 2)	26 Sept.	Lost in heavy weather in Home Waters.
713, 725, 817, 831, 843, 1018, 1030, 1079, 1125, 1260 (total 10)	2–5 Nov.	Lost in Operation INFATUATE (Walcheren).
551	7 Nov.	Lost in heavy weather, River Blackwater, Essex.
149	16 Nov.	Lost in India.
614	29 Nov.	Lost in heavy weather, English Channel.
1188	Dec.	Lost in Solomon Islands.
326	—	Lost in Mediterranean.
226, 254, 347, 440, 487, 696, 753 (total 7)	—	Cause and place unknown.
LANDING CRAFT ASSAULT		
(Hedgerow) (W.L. 12 tons)		
689	13 Mar.	Sank in Home Waters.
672, 811 (total 2)	2 Apr.	Foundered during exercises off E. Scotland.
671, 690, 965, 1072 (total 4)	June-July	Lost in Operation NEPTUNE (Normandy).
183, 258, 802 (total 3)	1 July	Lost in Mediterranean.
LANDING CRAFT EMERGENCY REPAIR		
(W.L. 10 tons)		
Nos. 5, 14, 21 (total 3)	May (date reported)	Cause and place unknown.
15	13 July.	
LANDING CRAFT FLAK		
(Mark II) (W.L. 500–540 tons)		
No. 1	17 Aug.	Blew up and sank, Operation NEPTUNE (Normandy).
LANDING CRAFT FLAK		
(Mark III) (W.L. 515–550 tons)		
No. 15	16–17 June	Mined in Convoy, Operation BRASSARD (Elba).

Class and Nos.	Date of Loss	How Lost and Where
LANDING CRAFT FLAK	1944	
(Mark IV,) (W.L. 500–510 tons)		
Nos. 31	5 Sept. (date reported)	Lost in Operation NEPTUNE (Normandy).
37, 38 (total 2)	1 Nov.	Lost in Operation INFATUATE (Walcheren).
LANDING CRAFT GUN (Large)		
(Mark III) (W.L. 500 tons)		
Nos. 1, 2 (total 2)	2 Nov.	Lost in Operation INFATUATE (Walcheren).
LANDING CRAFT GUN (Large)		
(Mark IV) (W.L. 530 tons)		
Nos. 764, 831, 1062 (total 3)	July-Aug.	Lost in Operation NEPTUNE (Normandy).
LANDING CRAFT GUN (Medium)		
(Mark I) (W.L. 381 tons)		
Nos. 101, 102 (total 2)	1 Nov.	Los. in Operation INFATUATE (Walcheren).
LANDING CRAFT HEADQUARTERS		
(W.L. 384 tons)		
No. 185	25 June	Sunk by mine, Operation NEPTUNE (Normandy).
LANDING CRAFT INFANTRY (Large)		
(W.L. 380–384 tons)		
No. 273	17 Mar.	Sunk by A/C, Anzio.
105	8 June	Torpedoed, Operation NEPTUNE (Normandy).
132	17 June	Lost and formally paid off.
99	14 Aug.	Sunk in Convoy, presumed by U/B, Operation NEPTUNE (Normandy).
102	11 Nov.	Damaged by gales and abandoned, Vis, Adriatic.
LANDING CRAFT INFANTRY (Small)		
(W.L. 110 tons)		
Nos. 511	2 Feb.	Beached at Portslade, Sussex. Total loss.
512, 517, 524, 531, 540 (total 5)	June	Lost in Operation NEPTUNE (Normandy).
537	June	Damaged beyond economical repair.
532	1 Nov.	Lost in Operation INFATUATE (Walcheren).
LANDING CRAFT MECHANISED		
(Mark I) (W.L. 30–37 tons)		
Nos. 192, 234, 254, 279, 282, 327, 329, 367 (total 8)	Feb. (date reported)	Lost in Home Waters.
76	Mar. (date reported)	Lost in E. Indies.
131, 182, 183, 207, 209 (total 5)	May (date reported)	
212, 215, 218, 219, 243, 272, 277, 285, 288, 324 (total 10)	May (date reported)	Lost overseas.
91	June (date reported)	Lost in E. Indies.
295	June (date reported)	Lost overseas.
127, 128, 165, 168, 180, 191, 203, 216, 226, 229, 231, 241, 251, 281, 316, 319, 330, 335, 337, 338, 345, 346, 348, 355, 357, 377, 382, 383, 408, 409, 419, 421, 425, 443, 444, 466 (total 36).	June–July	Lost in Operation NEPTUNE (Normandy).
138	7 July	Lost, English Channel.
263	11 Sept.	Wrecked on beach, Operation NEPTUNE (Normandy).
340, 424 (total 2)	19 Nov.	Lost overboard from JOHN L. MANSON in Mount's Bay.
LANDING CRAFT MECHANISED		
(Mark III) (W.L. 52 tons)		
Nos. 623, 910, 930, 1022, 1064, 1173, 1204 (total 7).	Jan. (approx.)	Lost in Operation SHINGLE (Anzio).
1313, 1314, 1373, 1378 (total 4)	Apr. (date reported)	Lost on passage from U.S.A. to India.
527, 534, 540, 588, 1029, 1045, 1071, 1083, 1123, 1171, 1205 (total 11).	May (date reported)	Lost overseas.
1380, 1381 (total 2)...	May (date reported)	Lost in Mediterranean.
1115, 1130 (total 2)...	June (date reported)	
577	June	Lost in Operation OVERLORD (Normandy).

Class and Nos.	Date of Loss	How Lost and Where
LANDING CRAFT MECHANISED (Mark III) (W.L. 52 tons)—*cont.*	1944	
531, 535, 568, 587, 627, 628, 631, 641, 908, 929, 1053, 1059, 1062, 1088, 1098, 1108, 1120, 1127, 1128, 1139, 1145, 1146, 1161, 1175, 1189, 1197, 1200, 1207, 1208, 1212, 1220, 1221, 1227, 1232, 1233, 1240, 1244, 1278, 1282, 1293, 1297, 1397 (total 42).	June–July	Lost in Operation NEPTUNE (Normandy).
618, 640 (total 2)	9 Aug.	Lost in Mediterranean.
1101	15 Nov.	Wrecked near Aden, en route to India.
525, 559, 591, 650, 907 (total 5)	—	Lost overseas, presumed during 1944.
LANDING CRAFT PERSONNEL (Large) (W.L. 8–11 tons)		
Nos. 66, 356, 373 (total 3)	Jan. (approx.)	Lost in Operation SHINGLE (Anzio).
152	24 Feb.	Wrecked during exercises in Home Waters.
541	28–29 Feb.	Lost off Isle of Wight.
360, 367 (total 2)	Apr. (date reported)	Lost during exercises at Mandapam.
323	14 Apr.	Destroyed in explosion at Bombay.
8, 263, 287, 577 (total 4)	May (date reported)	Lost overseas.
13, 14, 21–23, 40, 51, 121, 132, 139, 170, 175, 176, 187, 189, 197, 199, 208, 272, 280, 282, 285, 286, 289, 309, 312, 528, 556 (total 28).	June–July	Lost in Operation NEPTUNE (Normandy).
267	8 July	Sunk by mine off Cherbourg.
229, 298–300, 303–305, 308, 310 (total 9)	July	Lost in Home Waters.
84, 85, 88, 97, 98, 110, 118, 128, 137, 145, 146, 149, 162, 163, 198, 200, 230–233, 235, 238, 239, 241, 242, 246, 247, 269, 293, 294 (total 30)	Aug.–Sept.	Lost in Operation NEPTUNE (Normandy) while on loan to U.S. Navy.
348	15 Sept.	Destroyed by fire in India.
7, 18 (total 2)	6 Oct.	Lost in Home Waters.
52	11 Oct.	Lost by fire, Portsmouth Area.
133	5 Nov.	Lost in Schelde Area.
302	5 Nov.	Wrecked East of Ostend.
127, 134 (total 2)	Dec. (date reported)	Lost in Operation INFATUATE (Walcheren).
540, 760 (total 2)	—	Lost overseas, presumed during 1944.
LANDING CRAFT PERSONNEL (Ramped) (W.L. 9–11 tons)		
Nos. 616	22 Jan.	Broke adrift and badly holed in Home Waters.
781	14 Feb.	Lost in collision, Home Waters.
1026	23 Mar.	Sunk in Mediterranean.
866	14 Apr.	Destroyed by fire at Bombay.
614, 634, 663, 824, 844, 912, 913, 995 (total 8)	May (date reported)	Lost overseas.
584	May	Sunk in Home Waters.
643	May (approx.)	Lost at Naples.
723	June (date reported)	Lost in Mediterranean.
854	June (date reported)	Cause and place unknown.
966	June (date reported)	Damaged en route to Anzio.
970	June (date reported)	Lost in Home Waters.
867	June	Wrecked at Mandapam, Ceylon.
894, 896 (total 2)	June	Lost in Operation NEPTUNE (Normandy).
895	June	Damaged and sunk, Portsmouth area.
905	19 June	Lost in bad weather in Home Waters.
683	July (date reported)	Lost in action off coast of France.
971	28 July	Lost in collision in Home Waters.
999	26 Sept.	Sunk in gale in Home Waters.
1011	21 Oct.	Lost in collision in Home Waters.
805, 806 (total 2)	Nov (date reported)	Cause and place unknown.
652, 669 (total 2)	—	Lost in Home Waters, presumed during 1944.
640, 735, 978, 982, 987, 989, 991, 993, 1023 (total 9)	—	Lost overseas, presumed during 1944.
LANDING CRAFT PERSONNEL (Survey) (W.L. 9 tons)		
No. 154	July (date reported)	Cause and place unknown.

Class and Nos.	Date of Loss	How Lost and Where
LANDING CRAFT PERSONNEL .(Small) (W.L. 6 tons)	1944	
Nos. 60	25 Jan.	Wrecked in Azores.
76	13 Mar.	Lost on passage.
9	6 Apr.	Driven ashore at Weymouth.
74	May (date reported)	Lost overboard at Messina.
25, 50, 61, 73, 101, 135, 137 (total 7) ...	May (date reported)	Cause and place unknown.
136	June	Lost in Operation NEPTUNE (Normandy).
183	July (date reported)	Wrecked in Mediterranean.
129	10 Nov.	Lost by fire at Hythe.
1	—	Cause and place unknown.
LANDING CRAFT SUPPORT (Large) (Mark II) (W.L. 112 tons)		
Nos. 252, 256, 258 (total 3)	1 Nov.	Lost in Operation INFATUATE (Walcheren).
LANDING CRAFT SUPPORT (Medium) (Mark III) (W.L. 13·5 tons)		
Nos. 46	Jan. (approx.)	Lost in Operation SHINGLE (Anzio).
69	3 Mar.	Sunk during exercises off E. Scotland.
59	May (date reported)	Cause and place unknown.
75, 76, 80, 81, 83, 91, 99, 101, 103, 108, 114 (total 11)	June	Lost in Operation NEPTUNE (Normandy).
47	June	
54	1 July	Cause and place unknown.
42	25 Aug.	
49	—	
LANDING CRAFT TANK (Mark II) (W.L. 450–453 tons)		
No. 129	Nov. (date reported)	Cause and place unknown.
LANDING CRAFT TANK (Mark III) (W.L. 625–640 tons)		
Nos. 375	Feb. (date reported)	Sunk in Mediterranean.
390	9 July	Cause and place unknown.
7057, 7064 (total 2)	16 July	
387	17 July	Mined off W. Italy.
427	Aug.	Cause and place unknown.
377	Oct.	Lost, probably mined, on passage Marseilles to Maddalena.
480, 488, 491, 494, 7014, 7015 (total 6) ...	18—19 Oct.	Lost through stress of weather off Land's End.
7011	2 Nov.	Lost in Operation INFATUATE (Walcheren).
328	5 Dec.	Mined off W. Greece.
7089	6 Dec.	Hit obstruction in Boulogne Harbour. Total loss.
LANDING CRAFT TANK (Mark IV) (W.L. 611–640 tons)		
Nos. 1029	16 Jan.	Blew up, possibly mined, while at anchor off Skegness.
875	8 June	Sunk by enemy action.
967	13 June	Mined.
524, 715, 750, 809, 886, 947 (total 6) ...	June	Lost in Operation NEPTUNE (Normandy).
589	16 June	Destroyed to avoid capture, Mediterranean.
511	9 July	Broke back while in tow.
757	10 July	Formally paid off.
689	20 July	Destroyed by explosion.
1023	23 July	Damaged beyond economical repair.
901	24 July	Broke backs.
1039	5 Aug.	
1076	5 Aug.	Broke in two.
1092	10 Aug.	Broke back while in tow.
631	17 Aug.	Broke back.
1074	25 Aug.	Mined, English Channel.
943	Oct.	Sunk.
1045	25 Oct.	Broke in two while in tow, English Channel.
936	30 Oct.	Broke back through stress of weather off Lowestoft.
1171	23 Oct.	Sunk off N. European Coast.
789, 839, 1133 (total 3)	2 Nov.	Lost in Operation INFATUATE (Walcheren).
609	6 Nov.	Abandoned after damage by weather off Ostend.
976	7 Nov.	Abandoned with broken back, Schelde area.
1022	17 Nov.	Wrecked through stress of weather off Dungeness.

Class and Nos.	Date of Loss	How Lost and Where
LANDING CRAFT TANK (Mark V) (W.L. 291–311 tons)	1944	
Nos. 2498	June	Lost in Operation NEPTUNE (Normandy).
2049, 2229, 2307 (total 3)	6 June	Lost in Operation NEPTUNE (Normandy) while on loan to U.S. Navy.
2331	July	Broken back.
2461	Nov.	Capsized and sunk by gunfire, Bay of Bengal.
LANDING CRAFT TANK (Armoured) (Mark V) (W.L. 290–295 tons)		
Nos. 2039	June	Cause and place unknown.
2273, 2301, 2402 (total 3)	June	Lost in Operation NEPTUNE (Normandy) while on loan to U.S. Navy.
2428	June	Lost in Operation NEPTUNE (Normandy).
2263	15 July	Cause and place unknown.
2454	13 Oct.	Ran ashore in Lyme Bay, English Channel, in heavy gale. Wrecked.
LANDING CRAFT TANK (Rocket) (W.L. 600 tons)		
No. 457	5 Nov.	Mined off Ostend.
LANDING CRAFT VEHICLE (W.L. 10–11 tons)		
Nos. 894	Feb. (date reported)	Lost on service with R.A.S.C., C.T.C., Rothesay.
719	June	Cause and place unknown.
801	18 Oct.	Broke adrift and holed, Portsmouth area.
LANDING CRAFT VEHICLE (Personnel) (W.L. 10·5–13·5 tons)		
Nos. 1066	Feb.	Lost during exercises, Richborough area, Kent.
1016, 1029, 1031, 1033, 1044–1046, 1049, 1054, 1056, 1062, 1065, 1084, 1088, 1093, 1098, 1101, 1102, 1104, 1106, 1111, 1114, 1117, 1120–1122, 1124, 1129, 1132, 1133, 1139, 1146, 1153, 1155, 1157, 1159, 1165, 1170–1172, 1184, 1188, 1201, 1204, 1211, 1216, 1218, 1242, 1245, 1246, 1248, 1249, 1251, 1255, 1260, 1262, 1264 (total 57).	June (approx.)	Lost in Operation NEPTUNE (Normandy).
1288	13 July	Lost in Home Waters.
1103	20 Nov.	Abandoned at Chichester.
1199	25 Nov.	Sank, Portsmouth area.
1228	27 Nov.	Lost in Home Waters.
LANDING BARGES, EMERGENCY REPAIR (200 ton type)		
Nos. 8, 17, 25–27, 57, 60 (total 7)	19–25 June	Written off charge as result of damage caused in assault area during gale.
LANDING BARGES, OILER (200 ton type)		
Nos. 50	June	Cause and place unknown.
46, 56, 84 (total 3)	19–25 June	Written off charge as result of damage caused in assault area during gale.
87	11th July ⎫	Cause and place unknown.
53	9 Aug. ⎭	
(150 ton type)		
10	19–25 June	Written off charge as result of damage caused in assault area during gale.
73	9 Aug. ⎫	
4	17 Aug.	Cause and place unknown.
30	31 Aug. ⎭	
LANDING BARGES, VEHICLE (Mark I) (150 ton type)		
Nos. 367	17 Jan.	Wrecked on passage Dartmouth to Portland.
136, 149, 497 (total 3)	Feb. ⎫	
229, 266 (total 2)	Mar. (date reported)	Cause and place unknown.
52	7 June ⎭	
16, 51 (total 2)	12 June	Lost through stress of weather.
84	26 June ⎫	
121, 175 (total 2)	1 July ⎭	Cause and place unknown.
154	14 Aug.	Sank at moorings off Portsmouth.
83	19 Aug.	Sank in tow.

Class and Nos.	Date of Loss	How Lost and Where
LANDING BARGES, VEHICLE (Mark II) (200 ton type)	1944.	
Nos. 172, 176, 206, 232 (total 4)	19–25 June	Written off charge as result of damage caused in assault area during gale.
(150 ton type)		
16, 20, 51 (total 3)	June	Cause and place unknown.
3, 27, 49, 61, 67, 94, 95, 103, 209, 214 (total 10).	19–25 June	Written off charge as result of damage caused in assault area during gale.
19, 28, 116, 122 (total 4)	29 July	Cause and place unknown.
LANDING BARGES, WATER (200 ton type)		
Nos. 15	19–25 June	Written off charge as result of damage caused in assault area during gale.
(150 ton type)		
7	19–25 June	Written off charge as result of damage caused in assault area during dale.
14	29 Aug.	} Cause and place unknown.
11	12 Sept.	
RAMPED DUMB BARGES (100 ton type)		
Nos. 83	23 May	Sank on passage to Sheerness.
43, 65 (total 2)	1 July	Cause and place unknown.

Class	Name	Tonnage	Date of Completion	Date of Loss	How Lost and Where
				1945	
LANDING SHIPS TANK (Class II)	No. 364	2,750	7.12.42	22 Feb.	Torpedoed by U/B. off Ramsgate.
	178	2,750		24 Feb.	Mined on passage to Corfu, grounded and became total wreck.
	80	2,750	19.7.43	20 Mar.	Mined in English Channel and sank off Ostend.

Class and Nos.	Date of Loss	How Lost and Where
LANDING CRAFT ASSAULT (W.L. 11–13·5 tons)	1945	
Nos. 1161	26 Feb.	Lost through heavy weather at Leyte, Pacific.
1112, 1153 (total 2)	Mar. (date reported)	Presumed lost during 1945.
1472	27 Mar.	Lost at Leyte, Pacific.
1433	30 Mar.	Smashed by heavy seas. Admiralty Islands, S.W. Pacific.
1346, 1396 (total 2)	Apr. (date reported)	Lost in Mediterranean ; presumed during 1945.
841	22 Apr.	Sunk in operations off Holland.
1329, 1591 (total 2)	17 Aug.	Lost overboard from L.S.I. off India.
LANDING CRAFT ASSAULT (Obstruction Clearance) (W.L. 13·5 tons)		
1211	May (date reported)	Lost in Home Waters, presumed during 1945.
LANDING CRAFT MECHANISED (Mark I) (W.L. 30–37 tons)		
Nos. 136	Feb. (date reported)	Cause and place unknown.
270, 339, 359, 422 (total 4)	Feb. (date reported)	Lost from ASA LOTHROP.
354, 493 (total 2)	June (date reported)	Lost in operations on Arakan Coast, Burma.
LANDING CRAFT MECHANISED (Mark III) (W.L. 52 tons)		
Nos. 1131	23 Jan.	Lost in Arromanches Area, Normandy.
1011	Mar. (date reported)	Lost in Mediterranean.
1319, 1327 (total 2)	Apr.	Lost on Arakan Coast, Burma.
1092	June (date reported)	Cause and place unknown.

Class and Nos.	Date of Loss	How Lost and Where
LANDING CRAFT MECHANISED (Mark III) (W.L. 52 tons)—*cont.*	1945	
1185	July (date reported)	Lost, presumed during 1945.
LANDING CRAFT PERSONNEL (Large) (W.L. 8–11 tons)		
Nos. 11	18 Jan.	Lost on Passage from Brest to Cherbourg.
764	18 Mar.	Lost in Home Waters.
344, 378 (total 2)	29 May	Sunk at Akyab, Burma.
LANDING CRAFT PERSONNEL (Ramped) (W.L. 9–11 tons)		
Nos. 1018	.26 Jan.	Lost in Scheldt area.
707	22 Feb.	Lost by enemy action in Home Waters.
979	5 Mar.	Lost when in use as ship's boat in Eastern Theatre.
840	28 Mar.	Lost by enemy action in Home Waters.
738	9 Apr.	Lost during storm in Mediterranean.
832	June (date reported)	Lost in tow in Mediterranean.
965	July (date reported)	
LANDING CRAFT PERSONNEL (Mark II) (W.L. 3·8 tons)		
Nos. 1110, 1121 (total 2)	May	Lost in Aegean Operations.
1113	June (date reported)	Damaged in gale at Maddalena and written off.
LANDING CRAFT SUPPORT (Medium) (Mark II) (W.L. 12·5 tons)		
No. 30	June (date reported)	Lost in operations on Arakan Coast, Burma.
LANDING CRAFT SUPPORT (Medium) (Mark III) (W.L. 13·5 tons)		
No. 148	June (date reported)	Lost in operations on Arakan Coast, Burma.
LANDING CRAFT TANK (Mark III) (W.L. 625–640 tons)		
Nos. 492	6 Mar.	Capsized and sank, Red Sea.
357	29 May	Lost in Suda Bay, Crete, as result of explosion.
LANDING CRAFT TANK (Mark IV) (W.L. 611–640 tons)		
No. 1238	2 May	Mined in Rangoon River.
LANDING CRAFT VEHICLE (W.L. 10–11 tons)		
No. 814	30 Jan.	Lost in Home Waters.
802	2 Aug.	Lost in tow in Home Waters.
LANDING CRAFT VEHICLE (Personnel) (W.L. 10·5–13·5 tons)		
1191	Jan.	Cause and place unknown.
LANDING CRAFT VEHICLE (Personnel) (W.L. 10·5–13·5 tons)		
1358	Apr.	Lost by stranding, E. Mediterranean.
1167	15 July	Lost, Channel Islands.
LANDING BARGE, EMERGENCY REPAIR (200 ton type)		
Nos. 12, 30, 32–34 (total 5)	June (date reported)	Written off.
LANDING BARGE, KITCHEN		
No. 8	31 July	Sank in tow, English Channel
LANDING BARGES, OILER (200 ton type)		
Nos. 13, 37, 63, 69, 88, 96 (total 6)	June (date reported)	Written off.
(150 ton type)		
Nos. 17	20 Jan.	Swamped and sank in Arromanches Harbour during gale.
11, 21, 24, 26, 77, 82, 92, 95 (total 8) ...	June (date reported)	Written off.

Class and Nos.	Date and Loss	How Lost and Where
LANDING BARGE, VEHICLE	1945	
(Mark II) (200 ton type)		
Nos. 152	May (date reported)	
137, 140, 157, 170 (total 4)	June (date reported)	} Written off.
132	29 July	
(150 ton type)		
Nos. 1, 5, 9, 11, 31, 35, 42, 65, 72, 73, 75, 76, 99, 118, 211, 212 (total 16)	June (date reported)	Written off.
.LANDING BARGE, WATER		
(150 ton type)		
Nos. 1, 6 (total 2)	June (date reported)	Written off.
RAMPED DUMB BARGES		
(150 ton type)		
No. 114	June (date reported)	Written off.
59	26 Nov.	Sank in Edinburgh Channel.

II. SUMMARY OF LOSSES BY YEAR AND CLASS
LANDING SHIPS

Class	3 Sept., 1939 to 31 Dec. 1939	1940	1941	1942	1943	1944	1 Jan. 1945 to 15 Aug. 1945	Total	Total Displacement Tonnage lost
LANDING SHIPS INFANTRY—									
(LARGE)	—	—	—	1	—	3	—	4	8,570 (Light) 15,209
(SMALL)	—	—	—	—	—	1	—	1	2,938
LANDING SHIPS TANK—									
(MARK II)	—	—	—	—	3	7	3	13	35,750
FIGHTER DIRECTION TENDER	—	—	—	—	—	1	—	1	2,750
RAIDING CRAFT CARRIER ...	—	—	1	—	—	—	—	1	2,938
TOTAL NUMBERS	—	—	1	1	3	12	3	20	—
TOTAL TONNAGE :									
STANDARD DISPLACEMENT	—	—	—	—	8,250	22,000	8,250	—	38,500
LIGHT DISPLACEMENT ...	—	—	—	—	—	8,570	—	—	8,570
GROSS REGISTERED TONNAGE	—	—	2,938	9,890	—	8,257	—	—	21,085

LANDING CRAFT

Class	3 Sept., 1939 to 31 Dec., 1939	1940	1941	1942	1943	1944	1 Jan., 1945 to 15 Aug., 1945	Total
LANDING CRAFT—								
ASSAULT	—	10	22	59	15	244	10	360
(HEDGEROW)	—	—	—	—	—	10	—	10
(OBSTRUCTION CLEARANCE)	—	—	—	—	—	—	1	1
LANDING CRAFT EMERGENCY REPAIR	—	—	—	—	2	4	—	6
LANDING CRAFT FLAK—								
(MARK II)	—	—	—	1	—	1	—	2
(MARK III)	—	—	—	—	1	1	—	2
LANDING CRAFT GUN—								
(LARGE) (MARK III)	—	—	—	—	2	2	—	4
(LARGE) (MARK IV)	—	—	—	—	—	3	—	3
(MEDIUM)	—	—	—	—	—	2	—	2
LANDING CRAFT HEADQUARTERS	—	—	—	—	—	1	—	1
LANDING CRAFT INFANTRY—								
(LARGE)	—	—	—	—	4	5	—	9
(SMALL)	—	—	—	—	—	8	—	8
LANDING CRAFT MECHANISED—								
(MARK I)	—	10	12	39	7	66	7	141
(MARK III)	—	—	—	44	6	77	6	133
LANDING CRAFT PERSONNEL								
(LARGE)	—	1	14	37	14	90	4	160
(RAMPED)	—	—	—	19	19	40	7	85
(SURVEY)	—	—	—	—	—	1	—	1
(MEDIUM)	—	—	—	—	2	—	—	2
(SMALL)	—	—	—	—	1	15'	—	16
(MARK II)	—	—	—	—	—	—	3	3
LANDING CRAFT SUPPORT—								
(LARGE) (MARK I)	—	—	—	—	1	—	—	1
(LARGE) (MARK II)	—	—	—	—	—	3	—	3
(MEDIUM) (MARK I)	—	—	1	9	3	—	—	13
(MEDIUM) (MARK II)	—	—	—	1	—	—	1	2
(MEDIUM) (MARK III)	—	—	—	—	—	18	1	19
LANDING CRAFT TANK—								
(MARK I)	—	—	14	—	1	—	—	15
(MARK II)	—	—	6	9	3	1	—	19
(MARK III)	—	—	—	—	13	16	2	31
(MARK IV)	—	—	—	—	8	30	1	39
(MARK V)	—	—	—	8	8	6	—	22
(ARMOURED) (MARK V)	—	—	—	—	—	7	—	7
(ROCKET)	—	—	—	—	—	1	—	1
LANDING CRAFT VEHICLE	—	—	—	5	2	3	2	12
(PERSONNEL)	—	—	—	—	1	62	3	66
TOTAL	—	21	69	231	113	717	48	1,199
LANDING BARGES—								
(UNCLASSIFIED)	—	—	—	3	—	—	—	3
LANDING BARGES, EMERGENCY REPAIR	—	—	—	—	—	7	5	12
LANDING BARGE, KITCHEN	—	—	—	—	—	—	1	1
LANDING BARGES, OILER	—	—	—	—	—	10	15	25
LANDING BARGES, VEHICLE—								
(MARK I)	—	—	—	—	—	14	—	14
(MARK II)	—	—	—	—	—	21	22	43
LANDING BARGES, WATER	—	—	—	—	—	4	2	6
RAMPED DUMB BARGES	—	—	—	—	—	3	2	5
TOTAL	—	—	—	3	—	59	47	109
GRAND TOTAL LANDING CRAFT AND LANDING BARGES	—	21	69	234	113	776	95	1,308

INDEX

Section IV
BRITISH MERCHANT VESSELS LOST OR DAMAGED BY ENEMY ACTION DURING SECOND WORLD WAR

BRITISH MERCHANT VESSELS LOST OR DAMAGED BY ENEMY ACTION DURING SECOND WORLD WAR

3rd SEPTEMBER, 1939 TO 2nd SEPTEMBER, 1945

FOREWORD

This volume contains a list of all British Merchant and Fishing vessels lost or damaged by enemy action. The dates and positions given are, as a rule, those on which the vessels were attacked. In the case of ships lost other than on the actual date of attack, the fact has been noted in the remarks column together with any other relevant particulars.

The detailed information is as recorded in the Admiralty at 15th September, 1945.

British merchant ships commissioned for naval service or used as Royal Fleet Auxiliaries, are not included. Merchant vessels on charter to or requisitioned by the Admiralty are included, being distinguished by a * after their names in the name column.

Cases of minor or superficial damage to vessels have been omitted.

A table has also been included showing the monthly total of all non-enemy merchant shipping tonnage sunk correct to the nearest 1,000 tons, together with an analysis by cause ; and also a statement of casualties to personnel.

The following definition and abbreviations have been adopted :—

DEFINITION

British Merchant Vessels

Merchant vessels under the British Flag (i.e. those on United Kingdom, Dominion, Indian or Colonial Registers, and vessels on Bareboat Charter or on Requisition from other Flags).

ABBREVIATIONS

TYPE			
S.	Steamship	M.T.	Motor Trawler
M.	Motor Vessel	F.V.	Fishing Vessel
T-E.	Turbo Electric	Aux.	Sailing Vessel with auxiliary motor
S.B.	Sailing Barge		
S.V.	Sailing Vessel	Tank	Tanker
S.T.	Steam Trawler	O.R.	Oil Refinery
		Sch.	Schooner

CAUSE OF LOSS			
S.M.	Submarine	C.U.	Cause unknown or uncertain
A.C.	Aircraft		

OTHER			
Lt.	Light	B.	Bomb
L.H.	Lighthouse	G.	Gunfire
L.V.	Light Vessel	Nr.	Near
Pt.	Point	Est.	Estimated
m.	Miles	Approx.	Approximate
T.	Torpedo	*	Presumed

* After a Vessel's name in the *name* column indicates that she was on charter to or requisitioned by the Admiralty.

CONTENTS

LIST I

BRITISH MERCHANT VESSELS LOST BY ENEMY ACTION

Date	Name	Type	Gross tons	Position	Cause of loss	How lost	Remarks
SEPTEMBER, 1939							
3	ATHENIA	S.	13,581	56°44′N. 14°05′W.	S.M.	T.	
5	BOSNIA	S.	2,407	45°29′N. 09°45′W.	S.M.	T. & G.	
5	ROYAL SCEPTRE ...	S.	4,853	46°23′N. 14°59′W.	S.M.	T. & G.	
6	RIO CLARO ...	S.	4,086	46°30′N. 12°00′W.	S.M.	T. & G.	
6	MANAAR	S.	7,242	38°28′N. 10°50′W.	S.M.	T. & G.	
7	PUKKASTAN ...	S.	5,809	49°23′N. 07°49′W.	S.M.	T. & G.	
7	OLIVEGROVE ...	S.	4,060	49°05′N. 15°58′W.	S.M.	T.	
7	GARTAVON ...	S.	1,777	47°04′N. 11°32′W.	S.M.	G.	
8	WINKLEIGH ...	S.	5,055	48°06′N. 18°12′W.	S.M.	T.	
8	REGENT TIGER ...	M. Tank	10,177	49°57′N. 15°34′W.	S.M.	T.	
8	KENNEBEC... ...	S. Tank	5,548	49°18′N. 08°13′W.	S.M.	T. & G.	Wreckage sunk by H.M.S. on 9th Sept.
10	GOODWOOD ...	S.	2,796	1m. S.E. of Flamboro' Head (Approx.)	Mine	—	
10	MAGDAPUR... ...	S.	8,641	52°11′N. 01°43′E.	Mine	—	
11	BLAIRLOGIE ...	S.	4,425	54°58′N. 15°14′W.	S.M.	T. & G.	Abandoned and sunk in position 54°59′N. 15°09′W.
11	FIRBY	S.	4,869	59°40′N. 13°50′W.	S.M.	T. & G.	
11	INVERLIFFEY ...	M. Tank	9,456	48°14′N. 11°48′W.	S.M.	T. & G.	
13	NEPTUNIA*... ...	Tug	798	49°20′N. 14°40′W.	S.M.	T. & G.	
14	VANCOUVER CITY...	M.	4,955	51°23′N. 07°03′W.	S.M.	T.	
14	FANAD HEAD ...	S.	5,200	56°43′N. 15°21′W.	S.M.	T. & G.	
14	BRITISH INFLUENCE	M. Tank	8,431	49°43′N. 12°49′W.	S.M.	T. & G.	
15	CHEYENNE ...	M. Tank	8,826	50°20′N. 13°30′W.	S.M.	T. & G.	
15	TRURO	S.	974	58°20′N. 02°00′E.	S.M.	T. & G.	
16	AVIEMORE	S.	4,060	49°11′N. 13°38′W.	S.M.	T.	
16	ARKLESIDE ...	S.	1,567	48°00′N. 09°30′W.	S.M.	G.	
16	BRAMDEN ...	S.	1,594	51°22′N. 02°31′E.	Mine	—	
17	KAFIRISTAN ...	S.	5,193	50°16′N. 16°55′W.	S.M.	T.	
18	KENSINGTON COURT	S.	4,863	50°31′N. 08°27′W.	S.M.	G.	
22	AKENSIDE ...	S.	2,694	60°07′N. 04°37′E.	S.M.	T.	
24	HAZELSIDE ...	S.	4,646	51°17′N. 09°22′W.	S.M.	T. & G.	
30	CLEMENT	S.	5,051	09°05′S. 34°05′W.	Raider	—	" Admiral Graf Spee "
	Total... 30		153,634				
OCTOBER, 1939							
4	GLEN FARG ...	S.	876	58°52′N. 01°31′W.	S.M.	T. & G.	
5	STONEGATE ...	S.	5,044	31°10′N. 54°00′W.	Raider	—	" Deutschland "
5	NEWTON BEECH ...	S.	4,651	09°35′S. 06°30′W.	Raider	—	" Admiral Graf Spee "
7	ASHLEA	S.	4,222	09°S. 03°W. (Approx.)	Raider	—	" Admiral Graf Spee "
10	HUNTSMAN ...	S.	8,196	08°30′S. 05°15′W.	Raider	—	" Admiral Graf Spee "
13	HERONSPOOL ...	S.	5,202	50°13′N. 14°48′W.	S.M.	T.	
14	LOCHAVON ...	M.	9,205	50°25′N. 13°10′W.	S.M.	T.	
14	SNEATON ...	S.	3,678	49°05′N. 13°05′W.	S.M.	T. & G.	
17	YORKSHIRE... ...	S.	10,184	44°52′N. 14°31′W.	S.M.	T.	
17	CITY OF MANDALAY	S.	7,028	44°57′N. 13°36′W.	S.M.	T.	
17	CLAN CHISHOLM ...	S.	7,256	45°N. 15°W. (Approx.)	S.M.	T.	
20	SEA VENTURE ...	S.	2,327	60°50′N. 00°15′E.	S.M.	T. & G.	
21	ORSA	S.	1,478	150° 15m. from Flamboro' Head	Mine	—	

Date	Name	Type	Gross tons	Position	Cause of loss	How lost	Remarks
OCTOBER, 1939—(Contd.)							
22	WHITEMANTLE ...	S.	1,692	5 to 6m. E. of Withernsea Lt.	Mine	—	
22	TREVANION... ...	M.	5,299	19°40′S. 04°02′E.	Raider	—	" Admiral Graf Spee "
24	LEDBURY	S.	3,528	36°01′N. 07°22′W.	S.M.	G.	
24	MENIN RIDGE ...	S.	2,474	36°01′N. 07°22′W.	S.M.	T.	
24	TAFNA	S.	4,413	35°44′N. 07°23′W.	S.M.	T.	
27	BRONTE	S.	5,317	49°30′N. 12°15′W.	S.M.	T.	Sunk by H.M.S. on 30th October
29	MALABAR	S.	7,976	49°57′N. 07°37′W.	S.M.	T.	
30	CAIRNMONA ′...	S.	4,666	57°38′N. 01°45′W.	S.M.	T.	
	Total ... 21		104,712				
NOVEMBER, 1939							
9	CARMARTHEN COAST	S.	961	3m. off Seaham Harbour	Mine	—	
13	PONZANO	M.	1,346	51°29′N. 01°25′E.	Mine	—	
13	MATRA	S.	8,003	1m. E. of Tongue L.V.	Mine	—	
15	WOODTOWN ...	S.	794	½m. N.E. of N.E. Spit Buoy, near Margate	Mine	—	
15	AFRICA SHELL ...	M. Tank	706	10½m. S.W. × S. of Cape Zavora L.H.	Raider	—	" Admiral Graf Spee "
16	ARLINGTON COURT	S.	4,915	248° 320m. from Start Pt.	S.M.	T.	
About 17	PARKHILL	S.	500	North Sea	C.U.	—	
18	BLACKHILL ...	S.	2,492	145° 7½ cables from Longsand Head Buoy	Mine	—	
19	TORCHBEARER ...	S.	1,267	025° 2m. from Shipwash L.V.	Mine	—	
19	PENSILVA	S.	4,258	46°51′N. 11°36′W.	S.M.	T.	
19	DARINO	S.	1,351	44°12′N. 11°07′W.	S.M.	T.	
About 20	STANBROOK ...	S.	1,383	North Sea	C.U.	—	
About 20	BOWLING	S.	793	North Sea	C.U.	—	
21	GERALDUS	S.	2,495	3m. W.N.W. of Sunk L.V.	Mine	—	
22	LOWLAND	S.	974	2m. E.N.E. of N.E. Gunfleet Buoy	Mine	—	
23	HOOKWOOD ...	S.	1,537	3½m. E.N.E. of Tongue L.V.	Mine	—	
24	MANGALORE ...	S.	8,886	288° 1½m. from Spurn L.H.	Mine	—	
25	ROYSTON GRANGE...	S.	5,144	49°15′N. 09°00′W. (Approx.)	S.M.	T.	
25	USKMOUTH	S.	2,483	43°22′N. 11°27′W.	S.M.	T. & G.	
28	RUBISLAW ...	S.	1,041	1-1½m. E.N.E. of Tongue L.V.	Mine	—	
29	IONIAN	S.	3,114	132° 1½m. from Newarp L.V.	Mine	—	Abandoned in position 340° 4m. from Newarp L.V.
30	SHEAF CREST ...	S.	2,730	51°32′N. 01°26′E.	Mine	—	
	Total ... 22		57,173				
DECEMBER, 1939							
1	DALRYAN	S.	4,558	2 to 2½m. S.W. of Tongue L.V.	Mine	—	
2	SAN CALISTO ...	M. Tank	8,010	2½m. N.N.E. of Tongue L.V.	Mine	—	
2	DORIC STAR	S.	10,086	19°15′S. 05°05′E.	Raider	—	" Admiral Graf Spee "
3	TAIROA	S.	7,983	20°20′S. 03°05′E.	Raider	—	" Admiral Graf Spee "

Date	Name	Type	Gross tons	Position	Cause of loss	How lost	Remarks
DECEMBER, 1939—(Contd.)							
3	Moortoft	S.	875	North Sea	C.U.	—	
4	Horsted	S.	1,670	53°48'N. 00°16'E.	S.M.	T.	
5	Navasota ..: ...	S.	8,795	50°43'N. 10°16'W.	S.M.	T.	
7	Thomas Walton ...	S.	4,460	67°52'N. 14°28'E.	S.M.	T.	
7	Streonshalh ...	S.	3,895	25°00'S. 27°50'W.	Raider	—	" Admiral Graf Spee "
8	Merel	S.	1,088	Nr. Gull· L.V. off Ramsgate	Mine	—	
8	Brandon	S.	6,668	50°28'N. 08°26'W.	S.M.	T.	
8	Corea	S.	751	2½m. N.E. ¼ N. of Cromer Lt.	Mine	—	
9	San Alberto* ...	M. Tank	7,397	49°20'N. 09°45'W.	S.M.	T.	Sunk on 11th by H.M.S.
10	Willowpool ...	S.	4,815	3m. E. of Newarp L.V.	Mine	—	
12	Marwick Head ...	S.	496	½m. S. of N. Caister Buoy	Mine	—	
12	King Egbert ...	M.	4,535	4m. S.W. of Haisboro' L.V.	Mine	—	
13	Deptford ...	S.	4,101	½m. N.N.W. of Honningsvaag	S.M.	T.	
14	Inverlane ...	M. Tank	9,141	55°05'N. 01°07'W.	Mine	—	
16	Amble	S.	1,162	54°55'N. 01°03'W.	Mine	—	
17	Serenity	M.	487	8m. E.N.E. of Whitby	A.C.	B.	
19	City of Kobe ...	S.	4,373	52°35'N. 01°59'E.	Mine	—	
25	Stanholme ...	S.	2,473	51°20'N. 03°39'W.	Mine	—	
31	Box Hill ...	S.	5,677	53°32'N. 00°24'E.	Mine	—	
	Total ... 23		103,496				
JANUARY, 1940							
7	Cedrington Court	S.	5,160	2m. N.E. of North Goodwin L.V.	Mine	—	
7	Towneley ...	S.	2,888	1m. E.N.E. of N.E. Spit Buoy, nr. Margate	Mine	—	
9	Dunbar Castle ...	M.	10,002	51°23'N. 01°34'E.	Mine	—	
9	Oakgrove	S.	1,985	12 to 15m. S.E. of Cromer Knoll L.V.	A.C.	B.	
9	Gowrie	S.	689	4m. E. of Stonehaven	A.C.	B.	
10	Upminster ...	S.	1,013	53°03'N. 01°29'E.	A.C.	B.	
11	El Oso	S. Tank	7,267	280° 6m. from Bar L.V., Mersey	Mine	—	
11	Keynes	S.	1,706	53°47'N. 00°46'E.	A.C.	B.	Previously attacked in position 53°03'N. 01°40'E.
12	Granta	S.	2,719	53°13'N. 01°21'E.	Mine	—	
16	Inverdargle ...	M. Tank	9,456	51°16'N. 03°43'W.	Mine	—	
17	Cairnross	S.	5,494	276° 7 to 8m. from Bar L.V., Mersey	Mine	—	
17	Polzella	S.	4,751	Off Muckle Flugga, Shetlands	C.U.	—	
20	Caroni River ...	M. Tank	7,807	50°06'N. 05°01'W.	Mine	—	
21	Ferryhill ...	S.	1,086	005° 1½m. from St. Mary's L.V., off Tyne	Mine	—	
21	Protesilaus ...	S.	9,577	51°31'N. 04°04'W.	Mine	—	
23	Baltanglia ...	S.	1,523	55°35'N. 01°27'W.	S.M.	T.	
28	Eston	S.	1,487	Off Blyth	Mine	—	
29	Stanburn	S.	2,881	10m. S.E. × E.¼ S. of Flamboro' Head	A.C.	B.	
29	Leo Dawson ...	S.	4,330	North Sea	C.U..	—	
30	Giralda* ...	S.	2,178	3m. S.E. of Grimness, S. Ronaldsay, Orkneys	A.C.	B.	
30	Vaclite	S. Tank	5,026	49°20'N. 07°04'W.	S.M.	T.	
30	Bancrest	S.	4,450	58°53'N. 01°52'W.	A.C.	B.	

Date	Name	Type	Gross tons	Position	Cause of loss	How lost	Remarks
JANUARY, 1940—*(Contd.)*							
30	VOREDA	S. Tank	7,216	52°59′N. 01°59′E.	A.C.	B.	
30	HIGHWAVE	S.	1,178	1m. N.N.E. of Kentish Knock	A.C.	B.	
	Total ... 24		101,869				
FEBRUARY, 1940							
1	CREOFIELD	S. Tank	838	North Sea	C.U.	—	
2	ELLEN M.	M.	498	North Sea	C.U.	—	
2	PORTELET	S.	1,064	3 to 4m. S.W. × W. of New Smiths Knoll	Mine	—	
2	BRITISH COUNCILLOR	S. Tank	7,048	53°48′N. 00°34′E.	S.M.	T.	Sank on 3rd
3	ARMANISTAN ...	S.	6,805	38°15′N. 11°15′W.	S.M.	T.	
5	BEAVERBURN ...	S.	9,874	49°20′N. 10°07′W.	S.M.	T.	
7	MUNSTER	M.	4,305	53°36′N. 03°24′W.	Mine	—	
9	CHAGRES	S.	5,406	270° 5½m. from Bar L.V., Mersey	Mine	—	
9	AGNES ELLEN ...	S.	293	On voyage Holyhead to Workington	Mine	—	
13	BRITISH TRIUMPH...	M. Tank	8,501	53°06′N. 01°25′E.	Mine	—	
14	GRETAFIELD* ...	S. Tank	10,191	58°27′N. 02°33′W.	S.M.	T.	Beached, later total loss
14	TIBERTON	S.	5,225	North Sea	C.U.	—	
14	SULTAN STAR ...	S.	12,306	48°54′N. 10°03′W.	S.M.	T.	
14	LANGLEEFORD ...	S.	4,622	70m. N.W. of Fastnet	S.M.	T.	
17	BARON AILSA ...	S.	3,656	53°17′N. 01°12′E.	Mine	—	
17	PYRRHUS	S.	7,418	44°02′N. 10°18′W.	S.M.	T.	
21	LOCH MADDY ...	S.	4,996	070° 20m from Copinsay L.H., Orkneys	S.M.	T.	
22	BRITISH ENDEAVOUR	S. Tank	4,580	42°11′N. 11°35′W.	S.M.	T.	
24	ROYAL ARCHER ...	S.	2,266	56°06′N. 02°55′W.	Mine	—	
24	CLAN MORRISON* ...	S.	5,936	53°07′N. 01°22′E.	Mine	—	
24	JEVINGTON COURT...	S.	4,544	53°08′N. 01°22′E.	Mine	—	
	Total ... 21		110,372				
MARCH, 1940							
2	ALBANO	S.	1,176	128½° 7.6m. from Coquet Lt.	Mine	—	
3	CATO	S.	710	51°24′N. 03°33′W.	Mine	—	
4	PACIFIC RELIANCE	M.	6,717	50°23′N. 05°49′W.	S.M.	T.	
4	THURSTON	S.	3,072	32m. W. by N. of Trevose Head	S.M.*	T.*	
8	COUNSELLOR ...	S.	5,068	280° 6m. from Bar L.V., Mersey. (Approx.)	Mine	—	Sank in position 53°38′N. 03°23′W.
9	CHEVYCHASE ...	S.	2,719	53°18′N. 01°13′E.	Mine	—	
9	BORTHWICK ...	S.	1,097	51°44′N. 03°22′E.	Mine	—	
9 About	AKELD	S.	643	51°44′N. 03°22′E.	Mine	—	
11	ABBOTSFORD ...	S.	1,585	North Sea	C.U.	—	
12	GARDENIA	S.	3,745	53°04′N. 01°33′E.	Mine	—	
15	MELROSE	S.	1,589	51°21′N. 02°13′E.	Mine	—	
20	BARN HILL ...	S.	5,439	3m. S.S.W. of Beachy Head	A.C.	B.	
25	DAGHESTAN* ...	S. Tank	5,742	212° 9m. from Copinsay, Orkneys	S.M.	T.	
	Total ... 13		39,302				
APRIL, 1940							
9	THISTLEBRAE ...	S.	4,747	Trondheim	Seized	—	Taken in prize
10	BLYTHMOOR ...	S.	6,582	Narvik	C.U.	—	Sunk or seized

Date	Name	Type	Gross tons	Position	Cause of loss	How lost	Remarks
APRIL, 1940—(Contd.)							
12	THORLAND	S.	5,208	Sandefjord	Seized	—	Taken in prize
12	STANCLIFFE ...	S.	4,511	45m. N.E. of Unst Is., Shetlands	S.M.	T.	
15	SALERNO	S.	870	Sauda Fjord	Seized	—	Taken in prize
15	SALMON POOL ...	S.	4,803	Sauda Fjord	Seized	—	Taken in prize
15	MERSINGTON COURT	S.	5,141	Narvik	C.U.	—	Sunk or seized
15	NORTH CORNWALL	S.	4,304	Narvik	C.U.	—	Sunk or seized
17	SWAINBY	S.	4,935	065° 25m. from Muckle Flugga, Shetlands	S.M.	T.	
20	HAWNBY	S.	5,380	51°32′N. 01°13′E.	Mine	—	
20	MERSEY	S.	1,037	Nr. Midbrake Buoy, The Downs	Mine	—	
21	CEDARBANK ...	M.	5,159	62°49′N. 04°10′E.	S.M.	T.	
22	ROMANBY	S.	4,887	Narvik	C.U.	—	Sunk or seized
22	RIVERTON	S.	5,378	Narvik	C.U.	—	Sunk or seized
23	LOLWORTH* ...	S.	1,969	½m. N.W. of Elbow Buoy, off North Foreland	Mine	—	
24	STOKESLEY ...	S.	1,149	51°32′N. 01°16′E.	Mine	—	
24	RYDAL FORCE ...	S.	1,101	400 yds. S. of Gull L.V., Thames Estuary	Mine	—	
24	HAXBY	S.	5,207	31°30′N. 51°30′W.	Raider	—	
25	MARGAM ABBEY ...	S.	2,470	000° 9 cables from East Knob Buoy, Thames Estuary	Mine	—	
	Total ... 19		74,838				
MAY, 1940							
3	SCIENTIST	S.	6,199	20°00′S. 04°30′E. (Approx.)	Raider	—	
4	SAN TIBURCIO* ...	S. Tank	5,995	330° 4m. from Tarbet ˙Ness	Mine	—	
6	BRIGHTON	S.	5,359	51°03′N. 02°09′E.	Mine	—	
10	HENRY WOODALL...	S.	625	3m. E. of Withernsea	Mine	—	
11	TRINGA	S.	1,930	50°21′N. 02°55′E.	Mine	—	
12	ROEK	S.	1,041	51°54′N. 04°21′E.	Mine	—	
12	ST. DENIS	S.	2,435	Rotterdam	Scuttled	—	
13	CITY OF BRUSSELS...	S.	629	Brussels	Seized	—	
20	PEMBROKE COAST ...	M.	625	Harstad Harbour, Norway	A.C.	B.	
20	MAVIS	S.	935	Off No. 4 Green Buoy, Calais Roads	A.C.	B.	
21	FIRTH FISHER ...	S.	574	½m. E. of Boulogne Pier	Mine	—	
21	BAWTRY	S.	835	Off Dunkirk	A.C.	B.	Salved by Germans and taken in prize
21	HUBBASTONE ...	S.	873	Dieppe Harbour	A.C.	B.	Salved by Germans
21	MAID OF KENT ...	S.	2,693	Dieppe Harbour	A.C.	B.	
24	BRIGHTON	S.	2,391	Dieppe Quay	A.C.	B.	
25	SPINEL	M.	650	Dunkirk	A.C.	B.	Salved by Germans and taken in prize
27	SEQUACITY	M.	870	1½m. from No. 2 Buoy to E. of Calais	Shelled by shore battery	—	
27	WORTHTOWN ...	S.	868	Dunkirk	A.C.	B.	Salved by Germans and taken in prize
27	SHEAF MEAD ...	S.	5,008	43°48′N. 12°32′W.	S.M.	T.	
28	QUEEN OF THE CHANNEL	M.	1,162	51°15′N. 02°40′E.	A.C.	B.	
28	CARARE	S.	6,878	51°18′N. 03°45′W.	Mine	—	
28	ABUKIR	S.	694	51°20′N. 02°16′E.	E-Boat	T.	
28	MARJORY H. ...	M.	84	Dunkirk	Seized	—	Taken in prize
29	MONA'S QUEEN ...	S.	2,756	Off Dunkirk	Mine	—	
29	LORINA	S.	1,578	Dunkirk Roads	A.C.	B.	
29	CLAN MACALISTER ·	S.	6,787	Off Dunkirk	A.C.	B.	
29	FENELLA	S.	2,376	Dunkirk	A.C.	B.	
29	TELENA	M. Tank·	7,406	42°25′N. 09°08′W.	S.M.	G.	

Date	Name	Type	Gross tons	Position	Cause of loss	How lost	Remarks
MAY, 1940—(Contd.)							
30	NORMANNIA ...	S.	1,567	Off Dunkirk	A.C.	B.	
30	STANHALL	S.	4,831	48°59′N. 05°17′W.	S.M.	T.	
31	ORANGEMOOR ...	S.	5,775	49°43′N. 03°23′W.	S.M.	T.	
	Total ... 31		82,429				
JUNE, 1940							
1	SCOTIA	S.	3,454	51°07′N. 02°10′E.	A.C.	B.	
1	ORFORD	S.	20,043	Marseilles	A.C.	B.	
1	LARK	S.B.	67	Dunkirk	Abandoned	—	
1	ROYALTY	S.B.	101	Malo-les-Bains (Dunkirk)	Beached & abandoned	—	
1	DUCHESS	S.B.	91	Dunkirk	Beached & abandoned	—	
1	LADY ROSEBERY ...	S.B.	109	3m. E. of Dunkirk	Mine	—	
1	DORIS	S.B.	83	3m. E. of Dunkirk	Mine	—	
1	BARBARA JEAN ...	S.B.	144	Dunkirk	Blown up & abandoned	—	
1	AIDIE	S.B.	144	Dunkirk	Beached & set on fire	—	
1	ETHEL EVERARD ...	S.B.	190	Dunkirk	Beached & abandoned	—	
2	FOSSA*	Tug	105	Dunkirk	Stranded & abandoned	—	
2	ASTRONOMER* ...	S.	8,401	58°04′N. 02°12′W.	S.M.	T.	
2	PARIS	S.	1,790	51°11′N. 02°07′E.	A.C.	B.	
2	POLYCARP	S.	3,577	49°19′N. 05°35′W.	S.M.	T.	
5	SWEEP II	Sludge Vessel	145	138° 1.4m. from Landguard Pt., Felixstowe	Mine	—	
5	CAPABLE	M.	216	131° 2.8m. from Horsesand Fort, Spithead	Mine	—	
5	STANCOR	S.	798	58°48′N. 08°45′W.	S.M.	G.	
6	FRANCES MASSEY ...	S.	4,212	55°33′N. 08°26′W.	S.M.	T.	
6	HARCALO	S.	5,081	51°19′N. 01°32′E.	Mine	—	
8	HARDINGHAM ...	S.	5,415	51°34′N. 01°37′E.	Mine	—	
8	OILPIONEER* ...	M. Tank	5,666	67°44′N. 03°52′E.	Warship	—	" Admiral Hipper "
8	ORAMA	S.	19,840	67°44′N. 03°52′E.	Warship	—	" Admiral Hipper "
9	EMPIRE COMMERCE	S.	3,857	4 cables W. of N.E. Spit Buoy, nr. Margate	Mine	—	
9	DULWICH	S.	4,102	Off Villequier, River Seine	Beached & set on fire	—	Salved by Germans and taken in prize
11	ST. RONAIG ...	M.	509	132° 1m. from West Breakwater Lt., Newhaven	Mine	—	
11	BRUGES	S.	2,949	Off Le Havre	A.C.	B.	
12	BARON SALTOUN ...	S.	3,404	Outer Roads, Cherbourg	Mine	—	
12	WILLOWBANK ...	M.	5,041	44°16′N. 13°54′W.	S.M.	T.	
12	EARLSPARK... ...	S.	5,250	42°26′N. 11°33′W.	S.M.	T.	
12	BARBARA MARIE ...	S.	4,223	44°16′N. 13°54′W.	S.M.	T.	
12	TRAIN FERRY No. 2	S.	2,678	Le Havre	Beached & abandoned	—	
12	SWALLOW	M.	209	Paris	Damaged & abandoned	—	Taken in prize
12	INNISULVA	M.	264	Paris	Damaged & abandoned	—	
13	BRITISH INVENTOR	S. Tank	7,101	230° 5m. from St. Alban's Head	Mine	—	
14	BRITISH PETROL* ...	M. Tank	6,891	20°N. 50°W. (Approx.)	Raider	—	
14	BALMORALWOOD ...	S.	5,834	50°19′N. 10°28′W.	S.M.	T.	
15	ERIK BOYE ...	S.	2,238	50°37′N. 08°44′W.	S.M.	T.	
16	WELLINGTON STAR	M.	13,212	42°39′N. 17°01′W.	S.M.	T.	
17	TEIRESIAS	S.	7,405	47°07′N. 02°23′W.	A.C.	B.	
17	LANCASTRIA ...	S.	16,243	St. Nazaire	A.C.	B.	

Date	Name	Type	Gross tons	Position	Cause of loss	How lost	Remarks

JUNE, 1940—(Contd.)

Date	Name	Type	Gross tons	Position	Cause of loss	How lost	Remarks
18	NIAGARA	S.	13,415	35°53′S. 174°54′E.	Mine	—	
18	RONWYN	S.	1,766	Rochefort	Damaged & abandoned	—	
18	HESTER	S.	1,199	Rochefort	Damaged & abandoned	—	
18	DIDO	S.	3,554	Brest	Abandoned & seized	—	
19	ROSEBURN	S.	3,103	Off Dungeness	E-Boat	T. & G.	
19	BARON LOUDOUN ...	S.	3,164	45°00′N. 11°21′W.	S.M.	T.	
19	BRITISH MONARCH	S.	5,661	45°00′N. 11°21′W.	S.M.	T.	
19	THE MONARCH ...	S.	824	47°20′N. 04°40′W.	S.M.	T.	
20	STESSO	S.	2,290	Cardiff	A.C.	B.	
20	EMPIRE CONVEYOR	S.	5,911	56°16′N. 08°10′W.	S.M.	T.	
20	OTTERPOOL ...	S.	4,876	48°47′N. 07°50′W.	S.M.	T.	
21	LUFFWORTH ...	S.	279	Brest	Abandoned	—	Taken in prize
21	YARRAVILLE ...	S. Tank	8,627	39°40′N. 11°34′W.	S.M.	T.	
21	SAN FERNANDO ...	S. Tank	13,056	50°20′N. 10°24′W.	S.M.	T.	
24	ALBUERA	S.	3,477	2m. S.W. of Lydd Light Float	E-Boat	T.	
24	KINGFISHER ...	M.	276	50°30′N. 00°28′E.	E-Boat	T.	
25	WINDSORWOOD ...	S.	5,395	48°31′N. 14°50′W.	S.M.	T.	
25	SARANAC ...	S. Tank	12,049	48°24′N. 15°05′W.	S.M.	T. & G.	
27	LLANARTH ...	S.	5,053	47°30′N. 10°30′W.	S.M.	T.	
29	EMPIRE TOUCAN ...	S.	4,127	49°20′N. 13°52′W.	S.M.	T. & G.	
30	AVELONA STAR ...	S.	13,376	46°46′N. 12°17′W.	S.M.	T.	Sank 1st July
	Total ... 61		282,560				

JULY, 1940

Date	Name	Type	Gross tons	Position	Cause of loss	How lost	Remarks
1	BEIGNON	M.	5,218	47°20′N. 10°30′W. (Approx.)	S.M.	T.	
1	CLEARTON	S.	5,219	47°53′N. 09°30′W.	S.M.	T.	
2	AENEAS	S.	10,058	21m. S.E. of Start Pt.	A.C.	B.	
2	ARANDORA STAR ...	S.	15,501	55°20′N. 10°33′W.	S.M.	T.	
2	ATHELLAIRD ...	M. Tank	8,999	47°24′N. 16°49′W.	S.M.	T.	
3	BIJOU	S.B.	98	Mistley Quay, nr. Harwich	A.C.	B.	
4	ELMCREST	S.	4,343	13m. S. of Portland	E-Boat	T.	
4	DALLAS CITY ...	M.	4,952	50°09′N. 02°01′W.	A.C.	B.	
4	SILVERDIAL ...	Tug	55	Portland Harbour	A.C.	B. & G.	
4	COQUET MOUTH ...	Dredger	477	Off Amble, N. of Blyth	Mine	—	
5	DELAMBRE	S.	7,032	04°S. 26°W. (Approx.)	Raider	—	
5	MAGOG	S.	2,053	50°31′N. 11°05′W.	S.M.	T. & G.	
8	HUMBER ARM ...	S.	5,758	50°36′N. 09°24′W.	S.M.	T.	
9	AYLESBURY ...	S.	3,944	48°39′N. 13°33′W.	S.M.	T.	
10	TASCALUSA* ...	S. Tank	6,499	Falmouth Harbour	A.C.	B.	
10	WATERLOO	S.	1,905	2½m. N.E. of Smith's Knoll Buoy	A.C.	B.	
10	DAVISIAN	S.	6,433	18°00′N. 54°30′W. (Approx.)	Raider	—	
11	SEA GLORY ...	S.	1,964	North Atlantic	S.M.	T.	
11	CITY OF BAGDAD ...	S.	7,506	00°16′S. 90°00′E.	Raider	—	
11	MALLARD	S.	352	Between St. Catherine's Pt. and Beachy Head	E-Boat	T.	
12	HORNCHURCH ...	S.	2,162	Off Aldeburgh L.V.	A.C.	B.	
13	KING JOHN ...	M.	5,228	20°N. 60°W. (Approx.)	Raider	—	
13	KEMMENDINE ...	S.	7,769	04°S. 82°E. (Approx.)	Raider	—	
14	ISLAND QUEEN ...	S.	779	4 cables off A Buoy, Dover	A.C.	B. & G.	

Date	Name	Type	Gross tons	Position	Cause of loss	How lost	Remarks
JULY, 1940—(Contd.)							
About 14	GRACEFIELD ...	S.	4,631	13°S. 31°W. (Approx.)	Raider	—	
15	BELLEROCK ...	S.	1,199	51°20′N. 03°47′W.	Mine	—	
15	HEWORTH ...	S.	2,855	10m. S. of Aldeburgh L.V.	A.C.	B.	
15	CITY OF LIMERICK...	S.	1,359	48°39′N. 07°12′W.	A.C.	B.	
16	WENDOVER... ...	S.	5,487	23°S. 35°W. (Approx.)	Raider	—	
16	SCOTTISH MINSTREL	M. Tank	6,998	56°10′N. 10°20′W.	S.M.	T.	Sank on the 17th
17	MANIPUR ...	S.	8,652	58°41′N. 05°14′W.	S.M.	T.	
17	WOODBURY ...	S.	4,434	50°46′N. 13°56′W.	S.M.	T.	
17	FELLSIDE ...	S.	3,509	56°09′N. 12°30′W.	S.M.	T.	
19	PEARLMOOR ...	S.	4,581	55°23′N. 09°18′W.	S.M.	T.	
20	TROUTPOOL...	S.	4,886	54°40′N. 05°40′W.	Mine	—	
20	PULBOROUGH ...	S.	960	2½m. S.E. × S. of Dover Pier	A.C.	B.	
21	TERLINGS ...	S.	2,318	10m. S.W. of St. Catherine's Point, I.O.W.	A.C.	B.	
21	ELLAROY	S.	712	42°30′N. 12°36′W.	S.M.	G.	
23	THE LADY MOSTYN	M.	305	079° 1½m. from Formby L.V.	Mine	—	
25	CORHAVEN ...	S.	991	Off Dover	A.C.	B.	
25	POLGRANGE ...	S.	804	Off Dover	A.C.	B.	
25	LEO	S.	1,140	Off Dover	A.C.	B.	
25	HENRY MOON ...	S.	1,091	Off Sandgate	A.C.	B.	
25	PORTSLADE ...	S.	1,091	Off Sandgate	A.C.	B.	
26	LULONGA ...	S.	821	10m. S. of Shoreham	E-Boat	T.	
26	HAYTOR ...	S.	1,189	51°47′N. 01°48′E.	Mine	—	
26	BROADHURST ...	S.	1,013	14m. S. × W. of Shoreham	E-Boat	T.	
26	LONDON TRADER ...	S.	646	13m. S. × W. of Shoreham	E-Boat	T.	
26	ACCRA	M.	9,337	55°40′N. 16°28′W.	S.M.	T.	
26	VINEMOOR	M.	4,359	55°43′N. 16°25′W.	S.M.	T.	
27	DURDHAM	Sand Dredger	477	140¼° 1.54m. from Lavernock, Bristol Channel	Mine	—	
27	SALVESTRIA ...	S. Tank	11,938	042° 2.8 m. from Inchkeith L.H.	Mine	—	
27	SAMBRE ...	S.	5,260	56°37′N. 17°53′W.	S.M.	T.	
27	THIARA	M. Tank	10,364	56°37′N. 17°56′W.	S.M.	T.	
28	ORLOCK HEAD ...	S.	1,563	58°44′N. 04°21′W.	A.C.	B. & G.	Sank 320° 6.7 m. from Strathie Pt.
28	AUCKLAND STAR ...	M.	13,212	52°17′N. 12°32′W.	S.M.	T.	
29	GRONLAND	S.	1,264	Dover Harbour	A.C.	B.	Previously damaged by aircraft on 25th
29	OUSEBRIDGE ...	S.	5,601	Queen's Channel, Liverpool	Mine	—	
29	MOIDART ...	S.	1,262	51°59′N. 01°49′E.	Mine	—	
29	CLAN MONROE ...	S.	5,952	51°52′N. 01°48′E.	Mine	—	
29	CLAN MENZIES ...	S.	7,336	54°10′N. 12°00′W.	S.M.	T.	
30	JAMAICA PROGRESS	S.	5,475	56°26′N. 08°30′W.	S.M.	T.	
31	JERSEY CITY ...	S.	6,322	55°47′N. 09°18′W.	S.M.	T.	
31	DOMINGO DE LARRINAGA	S.	5,358	05°26′S. 18°06′W.	Raider	—	
	Total ... 64		271,056				
AUGUST, 1940							
2	CITY OF BRISBANE...	S.	8,006	Off S. Longsand Buoy, Thames Estuary	A.C.	B.	
3	STATIRA	M.	4,852	38m. N. of Stornaway	A.C.	B.	
3	WYCHWOOD ...	S.	2,794	52°00′N. 01°48′E.	Mine	—	
4	GERALDINE MARY...	S.	7,244	56°58′N. 15°55′W.	S.M.	T.	
4	KING ALFRED ...	S.	5,272	56°59′N. 17°38′W.	S.M.	T.	

9

Date	Name	Type	Gross tons	Position	Cause of loss	How lost	Remarks
AUGUST, 1940—(Contd.)							
4	Gogovale	S.	4,586	57°08′N. 16°26′W.	S.M.	T.	
5	Boma	S.	5,408	55°44′N. 08°04′W.	S.M.	T.	
7	Mohamed Ali el-Kebir	S.	7,527	55°22′N. 13°18′W.	S.M.	T.	
8	Upwey Grange ...	M.	9,130	54°20′N. 15°28′W.	S.M.	T.	
8	Holme Force* ...	S.	1,216	Off Newhaven	E-Boat	T.	
8	Fife Coast ...	M.	367	10 to 15m. W. of Beachy Head	E-Boat	T.	
8	Coquetdale* ...	S.	1,597	15m. W. of St. Catherine's Pt., I.O.W.	A.C.	B. & G.	
8	Empire Crusader	S.	1,042	15m. W. of St. Catherine's Pt., I.O.W.	A.C.	B.	
8	Ouse	S.	1,004	Off Newhaven	Collision	—	In avoiding torpedo from E-Boat
11	Llanfair	S.	4,966	54°48′N. 13°46′W.	S.M.	T.	
12	British Fame ...	M. Tank	8,406	37°44′N. 22°56′W.	S.M.	T.	
14	Betty	S.	2,339	260° 35m. from Tory Island	S.M.	T.	
15	Sylvafield* ...	M. Tank	5,709	56°39′N. 11°16′W.	S.M.	T.	
15	Brixton ...	S.	1,557	52°06′N. 01°49′E.	Mine	—	
16	Clan Macphee ...	S.	6,628	57°30′N. 17°14′W.	S.M.	T.	
16	Empire Merchant	M.	4,864	55°23′N. 13°24′W.	S.M.	T.	
16	City of Birmingham	S.	5,309	115° 5½m. from Spurn Pt.	Mine	— -	
16	Meath	S.	1,598	6 to 7 cables N.E. of Breakwater Lt., Holyhead	Mine	—	
18	Ampleforth ...	S.	4,576	56°10′N. 10°40′W.	S.M.	T.	
20	Turakina ...	S.	9,691	38°27′S. 167°35′E.	Raider	—	
21	Anglo Saxon ...	S.	5,596	26°10′N. 34°09′W.	Raider	—	
21	James No. 70 ...	Hopper Barge	182	Southampton	A.C.	B.	
22	Thorold	S.	1,689	2½m. S. of Smalls	A.C.	B. & G.	
23	Cumberland ...	S.	10,939	55°43′N. 07°33′W.	S.M.	T.	
23	Makalla	S.	6,677	58°17′N. 02°27′W.	A.C.	B.	
23	Llanishen ...	S.	5,053	58°17′N. 02°27′W.	A.C.	B.	
23	Severn Leigh ...	S.	5,242	54°31′N. 25°41′W.	S.M.	T.	
23	St. Dunstan	S.	5,681	55°43′N. 08°10′W.	S.M.	T.	Taken in tow but sank on 27th
23	Brookwood ...	S.	5,100	54°40′N. 27°57′W.	S.M.	T. & G.	
24	Blairmore... ...	S.	4,141	56°00′N. 27°30′W.	S.M.	T.	
24	La Brea	S. Tank	6,666	57°24′N. 11°21′W.	S.M.	T.	
24	King City	S.	4,744	17°S. 66°E. (Approx.)	Raider	—	
25	Yewcrest ...	S.	3,774	55°10′N. 25°02′W.	S.M.	G.	
25	Jamaica Pioneer	S.	5,471	57°05′N. 11°02′W.	S.M.	T.	
25	Pecten*	M. Tank	7,468	56°22′N. 07°55′W.	S.M.	T.	
25	Empire Merlin ...	S.	5,763	58°30′N. 10°15′W.	S.M.	T.	
25	Athelcrest ...	M. Tank	6,825	58°24′N. 11°25′W.	S.M.	T.	
25	Harpalyce ...	S.	5,169	58°52′N. 06°34′W.	S.M.	T.	
25	Goathland ...	S.	3,821	50°21′N. 15°08′W.	A.C.	B. & G.	
25	Fircrest	S.	5,394	58°52′N. 06°34′W.	S.M.	T.	
26	Ilvington Court...	S.	5,187	37°14′N. 21°52′W.	S.M.	T.	
26	Remuera ...	S.	11,445	57°50′N. 01°54′W.	A.C.	T.	
26	Cape York ...	M.	5,027	45° 10m. from Kinnaird Head	A.C.	T.	
26	British Commander	S. Tank	6,901	29°37′S. 45°50′E.	Raider	—	
28	Kyno	S.	3,946	58°06′N. 13°26′W.	S.M.	T.	
28	Dalblair	S.	4,608	56°06′N. 13°33′W.	S.M.	T.	
29	Empire Moose ...	S.	6,103	56°06′N. 14°00′W.	S.M.	T.	
29	Astra II	S.	2,393	56°09′N. 12°14′W.	S.M.	T.	
30	Chelsea ...	S.	4,804	59°45′N. 04°00′W.	S.M.	T.	
30	Mill Hill ...	S.	4,318	58°48′N. 06°49′W.	S.M.	T.	
31	Har Zion	S.	2,508	56°20′N. 10°00′W. (Approx.)	S.M.	T.	
	Total ... 56		278,323				

Date	Name	Type	Gross tons	Position	Cause of loss	How lost	Remarks
SEPTEMBER, 1940							
2	THORNLEA ...	S.	4,261	55°14'N. 16°40'W.	S.M.	T.	
2	CYMBELINE* ...	S. Tank	6,317	28°N. 35°W. (Approx.)	Raider	—	
3	ULVA	S.	1,401	55°45'N. 11°45'W.	S.M.	T.	
4	TITAN	S.	9,035	58°14'N. 15°50'W.	S.M.	T.	
4	LUIMNEACH ...	S.	1,074	47°50'N. 09°12'W.	S.M.	G.	
4	CORBROOK ...	S.	1,729	52°50'N. 02°09'E.	E-Boat	T.	
4	NEW LAMBTON ...	S.	2,709	52°50'N. 02°09'E.	E-Boat	T.	
4	JOSEPH SWAN ...	S.	1,571	52°50'N. 02°09'E.	E-Boat	T.	
4	FULHAM V ...	S.	1,562	52°50'N. 02°09'E.	E-Boat	T. & G.	
6	ST. GLEN	S.	4,647	57°25'N. 01°38'W.	A.C.	B.	
7	BECKTON	Tug	45	Beckton Gas Works, London River	A.C.	B.	
7	JOSE DE LARRINAGA	S.	5,303	58°30'N. 16°10'W.	S.M.	T.	
7	NEPTUNIAN ...	S.	5,155	58°27'N. 17°27'W.	S.M.	T.	
9	ATHELKING... ...	M. Tank	9,557	21°48'S. 67°40'E.	Raider	—	
9	MARDINIAN... ...	S.	2,434	56°37'N. 09°00'W.	S.M.	T.	
9	MINNIE DE LARRINAGA	S.	5,049	Port of London	A.C.	B.	
10	BENARTY	S.	5,800	18°40'S. 70°54'E.	Raider	—	
11	ALBIONIC	S.	2,468	North Atlantic	Raider*	—	
12	BENAVON	S.	5,872	26°S. 51°E. (Approx.)	Raider	—	
12	GOTHIC	S. Tank	2,444	130° 7,500 yds. from Spurn Pt.	Mine	—	
14	ST. AGNES	S.	5,199	41°27'N. 21°50'W.	S.M.	T. & G.	
15	EMPIRE VOLUNTEER	S.	5,319	56°43'N. 15°17'W. (Approx.)	S.M.	T.	
15	KENORDOC... ...	S.	1,780	57°42'N. 15°02'W.	S.M.	G.	
15	HALLAND	S.	1,264	070° 8m. from Dunbar	A.C.	B.	
15	NAILSEA RIVER ...	S.	5,548	4m. E. of Montrose	A.C.	T.	
16	ASKA	S.	8,323	55°15'N. 05°55'W.	A.C.	B.	
16	BIBURY	S.	4,616	12°N. 25°W. (Approx.)	Raider	—	
16	CITY OF MOBILE ...	S.	6,614	54°18'N. 05°16'W.	A.C.	B.	
17	CROWN ARUN ...	S.	2,372	58°02'N. 14°18'W.	S.M.	T.	
17	CITY OF BENARES	S.	11,081	56°43'N. 21°15'W.	S.M.	T.	
17	TREGENNA	S.	5,242	58°22'N. 15°42'W.	S.M.	T.	
17	MARINA	S.	5,088	56°46'N. 21°15'W.	S.M.	T.	
17	COMMISSAIRE RAMEL	S.	10,061	28°25'S. 74°27'E.	Raider	—	
18	MAGDALENA ...	S.	3,118	57°20'N. 20°16'W.	S.M.	T.	
19	SHELBRIT I ...	M. Tank	1,025	57°39'N. 03°56'W.	Mine	—	
20	INVERSHANNON* ...	M. Tank	9,154	55°40'N. 22°04'W. (Approx.)	S.M.	T.	Sank on 21st
20	EMPIRE ADVENTURE	S.	5,145	Off Islay	S.M.	T.	
20	NEW SEVILLA* ...	S. Tank	13,801	55°48'N. 07°22'W.	S.M.	T.	
20	BARON BLYTHSWOOD	S.	3,668	56°N. 23°W. (Approx.)	S.M.	T.	
21	FREDERICK S. FALES*	M. Tank	10,525	55°30'N. 13°40'W.	S.M.	T.	
21	CITY OF SIMLA ...	S.	10,138	55°55'N. 08°20'W.	S.M.	T.	
21	TORINIA* ...	M. Tank	10,364	55°N. 19°W. (Approx.)	S.M.	T.	
21	CANONESA	S.	8,286	54°55'N. 18°25'W.	S.M.	T.	
21	SCHOLAR	S.	3,940	55°11'N. 17°58'W.	S.M.	T.	Abandoned 54°38'N 16°40'W. on 24th
21	EMPIRE AIRMAN ...	S.	6,586	54°N. 18°W. (Approx.)	S.M.	T.	
21	BLAIRANGUS ...	S.	4,409	55°18'N. 22°21'W.	S.M.	T.	
21	ELMBANK	M.	5,156	55°20'N. 22°30'W.	S.M.	T.	
21	DALCAIRN	S.	4,608	55°N. 19°W. (Approx.)	S.M.	T.	
24	CONTINENTAL COASTER	S.	555	52°59'N. 02°10'E.	E-Boat	T.	
25	MABRITON	S.	6,694	56°12'N. 23°00'W.	S.M.	T.	
25	EURYMEDON ...	M.	6,223	53°34'N. 20°23'W.	S.M.	T.	Sank on 27th
25	SULAIRIA	S.	5,802	53°43'N. 20°10'W.	S.M.	T.	

Date	Name	Type	Gross tons	Position	Cause of loss	How lost	Remarks
SEPTEMBER, 1940—(Contd.)							
26	STRATFORD ...	S. Tank	4,753	54°50′N. 10°40′W.	S.M.	T.	
26	CORRIENTES ,..	S.	6,863	53°49′N. 24°19′W.	S.M.	T.	
26	PORT DENISON ...	S.	8,043	6m. N.E. of Peter-head	A.C.	T.	Sank on 27th
26	MANCHESTER BRIGADE	S.	6,042	54°53′N. 10°22′W.	S.M.	T.	
28	EMPIRE OCELOT ...	S.	5,759	54°37′N. 21°30′W.	S.M.	T.	Sank in position 54°55′N. 22°06′W.
28	DARCOILA	S.	4,084	North Atlantic	S.M.	T.	
28	DALVEEN	S.	5,193	58°10′N. 02°19′W.	A.C.	B.	
29	BASSA	S.	5,267	54°N. 21°W. (Approx.)	S.M.*	—	
30	HEMINGE	S.	2,499	53°26′N. 18°33′W.	S.M.	T.	
30	SAMALA	S.	5,390	46°N. 33°W. (Approx.)	S.M.*	—	
	Total ... 62		324,030				
OCTOBER, 1940							
1	HIGHLAND PATRIOT	S.	14,172	52°20′N. 19°04′W.	S.M.	T.	
2	KAYESON	S.	4,606	51°12′N. 24°22′W.	S.M.	T.	
2	LATYMER	S.	2,218	51°20′N. 10°30′W.	A.C.	B.	
3	LADY OF THE ISLES*	Cable ship	166	About 3m. E. of St. Anthony Pt., Nr. Falmouth	Mine	—	
4	SIRDAR	Tug	34	Cod's Reach, River Swale	A.C.	B.	
5	ADAPTITY	S.	372	51°44′N. 01°17′E. (Approx.)	Mine	—	
6	BENLAWERS ...	S.	5,943	53°20′N. 26°10′W.	S.M.	T.	
6	JERSEY QUEEN ...	S.	910	160° 1½ m. from St. Anthony Pt., Nr. Falmouth	Mine	—	
6	BRITISH GENERAL...	S. Tank	6,989	51°42′N. 24°03′W.	S.M.	T.	Sank on 7th.
8	BELLONA II ...	S.	840	4m. E. of Gourdon, Kincardineshire	A.C.	B.	
8	CONFIELD	S.	4,956	56°48′N. 10°17′W.	S.M.	T.	Sank on 9th
8	NATIA	S.	8,715	00°50′N. 32°24′W.	Raider	—	
9	GRAIGWEN	S.	3,697	58°11′N. 13°57′W.	S.M.	T.	
9	ALDERNEY QUEEN...	M.	633	Off Grassholm Island, N. Wales	A.C.	B. & G.	
11	PORT GISBORNE ...	M.	8,390	56°38′N. 16°40′W.	S.M.	T.	
12	ST. MALO	S.	5,779	57°58′N. 16°32′W.	S.M.	T.	
12	PACIFIC RANGER ...	M.	6,865	56°20′N. 11°43′W.	S.M.	T.	
13	STANGRANT... ...	S.	5,804	58°27′N. 12°36′W.	S.M.	T.	
14	HURUNUI	S.	9,331	58°58′N. 09°54′W.	S.M.	T.	
14	RECULVER (Trinity House Vessel)	M.	683	195° 1.2m. from Spurn Pt. L.H.	Mine	—	
15	THISTLEGARTH ...	S.	4,747	58°43′N. 15°00′W.	S.M.	T.	
15	BONHEUR	S.	5,327	57°10′N. 08°36′W.	S.M.	T.	
16	TREVISA	S.	1,813	57°28′N. 20°30′W.	S.M.	T.	
17	USKBRIDGE... ...	S.	2,715	60°40′N. 15°50′W.	S.M.	T.	
17	SCORESBY	S.	3,843	59°14′N. 17°51′W.	S.M.	T.	
17	LANGUEDOC ...	M. Tank	9,512	59°14′N. 17°51′W.	S.M.	T.	
17	FRANKRIG	S.	1,361	52°03′N. 01°48′E.	Mine	—	
17	HAUXLEY	S.	1,595	6m. N.N.W. of Smith's Knoll	E-Boat	T.	Sank on 18th
18	ASSYRIAN	S.	2,962	57°12′N. 10°43′W.	S.M.	T.	Sank on 19th
18	SANDSEND	S.	3,612	58°15′N. 21°29′W.	S.M.	T.	
18	BEATUS	S.	4,885	57°31′N. 13°10′W.	S.M.	T.	
18	EMPIRE MINIVER ...	S.	6,055	310° 250m. from Rathlin Head	S.M.	T.	
18	CREEKIRK	S.	3,917	57°30′N. 11°10′W. (Approx.)	S.M.	T.	
18	FISCUS ... ..,	S.	4,815	57°29′N. 11°10′W. (Approx.)	S.M.	T.	
18	SHEKATIKA... ...	S.	5,458	57°12′N. 11°08′W. (Approx.)	S.M.	T.	

Date	Name	Type	Gross tons	Position	Cause of loss	How lost	Remarks
OCTOBER, 1940—(Contd.)							
18	EMPIRE BRIGADE ...	S.	5,154	57°12′N. 10°43′W. (Approx.)	S.M.	T.	
19	WANDBY	S.	4,947	56°45′N. 17°07′W.	S.M.	T.	Sank on 21st
19	ARIDITY	M.	336	40 yds. N.E. of E. Oaze L.V.	Mine	—	
19	MATHERAN ...	S.	7,653	57°N. 17°W. (Approx.)	S.M.	T.	
19	LA ESTANCIA ...	S.	5,185	57°N. 17°W. (Approx.)	S.M.	T.	
19	CAPRELLA	M. Tank	8,230	56°37′N. 17°15′W.	S.M.	T.	
19	RUPERRA	S.	4,548	57°N. 16°W. (Approx.)	S.M.	T.	
19	SHIRAK	S. Tank	6,023	57°00′N. 16°35′W.	S.M.	T.	
19	SULACO	S.	5,389	57°25′N. 25°00′W.	S.M.	T.	
19	UGANDA	S.	4,966	56°37′N. 17°15′W.	S.M.	T.	
19	SITALA	M. Tank	6,218	150m. S.W. of Rockall	S.M.	T.	
19	CLINTONIA	S.	3,106	57°10′N. 11°20′W.	S.M.	T. & G.	
19	SEDGEPOOL ...	S.	5,556	57°20′N. 11°22′W.	S.M.	T.	
20	LOCH LOMOND ...	S.	5,452	56°00′N. 14°30′W.	S.M.	T.	
20	WHITFORD POINT ...	S.	5,026	56°38′N. 16°00′W.	S.M.	T.	
21	KERRY HEAD ...	S.	825	5m. due S. of Black-ball Head, Eire	A.C.	B.	
21	HOUSTON CITY ...	S.	4,935	225° ½m. from E. Oaze L.V.	Mine	—	
24	MATINA	S.	5,389	57°30′N. 16°31′W. (Approx.)	C.U.	—	
26	DOSINIA	M. Tank	8,053	Near Q.1 Black Buoy, Queens Channel, Mersey	Mine	—	
27	SUAVITY	M.	634	54°44′N. 01°05′W.	Mine	—	
28	DEVONIA	S.	98	51°23′N. 03°15′W.	Mine	—	
28	SHEAF FIELD ...	S.	2,719	2m. S.W. of Sunk L.V.	Mine	—	
28	SAGACITY	S.	490	148° 4,000 yds. from Spurn Main Lt.	Mine	—	
28	WYTHBURN. ...	S.	420	51°22′N. 03°15′W.	Mine	—	
28	EMPRESS OF BRITAIN	S.	42,348	55°16′N. 09°50′W.	S.M.	T.	Previously attacked by A.C. and set on fire on 26th in position 54°53′N. 10°49′W. Attacked again by S.M. as shown and sunk
29	G. W. HUMPHREYS	Sludge Vessel	1,500	E. Oaze Buoy, bearing E.S.E. about 2 cables	Mine	—	
30	RUTLAND	S.	1,437	57°14′N. 16°00′W. (Est.)	S.M.*	—	
31	HILLFERN	S.	1,535	35m. N.N.W. of Kinnaird Head	C.U.	—	
	Total ... 63		301,892				
NOVEMBER, 1940							
1	EMPIRE BISON ...	S.	5,612	59°30′N. 17°40′W.	S.M.	T.	
1	LETCHWORTH ...	S.	1,317	W. Oaze Buoy W. × N. 1 cable & Mouse L.V. S.S.W. 1 cable	A.C.	B.	
2	LEA	Tug	168	Tilbury Basin	Mine	—	
2	DEANBROOK ...	Tug	149	Tilbury Basin	Mine	—	
3	CASANARE	S.	5,376	53°58′N. 14°13′W.	S.M.	T.	
3	KILDALE	S.	3,877	57°45′N. 01°45′W.	A.C.	B.	
5	SCOTTISH MAIDEN ...	M. Tank	6,993	54°36′N. 14°23′W.	S.M.	T.	
5	MAIDAN	S.	7,908	52°26′N. 32°34′W. (Approx.)	Raider	—	" Admiral Scheer "
5	TREWELLARD ...	S.	5,201	52°26′N. 32°34′W. (Approx.)	Raider	—	" Admiral Scheer "
5	BEAVERFORD ...	S.	10,042	52°26′N. 32°34′W.	Raider	—	" Admiral Scheer "

Date	Name	Type	Gross tons	Position	Cause of loss	How lost	Remarks
NOVEMBER, 1940—(Contd.)							
5	HAIG ROSE ...	S.	1,117	Bristol Channel	C.U.	—	
5	KENBANE HEAD ...	S.	5,225	52°26′N: 32°34′W.	Raider	—	" Admiral Scheer "
5	MOPAN	S.	5,389	52°48′N. 32°15′W. (Approx.)	Raider	—	" Admiral Scheer "
5	FRESNO CITY ...	M.	4,955	51°47′N. 33°29′W.	Raider	—	" Admiral Scheer " Sank on 6th
6	NALON	S.	7,222	53°57′N. 15°03′W.	A.C.	B.	
6	CLAN MACKINLAY...	S.	6,365	58°33′N. 02°53′W.	A.C.	B.	
7	HERLAND ...	S.	2,645	146° 2 cables from Nore L.V.	Mine	—	
7	CAMBRIDGE... ...	S.	10,855	6m. E. of Wilson's Promontory Bass Strait, S.W. Pacific	Mine	—	
7	ASTROLOGER ...	S.	1,673	51°32′N. 01°06′E.	A.C.	B.	
9	BALTRADER ...	S.	1,699	51°41′N. 01°18′E.	Mine	- -	
11	AUTOMEDON ...	S.	7,528	04°18′N. 89°20′E.	Raider	—	
11	TREBARTHA ...	S.	4,597	4m. S.E. of Aberdeen	A.C.	B. & G.	
11	SKARV	S.	158	Bristol Channel	Mine*	—	
11	CREEMUIR	S.	3,997	10m. S.E. of Aberdeen	A.C.	T.	
11	BALMORE	S.	1,925	52°N. 17°W. (Approx.)	A.C.	B.	
12	ARGUS (Trinity House Vessel)	S.	661	199° 3 cables from S. Oaze Buoy	Mine	—	
13	CAPE ST. ANDREW...	S.	5,094	55°14′N. 10°29′W.	S.M.	T.	
13	EMPIRE WIND ...	S.	7,459	53°48′N. 15°52′W.	A.C.	B.	
13	LEON MARTIN ...	M. Tank	1,951	202° 5.2 cables from St. Anthony Pt., nr. Falmouth	Mine	—	
14	ST. CATHERINE ...	S.	1,216	½m. S. of Outer Buoy, Swept Channel, Aberdeen	A.C.	T.	
14	BUOYANT	M.	300	Off Skegness*	Mine	—	
15	KOHINUR	S.	5,168	04°24′N. 13°46′W.	S.M.	T.	
15	AMENITY	M.	297	53°33′N. 00°09′E.	Mine	—	
15	APAPA	M.	9,333	54°34′N. 16°47′W.	A.C.	B.	
15	BLUE GALLEON ...	S.	712	52°57′N. 01°56′E.	A.C.	B.	
16	FABIAN	S.	3,059	02°49′N. 15°29′W.	S.M.	T.	
16	PLANTER	S.	5,887	55°38′N. 08°28′W.	S.M.	T.	
17	ST. GERMAIN ...	M.	1,044	55°40′N. 08°40′W.	S.M.	T.	
18	LILIAN MOLLER ...	S.	4,866	North Atlantic	S.M.	T.	
18	CONGONIAN... ...	M. Tank	5,065	08°21′N. 16°12′W.	S.M.	T.	
18	ABILITY	Motor Barge	293	51°45′N. 01°11′E.	Mine	—	
18	NESTLEA	S.	4,274	50°38′N. 10°00′W.	A.C.	B. & G.	
18	NOWSHERA ...	S.	7,920	30°S. 90°E. (Approx.)	Raider	—	
20	MAIMOA	S.	10,123	31°50′S. 100°21′E.	Raider	—	
21	DAYDAWN	S.	4,768	56°30′N. 14°10′W.	S.M.	T.	
21	DAKOTIAN	S.	6,426	Dale Roads, Milford Haven	Mine	—	
21	CREE	S.	4,791	54°39′N. 18°50′W.	S.M.	T.	
21	PORT BRISBANE ...	S.	8,739	29°22′S. 95°36′E.	Raider	—	
22	JUSTITIA	S.	4,562	55°00′N. 13°10′W.	S.M.	T.	
22	BRADFYNE... ...	S.	4,740	55°04′N. 12°15′W.	S.M.	T.	
22	HERCULES	Tug	82	55°01′N. 01°23′W.	Mine	—	
22	PIKEPOOL	S.	3,683	23m.E.S.E. of Smalls Lt.	Mine*	—	
22	OAKCREST	S.	5,407	53°N. 17°W. (Approx.)	S.M.	T.	
23	BONAPARTE ...	Tug	38	Southampton	A.C.	B.	
23	LEISE MAERSK ...	M.	3,136	55°30′N. 11°00′W.	S.M.	T.	
23	KING IDWAL ...	S.	5,115	56°44′N. 19°13′W.	S.M.	T.	
23	TYMERIC	S.	5,228	57°00′N. 20°30′W.	S.M.	T.	
24	PRESERVER... ...	Salvage Vessel	630	054° 1 cable from No. 1 Buoy, Milford Haven	Mine	—	
24	RYAL	M.	367	51°32′N. 01°04′E.	Mine	—	
24	BEHAR	S.	6,100	51°42′N, 05°07′W.	Mine	—	Beached, later total loss

Date	Name	Type	Gross tons	Position	Cause of loss	How lost	Remarks
NOVEMBER, 1940—(Contd.)							
24	THOMAS M. ...	M.	310	Approx. 135° 1½m. from Yarmouth Harbour Entrance	Mine	—	
24	ALICE MARIE ...	S.	2,206	255° 8 cables from Knob L.V., Barrow Deep	Mine	—	
24	PORT HOBART ...	S.	7,448	24°44′N. 58°21′W.	Raider	—	" Admiral Scheer "
25	HOLMWOOD ...	S.	546	27m. W. × S. of Durham Pt., Chatham Is., S. Pacific	Raider	—	
25	T. C. C. HOPPER No. 3	Hopper Barge	698	54°40′N. 01°07′W.	Mine	—	
26	RANGITANE ...	M.	16,712	36°58′S. 175°22′W.	Raider	—	
27	DIPLOMAT	S.	8,240	55°42′N. 11°37′W.	S.M.	T.	
27	GLENMOOR* ...	M.	4,393	54°35′N. 14°31′W,	S.M.	T.	
28	ST. ELWYN ...	S.	4,940	55°30′N. 19°30′W.	S.M.	T.	
28	IRENE MARIA ...	S.	1,860	North Atlantic	S.M.*	—	
29	AID	Tug	134	8m. off Start Pt.	Warship	—	
29	B.H.C. No. 10 ...	Barge	290	8m. off Start Pt.	Warship	—	
29	ARACATACA... ...	S.	5,378	57°08′N. 20°50′W.	S.M.	T.	
	Total ... 73		303,682				
DECEMBER, 1940							
1	HER MAJESTY ...	Paddle Steamer	235	Southampton	A.C.	B.	
1	BRITISH OFFICER ...	S. Tank	6,990	About ½m. E. of North Pier Lt., Tyne	Mine	—	
1	PORT WELLINGTON	S.	8,301	32°10′S. 75°00′E. (Approx.)	Raider	—	
1	PALMELLA	S.	1,578	40°30′N. 13°30′W.	S.M.	T.	
1	TRIBESMAN ...	S.	6,242	15°N. 35°W. (Approx.)	Raider	—	" Admiral Scheer "
1	APPALACHEE ...	M. Tank	8,826	54°30′N. 20°00′W.	S.M.	T.	
2	CONCH*	M. Tank	8,376	55°40′N. 19°00′W.	S.M.	T.	
2	JEANNE M. ...	S.	2,465	39°19′N. 13°54′W.	S.M.	T.	
2	WILHELMINA ...	S.	7,135	55°55′N. 15°20′W.	S.M.	T.	
2	KAVAK	S.	2,782	55°00′N. 19°30′W.	S.M.	T.	
2	TASSO	S.	1,586	55°03′N. 18°04′W.	S.M.	T.	
2	STIRLINGSHIRE ...	M.	6,022	55°36′N. 16°22′W.	S.M.	T.	
2	GOODLEIGH... ...	S.	5,448	55°02′N. 18°45′W.	S.M.	T.	
2	VICTOR ROSS ...	M. Tank	12,247	56°04′N. 18°30′W.	S.M.	T.	
2	LADY GLANELY ...	M.	5,497	55°N. 20°W. (Approx.)	S.M.	T.	
2	VICTORIA CITY ...	S.	4,739	North Atlantic	S.M.	T.	
2	PACIFIC PRESIDENT	M.	7,113	56°04′N. 18°45′W. (Approx.)	S.M.	T.	
2	JOLLY GIRLS* ...	M.	483	101° 18 cables from North Pier Lt., Tyne	Mine	—	
3	W. HENDRIK ...	S.	4,360	56°26′N. 12°20′W.	A.C.	B.	
5	SILVERPINE ...	M.	5,066	54°14′N. 18°08′W.	S.M.	T.	
5	NIMBIN	M.	1,052	33°15′S. 151°47′E.	Mine	—	
5	EMPIRE STATESMAN	M.	5,306	North Atlantic	S.M.*	—	
6	SUPREMITY ...	M.	554	W.S.W. 3 cables from East Oaze L.V., Thames Estuary	Mine	—	
6	TRIONA	S.	4,413	Nauru	Raider	—	
7	KOMATA	S.	3,900	Nauru	Raider	—	
7	TRIADIC	M.	6,378	Nauru	Raider	—	
7	TRIASTER	M.	6,032	Nauru	Raider	—	
8	CALABRIA	S.	9,515	52°43′N. 18°07′W.	S.M.	T.	
8	ACTUALITY ...	M.	311	3m. S.W. of Mouse L.V.	Mine	—	
8	EMPIRE JAGUAR ...	S.	5,186	51°34′N. 17°35′W.	S.M.	T.	
9	ROYAL SOVEREIGN*	M.	1,527	51°24′N. 03°08′W.	Mine	—	
11	ROTORUA	S.	10,890	58°56′N. 11°20′W.	S.M.	T.	
14	WESTERN PRINCE...	M.	10,926	59°32′N. 17°47′W.	S.M.	T.	

Date	Name	Type	Gross tons	Position	Cause of loss	How lost	Remarks
DECEMBER, 1940—(Contd.)							
14	KYLEGLEN	S.	3,670	58°N. 25°W. (Approx.)	C.U.	—	
14	EUPHORBIA... ...	S.	3,380	North Atlantic	C.U.	—	
15	N. C. MONBERG ...	S.	2,301	52°40′N. 02°10′E.	E-Boat	T.	
17	INVER	S.	1,543	Off Southend	Mine	—	
17	MALRIX	S.	703	Off Southend	Mine	—	
17	BENEFICENT ...	S.	2,944	Off Southend	Mine	—	
17	AQUEITY ...	M.	370	Off Southend	Mine	—	
17	BELVEDERE ...	S.	869	Off Southend	Mine	—	
18	NAPIER STAR ...	S.	10,116	58°58′N. 23°13′W.	S.M.	T.	
18	DUQUESA	S.	8,651	00°57′N. 22°42′W.	Raider	—	" Admiral Scheer "
18	OSAGE	M. Tank	1,010	4m. N.E. of Arklow L.V., Co. Wicklow	A.C.	B.	
19	AMICUS	S.	3,660	54°10′N. 15°50′W.	S.M.	T.	
19	ARINIA	M. Tank	8,024	8m. E.S.E. of Southend Pier	Mine	—	
19	ISOLDA (L.V. Tender)	M.	734	Vicinity of Barrels Rock L.V., S. Wexford	A.C.	T.	
20	CARLTON	S.	5,162	54°30′N. 18°30′W.	S.M.	T. & G.	
21	SILVIO	S.	1,293	Liverpool	A.C.	B.	
21	INNISFALLEN ...	M.	3,071	Entrance Canada Dock, River Mersey	Mine	—	
21	T.I.C. 12	Barge	118	51°28′N. 00°46′E.	Mine	—	
21	SUN IX*	Tug	196	Between 1 and 2 buoys, Yantlet Channel, Thames Estuary	Mine	—	
21	RIVER THAMES* ...	Tug	88	51°28′N. 00°46′E.	Mine	—	
22	POOLGARTH ...	Tug	179	Off Canada Dock, S. Pier Head, Liverpool	Mine	—	
24	BRITISH PREMIER...	S. Tank	5,872	06°20′N. 13°20′W. (Approx.)	S.M.	T.	
25	JUMNA	S.	6,078	43°N. 20°W. (Approx.)	Raider	—	" Admiral Hipper "
26	WAIOTIRA ...	M.	12,823	58°05′N. 17°10′W.	S.M.	T.	Sank on 27th
27	KINNAIRD HEAD ...	S.	449	Off Southend	Mine	—	
27	ARABY	M.	4,936	9 cables W. of Nore L.V.	Mine	—	
27	ARDANBHAN ...	S.	4,980	59°16′N. 20°27′W.	S.M.	T.	
30	CALCIUM	S.	613	53°25′N. 03°45′W.	Mine	—	
	Total ... 61		265,314				
JANUARY, 1941							
2	NALGORA	S.	6,579	22°24′N. 21°11′W.	S.M.	T. & G.	
3	PINEWOOD	S.	2,466	1½m. S. of Pier, Southend	Mine	—	
5	SHAKESPEAR ...	S.	5,029	18°05′N. 21°10′W.	S.M.	G.	
6	LION*	Tug	87	320° 2½ cables from No. 5 Medway Buoy	Mine	—	
7	H. H. PETERSEN ...	S.	975	52°22′N. 02°05′E.	Mine	—	
6	EMPIRE THUNDER...	S.	5,965	59°14′N. 12°43′W.	S.M.	T.	
8	STRATHEARN (Trinity House Tender)	M.	683	51°45′N. 01°10′E.	Mine	—	
8	CLYTONEUS... ...	M.	6,278	56°23′N. 15°28′W.	A.C.	B.	
9	BASSANO	S.	4,843	57°57′N. 17°42′W.	S.M.	T.	
10	MIDDLESEX ...	S.	9,583	198° 0.8m. from Flatholm Is.	Mine	—	
11	BEACHY*	S.	1,600	53°29′N. 16°24′W.	A.C.	B.	
14	EUMAEUS	S.	7,472	08°55′N. 15°03′W.	S.M.	T.	
15	MANCUNIUM ...	Sludge Vessel	1,286	2m. N.E. of Bar L.V., Mersey	Mine	—	
16	OROPESA	S.	14,118	56°28′N. 12°00′W.	S.M.	T.	
16	ZEALANDIC ...	S.	10,578	58°28′N. 20°43′W.	S.M.	T.	
17	ALMEDA STAR ...	S.	14,935	58°16′N. 13°40′W.	S.M.	T.	
18	BRITISH UNION* ...	M. Tank	6,987	26°34′N. 30°58′W.	Raider	—	

Date	Name	Type	Gross tons	Position	Cause of loss	How lost	Remarks
JANUARY, 1941—(Contd.)							
19	BONNINGTON COURT	M.	4,909	275° 9.5 cables from Sunk L.V.	A.C.	B.	
20	FLORIAN	S.	3,174	North Atlantic	S.M.*	—	
20	STANPARK ...	S.	5,103	09°27′S. 03°00′W.	Raider	—	" Admiral Scheer "
21	TEMPLE MEAD ...	S.	4,427	54°14′N. 14°30′W.	A.C.	B.	
21	ENGLISHMAN* ...	Tug	487	40m. W. of Tory Island	A.C.	B.	
23	LURIGETHAN ...	S.	3,564	53°46′N. 16°00′W.	A.C.	B.	
23	LANGLEEGORSE ...	S.	4,524	53°19′N. 13°11′W.	A.C.	B.	
23	MOSTYN	S.	1,859	54°30′N. 14°52′W.	A.C.	B.	
24	CORHEATH	S.	1,096	270° 1m. from Botany Buoy, Thames Estuary	Mine	—	
24	MANDASOR	S.	5,144	04°18′S. 61°00′E.	Raider	—	
26	MERIONES	S.	7,557	52°53′N. 01°47′E.	A.C.	B.	
27	RINGWALL	S.	407	Irish Sea, S. of Isle of Man	Mine	—	
28	URLA	S.	5,198	54°54′N. 19°00′W.	S.M.	T.	
28	PANDION	S.	1,944	55°34′N. 10°22′W.	A.C.	B.	
28	GRELROSA	S.	4,574	55°12′N. 15°41′W.	A.C.	B.	
29	WEST WALES ...	S.	4,354	56°00′N. 15°23′W.	S.M.	T.	
29	RUSHPOOL	S.	5,125	56°00′N. 15°42′W.	S.M.	T.	
29	KING ROBERT ...	S.	5,886	56°00′N. 15°23′W.	S.M.	T.	
29	EURYLOCHUS ...	S.	5,723	08°15′N. 25°04′W.	Raider	—	
29	AFRIC STAR ...	S.	11,900	08°N. 25°W. (Approx.)	Raider	—	
29	W.B. WALKER ...	S. Tank	10,468	56°00′N. 15°23′W.	S.M.	T.	
31	PIZARRO	M.	1,367	49°03′N. 19°40′W.	S.M.	T.	
31	ROWANBANK ...	S.	5,159	57°00′N. 16°30′W.	A.C.	—	
31	SPEYBANK	M.	5,154	Indian Ocean	Raider	—	Taken in prize
	Total ... 41		208,567				
FEBRUARY, 1941							
2	EMPIRE ENGINEER	S.	5,358	54°N. 35°W. (Approx.)	S.M.*	—	
2	THE SULTAN ...	S.	824	51°43′N. 01°26′E.	A.C.	B.	
3	EMPIRE CITIZEN ...	S.	4,683	58°12′N. 23°22′W.	S.M.	T.	
4	DIONE II	S.	2,660	55°50′N. 10°30′W. (Approx.)	S.M.	G.	Previously attacked by A.C. on 3rd in position 55°40′N. 14°23′W.
4	GWYNWOOD ...	S.	1,177	Convoy anchorage, Humber	Mine	—	
5	RANEE	S.	5,060	Suez Canal	Mine	—	
6	MAPLECOURT ...	S.	3,388	55°39′N. 15°56′W.	S.M.	T.	
6	ANGULARITY ...	M.	501	Off East Coast between Ipswich and Newcastle	E-Boat	—	
7	BAY FISHER* ...	S.	575	3½m. N.E. of Bell Rock	A.C.	B.	
8	CANFORD CHINE ...	S.	3,364	Last seen in position 55°N. 15°W.	C.U.	—	
9	COURLAND	S.	1,325	35°53′N. 13°13′W.	S.M.	T.	
9	ESTRELLANO ...	S.	1,983	35°53′N. 13°13′W.	S.M.	T.	
9	VARNA	S.	1,514	35°42′N. 14°38′W.	A.C.	B.	Sank on 16th in position 44°55′N. 22°30′W.
9	BRITANNIC	S.	2,490	35°42′N. 14°38′W.	A.C.	B.	
9	JURA	S.	1,759	35°42′N. 14°38′W.	A.C.	B.	
9	DAGMAR I ...	S.	2,471	35°42′N. 14°38′W.	A.C.	B.	
10	BRANDENBURGH ...	S.	1,473	36°10′N. 16°38′W.	S.M.	T.	
11	ICELAND	S.	1,236	37°03′N. 19°50′W.	Raider	—	" Admiral Hipper "
12	WARLABY	S.	4,876	37°12′N. 21°20′W.	Raider	—	" Admiral Hipper "
12	WESTBURY ...	S.	4,712	37°10′N. 21°20′W.	Raider	—	" Admiral Hipper "
12	OSWESTRY GRANGE	S.	4,684	37°10′N. 21°20′W.	Raider	—	" Admiral Hipper "
12	SHREWSBURY ...	S.	4,542	36°46′N. 20°12′W.	Raider	—	" Admiral Hipper "
12	DERRYNANE ...	S.	4,896	37°12′N. 21°20′W.	Raider	—	" Admiral Hipper "

17

Date	Name	Type	Gross tons	Position	Cause of loss	How lost	Remarks
FEBRUARY, 1941—(Contd.)							
13	ARTHUR F. CORWIN	M. Tank	10,516	60°25′N. 17°11′W.	S.M.	T.	
About 13	CLEA*	M. Tank	8,074	North Western Approaches	S.M.	T.	
14	ELISABETH MARIE	S.	616	54°58′N. 12°30′W. (Approx.)	A.C.	B.	
15	ALNMOOR	S.	6,573	55°N. 13°W. (Est.)	C.U.	—	
15	BELCREST	S.	4,517	54°N. 21°W. (Approx.)	S.M.*	—	
15	HOLYSTONE ...	S.	5,462	Mid-North Atlantic	S.M.*	—	
16	GAIRSOPPA	S.	5,237	300m. S.W. of Galway Bay	S.M.	T.	
17	SIAMESE PRINCE ...	M.	8,456	59°53′N. 12°13′W.	S.M.	T.	
17	KYLE RONA ...	S.	307	Irish Sea	C.U.	—	
17	BEN REIN* ...	S.	156	Off Falmouth	Mine	—	
17	BLACK OSPREY ...	S.	5,589	61°30′N. 18°10′W. (Approx.)	S.M.	T.	
18	EMPIRE BLANDA ...	S.	5,693	North Atlantic	S.M.*	—	
18	SEAFORTH	M.	5,459	58°48′N. 18°17′W.	S.M.	T.	
18	EDWY R. BROWN...	M. Tank	10,455	61°N. 18°W. (Approx.)	S.M.	T.	
19	ALGARVE	S.	1,355	Nr. Sheringham Lt. Float	E-Boat	T.	
19	GRACIA	S.	5,642	59°39′N. 07°24′W. (Approx.)	A.C.	B.	
19	HOUSATONIC* ...	S. Tank	5,559	59°39′N. 07°24′W. (Approx.)	A.C.	B.	
20	BRITISH ADVOCATE	S. Tank	6,994	Indian Ocean (West of Seychelles)	Raider	—	" Admiral Scheer " Taken in prize
20	FORT MEDINE	S.	5,261	51°35′N. 03°56′W.	Mine	—	
20	RIGMOR	S.	1,278	49°54′N. 04°51′W.	A.C.	B.	
21	SCOTTISH STANDARD*	M. Tank	6,999	59°20′N. 16°12′W.	S.M.	T.	Previously attacked same day by A.C. in position 59°09′N. 16°18′W.
21	CANADIAN CRUISER	S.	7,178	06°36′S. 47°18′E.	Raider	—	" Admiral Scheer "
22	TRELAWNEY ...	S.	4,689	47°12′N. 40°13′W.	Raider	—	" Scharnhorst " or " Gneisenau "
22	LUSTROUS	S. Tank	6,156	47°12′N. 40°13′W.	Raider	—	" Scharnhorst " or " Gneisenau "
22	HARLESDEN ...	S.	5,483	47°12′N. 40°18′W. (Approx.)	Raider	—	" Scharnhorst " or " Gneisenau "
22	KANTARA	S.	3,237	47°12′N. 40°13′W. (Approx.)	Raider	—	" Scharnhorst " or " Gneisenau "
22	A. D. HUFF ...	S.	6,219	47°12′N. 40°13′W. (Approx.)	Raider	—	" Scharnhorst " or " Gneisenau "
23	ANGLO PERUVIAN ...	S.	5,457	59°30′N. 21°00′W.	S.M.	T.	
23	CAPE NELSON ...	S.	3,807	59°30′N. 21°00′W.	S.M.	T.	
23	MARSLEW	S.	4,542	59°18′N. 21°30′W.	S.M.	T.	
23	SHOAL FISHER ...	M.	698	50°10′N. 04°50′W.	Mine	—	
23	TEMPLE MOAT ...	S.	4,427	59°27′N. 20°20′W.	S.M.		
24	JONATHAN HOLT ...	S.	4,973	61°10′N. 11°55′W.	S.M.	T.	
24	LINARIA	S.	3,385	61°N. 25°W. (Approx.)	S.M.*	—	
24	NAILSEA LASS ...	S.	4,289	60m. S.W. of Fastnet	S.M.	T.	
24	SIRIKISHNA ...	S.	5,458	58°N. 21°W. (Approx.)	S.M.	T. & G.	
24	BRITISH GUNNER ...	S. Tank	6,894	61°09′N. 12°04′W.	S.M.	T.	
24	MANSEPOOL ...	S.	4,894	61°01′N. 12°00′W.	S.M.	T.	
24	HUNTINGDON ...	S.	10,946	58°25′N. 20°23′W.	S.M.	T.	
24	WAYNEGATE ...	S.	4,260	58°50′N. 21°47′W.	S.M.	T.	
25	GLOBE	S.B.	54	079° 6,100 yds. from Garrison Pt., Sheerness	Mine	—	
26	MINORCA	S.	1,123	53°04′N. 01°21′E.	E-Boat	T.	
26	MAHANADA ...	S.	7,181	54°07′N. 17°06′W.	A.C.	T.	
26	SWINBURNE ...	S.	4,659	54°00′N. 16°58′W.	A.C.	B.	
26	LLANWERN ...	S.	4,966	54°07′N. 17°06′W.	A.C.	B.	
27	BALTISTAN	S.	6,803	51°52′N. 19°55′W.	S.M.	T.	
27	STANWOLD	S.	1,020	10m. W.S.W. of Selsey	C.U.	—	

Date	Name	Type	Gross tons	Position	Cause of loss	How lost	Remarks
FEBRUARY, 1941—(Contd.)							
27	OLD CHARLTON ...	S.	1,562	51°57′N. 01°40′E.	A.C.	B.	
27	ANCHISES	S.	10,000	55°30′N. 13°17′W.	A.C.	B.	Again attacked by A.C. on the 28th and sunk
27	NOSS HEAD ...	S.	438	Vicinity of Gardenstown, E. Scotland	C.U.	—	
28	HOLMELEA	S.	4,223	54°24′N. 17°25′W.	S.M.	T.	
28	CABENDA	M.	534	51°34′N. 03°54′W.	Mine	—	
	Total ... 75		315,304				
MARCH, 1941							
1	PACIFIC	S.	6,034	180m. W.S.W. of Sydero Is., Faroes	S.M.	T.	
1	CADILLAC	S. Tank	12,062	59°44′N. 11°16′W.	S.M.	T.	
1	EFFNA	S.	6,461	61°30′N. 15°45′W. (Est.)	S.M.*	—	
2	CASTLEHILL ...	S.	690	East of Minehead	A.C.	B.	
3	PORT TOWNSVILLE	M.	8,661	52°05′N. 05°24′W.	A.C.	B.	Sank on 4th
4	ANONITY	M.	303	1½m. S.E. of Skegness Pier	Mine	—	
5	SILVERSTONE ...	Tug	58	3m. above Rochester Bridge, Medway	Mine*	—	
6	SUN VII*	Tug	202	060° 1 to 2m. from North Knob Buoy, Barrow Deep	Mine	—	
7	TERJE VIKEN ...	S. Tank	20,638	60°00′N. 12°50′W.	S.M.	T.	
7	ATHELBEACH ...	M. Tank	6,568	60°30′N. 13°30′W.	S.M.	T.	
7	DOTTEREL	S.	1,385	Off No. 6 Buoy, Southwold	E-Boat	T.	
7	KENTON	S.	1,047	52°57′N. 01°30′E.	E-Boat	T.	
7	CORDUFF	S.	2,345	Off No. 8 Buoy. Nr. Cromer	E-Boat	T.	
7	BOULDERPOOL ...	S.	4,805	52°58′N. 01°28′E. (Approx.)	E-Boat	T.	
7	FLASHLIGHT ...	S.	934	53°34′N. 00°49′E.	A.C.	B.	
7	DUNAFF HEAD ...	S.	5,258	60°33′N. 18°50′W.	S.M.	T.	
7	RYE	S.	1,048	Off Cromer	E-Boat	T.	
8	HINDPOOL	S.	4,897	20°51′N. 20°32′W.	S.M.	T.	
8	LAHORE	S.	5,304	21°03′N. 20°38′W.	S.M.	T.	
8	HARMODIUS ...	S.	5,229	20°35′N. 20°40′W.	S.M.	T.	
8	TIELBANK	S.	5,084	20°51′N. 20°32′W.	S.M.	T.	
8	NARDANA	S.	7,974	20°51′N. 20°32′W.	S.M.	T.	
8	TOGSTON	S.	1,547	305° 2m. from Smith's Knoll. (Approx.)	E-Boat	T.	
8	NORMAN QUEEN ...	S.	957	Off S. Haisboro' Buoy, E. of Cromer	E-Boat	T.	
10	CORINIA	S.	870	50°55′N. 00°35′E.	Mine	—	
10	SPARTA	S.	708	50°55′N. 00°35′E.	Mine	—	
10	WATERLAND ...	S.	1,107	50°55′N. 00°35′E.	Mine	—	
11	MEMNON	M.	7,506	20°41′N. 21°00′W.	S.M.	T.	
11	TREVETHOE ...	M.	5,257	52°46′N. 01°57′E.	E-Boat	T.	
12	EMPIRE FROST ...	S.	7,005	51°36′N. 05°40′W.	A.C.	B.	Attacked again on 13th whilst in tow and sank
13	TACOMA CITY ...	S.	4,738	104° 2¼ cables from Rock Ferry Lt., Mersey	Mine	—	
13	ULLAPOOL	S.	4,891	Off Princes Stage, Mersey	Mine	—	
13	BULLGER*	Tug	270	Druridge Bay, 16m. N. of Tyne	Mine	—	
14	WESTERN CHIEF ...	S.	5,759	58°52′N. 21°13′W.	S.M.	T.	
14	HERPORT	S.	2,633	53°15′N. 01°05′E.	Mine	—	
14	STANLEIGH* ...	S.	1,802	288° 12m. from Bar L.V., Mersey	A.C.	B.	
14	ARTEMISIA	S.	6,507	52°53′N. 01°39′E.	A.C.	B.	
15	BRITISH STRENGTH	M. Tank	7,139	42°N 43°W. (Approx.)	Raider	—	"Scharnhorst" or "Gneisenau"

Date	Name	Type	Gross tons	Position	Cause of loss	How lost	Remarks
MARCH, 1941—(Contd.)							
15	SIMNIA	M. Tank	6,197	40°28′N. 43°30′W.	Raider	—	" Gneisenau "
15	SAN CASIMIRO ...	M. Tank	8,046	39°58′N. 43°19′W.	Raider	—	" Gneisenau." Captured 15th. Scuttled 20th in position 45°12′N. 19°42′W.
15	ROYAL CROWN ...	S.	4,388	42°N. 43°W. (Approx.)	Raider	—	" Gneisenau "
15	MYSON	S.	4,564	42°N. 43°W. (Approx.)	Raider	—	" Scharnhorst "
15	RIO DORADO ...	S.	4,507	42°N. 43°W. (Approx.)	Raider	—	" Scharnhorst " or " Gneisenau "
15	ATHELFOAM ...	M. Tank	6,554	42°00′N. 43°25′W.	Raider	—	" Scharnhorst "
16	SARDINIAN PRINCE	S.	3,491	44°N. 43°W. (Approx.)	Raider	—	" Scharnhorst "
16	SILVERFIR	M.	4,347	42°N. 43°W. (Approx.)	Raider	—	" Gneisenau "
16	EMPIRE INDUSTRY	S.	3,721	42°N. 43°W. (Approx.)	Raider	—	" Scharnhorst "
16	DEMETERTON ...	S.	5,251	45°58′N. 44°00′W.	Raider	—	" Scharnhorst "
16	CHILEAN REEFER ...	M.	1,739	46°13′N. 44°45′W.	Raider	—	" Gneisenau "
16	VENETIA	S. Tank	5,728	61°00′N. 12°36′W.	S.M.	T.	
17	ANDALUSIAN ...	S.	3,082	14°33′N. 21°06′W.	S.M.	T.	
17	J. B. WHITE ...	S.	7,375	60°57′N. 12°27′W.	S.M.	T.	
17	MEDJERDA	S.	4,380	17°N. 21°W. (Est.)	S.M. *	—	
18	DAPHNE II... ...	S.	1,970	59 Buoy, off Humber	E-Boat	T.	
19	BENVORLICH ...	S.	5,193	54°48′N. 13°10′W.	A.C.	—	
20	SIR BEVOIS* ...	Tug	338	Plymouth	A.C.	B.	
20	CLAN OGILVY ...	S.	5,802	20°04′N. 25°45′W.	S.M.	T.	
21	BENWYVIS	S.	5,920	20°N. 26°W. (Approx.)	S.M.	T.	
21	JHELUM	S.	4,038	21°N. 25°W. (Approx.)	S.M.	T.	
21	LONDON II... ...	S.	1,260	51°23′N. 04°30′W.	A.C.	B.	
21	MILLISLE	S.	617	2m. E. of Helwick L.B., Bristol Channel	A.C.	—	
22	AGNITA	M. Tank	3,552	02°30′N. 25°00′W.	Raider	—	
22	ST. FINTAN ...	S.	495	7m. N.N.W. of Smalls (Approx.)	A.C.	—	
23	CHAMA	M. Tank	8,077	49°35′N. 19°13′W.	S.M.	T.	
About 24	KORANTON	S.	6,695	59°N. 27°W. (Approx.)	S.M.	—	
24	AGNETE MAERSK ...	S.	2,104	49°00′N. 22°55′W.	S.M.	G.	
25	ROSSMORE	S.	627	12m. N.E. of Godrevy Is.	A.C.	B.	
25	BEAVERBRAE ...	S.	9,956	60°12′N. 09°00′W.	A.C.	B.	
25	BRITANNIA	S.	8,799	07°24′N. 24°03′W.	Raider	—	
26	FARADAY*	Cable ship	5,533	038° 3m. from St. Anne's Head	A.C.	B.	
26	BRIER ROSE ...	S.	503	Irish Sea	C.U.	—	
26	SOMALI	S.	6,809	Off Blyth	A.C.	B.	Sank on 27th 1m. E. of Snoop Head, Sunderland
26	EMPIRE MERMAID	S.	6,381	58°36′N. 10°00′W.	A.C.	B.	Sank on 28th in position 57°33′N. 12°43′W.
27	CANADOLITE ...	M. Tank	11,309	05°N. 33°W. (Approx.)	Raider	—	Taken in prize.
27	MEG MERRILIES ...	S.	642	1m. S. of St. Govan's L.V.	A.C.	B.	
28	OLIVINE	S.	929	In Irish Sea or Bristol Channel	C.U.	—	
29	EMMA	Spritsail Barge	81	Rotherhithe	M.	—	
29	HYLTON	M.	5,197	60°02′N. 18°10′W.	S.M.	T.	
29	GERMANIC	S.	5,352	61°18′N. 22°05′W.	S.M.	T.	
29	OILTRADER ...	S. Tank	5,550	52°34′N. 02°01′E	A.C.	B.	

Date	Name	Type	Gross tons	Position	Cause of loss	How lost	Remarks
MARCH, 1941—*(Contd.)*							
30	EASTLEA	S.	4,267	North Atlantic	S.M.*	—	
30	COULTARN	S.	3,759	60°18′N. 29°28′W.	S.M.	T.	
30	UMONA	S.	3,767	About 90m. S.W. of Freetown	S.M.	T.	
	Total ... 83		364,575				
APRIL, 1941							
1	SAN CONRADO ...	M. Tank	7,982	325° 13m. from Smalls	A.C.	B.	
2	BRITISH RELIANCE	M. Tank	7,000	58°21′N. 28°30′W.	S.M.	T.	
2	BEAVERDALE ...	S.	9,957	60°50′N. 29°19′W.	S.M.	T. & G.	
2	HOMEFIELD ...	S.	5,324	Off Gavdo Is., E. Mediterranean	A.C.	B.	
2	FERMAIN	S.	759	50°35′N. 00°52′E.	A.C.	B.	
3	BRITISH VISCOUNT*	S. Tank	6,895	58°15′N. 27°30′W.	S.M.	T.	
3	ALDERPOOL ...	S.	4,313	58°21′N. 27°59′W.	S.M.	T.	
3	WESTPOOL	S.	5,724	58°12′N. 27°40′W.	S.M.	T.	
3	CAIRNIE	S.	250	6 to 8m. S. × W. of Tod Head	A.C.	B.	
3	GREENAWN ...	S.	784	North Sea, nr. Montrose	C.U.	—	
3	NORTHERN PRINCE	M.	10,917	Anti-Kithera Channel, E. Mediterranean	A.C.	B.	
4	ATHENIC	S.	5,351	58°32′N. 20°13′W.	S.M.	T.	
4	HARBLEDOWN ...	S.	5,414	58°30′N. 23°00′W.	S.M.	T.	
4	CONUS*	M. Tank	8,132	56°14′N. 31°19′W.	S.M.	T.	
4	WELCOMBE ...	S.	5,122	59°09′N. 22°00′W.	S.M.	T.	
4	MARLENE	S.	6,507	08°15′N. 14°19′W.	S.M.	T.	
4	SALVUS ...	S.	4,815	53°05′N. 01°27′E.	A.C.	B.	
5	ENA DE LARRINAGA	S.	5,200	01°10′N. 26°00′W.	S.M.	T.	
5	ST. CLEMENT ...	S.	450	57°19′N. 01°50′W.	A.C.	B.	
5	RATTRAY HEAD ...	S.	496	8m. E.N.E. of Aberdeen	A.C.	B.	
6	DUNSTAN	S.	5,149	59°09′N. 08°22′W.	A.C.	B.	
6	OLGA S. ...	M.	2,252	55°48′N. 09°45′W.	A.C.	B.	
6	CYPRIAN PRINCE ...	S.	1,988	Piraeus	A.C.	B.	
6	CLAN FRASER ...	S.	7,529	Piraeus	A.C.	B.	
6	CITY OF ROUBAIX	S.	7,108	Piraeus	A.C.	B.	
6	PATRIS	S.	1,706	Piraeus	A.C.	B.	
7	PORTADOC	S.	1,746	07°17′N. 16°53′W. (Approx.)	S.M.	T.	
7	ELISABETH	S.	945	5m. E.S.E. of Porthscatho, S.E. Cornwall	Mine	—	
8	HELENA MARGARETA	S.	3,316	33°00′N. 23°52′W.	S.M.	T.	
8	TWEED	S.	2,697	07°43′N. 15°11′W.	S.M.	T.	
8	HARPATHIAN ...	S.	4,671	32°22′N. 22°53′W.	S.M.	T.	
8	ESKDENE ...	S.	3,829	34°43′N. 24°21′W.	S.M.	T.	
8	AHAMO* ...	S. Tank	8,621	53°22′N. 00°59′E.	Mine	—	
9	DUFFIELD* ...	M. Tank	8,516	31°13′N. 23°24′W.	S.M.	T.	Previously attacked by S.M. on 8th in position 32°00′N. 23°24′W.
9	LUNULA	S. Tank	6,363	Thames Haven	Mine	—	
9	CRAFTSMAN... ...	S.	8,022	05°S. 20°W. (Approx.)	Raider	—	
9	DUDLEY ROSE* ...	S.	1,600	150° 4m. from Berry Head	A.C.	B.	
11	RETRIEVER ...	Cable Ship	674	264° 1m. from Aliki Rocks, off Phleva Is., Greece	A.C.	B.	
11	DRACO	S.	2,018	Tobruk	A.C.	B.	Again bombed 21st and became total loss
12	ST. HELENA ...	S.	4,313	07°50′N. 14°00′W.	S.M.	T.	

Date	Name	Type	Gross tons	Position	Cause of loss	How lost	Remarks
APRIL, 1941—(Contd.)							
12	MARIE MAERSK ...	M. Tank	8,271	Piraeus	A.C.	B.	
13	CORINTHIC ...	S.	4,823	08°10′N. 14°40′W.	S.M.	T.	
13	CITY OF KARACHI ...	S.	7,140	Volo, Greece	A.C.	B.	
14	CLAN CUMMING ...	S.	7,264	Gulf of Athens	Mine	—	
15	AURILLAC	S.	4,733	37°09′N. 18°42′W.	S.M.	T.	
15	GOALPARA	S.	5,314	Eleusis Bay, Piraeus	A.C.	B.	
15	QUILOA	S.	7,765	Eleusis Bay, Piraeus	A.C.	B.	
15	AQUILA	Tug	59	Hull	A.C.	B.	
16	SWEDRU	M.	5,379	55°21′N. 12°50′W.	A.C.	B.	
16	ANGLESEA ROSE ...	S.	1,151	50°25′N. 05°35′W.	A.C.	B.	
16	AMIENS*	S.	1,548	50°25′N. 05°35′W.	A.C.	B.	
17	EFFRA	S.	1,446	Nr. Cross Sand, L.V.	E-Boat	T.	
17	MONTALTO	S.	623	Rochester	A.C.	B.	
18	BRITISH SCIENCE ...	M. Tank	7,138	36°06′N. 24°00′E.	A.C.	T.	
20	EMPIRE ENDURANCE	S.	8,570	53°05′N. 23°14′W.	S.M.	T.	
21	BANKURA	S.	3,185	Tobruk	A.C.	B.	Subsequently further damaged by A.C. and became total loss
21	CALCHAS	S.	10,305	23°50′N. 27°00′W.	S.M.	T.	
21	URANIA	S.	1,953	Tobruk	C.U.	—	
22	CORONATION OF LEEDS	Steam Barge	87	Off Thames Haven	Mine	—	
23	SANTA CLARA VALLEY	M.	4,665	Nauplia Bay, Greece	A.C.	B.	
24	CAVALLO	S.	2,269	Nauplia, Greece	A.C.*	—	Sank on 25th
25	EMPIRE LIGHT ...	S.	6,828	02°S. 61°E. (Approx.)	Raider	—	
26	MOUNTPARK ...	S.	4,648	56°17′N. 12°21′W.	A.C.	B.	
27	BEACON GRANGE ...	M.	10,160	62°05′N. 16°26′W.	S.M.	T.	
27	CELTE	S.	943	61°20′N. 11°00′W.	A.C.	B.	
27	HENRI MORY ...	S.	2,564	330m. W.N.W. of Blaskets, nr. Achill Head	S.M.	T.	
28	PORT HARDY ...	S.	8,897	60°14′N. 15°20′W.	S.M.	T.	
28	OILFIELD	M. Tank	8,516	60°05′N. 16°00′W.	S.M.	T.	
28	CAPULET* ...	M. Tank	8,190	60°10′N. 17°00′W.	S.M.	T.	
28	AMBROSE FLEMING	S.	1,555	53°14′N. 01°08′E.	E-Boat	T.	
28	CLAN BUCHANAN ...	S.	7,266	05°24′N. 62°46′E.	Raider	—	
29	CITY OF NAGPUR ...	S.	10,146	52°30′N. 26°00′W.	S.M.*	—	
29	KALUA	S.	722	½m. N.N.E. of T.2 Buoy, Mouth of Tyne	A.C.	B.	
30	NERISSA	S.	5,583	55°57′N. 10°08′W.	S.M.	T.	
30	LASSELL	M.	7,417	12°55′N. 28°56′W.	S.M.	T.	
	Total ... 75		361,578				
MAY, 1941							
1	SAMSO	S.	1,494	08°35′N. 16°17′W.	S.M.	T.	
2	PARRACOMBE ...	S.	4,702	Mediterranean	Mine	—	
3	ARAYBANK	M.	7,258	Suda Bay, Crete	A.C.	B.	Again bombed on 16th and became total loss
3	WRAY CASTLE ...	S.	4,253	06°48′N. 13°55′W.	S.M.	T.	
3	CORBET	S.	468	248° 2 cables from Herculaneum Dock entrance, Liverpool	Mine	—	
3	BARNACLE	S.B.	138	Liverpool	A.C.	B.	
3	BONITA	Tug	65	Liverpool	A.C.	B.	
3	ELSTREE GRANGE	S.	6,598	Liverpool	A.C.	B.	
3	DOMINO	S.	1,453	Liverpool	A.C.	B.	
3	LUCE	Barge	143	Liverpool	A.C.	B.	
3	EUROPA	M.	10,224	Liverpool	A.C.	B.	
3	MALAKAND	S.	7,649	Liverpool	A.C.	B.	

Date	Name	Type	Gross tons	Position	Cause of loss	How lost	Remarks
MAY, 1941—(Contd.)							
3	EMILY BURTON ...	Motor Barge	58	Liverpool	A.C.	B.	
3	PIKE	S.B.	168	Liverpool	A.C.	B.	
3	LING	S.B.	164	Liverpool	A.C.	B.	
About							
3	WALTON	Steam Barge	82	Liverpool	A.C.	B.	
3	SILVERDALE ...	S.B.	176	Liverpool	A.C.	B.	
4	ROYSTON ...	S.	2,722	270° from 62C Buoy (Humber)	A.C.	B.	Taken in tow and sank on 5th in position 53°37′N. 00°39′E. (Approx.)
4	TREGOR	M.	222	6m. off Trevose Head	A.C.	B.	
4	PNEUMATIC ELEVATOR No. 11	—	295	Liverpool	A.C.	B.	
5	QUEEN MAUD ...	M.	4,976	07°54′N. 16°41′W.	S.M.	T.	
5	TRAFFIC	Steam Barge	155	Liverpool	A.C.	B.	
5	FAIR HEAD ...	S.	1,719	Belfast	A.C.	B.	
6	SURAT	M.	5,529	08°23′N. 15°13′W.	S.M.	T.	
6	OAKDENE	S.	4,255	06°19′N. 27°55′W.	S.M.	T.	
6	DUNKWA	M.	4,752	08°43′N. 17°13′W.	S.M.	T.	
7	IXION	S.	10,263	61°29′N. 22°40′W.	S.M.	T.	
7	BRITISH EMPEROR	S. Tank	3,663	08°30′N. 56°25′E.	Raider	—	
7	RIL IDA	S.	53	Hull	A.C.	B.	
7	BLUESTONE ...	S.	106	Greenock	A.C.	B.	
7	KILEENAN	Steam Barge	72	Liverpool	Mine	—	
7	IDA BURTON ...	S.B.	46	Liverpool	A.C.	B.	
8	MARTON	S.	4,969	Liverpool	A.C.	B.	
8	ROSE	Steam Barge	143	Liverpool	A.C.	B.	
8	TRENTINO	S.	3,079	Liverpool	A.C.	B.	
8	DELITE	S.B.	89	Hull	A.C.	B.	
8	LADORE	S.B.	91	Hull	A.C.	B.	
8	WHITAKERS No. II	S.B.	48	Hull	A.C.	B.	
8	IRISHMAN	Tug	99	Portsmouth Harbour	Mine	—	
8	RAMILLIES	S.	4,553	48°05′N. 32°26′W.	S.M.	T.	
8	RAWNSLEY ...	M.	4,998	34°59′N. 25°46′E.	A.C.	B.	Sank on 12th.
9	CITY OF WINCHESTER	S.	7,120	08°20′N. 26°14′W.	S.M.	T.	
9	GREGALIA	S.	5,802	60°24′N. 32°37′W.	S.M.	T.	
9	BENGORE HEAD ...	S.	2,609	60°45′N. 33°02′W.	S.M.	T.	
9	ESMOND	S.	4,976	60°45′N. 33°02′W.	S.M.	T.	
9	EMPIRE SONG ...	S.	9,228	Off Malta	Mine	—	
10	EMPIRE CARIBOU ...	S.	4,861	59°28′N. 35°44′W.	S.M.	T.	
10	CITY OF SHANGHAI	S.	5,828	06°40′N. 27°50′W.	S.M.	T.	
11	SOMERSET	S.	8,790	54°54′N. 16°20′W.	A.C.	B.	
12	FOWBERRY TOWER	S.	4,484	1m. S.W. x W. of Humber L.V.	A.C.	B.	
12	RICHARD DE LARRINAGA	S.	5,358	4 cables N. of 20 R. Buoy, Tyne	A.C.	B.	
13	BENVRACKIE ...	S.	6,434	00°49′N. 20°15′W.	S.M.	T.	
13	F	Hopper Barge	496	350 yds. S. of Dingle Oil Jetty	Mine	—	
13	SOMERSBY	S.	5,170	60°39′N. 26°13′W.	S.M.	T.	
14	RABAUL	M.	6,809	19°30′S. 04°30′E.	Raider	—	
14	DALESMAN	S.	6,343	Suda Bay, Crete	A.C.	B.	
15	BENVENUE	S.	5,920	04°27′N. 18°25′W.	S.M.	T.	
16	RODNEY STAR ...	S.	11,803	05°03′N. 19°02′W.	S.M.	T.	
16	ARCHANGEL ...	S.	2,448	57°55′N. 02°03′W.	A.C.	B.	
16	ETHEL RADCLIFFE	S.	5,673	Great Yarmouth	A.C.	B.	Previously damaged By E-Boat on 17th April
16	LOGICIAN	S.	5,993	Suda Bay, Crete	A.C.	B.	Again bombed on 25th and sank
17	STATESMAN ...	S.	7,939	56°44′N. 13°45′W.	A.C.	B.	
17	ELEONORA MAERSK*	M. Tank	10,694	Suda Bay, Crete	A.C.	B.	
18	PIAKO	S.	8,286	07°52′N. 14°57′W.	S.M.	T.	

Date	Name	Type	Gross tons	Position	Cause of loss	How lost	Remarks
MAY, 1941—(Contd.)							
18	BEGERIN	M.	483	295° 17m. from South Bishops	A.C.	B.	
19	EMPIRE RIDGE ...	S.	2,922	90m. W. of Bloody Foreland	S.M.	T.	
19	WINKFIELD ...	S.	5,279	1m. S.W. of B.4 Buoy, Thames Estuary	Mine	—	
19	CITY OF ROCHESTER	Paddle steamer	194	Acorn Yard, Rochester	A.C.	Parachute Mine	
20	DARLINGTON COURT	M.	4,974	57°28′N. 41°07′W.	S.M.	T.	
20	JAVANESE PRINCE...	M.	8,593	59°46′N. 10°45′W.	S.M.	T.	
20	STARCROSS	S.	4,662	51°45′N. 20°45′W.	S.M.	T.	Sunk by Escort.
20	HARPAGUS	S.	5,173	56°47′N. 40°55′W.	S.M.	T.	
20	NORMAN MONARCH	S.	4,718	56°41′N. 40°52′W.	S.M.	T.	
20	BRITISH SECURITY	M. Tank	8,470	57°28′N. 41°07′W.	S.M.	T.	
20	ROTHERMERE ...	S.	5,356	57°48′N. 41°36′W.	S.M.	T.	
20	COCKAPONSET ...	S.	5,996	57°28′N. 41°07′W.	S.M.	T.	
21	TEWKESBURY ...	S.	4,601	05°49′N. 24°09′W.	S.M.	T.	
21	MARCONI	S.	7,402	58°N. 41°W. (Approx.)	S.M.	T.	
22	BARNBY	S.	4,813	60°30′N. 34°12′W.	S.M.	T.	
22	BRITISH GRENADIER*	S. Tank	6,857	06°15′N. 12°59′W.	S.M.	T.	
23	VULCAIN	S.	4,362	09°20′N. 15°35′W.	S.M.	T.	
24	TRAFALGAR... ...	S.	4,530	25°S. 01°E. (Approx.)	Raider	—	
25	HELKA	S. Tank	3,471	E. Mediterranean	A.C.	B.	
26	COLONIAL	S.	5,108	09°13′N. 15°09′W.	S.M.	T.	
29	TABARISTAN ...	S.	6,251	06°32′N. 15°23′W.	S.M.	T.	
29	EMPIRE STORM ...	S.	7,290	55°00′N. 39°50′W.	S.M.	T.	
30	SILVERYEW ...	M.	6,373	16°42′N. 25°29′W.	S.M.	T.	
30	EMPIRE PROTECTOR	S.	6,181	06°00′N. 14°25′W.	S.M.	T.	
30	WESTAVON... ...	S.	2,842	51°36′N. 01°11′E.	Mine	—	
31	CLAN MACDOUGALL	M.	6,843	16°50′N. 25°10′W.	S.M.	T.	
31	GRAVELINES ...	S.	2,491	56°00′N. 11°13′W.	S.M.	T.	
31	SIRE...	S.	5,664	08°50′N. 15°30′W.	S.M.	T.	
	Total ... 92		386,953				
JUNE 1941							
1	SCOTTISH MONARCH	S.	4,719	12°58′N. 27°20′W.	S.M.	T.	
1	ALFRED JONES ...	M.	5,013	08°N. 15°W. (Approx.)	S.M.	T.	
2	MICHAEL E. ...	S.	7,628	48°50′N. 29°00′W.	S.M.	T.	
2	INVERSUIR	M. Tank	9,456	48°28′N. 28°20′W.	S.M.	T. & G.	
2	BEAUMANOIR ...	S.	2,477	180° 8 cables from 19 Buoy, Robin Hood's Bay	A.C.	B.	
2	PRINCE RUPERT CITY	S.	4,749	58°46′N. 04°41′W.	A.C.	B.	
3	ROYAL FUSILIER ...	S.	2,187	55°22′N. 01°21′W.	A.C.	B.	Sank 200° 4m. from May Is.
4	WELLFIELD* ...	M. Tank	6,054	48°34′N. 31°34′W.	S.M.	T.	
4	ROBERT HUGHES ...	Dredger	2,879	Entrance to Lagos, W. Africa	Mine	—	
4	TRECARREL... ...	S.	5,271	47°10′N. 31°00′W.	S.M.	T.	
6	TREGARTHEN ...	S.	5,201	46°17′N. 36°20′W.	S.M.	T.	
6	BARON LOVAT ...	S.	3,395	35°30′N. 11°30′W.	S.M.	T.	
6	SACRAMENTO VALLEY	S.	4,573	17°10′N. 30°10′W.	S.M.	T.	
6	GLEN HEAD ...	S.	2,011	35°40′N. 10°30′W.	A.C.	B.	
6	QUEENSBURY ...	S.	3,911	56°50′N. 02°07′W.	A.C.	B.	
7	KINGSTON HILL ...	S.	7,628	09°35′N. 29°40′W.	S.M.	T.	
7	BARON NAIRN ...	S.	3,164	47°36′N. 39°02′W.	S.M.	T.	
8	ELMDENE	S.	4,853	08°16′N. 16°50′W.	S.M.	T.	

24

Date	Name	Type	Gross tons	Position	Cause of loss	How lost	Remarks
JUNE, 1941—(Contd.)							
8	TREVARRACK ...	S.	5,270	48°46′N. 29°14′W.	S.M.	T.	
8	PHIDIAS	S.	5,623	48°25′N. 26°12′W.	S.M.	G.	
8	ADDA	M.	7,816	08°30′N. 14°39′W.	S.M.	T.	
9	DIANA ... , ...	S.	942	62°04′N. 13°40′W. (Approx.)	A.C.	B.	
9	SILVERPALM ...	M.	6,373	51°N. 26°W. (Approx.)	S.M.*	—	
9	DAGMAR	S.	844	50°35′N. 01°48′W.	A.C.	B.	
10	AINDERBY ...	S.	4,860	55°30′N. 12°10′W.	S.M.	T.	
10	ROYAL SCOT ...	S.	1,444	070° 5 cables from 62 Buoy, Humber entrance	Mine	—	
11	BARON CARNEGIE ...	S.	3,178	51°55′N. 05°34′W.	A.C.	T.	
11	MOORWOOD...	S.	2,056	At 20 C Buoy off Hartlepool	A.C.	T.	
12	EMPIRE DEW ...	M.	7,005	51°09′N. 30°16′W.	S.M.	T.	
12	CHINESE PRINCE ...	M.	8,593	56°12′N. 14°18′W.	S.M.	T.	
12	TRESILLIAN ...	S.	4,743	44°40′N. 45°30′W.	S.M.	T.	
13	DJURDJURA ...	S.	3,460	38°53′N. 23°11′W.	S.M.	T.	
13	KINGSTOWN ...	S.	628	9m. N.W. of S. Bishops Lt., Bristol Channel	A.C.	B.	
13	ST. LINDSAY ...	S.	5,370	51°N. 30°W. (Approx.)	S.M.*	—	
13	ST. PATRICK ...	S.	1,922	52°04′N. 05°25′W. (Approx.)	A.C.	B.	
13	SUSAN MAERSK ...	S.	2,355	North Atlantic	C.U	—	
17	TOTTENHAM ...	S.	4,762	07°38′S. 19°12′W.	Raider	—	
17	CATHRINE	M.	2,727	49°30′N. 16°00′W. (Approx.)	S.M.	T.	
18	NORFOLK	S.	10,948	57°17′N. 11°14′W.	S.M.	T.	
19	EMPIRE WARRIOR	S.	1,306	2¾m. off Guadiana Bar, Gulf of Cadiz	A.C.	B.	
21	GASFIRE	S.	3,001	About 10m. due E. of Southwold	Mine	—	
21	KENNETH HAWKSFIELD	S.	1,546	52°18′N. 01°59′E.	Mine	—	
22	BALZAC	S.	5,372	12°S. 29°W. (Approx.)	Raider	—	
23	HULL TRADER ...	S.	717	270° 1m. from No. 57 C. Buoy, Cromer (Approx.)	Mine	—	
23	TRELISSICK ...	S.	5,265	114° 3½m. from Sheringham Buoy, Cromer	A.C.	B.	
23	ARAKAKA* (Meteorological Vessel)	S.	2,379	47°N. 40°W. (Approx.)	S.M.*	—	
24	KINROSS	M.	4,956	55°23′N. 38°49′W.	S.M.	T.	
24	BROCKLEY HILL ...	S.	5,297	58°30′N. 38°20′W.	S.M.	T.	
25	DASHWOOD ...	S.	2,154	52°59′N. 01°52′E.	A.C.	B.	
26	MAREEBA	S.	3,472	10°N. 88°E. (Approx.)	Raider	—	
26	RIVER LUGAR ...	S.	5,423	24°N. 21°W. (Approx.)	S.M.	T.	
26	MALAYA II... ...	M.	8,651	59°56′N. 30°35′W.	S.M.	T.	
27	EMPIRE ABILITY ...	S.	7,603	23°50′N. 21°10′W.	S.M.	T.	
27	P.L.M.22 ...	S.	5,646	25°43′N. 22°47′W.	S.M.	T.	
28	AURIS*	M. Tank	8,030	34°27′N. 11°57′W.	S.M.	T.	
28	BARRHILL	S.	4,972	52°50′N. 01°46′E.	A.C.	B.	
29	RIO AZUL	S.	4,088	29°N. 25°W. (Approx.)	S.M.	T.	
29	GRAYBURN	S.	6,342	59°30′N. 18°07′W.	S.M.	T.	
29	CUSHENDALL ...	S.	626	56°57′N. 02°03′W.	A.C.	B.	
30	ST. ANSELM ...	S.	5,614	31°N. 26°W. (Approx.)	S.M.	T.	
	Total ... 60		268,548				

Date	Name	Type	Gross tons	Position	Cause of loss	How lost	Remarks
JULY, 1941							
1	HOMEFIRE ...	S.	1,262	53°05′N. 01°28′E.	A.C.	B.	
2	TORONTO CITY* ...	S.	2,486	47°03′N. 30°00′W.	S.M.*	—	
	(Meteorological Vessel)			(Approx.)			
3	ROSME	Sprit-sail Barge	82	51°34′N. 01°03′E.	Mine	—	
4	AUDITOR	S.	5,444	25°53′N. 28°23′W.	S.M.	T.	
4	LUNAN	S.	363	51°27′N. 03°10′W.	Mine	—	
4	BALFRON	S.	362	038° 3½m. from Ravenscar	A.C.	B.	
4	ROBERT L. HOLT ...	S.	2,918	24°15′N. 20°00′W. (Approx.)	C.U.	—	
5	ANSELM	S.	5,954	44°25′N. 28°35′W.	S.M.	T.	
5	BENCRUACHAN ...	S.	5,920	297° 9.8 cables from Mex High Lt. (off Alexandria)	Mine	—	
5	FOWEY ROSE ...	S.	470	51°51′N. 05°28′W.	A.C.	B.	
9	DESIGNER	S.	5,945	42°59′N. 31°40′W.	S.M.	T.	
9	INVERNESS ...	S.	4,897	42°46′N. 32°45′W.	S.M.	T.	
9	BLUE MERMAID ...	S.B.	97	185° 8m. from Clacton (Approx.)	Mine	—	
13	COLLINGDOC ...	S.	1,780	200° 4 cables from Southend Pier	Mine	—	
14	RUPERT DE LARRINAGA	S.	5,358	36°18′N. 21°11′W.	S.M.	T.	
15	FARFIELD	S.	468	250° 5m. from S. Stack	A.C.	B.	
17	GUELMA	S.	4,402	30°44′N. 17°33′W.	S.M.	T.	
19	HOLMSIDE	S.	3,433	19°00′N. 21°30′W.	S.M.	T.	
23	OMFLEET	Steam Barge	130	Hull	Mine	—	
24	MACON	S.	5,135	32°48′N. 26°12′W.	S.M.	T.	
26	HORN SHELL* ...	M. Tank	8,272	33°23′N. 22°18′W.	S.M.	T.	
26	BOTWEY	S.	5,106	55°42′N. 09°53′W. (Approx.)	S.M.	T.	
26	KELLWYN	S.	1,459	43°N. 17°W. (Approx.)	S.M.	T.	
27	HAWKINGE ...	S.	2,475	44°55′N. 17°44′W.	S.M.	T.	
28	ERATO	S.	1,335	43°10′N. 17°30′W.	S.M.	T.	
28	WROTHAM	S.	1,884	43°N. 17°W. (Approx.)	S.M.	T.	
28	LAPLAND	S.	1,330	40°36′N. 15°30′W.	S.M.	T.	
29	SHAHRISTAN ...	S.	6,935	35°19′N. 23°53′W. (Approx.)	S.M.	T.	
29	CHAUCER	S.	5,792	16°46′N. 38°01′W.	Raider	—	
30	ADAM'S BECK ...	S.	2,816	235° 1m. from 20 C. Buoy, Tyne	A.C.	B.	
	Total ... 30		94,310				
AUGUST, 1941							
2	TRIDENT	S.	4,317	Off 20 C Buoy, Tyne	A.C.	B.	
4	TUNISIA	S.	4,337	53°53′N. 18°10′W.	A.C.	B.	
5	KUMASIAN ...	S.	4,922	53°11′N. 15°38′W.	S.M.	T.	
5	SWIFTPOOL ...	S.	5,205	53°03′N. 16°00′W.	S.M.	T.	
5	HARLINGEN ...	S.	5,415	53°26′N. 15°40′W.	S.M.	T.	
5	BELGRAVIAN ...	S.	3,136	53°03′N. 15°54′W.	S.M.	T.	
5	CAPE RODNEY ...	S.	4,512	53°26′N. 15°40′W.	S.M.	T.	Sank on 9th in position 52°44′N. 11°41′W.
9	CORDENE	S.	2,345	53°01′N. 01°48′E.	A.C.	B.	
11	SIR RUSSELL ...	S.	1,548	349° 6 cables from No. 10 Buoy. Off Dungeness	E-Boat	T.	
11	EMPIRE HURST ...	S.	2,852	36°48′N. 09°50′W.	A.C.	B.	
14	AUSTRALIND ...	M.	5,020	04°13′S. 91°03′W.	Raider	—	
19	CISCAR	S.	1,809	49°10′N. 17°40′W.	S.M.	T.	
19	ALVA	S.	1,584	49°N. 17°W. (Approx.)	S.M.	T.	
19	AGUILA	S.	3,255	49°23′N. 17°56′W.	S.M.	T.	

Date	Name	Type	Gross tons	Position	Cause of loss	How lost	Remarks
AUGUST, 1941—(Contd.)							
19	Golden Grain ...	Motor Barge	101	51°35′N. 01°03′E.	Mine	—	
19	Devon	S.	9,036	05°S. 91°W. (Approx.)	Raider	—	
20	Turbo*	S. Tank	4,782	32°08′N. 31°57′E.	A.C.	T.	Seriously damaged Foundered in tow 5th April, 1942.
22	Empire Oak ...	Tug	482	40°43′N. 11°39′W. (Approx.)	S.M.	T.	
22	Clonlara	S.	1,203	40°43′N. 11°39′W. (Approx.)	S.M.	T.	
23	Stork	M.	787	40°43′N. 11°39′W. (Approx.)	S.M.	T.	
23	Aldergrove ...	S.	1,974	40°43′N. 11°39′W. (Approx.)	S.M.	T.	
24	Skagerak ...	S.	1,283	River Orwell, Harwich	Mine	—	
27	Tremoda	S.	4,736	53°36′N. 16°40′W. (Approx.)	S.M.	T.	Last seen on 28th in position 54°08′N. 15°28′W.
27	Saugor	S.	6,303	53°36′N. 16°40′W. (Approx.)	S.M.	T.	
27	Embassage ...	S.	4,954	54°N. 13°W. (Approx.)	S.M.	T.	
28	Otaio	M.	10,298	52°16′N. 17°50′W.	S.M.	T.	
	Total ... 26		96,196				
SEPTEMBER, 1941							
3	Fort Richepanse	M.	3,485	52°15′N. 21°10′W.	S.M.	T.	
5	Abbas Combe ...	S.	489	5m. N.N.W. of Bardsey Island	A.C.	B.	
7	Duncarron ...	S.	478	3m. East of Sheringham Buoy, Norfolk Coast	E-Boat	T.	
7	Marcrest ...	S.	4,224	090° 2m. from Yarmouth	A.C.	B.	
7	Empire Gunner ...	S.	4,492	52°08′N. 05°18′W.	A.C.	B.	
7	Trsat	S.	1,369	N.E. × E. 7m. from Kinnaird Head	A.C.	B.	
10	Empire Springbuck	S.	5,591	61°38′N. 40°40′W. (Approx.)	S.M.	T.	
10	Baron Pentland...	S.	3,410	61°15′N. 41°05′W.	S.M.	T.	
10	Sally Maersk ...	M.	3,252	61°40′N. 40°30′W.	S.M.	T.	
10	Murefte (Ferry) ...	S.	691	33°12′N. 34°55′E.	S.M.	G.	
10	Thistleglen ...	S.	4,748	61°59′N. 39°46′W.	S.M.	T.	
10	Empire Hudson ...	S.	7,465	61°28′N. 40°51′W.	S.M.	T.	
10	Muneric	S.	5,229	61°38′N. 40°40′W.	S.M.	T.	
10	Gypsum Queen ...	S.	3,915	63°05′N. 37°50′W.	S.M.	T.	
10	Bulysses	M. Tank	7,519	62°22′N. 38°22′W.	S.M.	T.	
11	Berury	S.	4,924	62°40′N. 38°50′W.	S.M.	T.	
11	Empire Crossbill	S.	5,463	63°14′N. 37°12′W.	S.M.	T.	
11	Stonepool ...	S.	4,815	63°05′N. 37°50′W.	S.M.	T.	
12	Tai Koo*	Tug	688	16°45′N. 40°05′E. (Approx.)	Mine	—	
13	Bloomfield* ...	S.	1,417	61°50′N. 06°00′W.	A.C.	B.	
15	Newbury	S.	5,102	54°39′N. 28°04′W.	S.M.	T.	
15	Daru	M.	3,854	51°56′N. 05°58′W.	A.C.	B.	
15	Flying Kite ...	Tug	260	Off Dalmuir Basin, Clyde	Mine	—	
15	Empire Eland ...	S.	5,613	54°N. 28°W. (Approx.)	S.M.*	—	
15	Birtley	S.	2,873	53°06′N. 01°17′E.	Mine	—	Sank on 16th in position 53°03′N. 01°18′E.
16	Jedmoor	M.	4,392	59°N. 10°W. (Approx.)	S.M.	T.	
17	Teddington ...	S.	4,762	53°04′N. 01°34′E.	E-Boat	T.	
19	T. J. Williams ...	S. Tank	8,211	61°34′N. 35°11′W.	S.M.	T.	

Date	Name	Type	Gross tons	Position	Cause of loss	How lost	Remarks
SEPTEMBER, 1941—(*Contd.*)							
19	EMPIRE BURTON ...	S.	6,966	61°30′N. 35°11′W.	S.M.	T.	
19	BRADGLEN	S.	4,741	230° 2m. from B.3 Buoy, Barrow Deep	Mine	—	
20	PORTSDOWN (Ferry)	S.	342	50°46′N. 01°06′W.	Mine	—	
20	CINGALESE PRINCE	M.	8,474	02°00′S. 25°30′W.	S.M.	T.	
20	FIONA SHELL ...	Storage Hulk	2,444	Gibraltar	Italian Assault Craft	—	
20	BALTALLINN ...	S.	1,303	49°07′N. 22°07′W.	S.M.	T.	
20	EMPIRE MOAT· ...	S.	2,922	48°07′N. 22°05′W. (Approx.)	S.M.	T.	
21	LISSA	S.	1,511	47°N. 22°W. (Approx.)	S.M.*	T.	
21	RUNA	S.	1,575	46°20′N. 22°23′W.	S.M.	T.	
21	RHINELAND ...	S.	1,381	47°N. 22°W. (Approx.)	S.M.*	T.	
21	VANCOUVER ...	S. Tank	5,729	51°51′N. 01°31′E.	Mine	—	
21	WALMER CASTLE*...	M.	906	47°16′N. 22°25′W.	A.C.	B.	
22	NICETO DE LARRINAGA	S.	5,591	27°32′N. 24°26′W.	S.M.	T.	
22	EDWARD BLYDEN...	M.	5,003	27°36′N. 24°29′W.	S.M.	T.	
22	SILVERBELLE ...	M.	5,302	25°45′N. 24°00′W.	S.M.	T.	Abandoned on 29th in position 26°30′N 23°14′W.
23	ST. CLAIR II	S.	3,753	30°25′N. 23°35′W.	S.M.	T.	
24	JOHN HOLT ...	S.	4,975	31°12′N. 23°32′W.	S.M.	T.	
24	LAFIAN	S.	4,876	31°12′N. 23°32′W.	S.M.	T.	
24	DIXCOVE	M.	3,790	31°12′N. 23°41′W.	S.M.	T.	
25	AVOCETA	S.	3,442	47°57′N. 24°05′W.	S.M.	T.	
25	EMPIRE STREAM ...	S.	2,922	46°03′N. 24°40′W. (Approx.)	S.M.	T.	
25	ERNA III	S.	1,590	51°45′N. 35°15′W. (Est.)	C.U.	—	
26	PETREL	S.	1,354	47°40′N. 23°28′W.	S.M.	T.	
26	LAPWING	S.	1,348	47°40′N. 23°30′W. (Approx.)	S.M.	T.	
26	CORTES	S.	1,374	47°48′N. 23°45′W. (Approx.)	S.M.	T.	
26	BRITISH PRINCE ...	M.	4,979	53°52′N. 00°25′E.	A.C.	B.	
27	MARGARETA ...	S.	3,103	50°15′N. 17°27′W.	S.M.	T.	
27	CERVANTES ...	S.	1,810	48°37′N. 20°01′W. (Approx.)	S.M.	T.	
27	IMPERIAL STAR ...	M.	12,427	37°31′N. 10°46′E.	A.C.	T.	
	Total ... 57		214,664				
OCTOBER, 1941.							
2	EMPIRE WAVE ...	S.	7,463	59°08′N. 32°26′W.	S.M.	T.	
2	SAN FLORENTINO*	S. Tank	12,842	52°42′N. 34°51′W.	S.M.	T.	Also torpedoed on 1st in position 52°50′N. 34°40′W.
2	HATASU	S.	3,198	600m. E. of Cape Race	S.M.	T.	
5	TYNEFIELD* ...	M. Tank	5,856	Suez Canal	Mine	—	
6	THISTLEGORM ...	S.	4,898	Anchorage F, Straits of Jubal, Suez	A.C.	B.	
8	ROSALIE MOLLER ...	S.	3,963	Anchorage H, Suez	A.C.	B.	
10	NAILSEA MANOR ...	S.	4,926	18°45′N. 21°18′W.	S.M.	T.	
12	CHEVINGTON ...	S.	1,537	52°59′N. 01°52′E.	E-Boat	T.	
12	GLYNN	S.	1,134	52°35′N. 01°56′E.	A.C.	B.	Sunk by gunfire from H.M.S.
15	EMPIRE HERON ...	S.	6,023	54°55′N. 27°15′W.	S.M.	T.	
15	SILVERCEDAR ...	M.	4,354	53°36′N. 30°00′W.	S.M.	T.	
15	VANCOUVER ISLAND	M.	9,472	53°37′N. 25°37′W.	S.M.	T.	
16	W. C. TEAGLE ...	S. Tank	9,551	57°N. 25°W. (Approx.)	S.M.	T.	
17	PASS OF BALMAHA*	S. Tank	758	31°14′N. 28°50′E.	S.M.	T.	

Date	Name	Type	Gross tons	Position	Cause of loss	How lost	Remarks
OCTOBER, 1941—(Contd.)							
18	MAHSEER	S.	7,911	51°41'N. 01°19'E.	Mine	—	
18	EMPIRE GHYLL ...	S.	2,011	221° 4 to 5 cables from B.7 Buoy, Barrow Deep	Mine	—	
19	BARON KELVIN ...	S.	3,081	100° 14m. from Tarifa	S.M.	T.	
19	INVERLEE*... ...	M. Tank	9,158	240° 30m. from Cape Spartel	S.M.	T.	
20	BRITISH MARINER...	S. Tank	6,996	07°43'N. 14°20'W.	S.M.	T.	
21	TREVERBYN ...	S.	5,281	51°N. 19°W. (Approx.)	S.M.	T.	
21	SERBINO ... ...,	S.	4,099	51°10'N. 19°20'W.	S.M.	T.	
24	CARSBRECK ...	S.	3,670	36°20'N. 10°50'W.	S.M.	T.	
24	ARIOSTO	S.	2,176	36°20'N. 10°50'W.	S.M.	T.	
24	ALHAMA	S.	1,352	35°42'N. 10°58'W. (Approx.)	S.M.	T.	
24	EMPIRE GUILLEMOT	S.	5,720	W. of Galeta Is., Mediterranean	A.C.	T.	
27	ANTIOPE	S.	4,545	53°13'N. 01°08'E.	A.C.	B.	
28	ULEA	S.	1,574	41°17'N. 21°40'W.	S.M.	T.	
28	HAZELSIDE ...	S.	5,297	23°10'S. 01°36'E.	S.M.	T.	
28	ROSLEA	S.	642	Off Belgian Coast	Captured and sunk	—	
29	SARASTONE ...	S.	2,473	37°05'N. 06°48'W.	A.C.	B.	
31	BRITISH FORTUNE	S. Tank	4,696	265° 1m. from Aldeburgh Lt. Buoy	A.C.	B.	
31	KING MALCOLM ...	M.	5,120	Last seen in position 47°40'N. 51°15'W.	S.M.*	—	
	Total ... 32		151,777				
NOVEMBER, 1941.							
1	BRADFORD CITY ...	M.	4,953	22°59'S. 09°49'E.	S.M.	T.	
2	MARIE DAWN ...	S.	2,157	20m. from Spurn Pt.	A.C.	B.	Sank on 3rd, 2m. S.W. of H.2 Buoy, Humber
2	LARPOOL	S.	3,872	250m. E.S.E. of Cape Race	S.M.	T.	
2	BRYNMILL	S.	743	210° 4m. from E. Dudgeon Buoy	A.C.	—	Sank 5m. W. of E. Dudgeon Bell Buoy
2	FOREMOST 45 ...	Hopper Barge	824	51°21'N. 03°17'W.	Mine	—	
3	FLYNDERBORG ...	S.	2,022	51°21'N. 51°45'W.	S.M.	T.	
3	GRETAVALE ...	S.	4,586	51°21'N. 51°45'W.	S.M.	T.	
3	EMPIRE GEMSBUCK	S.	5,626	52°18'N. 53°05'W.	S.M.	T.	
3	EVEROJA	S.	4,830	077° 80m. from Belle Isle	S.M.	T.	Sank on 4th
About 3	ROSE SCHIAFFINO ...	S.	3,349	Vicinity Newfoundland, N. Atlantic	S.M.*	---	
4	BRITISHER ...	S.	68	Off Maplin Lt., Thames Estuary	Mine*	—	
7	NOTTINGHAM ...	M.	8,532	53°24'N. 31°51'W.	S.M.	T.	
12	PERU	M.	6,961	01°30'N. 13°20'W.	S.M.	T.	
12	MAURITA	S.	201	Hilbre Swash, Dee Estuary, Liverpool Bay	Mine	—	
14	EMPIRE PELICAN ...	S.	6,463	Between Galeta Is. and Tunisian Coast	A.C.	T.	
15	EMPIRE DEFENDER	S.	5,649	18m. S. of Galeta Is., Mediterranean	A.C.	T.	
15	CORHAMPTON ...	S.	2,495	26m. N.E. of Spurn Head	A.C.	B.	Sank on 16th whilst in tow in position 53°53'N. 00°26'E.
17	BOVEY TRACEY ...	S.	1,212	52°28'N. 02°05'E.	A.C.	B.	
19	ARUBA	S.	1,159	52°51'N. 02°07'E.	E-Boat	T.	
19	WALDINGE	S.	2,462	52°56'N. 02°01'E.	E-Boat	T.	Sank on 20th
24	VIRGILIA	S. Tank	5,723	3m. N.E. of Hearty Knoll Buoy	E-Boat	T.	

Date	Name	Type	Gross tons	Position	Cause of loss	How lost	Remarks
NOVEMBER, 1941—(Contd.)							
29	THORNLIEBANK ...	S.	5,569	41°50′N. 29°48′W.	S.M.	T.	
29	ASPERITY	S. Tank	699	53°11′N. 01°07′E.	E-Boat	T.	
29	CORMARSH ...	S.	2,848	53°16′N. 01°04′E.	E-Boat	T.	
30	ASHBY	S.	4,868	36°54′N. 29°51′W.	S.M.	T.	
30	EMPIRE NEWCOMEN	S.	2,840	5m. S. of Dudgeon Lt., off Cromer	E-Boat	T.	
	Total ... 26		90,711				
DECEMBER, 1941							
2	GRELHEAD	S.	4,274	2m. from Punta Negri, Morocco	C.U.	—	
2	BRITISH CAPTAIN ...	S. Tank	6,968	52°13′N. 01°55′E.	Mine	—	
3	MACLAREN	S.	2,330	51°21′N. 03°17′W.	Mine	—	
6	GREENLAND ...	S.	1,281	52°14′N. 01°56′E.	Mine	—	Sank in position 52°14′N. 02°06′E.
6	SCOTTISH TRADER...	S.	4,016	N. Atlantic, S. of Iceland	S.M.	—	
7	WELSH PRINCE ...	S.	5,148	110° 5 cables from No. 59 Buoy, vicinity of Spurn Head	Mine	—	Abandoned in position 53°24′N. 00°59′E.
7	SEVERN TRANSPORT	M.	119	51°27′N. 03°04′W.	Mine	—	
8	FIREGLOW ...	S.	1,261	3m. S. of Dudgeon Buoy	Mine	—	Sank in position 53°19′N. 01°05′E.
8	EDITH MOLLER* ...	Tender	645	S. of Amoy	Captured	—	
8	MIN-WO	Tug	287	Hankow	Seized	—	
8	WANTUNG ...	S.	1,061	Shanghai	Seized	—	
8	KINTANG	S.	435	Shanghai	Seized	—	
8	HSIN TSEANGTAH ...	S.	933	Shanghai	Seized	—	
8	SCOT I	Tug	274	Shanghai	Seized	—	
8	MERRY MOLLER ...	Tug	382	Shanghai	Seized	—	
8	DIANA MOLLER ...	Tug	252	Shanghai	Seized	—	
8	CHRISTINE MOLLER	Salvage Tug	800	Shanghai	Seized	—	
8	JESSIE MOLLER ...	Salvage Vessel	530	Shanghai	Seized	—	
8	READY MOLLER ..	Tug	268	Off Amoy	Captured	—	
8	CHEKIANG	S.	2,172	Wangpu River, N. China	Seized	—	
8	MARY MOLLER ...	S.	2,698	Wangpu River, N. China	Seized	—	
8	KIA-WO	S.	1,311	Ichang	Seized	—	
8	ANALOCK ...	S.	6,638	China Seas	Seized	—	On charter to Japan.
8	KIANG-WO	S.	2,209	China Seas	Seized	—	Two crew reported prisoners of war in Japan
8	DESLOCK	S.	5,015	China Seas	Seized	—	On charter to Japan.
8	TUNG ON	S.	1,950	China Seas	C.U.	—	Sunk, seized or captured
8	FEDERLOCK ...	S.	6,607	China Seas	Seized	—	On charter to Japan.
8	MACAU	S.	1,665	China Seas	C.U.	—	Sunk, seized or captured
8	HATTERLOCK ...	S.	5,138	China Seas	Seized	—	} On charter to Japan
8	MUNLOCK	S.	5,240	China Seas	Seized	—	
8	ST. QUENTIN ...	S.	3,528	China Seas	Seized	—	
8	VITORLOCK ...	S.	5,030	China Seas	Seized	—	
8	WENCHOW	S.	3,113	China Seas	Seized	—	} Masters prisoners of war
8	WOOSUNG	S.	3,426	China Seas	Seized	—	
8	HSIN CHANG WO ...	S.	582	Ichang	Seized	—	
8	SIANGTAN	S.	1,195	Ichang	Seized	—	} Crew prisoners of war
8	SHASI	S.	1,327	In Yangtsze River	Seized	—	
8	SUI-TAI	S.	1,816	Shanghai	C.U.	—	Sunk, seized or captured
8	KONG SO	S.	789	Tinghai	Seized	—	Master prisoner of war

Date	Name	Type	Gross tons	Position	Cause of loss	How lost	Remarks
DECEMBER, 1941—*(Contd.)*							
8	CHUEN CHOW ...	S.	1,088	Far Eastern Waters	C.U.	—	⎫
8	CHUNG ON ...	S.	968	Far Eastern Waters	C.U.	—	⎪
8	FOOK ON	M.	738	Far Eastern Waters	C.U.	—	⎪
8	KWONG FOOK CHEUNG	S.	881	Far Eastern Waters	C.U.	—	⎪
8	LING KONG	S.	850	Far Eastern Waters	C.U.	—	⎬ Sunk, seized or cap-
8	ON LEE*	S.	1,026	Far Eastern Waters	C.U.	—	tured
8	TAI HING	S.	1,068	Far Eastern Waters	C.U.	—	⎪
8	TAI LEE	S.	1,423	Far Eastern Waters	C.U.	—	⎪
8	TAI MING* ...	S.	649	Far Eastern Waters	C.U.	—	⎪
8	TIN YAT	S.	942	Far Eastern Waters	C.U.	—	⎪
8	TAISHAN*	S.	3,174	Far Eastern Waters	C.U.	—	⎭
8	CHANGSHA	S.	2,482	China Seas	Seized	—	
8	KAU TUNG	S.	1,665	China Seas	C.U.	—	⎫
8	KWONG SAI ...	S.	1,309	China Seas	C.U.	—	⎬ Sunk, seized or
8	KWONG TUNG ...	S.	1,218	China Seas	C.U.	—	⎭ captured
8	KUT-WO	S.	2,665	China Seas	Seized	—	
8	LOONGWO	S.	3,923	China Seas	Seized	—	
8	KINSHAN	S.	2,733	China Seas	C.U.	—	Sunk, seized or cap- tured
8	PAOWO	S.	2,517	China Seas	Seized	—	Chief Engineer prisoner of war
8	SAGRES	S.	2,333	China Seas	Seized	—	
8	WUHU	S.	2,938	China Seas	Seized	—	
8	FATSHAN	S.	2,639	Canton	Seized	—	
8	CARMEN MOLLER ...	Tug	366	S. of Amoy	Captured	—	
8	ELSIE MOLLER ...	Tug	1,136	Off Amoy	Captured	—	
8	HSIN PEKING ...	S.	2,104	On voyage Tongku to Hong Kong	Captured	—	
8	KIANGSU	S.	2,676	Off Amoy	Captured	—	
8	MARIE MOLLER ...	Tug	593	Off Ningpo	Captured	—	
8	NANNING ...	S.	2,486	Hong Kong	Seized	—	
8	ST. DOMINIC* ...	Tug	451	S. of Saddle Is., China Seas	C.U.	—	
8	SOOCHOW	S.	2,604	Hong Kong	Scuttled	—	Salved by Japanese
9	BENNEVIS	S.	5,356	Off Hong Kong	Captured	—	
10	KIRNWOOD ...	S.	3,829	56°57′N. 16°35′W.	S.M.	T.	
10	KURDISTAN ...	S.	5,844	56°51′N. 16°36′W.	S.M.	T.	Sank on 11th
10	HARELDAWINS ...	S.	1,523	Off Luzon Is., Philip- pines	C.U.	—	
12	DROMORE CASTLE ...	S.	5,242	20m. S.S.E. of Hum- ber	Mine	—	
12	KALGAN	S.	2,655	Bangkok	Seized	—	
12	CAMBAY PRINCE ...	S.	455	Bleak Pier, Hong Kong	Scuttled	—	
12	SHINAI	S.	2,410	Kuching, N. Borneo	Seized	—	
14	ST. VINCENT DE PAUL	S.	1,339	Hong Kong	C.U.	—	
15	EMPIRE BARRACUDA	S.	4,972	35°30′N. 06°17′W.	S.M.	T.	
19	RUCKINGE	S.	2,869	38°20′N. 17°15′W.	S.M.	T.	
20	SUMATRA	S.	984	Hong Kong	Seized	—	Sunk by gunfire by H.M.S. on 20th. Subsequently salved by Japanese
21	BENMACDHUI	S.	6,869	53°40′N. 00°30′E.	Mine	—	
23	SHUNTIEN* ...	S.	3,059	32°06′N. 24°46′E.	S.M.	T.	
24	MARGARET ...	M.	248	Kuching, N. Borneo	Seized	—	
24	REJANG ...	M.	288	Kuching, N. Borneo	Seized	—	
24	GLADYS	S.	358	Kuching, N. Borneo	Seized	—	
24	KIM CHIN SENG ...	Motor Lighter	165	Kuching, N. Borneo	Seized	—	
24	PHENIX*	S. Tank	5,907	Haifa Harbour	Mine	—	
24	STANMOUNT ...	S. Tank	4,468	350° 1m. from No. 6 Buoy, Yarmouth	Mine	—	
24	MERCHANT	S.	4,615	354° 1¼m. from No. 6 Buoy, Yarmouth	Mine	—	
24	FORAFRIC	M.	3,475	In Celebes Sea, S. of Philippine Is.	A.C.	B.	
25	APOBY	S.	2,790	Hong Kong	Scuttled	—	

Date	Name	Type	Gross tons	Position	Cause of loss	How lost	Remarks
DECEMBER, 1941—(Contd.)							
25	ARIADNE MOLLER	S.	1,840	Hong Kong	Scuttled	—	
25	CHENGTU	S.	2,219	Hong Kong	Scuttled	—	Salved by Japanese
25	ETHEL MOLLER ...	Salvage Vessel	912	Hong Kong	Scuttled	—	Salved by Japanese
25	FAUSANG	S.	2,256	Hong Kong	Scuttled	—	
25	HINSANG	M.	4,644	Hong Kong	Scuttled	—	Salved by Japanese
25	KANCHOW	S.	2,001	Hong Kong	Scuttled	—	
25	JOSEPHINE MOLLER	Tug	1,274	Hong Kong	Scuttled	—	
25	KATHLEEN MOLLER	Salvage Vessel	1,487	Hong Kong	Scuttled	—	
25	JOAN MOLLER	S.	2,232	Hong Kong	Scuttled	—	Salved by Japanese
25	MING SANG ...	S.	3,420	Hong Kong	Scuttled	—	Salved by Japanese
25	SHRIVATI	M.	389	Hong Kong	Scuttled	—	
25	SHUN CHIH ...	S.	1,881	Hong Kong	Scuttled	—	
25	HSIN FUHLE ...	Tug	184	Hong Kong	Scuttled	—	
25	PATRICIA MOLLER*	Tug	390	Hong Kong	Scuttled	—	
25	GERTRUDE MOLLER*	Tug	92	Hong Kong	Scuttled	—	
25	SHINHWA	S.	1,460	Off Hong Kong	Captured	—	
25	CORMEAD	S.	2,848	350° 3m. from No. 5 Buoy, Lowestoft	Mine	—	Sank on 26th in position 52°25′N. 02°13′E.
25	YAT SHING	S.	2,284	Hong Kong	Scuttled	—	
26	TANTALUS	M.	7,724	Off Manila	A.C.	—	
27	J. B. PADDON ...	S.	570	53°55′N. 00°16′E.	A.C.	B.	
28	VOLO	S.	1,587	31°45′N. 26°48′E.	S.M.	T.	
28	KAIPING	S.	2,563	Manila Bay	A.C.	—	
28	HAI KWANG ...	M. Tank	905	Manila Bay	A.C.	—	
28	SEISTAN	S.	2,455	Manila Bay	A.C.	—	
About 29	SUBOK	M.	148	Labuan	Seized	—	
About 29	JITRA	M.	122	Labuan	Seized	—	
29	HENRY KESWICK ...	Tug	671	Corregidor, Philippines	C.U.	—	
31	CARDITA	M. Tank	8,237	59°18′N. 12°50′W.	S.M.	T.	Sank 3rd Jan., 1942
	Total ... 120		270,873				
JANUARY, 1942							
1	PENRHOS	S.	187	243° 1m. from N. Constable Buoy, Liverpool Bay (Approx.)	Mine	—	
1	KENTWOOD... ...	S.	2,180	Nr. 56 Buoy, Hearty Knoll Channel	Mine	—	Sank in tow 2 cables N.E. of 56 Buoy, off Yarmouth
2	WAZIRISTAN ...	S.	5,135	74°09′N. 19°10′E.	S.M.*	—	
3	CORFEN	S.	1,848	1½m. N.E. of B.8 Buoy, Barrow Deep	Mine	—	Sank in tow in position 51°50′N. 01° 27′E.
3	ROBERT	S.	1,272	160° 1.5m. from 54 E. Buoy, off Lowestoft	Mine	—	Sank on 4th in position 52°17′N. 02° 00′E.
4	KWANGTUNG ...	S.	2,626	09°12′S. 111°10′E.	S.M.	G.	
6	NORWICH TRADER...	S.	217	51°55′N. 01°32′E.	Mine*	—	
10	BARON ERSKINE ...	S.	3,657	59°15′N. 18°30′W.	S.M.*	—	
11	CYCLOPS	S.	9,076	41°51′N. 63°48′W.	S.M.	T.	
11	WULIN	M.	2,515	In Muar River, Johore State	A.C.	B.	
11	BAYNAIN	S.	659	Off Tarakan, Dutch East Indies	C.U.	—	Sunk, seized or captured
About 11	BORDERDENE ...	S.	122	51°18′N. 03°03′W. (Approx.)	Mine	—	
12	QUICKSTEP... ...	S.	2,722	51°46′N. 01°26′E.	Mine	—	
12	CALEDONIAN MONARCH	S.	5,851	57°N. 26°W. (Approx.)	S.M.*	—	
13	LERWICK	S.	5,626	54°26′N. 00°24′W.	A.C.	B.	

Date	Name	Type	Gross tons	Position	Cause of loss	How lost	Remarks
JANUARY, 1942—(Contd.)							
14	JALARAJAN ...	S.	5,102	00°12′S. 97°00′E.	S.M.	T.	
14	EMPIRE SURF ...	S.	6,641	58°42′N. 19°16′W.	S.M.	T.	
14	DAYROSE	S.	4,113	46°32′N. 53°00′W.	S.M.	T.	
14	MERCIA	Tug	94	51°31′N. 02°47′W.	Mine	—	
15	COIMBRA	S. Tank	6,768	40°25′N. 72°21′W.	S.M.	T.	
15	DIALA	M. Tank	8,106	44°50′N. 46°50′W.	S.M.	T.	Derelict, last seen in position 47°N. 37°W. on 19th March
15	EMPIRE BAY ...	S.	2,824	Tees Bay	A.C.	B.	
17	CULEBRA	S.	3,044	40°N. 50°W. (Est.)	S.M.	T. & G.	
19	LADY HAWKINS ...	S.	7,989	35°00′N. 72°30′W. (Approx.)	S.M.	T.	
19	H.K.D.	S.B.	65	130° ½m. from Van Meerlant Wreck Buoy, Thames Estuary	Mine	—	
22	ATHELCROWN ...	M. Tank	11,999	45°06′N. 40°56′W.	S.M.	T.	
22	CHAK-SANG... ...	S.	2,358	15°42′N. 95°02′E.	S.M.	G.	
23	THIRLBY	S.	4,887	43°20′N. 66°15′W. (Approx.)	S.M.	T.	
24	EMPIRE WILDEBEESTE	S.	5,631	39°30′N. 59°54′W.	S.M.	T.	
24	EMPIRE GEM ...	M. Tank	8,139	35°06′N. 74°58′W.	S.M.	T.	Sank in position 35°02′N. 75°33′W. (Approx.)
25	SWYNFLEET ...	S.	1,168	51°55′N. 01°19′E.	Mine	—	
26	TRAVELLER... ...	S.	3,963	40°N. 61°45′W. (Est.)	S.M.*	—	
26	REFAST	S. Tank	5,189	42°41′N. 53°02′W.	S.M.	T.	
29	GIANG SENG ...	S.	1,811	Dutch East Indies	C.U.	—	Sunk, seized or captured
30	JALATARANG ...	S.	2,498	12°59′N. 81°00′E.	S.M.	T. & G.	
30	JALAPALAKA ...	S.	4,215	13°00′N. 81°08′E.	S.M.	G.	
31	SAN ARCADIO ...	M. Tank	7,419	38°10′N. 63°50′W.	S.M.	T. & G.	
	Total ... 37		147,716				
FEBRUARY, 1942							
1	TACOMA STAR ...	S.	7,924	37°33′N. 69°21′W.	S.M.	T.	
3	NORAH MOLLER ...	M.	4,433	Banka Strait	A.C.	B.	
3	KATONG	S.	1,461	4m. from Bar L.V., Palembang	A.C.	G.	
3	LOCH RANZA ...	S.	4,958	00°37′N. 104°14′E.	A.C.	B.	
3	PINNA*	S. Tank	6,121	00°52′S. 104°19′E.	A.C.	B.	Again attacked on 4th and sunk
4	MONTROLITE ...	M. Tank	11,309	35°14′N. 60°05′W.	S.M.	T.	
4	SILVERAY	M.	4,535	43°54′N. 64°16′W.	S.M.	T.	
5	CORLAND	S.	3,431	53°43′N. 00°36′E.	A.C.	B.	
5	EMPRESS OF ASIA...	S.	16,909	Approaches to Singapore	A.C.	B.	
6	OPAWA	M.	10,354	38°21′N. 61°13′W.	S.M.*	—	
7	EMPIRE SUN ...	S.	6,952	44°07′N. 64°16′W.	S.M.	T.	
8	OCEAN VENTURE ...	S.	7,174	37°05′N. 74°46′W.	S.M.	T.	
9	EMPIRE FUSILIER ...	S.	5,408	44°45′N. 47°25′W.	S.M.	T.	
10	VICTOLITE	M. Tank	11,410	36°12′N. 67°14′W.	S.M.	T.	
11	WANYUAN* ...	S.	674	Singapore	Seized	—	Previously immobilised
13	DERRYMORE ...	M.	4,799	05°18′S. 106°20′E.	S.M.	T.	
13	SUBADAR	S.	5,424	Banka Strait	A.C.	B.	
13	HOSANG	S.	5,698	Palembang	Seized	—	Damaged by A.C.
14	BIELA	S.	5,298	42°55′N. 45°40′W.	S.M.	T.	
14	KAMUNING... ...	S.	2,076	08°35′N. 81°44′E.	S.M.	T. & G.	
14	CLAN CHATTAN ...	S.	7,262	35°01′N. 20°11′E.	A.C.	B.	
14	ROWALLAN CASTLE	M.	7,798	34°54′N. 19°40′E.	A.C.	B.	Sunk by H.M.S.

Date	Name	Type	Gross tons	Position	Cause of loss	How lost	Remarks
FEBRUARY, 1942—(*Contd.*)							
15	REDANG	S.	531	Far Eastern Waters	C.U.	—	Sunk, seized or captured
15	JOHANNE JUSTESEN	S.	4,681	09°04'N. 75°58'E.	S.M.	T.	
15	EMPIRE SPRING ...	M.	6,946	42°N. 55°W. (Approx.)	S.M.*	—	
15	RHU*	M.	254	Singapore	Seized	—	
16	BAGAN (Ferry) ...	S.	244	Palembang	Scuttled	—	
16	SOMME	S.	5,265	40°N. 55°W. (Approx.)	S.M.	T.	
16	ORANJESTAD ...	S. Tank	2,396	At anchor off San Nicholas, Aruba	S.M.	T.	
16	SAN NICOLAS ...	S. Tank	2,391	25m. S.W. of Punta Macolla, Gulf of Venezuela	S.M.	T.	
16	TIA JUANA ...	S. Tank	2,395	25m. S.W. of Punta Macolla, Gulf of Venezuela	S.M.	T.	
16	BRUNEI	M.	101	Singapore	Scuttled	— -	
16	TALTHYBIUS ...	S.	10,254	Singapore	Seized	...	Previously damaged by A.C. on 3rd
17	TATUNG	S.	1,560	Tanjong Batoe	Seized	—	Previously immobilised
19	EMPIRE SEAL ...	M.	7,965	43°14'N. 64°45'W.	S.M.	T.	
19	EMPIRE COMET ...	M.	6,914	58°15'N. 17°10'W.	S.M.*	—	
19	BRITISH MOTORIST*	M. Tank	6,891	Port Darwin	A.C.	B.	
19	ZEALANDIA ...	S.	6,683	Port Darwin	A.C.	B.	
19	NEPTUNA*	M.	5,952	Port Darwin	A.C.	B.	
20	BHIMA	M.	5,280	07°47'N. 73°31'E.	S.M.	T.	
20	SCOTTISH STAR ...	S.	7,224	13°24'N. 49°36'W.	S.M.	T.	
20	KOOLAMA	M.	4,068.	Off Wyndham, W. Australia	A.C.	B.	
21	CIRCE SHELL* ...	M. Tank	8,207	11°03'N. 62°03'W.	S.M.	T. & G.	
22	GEORGE L. TORIAN	S.	1,754	09°13'N. 59°04'W.	S.M.	T.	
22	KARS	M. Tank	8,888	44°15'N. 63°25'W.	S.M.	T.	
22	ADELLEN*	M. Tank	7,984	49°20'N. 38°15'W.	S.M.	T.	
22	HANNE	S.	1,360	31°57'N. 25°26'E.	A.C.	B.	
22	BINTANG	M.	2,825	31°50'N. 26°01'E.	A.C.	B.	
23	LENNOX	S.	1,904	09°15'N. 58°30'W.	S.M.	T.	
23	EMPIRE HAIL ...	S.	7,005	44°48'N. 40°21'W.	S.M.	T.	
24	EMPIRE CELT ...	S. Tank	8,032	43°50'N. 43°38'W.	S.M.	T.	Remained afloat. Date and position of sinking uncertain
24	ANADARA	M. Tank	8,009	43°45'N. 42°15'W. (Est.)	S.M.	T.	
24	INVERARDER* ...	S. Tank	5,578	44°34'N. 42°37'W.	S.M.	T.	
24	WHITE CREST ...	S.	4,365	43°45'N. 42°15'W. (Approx.)	S.M.*	—	
24	LA CARRIERE* ...	S. Tank	5,685	16°53'N. 67°05'W.	S.M.	T.	Sank on 25th after second attack
27	MACGREGOR ...	S.	2,498	19°50'N. 69°40'W. (Approx.)	S.M.	G.	
27	NAM YONG... ...	S.	1,345	Indian Ocean	C.U.	—·	Sunk or captured
27	FERNSIDE	S.	269	Off Banff*	A.C.*	—	
28	CITY OF MANCHESTER	S.	8,917	08°16'S. 108°52'E.	S.M.	T. & G.	
	Total ... 59		314,028				
MARCH, 1942							
1	CARPERBY	S.	4,890	39°57'N. 55°40'W.	S.M.	T.	
1	AUDACITY	S. Tank	589	53°33'N. 00°22'E.	Mine	—	
1	POLGARTH	S.	794	2m. S.S.W. of Aldeburgh Lt. Float	Mine	—	

Date	Name	Type	Gross tons	Position	Cause of loss	How lost	Remarks
MARCH, 1942—(*Contd.*)							
2	SHINYU	S.	1,615	Sourabaya	C.U.	—	⎫
2	KULIT	M. Tank	213	Sumatra	C.U.	—	⎪
2	SISUNTHON NAWA...	S.	3,286	Sourabaya	C.U.	—	Sunk or seized
2	RIBOT	M. Tank	237	Sumatra	C.U.	—	
2	TAIYUAN	S.	2,994	Sourabaya	C.U.	—	⎭
3	HELENUS	S.	7,366	06°01′N. 12°02′W.	S.M.	T.	
3	RASA	M.	217	D.E.I. Waters	C.U.	—	⎫
3	RIMAU	M.	214	D.E.I. Waters	C.U.	—	⎪
3	PETALING	M.	168	D.E.I. Waters	C.U.	—	⎪
3	PANDAI	M.	166	D.E.I. Waters	C.U.	—	Sunk, seized or captured
3	RIMBA	M.	139	D.E.I. Waters	C.U.	—	⎬ tured
3	INTAN	M.	117	D.E.I. Waters	C.U.	—	⎪
3	RENGAM	M.	185	D.E.I. Waters	C.U.	—	⎭
3	PHASIANELLA ...	M. Tank	855	Batavia	Scuttled	—	
4	FRUMENTON ...	S.	6,675	170° ½m. from 54 E. Buoy, off Orfordness	Mine	—	
5	IPOH	S.	1,279	Batavia	C.U.	—	⎫ Sunk or seized
5	KINTA	S.	1,220	Batavia	C.U.	—	⎬
5	AUBY	S.	636	D.E.I. Waters	C.U.	—	Sunk, seized or captured
5	BENMOHR ...	S.	5,920	06°05′N. 14°15′W.	S.M.	T.	
5	AMPANG	S.	213	D.E.I. Waters	C.U.	—	Sunk, seized or captured
5	RAWANG	S.	198	Malayan Waters	Scuttled	—	Salved by Japanese
5	RANTAU	M.	197	Banka Strait	C.U.	—	⎫
5	RELAU	M.	223	Banka Strait	C.U.	—	⎬ Sunk or captured
5	ROMPIN	M.	189	Banka Strait	C.U.	—	⎭
6	MELPOMENE ...	S. Tank	7,011	23°35′N. 62°39′W.	S.M.	T.	
7	CHAUK	S.	419	Rangoon	Scuttled	—	
7	UNIWALECO ...	S. Tank	9,755	13°23′N. 62°04′W.	S.M.	T.	
7	MINBU	S.	139	Rangoon	Scuttled	—	
7	LANYWA	S.	52	Bassein Creek, Burma	C.U.	—	
7	NYOUNGHLA ...	S.	382	Rangoon	Scuttled	—	
7	SADAING ...	Launch	266	Rangoon	Scuttled	—	
8	HENGIST ...	S.	984	59°31′N. 10°15′W.	S.M.	T.	
8	BALUCHISTAN ...	S.	6,992	04°13′N. 08°32′W.	S.M.	T. & G.	
10	LAKSHIMI GOVINDA	S.V.	235	13°22′N. 87°27′E.	S.M.	G.	
11	CHILKA	S.	4,360	Indian Ocean, Off Padang, Sumatra	S.M.	G.	
11	HORSEFERRY ...	S.	951	52°52′N. 02°10′E.	E-Boat	T.	
13	DAYTONIAN ...	S.	6,434	26°33′N. 74°43′W.	S.M.	T. & G.	
14	BRITISH RESOURCE	M. Tank	7,209	36°04′N. 65°38′W.	S.M.	T.	
15	MANAQUI	S.	2,802	17°15′N. 61°00′W.	S.M.*	—	
15	SARNIADOC ...	S.	1,940	15°45′N. 65°00′W. (Approx.)	S.M.*	—	
15	ATHELQUEEN ...	M. Tank	8,780	26°50′N. 75°40′W.	S.M.	T. & G.	
15	DAGO	S.	1,757	39°19′N. 09°26′W.	A.C.	B.	
16	BARON NEWLANDS	S.	3,386	04°35′N. 08°32′W.	S.M.	T.	
16	STANGARTH... ...	S.	5,966	22°N. 65°W. (Approx.)	S.M.*	—	
16	CRESSDENE ...	S.	4,270	52°08′N. 01°52′E.	Mine	—	
17	ILE DE BATZ ...	S.	5,755	04°04′N. 08°04′W.	S.M.	T.	
17	SAN DEMETRIO ...	M. Tank	8,073	37°03′N. 73°50′W.	S.M.	T.	
17	SCOTTISH PRINCE ...	M.	4,917	04°10′N. 08°00′W.	S.M.	T.	
17	ALLENDE	S.	5,081	04°00′N. 07°44′W. (Approx.)	S.M.	T.	
22	THURSOBANK ...	S.	5,575	38°05′N. 68°30′W.	S.M.	T.	
23	PEDER BOGEN* ...	S. Tank	9,741	24°41′N. 57°44′W.	S.M.	T.	
23	BRITISH PRUDENCE*	M. Tank	8,620	45°28′N. 56°13′W.	S.M.	T.	

Date	Name	Type	Gross tons	Position	Cause of loss	How lost	Remarks
MARCH, 1942—(Contd.)							
23	EMPIRE STEEL ...	M. Tank	8,138	37°45'N. 63°17'W.	S.M.	T. & G.	
23	CLAN CAMPBELL ...	S.	7,255	245° 8m. from Filfola Is., Nr. Malta	A.C.	B.	
25	NARRAGANSETT ...	M. Tank	10,389	34°46'N. 67°40'W.	S.M.	T.	
25	TREDINNICK ...	S.	4,589	27°15'N. 49°15'W. (Approx.)	S.M.*	—	
26	PAMPAS	M.	5,415	Malta	A.C.	B.	
28	EMPIRE RANGER ...	S.	7,008	72°10'N. 30°00'E.	A.C.	B.	
28	WELLPARK	S.	4,649	25°S. 10°W. (Est.)	Raider	—	
29	HERTFORD ...	S.	10,923	40°50'N. 63°31'W.	S.M.	T.	
30	MUNCASTER CASTLE	M.	5,853	02°02'N. 12°02'W.	S.M.	T.	
30	INDUNA	S.	5,086	70°55'N. 37°18'E.	S.M.	T.	
31	EASTMOOR	S.	5,812	37°33'N. 68°18'W.	S.M.	T.	
ˋ31	SAN GERARDO* ...	S. Tank	12,915	36°N. 67°W. (Approx.)	S.M.	T.	
	Total ... 67		250,679				
APRIL, 1942							
1	RIO BLANCO ...	S.	4,086	35°16'N. 74°18'W.	S.M.	T.	
1	WILLESDEN ...	S.	4,563	16°S. 16°W. (Est.)	Raider	—	
1	LOCH DON	S.	5,249	37°05'N. 61°40'W.	S.M.	T.	
1	ROBERT W. POMEROY	S.	1,750	53°10'N. 01°10'E.	Mine	—	
2	CLAN ROSS... ...	S.	5,897	15°58'N. 68°24'E.	S.M.	T.	
2	GLENSHIEL ...	M.	9,415	01°00'S. 78°11'E.	S.M.	T.	
3	NEW WESTMINSTER CITY	S.	4,747	Murmansk	A.C.	B.	
3	EMPIRE STARLIGHT	S.	6,850	Murmansk Harbour	A.C.	B.	Bombed again on 15th and repeatedly thereafter until 1st June, when ship became a total loss
5	HARPASA	S.	5,082	19°19'N. 85°46'E.	A.C.	B.	
6	SILKSWORTH ...	S. ·	4,921	Off Puri, Bay of Bengal	Warship	—	
6	AUTOLYCUS ...	S.	7,621	19°40'N. 86°50'E.	Warship	—	
6	DARDANUS ...	S.	7,726	16°00'N. 82°20'E.	Warship	—	
6	GANDARA ...	S.	5,281	16°00'N. 82°20'E.	Warship	—	
6	GANGES	S.	6,246	17°48'N. 84°09'E.	Warship	—	
6	MALDA	S.	9,066	19°45'N. 86°27'E.	Warship	—	
6	INDORA	S.	6,622	Bay of Bengal	Warship	—	
6	TAKSANG	S.	3,471	17°52'N. 83°40'E.	Warship	—	
6	SHINKUANG ...	S.	2,441	Bay of Bengal	Warship	—	
6	SINKIANG	S.	2,646	Bay of Bengal	A.C.	B.	
7	FULTALA	M.	5,051	06°52'N. 76°54'E.	S.M.	T.	
7	BRITISH SPLENDOUR	M. Tank	7,138	35°07'N. 75°19'W.	S.M.	T.	
7	BAHADUR	S.	5,424	19°44'N. 68°28'E.	S.M.	T. & G.	
9	YU SANG	S.	3,357	Marivales Harbour, Philippine Is.	A.C.	B.	
9	BRITISH SERGEANT	S. Tank	5,868	08°00'N. 81°38'E.	A.C.	B.	
9	ATHELSTANE* ...	S. Tank	6,571	07°30'N. 81°56'E.	A.C.	B.	
9	SAGAING	S.	7,958	Trincomalee	A.C.*	—	
10	KIRKPOOL	S.	4,842	33°S. 07°W. (Approx.)	Raider	—	
10	SAN DELFINO ...	M. Tank	8,072	35°35'N. 75°06'W.	S.M.	T.	
10	EMPIRE PRAIRIE ...	S.	7,010	35°N. 60°W. (Approx.)	S.M.*	—	
11	ULYSSES	S.	14,647	34°23'N. 75°35'W.	S.M.	T.	
11	EMPIRE COWPER ...	S.	7,164	71°01'N. 36°00'E.	A.C.	B.	
13	EMPIRE PROGRESS	S.	5,249	40°29'N. 52°35'W.	S.M.	T.	
13	HARPALION... ...	S.	5,486	73°33'N. 27°19'E.	A.C.	B.	
14	EMPIRE AMETHYST	S. Tank	8,032	16°N. 72°W. (Approx.)	S.M.*	—	

Date	Name	Type	Gross tons	Position	Cause of loss	How lost	Remarks
APRIL, 1942—*(Contd.)*							
14	EMPIRE THRUSH ...	S.	6,160	35°08′N. 75°18′W.	S.M.	T.	
14	LANCASTER CASTLE	S.	5,172	Anchored in River at Murmansk	A.C.	B.	
16	EMPIRE HOWARD ...	S.	6,985	73°48′N. 21°32′E.	S.M.	T.	
16	CASPIA	S. Tank	6,018	10m. S. of Beirut	S.M.	T.	
18	MEGOHM	Dredger	124	River Irrawaddy	C.U.	—	
19	PATELLA*	M. Tank	7,468	23°S. 20°W. (Approx.)	Raider	—	
20	EMPIRE DRYDEN ...	S.	7,164	34°21′N. 69°00′W.	S.M.	T.	
20	HARPAGON	S.	5,719	34°35′N. 65°50′W.	S.M.	T.	
20	VINELAND	S.	5,587	23°05′N. 72°20′W.	S.M.	T.	
20	PLAWSWORTH ...	S.	1,489	¼m. S. of Aldeburgh Buoy	Mine	—	
22	DERRYHEEN ...	S.	7,217	31°20′N. 70°55′W.	S.M.	T.	
23	KIRKLAND	S.	1,361	31°51′N. 26°37′E.	S.M.	T.	
23	JERSEY	M.	4,986	Suez	Mine	—	
23	CHATWOOD	S.	2,768	53°19′N. 01°00′E.	Mine	—	
24	EMPIRE DRUM ...	M.	7,244	37°00′N. 69°15′W.	S.M.	T.	
25	MODESTA	S.	3,849	33°40′N. 63°10′W. (Approx.)	S.M.	T.	
29	ATHELEMPRESS* ...	M. Tank	8,941	13°21′N. 56°15′W.	S.M.	T. & G.	
29	ALLIANCE*	Tug	81	022° 9.5 cables from Famagusta Lt., off Cyprus	Mine	—	
	Total ... 52		292,882				
MAY, 1942							
About							
1	MILDRED PAULINE	Sch.	300	Off Nova Scotia	S.M.	G.	
1	JAMES E. NEWSOM...	Sch.	671	35°50′N. 59°40′W.	S.M.	G.	
2	UNIQUE	S.B.	51	51°38′N. 01°00′E.	Mine	—	
2	CAPE CORSO ...	S.	3,807	73°02′N. 19°46′E.	A.C.	T.	
2	BOTAVON	S.	5,848	73°02′N. 19°46′E.	A.C.	T.	
2	JUTLAND	S.	6,153	73°02′N. 19°46′E.	A.C.	T.	
2	CALDERON	S.	1,374	31°05′N. 29°07′E.	A.C.	B.	
3	BRITISH WORKMAN	S. Tank	6,994	44°07′N. 51°53′W.	S.M.	T.	
3	OCEAN VENUS ...	S.	7,174	28°23′N. 80°21′W.	S.M.	T.	
4	FLORENCE M. DOUGLAS	Sch.	119	07°55′N. 58°10′W.	S.M.	G.	
5	KHODAUNG ...	M. Tank	254	River Irrawaddy	C.U.	—	Destroyed by fire
5	STANBANK	S.	5,966	34°55′N. 61°47′W.	S.M.	T.	
5	LADY DRAKE ...	S.	7,985	35°43′N. 64°43′W.	S.M.	T.	
6	ROYAL LADY ...	M.	195	Gozo, Mediterranean	A.C.	B.	
6	EMPIRE BUFFALO ...	S.	6,404	19°14′N. 82°34′W.	S.M.	T.	
8	MONT LOUIS ...	S.	1,905	08°23′N. 58°44′W.	S.M.	T.	
9	CALGAROLITE ...	M. Tank	11,941	19°24′N. 82°30′W.	S.M.	T. & G.	
10	CLAN SKENE ...	S.	5,214	31°43′N. 70°43′W.	S.M.	T.	
10	KITTY'S BROOK ...	S.	4,031	42°56′N. 63°59′W.	S.M.	T.	
10	NANKIN	S.	7,131	26°43′S. 89°56′E.	Raider	—	Taken in prize
10	RAMB IV (Hospital Ship)	M.	3,676	31°17′N. 29°23′E.	A.C.	B.	
11	EMPIRE DELL ...	S.	7,065	53°00′N. 29°57′W.	S.M.	T.	
11	CAPE OF GOOD HOPE	M.	4,963	22°48′N. 58°43′W.	S.M.	T. & G.	
12	CRISTALES	S.	5,389	52°55′N. 29°50′W.	S.M.	T.	
12	LLANOVER	S.	4,959	52°50′N. 29°04′W.	S.M.	T.	
12	NICOYA	S.	5,364	49°19′N. 64°51′W.	S.M.	T.	
12	DENPARK	S.	3,491	22°28′N. 28°10′W.	S.M.	T.	
13	BATNA	S.	4,399	52°09′N. 33°56′W.	S.M.	T.	
13	BRITISH COLONY* ...	S. Tank	6,917	13°12′N. 58°10′W.	S.M.	T.	
13	CITY OF MELBOURNE	S.	6,630	15°00′N. 54°40′W.	S.M.	T.	

Date	Name	Type	Gross tons	Position	Cause of loss	How lost	Remarks
MAY, 1942—(Contd.)							
15	SOUDAN	S.	6,677	36°10'S. 20°22'E.	Mine	—	
16	ARDUITY	M.	304	53°22'N. 00°30'E.	Mine	— —	
17	SAN VICTORIO ...	M. Tank	8,136	11°40'N. 62°33'W.	S.M.	T.	
17	PEISANDER. ...	M.	6,225	37°24'N. 65°38'W.	S.M.	T.	
17	FORT QU'APPELLE...	S.	7,121	39°50'N. 63°30'W.	S.M.	T.	
17	BARRDALE	S.	5,072	15°15'N. 52°27'W.	S.M.	T.	
20	TORONDOC	S.	1,927	14°45'N. 62°15'W. (Est.)	S.M.*	—	
20	EOCENE	S. Tank	4,216	31°56'N. 25°14'E.	S.M.	T.	
20	DARINA	M. Tank	8,113	29°17'N. 54°25'W.	S.M.	T.	
21	NEW BRUNSWICK ...	S.	6,529	36°53'N. 22°55'W.	S.M.	T.	
21	TROISDOC	S.	1,925	18°15'N. 79°20'W.	S.M.	T.	
22	FRANK B. BAIRD ...	S.	1,748	28°03'N. 58°50'W.	S.M.	G.	
23	MARGOT	S.	4,545	39°N. 68°W. (Approx.)	S.M.	T.	
24	ZURICHMOOR ...	S.	4,455	39°30'N. 66°00'W.	S.M.*	—	
27	ATHELKNIGHT ...	M. Tank	8,940	27°50'N. 46°00'W.	S.M.	T. & G.	
27	EMPIRE PURCELL ...	S.	7,049	74°00'N. 26°08'E.	A.C.	B.	
27	EMPIRE LAWRENCE	S.	7,457	74°00'N. 25°10'E. (Approx.)	A.C.	B.	
27	LOWTHER CASTLE...	S.	5,171	60m. E.S.E. of Bear Is. (Approx.)	A.C.	T.	
28	WESTERN HEAD ...	S.	2,599	19°57'N. 74°18'W.	S.M.	T.	
28	MENTOR	S.	7,383	24°11'N. 87°02'W.	S.M.	T.	
28	NORMAN PRINCE ...	S.	1,913	14°40'N. 62°15'W.	S.M.	T.	
28	YORKMOOR ...	S.	4,457	29°30'N. 72°29'W.	S.M.	G.	
29	CHARLBURY ...	S.	4,836	06°22'S. 29°44'W.	S.M.	T. & G.	
29	ALLISTER	S.	1,597	18°23'N. 81°13'W.	S.M.	T.	
30	LIVERPOOL PACKET	S.	1,188	43°20'N. 66°20'W. (Approx.)	S.M.	T.	
31	FRED W. GREEN ... (Derrick Ship)	S.	2,292	30°20'N. 62°00'W.	S.M.	T.	
	Total ... 56		258,245				
JUNE, 1942							
1	WESTMORELAND ...	S.	8,967	35°55'N. 63°35'W.	S.M.	T.	
2	MATTAWIN ...	M.	6,919	40°14'N. 66°01'W.	S.M.	T.	
2	CITY OF BREMEN ...	S.	903	49°57'N. 11°35'W.	A.C.	B.	
3	LILLIAN	Sch.	80	12°25'N. 59°30'W.	S.M.	G.	
3	IRON CHIEFTAIN ...	S.	4,812	33°55'S. 151°50'E.	S.M.	T.	
4	IRON CROWN ...	S.	3,353	38°17'S. 149°44'E.	S.M.	T.	
4	GEMSTONE	S.	4,986	01°52'N. 26°38'W.	Raider	—	
5	ELYSIA	S.	6,757	27°33'S. 37°05'E.	Raider	T.	Sank on 9th
7	CHILE	M.	6,956	04°17'N. 13°48'W.	S.M.	T.	
8	ROSENBORG ...	S.	1,512	18°47'N. 85°05'W.	S.M.	G.	
8	KING LUD	M.	5,224	20°S. 40°E. (Approx.)	S.M.*	—	
10	EMPIRE CLOUGH ...	S.	6,147	51°50'N. 35°00'W. (Approx.)	S.M.	T.	
10	RAMSAY	S.	4,855	51°53'N. 34°59'W.	S.M.	T.	
10	ARDENVOHR ...	M.	5,025	12°45'N. 80°20'W.	S.M.	T.	
10	SURREY	S.	8,581	12°45'N. 80°20'W.	S.M.	T.	
10	HAVRE	S.	2,073	Between Alexandria and Matruh	S.M.	T.	
10	PORT MONTREAL ...	M.	5,882	12°17'N. 80°20'W.	S.M.	T.	
11	GEO. H. JONES ...	S. Tank	6,914	45°40'N. 22°40'W.	S.M.	T.	
11	PONTYPRIDD ...	S.	4,458	49°50'N. 41°37'W.	S.M.	T.	
11	FORT GOOD HOPE ...	S.	7,130	10°19'N. 80°16'W.	S.M.	T.	
11	MAHRONDA ...	S.	7,926	14°37'S. 40°58'E.	S.M.	T.	
11	LYLEPARK	S.	5,186	14°S. 10°W. (Approx.)	Raider	—	
12	DARTFORD	S.	4,093	49°19'N. 41°33'W.	S.M.	T.	
12	CLIFTON HALL ...	M.	5,063	16°25'S. 40°10'E.	S.M.	T.	
12	HARDWICKE GRANGE	S.	9,005	25°45'N. 65°45'W.	S.M.	T.	

Date	Name	Type	Gross tons	Position	Cause of loss	How lost	Remarks
JUNE, 1942—(Contd.)							
13	CLAN MACQUARRIE	S.	6,471	05°30′N. 23°30′W.	S.M.	T. & G.	
14	DUTCH PRINCESS ...	Sch.	125	13°46′N. 60°06′W.	S.M.	G.	
14	BHUTAN	S.	6,104	34°00′N. 23°40′E. (Approx.)	A.C.	B.	
14	ETRIB	S.	1,943	43°18′N. 17°38′W.	S.M.	T.	
14	PELAYO	M.	1,346	43°18′N. 17°38′W.	S.M.	T.	
15	CITY OF OXFORD ...	S.	2,759	43°32′N. 18°12′W.	S.M.	T.	
15	THURSO	S.	2,436	43°41′N. 18°02′W.	S.M.	T.	
15	KENTUCKY* ...	S. Tank	9,308	36°37′N. 12°10′E.	A.C.	B.	
15	BURDWAN	S.	6,069	35m. S. of Pantellaria Island	A.C.	B.	
16	PORT NICHOLSON ...	S.	8,402	42°11′N. 69°25′W.	S.M.	T.	
17	MACDHUI	M.	4,561	Port Moresby	A.C.	—	Again attacked on 18th and capsized. Later became total loss
18	MOTOREX ...	M. Tank	1,958	10°10′N. 81°30′W.	S.M.	T. & G.	
19	DALRIADA*	S.	973	Edinburgh Channel, Thames Estuary	Mine	—	
20	AFON DULAIS ...	S.	988	50°04′N. 00°23′W.	Mine	—	
24	WILLIMANTIC ...	S.	4,558	25°55′N. 51°58′W.	S.M.	G.	
25	ANGLO CANADIAN ...	M.	5,268	25°12′N. 55°31′W.	S.M.	T.	
26	PUTNEY HILL ...	M.	5,216	24°20′N. 63°16′W.	S.M.	T. & G.	
28	MONA MARIE ...	Sch.	126	12°22′N. 60°10′W.	S.M.	—	
28	QUEEN VICTORIA ...	M.	4,937	21°15′S. 40°30′E. (Approx.)	S.M.*	—	
28	ZEALAND	S.	1,433	32°27′N. 34°43′E.	S.M.	T.	
29	EMPIRE MICA ...	S. Tank	8,032	29°25′N. 85°17′W.	S.M.	T.	
29	WAIWERA	M.	12,435	45°49′N. 34°29′W.	S.M.	T.	
30	AIRCREST	S.	5,237	31°49′N. 34°34′E.	A.C.	T.	
	Total ... 48		233,492				
JULY, 1942							
1	MARILYSE MOLLER	S.	786	31°22′N. 33°44′E.	S.M.	T.	
4	NAVARINO ...	S.	4,841	75°57′N. 27°14′E.	A.C.	T.	
5	BOLTON CASTLE ...	S.	5,203	76°40′N. 36°30′E.	A.C.	B.	
5	RIVER AFTON ...	S.	5,479	75°57′N. 43°00′E.	S.M.	T.	
5	AVILA STAR ...	S.	14,443	38°04′N. 22°46′W.	S.M.	T.	
5	EARLSTON ...	S.	7,195	74°54′N. 37°40′E.	S.M.	T.	
5	ZAAFARAN* ... (Rescue Ship)	S.	1,559	75°05′N. 43°40′E.	A.C.	B.	
5	EMPIRE BYRON ...	S.	6,645	76°18′N. 33°30′E.	S.M.	T.	
6	MUNDRA	S.	7,341	28°45′S. 32°20′E.	S.M.	T. & G.	
6	DINARIC	S.	2,555	49°30′N. 66°30′W.	S.M.	T.	Sank on 9th in position 49°28′N. 65° 38′W.
7	UMTATA	S.	8,141	25°35′N. 80°02′W.	S.M.*	—	
7	HARTLEBURY ...	S.	5,082	72°30′N. 52°00′E. (Approx.)	S.M.	T.	
8	HARTISMERE ...	S.	5,498	18°00′S. 41°22′E.	S.M.	T. & G.	
9	EMPIRE EXPLORER	S.	5,345	11°40′N. 60°55′W.	S.M.	T. & G.	
9	POMELLA	M. Tank	6,766	50°19′N. 03°00′W.	E-Boat	T.	
9	GRIPFAST*	S.	1,109	50°26′N. 02°59′W.	A.C.	B.	
9	CAPE VERDE ...	M.	6,914	11°32′N. 60°17′W.	S.M.	T.	
11	PORT HUNTER ...	S.	8,826	31°N. 24°W. (Approx.)	S.M.	T.	
11	CORTONA	S.	7,093	32°45′N. 24°45′W.	S.M.	T.	
12	SHAFTESBURY ...	S.	4,284	31°42′N. 25°30′W.	S.M.	T.	
12	SIRIS	S.	5,242	31°20′N. 24°48′W.	S.M.	T. & G.	
12	HAURAKI	M.	7,113	17°32′S. 80°25′E.	Raider	—	
13	SITHONIA	S.	6,723	29°N. 25°W. (Approx.)	S.M.	T.	
14	BRITISH YEOMAN* ...	S. Tank	6,990	26°42′N. 24°20′W.	S.M.	T.	
15	EMPIRE ATTENDANT	S.	7,524	23°48′N. 21°51′W.	S.M.	T.	

Date	Name	Type	Gross tons	Position	Cause of loss	How lost	Remarks
JULY, 1942—(*Contd.*)							
16	GLOUCESTER CASTLE	S.	8,006	08°S. 01°E. (Est.)	Raider	—	
18	GLACIER	Sch.	130	10°50′N. 58°58′W.	S.M.	G.	
18	COMRADE	Sch.	110	11°20′N. 58°50′W.	S.M.	G.	
19	EMPIRE HAWKSBILL	S.	5,724	42°29′N. 25°26′W.	S.M.	T.	
19	LAVINGTON COURT	S.	5,372	42°38′N. 25°28′W.	S.M.	T.	Foundered in tow 1st August in position 49°40′N. 18° 04′W.
20	FREDERIKA LENSEN	S.	4,367	49°22′N. 65°12′W.	S.M.	T.	
20	INDUS	M.	5,187	26°44′S. 82°50′E.	Raider	—	
21	DONOVANIA ...	M. Tank	8,149	10°56′N. 61°10′W.	S.M.	T.	
23	GARMULA	S.	5,254	05°32′N. 14°45′W.	S.M.	T.	
25	BROOMPARK ...	S.	5,136	49°02′N. 40°26′W.	S.M.	T.	Sank in tow on 1st August in position 47°42′N. 51°55′W.
26	EMPIRE RAINBOW...	M.	6,942	47°08′N. 42°57′W.	S.M.	T.	
27	ELMWOOD ...	S.	7,167	04°48′N. 22°00′W.	S.M.	T.	
27	WEIRBANK	M.	5,150	11°29′N. 58°51′W.	S.M.	T.	
29	PACIFIC PIONEER ...	M.	6,734	43°30′N. 60°35′W.	S.M.	T.	
29	PRESCODOC ...	S.	1,938	08°50′N. 59°05′W.	S.M.	T.	
30	DANMARK	M.	8,391	07°00′N. 24°19′W.	S.M.	T. & G.	
	Total ... 41		232,454				
AUGUST, 1942							
1	CLAN MACNAUGHTON	S.	6,088	11°54′N. 54°25′W.	S.M.	T.	
2	FLORA II	S.	1,218	62°45′N. 19°07′W.	S.M.	T.	
2	TREMINNARD ...	S.	4,694	10°40′N. 57°07′W.	S.M.	T.	
3	TRICULA	M. Tank	6,221	11°35′N. 56°51′W.	S.M.	T.	
3	LOCHKATRINE ...	M.	9,419	45°52′N. 46°44′W.	S.M.	T.	
4	RICHMOND CASTLE	M.	7,798	50°25′N. 35°05′W.	S.M.	T.	
4	EMPIRE ARNOLD ...	S.	7,045	10°45′N. 52°30′W.	S.M.	T.	
5	ARLETTA	S. Tank	4,870	44°44′N. 55°22′W.	S.M.	T.	
6	MAMUTU	M.	300	09°11′S. 144°12′E.	S.M.	G.	
8	RADCHURCH ...	S.	3,701	56°15′N. 32°00′W. (Approx.)	S.M.*	—	
8	TREHATA	S.	4,817	56°30′N. 32°14′W.	S.M.	T.	
8	KELSO	S.	3,956	56°30′N. 32°14′W.	S.M.	T.	
8	ANNEBERG	S.	2,537	56°30′N. 32°14′W.	S.M.	T.	Sunk by escort
9	SAN. EMILIANO ...	M. Tank	8,071	07°22′N. 54°08′W.	S.M.	T.	
9	DALHOUSIE ...	M.	7,072	20°22′S. 24°40′W.	Raider	—	
10	MEDON	M.	5,445	09°26′N. 38°28′W.	S.M.	T. & G.	
10	EMPIRE REINDEER	S.	6,259	57°00′N. 22°30′W.	S.M.	T.	
10	OREGON	M.	6,008	57°05′N. 22°41′W.	S.M.	T.	
10	CAPE RACE ...	S.	3,807	56°45′N. 22°50′W.	S.M.	T.	
10	VIVIAN P. SMITH ...	S.V.	130	21°50′N. 68°40′W.	S.M.	G.	
11	VIMEIRA	S. Tank	5,728	10°03′N. 28°55′W.	S.M.	T. & G.	
12	OHIO*	S. Tank	9,514	Between Cap Bon and Malta	A.C.	B.	First attacked by S.M. on 12th 75m. N. of Cap Bon, then continuously attacked by A.C. until arrival at Malta on 15th, when vessel became a total loss
12	CLAN FERGUSON ...	S.	7,347	20m. N. of Zembra Is., Mediterranean	A.C.	T.	
12	DEUCALION... ...	M.	7,516	37°56′N. 08°40′E.	A.C.	B.	Subsequently torpedoed by A.C. on same date in position 270° 5m. from Cani Rocks and sank
12	EMPIRE HOPE ...	M.	12,688	Off Galeta Is., Mediterranean	A.C.	B.	Sunk by Escort

Date	Name	Type	Gross tons	Position	Cause of loss	How lost	Remarks
AUGUST, 1942—(Contd.)							
13	GLENORCHY	M.	8,982	5m. N.W. of Kelibia Lt., Tunisia	E-Boat	T.	
13	WAIRANGI	M.	12,436	36°34'N. 11°15'E.	E-Boat	T.	
13	DORSET	M.	10,624	36°12'N. 12°49'E.	A.C.	B.	
13	WAIMARAMA	M.	12,843	36°25'N. 12°00'E.	A.C.	B.	
14	SYLVIA DE LARRINAGA	S.	5,218	10°49'N. 33°35'W.	S.M.	T.	
14	EMPIRE CORPORAL	S. Tank	6,972	21°45'N. 76°10'W.	S.M.	T.	
14	MICHAEL JEBSEN	S.	2,323	21°45'N. 76°10'W.	S.M.	T.	
17	PRINCESS MARGUERITE	S.	5,875	32°03'N. 32°47'E.	S.M.	T.	
17	FORT LA REINE	S.	7,133	18°30'N. 75°20'W.	S.M.	T.	
18	HATARANA	S.	7,522	41°07'N. 20°32'W.	S.M.	T.	
18	EMPIRE BEDE	M.	6,959	19°41'N. 76°50'W.	S.M.	T.	
18	HAMLA	S.	4,416	04°S. 24°W. (Est.)	Raider	--	
About 18	ARABISTAN	S.	5,874	11°30'S. 26°00'W. (Approx.)	Raider		
19	SEA GULL D.	Lugger	75	11°38'N. 67°42'W.	S.M.	G.	
19	CITY OF MANILA	S.	7,452	43°21'N. 18°20'W.	S.M.	T.	
19	BRITISH CONSUL*	S. Tank	6,940	11°58'N. 62°38'W.	S.M.	T.	
19	CRESSINGTON COURT	M.	4,971	07°58'N. 46°00'W.	S.M.	T.	
19	EMPIRE CLOUD ·	S.	5,969	11°58'N. 62°38'W.	S.M.	T.	Sank in tow on 21st in position 10°54'N. 62°10'W.
21	CITY OF WELLINGTON	S.	5,733	07°29'N. 14°40'W.	S.M.	T.	
24	KATVALDIS	S.	3,163	48°55'N. 35°10'W.	S.M.	T.	
24	SHEAF MOUNT	S.	5,017	48°55'N. 35°10'W.	S.M.	T.	
25	EMPIRE BREEZE	S.	7,457	49°22'N. 35°52'W.	S.M.	T.	
25	HARMONIDES	S.	5,237	01°47'N. 77°27'E.	S.M.	T.	
25	AMAKURA	S.	1,987	17°46'N. 75°52'W.	S.M.	T.	
25	VIKING STAR	S.	6,445	06°00'N. 14°00'W. (Approx.)	S.M.	T.	
26	CLAN MACWHIRTER	S.	5,941	35°45'N. 18°45'W.	S.M.	T.	
26	BEECHWOOD	S.	4,897	05°30'N. 14°04'W.	S.M.	T.	
26	EMPIRE KUMARI	S.	6,288	31°58'N. 34°21'E.	S.M.	T.	Towed to Haifa; became a total loss
28	SAN FABIAN	S. Tank	13,031	18°09'N. 74°38'W.	S.M.	T.	
28	CITY OF CARDIFF	S.	5,661	40°20'N. 16°02'W.	S.M.	T.	Sank on 29th
31	WINAMAC	S. Tank	8,621	10°36'N. 54°34'W,	S.M.	T.	
	Total ... 56		344,311				
SEPTEMBER, 1942							
1	ILORIN	S.	815	05°N. 01°W. (Approx.)	S.M.	T.	
1	GAZCON	S.	4,224	13°01'N. 50°30'E.	S.M.	T.	
2	OCEAN MIGHT	S.	7,173	00°57'N. 04°11'W.	S.M.	T.	
3	PENROSE	S.	4,393	38°N. 09°W. (Approx.)	S.M.	T.	
3	HOLLINSIDE	S.	4,172	38°N. 09°W. (Approx.)	S.M.	T.	
3	DONALD STEWART	S.	1,781	50°32'N. 58°46'W.	S.M.	T.	
5	SAGANAGA	S.	5,454	47°35'N. 52°59'W.	S.M.	T.	
5	LORD STRATHCONA	S.	7,335	47°35'N. 52°59'W.	S.M.	T.	
5	MYRMIDON	M.	6,278	00°45'N. 06°27'W.	S.M.	T.	
6	HELEN FORSEY	Aux. Sch.	167	28°35'N. 57°35'W.	S.M.	G.	
6	TUSCAN STAR	M.	11,449	01°34'N. 11°39'W.	S.M.	T.	
6	ANSHUN	M.	3,188	Milne Bay, New Guinea	Warship	—	
6	JOHN A. HOLLOWAY	S.	1,745	14°10'N. 71°30'W.	S.M.	T.	
7	OAKTON	S.	1,727	48°50'N. 63°46'W.	S.M.	T.	
9	HARESFIELD	S.	5,299	13°05'N. 54°35'E.	S.M.	T.	
10	EMPIRE OIL	S. Tank	8,029	51°23'N. 28°13'W.	S.M.	T.	

Date	Name	Type	Gross tons	Position	Cause of loss	How lost	Remarks
SEPTEMBER, 1942—(Contd.)							
11	EMPIRE MOONBEAM	S.	6,849	48°55′N. 33°38′W.	S.M.	T.	
11	HEKTORIA	S. Tank	13,797	48°55′N. 33°38′W.	S.M.	T.	
11	EMPIRE DAWN ...	M.	7,241	34°S. 02°E. (Approx.)	Raider	—	
12	TREVILLEY ...	M.	5,296	04°30′S. 07°50′W.	S.M.	T. & G.	
12	LACONIA	S.	19,695	05°05′S. 11°38′W.	S.M.	T.	
13	OCEAN VANGUARD	S.	7,174	10°43′N. 60°11′W.	S.M.	T.	
13	EMPIRE LUGARD ...	M.	7,241	12°07′N. 63°32′W.	S.M.	T.	
13	EMPIRE STEVENSON	S.	6,209	76°10′N. 10°05′E.	A.C.	T.	
13	EMPIRE BEAUMONT	S.	7,044	76°10′N. 10°05′E.	A.C.	T.	
14	ATHELTEMPLAR* ...	M. Tank	8,992	76°10′N. 18°00′E.	S.M.	T.	
14	HARBOROUGH ...	S.	5,415	10°03′N. 60°20′W.	S.M.	T. & G.	
15	KIOTO	S.	3,297	11°05′N. 60°46′W.	S.M.	T.	
16	OCEAN HONOUR ...	S.	7,173	12°48′N. 50°50′E.	S.M.	T. & G.	
17	PETERTON ...	S.	5,221	18°45′N. 29°15′W.	S.M.	T.	
18	FERNWOOD ...	S.	1,892	Dartmouth	A.C.	B.	
18	NORFOLK	S.	1,901	08°36′N. 59°20′W.	S.M.	T.	
19	QUEBEC CITY ...	S.	4,745	02°12′S. 17°36′W.	S.M.	T. & G.	
20	REEDPOOL ...	S.	4,838	08°58′N. 57°34′W.	S.M.	T.	
20	EMPIRE HARTEBEESTE	S.	5,676	56°20′N. 38°10′W.	S.M.	T.	
22	TENNESSEE... ...	S.	2,342	58°40′N. 33°41′W.	S.M.	T.	
22	ATHELSULTAN ...	M. Tank	8,882	58°24′N. 33°38′W.	S.M.	T.	
22	OCEAN VOICE ...	S.	7,174	71°23′N. 11°03′W.	S.M.*	—	Sunk by H.M.S
23	BRUYERE	S.	5,335	04°55′N. 17°16′W.	S.M.	T.	
25	EMPIRE BELL ...	S.	1,744	62°19′N. 15°27′W.	S.M.	T.	
25	BOSTON	S.	4,989	54°23′N. 27°54′W.	S.M.	T.	
25	NEW YORK ...	S.	4,989	54°34′N. 25°44′W. (Approx.)	S.M.	T.	
26	YORKTOWN ...	S.	1,547	55°10′N. 18°50′W.	S.M.	T.	
28	REGISTAN	S.	6,008	12°37′N. 57°10′W.	S.M.	T.	
28	LIFLAND	S.	2,254	56°40′N. 30°30′W. (Est.)	S.M.*	- -	
29	EMPIRE AVOCET ...	S.	6,015	04°05′N. 13°23′W.	S.M.	T.	
29	BARON OGILVY ...	S.	3,391	02°30′N. 14°30′W.	S.M.	T.	
30	ALIPORE	S.	5,273	07°09′N. 54°23′W.	S.M.	T. & G.	
30	KUMSANG	S.	5,447	04°07′N. 13°40′W.	S.M.	T.	
30	SIAM II	M.	6,637	03°25′N. 15°46′W.	S.M.	T.	
	Total ... 50		274,952				
OCTOBER, 1942							
1	EMPIRE TENNYSON	S.	2,880	09°27′N. 60°05′W.	S.M.	T.	
6	ANDALUCIA STAR ...	S.	14,943	06°38′N. 15°46′W.	S.M.	T.	
7	MANON	S.	5,597	15°00′N. 80°30′E.	S.M.	T.	
7	SHEAF WATER ...	S.	2,730	53°06′N. 01°25′E.	E-Boat	T.	
7	IGHTHAM	S.	1,337	53°32′N. 00°45′E.	Mine	—	Sank in position 55° 33′N. 00°26′E.
7	ILSE	S.	2,874	53°06′N. 01°25′E.	E-Boat	T.	
7	JESSIE MAERSK ...	S.	1,972	53°06′N. 01°25′E.	E-Boat	T.	
7	BORINGIA	M.	5,821	35°09′S. 16°32′E.	S.M.	T.	
8	GLENDENE ...	S.	4,413	04°29′N. 17°41′W.	S.M.	T.	
8	CITY OF ATHENS ...	S.	6,558	33°40′S. 17°03′E.	S.M.	T.	
8	CLAN MACTAVISH ...	S.	7,631	34°53′S. 16°45′E.	S.M.	T.	
8	SARTHE	S.	5,271	34°50′S. 18°40′E. (Approx.)	S.M.	T.	
9	PENNINGTON COURT	S.	6,098	58°18′N. 27°55′W.	S.M.	T.	
9	CAROLUS	S.	2,375	48°47′N. 68°10′W.	S.M.	T.	
9	ORONSAY	S.	20,043	04°29′N. 2·°52′W.	S.M.	T.	
10	DUCHESS OF ATHOLL	S.	20,119	07°03′N. 11°12′W.	S.M.	T.	
10	ORCADES	S.	23,456	35°51′S. 14°40′E.	S.M.	T.	
11	AGAPENOR	S.	7,392	06°53′N. 15°23′W.	S.M.	T.	
11	WATERTON	S.	2,140	47°07′N. 59°54′W.	S.M.	T.	
13	EMPIRE NOMAD ...	S.	7,167	37°50′S. 18°16′E.	S.M.	T.	
13	ASHWORTH	S.	5,227	53°05′N. 44°06′W.	S.M.	T.	

Date	Name	Type	Gross tons	Position	Cause of loss	How lost	Remarks
OCTOBER, 1942 *(Contd.)*							
13	STORNEST	S.	4,265	54°25′N. 27°42′W.	S.M.	T.	
13	SOUTHERN EMPRESS*	S. O.R.	12,398	53°40′N. 40°40′W.	S.M.	T.	
14	EMPIRE MERSEY ...	S.	5,791	54°00′N. 40°15′W.	S.M.	T.	
14	CARIBOU	S.	2,222	47°19′N. 59°29′W.	S.M.	T.	
16	NEWTON PINE ...	S.	4,212	55°N. 30°W. (Est.)	S.M.*	—	
16	CASTLE HARBOUR*	S.	730	11°00′N. 61°10′W.	S.M.	T.	
17	EMPIRE CHAUCER ...	S.	5,970	40°20′S. 18°30′E.	S.M.	T.	
19	ROTHLEY	M.	4,996	13°34′N. 54°34′W.	S.M.	T.	
19	SCALARIA	S. Tank	5,683	Ras Gharib, Red Sea	A.C.	T. & B.	
22	DONAX	M. Tank	8,036	49°51′N. 27°58′W.	S.M.	T.	Abandoned and sank on 29th
22	OCEAN VINTAGE ...	S.	7,174	21°37′N. 60°06′E.	S.M.	T.	
22	WINNIPEG II ...	S.	9,807	49°51′N. 27°58′W.	S.M.	T.	
22	EMPIRE TURNSTONE	S.	6,113	54°40′N. 28°00′W.	S.M.	T.	
23	CITY OF JOHANNESBURG	S.	5,669	33°20′S. 29°30′E.	S.M.	T.	
23	EMPIRE STAR	M.	12,656	48°14′N. 26°22′W.	S.M.	T.	
24	HOLMPARK	S.	5,780	13°11′N. 47°00′W.	S.M.	T.	
26	ANGLO MAERSK ...	M. Tank	7,705	27°50′N. 22°15′W.	S.M.	T.	Again attacked on 27th in position 27° 15′N. 18°50′W. and sank
27	PACIFIC STAR ...	S.	7,951	29°16′N. 20°57′W.	S.M.	T.	Abandoned on 28th in position 29°21′N 19°28′W. Last seen on 30th sinking.
27	SOURABAYA* ...	S. Tank	10,107	54°32′N. 31°02′W.	S.M.	T.	
27	STENTOR	M.	6,148	29°13′N. 20°53′W.	S.M.	T.	
28	HOPECASTLE ...	M.	5,178	31°39′N. 19°35′W.	S.M.	T.	
28	NAGPORE	S.	5,283	31°30′N. 19°36′W.	S.M.	T. & G.	
29	PRIMROSE HILL ...	S.	7,628	18°58′N. 28°40′W.	S.M.	T.	
29	BULLMOUTH* ...	M. Tank	7,519	33°20′N. 18°25′W.	S.M.	T.	
29	BIC ISLAND ...	S.	4,000	55°05′N. 23°27′W.	S.M.	T.	
29	BARRWHIN	S.	4,998	55°02′N. 22°45′W.	S.M.	T.	
29	ROSS	M.	4,978	38°51′S. 21°40′E.	S.M.	T.	
29	LAPLACE	S.	7,327	40°33′S. 21°35′E.	S.M.	T.	
29	ABOSSO	M.	11,330	48°30′N. 28°50′W.	S.M.	T.	
29	BRITTANY	M.	4,772	33°29′N. 18°32′W.	S.M.	T.	
29	CORINALDO ...	S.	7,131	33°20′N. 18°12′W.	S.M.	T.	
30	TASMANIA	M.	6,405	36°06′N. 16°59′W.	S.M.	T.	
30	BARON VERNON ...	S.	3,642	36°06′N. 16°59′W.	S.M.	T.	
30	PRESIDENT DOUMER	M.	11,898	35°08′N. 16°44′W.	S.M.	T.	
30	MARYLYN	S.	4,555	00°46′S. 32°42′W.	S.M.	T.	
30	SILVERWILLOW ...	M.	6,373	35°08′N. 16°44′W.	S.M.	T.	Abandoned 5th November. Foundered 11th November in position 37°24′N. 10°45′W.
31	ALDINGTON COURT	M.	4,891	30°20′S. 02°10′W.	S.M.	T.	
31	EMPIRE GUIDON ...	S.	7,041	30°10′S. 33°50′E.	S.M.	T.	
	Total ... 59		404,406				
NOVEMBER, 1942							
1	ELMDALE	S.	4,872	00°17′N. 34°55′W.	S.M.	T.	
1	MENDOZA	S.	8,233	29°20′S. 32°13′E.	S.M.	T.	
2	LLANDILO	S.	4,966	27°03′S. 02°59′W.	S.M.	T.	
2	REYNOLDS	S.	5,113	29°S. 41°E. (Approx.)	Raider	—	
2	EMPIRE ZEAL ...	S.	7,009	00°30′S. 30°45′W.	S.M.	T. & G.	
2	ROSE CASTLE ...	S.	7,803	47°36′N. 52°58′W.	S.M.	T.	
2	P.L.M.27	S.	5,633	47°36′N. 52°58′W.	S.M.	T.	
2	EMPIRE SUNRISE ...	S.	7,459	51°50′N. 46°25′W.	S.M.	T.	
2	EMPIRE LEOPARD ...	S.	5,676	52°26′N. 45°22′W.	S.M.	T.	
2	HARTINGTON ...	S.	5,496	52°30′N. 45°30′W. (Approx.)	S.M.	T.	

Date	Name	Type	Gross tons	Position	Cause of loss	How lost	Remarks
NOVEMBER, 1942—*(Contd.)*							
2	Maritima	S.	5,801	52°20′N. 45°40′W.	S.M.	T.	
2	Dalcroy	S.	4,558	52°30′N. 45°30′W. (Approx.)	S.M.	T.	
2	Empire Antelope	S.	4,945	52°26′N. 45°22′W.	S.M.	T.	
2	Empire Gilbert ...	S.	6,640	Off E. Coast of Iceland	S.M.*	—	
3	Gypsum Empress...	S.	4,034	12°27′N. 64°04′W.	S.M.	T.	
3	Chr. J. Kampmann	S.	2,260	12°06′N. 62°42′W.	S.M.	T.	
3	Dagomba	M.	3,845	02°30′N. 19°00′W.	S.M.	T.	
3	Jeypore	S.	5,318	55°30′N. 40°16′W.	S.M.	T.	
3	Empire Lynx ...	S.	6,379	55°20′N. 40°01′W.	S.M.	T.	
3	Hatimura	S.	6,690	55°38′N. 39°52′W.	S.M.	T.	
4	Trekieve	S.	5,244	25°46′S. 33°48′E.	S.M.	T.	
4	Daleby	S.	4,640	57°N. 36°W. (Approx.)	S.M.	T.	
4	Oued Grou ...	S.	792	04°33′N. 04°49′E.	S.M.	T.	
5	La Cordillera ...	M.	5,185	12°02′N. 58°04′W.	S.M.	T.	
5	New Toronto ...	S.	6,568	05°57′N. 02°30′E.	S.M.	T.	
6	Arica	S.	5,431	10°58′N. 60°52′W.	S.M.	T.	
6	Ocean Justice ...	S.	7,173	10°06′N. 60°00′W.	S.M.	T.	
6	City of Cairo ...	S.	8,034	23°30′S. 05°30′W.	S.M.	T.	
7	Roxby	S.	4,252	49°35′N. 30°32′W.	S.M.	T.	
7	D'Entrecasteaux	S.	7,291	15°30′N. 57°00′W.	S.M.	T.	
7	Lindenhall ...	S.	5,248	11°34′N. 63°26′W.	S.M.	T.	
7	Glenlea	S.	4,252	50°N. 30°W. (Approx.)	S.M.	T.	
9	Cerinthus ...	S. Tank	3,878	12°27′N. 27°45′W.	S.M.	T. & G.	
9	Ardeola	S.	2,609	Off Bizerta	Captured	—	
9	Tadorna	S.	1,947	1¼m. N. of Bizerta	Captured	—	
10	Garlinge*	S.	2,012	21m. N. of Cape Ivi, Algeria	S.M.	T.	
10	Start Point ...	S.	5,293	13°12′N. 27°27′W.	S.M.	T.	
11	Nurmahal ...	S.	5,419	14°45′N. 55°45′W. (Est.)	S.M.*	—	
11	City of Ripon ...	S.	6,368	08°40′N. 59°20′W.	S.M.	T.	
11	Viceroy of India	T.-E.	19,627	36°26′N. 00°24′W.	S.M.	T.	
11	Awatea	S.	13,482	1m. N. of Bougie Breakwater, Algeria	A.C.	T. & B.	
11	Cathay	S.	15,225	Bougie, Algeria	A.C.	B.	Sank on 12th
12	Browning ...	S.	5,332	35°53′N. 00°33′W.	S.M.	T.	
13	Louise Moller ...	S.	3,764	30°50′S. 35°54′E.	S.M.	T.	
13	Maron	M.	6,487	36°27′N. 00°58′W.	S.M.	T.	
14	Warwick Castle...	M.	20,107	39°16′N. 13°25′W.	S.M.	T.	
14	Narkunda ...	S.	16,632	36°52′N. 05°01′E.	A.C.	B.	
14	Empire Sky ...	S.	7,455	Off N. Russian Coast	C.U.	—	
15	King Arthur ...	M.	5,224	10°30′N. 59°50′W.	S.M.	T.	
15	Ettrick	M.	11,279	36°13′N. 07°54′W.	S.M.	T.	
15	Irish Pine ...	S.	5,621	Off New York	S.M.*	—	
15	Linwood	S.	992	¼m. East of Longsand Buoy, Thames Estuary	Mine	—	
16	Clan MacTaggart	S.	7,622	36°08′N. 07°23′W.	S.M.	T.	
17	City of Corinth...	S.	5,318	10°55′N. 61°01′W.	S.M.	T.	
17	Widestone ...	S.	3,192	54°30′N. 37°10′W.	S.M.	T.	
18	President Sergent	S. Tank	5,344	54°07′N. 38°26′W.	S.M.	T.	
18	Tower Grange ...	M.	5,226	06°20′N. 49°10′W.	S.M.	T.	
19	Yewforest ...	S.	815	120° 11m. from Eddystone Lt. (Approx.)	E-Boat	T.	
19	Birgitte	S.	1,595	118° 5½m. from Eddystone Lt.	E-Boat	T.	
19	Scottish Chief* ...	S. Tank	7,006	30°39′S. 34°41′E.	S.M.	T.	
20	Grangepark ...	S.	5,132	35°55′N. 10°14′W.	S.M.	T.	
21	Empire Starling...	S.	6,060	13°05′N. 56°20′W.	S.M.	T.	
21	Empire Sailor ...	M.	6,140	43°53′N. 55°12′W.	S.M.	T.	
23	Cranfield ...	S.	5,332	08°26′N. 76°42′E.	S.M.	T.	
23	Tilawa	S.	10,006	07°36′N. 61°08′E.	S.M.	T.	Again attacked in position 07°45 N. 61°10′E.

Date	Name	Type	Gross tons	Position	Cause of loss	How lost	Remarks
NOVEMBER, 1942—(Contd.)							
23	Goolistan	S.	5,851	75°30′N. 08°00′E.	S.M.*	T.	
23	Benlomond ...	S.	6,630	00°30′N. 38°45′W. (Est.)	S.M.	T.	
24	Trentbank ...	S.	5,060	10m. N. of Cap Tenes, Algeria	A.C.	T.	
24	Dorington Court	S.	5,281	27°00′S. 34°45′E.	S.M.	T. & G.	Sunk by gunfire after being abandoned.
26	Barberrys ...	S.	5,170	50°36′N. 47°10′W.	S.M.	T.	
26	Ocean Crusader...	S.	7,178	50°30′N. 45°30′W.	S.M.*	—	
26	Clan Macfadyen...	S.	6,191	08°57′N. 59°48′W.	S.M.	T.	
28	Empire Cromwell	S.	5,970	09°00′N. 58°30′W.	S.M.	T.	
28	Nova Scotia ...	S.	6,796	28°30′S. 33°00′E.	S.M.	T.	
30	Llandaff Castle...	S.	10,799	27°20′S. 33°40′E.	S.M.	T.	
30	Trevalgan ...	M.	5,299	09°40′N. 59°15′W.	S.M.	T.	
	Total ... 76		474,606				
DECEMBER, 1942							
2	Solon II	S.	4,561	07°45′N. 56°30′W. (Approx.)	S.M.	T.	
2	City of Bath ...	S.	5,079	09°29′N. 59°30′W.	S.M.	T.	
2	Wallsend ...	S.	3,157	20°08′N. 25°50′W.	S.M.	T.	
3	Empire Dabchick	S.	6,089	43°00′N. 58°17′W.	S.M.	T.	
3	Gatinais	M.	383	190° 5m. from Start Pt.	E-Boat	T.	
5	Teesbank	M.	5,136	03°33′N. 29°35′W.	S.M.	T.	
6	Ceramic	S.	18,713	40°30′N. 40°20′W.	S.M.	T.	
7	Henry Stanley ...	M.	5,026	40°35′N. 39°40′W.	S.M.	—	
7	Peter Maersk ...	M.	5,476	39°47′N. 41°00′W.	S.M.	T.	
8	Nigerian ...	S.	5,423	09°17′N. 59°00′W.	S.M.	T.	
8	Empire Spenser ...	M. Tank	8,194	57°04′N. 36°01′W.	S.M.	T.	
9	Charles L.D. ...	M.	5,273	59°02′N. 30°45′W.	S.M.	T.	
12	Ripley	M.	4,997	00°35′S. 32°17′W.	S.M.	T.	
12	Empire Gull ...	S.	6,408	26°S. 35°E. (Approx.)	S.M.	T.	
12	Empire Hawk ...	S.	5,033	05°56′N. 39°50′W.	S.M.	T.	
12	Avonwood ...	S.	1,056	3m. from No. 4 Buoy, off Lowestoft	E-Boat	T.	
12	Glen Tilt ...	S.	871	3m. from No. 4 Buoy, off Lowestoft	E-Boat	T.	
12	Lindisfarne ...	S.	999	3m. from No. 4 Buoy, off Lowestoft	E-Boat	T.	
12	Knitsley	S.	2,272	1½m. N. of No. 4 Buoy, Lowestoft	E-Boat	T.	
13	City of Bombay ...	S.	7,140	02°43′S. 29°06′W.	S.M.	T.	
14	Edencrag* ...	S.	1,592	35°49′N. 01°25′W.	S.M.*	—	
14	Orfor ...	S.	6,578	16°N. 50°W. (Approx.)	S.M.	T.	
15	Hannah Moller ...	S.	2,931	Benghazi	A.C.	B.	
16	East Wales ...	S.	4,358	00°24′N. 31°27′W.	S.M.	T.	
16	Observer ...	S.	5,881	05°30′S. 31°00′W.	S.M.	T.	
18	Bretwalda ...	S.	4,906	44°35′N. 16°28′W.	S.M.	T.	
19	Bankside	Aux. S.B.	77	Nr. Maplin Spit, Thames Estuary	Mine	—	
20	Otina	M. Tank	6,217	47°40′N. 33°06′W.	S.M.	T.	
21	Queen City ...	S.	4,814	00°49′S. 41°34′W.	S.M.	T. & G.	
21	Strathallan ...	S.	23,722	36°52′N. 00°34′W.	S.M.	T.	
21	Montreal City ...	S.	3,066	50°23′N. 38°00′W.	S.M.	T.	
26	Empire Union ...	S.	5,952	47°30′N. 24°30′W.	S.M.	T.	
27	Empire March ...	S.	7,040	40°S. 05°W. (Approx.)	Raider*	—	
27	King Edward ...	S.	5,224	47°25′N. 25°20′W.	S.M.	T.	
27	Melrose Abbey ...	S.	2,473	47°30′N. 24°30′W.	S.M.	T.	
27	Oakbank ...	M.	5,154	00°46′S. 37°58′W.	S.M.	T.	
27	Gertrude May ...	S.B.	72	51°45′N. 01°19′E. (Approx.)	Mine	—	
28	Lynton Grange ...	S.	5,029	43°23′N. 27°14′W.	S.M.	T.	

Date	Name	Type	Gross tons	Position	Cause of loss	How lost	Remarks
DECEMBER, 1942—(Contd.)							
28	ZARIAN	S.	4,871	43°23′N. 27°14′W.	S.M.	T.	
28	BARON COCHRANE...	S.	3,385	43°23′N. 27°14′W.	S.M.	T.	
28	EMPIRE SHACKLETON	S.	7,068	43°20′N. 27°18′W.	S.M.	T.	
28	MELMORE HEAD ...	S.	5,273	43°27′N. 27°15′W.	S.M.	T.	
28	VILLE DE ROUEN ...	S.	5,598	43°25′N. 27°15′W.	S.M.	T.	
28	TREWORLAS ...	S.	4,692	10°52′N. 60°45′W.	S.M.	T.	
28	EMPIRE WAGTAIL...	S.	4,893	43°17′N. 27°22′W. (Approx.)	S.M.	T.	
	Total ... 45		232,152				
JANUARY, 1943							
2	EMPIRE METAL ...	M. Tank	8,201	Bone Harbour	A.C.	B.	
2	ST. MERRIEL ...	S.	4,980	Bone Harbour	A.C.	B.	
3	BARON DECHMONT	S.	3,675	03°11′S. 38°41′W.	S.M.	T.	
3	BRITISH VIGILANCE	M. Tank	8,093	20°58′N. 44°40′W.	S.M.	T.	
7	BENALBANACH	S.	7,153	37°07′N. 04°38′E.	A.C.	T.	
8	YORKWOOD... ...	S.	5,401	04°10′S. 35°30′W.	S.M.	T.	
8	OLTENIA II* ...	S. Tank	6,394	27°59′N. 28°50′W.	S.M.	T.	
9	EMPIRE LYTTON ...	S. Tank	9,807	28°08′N. 28°20′W.	S.M.	T.	
9	WILLIAM WILBERFORCE	M.	5,004	29°20′N. 26°53′W.	S.M.	T.	
10	OCEAN VAGABOND...	S.	7,174	57°17′N. 20°11′W.	S.M.	T.	
10	BRITISH DOMINION	M. Tank	6,983	30°30′N. 19°55′W.	S.M.	T.	
11	C. S. FLIGHT ...	Sch.	67	12°25′N. 63°00′W.	S.M.*	—	
13	AILSA	S.B.	67	½m. N.E. of Whittaker Beacon, Burnham-on-Crouch	Mine	—	
15	OCEAN COURAGE ...	S.	7,173	10°52′N. 23°28′W.	S.M.	T.	
17	KALINGO	S.	2,051	34°07′S. 153°15′E.	S.M.	T.	
20	HAMPTON LODGE*	S.	3,645	36°44′N. 01°50′E.	A.C.	B	Sank on 21st
23	LACKENBY	S.	5,112	55°N. 47°W. (Approx.)	S.M.*	—	
28	RESOLUTE	S.B.	76	51°47′N. 01°14′E.	Mine*	—	
	Total ... 18		91,056				
FEBRUARY, 1943							
3	RHEXENOR	S.	7,957	24°59′N. 43°37′W.	S.M.	T. & G.	
3	INVERILEN	M. Tank	9,456	56°35′N. 23°30′W.	S.M.	T.	
3	CORDELIA*... ...	M. Tank	8,190	56°37′N. 22°58′W.	S.M.	T.	
7	TOWARD*	S.	1,571	55°13′N. 26°22′W.	S.M.	T.	
7	IRON KNIGHT ...	S.	4,812	36°51′S. 150°38′E.	S.M.	T.	
7	EMPIRE WEBSTER...	S.	7,043	36°47′N. 01°37′E.	S.M.	T.	
7	AFRIKA	M.	8,597	55°16′N. 26°31′W.	S.M.	T.	
7	HARMALA	S.	5,730	55°14′N. 26°37′W.	S.M.	T.	
7	BALTONIA*... ...	S.	2,013	35°58′N. 05°59′W.	Mine	—	
7	MARY SLESSOR ...	M.	5,027	35°58′N. 05°59′W.	Mine	—	
7	EMPIRE MORDRED...	S.	7,024	35°58′N. 05°59′W.	Mine	—	
7	EMPIRE BANNER ...	S.	6,699	36°48′N. 01°32′E.	S.M.	T.	
8	NEWTON ASH ...	S.	4,625	56°25′N. 22°26′W.	S.M.	T.	
10	QUEEN ANNE ...	M.	4,937	34°53′S. 19°51′E.	S.M.	T.	
11	HELMSPEY	S.	4,764	34°22′S. 24°54′E.	S.M.	T.	
17	LLANASHE	S.	4,836	34°00′S. 28°30′E.	S.M.	T.	
21	KYLECLARE ...	S.	700	41°45′N. 11°45′W. (Est.)	S.M.*	—	
21	EMPIRE TRADER ...	S.	9,990	48°25′N. 30°10′W.	S.M.	T.	
21	RADHURST	S.	3,454	48°50′N. 47°00′W. (Est.)	S.M.*	T.	
22	ROXBURGH CASTLE	M.	7,801	38°12′N. 26°22′W.	S.M.	T.	

Date	Name	Type	Gross tons	Position	Cause of loss	How lost	Remarks
FEBRUARY, 1943 — (Contd.)							
22	EMPIRE REDSHANK	S.	6,615	47°00'N. 34°30'W.	S.M.	T.	
23	ATHELPRINCESS ...	M. Tank	8,882	32°02'N. 24°38'W.	S.M.	T.	
23	EMPIRE NORSEMAN	S. Tank	9,811	31°18'N. 27°20'W.	S.M.	T.	
23	FINTRA	S.	2,089	36°57'N. 03°41'E.	S.M.	T.	
23	EULIMA	M. Tank	6,207	46°48'N. 36°18'W.	S.M.	T.	
25	MANCHESTER MERCHANT	S.	7,264	45°10'N. 43°23'W.	S.M.	T.	
25	STOCKPORT* ...	S.	1,683	45°N. 44°W. (Est.)	S.M.*	T.	
27	ST. MARGARET ...	S.	4,312	27°38'N. 43°23'W.	S.M.	T.	
27	MODAVIA	M.	4,858	090° 14m. from Berry Head (Lyme Bay)	E-Boat	T.	
	Total ... 29		166,947				
MARCH, 1943							
3	CITY OF PRETORIA	S.	8,049	41°45'N. 42°30'W. (Est.)	S.M.*	T.	
3	NIRPURA	S.	5,961	32°47'S. 29°47'E.	S.M.	T.	
3	EMPIRE MAHSEER...	S.	5,087	32°01'S. 30°48'E.	S.M.	T.	
4	CALIFORNIA STAR ...	M.	8,300	42°32'N. 37°20'W.	S.M.	T.	
4	MARIETTA E. ...	S.	7,628	31°49'S. 31°11'E.	S.M.	T.	
5	FIDRA	S.	1,574	43°50'N. 14°50'W.	S.M.	T.	
5	EMPIRE TOWER ...	S.	4,378	43°50'N. 14°46'W.	S.M.	T.	
5	TREFUSIS	S.	5,299	43°50'N. 14°46'W.	S.M.	T.	
5	GER-Y-BRYN ...	S.	5,108	43°50'N. 14°45'W.	S.M.	T.	
6	EGYPTIAN	S.	2,868	56°25'N. 37°38'W.	S.M.	T.	
6	FORT BATTLE RIVER	S.	7,133	36°33'N. 10°22'W.	S.M.	T.	
7	BARON KINNAIRD...	S.	3,355	50°N. 40°W. (Est.)	S.M.*	—	
7	EMPIRE LIGHT ...	M. Tank	6,537	53°57'N. 46°14'W.	S.M.	T.	
7	SABOR	S.	5,212	34°30'S. 23°10'E.	S.M.	T.	
8	FORT LAMY ...	S.	5,242	58°30'N. 31°00'W. (Approx.)	S.M.	T.	
8	GUIDO	S.	3,921	58°08'N. 32°20'W.	S.M.	T.	
9	ROSEWOOD ...	M. Tank	5,989	58°37'N. 22°32'W.	S.M.	T.	
9	KELVINBANK ...	M.	3,872	07°24'N. 52°11'W.	S.M.	T.	
9	CLARISSA RADCLIFFE	S.	5,754	42°N. 62°W. (Est.)	S.M.*	—	
10	NAILSEA COURT ...	S.	4,946	58°45'N. 21°57'W.	S.M.	T.	
10	TUCURINCA ...	S.	5,412	51°00'N. 30°10'W.	S.M.	T.	
11	EMPIRE LAKELAND	S.	7,015	58°N. 15°W. (Est.)	S.M.*	—	
11	EMPIRE IMPALA ...	S.	6,116	58°N. 15°W. (Est.)	S.M.*	—	
11	AELYBRYN	S.	4,986	28°30'S. 34°00'E.	S.M.	T.	
11	LEADGATE	S.	2,125	58°N. 15°W. (Est.)	S.M.*	—	
13	EMPRESS OF CANADA	S.	21,517	01°13'S. 09°57'W.	S.M.	T.	
13	MARCELLA	S.	4,592	42°45'N. 13°31'W.	S.M.	T.	
13	OPORTO	S.	2,352	42°45'N. 13°31'W.	S.M.	T.	
13	CLAN ALPINE ...	S.	5,442	42°45'N. 13°31'W.	S.M.	T.	Sunk by Escort
13	OCEAN FREEDOM ...	S.	7,173	Murmansk	A.C.	B.	
15	OCEAN SEAMAN ...	S.	7,178	36°55'N. 01°59'E.	S.M.	T.	
16	HADLEIGH	S.	5,222	36°10'N. 00°30'W.	S.M.	T.	
17	CORACERO	S.	7,252	51°04'N. 33°20'W.	S.M.	T.	
17	SOUTHERN PRINCESS	S. Tank	12,156	50°36'N. 34°30'W.	S.M.	T.	
17	KINGSBURY ...	S.	4,898	51°55'N. 32°41'W.	S.M.	T.	
17	FORT CEDAR LAKE	S.	7,134	52°14'N. 32°15'W.	S.M.	T.	
17	KING GRUFFYDD ...	S.	5,072	51°55'N. 32°41'W.	S.M.	T.	
17	ZOUAVE	S.	4,256	52°25'N. 30°15'W.	S.M.	T.	
17	PORT AUCKLAND ...	S.	8,789	52°25'N. 30°15'W.	S.M.	T.	
17	NARIVA	S.	8,714	50°40'N. 34°10'W.	S.M.	T.	
18	CANADIAN STAR ...	M.	8,293	53°24'N. 28°34'W.	S.M.	T.	
18	DAFILA	S.	1,940	32°59'N. 22°21'E.	S.M.	T.	
18	KAYING	S.	2,626	32°59'N. 22°21'E.	S.M.	T.	
19	LULWORTH HILL ...	S.	7,628	10°10S. 01°00'E. (Approx.)	S.M.	T.	
19	GLENDAIOUGH ...	S.	868	53°16'N. 01°03'W.	Mine	—	

47

Date	Name	Type	Gross tons	Position	Cause of loss	How lost	Remarks
MARCH, 1943—*(Contd.:)*							
19	OCEAN VOYAGER ...	S.	7,174	Tripoli Harbour	A.C.	B.	Sank on 20th
20	FORT MUMFORD ...	S.	7,132	10°N. 71°E. (Approx.)	S.M.	T.	
21	CITY OF CHRISTCHURCH	S.	6,009	39°35′N. 12°46′W.	A.C.	B.	Sank on 22nd in position 38°42′N. 10°14′W.
23	WINDSOR CASTLE ...	S.	19,141	37°28′N. 01°10′E.	A.C.	T.	
26	EMPIRE STANDARD	S.	7,047	Algiers Harbour	A.C.	B.	
26	CITY OF PERTH ...	S.	6,415	35°50′N. 01°41′W.	S.M.	T.	
27	EMPIRE ROWAN ...	M.	9,545	37°16′N. 06°54′E.	A.C.	T.	
27	CITY OF GUILDFORD	S.	5,157	33°00′N. 22°50′E.	S.M.	T.	
28	SILVERBEECH ...	M.	5,319	25°20′N. 15°55′W.	S.M.	T.	
28	LAGOSIAN	S.	5,449	25°35′N. 15°43′W.	S.M.	T.	
29	CELTIC STAR ...	S.	5,575	04°16′N. 17°44′W.	S.M.	T.	
29	UMARIA	S.	6,852	46°44′N. 16°38′W.	S.M.	T.	Sank on 30th
29	EMPIRE WHALE ...	S.	6,159	46°44′N. 16°38′W.	S.M.	T.	
29	NAGARA	S.	8,791	46°50′N. 16°40′W.	S.M.	T.	
30	EMPIRE BOWMAN ...	S.	7,031	47°26′N. 15°53′W.	S.M.	T.	
30	FORT A LA CORNE...	S.	7,133	36°52′N. 01°47′E.	S.M.	T.	
	Total ... 61		384,898				
APRIL, 1943							
2	GOGRA	S.	5,190	41°02′N. 15°39′W.	S.M.	T.	
2	KATHA	S.	4,357	41°02′N. 15°39′W.	S.M.	T.	
2	CITY OF BARODA ...	S.	7,129	26°56′S. 15°21′E.	S.M.	T.	
2	MELBOURNE STAR...	M.	12,806	28°05′N. 57°30′W. (Est.)	S.M.	T.	
5	BRITISH ARDOUR*	S. Tank	7,124	58°08′N. 33°04′W.	S.M.	T.	
5	ALOE	S.	5,047	32°37′S. 37°50′E.	S.M.	T.	
5	SHILLONG	M.	5,529	57°10′N. 35°30′W.	S.M.	T.	
5	WAROONGA ...	S.	9,365	57°10′N. 35°30′W.	S.M.	T.	Sank on 6th
6	JOSEFINA THORDEN	M. Tank	6,620	Near Sunk Head Buoy, Thames Estuary	Mine	—	Beached ; later became total loss
10	RUNO	S.	1,858	32°15′N. 23°55′E.	S.M.*	T.	
11	EMPIRE WHIMBREL	S.	5,983	02°31′N. 15°55′W.	S.M.	T. & G.	
11	LANCASTRIAN PRINCE	S.	1,914	50°18′N. 42°48′W.	S.M.	T.	
12	FRESNO CITY ...	M.	7,261	54°15′N. 30°00′W.	S.M.	T.	
12	PACIFIC GROVE ...	M.	7,117	54°10′N. 30°00′W.	S.M.	T.	
14	STANLAKE*... ...	S.	1,742	060° 12m. from Lizard Head	E-Boat	T.	
17	FORT RAMPART ...	S.	7,134	47°22′N. 21°58′W.	S.M.	T.	
17	DYNAMO	S.	809	Near B.8 Buoy, Barrow Deep	Mine	—	
18	MANAAR	S.	8,007	30°59′S. 33°00′E.	S.M.	T. & G.	
18	EMPIRE BRUCE ...	S.	7,459	06°40′N. 13°17′W.	S.M.	T.	
18	CORBIS	M. Tank	8,132	34°56′S. 34°03′E.	S.M.	T.	
21	WANSTEAD ...	S.	5,486	55°46′N. 45°14′W.	S.M.	T.	
21	ASHANTIAN ...	S.	4,917	55°50′N. 44°00′W.	S.M.	T.	
22	AMERIKA	M.	10,218	57°30′N. 42°50′W.	S.M.	T	
24	KOWARRA	S.	2,125	24°26′S. 153°44′E.	S.M.	T.	
24	ROSENBORG ...	S.	1,997	61°N. 15°W. (Approx.)	S.M.	T.	
25	DORYSSA	M. Tank	8,078	37°03′S. 24°03′E.	S.M.	T. & G	
25	LIMERICK	M.	8,724	28°54′S. 153°54′E.	S.M.	T.	
29	WOLLONGBAR ...	S.	2,239	31°17′S. 153°07′E.	S.M.	T.	
30	NAGINA	S.	6,551	07°19′N. 13°50′W.	S.M.	T.	
30	CORABELLA ...	S.	5,682	07°15′N. 13°49′W.	S.M.	T.	
30	BANDAR SHAHPOUR	S.	5,236	07°15′N. 13°49′W.	S.M.	T.	
30	PORT VICTOR ...	M.	12,411	47°49′N. 22°02′W.	S.M.	T.	
	Total ... 32		194,247				

Date	Name	Type	Gross tons	Position	Cause of loss	How lost	Remarks
MAY, 1943							
1	CLAN MACPHERSON	S.	6,940	07°58'N. 14°14'W.	S.M.	T.	
1	CITY OF SINGAPORE	S.	6,555	07°55'N. 14°16'W.	S.M.	T.	
1	BRITISH TRUST* ...	M. Tank	8,466	32°40'N. 19°53'E.	A.C.	T.	
1	ERINPURA ...	S.	5,143	32°40'N. 19°53'E.	A.C.	B.	
5	HARBURY	S.	5,081	55°01'N. 42°59'W.	S.M.	T.	
5	SELVISTAN	S.	5,136	53°10'N. 44°40'W.	S.M.	T.	
5	NORTH BRITAIN ...	S.	4,635	55°08'N. 42°43'W.	S.M.	T.	
5	HARPERLEY	S.	4,586	55°00'N. 42°58'W.	S.M.	T.	
5	BRISTOL CITY ...	S.	2,864	54°00'N. 43°55'W.	S.M.	T.	
5	WENTWORTH ...	S.	5,213	53°59'N. 43°55'W.	S.M.	T.	
5	DOLIUS	M.	5,507	54°00'N. 43°35'W.	S.M.	T.	
5	GHARINDA	S.	5,306	53°10'N. 44°40'W.	S.M.	T.	
5	LORIENT	S.	4,737	54°N. 44°W. (Approx.)	S.M.*	T.	
5	HOLMBURY ...	S.	4,566	04°30'N. 10°20'W.	S.M.	T. & G.	
8	CAMERATA	S.	4,875	Gibraltar	Italian Assault Craft	—	
8	KANBE	S.	6,244	Off Liberian Coast	S.M.	T.	
11	NAILSEA MEADOW...	S.	4,962	32°04'S. 29°13'E.	S.M.	T.	
11	ANTIGONE ...	S.	4,545	40°30'N. 32°30'W.	S.M.	T.	
11	TINHOW ...	S.	5,232	25°15'S. 33°30'E.	S.M.	T.	
12	DORSET COAST ...	M.	646	Algiers	A.C.	B.	
12	FORT CONCORD ...	S.	7,138	46°05'N. 25°20'W.	S.M.	T.	
13	CENTAUR* (Hospital Ship)	M.	3,222	27°17'S. 154°05'E.	S.M.	T.	
15	IRISH OAK	S.	5,589	47°51'N. 25°53'W.	S.M.	T.	
17	NORTHMOOR ...	M.	4,392	28°27'S. 32°43'E.	S.M.	T.	
17	AYMERIC	S.	5,196	59°42'N. 41°39'W.	S.M.	T.	
18	EMPIRE EVE* ...	S.	5,979	36°37'N. 00°46'E.	S.M.	T.	
19	ANGELUS	S.V.	255	38°40'N. 64°00'W.	S.M.	G.	
22	ALPERA	S.	1,777	300° 15m. from Cape St. Vincent	A.C.	B.	
29	HOPETARN ...	M.	5,231	30°50'S. 39°32'E.	S.M.	T.	
30	LLANCARVAN ...	S.	4,910	2m. S. of Cape St. Vincent	A.C.	B.	
31	CATFORD	S.	1,568	53°37'N. 00°42'E.	Mine	—	
	Total ... 31		146,496				
JUNE, 1943							
5	DUMRA	M.	2,304	28°15'S. 33°20'E.	S.M.	T.	
6	HARRIER	S.	193	29°S. 34°E. (Approx.)	S.M.*	—	
14	EMPIRE MAIDEN ...	S. Tank	813	Pantellaria Island	A.C.	B.	
15	ATHELMONARCH* ...	M. Tank	8,995	32°20'N. 34°39'E.	S.M.	T.	
15	SAN ERNESTO ...	M. Tank	8,078	09°18'S. 80°20'E.	S.M.	T. & G.	
17	YOMA	S.	8,131	33°03'N. 22°04'E.	S.M.	T.	
21	BRINKBURN ...	S.	1,598	36°53'N. 02°22'E.	S.M.*	T.	
23	VOLTURNO	S.	3,424	2m. W.N.W. of Cape St. Vincent	A.C.	B.	
23	SHETLAND	S.	1,846	2½m. W.N.W. of Cape St. Vincent	A.C.	B.	
24	BRITISH VENTURE...	S. Tank	4,696	25°13'N. 58°02'E.	S.M.	T.	
28	VERNON CITY ...	S.	4,748	04°30'S. 27°20'W.	S.M.	T.	
	Total ... 11		44,826				
JULY, 1943							
2	HOIHOW	S.	2,798	19°30'S. 55°30'E. (Approx.)	S.M.	T.	
2	EMPIRE KOHINOOR	S.	5,225	06°20'N. 16°30'W.	S.M.	T.	Torpedoed again on 3rd and sunk

Date	Name	Type	Gross tons	Position	Cause of loss	How lost	Remarks
JULY, 1943 —(*Contd.*)							
4	St. Essylt ...	M.	5,634	36°44'N. 01°31'E.	S.M.	T.	
4	City of Venice ...	S.	8,762	36°44'N. 01°31'E.	S.M.	T.	
5	Devis	M.	6,054	37°01'N. 04°10'E.	S.M.*	T.	
6	Jasper Park ...	S.	7,129	32°52'S. 42°15'E.	S.M.	T.	
6	Shahjehan ...	S.	5,454	33°01'N. 21°32'E.	S.M.	T.	Sank on 7th in position 32°51'N. 21° 10'E.
7	Leana	S.	4,743	25°06'S. 35°33'E.	S.M.	T. & G.	
9	Manchester Citizen	S.	5,343	05°50'N. 02°22'E.	S.M.	T.	
10	Talamba ... ... (Hospital Ship)	S.	8,018	36°55'N. 15°13'E.	A.C.	B.	
11	California ...	S.	16,792	41°15'N. 15°24'W.	A.C.	B.	
11	Duchess of York	S.	20,021	41°18'N. 15°24'W.	A.C.	B.	
12	Rahmani	S.	5,463	14°52'N. 52°06'E.	S.M.	T.	
12	Ocean Peace ...	S.	7,173	36°55'N. 15°13'E.	A.C.	B.	
14	Harvard	Aux. Sch.	114	10°05'N. 60°20'W.	S.M.	G.	
15	Harmonic	S.	4,558	23°S. 33°W. (Approx.)	S.M.	T.	
15	Gilbert B. Walters	Sch.	176	09°40'N. 59°50'W.	S.M.	G.	
15	Empire Lake* ...	S.	2,852	21°27'S. 51°47'E.	S.M.	T.	
15	J. B. W.	S.B.	72	N. of N.E. Maplin Buoy, Burnham-on-Crouch	Mine*	—.	
16	Fort Franklin ...	S.	7,135	22°36'S. 51°22'E.	S.M.	T.	
16	City of Canton ...	S.	6,692	13°52'S. 41°10'E.	S.M.	T.	Sank on 17th
18	Incomati	M.	7,369	03°09'N. 04°15'E.	S.M.	T. & G.	
20	Fort Pelly ...	S.	7,131	Augusta, Sicily	A.C.	B.	
21	Empire Florizel...	S.	7,056	Off Augusta, Sicily	A.C.	B.	
24	Henzada	S.	4,161	25°15'S. 44°08'W.	S.M.	T.	
24	Fort Chilcotin ...	S.	7,133	15°03'S. 32°35'W.	S.M.	T.	
26	Fishpool	M.	4,950	Syracuse, Sicily	A.C.	B.	
26	El Argentino ...	M.	9,501	39°50'N. 13°38'W.	A.C.	B.	
27	Halizones ...	S.	5,298	38°04'N. 12°59'W.	A.C.	B.	Sank on 30th in position 37°22'N. 13°03'W.
29	Cornish City ...	M.	4,952	27°20'S. 52°10'E.	S.M.	T.	
	Total ... 30		187,759				
AUGUST, 1943							
1	Uskside	S.	2,708	Palermo	A.C.	B.	
2	City of Oran ...	S.	7,323	13°45'S. 41°16'E.	S.M.	T.	Sunk by Escort on 3rd
4	Dalfram	S.	4,558	20°53'S. 56°43'E.	S.M.	T.	
6	Fort Halkett ...	S.	7,133	09°30'S. 26°50'W.	S.M.	T.	
6	Macumba	S.	2,526	11°30'S. 134°40'E.	A.C.	B.	
7	Contractor ...	S.	6,004	37°15'N. 07°21'E.	S.M.*	T.	
7	Umvuma	S.	4,419	20°18'S. 57°14'E.	S.M.	T.	
11	Clan MacArthur	S.	10,528	23°00'S. 53°11'E.	S.M.	T.	
15	Warfield	S.	6,070	39°59'N. 12°58'W.	A.C.	B.	
16	Empire Kestrel ...	S.	2,689	37°10'N. 04°35'E.	A.C.	T.	
17	Empire Stanley ...	M.	6,921	27°08'S. 48°15'E.	S.M.	T.	
19	Sai On	S.	1,950	Macau (Portuguese China)	Seized	—	
20	Namaz	Sch.	50	33°42'N. 34°43'E.	S.M.	—	
20	Panikos	Sch.	21	33°42'N. 34°43'E.	S.M.	—	
	Total ... 14		62,900				
SEPTEMBER, 1943							
6	Sellinge*	S.	2,327	Off Hurd Bank, Malta	Mine	—	
9	Larchbank ...	M.	5,151	07°38'N. 74°00'E.	S.M.	T.	
13	Newfoundland (Hospital Ship)	S.	6,791	40°13'N. 14°21'E.	A.C.	B.	Sunk on 14th by gunfire
13	Fort Babine ...	S.	7,135	41°31'N. 14°39'W.	A.C.	B.	

Date	Name	Type	Gross tons	Position	Cause of loss	How lost	Remarks
SEPTEMBER, 1943—(Contd.)							
19	Fort Longueuil ...	S.	7,128	10°S. 68°E. (Est.)	S.M.*	T.	
20	St. Usk	S.	5,472	16°30'S. 29°28'W.	S.M.	T.	
20	Almenara ...	S.	1,851	20 to 25m. S.S.E. of Taranto	Mine	—	
23	Fort Jemseg ...	S.	7,134	53°18'N. 40°24'W.	S.M.	T.	
29	Banffshire ...	S.	6,479	09°26'N. 71°20'E.	S.M.	T.	
30	Empire Commerce	M. Tank	3,722	37°19'N. 06°40'E.	S.M.	T.	
30	Fort Howe ...	S.	7,133	37°19'N. 06°40'E.	S.M.	T.	
	Total ... 11		60,323				
OCTOBER, 1943							
1	Tahsinia	M.	7,267	06°51'N. 73°48'E.	S.M.	T. & G.	
1	Stanmore	S.	4,970	36°41'N. 01°10'E.	S.M.	T.	
2	Haiching	S.	2,183	18°46'N. 71°55'E.	S.M.	T.	
4	Fort Fitzgerald...	S.	7,133	36°42'N. 01°17'E.	A.C.	T.	
11	Ocean Viking ...	S.	7,174	40°20'N. 17°00'E.	Mine	—	
11	Jalabala	S.	3,610	11°40'N. 75°19'E.	S.M.	T.	
16	Essex Lance ...	S.	6,625	57°53'N. 28°00'W.	S.M.	T.	
19	Penolver	S.	3,721	47°19'N. 52°27'W.	Mine	—	
21	Saltwick	S.	3,775	36°55'N. 01°36'E.	A.C.	T.	
24	Congella	M.	4,533	01°02'N. 71°14'E.	S.M.	G.	
31	New Columbia ...	S.	6,574	04°25'N. 05°03'E.	S.M.	T.	
	Total ... 11		57,565				
NOVEMBER, 1943							
2	Baron Semple ...	S.	4,573	05°S. 21°W. (Est.)	S.M.*	—	
2	Dona Isabel ...	S.	1,179	16m. W.S.W. of Dungeness	E-Boat	T.	
2	Master Standfast	M.	150	North Sea area	Captured	—	
2	Storaa	S.	1,967	Off Hastings	E-Boat	T.	
2	Foam Queen ...	S.	811	Between Dungeness and Beachy Head	E-Boat	T.	
4	British Progress	S. Tank	4,581	52°55'N. 02°00'E. (Approx.)	E-Boat	T.	Towed to port but subsequently broken up
10	Sambo	S.	7,176	12°28'N. 43°31'E.	S.M.	T.	
11	Birchbank ...	M.	5,151	36°10'N. 00°06'W.	A.C.	T.	
11	Indian Prince ...	M.	8,587	36°13'N. 00°05'W.	A.C.	T.	
13	Cormount	S.	2,841	Off Harwich	Mine	—	
18	Sambridge ...	S.	7,176	11°25'N. 47°25'E.	S.M.	T.	
18	Empire Dunstan...	S.	2,887	39°24'N. 17°40'E.	S.M.	T.	
21	Marsa	S.	4,405	46°40'N. 18°18'W.	A.C.	B.	
26	Morar	S.	1,507	51°50'N. 01°34'E.	Mine	—	
26	Rohna	S.	8,602	36°56'N. 05°20'E.	A.C.	B.	
	Total ... 15		61,593				
DECEMBER, 1943							
2	Testbank	S.	5,083	Bari	A.C.	—	} Blew up or caught fire following explosion of ammunition ship
2	Devon Coast ...	M.	646	Bari	A.C.	—	
2	Lars Kruse ...	S.	1,807	Bari	A.C.	—	
2	Fort Athabaska ...	S.	7,132	Bari	A.C.	—	
9	Cap Padaran ...	S.	8,009	39°15'N. 17°30'E.	S.M.	T.	
13	Daisy Moller ...	S.	4,087	16°21'N. 82°13'E.	S.M.	T.	
17	Kingswood ...	S.	5,080	05°57'N. 01°43'E.	S.M.	T.	
19	Phemius	S.	7,406	05°01'N. 00°17'W.	S.M.	T.	
23	Peshawur	S.	7,934	11°14'N. 80°11'E.	S.M.	T.	
24	Dumana	M.	8,427	04°27'N. 06°58'W.	S.M.	T.	
	Total ... 10		55,611				

Date	Name	Type	Gross tons	Position	Cause of loss	How lost	Remarks
JANUARY, 1944							
3	Empire Housman...	M.	7,359	60°50′N. 22°07′W.	S.M.	T.	Previously torpedoed on 31st December. Torpedoed again 3rd January in position shown. Sank on 5th
6	Polperro	M.	403	49°57′N. 05°28′W. (Approx.)	E-Boat	T.	
6	Underwood ...	M.	1,990	49°57′N. 05°28′W. (Approx.)	E-Boat	T.	
10	Ocean Hunter ...	S.	7,178	36°07′N. 00°11′W.	A.C.	T.	
16	Perseus	S.	10,286	12°00′N. 80°14′E.	S.M.	T.	
20	Fort Buckingham	S.	7,122	08°50′N. 66°25′E. (Est.)	S.M.	T.	
24	St. David (Hospital Carrier)	S.	2,702	41°10′N. 12°21′E.	A.C.	B.	
25	Fort La Maune ...	S.	7,130	13°04′N. 56°30′E.	S.M.	T.	
25	Fort Bellingham	S.	7,153	73°25′N. 25°10′E.	S.M.	T.	
26	Samouri	S.	7,219	13°04′N. 55°45′E.	S.M.	T.	
26	Surada	S.	5,427	13°00′N. 55°15′E.	S.M.	T.	
31	Emerald	S.	806	S.E. of Beachy Head	E-Boat	T.	
31	Caleb Sprague ...	S.	1,813	10m. S.E. of Beachy Head	E-Boat	T.	
	Total ... 13		66,588				
FEBRUARY, 1944							
7	Margit*	S.	1,735	61°30′N. 10°30′W. (Est.)	S.M.*	—	
10	El Grillo* ...	S. Tank	7,264	Seidis Fjord, Iceland	A.C.	B.	
12	Khedive Ismail ...	S.	7,513	00°57′N. 72°16′E.	S.M.	T.	
15	Fort St. Nicholas	S.	7,154	40°34′N. 14°37′E.	S.M.	T.	
22	British Chivalry	S. Tank	7,118	00°50′S. 68°00′E.	S.M.	T.	
23	San Alvaro ...	M. Tank	7,385	13°46′N. 48°55′E.	S.M.	T.	
24	Philipp M. ...	S.	2,085	Nr. Hearty Knoll Buoy, off Gt. Yarmouth	E-Boat	T.	
26	Silvermaple ...	M.	5,313	04°44′N. 03°20′W.	S.M.	T.	
26	Sutlej	M.	5,189	08°S. 70°E. (Approx.)	S.M.	T.	
29	Palma	M.	5,419	05°51′N. 79°58′E.	S.M.	T.	
29	Ascot	S.	7,005	05°S. 63°E. (Approx.)	S.M.	T. & G.	
	Total ... 11		63,180				
MARCH, 1944							
3	Fort McLeod ...	S.	7,127	02°01′N. 77°06′E.	S.M.	T. & G.	
4	Empire Tourist ...	S.	7,062	73°25′N. 22°11′E.	S.M.	T.	
5	John Holt ...	S.	4,964	03°56′N. 07°36′E.	S.M.	T.	
9	Behar	M.	7,840	20°32′S. 87°10′E.	Raider	—	
16	El Madina ...	S.	3,962	20°54′N. 89°36′E.	S.M.	T.	
18	Nancy Moller ...	S.	3,916	02°14′N. 78°25′E.	S.M.	T.	
20	Matadian	S. Tank	4,275	05°07′N. 04°47′E.	S.M.	T.	
22	Watuka	S.	1,621	44°30′N. 62°51′W.	S.M.	T.	
27	Tulagi*	M.	2,281	11°00′S. 78°40′E.	S.M.	T.	
30	City of Adelaide	S.	6,589	12°01′S. 80°27′E.	S.M.	T. & G.	
	Total ... 10		49,637				
APRIL, 1944							
1	Dahomian	S.	5,277	34°25′S. 18°19′E.	S.M.	T.	
8	Nebraska	S.	8,262	11°55′S. 19°52′W.	S.M.	T.	
20	Royal Star ...	S.	7,900	37°02′N. 03°41′E.	A.C.	T.	
	Total ... 3		21,439				

Date	Name	Type	Gross tons	Position	Cause of loss	How lost	Remarks
MAY, 1944							
1	JANETA	S.	5,312	18°10′S. 20°00′W.	S.M.	T.	
6	ANADYR	S.	5,321	10°55′S. 27°30′W.	S.M.	T.	
11	EMPIRE HEATH ...	S.	6,644	19°S. 31°W.	S.M.	T.	
19	FORT MISSANABIE...	S.	7,147	38°20′N. 16°28′E.	S.M.	T.	
30	NORDEFLINGE* ...	S.	2,873	37°02′N. 03°47′E.	A.C.	B.	
	Total ... 5		27,297				
JUNE, 1944							
5	HELEN MOLLER ...	S.	5,259	04°28′S. 74°45′E.	S.M.	T.	
6	SAMBUT	S.	7,219	51°08′N. 01°33′E.	C.U.	--	
10	DUNGRANGE ...	S.	621	S. of St. Catherine's Pt., I.O.W.	E-Boat	T.	
10	BRACKENFIELD ...	S.	657	50m. S. of Nab. L.V.	E-Boat	T.	
10	ASHANTI	M.	534	Off St. Catherine's Pt., I.O.W.	E-Boat	T.	
16	COLUMBINE... ...	S.	3,268	32°44′S. 17°22′E.	S.M.	T.	
16	ALERT (Trinity House Vessel)	S.	793	49°25′N. 00°40′W.	Mine	---	
18	ALBERT C. FIELD...	S.	1,764	50°28′N. 01°46′W.	A.C.	T.	
20	WESTDALE	S.	424	49°24′N. 00°38′W.	Mine	---	
22	DUNVEGAN HEAD...	S.	638	Off Assault Beaches, Normandy	C.U.	---	
24	FORT NORFOLK ...	S.	7,131	Off Assault Beaches, Normandy	Mine	---	
24	EMPIRE LOUGH ...	S.	2,824	51°06′N. 01°16′E.	C.U.	---	
24	DERRYCUNIHY ...	M.	7,093	Off Assault Beaches, Normandy	Mine	---	
28	MAID OF ORLEANS	S.	2,386	50°10′N. 00°40′W.	S.M.	T.	
29	NELLORE	S.	6,942	07°51′S. 75°20′E.	S.M.	T.	
29	EMPIRE PORTIA ...	S.	7,058	50°33′N. 00°35′W.	S.M.	T.	
	Total ... 16		54,611				
JULY, 1944							
2	EMPIRE BROADSWORD	S.	7,177	49°25′N. 00°54′W.	Mine	---	
5	GLENDINNING ...	S.	1,927	50°32′N. 00°22′W.	S.M.	T.	
9	SHAHZADA	S.	5,454	15°30′N. 65°30′E.	S.M.	T.	
12	NAJA	Tug	72	Upper Pool, Wapping, London	Flying Bomb	---	
14	DIRECTOR	S.	5,107	24°30′S. 35°44′E.	S.M.	T.	
15	TANDA	S.	7,174	13°22′N. 74°09′E.	S.M.	T.	
19	KING FREDERICK ...	S.	5,265	09°29′N. 71°45′E.	S.M.	T.	
20	No. 36	Hopper Barge	772	Cherbourg	Mine	---	
30	SAMWAKE	S.	7,219	50°40′N. 00°31′E. (Approx.)	E-Boat	T.	
	Total ... 9		40,167				
AUGUST, 1944							
4	T.C.C. HOPPER No. 1	Hopper Barge	604	Cherbourg	Mine	--	
5	EMPIRE CITY ...	M.	7,295	11°33′S. 41°25′E.	S.M.	T.	
7	EMPIRE DAY ...	M.	7,242	07°06′S. 42°00′E.	S.M.	T.	
7	AMSTERDAM (Hospital Carrier)	S.	4,220	49°25′N. 00°35′W.	Mine*	---	
13	RADBURY	S.	3,614	24°20′S. 41°45′E.	S.M.	T.	
16	EMPIRE LANCER ...	S.	7,037	15°S. 45°E. (Approx.)	S.M.	T.	
17	IDDESLEIGH ...	S.	5,205	¾m. S. of 90 Buoy. Off Langrune, Assault area, Normandy	One man torpedo	---	Previously damaged by torpedo on 10th
18	NAIRUNG	S.	5,414	15°S. 42°E. (Est.)	S.M.*	T.	
19	WAYFARER	S.	5,068	14°30′S. 42°20′E. (Est.)	S.M.	T.	

Date	Name	Type	Gross tons	Position	Cause of loss	How lost	Remarks
AUGUST, 1944—(Contd.)							
19	St. Enogat ...	S.	2,360	50°16′N. 00°50′W. (Approx.)	S.M.*	T.	
20	Berwickshire ...	S.	7,464	30°58′S. 38°50′E.	S.M.	T.	
20	Coral	S.	638	50°13′N. 00°48′W.	S.M.	T.	
23	Fort Yale ...	S.	7,134	50°23′N. 00°55′W.	S.M.	T.	Previously damaged by mine on 8th
24	Empire Rosebery	S. Tank	2,370	49°22′N. 00°36′W.	Mine	—	
25	Orminster ...	S.	5,712	50°09′N. 00°44′W.	S.M.	T.	
26	Ashmun J. Clough	S.	1,791	50°10′N. 01°41′W.	S.M.	T.	
31	Troilus	S.	7,422	14°10′N. 61°04′E.	S.M.	T.	
	Total ... 17		80,590				
SEPTEMBER, 1944							
3	Livingston ...	S.	2,140	46°15′N. 58°05′W.	S.M.	T.	
8	Empire Heritage	S. Tank	15,702	55°27′N. 08°01′W.	S.M.	T.	
8	Pinto	M.	1,346	55°27′N. 08°01′W.	S.M.	T.	
29	Samsuva	S.	7,219	72°58′N. 23°59′E.	S.M.	T.	
	Total ... 4		26,407				
OCTOBER, 1944							
26	Rouseville ...	M. Tank	1,155	49°26′N. 00°36′E. In River Seine, off Vieux Port	Mine	—	
NOVEMBER, 1944							
2	Rio Bravo ...	M. Tank	1,141	Ostend Roads	E-Boat	T.	
5	Marion Moller ...	S.	3,827	10°40′N. 81°10′E.	S.M.	T.	
10	Shirvan	S. Tank	6,017	64°08′N. 22°50′W. (Approx.)	S.M.	T.	
10	Empire Wold* ...	Tug	269	64°08′N. 22°38′W.	S.M.*	—	
	Total .. 4		11,254				
DECEMBER, 1944							
1	Empire Dace (Ferry)	S.	716	Entrance to Misso-longhi, Greece	Mine	—	
3	Cornwallis ...	S.	5,458	43°59′N. 68°20′W. (Approx.)	S.M.	T.	
7	Samsip	S.	7,219	298° 1m. from N.F.11 Buoy, Scheldt Estuary	Mine	—	Sunk by gunfire
15	Fort Maisonneuve	S.	7,128	105° 8.5m. from N.F.14 Buoy, Scheldt Estuary	Mine	—	
18	Silverlaurel ...	S.	6,142	50°07′N. 04°40′W.	S.M.	T.	
23	Dumfries	S.	5,149	50°23′N. 01°43′W.	S.M.*	T.	
23	Slemish	S.	1,536	49°45′N. 01°42′W.	S.M.*	T.	
23	Tid 70	Tug	50	50°12′N. 00°52′W.	Mine	—	
24	Empire Path ...	S.	6,140	51°22′N. 02°52′E.	Mine	—	
28	Empire Javelin ...	S.	7,177	50°04′N. 01°00′W.	S.M.	T.	
	Total ... 10		46,715				
JANUARY, 1945							
10	Blackheath ...	S.	4,637	35°49′N. 06°03′W.	S.M.*	T.	
11	Normandy Coast...	S.	1,428	53°19′N. 04°48′W.	S.M.	T.	
14	Athelviking ...	M. Tank	8,779	44°20′N. 63°24′W.	S.M.	T.	

Date	Name	Type	Gross tons	Position	Cause of loss	How lost	Remarks
JANUARY, 1945—(*Contd.*)							
14	BRITISH FREEDOM*	M. Tank	6,985	44°28′N. 63°28′W.	S.M.	T.	
15	MAJA	M. Tank	8,181	53°40′N. 05°14′W.	S.M.	T.	
15	D	Hopper Barge	262	109° 1.53m. from Eastham Pumping Chimney, Mersey	Mine	—	
15	DALEMOOR ...	S.	5,835	53°22′N. 00°50′E. (Approx.)	Mine	—	
18	SAMVERN	S.	7,219	51°22′N. 03°02′E.	Mine	—	
22	HALO	S.	2,365	51°22′N. 02°24′E. (Approx.)	E-Boat	T.	
	Total ... 9		45,691				
FEBRUARY, 1945							
6	EVERLEIGH ...	S.	5,222	50°30′N. 01°48′W.	S.M.	T.	
17	REGENT LION ...	M. Tank	9,551	35°56′N. 05°45′W.	▸ S.M.	T.	
22	ALEXANDER KENNEDY	S.	1,313	50°06′N. 04°50′W.	S.M.*	T.	
22	GOODWOOD ...	S.	2,780	52°53′N. 02°12′E. (Approx.)	E-Boat	T.	
22	BLACKTOFT ...	S.	1,109	52°52′N. 02°36′E.	E-Boat	T.	
23	POINT PLEASANT PARK	S.	7,136	29°42′S. 09°58′E.	S.M.	T. & G.	
24	ORISKANY	S.	1,644	50°05′N. 05°51′W.	S.M.	T.	
24	ALERT*	Cable Ship	941	51°21′N. 01°37′E.	C.U.	—	
25	EGHOLM	S.	1,317	55°50′N. 01°52′W.	S.M.*	T.	
26	AURETTA	S.	4,571	51°24′N. 02°49′E.	Mine	—	
27	SAMPA	S.	7,219	9m. N. of Ostend (Approx.)	Mine	—	
28	NORFOLK COAST ...	M.	646	51°58′N. 05°25′W.	S.M..	T.	
	Total ... 12		43,449				
MARCH, 1945							
2	KING EDGAR ...	M.	4,536	52°05′N. 05°42′W.	S.M.	T.	
8	LORNASTON ...	S	4,934	50°35′N. 00°03′W.	S.M.*	T.	
10	BARON JEDBURGH...	S.	3,656	10°02′S. 25°00′W.	S.M.	T.	
13	TABER PARK ...	S.	2,878	52°22′N. 01°53′E.	Midget S.M.*	—	
16	INGER TOFT ...	S.	2,190	57°25′N. 06°52′W.	S.M.	T.	
19	SAMSELBU	S.	7,253	51°23′N. 03°06′E.	Mine	—	
19	EMPIRE BLESSING...	S.	7,062	51°24′N. 03°17 E.	Mine	—	
19	CRICHTOUN ...	S.	1,097	Off Lowestoft	E-Boat	T.	
19	ROGATE	S.	2,871	070° 3m. from No. 4 Buoy (off Lowestoft)	E-Boat	T.	
22	EMPIRE KINGSLEY...	S.	6,996	50°08′N. 05°51′W.	S.M.	T.	
26	NEWLANDS ...	S.	1,556	51°28′N. 01°25′E. (Approx.)	Midget S.M.	—	
30	JIM	S.	833	52°08′N. 01°40′E.	Midget S.M.*	—	
	Total ... 12		45,862				
APRIL, 1945							
5	GASRAY	S.	1,406	2m. from St. Abb's Head	S.M.	T.	
6	CUBA	S.	11,420	50°36′N. 00°57′W.	S.M.	T.	
9	SAMIDA ...	S.	7,219	50°57′N. 01°03′E. (Approx.)	S.M.	T.	
16	MONARCH*. .	Cable Ship	1,150	52°08′N. 01°52′E.	S.M.*	T.	
16	ATHELDUKE .	M. Tank	8,966	55°39′N. 01°31′W.	S.M.	T.	

Date	Name	Type	Gross tons	Position	Cause of loss	How lost	Remarks
APRIL, 1945—*(Contd.)*							
16	GOLD SHELL ...	M. Tank	8,208	51°22′N. 02°55′E.	Mine	—	
18	EMPIRE GOLD ...	S. Tank	8,028	47°47′N. 06°26′W.	S.M.	T.	
18	FILLEIGH	S.	4,856	51°20′N. 01°42′E.	S.M.	T.	
24	MONMOUTH COAST...	S.	878	80m. from Sligo	S.M.*	T.	
	Total ... 9		52,131				
MAY, 1945							
7	AVONDALE PARK ...	S.	2,878	1m. S.E. of May Is., Firth of Forth	S.M.	T.	

LIST II

BRITISH FISHING VESSELS LOST BY ENEMY ACTION

Date	Name	Type	Gross tons	Position	Cause of loss	How lost	Remarks
SEPTEMBER, 1939							
13	DAVARA	S.T.	291	21m. N.W. × N. of Tory Is.	S.M.	G.	
16	RUDYARD KIPLING	S.T.	333	53°50′N. 11°10′W.	S.M.	Time Bombs	
18	ARLITA	S.T.	326	57°51′N. 09°28′W.	S.M.	G.	
18	LORD MINTO	S.T.	295	57°51′N. 09°28′W.	S.M.	G.	
24	CALDEW	S.T.	287	60°47′N. 06°20′W.	S.M.	G.	
	Total ... 5		1,532				
OCTOBER, 1939							
28	ST. NIDAN ...	S.T.	565	60°N. 05°W. (Approx.)	S.M.	G. and explosive charge	
28	LYNX II ...	S.T.	250	60°N. 05°W. (Approx.)	S.M.	G.	
	Total ... 2		815				
NOVEMBER, 1939							
12	CRESSWELL	S.T.	275	18m. N.W. × N. of Flannan Is., Outer Hebrides	S.M.	G.	
18	WIGMORE ...	S.T.	345	25m. N. × W. of Rattray Head	S.M.	T.	
20	SEA SWEEPER ...	S.T.	329	25m. N.W. × W. of Tory Is.	S.M.	G.	
20	DELPHINE ...	S.T.	250	18m. N. × E. of Tory Is.	S.M.	G.	
20	THOMAS HANKINS...	S.T.	276	14m. N.W. of Tory Is.	S.M.	G.	
21	SULBY ...	S.T.	287	75m. N.W. of Rathlin Is.	S.M.	G.	
21	WILLIAM HUMPHRIES	S.T.	276	75m. N.W. of Rathlin Is.	S.M.	G.	
	Total ... 7		2,038				
DECEMBER, 1939							
17	PEARL ...	S.T.	198	65m. E. ½S. of Outer Dowsing L.V.	A.C.	B.	
17	COMPAGANUS ...	S.T.	270	150m. E. × N. of May Is.	A.C.	B.	
17	ISABELLA GREIG ...	S.T.	210	145m. E. × N. of May Is.	A.C.	B.	
17	TRINITY N.B. ...	S.T.	203	57°50′N. 01°30′W.	A.C.	B.	
18	ACTIVE ...	S.T.	185	48m. N.N.W. of Rattray Head	A.C.	T.	
18	ZELOS ...	S.T.	227	112m. E. × N. of May Is.	A.C.	B.	
19	DANEDEN ...	S.T.	210	12m. E.S.E. of Fetlar, Shetlands	A.C.	B.	
19	RIVER EARN ...	S.T.	202	58°30′N. 02°00′E.	A.C.	B.	
28	BARBARA ROBERTSON	S.T.	325	35m. N.W. of Butt of Lewis	S.M.	G.	
28	RESERCHO ...	S.T.	258	6m. S.E. × E. of Flamboro' Head	Mine	—	
	Total ... 10		2,288				

Date	Name	Type	Gross tons	Position	Cause of loss	How lost	Remarks
JANUARY, 1940							
6	Eta	M.T.	81	6m. N. ¼W. of Outer Gabbard L.V.	Mine	—	
11	Lucida	S.T.	251	55°00′N. 00°53′W.	Mine	—	
11	Croxton ...	S.T.	195	53°20′N. 02°40′E.	A.C.	B.	
12	William Ivey ...	S.T.	202	15 to 16m. N. ¼E. of Longstone L.H.	A.C.	B.	
15	Newhaven... ...	S.T.	162	18m. S.S.E. of Lowestoft (Est.)	Mine	—	
	Total ... 5		891				
FEBRUARY, 1940							
10	Theresa Boyle ...	S.T.	224	115m. E. × N. of Aberdeen	A.C.	B.	
11	Togimo	S.T.	290	50°40′N. 11°02′W.	S.M.	G.	
27	Ben Attow ...	S.T.	156	7m. E. ¼S. of May Is.	Mine	—	
	Total ... 3		670				
MARCH, 1940							
10	Leukos	S.T.	216	N.W. of Tory Is.	C.U.	—	
11	Halifax	S.T.	165	3m. S.E. of Aldeburgh L.V.	Mine	—	
	Total ... 2		381				
APRIL, 1940							
3	Gorspen	S.T.	208	31m. N.E. of Outer Skerries	A.C.	B.	
3	Sansonnet... ...	S.T.	212	18m. E. × S. of Muckle Flugga	A.C.	B.	
	Total ... 2		420				
MAY, 1940							
22	Teaser	Motor Fishing Smack	9	400 yds. W. of Tollesbury Pier, R. Blackwater, Essex	Mine	—	
About 30	Corennie	S.T.	203	North Sea	C.U.	—	
	Total ... 2		212				
JUNE, 1940							
1	Slasher	S.T.	195	70m. N.E. ¼E. of Humber	A.C.	B.	
1	Renown	F.V.	9	Near Sandetti L.V.	Mine	—	
2	Greynight ...	S.T.	96	54°40′N. 01°30′E.	A.C.	B. & G.	
3	Ocean Lassie ...	Drifter	96	055° 2¾ cables from Outer Ridge Buoy, Harwich	Mine	—	
10	River Ness ...	S.T.	203	8m. N.E. × N. of Skerries	A.C.	B.	
28	Castleton ...	S.T.	211	Vicinity of Orkneys	C.U.	—	
	Total ... 6		810				
JULY, 1940							
4	Remembrance ...	F.V.	7	51°53′N. 01°22′E.	Mine	—	
12	Volante ...	S.T.	255	10m. E. of Hvalbam, Iceland	A.C.	B.	
29	Leach's Romance	F.V.	44	10½m. due S. of Kemp Town	Mine	—	
	Total ... 3		306				

Date	Name	Type	Gross tons	Position	Cause of loss	How lost	Remarks
AUGUST, 1940							
18	Valeria	S.T.	189	035° 8m. from Smalls	A.C.	B.	
28	Flavia	S.T.	202	North Sea	C.U.	—	
	Total ... 2		391				
SEPTEMBER, 1940							
7	Salacon	S.T.	211	114° 5.3m. from Spurn Pt. L.H.	Mine	—	
11	Beathwood ...	S.T.	209	1m. E. of Montrose Coast Guard Look-out	A.C.	B.	
11	Respondo	S.T.	209	Off Old Head of Kin-sale	C.U.	—	
24	Bass Rock ...	S.T.	169	Off Old Head of Kin-sale	A.C.	B.	
	Total ... 4		798				
OCTOBER, 1940							
16	Pride	Motor F.V.	25	Off Scarborough	Mine	—	
17	Albatross ...	F.V.	15	Off Grimsby	Mine	—	
25	Encourage ...	Motor F.V.	45	210° 6½ cables from Breakwater Fort, Plymouth	Mine	—	
25	Windsor	S.T.	222	174° 2.1m. from Spurn Pt.	Mine	—	
25	Carlton	Steam Drifter	207	131¼° 3.5m. from Spurn Pt.	Mine	—	
	Total ... 5		514				
NOVEMBER, 1940							
12	Lord Haldane ...	S.T.	91	Neighbourhood of Bristol Channel	C.U.	—	
DECEMBER, 1940							
2	Kilgerran Castle	S.T.	276	51°21′N. 08°35′W.	A.C.	B.	
17	Carry On	Steam Drifter	93	E. of Nore Sand L.V.	Mine	—	
	Total ... 2		369				
JANUARY, 1941							
12	Strathrye... ...	S.T.	212	50°35′N. 03°59′W.	Mine	—	
12	Oyama	S.T.	340	North Atlantic	C.U.	—	
27	Caerphilly Castle	S.T.	275	52°35′N. 12°00′W.	A.C.	B.	
	Total ... 3		827				
FEBRUARY, 1941							
11	John Dunkin ...	S.T.	202	13m. N. × E. of Buckie	A.C.	B.	
11	Eamont	S.T.	227	58°15′N. 03°26′W.	A.C.	B.	
16	Thomas Deas ...	S.T.	276	273° 4m. from Spurn Pt.	Mine	—	
16	Naniwa	S.T.	340	52°15′N. 12°30′W.	A.C.	B.	
	Total ... 4		1,045				
MARCH, 1941							
11	Aberdeen	S.T.	163	Cardigan Bay	A.C.	B. & G.	
14	Peaceful Star ...	Steam Drifter	94	17m. E.S.E. of Rock-abill L.H.	A.C.	B.	
20	Joan Margaret*...	F.V.	25	River Humber	Mine	—	
20	Bianca	S.T.	174	Irish Sea	A.C.	T.	
23	Elmira	S.T.	197	59°55′N. 03°40′W.	A.C.	B.	

Date	Name	Type	Gross tons	Position	Cause of loss	How lost	Remarks
MARCH, 1941—(Contd.)							
25	ALASKAN	F.V.	21	54°49′N. 01°07′W.	Mine	—	
26	MILLIMUMUL ...	S.T.	287	Nr. Newcastle, N.S.W.	Mine	—	
27	KINCLAVEN ...	S.T.	178	Off Faroes	C.U.	—	
28	KESTREL ..: ...	S.T.	75	N.E. of N. Lundy Lt.	A.C.	B.	
29	KIMBERLEY ...	S.T.	190	Near 62D Buoy, 22m. S.E.of Flamborough Head	A.C.	B.	
29	EXETER	S.T.	165	5m. S.W. of Bally-cotton	A.C.	B.	
29	HORACE E. NUTTEN	S.T.	209	Moray Firth	C.U.	—	
30	NISUS	S.T.	210	Faroese Waters	C.U.	—	
31	HELPMATE ...	Steam Drifter	76	Off Newlyn, Cornwall	C.U.	—	
31	ONTARIO	S.T.	208	60°15′N. 11°00′W.	A.C.	B. & G.	
	Total ... 15		2,272				
APRIL, 1941							
4	WHITBY	S.T.	164	3m. S.S.E. of Black-water L.V.	A.C.	B.	
6	DANELAND... ...	S.T.	289	30m. N. ¼W. of Rath-lin O'Birne Is.	A.C.	B.	
7	SYLVIA	S.T.	213	61°27′N. 05°48′W.	A.C.	B.	
26	COMMANDER HORTON	S.T.	227	Off Iceland	C.U.	—	
	Total ... 4		893				
MAY, 1941							
7	WATERLILY ...	F.V.	12	Bessom Creek, West Mersea	A.C.	B.	
8	WELCOME HOME ...	Ketch	38	Hull	A.C.	B.	
9	TANKERTON TOWERS	S.T.	97	Off St. Goven's L.V.	A.C.	B.	
13	FORT RONA ...	S.T.	203	15m. W.S.W. of Bardsey Is.	A.C.	B.	
	Total ... 4		350				
JUNE, 1941							
5	LAVINIA L.* ...	Steam Drifter	73	Sheerness	A.C.	B.	
15	AUDACIOUS ...	F.V.	7	51°28′N. 00°51′E.	Mine	—	
18	DORIS II	F.V.	6	Off Sheerness	Mine*	—	
	Total ... 3		86				
JULY, 1941							
1	STRATHGAIRN ...	S.T.	211	20m. S.W. of Barra Head (Approx.)	Mine	—	
6	WESTFIELD... ...	S.T.	140	Off St. Goven's Head	A.C.*	—	
10	ISABELLA FOWLIE...	S.T.	196	7m. E.N.E. of Long-stone	A.C.	B.	
17	BEN GLAMAIR ...	S.T.	198	Vicinity of Dunstan-burgh	C.U.	—	
27	BEN STROME ...	S.T.	198	15m. S.E. of Fuglo Is., Faroes	A.C.	B.	
28	STRATHLOCHY ...	S.T.	212	180m. N.W. of Rosa Head, Orkneys	A.C.	B.	
	Total ... 6		1,155				
AUGUST, 1941							
4	ROBERT MAX ...	F.V.	172	36°47′N. 21°15′W.	S.M.	G.	
8	OCEAN VICTOR ...	S.T.	202	Off Iceland	A.C.*	—	

Date	Name	Type	Gross tons	Position	Cause of loss	How lost	Remarks
AUGUST, 1941—(Contd.)							
12	EXPRESS	Motor Fishing Smack	16	1m. S.W. of E. Spaniard Buoy, off Whitstable	Mine	—	
20	JULIET	S.T.	173	30m. S. of Old Head of Kinsale	A.C.	B.	
30	LADYLOVE	S.T.	230	Off Iceland*	C.U.	—	
	Total ... 5		793				
SEPTEMBER, 1941							
7	OPHIR II	S.T.	213	About 15m. from Spurn Pt. in Northern Approach Channel	Mine	—	
8	KING ERIK ...	S.T.	228	Off Iceland	C.U.	—	
19	GLEN ALVA ...	F.V.	6	Off Jenkins Buoy, Southend	Mine	—	
28	MURIELLE	S.T.	96	Approx. 9m. S.W. × S. of Morecambe L.V.	Mine	—	Sank 3m. W. × N. of Blackpool Tower whilst in tow
	Total ... 4		543				
NOVEMBER, 1941							
2	CALIPH	S.T.	226	12m. S. of Old Head of Kinsale	A.C.	B.	
8	CRADOCK	S.T.	204	14m. N.N.E. of St. Abb's Head	A.C.	B.	
16	FERNBANK	S.T.	211	12m. N.W. of Myggenaes, Faroes	A.C.	B.	
	Total ... 3		641				
DECEMBER, 1941							
1	ST. LEONARD No. 1	S.T.	210	60°58′N. 01°10′W. (Approx.)	A.C.	B.	
8	LORD SHREWSBURY	S.T.	167	Entrance to River Humber	Mine*	—	
10	KINCORTH	Steam Drifter	148	082° 7m. from Lynas Pt.	Mine	—	
19	MOUETTE	F.V.	3	Blue Anchor Bay, Minehead	Mine	—	
	Total ... 4		528				
JANUARY, 1942							
29	BRACONBUSH ...	S.T.	204	Off Duncansby Head	Mine*	—	
FEBRUARY, 1942							
22	BELLEVUE	S.T.	156	Off Turnberry L.H. Near Ailsa Craig (Est.)	C.U.	—	
MAY, 1942							
4	LITTLE EXPRESS ...	F.V.	9	½m. S.E. of West Pansand Buoy, Kentish Flats	Mine	—	
14	OUR JANIE... ...	F.V.	19	Brixham	A.C.	—	
	Total ... 2		28				

Date	Name	Type	Gross tons	Position	Cause of loss	How lost	Remarks
JUNE, 1942							
17	MAGGIE	F.V.	6	25m. N.N.E. of N. Foreland	Mine	—	
About 25	BROMELIA ..., ...	S.T.	242	Off Iceland	C.U.	—	
	Total ... 2		248				
JULY, 1942							
2	WHINNYFOLD ...	S.T.	210	15m. S.E. of Langanaes L.V., Iceland	A.C.	B.	
25	LUCILLE M. ...	Motor F.V.	54	42°02′N. 65°38′W.	S.M.	G.	
	Total ... 2		264				
AUGUST, 1942							
2	DUREENBEE ...	S.T.	223	35°55′S. 150°30′E.	S.M.	G.	
About 6	BOMBAY	S.T.	229	62°N. 18°W. (Est.)	C.U.	—	
	Total ... 2		452				
DECEMBER, 1942							
About 25	BEN SCREEL ...	S.T.	195	Off St. Abb's Head	Mine*	—	
MARCH, 1943							
17	E.V.G. (No. RX. 152)	F.V.	16	5m. S. of Rye	Mine	—	
APRIL, 1943							
10	BOY BILLY ...	F.V.	5	235° 6m. from Dungeness	Mine	—	
JUNE, 1943							
26	CRYSTAL	S.T.	149	12m. off Scarborough	Mine	—	
SEPTEMBER, 1943							
1	STRATHLYON ...	S.T.	218	Off Iceland	Mine*	—	
JANUARY, 1944							
30	ALONSO	S.T.	172	North Sea Fishing Grounds	C.U.	—	
JULY, 1944							
5	NOREEN MARY ...	S.T.	207	58°30′N. 05°23′W.	S.M.	G.	
27	ROCHESTER ...	S.T.	165	53°54′N. 00°42′E. (Est.)	Mine	—	
	Total ... 2		372				

Date	Name	Type	Gross tons	Position	Cause of loss	How lost	Remarks
FEBRUARY, 1945							
25	AQUARIUS	S.T.	187	15m. S.E. × E. of Outer Dowsing L.V. (Approx.)	Mine	—	
APRIL, 1945							
20	ETHEL CRAWFORD...	S.T.	200	55°13′N. 05°14′W.	Mine	—	

LIST III

BRITISH MERCHANT AND FISHING VESSELS DAMAGED BY ENEMY ACTION BUT NOT LOST

(Vessels only superficially damaged have not been included).

Date	Name	Type	Gross tons	Position	Cause of damage	How damaged	Remarks
SEPTEMBER, 1939							
16	CITY OF PARIS ...	S.	10,902	52°14'N. 01°43'E.	Mine	--	
21	TEAKWOOD ...	S. Tank	6,014	49°39'N. 06°39'W.	S.M.	T.	
OCTOBER, 1939							
5	MARWARRI	S.	8,063	190° 3½m. from Scar-weather L.V.	Mine	—	
6	LOCHGOIL	M.	9,462	51°24'N. 04°00'W.	Mine	—	
13	STONEPOOL ...	S.	4,803	48°40'N. 15°30'W. (Approx.)	S.M.	G.	
NOVEMBER, 1939							
18	JAMES J. MAGUIRE	M. Tank	10,525	51°46'N. 01°40'E.	Mine	—	
23	DAVISIAN	S.	6,433	Off Nore L.V.	Mine	—	
24	SUSSEX	M.	11,063	S.E. of Southend	Mine	—	
DECEMBER, 1939							
2	ESKDENE	S.	3,829	56°30'N. 01°40'W. (Approx.)	C.U.	—	Mine or S.M. T.
14	ATHELTEMPLAR ...	M. Tank	8,939	55°05'N. 01°07'W.	Mine	—	
17	AGNITA	M. Tank	3,552	50°42'N. 00°44'E.	A.C.	B.	
17	EILEEN WRAY ...	S.T.	227	Off Hartlepool	A.C.	B. & G.	
17	CRAIGIELEA ...	S.T.	211	90m. N.E. × E. ½E. of Aberdeen	A.C.	B. & G.	
18	ASTROS	S.T.	275	115m. E. × N. of May Island	A.C.	B.	
18	NEW CHOICE ...	S.T.	236	115m. E. × N. of May Island	A.C.	B. & G.	
18	ETRURIA	S.T.	373	20m. S.E. ½E. of Duncansby Head	A.C.	B. & G.	
19	STAR OF SCOTLAND	S.T.	203	10m. S.E. of Fetlar Is., Shetlands	A.C.	B. & G.	
21	DOSINIA	M. Tank	8,053	½m. S.W. of Hais-boro' L.V.	Mine	--	
22	GRYFEVALE ...	S.	4,434	3m. E. of Tyne Piers	Mine	—	
26	ADELLEN ...	M. Tank	7,984	51°30'N. 01°43'E.	Mine	--	
28	SAN DELFINO ...	M. Tank	8,072	In Humber	Mine	—	
JANUARY, 1940							
6	CITY OF MARSEILLES	S.	8,317	1½m. S.E. of No. 1 Black Buoy, River Tay	Mine	—	
9	CHRYSOLITE ...	S.T..	251	8m. N.W. × N. of Smith's Knoll L.V.	A.C.	B. & G.	
9	RECULVER (Trinity House Vessel)	M.	683	Off Great Yarmouth	A.C.	B. & G.	
9	NORTHWOOD ...	S.	1,146	Off Whitby	A.C.	B. & G.	

Date	Name	Type	Gross tons	Position	Cause of damage	How damaged	Remarks
JANUARY, 1940—(*Contd.*)							
11	FLAVIA	S.T.	202	90m. N.E. × E. of Buchanness	A.C.	B. & G.	
11	PITWINES	S.	932	25m. S.E. × S. of Flamboro' Head	A.C.	B. & G.	
12	PERSIAN EMPIRE ...	S.T.	195	7m. E. × N. of Filey	A.C.	B.	
12	BLYTHMOOR ...	S.	6,582	54°16′N. 00°10′W.	A.C.	B.	
15	GRACIA	S.	5,642	5m. W.S.W. of Bar L.V., Mersey	Mine	—	
15	KILDALE	S.	3,877	2m. E. of S. Shiphead Buoy, off the Naze	Mine	—	
29	IMPERIAL MONARCH	S.	5,831	062° 10m. from Scurdyness	A.C.	B. & G.	
29	GRIPFAST	S.	1,109	10m. S.E. × E. ½S. of Flamboro' Head	A.C.	B. & G.	
30	ROYAL CROWN ...	S.	4,364	15m. S. of Smith's Knoll L.V.	A.C.	B. & G.	
30	JERSEY QUEEN	S.	910	53°06′N. 01°30′E.	A.C.	B. & G.	
FEBRUARY, 1940							
3	KILDALE	S.	3,877	53°47′N. 00°34′E.	A.C.	B. & G.	
3	YEWDALE	S.	823	4m. N.N.E. of Scarborough	A.C.	B. & G.	
3	BEECHWOOD ...	S.	4,897	3m. E. of Smith's Knoll L.V.	A.C.	B. & G.	
3	HARLEY	S.	400	8m. S.S.E. of Flamboro' Head	A.C.	B. & G.	
3	NEWMINSTER ...	S.	967	54°49′N. 01°03′E.	A.C.	B. & G.	
3	ROSE OF ENGLAND	S.T.	223	5 to 6m. E. of Scarborough Castle	A.C.	B. & G.	
3	NAIRANA	S.T.	225	54°00′N. 02°20′E.	A.C.	B. & G.	
9	BOSTON TRADER ...	M.	371	½m. S.E. × S. of Blakeney Bell Buoy	A.C.	B. & G.	
9	FOREMOST 102 ...	Hopper Barge	833	4m. W. of Bell Rock	A.C.	B. & G.	
9	CLINTONIA	S.	3,106	2m. E. of Flamboro' Head	A.C.	B. & G.	
9	LAURIESTON ...	S.	1,304	7m. E. of Coquet Island	A.C.	B. & G.	
9	CREE	S.	4,791	5m. E. of Rattray Head	A.C.	B. & G.	
9	LOWDOCK	S.T.	276	2½m. E. of Scarborough	A.C.	B. & G.	
11	IMPERIAL TRANSPORT	M. Tank	8,022	59°N. 12°W. (Approx.)	S.M.	T.	
MARCH, 1940							
2	DOMALA	M.	8,441	30m. E. of St. Catherine's Pt., I.O.W.	A.C.	B.	
4	CHARLES F. MEYER	M. Tank	10,516	50°28′N. 00°16′E.	Mine	—	
17	EMERALD	S.T.	150	80m. E. × N. of Spurn Lt.	A.C.	G.	
20	THISTLEBRAE ...	S.	4,747	North Sea	A.C.	B.	
20	NORTHERN COAST...	S.	1,211	58°53′N. 02°00′W. (Approx.)	A.C.	B. & G.	Attacked again on 29th
28	PRINCESS ROYAL ...	S.T.	213	40m. S.S.W. of Bressay Lt., Shetlands	A.C.	B. & G.	
29	NORTHERN COAST...	S.	1,211	10m. N.N.E. of Kinnaird Head	A.C.	B. & G.	Previously attacked on 20th
APRIL, 1940							
20	WESTERN PRINCE...	M.	10,926	Near Edinburgh Channel L.V., Thames Estuary	A.C.	G.	
25	SEMINOLE	M. Tank	10,389	51°29′N. 04°07′W.	Mine	—	

Date	Name	Type	Gross tons	Position	Cause of damage	How damaged	Remarks
APRIL, 1940—(Contd.)							
26	CREE	S.	4,791	52°53'N. 02°19'E.	Mine	—	
27	SCOTTISH AMERICAN	S. Tank	6,999	58°41'N. 04°40'W.	S.M.	T.	
27	DELIUS	M.	6,065	Romsdalsfjord	A.C.	B.	Attack continued on 28th
MAY, 1940							
20	BALTEAKO	S.	1,328	Narvik	A.C.	B.	
22	DUNSTER GRANGE...	M.	9,494	49°20'N. 08°40'W.	S.M.	T. & G.	
26	YEWDALE	S.	823	French Channel Coast	Shelled by shore battery	—	Shelled again and attacked by A.C. on 28th
27	BIARRITZ	S.	2,388	Dunkirk	Shelled by shore battery	—	
30	FULHAM IV ...	S.	1,584	Off Orfordness	A.C.	B.	
30	PRINCESS MAUD ...	S.	2,883	Off Gravelines	Shelled by shore battery	—	
JUNE, 1940							
1	PRAGUE	S.	4,220	115° 13m. from N. Foreland	A.C.	B.	
2	KATREEN	S.T.	104	54°30'N. 01°40'E.	A.C.	B. & G.	
2	ROYAL DAFFODIL ...	M.	2,060	51°13'N. 02°00'E.	A.C.	B. & G.	
3	WORTHING (Hospital Ship)	S.	2,294	Off Dunkirk	A.C.	B.	
7	EROS	T.-E.	5,888	55°33'N. 08°26'W.	S.M.	T.	
11	ATHELPRINCE ...	M. Tank	8,782	43°24'N. 13°20'W.	S.M.	T.	
19	GOLDEN GRAIN ...	M. Barge	101	Felixstowe	A.C.	—	
24	CLAN ROSS... ...	S.	5,897	43°54'N. 01°53'W.	A.C.	B.	
30	CLAN OGILVY ...	S.	5,802	46°17'N. 14°35'W.	S.M.	T.	
30	HELDER	S.	979	Off St. Catherine's Pt., I.O.W.	E.-Boat	T. & G.	
JULY, 1940							
1	ZARIAN	S.	4,871	48°03'N. 11°11'W.	S.M.	T.	
2	BARON RUTHVEN ...	S.	3,178	50°25'N. 01°27'W.	A.C.	B.	
4	BRITISH CORPORAL	S. Tank	6,972	50°13'N. 02°35'W. (Approx.)	E.-Boat	T.	
4	FAIRWATER ...	S.	4,108	50°16'N. 02°14'W.	A.C.	B. & G.	
4	FLIMSTON	S.	4,674	Off Portland	A.C.	B.	
4	ANTONIO	S.	5,225	20m. S.S.W. of Portland Bill	A.C.	B.	
4	EASTMOOR	S.	5,812	314° 12m. from Portland Bill	A.C.	B.	
4	ARGOS HILL ...	S.	7,178	Off Portland	A.C.	B. & G.	
4	CITY OF MELBOURNE	S.	6,630	In Portland Harbour	A.C.	B.	
4	KING FREDERICK ...	S.	5,106	50°10'N. 02°33'W.	A.C.	B.	
4	IRENE MARIA ...	S.	1,860	50°30'N. 02°00'W. (Approx.)	A.C.	B.	
4	BRIARWOOD ...	S.	4,019	Off Portland	A.C.	B.	
4	LIFLAND	S.	2,254	Off Portland	A.C.	B.	
4	EAST WALES ...	S.	4,358	In Portland Harbour	A.C.	B.	
4	WILLIAM WILBERFORCE	M.	5,004	In Portland Harbour	A.C.	B.	
5	HARTLEPOOL ...	S.	5,500	16m. S.S.W. of Portland Lt.	E.-Boat	T.	
6	APRICITY	M.	402	South of Portland Bill	A.C.	B.	Previously attacked by aircraft on 4th
8	EASTWOOD	S.	1,551	1m. N. of 20D Buoy, Hartlepool	A.C.	B.	
8	CORUNDUM ...	S.	929	7m. S.W. of Folkestone	A.C.	B.	
9	SAN FELIPE ...	S.	5,919	Roath Docks, Cardiff	A.C.	B.	

Date	Name	Type	Gross tons	Position	Cause of damage	How damaged	Remarks
JULY, 1940—*(Contd.)*							
9	KENNETH HAWKSFIELD	S.	1,546	Dover Area	A.C.	B.	
9	POLGRANGE ...	S.	804	51°46′N. 01°46′E.	A.C.	B. & G.	
9	EMPIRE DAFFODIL	M.	398	13m. S.S.W. of Portland	A.C.	B.	
10	BRITISH CHANCELLOR	S. Tank	7,085	Off Falmouth	A.C.	B.	
11	KYLEMOUNT ...	S.	704	10m. W. of Dartmouth	A.C.	B.	
11	PERU	M.	6,961	Portland Harbour	A.C.	B.	
11	ELEANOR BROOKE...	S.	1,037	Portland	A.C.	B.	
12	JOSEWYN	S.	1,926	8m. W.N.W. of St. Catherine's Pt., I.O.W.	A.C.	B. & G.	
14	MONS	S.	641	1½m. S. of Dover Pier	A.C.	B. & G.	
18	LODDON	S.T.	200	51°05′ N. 08°35′ W.	A.C.	B.	
18	GENERTON	S.	4,797	North Sea	A.C.	B.	
20	WESTOWN	S.	710	Off Dover	A.C.	B.	
22	SWYNFLEET ...	S.	1,168	53°33′N. 00°56′E.	A.C.	B.	
24	ALERT (Trinity House Vessel)	S.	793	Nr. S. Goodwin L.V.	A.C.	B. & G.	
25	TAMWORTH ...	S.	1,332	Off Dover	A.C.	B.	
25	NEWMINSTER ...	S.	967	Off Dover	A.C.	B.	
25	HODDER	S.	1,016	Off Dover	A.C.	B.	
25	SUMMITY	M.	554	Off Dover	A.C.	B.	
25	GRONLAND	S.	1,264	Off Dover	A.C.	B. & G.	Attacked again by aircraft on 29th and sunk
27	WESTAVON	S.	2,842	52°01′N. 01°51′E.	A.C.	B.	
28	MATHURA	S.	8,890	Aden	A.C.	B.	
AUGUST, 1940							
1	CITY OF CANBERRA	S.	7,484	52°06′N. 01°52′E.	Mine	—	
1	KERRY HEAD ...	S.	825	4m. E.S.E. of Old Head of Kinsale (Approx.)	A.C.	B.	
1	GOTHIC	S. Tank	2,444	310° 12m. from Flamboro' Head	A.C.	B.	
1	HIGHLANDER ...	S.	1,216	56°56′N. 02°04′W.	A.C.	B. & G.	
2	ALEXIA	M. Tank	8,016	55°30′N. 15°30′W.	S.M.	T. & G.	
2	LUCERNA	M. Tank	6,556	55°18′N. 16°39′W.	S.M.	T.	
4	WHITE CREST ...	S.	4,365	Off Cape Wrath	A.C.	B.	
8	POLLY M.	M.	380	190° 15m. from Newhaven	E-Boat	G.	
8	SCHELDT	M.	497	15m. W. of St. Catherine's Pt., I.O.W.	A.C.	B.	
8	BALMAHA	S.	1,428	15m. W. of St. Catherine's Pt., I.O.W.	A.C.	B.	
8	JOHN M.	M.	500	10m. S. of Needles, I.O.W.	E-Boat	G.	Also bombed by aircraft
10	BLAIRCLOVA ...	S.	5,083	20m. N.N.E. of Holyhead	A.C.	B.	
11	KIRNWOOD ...	S.	3,829	52°27′N. 02°10′E.	A.C.	B.	
11	OILTRADER ...	S. Tank	5,550	071° 3½m. from Shipwash L.V.	A.C.	B.	
12	ERMINE	S.T.	181	Off Smalls	A.C.	B. & G.	
12	KERNEVAL	S.T.	172	Off Smalls	A.C.	B. & G.	
12	RIVER YTHAN ...	S.T.	161	Off Smalls	A.C.	B. & G.	
16	CLAN FORBES ...	S.	7,529	Tilbury Dock	A.C.	B.	
16	LOCH RYAN ...	Aux.	210	40m. N.W. × N. of Longships Lt.	A.C.	B. & G.	
17	ST. PATRICK ...	S.	1,922	St. George's Channel	A.C.	B. & G.	
17	YEWKYLE	S.	824	52°27′N. 05°45′W.	A.C.	B. & G.	
18	LYSTER	Dredger	619	Brunswick Dock, Liverpool	A.C.	B.	
19	WALDINGE	S.	2,462	Milford Haven	A.C.	B.	

Date	Name	Type	Gross ·tons	Position	Cause of damage	How damaged	Remarks
AUGUST, 1940—(Contd.)							
20	MACVILLE	S.	666	Blacksod Bay	A.C.	B.	
20	PEEBLES	M.	4,982	20m. E. of Tuskar Rock, Irish Sea	A.C.	B. & G.	
20	OUR MAGGIE ...	M.T.	17	Brixham	A.C.	B.	
21	ALACRITY	M.	554	Falmouth	A.C.	B.	
21	WOLSELEY	S.T.	159	9m. W. of Smalls Lt. (Approx.)	A.C.	G.	
23	BEACON GRANGE ...	M.	10,119	58°17'N. 02°27'W.	A.C.	B.	
23	HAVILDAR	S.	5,407	55°39'N. 07°18'W.	S.M.	T.	
23	OVERTON	S.	426	Off Bardsey Island	A.C.	B.	
25	STAKESBY	S.	3,900	23m. N. of Butt of Lewis	S.M.	T.	
25	HAMPSHIRE COAST	M.	485	6m. S.W. of St. Ann's Lt.	A.C.	B. & G.	
25	OSSIAN	S.	1,514	51°39'N. 05°51'W.	A.C.	B. & G.	
25	SANFRY	S.	946	50°26'N. 00°22'W.	A.C.	B.	Subsequently attacked by E-Boat on 26th
26	CITY OF HANKOW...	S.	7,360	Off Peterhead	A.C.	B.	
27	SIR JOHN HAWKINS	S.	930	Plymouth	A.C.	B.	
28	HARTISMERE ...	S.	5,498	56°04'N. 13°06'W.	S.M.	T.	
29	BALTISTAN ...	S.	6,803	55°06'N. 15°39'W.	A.C.	G.	
30	S.H.3	Hopper Barge	389	Victoria Dock, Hull	A.C.	B.	
30	ANADARA	M. Tank	8,009	56°15'N. 09°10'W.	S.M.	T.	
31	CORNWALL	S.	11,288	258° 6m. from Elephonisi Island (S. of Crete)	A.C.	B.	
31	BRITISH ENERGY ...	M. Tank	7,209	Birkenhead	A.C.	B.	
31	ATHELVISCOUNT ...	M. Tank	8,882	Cammell Laird Yd., River Mersey	A.C.	B.	
SEPTEMBER, 1940							
2	LAGOSIAN	S.	5,412	13m. E.S.E. of Peterhead	A.C.	B.	
2	ASHBY	S.	4,868	Off Rattray Head	A.C.	B.	
4	EWELL	S.	1,350	North Sea	E-Boat	G.	
5	MELBOURNE STAR...	M.	12,806	53°27'N. 15°12'W.	A.C.	B. & G.	
6	GANNET	S.	1,336	57°25'N. 01°45'W.	A.C.	B.	
6	IWATE	S.T.	314	53°30'N. 14°00'W.	A.C.	G.	
6	ILFRACOMBE ...	S.T.	165	51°20'N. 11°22'W.	A.C.	G.	
7	BARONESA	S.	8,663	Port of London	A.C.	B.	
7	GOTHLAND	S.	1,286	Port of London	A.C.	B.	
7	BENNEVIS	S.	5,264	Port of London	A.C.	B.	
7	UMGENI	S.	8,180	Port of London	A.C.	B.	
7	GLENSTRAE... ...	S.	9,460	Port of London	A.C.	B.	
7	KNITSLEY	S.	2,272	Port of London	A.C.	B.	
7	UMTALI	S.	8,162	Port of London	A.C.	B.	Attacked again by aircraft on 11th
7	INANDA	S.	5,985	Port of London	A.C.	B.	Attacked again by aircraft on 8th and 9th
7	INKOSI	S.	6,618	Port of London	A.C.	B.	
7	FRUMENTON ...	S.	6,675	Port of London	A.C.	B.	
7	HETTON	S.	2,714	Port of London	A.C.	B.	
7	EASTWOOD	S.	1,551	Port of London	A.C.	B.	
7	WILLIAM CASH ...	S.	1,186	Port of London	A.C.	B.	
7	OTAIO	M.	10,298	Port of London	A.C.	B.	
8	TYNEMOUTH ...	S.	3,168	Port of London	A.C.	B.	
8	SHERWOOD... ...	S.	1,530	Port of London	A.C.	B.	
9	RYAL	M.	367	Port of London	A.C.	B.	
11	NORMAN QUEEN ...	S.	957	Port of London	A.C.	B.	
11	ALEXIA	M. Tank	8,016	57°56'N. 02°02'E.	A.C.	B.	
11	HARPENDEN ...	S.	4,678	55°34'N. 15°56'W.	S.M.	T.	
12	GLENROY	M.	9,809	Liverpool	A.C.	B.	
12	TINTERN ABBEY ...	S.	2,471	270° 6m. from Chicken Rock, Isle of Man	A.C.	B. & G.	

Date	Name	Type	Gross tons	Position	Cause of damage	How damaged	Remarks
SEPTEMBER, 1940—*(Contd.)*							
13	INISHTRAHULL ...	S.	869	Belfast Lough	A.C.	B.	
15	CORONDA	S. Tank	7,503	58°07′N. 09°24′W.	A.C.	B.	
15	REGENT LION ...	M. Tank	9,551	N. Channel, off Mull of Kintyre	A.C.	B. & G.	
15	STANWOLD	S.	1,020	Southampton	A.C.	B.	
15	WEST HARSHAW ...	S.	5,756	North Channel, Irish Sea	A.C.	B. & G.	
18	RUDMORE	S.	969	Gravesend Reach	A.C.	B.	
18	LING	S.B.	164	N. Morpeth Docks, Liverpool	A.C.	B.	
19	WEST KEDRON ...	S.	5,621	North Channel, Irish Sea	A.C.	B. & G.	
20	BHIMA	M.	5,280	13°57′N. 42°53′E.	A.C.	B.	
21	BROOMPARK ...	S.	5,136	55°08′N. 18°30′W.	S.M.	T.	
21	ENCHANTRESS ...	S.B.	56	London Docks	A.C.	B.	
22	COLLEGIAN	S.	7,886	320m. W. of Malin Head	S.M.	G.	
23	CORINIA	S.	870	Gravesend Reach	A.C.	B.	
23	PACIFIC GROVE ...	M.	7,117	5m. N.W. of Tory Island	A.C.	B. & G.	
26	ASHANTIAN ...	S.	4,917	55°10′N. 11°00′W. (Approx.)	S.M.	T.	
26	WELSH PRINCE ...	S.	5,148	57°37′N. 01°34′W.	A.C.	B.	
26	DIPLOMAT	S.	8,240	Brunswick Dock, Liverpool	A.C.	B.	
26	PETERTON	S.	5,221	Brunswick Dock, Liverpool	A.C.	B.	
26	WELLINGTON ...	Tug	285	Liverpool	A.C.	B.	
26	WEST KEDRON ...	S.	5,621	Liverpool	A.C.	B.	
26	SUVA	S.	4,873	57°30′N. 01°32′W.	A.C.	B.	
28	QUEEN CITY ...	S.	4,814	58°10′N. 02°19′W.	A.C.	B.	
30	SUSSEX	M.	11,063	54°20′N. 15°32′W.	A.C.	B. & G.	
30	MOUNTPARK ...	S.	4,648	57°24′N. 01°35′W.	A.C.	B.	
30	EMPIRE SUCCESS ...	S.	6,009	5m. E. of Peterhead	A.C.	B.	
30	BARON VERNON ...	S.	3,642	52°40′N. 17°56′W.	A.C.	B. & G.	
30	KERMA	S.	4,333	57°24′N. 01°35′W.	A.C.	B.	
30	HENRY DUNDAS ...	M. Tank	10,448	Mersey River Anchorage	A.C.	B.	
OCTOBER, 1940							
2	TREHATA	S.	4,817	Off Peterhead	A.C.	B.	
3	FRAMLINGHAM ...	S.T.	169	20m. S. of Fastnet	A.C.	B.	
3	IWATE	S.T.	314	5m. N.W. of Mizzen Hd.	A.C.	B. & G.	
5	ORTOLAN	S.	489	Free Trade Wharf, Stepney	A.C.	B.	
6	HULL TRADER ...	S.	717	London Docks	A.C.	B.	
6	FIRECREST	S.	538	2½m. S.W. of Sunk L.V., Thames Estuary	A.C.	B. & G.	
8	ORONSAY	S.	20,043	56°N. 10°W. (Approx.)	A.C.	B. & G.	
10	TILL	M.	367	51°36′N. 01°12′E.	Mine	—	
11	THYRA II	S.	1,088	Off East Barrow L.V., Thames Estuary	Mine	—	
11	CLAN MACTAGGART	S.	7,622	Liverpool	A.C.	B.	
11	CLAN CUMMING ...	S.	7,264	Liverpool	A.C.	B.	
11	HIGHLAND CHIEFTAIN	M.	14,135	Liverpool	A.C.	B.	
11	VIRGILIA	S. Tank	5,723	Liverpool	A.C.	B.	
11	INVER	S.	1,543	Straits of Dover	Shelled by Shore Battery	—	
11	BANNTHORN ...	S.	429	Rathlin O'Birne Sound, Eire	A.C.	G.	
12	STARLING	S.	1,320	4m. S.W. of San Sebastian Lt.	A.C.	B. & G.	

Date	Name	Type	Gross tons	Position	Cause of damage	How damaged	Remarks
OCTOBER, 1940—(Contd.)							
12	LONGSCAR	S.T.	215	Off Hartlepool	A.C.	B.	
13	CARGO FLEET No. 2	Hopper Barge	1,130	1 cable W. of Datum Buoy, off Tees	Mine	—	
15	BRITISH GLORY ...	M. Tank	6,993	57°10′N. 08°36′W.	S.M.	T.	
16	ACTIVITY	M.	358	51°31′N. 00°55′E.	Mine	—	
17	ETHYLENE	S.	936	½m. N.N.E. of East Oaze Lt. Buoy	Mine	—	
17	GEORGE BALFOUR...	S.	1,570	230° 12,900 yds. from Aldeburgh L.V.	Mine	—	
17	P.L.M. 14	S.	3,754	52°52′N. 02°06′E.	E-Boat	T.	
17	GASFIRE	S.	2,972	52°52′N. 02°06′E.	E-Boat	T.	
17	CARSBRECK ...	S.	3,670	58°46′N. 14°11′W.	S.M.	T.	
18	KING ATHELSTAN ...	S.T.	159	About 15m. off Mizzen Head	A.C.	B. & G.	
18	BLAIRSPEY	S.	4,155	57°55′N. 11°10′W.	S.M.	T.	Torpedoed again on 19th
20	CONAKRIAN... ...	S.	4,876	130° 9m. from Girdleness	A.C.	T.	
20	ATHELMONARCH ...	M. Tank	8,995	56°45′N. 15°58′W.	S.M.	T.	
20	CITY OF ROUBAIX...	S.	7,108	Alexandria Dock, Liverpool	A.C.	B.	
23	EMPIRE ABILITY ...	S.	7,603	Gareloch	A.C.	B.	
25	JANET	Motor F.V.	25	Montrose Quay	A.C.	B.	
27	ALFRED JONES ...	M.	5,013	56°00′N. 12°08′W.	A.C.	B.	
27	CONISTER	S.	411	Queen's Dock, Liverpool	A.C.	B.	
27	NEWLANDS ...	S.	1,556	45°10′N. 10°00′W.	A.C.	B.	
31	STARSTONE ...	S.	5,702	54°12′N. 15°32′W.	A.C.	B.	
NOVEMBER, 1940							
3	EROS	T.E.	5,888	57°48′N. 01°54′W.	A.C.	T.	
3	WINDSOR CASTLE ...	S.	19,141	54°12′N. 13°18′W.	A.C.	B.	
3	CAIRNGORM... ...	M.	394	Bristol Channel	Mine	—	
5	SAN DEMETRIO ...	M. Tank	8,073	52°48′N. 32°15′W.	Raider	—	
5	ANDALUSIAN ...	S.	3,082	North Atlantic	Raider	—	
6	HARBOROUGH ...	S.	5,415	076° 9m. from Noss Head	A.C.	B.	
7	DAGO II	S.	1,993	51°32′N. 01°06′E.	A.C.	B.	
7	MEDEE	S.	2,163	51°10′N. 01°12′E.	A.C.	B.	
8	EMPIRE DORADO ...	S.	5,595	55°07′N. 16°50′W.	A.C.	B.	
8	FIREGLOW	S.	1,261	S.W. of Swin Buoy, Thames Estuary	A.C.	B. & G.	
8	EWELL	S.	1,350	51°43′N. 01°23′E.	A.C.	B. & G.	
8	CATFORD	S.	1,568	S.W. of Swin Buoy, Thames Estuary	A.C.	G.	
9	EMPRESS OF JAPAN	S.	26,032	53°54′N. 14°28′W.	A.C.	B.	
9	BEAL	M.	504	Off Tees	Mine	—	
9	SHELBRIT II ...	M. Tank	695	Alongside Cleveland Wharf, Shoreham	A.C.	B.	
11	CORSEA	S.	2,764	Barrow Deep	A.C.	B.	
11	COLONEL CROMPTON	S.	1,495	Barrow Deep	A.C.	B.	
11	PITWINES	S.	932	N.E. of Yarmouth	A.C.	B.	
11	CORDUFF	S.	2,345	Barrow Deep Channel	A.C.	B.	
11	HARLAW	S.	1,141	Off Aberdeen	A.C.	B.	
11	GRIT	M.	501	200 yds. S.W. × S. of Margate Buoy	Mine	—	
11	IWATE	S.T.	314	35m. S. × W. of Old Head of Kinsale	A.C.	B. & G.	
13	BRITISH PRESTIGE...	M. Tank	7,106	Off Humber Boom	Mine	—	
14	FAIRY	M.	207	Nr. Chequer Buoy, off Mouth of Humber	Mine	—	
14	FISHPOOL	M.	4,950	55°00′N. 17°04′W. (Approx.)	A.C.	B.	

Date	Name	Type	Gross tons	Position	Cause of damage	How damaged	Remarks
NOVEMBER, 1940—(Contd.)							
16	SHERBROOKE	S.	2,052	8m. S.E. of Orford-ness	A.C.	B. & G.	
16	DAGENHAM	S.	2,178	2½ cables E.N.E. of Mouse L.V.	Mine*	—	
18	S.N.A.8	S.	2,569	Off Swin L.V.	A.C.	B.	
18	LANGLEETARN	S.	4,908	Thames Estuary	A.C.	B.	
18	BIELA	S.	5,298	52°26′N. 16°31′W.	A.C.	B.	
18	EL NAWRAS	S. Tank	323	Alexandria	A.C.	B.	
19	FOLDA	S.	1,165	51°47′N. 01°30′E.	A.C.	B.	
20	CHESAPEAKE	M. Tank	8,955	Off Lizard	A.C.	B. & G.	
22	ZAHRA	S. Tank	821	Alexandria	A.C.	B.	
23	LLANDOVERY CASTLE	S.	10,640	Southampton	A.C.	B.	
23	DUCHESS OF CORNWALL	S.	302	Alongside Royal Pier, Southampton	A.C.	B.	
24	CAMROUX IV	M.	590	045° 1m. from East Oaze L.V.	Mine	—	Previously slightly damaged by air-craft on 20th
24	LENT LILY	M.T.	44	6m. E.S.E. of Wolf Rock	E-Boat*	G.	
27	GALACUM	S.	585	51°34′N. 01°09′E.	Mine	—	
27	CHARMOUTH	S.T.	195	Off Milford Haven	A.C.	B. & G.	
27	RATTRAY	S.T.	182	Off Milford Haven	A.C.	G.	
27	CHARLES F. MEYER	M. Tank	10,516	56°00′N. 13°52′W.	S.M.	T.	
28	SKIPJACK	S.	1,167	Dover	Shelled by Shore Battery	—	
29	FERMAIN	S.	759	Dover	Shelled by Shore Battery	—	
DECEMBER, 1940							
1	LOCH RANZA	S.	4,958	54°37′N. 18°54′W.	S.M.	T.	
2	DUNSLEY	S.	3,862	54°41′N. 18°41′W.	S.M.	G.	
3	ROBRIX	M.	292	110° 2m. from Spurn Pt. L.H.	Mine	—	
3	WILLIAM DOWNES	S.T.	275	5m. W.N.W. of Skel-ligs	A.C.	B. & G.	
3	SLEBECH	S.T.	222	5m. W.N.W. of Skel-ligs	A.C.	G.	
3	QUEBEC CITY	S.	4,745	North Atlantic, off Irish Coast	A.C.	G.	
5	WATERLAND	S.	1,107	Dover	Shelled by Shore Battery	—	
7	YEWARCH	S.	827	Off Dudgeon Buoy, Humber	A.C.	B. & G.	
7	HERTFORD	S.	10,923	35°30′S. 135°25′E.	Mine	—	
8	TREVERBYN	S.	5,281	59°00′N. 14°24′W.	A.C.	B. & G.	
11	SAXON QUEEN	M.	482	Near Sunk Head Buoy, Thames Es-tuary	A.C.	B.	
13	ORARI	M.	10,350	49°50′N. 20°55′W.	S.M.	T.	
14	EMPIRE RAZORBILL	S.	5,118	59°31′N. 13°15′W.	S.M.	G.	
16	BIC ISLAND	S.	3,921	54°12′N. 17°45′W.	A.C.	B.	
18	TWEED	S.	2,697	53°40′N. 04°40′W.	A.C.	B. & G.	
20	OVERDALE	Hopper Barge	315	Liverpool	A.C.	B.	
20/21	EUROPA	M.	10,224	Liverpool	A.C.	B.	
20/21	LAPLACE	S.	7,327	Liverpool	A.C.	B.	
20/21	EASTERN PRINCE	M.	10,926	Liverpool	A.C.	—	
20/21	JOHN A. BROWN	M. Tank	10,455	Liverpool	A.C.	B.	Also struck a mine on same date
20/21	ROXBURGH CASTLE	M.	7,801	Liverpool	A.C.	B.	
21	ALPERA	S.	1,777	Liverpool	A.C.	B.	
21	CITY OF CORINTH	S.	5,318	Liverpool	A.C.	B.	
21	DEMETERTON	S.	5,251	Liverpool	A.C.	B.	

Date	Name	Type	Gross tons	Position	Cause of damage	How damaged	Remarks
DECEMBER, 1940—*(Contd.)*							
21/22	LLANGIBBY CASTLE	M.	11,951	Liverpool	A.C.	B.	
21/22	MAHRONDA ...	S.	7,926	Liverpool	A.C.	B.	
21/22	DEUCALION... ...	M.	7,516	Liverpool	A.C.	B.	
22	ELAX	M. Tank	7,403	Off No. 10 Buoy, Liverpool	Mine	—	
22	PARDO	M.	5,400	Liverpool	A.C.	B.	
22	LLANDILO ...	S.	4,966	Between Nos. 2 and 3 Yantlet Buoys, Thames Estuary	Mine	—	
22	ALMEDA STAR ...	S.	14,935	Liverpool	A.C.	B.	
22	No. 9	Hopper Barge	671	Liverpool	A.C.	B.	
23	PACIFIC PIONEER ...	M.	6,734	Manchester	A.C.	B.	
23	IWATE	S.T.	314	52°55′N. 12°20′W.	A.C.	B. & G.	
23	FLYNDERBORG ...	S.	2,022	Oban	A.C.	B. & G.	
23	LUPINA	Drifter	88	Oban	A.C.	B.	
24	PETERTON	S.	5,221	54°51′N. 13°13′W.	A.C.	B. & G.	
25	EMPIRE TROOPER ...	S.	13,994	43°58′N. 24°15′W.	Raider	—	
27	LADY CONNAUGHT...	S.	2,284	53°37′N. 03°43′W.	Mine	—	
27	VICTORIA	S.	1,641	290° 8m. from Bar L.V., Mersey	Mine	—	
28	LOCHEE	M.	964	4m. N.E. × N. of Bar L.V., Mersey	Mine	—	
28	CANUTE	Tug	271	Southampton	A.C.	B.	
29	TREVARRACK ...	S.	5,270	55°34′N. 09°30′W.	A.C.	B. & G.	
29	CATRINE	M.	5,218	Liverpool Bay	Mine	—	Struck a second mine on 30th near Q.1 Buoy Queen's Channel, Liverpool
30	DORCASIA	M. Tank	8,053	250° 3m. from Bar L.V., Mersey	Mine	—	
31	BRITISH ZEAL ...	M. Tank	8,532	15°40′N. 20°43′W.	S.M.	T.	
JANUARY, 1941							
1	ATTENDANT ...	S.	1,016	1 cable E. of 9 Buoy, Sheerness	Mine	—	
2	LOCH DEE ...	S.	5,252	Cardiff	A.C.	B.	
5	TEMPLE MOAT ...	S.	4,427	55°29′N. 18°55′W.	A.C.	B. & G.	
9	DORSET COAST ...	M.	646	51°24′N. 03°08′W.	Mine	—	
11	BRITISH FIDELITY...	M. Tank	8,465	51°22′N. 03°05′W.	Mine	—	
11	GREYFRIARS ...	S.	1,142	1m. W. of 59A Buoy, off Grimsby	A.C.	B.	
13	WOOLER	M.	507	Victoria Wharf, Plymouth	A.C.	B.	
15	MAYWOOD	S.	1,823	51°21′N. 03°16′W.	Mine	—	
15	KARRI	M.	354	2m. N. of Bar L.V., Mersey	Mine	—	
15	STALKER	S.T.	197	Hawke Roads, Grimsby	A.C.	B.	
16	GLADONIA	M.	360	Off Sunk L.V., Thames Estuary	A.C.	B.	
16	ROMSEY	S.	509	51°41′N. 05°09′W.	Mine	—	
16	SKJOLD	S.	1,345	N. of Lundy Island	A.C.	B.	
16	LLANWERN ...	S.	4,966	Avonmouth	A.C.	B.	
16/17	ESSEX	M.	11,063	Malta	A.C.	B.	
17	ATHELDUKE ...	M. Tank	8,966	51°21′N. 03°20′W.	Mine	—	
19	CLAN CUMMING ...	S.	7,264	Off Piræus	S.M.	T.	
19	ZELO	S.	2,294	Off Sunk L.V., Thames Estuary	A.C.	B.	
20	VASCO	S.	2,878	Athens	A.C.	B.	
20	TREGARTHEN ...	S.	5,201	55°54′N. 07°00′W.	A.C.	B.	
22	JAMAICA PLANTER...	M.	4,098	196° 2,500 yds. from Nell's Pt., Barry Island	Mine	—	
24	TASMANIA	M.	6,405	090° 11½m. from Rattray Head	Mine*	—	

Date	Name	Type	Gross tons	Position	Cause of damage	How damaged	Remarks
JANUARY, 1941—(*Contd.*)							
26	GWYNWOOD ...	S.	1,177	Abreast No. B.3 Buoy, Barrow Deep	A.C.	B.	
26	CATFORD	S.	1,568	Off Oaze Bank	Mine	—	
26	GRANGETOFT ...	S.	975	Off B.4 Buoy, Barrow Deep	A.C.	B. & G.	
26	SANDHILL	M.	586	53°43′N. 03°15′W.	Mine	—	
28	TAFELBERG... ...	S. O.R.	13,640	51°21′N. 03°16′W.	Mine	—	Reconstructed as tanker and renamed EMPIRE HERITAGE
28	BARON RENFREW ...	S.	3,635	55°50′N. 10°18′W.	A.C.	B.	
29	WESTMORELAND ...	S.	8,967	270° 3m. from Bar L.V., Mersey	Mine	—	
31	DORSETSHIRE (Hospital Ship)	M.	9,717	Gulf of Sollum	A.C.	B.	Attacked again on 1st February
31	DESMOULEA ...	M. Tank	8,120	35°31′N. 02°34′E.	Destroyer or E-Boat	T.	
FEBRUARY, 1941							
2	WAZIRISTAN ...	S.	5,135	61°21′N. 11°12′W.	A.C.	B.	
3	DERWENTHALL ...	M.	4,934	Suez Canal	Mine	—	
3	CALYX	M.	212	8m. N.E. of Bar L.V., Mersey	Mine	—	
7	SCOTTISH CO-OPERATOR	M.	513	2m. S.W. of Workington Pier, Solway Firth	Mine	—	
9	CRISTA	M.	2,590	Tobruk Harbour	Mine	—	
10	BENMACDHUI ...	S.	6,869	52°42′N. 02°00′E.	A.C.	B.	
11	CANTICK HEAD ...	S.	488	30m. N.W. of Kinnaird Head	A.C.	G.	
12	LORNASTON ...	S.	4,934	37°12′N. 21°20′W.	Raider	—	
13	WESTCLIFFE HALL...	S.	1,900	010° 2¼m. from Whitby High Lt.	A.C.	B.	
13	CAPE RODNEY ...	S.	4,512	Off Girdleness	A.C.	B.	
14	MOORLANDS ...	S.	420	2m. N. of Sands End Bay, off Banff	A.C.	B. & G.	Bombed again on 20th in Buckie Harbour
15	STOCK FORCE ...	S.	983	Nr. Outer Dowsing Float, Humber	A.C.	B.	
19	FULHAM II... ...	S.	1,596	Off Tyne Piers	Mine	—	
19	ATHELSULTAN ...	M. Tank	8,882	120° 2¼m. from May Island	A.C.	B.	
19/20	QUEENFORTH ...	Tug	204	Swansea	A.C.	B.	
20	D. L. HARPER ...	M. Tank	12,223	58°50′N. 12°12′W.	A.C.	B.	
20	SCARBOROUGH ...	S.T.	162	52°15′N. 11°45′W.	A.C.	B. & G.	
20	BRITISH SPLENDOUR	M. Tank	7,138	1½m. S. of Black Head, Nr. Lizard	A.C.	B.	
20	ST. ROSARIO ...	S.	4,312	58°50′N. 11°40′W.	A.C.	B. & G.	Bombed again on 22nd in position 59°40′N. 12°40′W.
20	ROSENBORG ...	S.	1,997	58°49′N. 11°40′W.	A.C.	B. & G.	
22	LUXOR	M. Tank	6,554	Swansea	A.C.	B.	
22	KINGSTON HILL ...	S.	7,628	59°44′N. 12°33′W.	A.C.	B.	
22	KEILA	S.	3,621	59°44′N. 12°33′W.	A.C.	B.	
25	TYNEFIELD ...	M. Tank	5,856	Tobruk	A.C.	B.	
26	EMPIRE STEELHEAD	S.	7,744	080° 10m. from Cromarty	A.C.	B. & G.	
26	DIALA	M. Tank	8,106	55°50′N. 14°00′W.	S.M.	T.	
26	MELMORE HEAD ...	S.	5,273	55°07′N. 16°00′W.	A.C.	B.	
26	LEEDS CITY ...	S.	4,758	54°00′N. 17°45′W.	A.C.	B.	
26	HOPTON	S.T.	202	6m. E.S.E. of Girdleness	A.C.	B. & G.	
27	BLACKTOFT ...	S.	1,109	51°57′N. 01°40′E.	A.C.	B.	
27	CAPE CLEAR ...	M.	5,085	53°27′N. 04°01′W.	Mine	—	
27	NEWLANDS ...	S.	1,556	Barrow Deep	A.C.	B.	

Date	Name	Type	Gross tons	Position	Cause of damage	How damaged	Remarks
MARCH, 1941							
1	FORTHBANK ...	S.	5,057	57°53′N. 01°57′W.	A.C.	B.	
1	EMPIRE SIMBA ...	S.	5,691	52°21′N. 05°23′W.	A.C.	B.	
1	ATHELTEMPLAR ...	M. Tank	8,949	57°04′N. 01°50′W.	A.C.	B.	
4	RUTH II	M.	321	2 cables N.N.E. of Bar L.V., Mersey	Mine	—	
4	EAST COAST ...	S.T.	192	Off Fastnet	A.C.	B. & G.	
4	ANGLIAN COAST ...	M.	594	075° 2 cables from Bar L.V., Mersey	Mine	—	
4	LYNDIS KITWOOD...	Pilot Cutter	20	Off Skegness	Mine	—	
6	EILIAN HILL ...	S.	781	Off Nell's Point, Barry Island	Mine	—	
7	DELILIAN	S.	6,423	60°28′N. 13°38′W.	S.M.	T.	
9	ESMOND	S.	4,976	57°21′N. 01°38′W.	A.C.	B.	
9	SYLVIA BEALE ...	S.	1,040	5m. E.N.E. of Dungeness	A.C.	B.	
11	ROYAL STAR ...	S.	7,900	Stonehaven	A.C.	B. & G.	
11/12	CONTRACTOR ...	S.	6,004	Manchester	A.C.	B.	
11/12	NOVELIST	S.	6,133	Manchester	A.C.	B.	
11/12	MARKHOR	S.	7,917	Manchester	A.C.	B.	
12	CAMROUX I ...	M.	324	Off Blyth	Mine	—	
12	ESSEX LANCE ...	S.	6,625	51°03′N. 01°38′E.	A.C.	B. & G.	
12/13	CATRINE	M.	5,218	Liverpool	A.C.	B.	
12/13	IMPERIAL STAR ...	M.	12,427	Liverpool	A.C.	B.	
12/13	ELAX	M. Tank	7,403	Liverpool	A.C.	B.	
12/13	EL MIRLO	M. Tank	8,092	Liverpool	A.C.	B.	
13	NGATIRA	M.	525	51°21′N. 03°17′W.	Mine	—	
13	WEARWOOD ...	S.	4,597	Liverpool	A.C.	B.	
13	MYRMIDON	M.	6,278	Liverpool	Mine	—	
13	MOUNTSTEWART ...	S.	1,099	Liverpool	A.C.	B.	
13/14	CLERMISTON ...	S.	1,448	Glasgow	A.C.	B.	
13/14	TREVARRACK ...	S.	5,270	Clyde	A.C.	B.	
14	MINEGARTH ...	Tug	179	Liverpool	A.C.	B.	
14	SCOTTISH CHIEF ...	S. Tank	7,006	Liverpool	A.C.	B.	
14	EMPIRE SIMBA ...	S.	5,691	Liverpool	Mine	—	
15	WARRIOR	Tug	249	Clyde	Mine	—	
15	ERODONA	M. Tank	6,207	61°20′N. 17°00′W.	S.M.	T.	
16	FRANCHE COMTE ...	M. Tank	9,314	61°15′N. 12°30′W.	S.M.	T.	
17	CORMEAD	S.	2,848	52°20′N. 02°00′E.	A.C.	B. & G.	
17	PIONEER (Trinity House Vessel)	Pilot Cutter	281	B.3 Buoy, Thames Estuary	A.C.	B. & G.	
19	NAILSEA MEADOW...	S.	4,962	Victoria Dock, London	A.C.	B.	
19	TOTTENHAM ...	S.	4,762	Southend Anchorage	Mine	—	
19/20	TELESFORA DE LARRINAGA	S.	5,780	Victoria Dock, London	A.C.	B.	
19/20	LINDENHALL ...	S.	5,248	Victoria Dock, London	Mine	—	
20	CHARLIGHT ...	Tug	40	Off Le Bas Wharf, Millwall	A.C.	B.	
20	MARI II	S.	1,395	Plymouth	A.C.	B.	
21	HALO	S.	2,365	Off Beckton Pier	Mine	—	
22	DASHWOOD ...	S.	2,154	Barrow Deep	A.C.	B.	
23	CITY OF LINCOLN ...	S.	8,039	Grand Harbour, Malta	A.C.	B.	
23	PERTHSHIRE ...	S.	10,496	Grand Harbour, Malta	A.C.	B.	
23	SAMURAI	S.T.	221	30m. N.N.W. of St. Kilda	A.C.	B. & G.	
24	MARIE MAERSK ...	M. Tank	8,271	Eastern Mediterranean	A.C.	B.	
26	KINGSWAY	S.T.	211	10m. E. of Bell Rock	A.C.	B.	
26	BALUCHISTAN ...	S.	6,992	Eastern Mediterranean	A.C.	B.	
26	THE LADY BELLE...	S.	331	10m. S. of Grassholm Island	A.C.	B. & G.	

Date	Name	Type	Gross tons	Position	Cause of damage	How damaged	Remarks
MARCH, 1941—(Contd.)							
27	PALMSTONE ...	Salvage Vessel	430	2m. S.E. of St. Goven's L.V.	A.C.	B.	
27	FORT DEE	S.T.	212	61°31'N. 05°04'W.	A.C.	B. & G.	
28	STAFFORDSHIRE ...	M.	10,683	59°30'N. 10°18'W.	A.C.	B.	
29	GRENAA	S.	1,262	Off Rotherhithe	Mine	—	
31	RATTRAY	S.T.	182	2m. S.E. × E. of Hook Pt.	A.C.	B. & G.	
APRIL, 1941							
1	ADELLEN	M. Tank	7,984	7 cables from Sea Buoy, Milford Haven	A.C.	B.	
1	CHESAPEAKE ...	M. Tank	8,955	10m. S.W. of St. Goven's Head	A.C.	B. & G.	Also attacked earlier same day 15m. N. of Smalls
2	MELROSE ABBEY ...	S.	1,908	River Ythan (N. of Aberdeen)	Mine	—	
2	WILD ROSE ...	S.	873	12m. S.E. of Tuskar L.H.	A.C.	B.	
3	GEDDINGTON COURT	S.	6,903	56°25'N. 02°13'W.	A.C.	B.	
3	ASSUAN	S.	499	56°42'N. 02°26'W.	A.C.	B. & G.	
4	CAPE VERDE ...	M.	6,914	52°12'N. 05°42'W.	A.C.	B. & G.	
6	GLENFINLAS ...	S.	7,572	52°01'N. 01°47'E. (Approx.)	A.C.	B. & G.	
6	CINGALESE PRINCE	M.	8,474	Piraeus	A.C.	B.	
6	DEVIS	M.	6,054	Piraeus	A.C.	B.	
7	KIRNWOOD ...	S.	3,829	51°47'N. 01°30'E.	A.C.	B. & G.	
8	CORMARSH ...	S.	2,848	Off Sheringham Buoy	A.C.	B.	
8	CHAUCER	S.	5,792	Nr. Humber L.V.	A.C.	B.	Attacked again on 9th
9	KYLEGORM ...	S.	622	245° 4m. from St. Ann's Head	A.C.	B.	
9	BRITISH WORKMAN	S. Tank	6,994	58°31'N. 02°40'W.	A.C.	B. & G.	
9	ABERHILL	S.	1,516	54°37'N. 00°48'W.	A.C.	B. & G.	
9	PERSIA	Tug	165	Shellhaven, London	Mine	—	
9	BRITISH STATESMAN	S. Tank	6,991	Off Harwich	A.C.	B.	
9	PANDORIAN ...	S.	4,159	140° 15m. from Duncansby Head	A.C.	B.	
10	THIRLBY	S.	4,887	140m. N.N.W. of Butt of Lewis	A.C.	B. & G.	
10	BUSIRIS	S.	943	Off Runnelstone, Mounts Bay	A.C.	B.	
12	DARTFORD	S.	4,093	1½m. S. of Mumbles Lt.	A.C.	B.	
13	BARON BELHAVEN	S.	6,591	51°33'N. 05°32'W.	A.C.	B.	
16	KING ATHELSTAN ...	S.T.	159	3m. off Ballinskelligs	A.C.	B.	
17	ETHEL RADCLIFFE	S.	5,673	Near Cross Sands L.V., off Great Yarmouth	E-Boat	T.	Subsequently sunk by A.C. on May 16th
18	SCOTTISH MUSICIAN	M. Tank	6,998	205° 3m. from St. Ann's Head	A.C.	B.	
20	R. S. JACKSON ...	Spritsail Barge	60	London	A.C.	B.	
21	BRITISH LORD ...	S. Tank	6,098	34°35'N. 23°32'E.	A.C.	B.	
21	BRITISH RENOWN ...	M. Tank	6,997	3m. S.E. of Dartmouth	A.C.	B.	
21	REGENCY	Tug	76	Off Ford's, Dagenham	Mine	—	
21	ALPHA	F.V.	11	Whittaker Channel, Essex	Mine	—	
21	MAIDSTONE ...	S.	688	Plymouth	A.C.	B.	
22	ANTONIO	S.	5,225	Off T.2 Buoy, Tyne	A.C.	B.	
22	CROHAM	S.	391	Peterhead	A.C.	B.	
23	MISS ELAINE ...	Salvage Vessel	364	Plymouth	A.C.	B.	
24	DOLIUS	M.	5,507	56°35'N. 02°11'W.	A.C.	B. & G.	
26	SCOTTISH PRINCE ...	M.	4,917	36°07'N. 24°30'E.	A.C.	B.	

Date	Name	Type	Gross tons	Position	Cause of damage	How damaged	Remarks
APRIL, 1941—*(Contd.)*							
28	MARIE DAWN ...	S.	2,157	Off Sheringham Buoy	A.C.	B. & G.	
28	EMPIRE STRAIT ...	S.	2,824	Off Yarmouth	A.C.	B.	
29	CORGLEN	S.	2,822	½m. N.N.E. of T.2 Buoy, Tyne	A.C.	B.	
29	PROWESS	M.	207	Off Projector Buoy, Humber	Mine	—	
MAY, 1941							
1	SEA FISHER ...	S.	2,950	55°34'N. 01°28'W.	Mine*	—	
3	TACOMA STAR ...	S.	7,924	Liverpool	A.C.	B.	
3	CANTAL	S.	3,178	Liverpool	A.C.	—	
3/4	BARONESA ...	S.	8,663	Liverpool	A.C.	B.	
3/4	LOBOS	M.	6,479	Liverpool	A.C.	B.	
3/4	WAPITI	Tug	208	Liverpool	A.C.	B.	
3/4	MAHOUT	S.	7,921	Liverpool	A.C.	—	
3/4	SAN FABIAN ...	S. Tank	13,031	Stanlow, Liverpool	A.C.	B.	
3/4	BUSIRIS	S.	943	Liverpool	A.C.	B.	
3/4	LIMPET	S.B.	164	Liverpool	A.C.	B.	
3/4	OYSTER	S.B.	133	Liverpool	A.C.	—	
3/4	CLAM	S.B.	159	Liverpool	A.C.	B.	
3/4	GLITTO	S.B.	166	Liverpool	A.C.	B.	
4	BISON	Tug	274	Liverpool	A.C.	B.	
4	TALTHYBIUS ...	S.	10,254	Liverpool	A.C.	B.	Bombed again on the 8th
4	HORNBY	Tug	201	Liverpool	A.C.	—	
4	ENID BLANCH ...	Tug	99	Liverpool	A.C.	—	
4	No. 33	Hopper Barge	718	Liverpool	A.C.	B.	
4	ROXBURGH CASTLE	M.	7,801	Liverpool	A.C.	B.	
4/5	BONGO	S.B.	46	LIVERPOOL	A.C.	B.	
5	SHEPPERTON FERRY	S.	2,839	Belfast	A.C.	B.	
5	SILVERSANDAL ...	M.	6,770	Liverpool	A.C.	B.	Previously slightly damaged on 3rd
5	CLAN MACINNES ...	S.	4,672	Liverpool	A.C.	B.	
5	CAPE BRETON ...	S.	6,044	Belfast	A.C.	B.	
6	INDUSTRIA ...	S.	4,861	Liverpool	A.C.	B.	
8	ROYAL DAFFODIL II (Ferry)	M.	591	Liverpool	A.C.	B.	
8	BARON INCHCAPE ...	S.	7,005	Liverpool	A.C.	B.	Previously slightly damaged between 3rd and 6th
8	No. 20	Camel Barge	703	Liverpool	A.C.	B.	
9	OSTREVENT... ...	S.	1,737	E. of Helwick L.V.	A.C.	B.	
9	EMPIRE CLOUD ...	S.	5,969	61°00'N. 32°30'W.	S.M.	T.	
9	ALEXANDRA ...	S.B.	84	Hull	A.C.	B.	
9	DAN-Y-BRYN ...	S.	5,117	Hull	A.C.	B.	
9	CASTILIAN ...	S.	3,067	Hull	A.C.	B.	
9	FISHPOOL ...	M.	4,950	Barrow	A.C.	B.	
9/10	SAN ROBERTO ...	S. Tank	5,890	22m. E. × N. of Spurn Pt.	A.C.	B.	
9/10	BRITISH STATESMAN	S. Tank	6,991	22m. E. × N. of Spurn Pt.	A.C.	B.	
10	AELYBRYN	S.	4,986	59°23'N. 35°25'W.	S.M.	T.	
10	TOWER FIELD ...	S.	4,241	Off Outer Dowsing Buoy	A.C.	B.	
10	HENRY WARD ...	Sludge Vessel	1,438	In Dry Dock, Green & Silley Weir, London	A.C.	B.	
11	CAITHNESS ...	M.	4,970	52°03'N. 05°24'W.	A.C.	B.	
11	DENCADE	Tug	58	Brixham	A.C.	B.	
11	SILVER LINING ...	F.V.	40	Brixham	A.C.	B.	
13	LOTTINGE	S.	2,468	Off Tyne	A.C.	B. & G.	
14	CAPE HORN ...	M.	5,643	Port Said	A.C.	B. & G.	
16	JOFFRE ROSE ...	S.	715	Off St. David's Head	A.C.	B. & G.	Bombed again on 18th in Dale Bay
16	OBSIDIAN	S.	811	52°06'N. 05°25'W.	A.C.	B. & G.	

Date	Name	Type	Gross tons	Position	Cause of damage	How damaged	Remarks
MAY, 1941—(*Contd.*)							
17	Arthur Wright ...	S.	1,091	5m. S. of Shoreham	A.C.	B. & G.	
17	Aba (Hospital Ship)	M.	7,938	50m. S. of Crete	A.C.	B.	
18	Eskburn	S.	472	Off Blyth	A.C.	B.	
19	Dixcove	M.	3,790	51°36′N. 01°11′E.	Mine	—	
20	San Felix ...	S. Tank	13,037	57°32′N. 40°21′W.	S.M.	T.	
22	Empire Progress...	S.	5,249	3m. S.W. of Needles	A.C.	B. & G.	
24	Octane	M. Tank	2,034	50°08′N. 05°02′W.	Mine	—	
24	Sarnia	S.	711	Milford Haven	A.C.	B. & G.	
24	Cressdene ...	S.	4,270	Mumbles Roads	A.C.	B. & G.	
26	Gros Pierre ...	S.	297	Off Sunderland	A.C.	B.	
26	H. E. Stroud ...	S.T.	214	135° 10m. from Lamb Head, Stromsay	A.C.	B. & G.	
30	Kyleclare ...	S.	700	Off Limerick	A.C.	B.	
30	Sangara	M.	5,445	Accra Harbour	S.M.	T.	
JUNE, 1941							
2	Ben Screel ...	S.T.	195	55°30′N. 01°30′W.	A.C.	B.	
3	Dennis Rose ...	S.	1,600	About 5m. W. × S. of Start Pt.	A.C.	B.	
6	Emulator	S.T.	168	7 to 8m. E. of Scarborough	A.C.	B.	
8	Ensis	M. Tank	6,207	48°46′N. 29°14′W.	S.M.	T.	
8/9	Remagio ...	S.T.	174	Nr. Bamburgh	A.C.	B.	
10	Clearpool ...	S.	5,404	Off 18B Buoy, Scarborough	A.C.	B. & G.	
10	Durenda	M.	7,241	Approaching Port Said	A.C.	B.	
11	Westburn ...	S.	2,842	3m. N. of Skinningrove, off Hartlepool	A.C.	B.	
13	Empire Creek ...	S.	332	57°16′N. 01°43′W.	A.C.	B.	
13	Dalemoor	S.	5,796	57°04′N. 01°51′W.	A.C.	B.	
16	Atlantic ...	S.T.	167	3m. S.E. of Eddystone	A.C.	B.	
17	Jim	S.	833	Off T.2 Buoy, Tyne	A.C.	B.	
20	Inverarder ...	S. Tank	5,578	Off Isle of Wight	A.C.	B.	
20	Ilse	S.	2,844	W. side of Hartlepool Approach Channel	Mine	—	
20	Cormount ...	S.	2,841	Off Outer Dowsing L.V.	A.C.	T.	
23	Camroux 11 ...	M.	324	1m. N.E. of No. 17 Buoy, Flamboro' Head	Mine	—	
23	Tolworth	S.	1,351	53°05′N. 01°25′E.	A.C.	B.	
24	Levenwood ...	S.	803	Tees Bay	A.C.	B.	
25	Isle of Wight ...	S.T.	176	Off Scarborough	A.C.	B.	
29	Silverlaurel ...	S.	6,142	King George Dock, Hull	A.C.	B.	
29	Empire Meteor ...	S.	7,457	53°05′N. 01°30′E.	A.C.	B.	
30	Empire Larch ...	Tug	487	Off Gt. Yarmouth	A.C.	B.	
JULY, 1941							
1	Highwood ...	S.	1,177	Barry	A.C.	B.	
1	Jamaica Planter...	M.	4,098	Barry	A.C.	B.	
4	Goldfinch ...	M.	454	270° 10m. from St. Bee's Head, Solway Firth	Mine	—	
5	North Devon ...	S.	3,658	Off Sheringham	A.C.	B.	
11	River Trent ...	M.	246	53°00′N. 01°15′E.	Mine	—	
13	Scorton	S.	4,813	2m. off 57C Buoy, Smith's Knoll	A.C.	B.	
14	Georgic	M.	27,759	Suez Bay	A.C.	B.	
16	Elizabete	S.	2,039	Between 20C Buoy and T.2 Buoy, Tyne	A.C.	B.	

Date	Name	Type	Gross tons	Position	Cause of damage	How damaged	Remarks
JULY, 1941—(Contd.)							
17	EMERALD QUEEN ...	M.	481	54°39′N. 00°48′W.	A.C.	B.	
18	PILAR DE LARRINAGA	S.	7,046	54°23′N. 16°53′W.	A.C.	B. & G.	
20	CANADIAN STAR ...	M.	8,293	49°15′N. 21°00′W.	S.M.	G.	
20	UMVUMA	S.	4,419	Nr. 57 Buoy, off Humber	A.C.	B.	
23	ADAMANT	Barge	80	Hull	Mine	- -	
23	SOAVITA	Barge	80	Hull	Mine	—	
24	SYDNEY STAR ...	M.	12,696	Mediterranean	E-Boat	T.	
26	ATLANTIC CITY ...	M.	5,133	55°42′N. 09°58′W.	S.M.	T.	
31	ONWARD	S.T.	209	20m. E. of Nolso, Faroes	A.C.	B. & G.	
AUGUST, 1941							
2	KOOLGA	S.	1,110	Nr. 54D Buoy, Smith's Knoll	A.C.	B.	
3	DESMOULEA ...	M. Tank	8,120	Off W. Beacon, Suez	A.C.	T.	
8	GOLD SHELL ...	M. Tank	8,208	53°05′N. 01°32′E.	A.C.	B.	
9	GLENDALOUGH ...	S.	868	52°59′N. 01°53′E.	A.C.	B.	
12	EAGLESCLIFFE HALL	S.	1,900	2m. E. of Sunderland (Approx.)	A.C.	B.	
17	KINDERSLEY ...	S.	1,999	3m. S.E. × E. of B.1 Buoy, off Blyth	A.C.	B.	
20	DALEWOOD ...	S.	2,774	53°11′N. 01°05′E.	E-Boat	T.	
22	DURHAM	M.	10,893	W. of Pantellaria	Mine	—	
28	DONOVANIA ...	M. Tank	8,149	3m. S.S.W. of St. Ann's Head	A.C.	B.	
SEPTEMBER, 1941							
3/4	HARPALYCUS ...	S.	5,629	Off Ashrafi Reef, Gulf of Suez	A.C.	B.	
6	STANMOUNT ...	S. Tank	4,468	Off Gt. Yarmouth	A.C.	B.	
7	NAIRANA	S.T.	225	7 to 8m. off Myggenaes, Faroes	A.C.	B.	
10	TAHCHEE	S. Tank	6,508	61°15′N. 41°05′W.	S.M.	T.	
11	CORMEAD	S.	2,848	52°33′N. 02°05′E.	A.C.	B.	Attacked again on 12th
11	WAR GREY ...	S.T.	246	Off Sunderland	A.C.	B.	
15	PONTFIELD ...	M. Tank	8,290	53°03′N. 01°20′E.	Mine	—	
15	ATLANTIC COCK ...	Tug	182	Off Dalmuir Basin, Clyde	Mine	—	
17	TETELA	S.	5,389	53°04′N. 01°34′E.	E-Boat	T.	
19	PRESTATYN ROSE ...	S.	1,151	3m. N.E. of Sunk Buoy, off Harwich	A.C.	B.	
20	DURHAM	M.	10,893	Gibraltar	Italian Assault Craft	—	
24	DALTONHALL ...	M.	7,253	51°45′N. 05°16′W.	Mine	—	
26	ORIOLE	M.	489	Off S. Bishops, Cardigan Bay	Mine	—	
30	CEDARWOOD ...	S.	899	Off Dover	A.C.	B.	
OCTOBER, 1941							
1	SERENITY	M.	557	10m. S.E. × E. of St. Goven's L.V.	A.C.	B. & G.	
2	SOUTHPORT ...	S.	572	South Shields	A.C.	B.	
6	SALAMAUA	M.	6,676	Anchorage, Straits of Jubal, Suez	A.C.	B.	
7	SVEND FOYN ...	S. O.R.	14,795	60°37′N. 21°44′W.	S.M.	T.	
11	ICEMAID	S.	1,964	Nr. Shipwash L.V., off Harwich	Mine	—	

Date	Name	Type	Gross tons	Position	Cause of damage	How damaged	Remarks
OCTOBER, 1941—(Contd.)							
16	Edenvale	M.	444	Off Old Head of Kinsale	A.C.	B.	
20	Cordelia	M. Tank	8,190	In convoy Anchorage, Milford	Mine	—	
NOVEMBER, 1941							
1	Kingsland ...	S.	3,669	North Sea	A.C.	B.	
2	Thyra III ...	S.	828	Great Yarmouth Roads	A.C.	B.	
2	Agility	S. Tank	522	Great Yarmouth Roads	A.C.	B.	
5	Glencree	S.	481	15m. S.W. of Bishops Lt.	A.C.	B. & G.	
8	Gaslight	S.	1,696	2 cables S.E. of S.1 Buoy, off Sunderland	A.C.	B.	
12	Ben Screel ...	S.T.	195	14m. N.E. × N. of St. Abb's Head	A.C.	B.	
24	Blairnevis ...	S.	4,155	52°20′N. 01°59′E.	E-Boat	T.	
24	Ardenza	S.	933	10m. S.E. of Orfordness	A.C.	B.	
DECEMBER, 1941							
10	Anshun	M.	3,188	Manila Harbour	A.C.	B.	
10	Anhui	S.	3,494	Outer Harbour, Manila	A.C.	B.	
13	Myriel	S. Tank	3,560	31°03′N. 29°00′E.	S.M.	T.	
19	Lucellum	M. Tank	9,425	270° 5m. from Bardsey Island	A.C.	B.	
22	Nam Yong... ...	S.	1,345	Port Swettenham, Malaya	A.C.	B.	
24	Eastwood	S.	1,551	270° 2½m. from Aldeburgh Lt.	Mine	—	
25	Charles Parsons...	S.	1,554	8m. N. of Hartlepool (Approx.)	A.C.	B.	
25	Sheaf Mount ...	S.	5,017	North Atlantic	A.C.	B.	
JANUARY, 1942							
5	Scottish Musician	M. Tank	6,998	52°16′N. 01°59′E.	Mine	—	
5	Largo	S.	2,209	1m. S.E. × E. of 54E Buoy, off Southwold	Mine	—	
6	Loddon	S.T.	200	N.W. of 18D Buoy, off Whitby	A.C.	B.	
8	Craig-an-Eran ...	S.T.	202	Off Old Head of Kinsale	A.C.	B. & G.	
13	Empire Masefield	S.	7,023	54°22′N. 00°19′W.	A.C.	B.	
16	Toorak	S. Tank	8,627	47°54′N. 52°11′W.	S.M.	T.	
16	Llangibby Castle	M.	11,951	46°04′N. 19°06′W.	S.M.	T.	
17	Harmatris... ...	S.	5,395	69°16′N. 36°00′E.	S.M.	T.	
28	Idar	S.	391	10°12′N. 80°13′E.	S.M.	G.	Also set on fire by boarding party
29	Fairnilee	Tug	226	Falmouth	A.C.	B.	
29	Northgate Scot ...	Tug	174	Falmouth	A.C.	B.	
31	Empire Redshank	S.	6,615	63°24′N. 02°24′W.	A.C.	B. & G.	
31	Longwood ...	M. Tank	9,463	290° 20m. from Outer Buoy, Colombo	S.M.	T.	
FEBRUARY, 1942							
1	Sedulity	M.	490	Off Cromer	A.C.	B. & G.	
3	Spondilus	M. Tank	7,402	06°16′N. 79°38′E.	S.M.	T. & G.	

Date	Name	Type	Gross tons	Position	Cause of damage	How damaged	Remarks
FEBRUARY, 1942—(*Contd.*)							
3	MADURA	S.	9,032	Dutch East Indies	A.C.	B.	
4	AQUARIUS	S.T.	187	5m. E. × N. of Aberdeen	A.C.	B. & G.	
5	HELDER	S.	979	3½m. E. of Humber Light Float	A.C.	B. & G.	
6	BLUSH ROSE ...	S.	645	3m. S. of St. Ann's Head	A.C.	B.	
10	LIEUTENANT ROBERT MORY	S.	3,176	5m. W. of Trevose Head	A.C.	B.	
12 About	JALAVIHAR	S.	5,330	Off Singapore	A.C.	B. & G.	
12	ANGLO INDIAN ...	S.	5,609	Dutch East Indies	A.C.	B.	
12	EMPIRE STAR ...	M.	12,656	Durian Straits, Dutch East Indies	A.C.	B.	
13	CLAN CAMPBELL ...	S.	7,255	32°22′N. 24°22′E.	A.C.	B.	
15	EMPIRE HEAD ...	M.	489	34°42′N. 00°54′W.	A.C.	B.	
16	PEDERNALES ...	S. Tank	4,317	Off San Nicholas, Aruba	S.M.	T.	
18	BRITISH CONSUL ...	S. Tank	6,940	10°37′N. 61°34′W.	S.M.	T.	
19	BAROSSA	S.	4,239	Port Darwin	A.C.	B.	
19	MANUNDA (Hospital Ship)	M.	9,115	Port Darwin	A.C.	B. & G.	
20	JALAKRISHNA ...	S.	4,991	Dutch East Indies	A.C.	B.	
22	ENSEIGNE MARIE ST. GERMAIN	S.	3,139	Off Yarmouth	Mine	—	
24	DILOMA	M. Tank	8,146	43°51′N. 43°41′W.	S.M.	T.	
28	BRITISH JUDGE ...	S. Tank	6,735	10m. S. of Princes Island, Dutch East Indies	S.M.	T.	
MARCH, 1942							
5	ALACRITY	M.	554	7m. N.W. of Bishop Rock	A.C.	B.	
7	CERION	M.	2,588	Tobruk	A.C.	B.	
9	LADY NELSON ...	S.	7,970	Castries Harbour, St. Lucia, W. Indies	S.M.	T.	
9	UMTATA	S.	8,141	Castries Harbour, St. Lucia, W. Indies	S.M.	T.	
17	CRISTA	M.	2,590	32°21′N. 25°00′E.	S.M.	T.	
21	ATHELVISCOUNT ...	M. Tank	8,882	38°46′N. 55°44′W.	S.M.	T.	
21	SAN CIRILO ...	M. Tank	8,012	00°40′N. 79°40′E.	S.M.	T.	
24	LANCASTER CASTLE	S.	5,172	Murmansk	A.C.	B.	
25	IMPERIAL TRANSPORT	M. Tank	8,022	46°26′N. 41°30′W.	S.M.	T.	
27	DESTRO	S.	3,553	Tobruk	A.C.	B.	
29	OLTENIA II ...	S. Tank	6,394	18°36′N. 85°33′E.	A.C.	B.	
APRIL, 1942							
5	BENLEDI	S.	5,943	Colombo	A.C.	B.	
6	ANGLO CANADIAN ...	M.	5,268	Vizagapatam Roads, Bay of Bengal	A.C.	B.	
6	ELMDALE	S.	4,872	06°52′N. 78°50′E.	S.M.	G.	
7	SOMERSETSHIRE (Hospital Ship)	M.	9,716	32°13′N. 26°34′E.	S.M.	T.	
9	EMPIRE MOONRISE...	S.	6,854	Colombo	A.C.	B.	
15	GOLLY	S.	627	Malta	A.C.	B.	Again damaged by aircraft on 4th May
MAY, 1942							
1	THISTLEFORD ...	S.	4,781	Port Said	A.C.	B.	
1	LA PAZ	M.	6,548	28°15′N. 80°20′W.	S.M.	T.	

Date	Name	Type	Gross tons	Position	Cause of damage	How damaged	Remarks
MAY, 1942—(Contd.)							
2	DALFRAM	S.	4,558	34°10′S. 17°49′E.	Mine	—	
3	GEO. W. McKNIGHT	M. Tank	12,502	11°18′N. 61°19′W.	S.M.	T. & G.	
4	ECLIPSE	S. Tank	9,767	26°30′N. 80°00′W.	S.M.	T.	
11	BEN IVER	S.T.	197	59°39′N. 09°25′W.	Mine	—	
12	FANO	S.	1,889	Southampton	A.C.	B.	
14	OUR MAGGIE ...	M.T.	17	Brixham Harbour	A.C.	B.	
14	DENCADE	Tug	58	Brixham Harbour	A.C.	B.	
14	BREADWINNER ...	M.T.	59	Brixham Harbour	A.C.	B.	
18	SAN ELISEO ...	M. Tank	8,042	15°30′N. 54°16′W.	S.M.	T.	Further attacks on 19th in positions 14°42′N. 55°02′W. and 14°20′N. 56°22′W.
20	E. P. THERIAULT ...	Sch.	326	24°30′N. 83°55′W.	S.M.	G. and time bombs	
30	BRITISH LOYALTY...	M. Tank	6,993	037° 5 cables from Antsivana L.H., Diego Suarez,Madagascar	S.M.	T.	
JUNE, 1942							
12	CITY OF CALCUTTA...	S.	8,063	Off Mersa Matruh, Mediterranean	A.C.	B.	
14	POTARO	M.	5,410	450m. E. of Malta	A.C.	B.	
16	ORARI	M.	10,350	Entrance to Malta	Mine	—	
20	FORT CAMOSUN ...	S.	7,100	47°22′N. 125°30′W.	S.M.	T.	
22	RECTOR	Tug	106	Southampton	A.C.	B.	
27	BRITISH FREEDOM...	M. Tank	6,985	34°45′N. 75°22′W.	S.M.	T.	
JULY, 1942							
7	MANX KING ...	S.T.	235	10m. N.E. of Fuglo Head, Faroes	A.C.	B. & G.	
14	SHUNA	S.	1,575	Gibraltar	Mine	—	Limpet*
14	EMPIRE SNIPE ...	S.	2,497	120° 1½m. from North Mole Lt., Gibraltar	Mine	—	Limpet*
14	BARON DOUGLAS ...	S.	3,899	343° 14 cables from North Mole Lt., Gibraltar	Mine	—	Limpet
18	SAN GASPAR ...	S. Tank	12,910	10°30′N. 60°27′W.	S.M.	T.	
22	ALLARA	S.	3,279	33°03′S. 152°22′E.	S.M.	T.	
25	BRITISH MERIT ...	M. Tank	8,093	49°03′N. 40°36′W.	S.M.	T.	
AUGUST, 1942							
3	G. S. WALDEN ...	M. Tank	10,627	45°45′N. 47°17′W.	S.M.	T.	
3	EL CIERVO ...	S. Tank	5,841	229° 7m. from Start Pt.	A.C.	T.	
4	KATOOMBA ...	S.	9,424	300m. E.S.E. of Albany, S.W. Pacific	S.M.	G.	
9	ALEXIA	M. Tank	8,016	16°50′N. 60°40′W.	S.M.	T.	Attacked again in position 16°47′N. 60°27′W.
12	BRISBANE STAR ...	M.	12,791	Off Skuki Channel, Mediterranean	A.C.	T.	
13	ROCHESTER CASTLE	M.	7,795	36°28′N. 11°47′E.	E-Boat	T.	Also bombed by A.C.
14	STANDELLA ...	M. Tank	6,197	21°41′N. 76°09′W.	S.M.	T.	
17	LAGUNA	M.	6,466	18°45′N. 75°04′W.	S.M.	T.	
25	KYLOE	S.	2,820	52°27′N. 02°01′E.	Mine	—	
29	MALAITA	M.	3,310	09°50′S. 142°55′E.	S.M.	T.	

Date	Name	Type	Gross tons	Position	Cause of damage	How damaged	Remarks
SEPTEMBER, 1942							
8	Nephrite	S.	927	4½m. E. of Ramsgate	A.C.	B.	
10	F. J. Wolfe ...	M. Tank	12,190	51°30′N. 28°25′W.	S.M.	T.	
11	Cornwallis ...	S.	5,458	13°05′N. 59°36′W.	S.M.	T.	
15	Ravens Point ...	S.	1,787	330° 7 cables from North Mole Lt., Gibraltar	Mine	—	Limpet
16	Essex Lance ...	S.	6,625	49°03′N. 67°08′W.	S.M.	T.	
29	Ocean Vagabond...	S.	7,174	47°31′N. 52°27′W.	S.M.	T.	
OCTOBER, 1942							
13	Martaban	S.	4,161	06°31′N. 82°03′E.	S.M.	T.	
14	George Balfour...	S.	1,570	Vicinity of 58 Buoy, S.E. of Dudgeon Shoal	E-Boat	T.	
NOVEMBER, 1942							
8	Benalder	S.	5,161	04°19′N. 02°44′W.	S.M.	T.	
8	Capo Olmo ...	S.	4,712	10°56′N. 61°14′W.	S.M.	T.	
9	Wandle	S.	1,482	2m. N. of 3C Buoy, Lowestoft	E-Boat	T.	
13	Glenfinlas ...	S.	7,479	Bougie Harbour	A.C.	B.	
14	Lalande	S.	7,453	36°08′N. 03°46′W.	S.M.	T.	
15	Adviser	S.	6,348	32°03′S. 33°52′E.	S.M.	T.	
21	Forest	M.	4,998	Bougie	A.C.	B.	Again bombed at Gibraltar on 11th Dec.
21	British Promise ...	M. Tank	8,443	43°53′N. 55°02′W.	S.M.	T.	
21	British Renown...	M. Tank	6,997	43°53′N. 55°02′W.	S.M.	T.	
23	Scythia ...! ...	S.	19,761	Off Algiers	A.C.	T.	
28	Empire Glade ...	M.	7,006	17°16′N. 48°44′W.	S.M.	G.	
DECEMBER, 1942							
1	Hindustan ...	M.	5,245	Bone	A.C.	B.	
6	Ousel	S.	1,533	Philippeville	A.C.	B. & G.	Attacked again on 11th
12	Empire Centaur...	S.	7,041	Algiers Bay	Italian Assault Craft	--	
12	Harmattan ...	S.	4,558	36°48′N. 03°04′E.	S.M.	T.	
12	Ocean Vanquisher	S.	7,174	36°48′N. 03°04′E.	S.M.	T.	
13	Hororata	S.	13,945	42°03′N. 34°33′W.	S.M.	T.	
15	Period	S.	2,791	Timor Sea	A.C.	B.	
16	Regent Lion ...	M. Tank	9,551	50°49′N. 24°07′W.	S.M.	T.	
22	Cameronia... ...	S.	16,297	37°03′N. 05°24′E.	A.C.	T.	
27	Scottish Heather	S. Tank	7,087	46°15′N. 26°20′W.	S.M.	T.	
JANUARY, 1943							
1	Novelist	·S.	6,133	Bone Harbour	A.C.	B.	
1	Harpalyce ...	M.	7,269	Bone Harbour	A.C.	B.	
2	Dalhanna... ...	S.	5,571	Bone Harbour	A.C.	B.	
7	Ville de Stras-bourg	S.	7,159	37°04′N. 04°06′E.	S.M.*	T.	Subsequently bombed in Algiers Harbour
10	San Cipriano ...	M. Tank	7,966	Off Veleki Point, Kola Inlet	A.C.	B.	
17	Recorder	S.	5,982	Bone	A.C.	B.	
21	Ocean Rider ...	S.	7,178	4½m. W. of Cape Caxine, Algiers	A.C.	T.	

Date	Name	Type	Gross tons	Position	Cause of damage	How damaged	Remarks
FEBRUARY, 1943							
6	FORT BABINE ...	S.	7,135	36°15′N. 00°15′E.	A.C.	T.	
23	BRITISH FORTITUDE	M. Tank	8,482	31°10′N. 27°30′W.	S.M.	T.	
26	EMPIRE PORTIA ...	S.	7,058	69°17′N. 33°20′E.	A.C.	B.	
27	SEMINOLE	M. Tank	10,389	35°53′N. 02°33′W.	S.M.	T.	
MARCH, 1943							
4	SHEAF CROWN ...	S.	4,868	31°49′S. 31°11′E.	S.M.	T.	
4	CHATEAUROUX ...	S.	4,765	41°10′N. 15°10′W.	A.C.	B.	
6	FORT PASKOYAC ...	S.	7,134	36°27′N. 10°17′W.	S.M.	T.	
6	EMPIRE KINSMAN...	S.	6,744	Murmansk	A.C.	B.	
9	FORT NORMAN ...	S.	7,133	36°51′N. 01°09′E.	S.M.	T.	
9	EMPIRE STANDARD	S.	7,047	36°51′N. 01°09′E.	S.M.	T.	
9	COULMORE	S.	3,670	58°48′N. 22°00′W.	S.M.	T.	
14	DUCHESS OF YORK	S.	20,021	305m. S.W. × W. of Cape Finisterre	A.C.	B.	
16	MERCHANT PRINCE	M.	5,229	36°10′N. 00°30′W.	S.M.	T.	
26	BECKENHAM ...	S.	4,636	32°56′N. 13°19′E.	Mine	—	
29	OCEAN VICEROY ...	S.	7,174	46°44′N. 16°38′W.	S.M.	T.	
APRIL, 1943							
4	DOVER HILL ...	S.	5,815	Mishukov Anchorage, Kola Inlet	A.C.	B.	
4	BRITISH GOVERNOR	S. Tank	6,840	Mishukov Anchorage, Kola Inlet	A.C.	B.	
11	NOORA	S.	1,072	Port Harvey, Australia	A.C.	B.	
11	HANYANG ...	S.	2,876	15m. E. of Oro Bay, New Guinea	A.C.	B.	
14	GORGON	M.	3,533	Milne Bay, New Guinea	A.C.	B.	
23	SILVERMAPLE ...	M.	5,313	59°05′N. 35°40′W.	S.M.	T.	
26	EMPIRE MORN ...	S.	7,092	33°52′N. 07°50′W.	Mine*	—	
MAY, 1943							
8	MAHSUD	S.	7,540	Gibraltar	Italian Assault Craft	—	
9	ISLANDER	S.	1,598	Near Cape Arnhem, Northern Territory, Australia	A.C.	B.	
12	ORMISTON	S.	5,832	30°16′S. 153°23′E.	S.M.	T.	
15	CORMULL	S.	2,865	¼ cable W. of No. 7 Buoy, 14m. N.E. of Yarmouth	Mine	—	
18	FORT ANNE ...	S.	7,134	36°35′N. 01°01′E.	S.M.	T.	
24	DENEWOOD... ...	S.	7,280	River Wear, Sunderland	A.C.	B.	
24	EMPIRE DEED ...	S.	6,766	Sunderland	A.C.	B.	
JUNE, 1943							
2	STANDELLA ...	M. Tank	6,197	07°25′N. 13°26′W.	S.M.	T.	
18	LALANDE	S.	7,453	220° 16m. from Cape Espichel, Portugal	A.C.	B.	
JULY, 1943							
9	STANHOPE	S.	2,337	37°10′N. 09°00′W.	A.C.	B.	
12	PORT FAIRY ...	M.	8,337	37°18′N. 14°37′W.	A.C.	B.	
12	DORSETSHIRE ... (Hospital ship)	M.	9,717	286° 13m. from Cape Passaro Lt., Sicily	A.C.	B.	

Date	Name	Type	Gross tons	Position	Cause of damage	How damaged	Remarks
JULY, 1943—(Contd.)							
15	TWICKENHAM ...	S.	4,762	28°36'N. 13°18'W.	S.M.	T.	
16	KAIPARA	M.	5,882	13°30'N. 17°43'W.	S.M.	T.	
19	KAITUNA	M.	4,914	35°15'N. 35°35'E.	Mine	—	Limpet
21	OCEAN VIRTUE ...	S.	7,174	Augusta, Sicily	A.C.	B.	
22	EMPIRE MOON ...	S.	7,472	36°43'N. 15°20'E.	S.M.	T.	
24	LLANDAFF ...	S.	4,825	20m. N.E. of Kildin Island, entrance to Kola Inlet	A.C.	B.	
26	EMPIRE BRUTUS ...	S.	7,233	39°50'N. 13°38'W.	A.C.	B.	
27	EMPIRE HIGHWAY...	M.	7,166	38°04'N. 12°59'W.	A.C.	B.	
29	EMPIRE DARWIN ...	S.	6,765	44°52'N. 16°00'W.	A.C.	B.	
AUGUST, 1943							
4	STANRIDGE ...	S.	5,975	Gibraltar	Italian Assault Craft	—	
13	EMPIRE HAVEN ...	S.	6,852	36°15'N. 02°23'W.	A.C.	T.	
15	BARON FAIRLIE ...	S.	6,706	39°59'N. 12°58'W.	A.C.	B.	
15	OCEAN FAITH ...	S.	7,173	39°05'N. 12°54'W.	A.C.	B.	
23	SPEEDFAST	S.	1,898	Palermo	A.C.	B.	
SEPTEMBER, 1943							
6	FORT DREW ...	S.	7,134	35°52'N. 14°47'E.	Mine	—	
12	LYMINGE	S.	2,499	Off Salerno	A.C.	B.	
25	NAIRANA	S.T.	225	53°54'N. 00°30'E.	A.C.	B.	
OCTOBER, 1943							
4	SAMITE	S.	7,219	36°42'N. 01°17'E.	A.C.	B.	
7	LAURELWOOD ...	M. Tank	7,347	Off Taranto	Mine	—	
20	BRITISH PURPOSE...	M. Tank	5,845	11°49'N. 74°54'E.	S.M.	T.	
23	KERLOGUE	M.	335	100m. S. of Ireland	A.C.	B.	
NOVEMBER, 1943							
4	FIRELIGHT	S.	2,841	52°55'N. 02°00'E. (Approx.)	E.Bt.	T.	
21	DELIUS	M.	6,065	46°46'N. 18°30'W.	A.C.	B.	
DECEMBER, 1943							
2	CRISTA	M.	2,590	Bari	A.C.	—	⎫ Damaged by bombs or by debris following explosion of ammunition ship
2	FORT LAJOIE ...	S.	7,134	Bari	A.C.	—	
2	BRITTANY COAST ...	S.	1,389	Bari	A.C.	—	
3	FORT CAMOSUN ...	S.	7,126	11°23'N. 46°03'E.	S.M.	T.	
5	CLAN MATHESON ...	S.	5,613	Calcutta	A.C.	B.	
31	TORNUS	M. Tank	8,054	19°45'N. 59°10'E.	S.M.	T. & G.	
31	EMPIRE HOUSMAN...	M.	7,359	60°30'N. 24°35'W.	S.M.	T.	Torpedoed again on 3rd Jan., 1944, and sunk
JANUARY, 1944							
2	LARGS BAY ...	S.	14,182	Approaches to Naples	Mine	—	
11	TRIONA	S.	7,283	00°03'N. 80°43'E.	S.M.	T.	
24	LEINSTER ... ... (Hospital Carrier)	M.	4,303	41°19'N. 12°36'E.	A.C.	B.	
24	ST. ANDREW ... (Hospital Carrier)	S.	2,702	41°10'N. 12°26'E.	A.C.	B.	
29	FORT LOUISBOURG	S.	7,130	Surrey Commercial Dock, London	A.C.	B.	

Date	Name	Type	Gross tons	Position	Cause of damage	How damaged	Remarks
FEBRUARY, 1944							
9	KELMSCOTT	S.	7,039	47°31′N. 52°23′W.	S.M.	T.	
11	ASPHALION	S.	6,274	17°28′N. 83°32′E.	S.M.	T.	
12	CORFIRTH ...	S.	1,803	170° 1m. from Ajaccio	Mine	—	
20	NOLISEMENT	S.	5,084	270° 3¼m. from Monopoli L.H.	Mine	—	
29	ENSIS	M. Tank	6,207	35°36′N. 35°33′E.	S.M.	T.	
MARCH, 1944							
6	CORUNDUM	S.	929	Off Dover	Shelled by Shore Batteries	—	
9	BRITISH LOYALTY...	M. Tank	6,993	Addu Atoll Harbour	S.M.	T.	
15	ABA (Hospital Ship)	M.	7,938	Naples	A.C.	B.	
APRIL, 1944							
20	SAMITE	S.	7,219	37°02′N. 03°41′E.	A.C.	T.	
MAY, 1944							
14	G. S. WALDEN	M. Tank	10,627	36°45′N. 00°55′E.	S.M.	T.	
14	FORT FIDLER	S.	7,127	36°45′N. 00°55′E.	S.M.	T.	
JUNE, 1944							
7	ST. JULIEN... (Hospital Carrier)	S.	1,952	49°35′N. 00°32′W.	Mine	—	
7	DINARD (Hospital Carrier)	S.	2,313	49°35′N. 00°35′W.	Mine	—	
11	FORT MCPHERSON...	S.	7,132	50°02′N. 00°36′W.	A.C.	B.	
12	BRITISH ENGINEER	S. Tank	6,993	50°10′N. 00°59′W.	Mine	—	
13	THE VICEROY	S.	824	Off Assault Beaches, Normandy	Mine	—	
23	EMPIRE TRISTRAM...	S.	7,167	Surrey Commercial Dock, London	Flying bomb	—	Again hit by Flying bomb on 12th July
24	GURDEN GATES	S.	1,791	Off Folkestone	Shelled by shore battery	—	
27	SHELL SPIRIT 1	M. Tank	440	Beckton	Flying bomb	—	
28	DALEGARTH FORCE	S.	825	1m. S.W. of Dover	Shelled by shore battery	—	
28	VIKING	S.	1,957	Rotherhithe	Flying bomb	—	
28	JACOB	Tug	65	Rotherhithe	Flying bomb	—	
28	TORO	Tug	87	Rotherhithe	Flying bomb	—	
JULY, 1944							
6	EMPIRE HALBERD...	S.	7,177	006° 3.8 miles from Longships Lt.	Mine	—	
8	EMPIRE BRUTUS ...	S.	7,233	075° 2¼ cables from Juno L.V., Normandy	Mine	—	
17	ORANMORE ...	S.	495	49°37′N. 00°28′W.	Mine	—	
19	ABBOTSBURY	Tug	92	Albert Dock Hoists, R. Thames	Flying bomb	—	
24	SAMNEVA ...	S.	7,219	50°14′N. 00°47′W.	S.M.	T.	
26	FORT MCPHERSON...	S.	7,132	Victoria Dock, London	Flying bomb	—	

Date	Name	Type	Gross tons	Position	Cause of damage	How damaged	Remarks
JULY, 1944—(Contd.)							
27	FORT PERROT ...	S.	7,171	50°50′N. 00°44′E.	E-Boat	T.	
27	EMPIRE BEATRICE...	S.	7,046	50°55′N. 01°02′E.	E-Boat	T.	
30	ASCANIUS	S.	10,048	50°15′N. 00°48′W.	S.M.	T.	
30	OCEAN COURIER ...	S.	7,178	50°42′N. 00°36′W.	E-Boat	T.	
30	FORT DEARBORN ...	S.	7,160	50°40′N. 00°31′E. (Approx.)	E-Boat	T.	
30	FORT KASKASKIA ...	S.	7,187	50°38′N. 00°27′E.	E-Boat	T.	
30	OCEAN VOLGA ...	S.	7,174	50°41′N. 00°32′E.	E-Boat	T.	
AUGUST, 1944							
3	SAMLONG	S.	7,219	49°24′N. 00°28′W.	One man torpedo	---	
3	FORT LAC LA RONGE	S.	7,131	49°22′N. 00°21′W.	One man torpedo	-—	
4	SAMSYLARNA ...	S.	7,100	33°05′N. 20°16′E.	A.C.	T.	
8	FORT YALE ...	S.	7,134	49°26′N. 00°33′W. (Approx.)	Mine	---	Torpedoed on 23rd August and sunk
10	IDDESLEIGH ...	S.	5,205	½m. from 90 Buoy, Sword Beach, Normandy	S.M.*	T.	Torpedoed again on 17th August and became a total loss
18	FORT GLOUCESTER...	S.	7,127	082° 10¼m. from Dungeness	E-Boat	T.	
18	SAMDEL	S.	7,219	West India Dock, London	Flying bomb	—	
19	HARPAGUS	M.	7,271	1½m. N. of W. Breakwater, Arromanches Harbour	Mine*	—	
20	DARONIA	M. Tank	8,139	31°10′S. 38°00′E.	S.M.	T.	
SEPTEMBER, 1944							
21	MORIALTA	M.	1,379	42°55′N. 05°30′E.	Mine	—	
23	WOLSELEY	S.T.	159	22m. E.N.E. of Gt. Yarmouth	Mine	—	
OCTOBER, 1944							
4	COTTON VALLEY ...	M. Tank	1,179	190° 6m. from Port du Bouc	Mine	—	
21	GUERNSEY QUEEN	M.	567	Entrance to Boulogne	Mine	—	
NOVEMBER, 1944							
2	FORT THOMPSON ...	S.	7,134	48°55′N. 67°41′W.	S.M.	T.	
10	FORT LA BAYE ...	S.	7,162	31°25′N. 32°23′E.	Mine	---	
12	FAIRPLAY I ...	Salvage Tug	162	Ostend Harbour	Mine	—	
21	EMPIRE CUTLASS ...	S.	7,177	294° 700 yds. from Digue Nord Lt., Le Havre	S.M.	T.	
DECEMBER, 1944							
20	EMPIRE OSBORNE...	S.	2,906	190° 3½m. from Cap de la Heve, R. Seine (Approx.)	Mine	—	
21	SAMTUCKY	S.	7,219	44°22′N. 63°23′W.	S.M.	T.	
JANUARY, 1945							
4	NIPIWAN PARK ...	M. Tank	2,373	44°30′N. 63°00′W.	S.M.	T.	

Date	Name	Type	Gross tons	Position	Cause of damage	How damaged	Remarks
FEBRUARY, 1945							
19	City of Lincoln ...	S.	8,039	300° 8 cables from 14 Buoy, off Humber	Mine	—	
22	Skjold	S.	1,345	52°53′N. 02°08′E.	E-Boat	G.	
28	Cydonia	S.	3,517	53°17′N. 00°57′E.	Mine	—	
MARCH, 1945							
6	Empire Geraint...	S.	6,991	090° 1m. from St. Goven's Lt., off Milford Haven	S.M.	T.	
8	Kyle Castle ...	S.	845	Granville ⎫	Damaged	—	
8	Parkwood ...	S.	1,049	Granville ⎪	in	—	
8	Nephrite	S.	927	Granville ⎬	sea-borne	—	
8	Eskwood	S.	791	Granville ⎭	raid	—	
APRIL, 1945							
11	Port Wyndham ...	M.	8,580	Off Outer Lade Buoy, Dungeness	Midget S.M.*	—	
15	Conakrian... ...	S.	4,876	51°20′N. 02°36′E.	Mine	—	
23	Riverton	S.	7,345	50°25′N. 05°25′W.	S.M.	T.	
30	Samclyde	S.	7,219	40°22′N. 22°51′E.	Mine	—	
MAY, 1945							
4	Empire Unity ...	M. Tank	6,386	64°23′N. 22°37′W.	S.M.*	T.	

LIST IV

BRITISH MERCHANT AND FISHING VESSELS LOST BY MISCELLANEOUS WAR CAUSES OTHER THAN ENEMY ACTION

(*Note :* The majority of these vessels were lost by striking British or Allied mines. Though their loss was due to war causes it could not be attributed to enemy action.

BRITISH

Date	Name	Type	Gross tons	Position
13 November, 1939	SIRDHANA	S.	7,745	Off Singapore
6 January, 1940	BRITISH LIBERTY	M. Tank	8,485	4m. N.E. of Dyck L.V.
6 June, 1940	LAPWING	S.T.	217	54°00'N. 01°10'E.
9 September, 1940	JOHN BAPTISH	S.T.	290	S. of Coningbeg L.V.
23 September, 1940	TACOMA	M.	5,905	Dakar
24 November, 1940	ALMA DAWSON	S.	3,985	55°32'N. 06°44'W.
25 November, 1940	PATRIA	S.	11,885	Haifa Anchorage
11 December, 1940	ROBINIA	S.T.	208	65°20'N. 12°40'W.
6 January, 1941	GADRA	S.T.	219	1½m. off Myling Head, Faroes
11 January, 1941	ORIOLE	F.V.	172	2½m. N. of Stakken North Pt., Faroes
31 January, 1941	BOTUSK	S.	3,091	Off North Rona Island
16 February, 1941	EMPIRE OTTER	S. Tank	4,670	25m. S.W. of Hartland Pt.
27 February, 1941	CHRISTABELLE	S.T.	203	61°27'N. 06°05'W.
8 June, 1941	HOPTON	S.T.	202	Off Iceland
13 July, 1941	PEGASUS	S. Tank	3,597	Beirut, Syria
8 December, 1941	GERTIE	S.	341	Off Tuskar Lt.
24 January, 1942	TAI SANG	S.	3,555	00°55'N. 103°35'E.
27 January, 1942	HARPA	M. Tank	3,007	Main Strait, Singapore
5 April, 1942	EMPIRE BEACON	M.	872	250° 6m. from St. Ann's Head
12 July, 1942	HERON	S.T.	223	Nr. Faroes Bank
4 October, 1942	ATHELBRAE	S. Tank	681	10°02'N. 61°51'W.
1 January, 1943	EMPIRE PANTHER ...	S.	5,600	8m. off Strumble Head
24 July, 1944	PORTSEA	S.	1,583	43°28'N. 13°44'E.
24 July, 1944	AUK	S.	1,338	43°48'N. 13°44'E.
7 December, 1944	GLENMAROON	S.	745	54°05'N. 03°53'W.
12 April, 1945	FALMOUTH	S.T.	165	6m. E.N.E. of No. 62 F. Buoy, off Humber
28 April, 1945	DINORAH	S.T.	192	Off Bridlington
1 May, 1945	NEURALIA	S.	9,182	40°11'N. 17°44'E.
24 July, 1945	GOZO	S.T.	172	Off Old Head of Kinsale

APPENDIX A

CASUALTIES TO PERSONNEL OF BRITISH MERCHANT SHIPS

(1)   Deaths (at sea or ashore) and supposed deaths (at sea) which have been notified to the Registrar General of Shipping and Seamen and recorded as due to enemy action or other causes arising out of the war, comprising :

(1) seamen of all nationalities who served in British ships, and

(2) British seamen who served in foreign ships chartered or requisitioned by His Majesty's Government, from the outbreak of war to 31st August, 1945, were as follows :—

In Merchant Vessels	In Fishing Vessels	Total
29,180	814	29,994

APPENDIX B

Table showing Number and Gross Tonnage of British, Allied and Neutral Merchant and Fishing Vessels lost through Enemy Action during each month of the war, 3rd September, 1939, to 2nd September, 1945, inclusive, showing cause of loss.

(Thousands of Tons)

Month	U-BOAT No.	U-BOAT Gross tonnage	MINE No.	MINE Gross tonnage	SURFACE CRAFT No.	SURFACE CRAFT Gross tonnage	AIRCRAFT No.	AIRCRAFT Gross tonnage	CAUSE UNCERTAIN No.	CAUSE UNCERTAIN Gross tonnage	TOTAL No.	TOTAL Gross tonnage
1939												
SEPT. ...	40	153	9	31	1	5	—	—	—	—	50	189
OCT. ...	27	135	10	29	8	32	—	—	—	—	45	196
NOV. ...	18	61	27	108	2	2	—	—	3	3	50	174
DEC. ...	18	72	37	89	4	22	10	3	1	1	70	187
TOTAL ...	103	421	83	257	15	61	10	3	4	4	215	746
1940												
JAN. ...	31	91	23	81	—	—	12	25	4	16	70	213
FEB. ...	35	153	14	51	1	2	2	1	4	8	56	215
MARCH ...	15	47	16	37	—	—	5	7	3	7	39	98
APRIL ...	6	31	11	20	2	6	4	6	20	74	43	137
MAY ...	10	48	18	48	2	7	36	154	14	17	80	274
JUNE ...	58	284	22	86	9	61	25	106	20	35	134	572
JULY ...	38	196	14	35	17	81	33	70	—	—	102	382
AUGUST ...	56	268	5	12	13	63	15	53	2	1	91	397
SEPT. ...	59	295	7	8	17	88	14	56	—	—	97	447
OCT. ...	63	352	23	33	5	32	6	9	6	17	103	443
NOV. ...	32	147	24	47	19	115	18	66	2	1	95	376
DEC. ...	37	213	24	54	11	64	7	15	3	12	82	358
TOTAL ...	440	2,125	201	512	96	519	177	568	78	188	992	3,912
1941												
JAN. ...	21	127	10	17	12	94	20	78	—	—	63	316
FEB. ...	38	195	9	17	21	89	27	89	6	12	101	402
MARCH ...	41	243	19	23	32	156	40	113	7	2	139	537
APRIL ...	43	249	6	25	9	48	84	296	13	36	155	654
MAY ...	58	326	8	23	3	15	55	136	—	—	124	500
JUNE ...	61	310	9	14	4	18	25	62	9	27	108	431
JULY ...	22	94	7	9	1	6	11	9	3	3	44	121
AUGUST ...	23	80	3	2	5	25	9	24	—	—	40	131
SEPT. ...	53	203	9	14	5	16	12	41	4	12	83	286
OCT. ...	32	157	4	20	2	3	10	35	3	4	51	219
NOV. ...	12	62	5	2	7	17	10	23	—	—	34	104
DEC. ...	25	116	19	64	1	6	20	64	122	236	187	486
TOTAL ...	429	2,162	108	230	102	493	323	970	167	332	1,129	4,187

Month	U-BOAT		MINE		SURFACE CRAFT		AIRCRAFT		CAUSE UNCERTAIN		TOTAL	
	No.	Gross tonnage	No.	Gross tonnage	No.	Gross tonnage	No.	Gross tonnage	No.	Gross tonnage	No.	Gross tonnage
1942												
JAN. ...	62	328	11	10	1	3	15	57	9	20	98	418
FEB. ...	82	470	2	7	—	—	29	139	17	36	130	652
MARCH ...	94	532	5	17	10	23	12	48	103	169	224	789
APRIL ...	75	438	8	15	25	131	16	83	4	6	128	673
MAY ...	125	607	6	18	3	20	14	59	—	—	148	704
JUNE ...	144	700	7	20	7	49	11	54	—	—	169	823
JULY ...	96	476	2	9	11	54	18	74	—	—	127	613
AUGUST ...	108	544	—	—	8	59	6	61	2	1	124	665
SEPT. ...	98	486	—	—	4	24	12	58	—	—	114	568
OCT. ...	93	614	3	5	3	8	1	6	—	—	100	633
NOV. ...	117	718	1	1	5	10	7	62	4	16	134	807
DEC. ...	61	337	3	1	8	19	2	4	—	—	74	361
TOTAL ...	1,155	6,250	48	103	85	400	143	705	139	248	1,570	7,706
1943												
JAN. ...	37	203	5	19	—	—	6	26	2	6	50	254
FEB. ...	63	359	7	34	1	5	—	—	1	5	72	403
MARCH ...	108	627	2	1	—	—	10	65	—	—	120	693
APRIL ...	56	328	5	12	1	2	2	3	—	—	64	345
MAY ...	50	265	1	2	—	—	5	21	2	12	58	300
JUNE ...	20	96	5	4	2	18	3	6	—	—	30	124
JULY ...	45	245	—	—	1	7	13	106	—	—	59	358
AUGUST ...	16	86	—	—	1	8	5	14	3	19	25	127
SEPT. ...	20	119	3	4	—	—	4	23	2	1	29	147
OCT. ...	20	97	5	20	—	—	4	23	—	—	29	140
NOV. ...	14	67	3	7	4	8	7	62	—	—	28	144
DEC. ...	13	87	1	6	—	—	17	75	—	—	31	168
TOTAL ...	462	2,579	37	109	10	48	76	424	10	43	595	3,203
1944												
JAN. ...	13	92	1	7	5	7	4	24	1	1	24	130
FEB. ...	18	93	—	—	1	2	3	22	—	—	22	117
MARCH ...	23	143	1	7	2	8	—	—	—	—	26	158
APRIL ...	9	62	—	—	—	—	3	20	—	—	12	82
MAY ...	4	24	—	—	—	—	1	3	—	—	5	27
JUNE ...	11	58	6	25	3	2	2	9	3	10	25	104
JULY ...	12	63	3	8	1	7	—	—	—	—	16	79
AUGUST ...	18	99	3	7	—	—	—	—	3	13	24	119
SEPT. ...	7	43	1	2	—	—	—	—	—	—	8	45
OCT. ...	1	7	2	4	—	—	—	—	—	—	3	11
NOV. ...	7	30	—	—	1	1	1	7	—	—	9	38
DEC. ...	9	59	8	35	—	—	5	36	1	4	23	134
TOTAL ...	132	773	25	95	13	27	19	121	8	28	197	1,044
1945												
JAN. ...	11	57	4	17	1	2	1	7	—	—	17	83
FEB. ...	15	65	5	18	2	4	1	7	1	1	24	95
MARCH ...	12	58	6	36	2	4	—	—	4	6	24	104
APRIL ...	13	73	4	8	—	—	3	23	—	—	20	104
MAY ...	3	10	—	—	—	—	—	—	—	—	3	10
JUNE to SEPT. ...	Nil	Nil	Nil	Nil	Nil	Nil	Nil	Nil	Nil	Nil	Nil	Nil
TOTAL ...	54	263	19	79	5	10	5	37	5	7	88	396
GRAND TOTAL 3rd SEPT., 1939 to 2nd SEPT., 1945	2,775	14,573	521	1,385	326	1,558	753	2,828	411	850	4,786	21,194

PART IX

INDEX OF VESSELS LOST OR DAMAGED

Of further interest . . .

Encyclopaedia of the
Modern Royal Navy
3rd edition

Having learned several lessons the hard way during the Falklands conflict, the Royal Navy today is steadily being refitted and re-equipped with new ships, new weapons systems, more fire- and blast-resistant materials and new sonars and sensors to make it an even harder-hitting force, primarily in the anti-submarine role, within NATO. In this completely revised third edition of his highly acclaimed reference work on all aspects of the modern Royal Navy, **Paul Beaver** examines these changes in depth.

The book explains the role and organization of every aspect of the Royal Navy including the Fleet Air Arm, the Royal Marines, the Royal Fleet Auxiliary, the Royal Maritime Auxiliary, the Royal Naval Auxiliary, the WRNS, QARNNS, RNR, WRNR and even the Sea Cadets.

Every vessel, aircraft and weapon in use by the Royal Navy and the auxiliary service is covered, complete with specifications, scale drawings and photographs. Uniforms, badges and insignia are all described and illustrated, including the variety of specialist and protective clothing necessary in modern naval operations.

Virtually everything you could wish to know about the Royal Navy today is to be found in the pages of this fascinating volume, which has been compiled with the help of serving officers and Ministry of Defence officials to ensure complete accuracy.

Paul Beaver is a professional journalist and writer specializing in naval subjects. He is the author of several other PSL books, including *Modern Royal Navy Warships* and *Modern Military Helicopters*.